KT-160-293

Criminal Law

··

Fifteenth Edition

Michael J. Allen

*LLB, LLM, Barrister, former Commissioner at the Criminal Cases
Review Commission (2002–2012) and former Professor of Law at
Newcastle Law School (1996–2002)*

Ian Edwards

PhD, LLB, BA, Senior Lecturer at the University of East Anglia

OXFORD

UNIVERSITY PRESS

OXFORD

UNIVERSITY PRESS

Great Clarendon Street, Oxford, OX2 6DP,
United Kingdom

Oxford University Press is a department of the University of Oxford.
It furthers the University's objective of excellence in research, scholarship,
and education by publishing worldwide. Oxford is a registered trade mark of
Oxford University Press in the UK and in certain other countries

© Michael J. Allen and Ian Edwards 2019

The moral rights of the authors have been asserted

Twelfth edition 2013
Thirteenth edition 2015
Fourteenth edition 2017

Impression: 1

All rights reserved. No part of this publication may be reproduced, stored in
a retrieval system, or transmitted, in any form or by any means, without the
prior permission in writing of Oxford University Press, or as expressly permitted
by law, by licence or under terms agreed with the appropriate reprographics
rights organization. Enquiries concerning reproduction outside the scope of the
above should be sent to the Rights Department, Oxford University Press, at the
address above

You must not circulate this work in any other form
and you must impose this same condition on any acquirer

Public sector information reproduced under Open Government Licence v3.0
(http://www.nationalarchives.gov.uk/doc/open-government-licence/open-government-licence.htm)

Published in the United States of America by Oxford University Press
198 Madison Avenue, New York, NY 10016, United States of America

British Library Cataloguing in Publication Data
Data available

Library of Congress Control Number: 2019941640

ISBN 978–0–19–883193–8

Printed in Great Britain by
Bell & Bain Ltd., Glasgow

Links to third party websites are provided by Oxford in good faith and
for information only. Oxford disclaims any responsibility for the materials
contained in any third party website referenced in this work.

OUTLINE CONTENTS

DETAILED CONTENTS

NEW TO THIS EDITION

Key revisions in the fifteenth edition include:

- Analysis of the latest case law developments and legislation including: *Ivey* v *Genting Casinos UK Ltd* [2017] UKSC 67 and *DPP* v *Patterson* [2017] EWHC Admin 2820 (on dishonesty); *Wallace (Berlinah)* [2018] EWCA Crim 690 (on liability for causing another's suicide); *Lane and Letts* [2018] UKSC 36 (on the presumption of *mens rea*); *Loake* v *CPS* [2018] 1 Cr App R 16 (on the basis of the insanity defence); *Taj (Simon)* [2018] EWCA Crim 1743 (on intoxication, mistaken belief, and self-defence); *Petgrave* [2019] RTR 6 (on the tests for duress of circumstances); *Ray (Steven)* [2017] EWCA Crim 1391 (on the proper interpretation of the 'householder' defence); *Crilly* [2018] EWCA Crim 168 (on 'joint enterprise'); *Golds* [2016] UKSC 61, *Squelch* [2017] EWCA Crim 204, *Conroy* [2017] EWCA Crim 81, and *Kay* [2017] 4 WLR 121 (on diminished responsibility); *Rejmanski* [2017] EWCA Crim 2061 (on loss of control); *Rose (Honey)* [2018] QB 328 (on gross negligence manslaughter); *BM* [2018] EWCA Crim 560 (on consent and body modification); *Gimbert* [2018] EWCA Crim 2190 and *Darroux* [2018] EWCA Crim 1009 (on theft);

- Updated references to the latest policy guidance from the CPS and to the Sentencing Council's latest sentencing guidelines;

- A revised first chapter that offers students an in-depth contextual understanding of the principles underpinning the law, key aspects of criminal procedure, and the social contexts in which the criminal law functions;

- Revised and updated '*Law in context*' features offering students topical contextual insights into the law under discussion, including a new feature in Chapter 11 on 'procedure and evidence in rape trials'.

PREFACE

Criminal law is a subject of great complexity which students find both fascinating and frustrating. The complexity is in large part caused by the uncertainty created by judges, in courts at all levels, who sometimes fail to understand or adhere to fundamental principles and Parliament which all too often legislates in haste, leaving the rest of us to make sense of the legislation. The subject can be both challenging and potentially exasperating.

Traditionally textbooks on criminal law provide more detail than students require and may, themselves, add to the confusion. This book seeks to state clearly both the principles fundamental to criminal liability and the law's current state in the areas covered in most criminal law courses. In addition it highlights areas where there are doubts, problems, or confusion. It is hoped that this book will help students both to meet the intellectual challenge which criminal law presents them and safely to negotiate those areas where frustration might creep in.

In the two years since the fourteenth edition of this book was published there have been numerous developments in both statutory and case law. New cases have been incorporated into most chapters, and an updated Chapter 1 continues to situate the substantive law in its wider social, political, and legal contexts. Notable developments include the Supreme Court's revisiting of the meaning of dishonesty in *Ivey* v *Genting Casinos UK Ltd* [2017] UKSC 67 and Court of Appeal cases on criminal liability for causing another's suicide (*Wallace (Berlinah)* [2018] EWCA Crim 690) and consent as a defence in cases of body modification (*BM* [2018] EWCA Crim 560).

In earlier editions, presentational devices were developed which were designed to improve the visual impact of the text and to reinforce understanding by highlighting statutory provisions, quotations, key cases, examples, questions, and tables to highlight the *actus reus* and *mens rea* elements of the major offences. These have been retained and further developed for this edition, with the addition of a summary of 'key points' at the end of each chapter, as well as enhanced 'law in context' sections in Chapters 2–15 to highlight some of the wider contexts in which the substantive law can be seen.

Thanks are due to all the editorial staff at OUP who have assisted with its production.

The law is stated as it was on 1 January 2019.

Michael J. Allen
Ian Edwards

GUIDE TO THE ONLINE RESOURCES

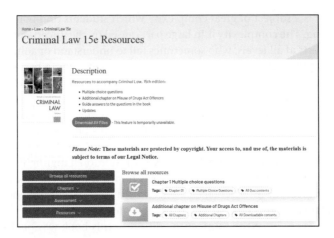

The online resources which accompany this book provide extra resources which are free to use and designed to help support your legal learning and development.

 www.oup.com/uk/allen_edwards15e/

Multiple-choice questions

A selection of multiple-choice questions, arranged by chapter, allows you to quickly assess your knowledge of the various topics in criminal law.

Additional chapter

An additional chapter on Misuse of Drugs Act offences is available for those studying this topic and those keen to expand their legal knowledge.

Guidance on answering questions

Guidance on how to answer the questions provided throughout the book will help you to think more deeply about the issues at hand.

Updates

An indispensable resource, providing access to recent cases and development in the laws that have occurred since publication of the book.

TABLE OF CASES

TABLE OF LEGISLATION

TABLE OF STATUTORY INSTRUMENTS AND CIRCULARS

1

....

Criminal law in context

1.1 Substantive criminal law

This book is about the substantive criminal law: the law that determines what is or is not a crime. It is not primarily concerned with why certain conduct is defined as criminal; that is a matter of moral philosophy. Neither is it focused on the reasons why people commit crimes; that is a matter for criminologists to ponder. Likewise, the procedures by which criminals are arrested, prosecuted, convicted, and sentenced are outside the remit of this book. Similarly, the study of punishment and the efficacy of the various sentencing options available to the courts is a matter for penologists to consider. However, we can better understand the substantive criminal law if we learn from and about these related academic disciplines. **Moral philosophy** underpins the decisions about what should be criminalised. **Criminology** provides insights into how much crime there is, who commits it and why, and who are the victims. Having some understanding of **criminal procedure** will help us appreciate the reality of the substantive criminal law, and the practical operation of the criminal process. Insights from **penology** will help us understand what does and what *should* happen to offenders after conviction. So while the book's focus is on the substantive criminal law, be ready to think more broadly about the substantive law in context.

The criminal law is a complex and expansive subject. Before studying it, however, we need to place it in context by considering questions such as the following: What is a crime? What purposes or functions does the criminal law serve? Why is particular conduct classified as criminal?

1.2 Defining a crime

A crime may be defined as an act (or omission or a state of affairs) which contravenes the law and which can be followed by prosecution in criminal proceedings with the attendant consequence, following conviction, of punishment. This definition reveals nothing of the characteristics of acts that are defined as criminal. Indeed the same act may give rise to both criminal and civil liability. For example, if D punches P he may be guilty of assault, a crime. The same act also constitutes the tort of assault, which is a form of trespass to the person and D, if successfully sued by P, would be liable to pay damages. Likewise, if D sets fire to P's house he may be guilty of the crime of arson. P could also sue him for the tort of trespass to his property.

When Parliament passes legislation making a particular act criminal, the nature of that act does not change but the consequences of performing it do. For example, until 1930 it was not an offence to take and drive away a motor vehicle without the owner's consent. Section 28 of the Road Traffic Act 1930 made this an offence and in 1968 Parliament extended this offence to cover the taking of any 'conveyance' thus including, for example, boats (see s. 12 of the Theft Act 1968). Similarly, until 1978 it was not an offence for a diner in a restaurant to make off without paying for the meal he had consumed. The mischief of customers making off without paying their bills where payment on the spot was expected was dealt with in s. 3 of the Theft Act 1978. In both these cases, the relevant act remains the same and the actor continues to be civilly liable for trespass and debt respectively. Parliament's legislative intervention, however, has meant that both these acts may also result in criminal liability.

By the same token, if Parliament enacts legislation that abolishes a particular crime, the nature of the act which previously constituted a crime remains the same; only the consequences of performing that act change. For example, s. 1 of the Sexual Offences Act 1967 provided that it would no longer be an offence for a man over the age of 21 to commit buggery or gross indecency in private with another man over that age who consented to the act. The nature of these acts did not change after 1967 but the consequence of committing them in particular circumstances changed as the criminal sanction was removed.

A simple definition of crime is thus of limited use. It only indicates which acts are criminal by reference to consequences which may ensue from their commission; it tells us nothing about the function of the criminal law or why particular conduct is classified as criminal. The definition, therefore, is essentially concerned with the legal consequences of the act.

1.3 The functions of the criminal law

The main function of the criminal law is largely to set the parameters within which the criminal justice system operates. There are two aspects to this. First, the criminal justice system is a tool of social control representing the agglomeration of powers, procedures, and sanctions which surround the criminal law. The police are empowered to investigate crime, search for evidence, arrest suspected offenders, and question them. The courts are empowered to try persons charged with committing crimes and, if convicted, to sentence them. In setting the parameters within which this coercive State apparatus operates, the criminal law plays a central role; a person may only be arrested where he is suspected of committing a crime; the police may only search for evidence which points towards the commission of a crime; the courts may only try and sentence persons who are charged with, and then convicted of, committing crimes. It is therefore crucial to define clearly what acts, omissions, or states of affairs amount to crimes: all the other powers, procedures, and sanctions of the criminal justice system are dependent upon these definitions. The criminal law, accordingly, limits and controls the legitimate exercise by the State of its coercive power. Secondly, the criminal law operates as a guide to the citizen indicating the limits of legitimate behaviour and predicting the consequences of infraction of the criminal law. The criminal law guides us in making decisions in life, by communicating to us the disapproval and punishment that will result from particular paths we might choose, such as using violence, possessing prohibited drugs, or driving at high speed on a motorway.

If the State's power is to be effectively limited and if the citizen is to be able confidently to make rational choices regarding his behaviour, the criminal law must be clear, relatively stable, and accessible—that is, knowable in advance. From the outset, we should question whether English criminal law meets these standards. Throughout this book judicial decisions on the content and ambit of the substantive criminal law will be subjected to criticism. There is a tendency for judges to lose sight of the wider role which the criminal law serves in their understandable desire to see persons whom they regard as 'undesirable characters' locked behind bars. Judges do not always make explicit the factors that have led to their decisions. Note also that, even at appellate level, judges can make errors and misunderstand key principles of criminal law. As we will see throughout the book, the House of Lords and Supreme Court have, on several occasions, overturned key decisions of the Court of Appeal, House of Lords, and Privy Council (e.g. in *R v Jogee* [2016] UKSC 8 the Supreme Court ruled that an earlier Privy Council decision, *Chan Wing-Siu* [1985] AC 168, had introduced a new principle concerning accessorial liability that was based on an incomplete and erroneous reading of the previous case law, coupled with generalised and questionable policy arguments: see **Chapter 7**).

But criticism should not be confined to the judiciary; the legislature also deserves criticism for its hyperactivity in creating new crimes and doing so by means of poorly drafted statutory provisions. The courts regularly bemoan the complexity of the legislation they are called upon to interpret and apply, as well as the difficulty of tracking the state of statutory provisions that may be subject to countless amendments by various subsequent provisions with no attempt at consolidation. In *Chambers* [2008] EWCA Crim 2467, Toulson LJ launched a broadside at the legislature criticising both the volume and form of criminal statutory provisions.

D had been prosecuted by Her Majesty's Revenue and Customs for fraudulent evasion of duty contrary to s. 170(1)(b) of the Customs and Excise Management Act 1979. This offence is aimed at smugglers but regulations made under the Act dealt with the circumstances in which a confiscation order could be made for evading duty. D pleaded guilty and was made subject to a confiscation order which he appealed. The prosecution relied upon the Excise Goods Regulations 1992 to contend that D's actions were caught by the legislation. At the Court of Appeal, the Court having issued a draft judgment for the parties to consider in advance of judgment being delivered, a lawyer at the Revenue and Customs Prosecution Office noticed that the 1992 Regulations had been superseded by the Tobacco Product Regulations 2001, some five years before Mr Chambers' actions which formed the subject of the prosecution. These changed the basis upon which a confiscation order would be assessed. Quashing the confiscation order the Court of Appeal complained of the problem of criminal legislation being one of 'substantial constitutional importance', stating:

64 This case also provides an example of a wider problem. It is a maxim that ignorance of the law is no excuse, but it is profoundly unsatisfactory if the law itself is not practically accessible. To a worryingly large extent, statutory law is not practically accessible today, even to the courts whose constitutional duty it is to interpret and enforce it. There are four principal reasons.

65 First, the majority of legislation is secondary legislation.

66 Secondly, the volume of legislation has increased very greatly over the last 40 years. The Law Commission's Report on Post-Legislative Scrutiny, (2006) Law Com 302, gave some figures in Appendix C. In 2005 there were 2,868 pages of new Public General Acts and approximately 13,000 pages of new Statutory Instruments, making a total well in excess of 15,000 pages (which is equivalent to over 300 pages a week) excluding European Directives and European Regulations, which were responsible for over 5,000 additional pages of legislation.

67 Thirdly, on many subjects the legislation cannot be found in a single place, but in a patchwork of primary and secondary legislation.

68 Fourthly, there is no comprehensive statute law database with hyperlinks which would enable an intelligent person, by using a search engine, to find out all the legislation on a particular topic. This means that the courts are in many cases unable to discover what the law is, or was at the date with which the court is concerned, and are entirely dependent on the parties for being able to inform them what were the relevant statutory provisions which the court has to apply. This [is a] lamentable state of affairs . . .

While ignorance of the law may be no excuse, there is a responsibility upon the State to make the law accessible to its citizens if it wishes them to behave lawfully. Unfortunately, there is no Criminal Code in English law that sets out in a single document all the key principles, offences, and defences of substantive law. Other jurisdictions do have such a Code (e.g. Germany (https://www.gesetze-im-internet. de/englisch_stgb/) and Canada (http://laws-lois.justice.gc.ca/eng/acts/C-46/)). The Law Commission has proposed such a Code, but it is unlikely to be implemented: comprehensive criminal law reform is not a priority for contemporary British governments (Law Commission, *Legislating the Criminal Code*, http://www.lawcom.gov. uk/project/legislating-the-criminal-code/).

1.3.1 Criminal law and political populism

Why has the British Parliament been eager to expand the substantive criminal law and deploy it so extensively? We can see the expansion of substantive criminal law as a series of responses to immediate political pressures and sometimes to what criminologists call 'moral panics'. In his 1972 book, *Folk Devils and Moral Panics*, sociologist Stanley Cohen described how moral panics occur when a 'condition, episode, person or group of persons emerges to become defined as a threat to societal values and interests' (p. 9). Cohen argued that the mass media play a central role in stoking public fears about particular groups in society or particular types of behaviour and those fears put pressure on governments to respond to the perceived threat by enacting new criminal laws.

Legislation resulting from 'moral panics' can lack coherence and clarity. For example, the Dangerous Dogs Act 1991 (DDA 1991) was a direct response to widely reported attacks by particular breeds of dogs on young children, causing serious injury and in some cases death. The Government enacted the DDA 1991 to address apparent public concern about these attacks and made it a criminal offence amongst other things to own (without special exemption) particular breeds of dog, or allow them to be in a public place without being muzzled and kept on a lead. Since its introduction the legislation has been repeatedly criticised for lacking clarity and coherence, mainly for being breed-specific in its focus rather than addressing the dangerous behaviour of any dog, regardless of its breed. The haste with which it was enacted and the lack of attention given by the Government to the *reality* of the problem of 'dangerous dogs' (as distinct from how the perceived problem was being reported in the tabloid media) meant that the legislation was flawed.

More recently the Psychoactive Substances Act 2016 (PSA 2016) has criminalised activities concerning so-called 'legal highs', synthetic psychoactive substances producing effects similar to drugs such as cannabis, cocaine, amphetamine, and MDMA ('ecstasy'). Consumption of 'legal highs' has reportedly led to a number of deaths (Centre for Social Justice *Ambitious for Recovery: Tackling Drug and Alcohol Addiction in the UK* (2014) http://www.centreforsocialjustice.org.uk/library/ambitious-recovery-tackling-drug-alcohol-addiction-uk). The substances were frequently sold in 'head shops' and were generally untested for safety. The Government responded by passing the PSA 2016 which creates several new offences in respect of 'legal highs', each punishable with imprisonment. The Act does not criminalise mere possession of psychoactive substances, other than in a custodial institution (where such substances have been prevalent) but it does criminalise possession with intent to supply, as well as the importation and export of such substances. Amongst other things, the Act also criminalises the intentional supply of such a substance to another person if the supplier knows or is reckless as to whether the substance is likely to be consumed by another person for its psychoactive effects. The Act gives the police additional powers to deal with the sale of 'legal highs' through 'head shops' (s. 13).

What started as a response to the social problem of 'legal highs', culminated in a controversially broad and potentially ambiguous Act. The final Act contains 63 sections and five schedules. In Parliament, there was debate about which substances should be defined as 'psychoactive'. Section 1 of the Act defines a 'psychoactive substance' as one which 'produces a psychoactive effect in a person if, by stimulating or depressing the person's central nervous system, it affects the person's mental functioning or emotional state'. When you think about the substances that we consume each day, you can see the potential breadth of this definition. Many types of food and drink (including tea, coffee, alcohol, and sugar) will affect our mental functioning or emotional state as a result of stimulating or depressing our central nervous systems! The Act specifically lists alcohol, nicotine, food, and caffeinated drinks as exemptions to the new laws. The Home Office has issued guidance for retailers (*Psychoactive Substances Act 2016: Guidance for Retailers* (2016): https://www.gov.uk/government/publications/psychoactive-substances-act-guidance-for-retailers/psychoactive-substances-act-2016-guidance-for-retailers) in which it acknowledges that it may be difficult for retailers to know whether a particular substance is covered by the Act and therefore whether the retailers should be selling it. Several Parliamentarians noted that alkyl nitrate capsules (more commonly known as 'poppers' and popular amongst gay men for enhancing sexual pleasure) would be covered by the bill and therefore it was likely to have a particular effect on some people who are not part of the social problem of 'legal highs' that the legislation was intended to address. In the end, the Home Office announced in a letter that 'poppers' would not fall within the definition of 'psychoactive', by virtue of the substance's effect on stimulating or depressing the central nervous system being *indirect* rather than *direct* (*The Independent*, 'Legal Highs Will Not Be Banned Despite Legal Highs Crackdown, Government Says' (22 March 2016)).

Each British political party tends to have particular views about the functions and appropriate boundaries of the criminal law. Historically, the Conservative Party has tended to emphasise the importance of 'law and order', bolstering police powers, toughening punishments, and using the criminal law widely to respond to particular social issues. By contrast the Labour Party has tended to focus on addressing social issues related to criminality, such as unemployment, poverty, and education, rather than using the criminal law and imprisonment as a blunt instrument to repress crime. These are broad-brush statements of course, and both main parties have had periods when they adopted the approach that is historically associated with the other. For example, the Conservative Government in 1990 stated boldly in a White Paper (*Crime, Justice and Protecting the Public* (Cmnd 965, 1990)) that 'prison can be an expensive way of making bad people worse' (para. 2.7) and legislated thereafter to restrict the use of harsh, deterrent sentences (in the Criminal Justice Act 1991: see **1.3.4.6**). Before becoming Prime Minister, Tony Blair adopted a now-famous slogan, arguing that society needs to be 'tough on crime, tough on the causes of crime' (*The New Statesman*, 29 January 1993) (a slogan that led *The Times* newspaper to declare in an editorial that he had 'parked his tanks' on the Conservatives' lawn: *The Times*, 2 October 1993) and under his premiership the criminal law expanded rapidly in breadth and reach (Ashworth, 'Is the Criminal Law a Lost Cause?' (2000) 116 LQR 225–56, 225). The other main parties have their own views on the use of the substantive criminal law. The Liberal Democrats, rooting their policies in liberalism, tend to argue that the State should not intervene in citizens' lives any more than is necessary to prevent harm. For example, they have called for a re-examination of the country's approach to drugs regulation, including the legalisation of cannabis possession for adults' personal use and the introduction of a regulated cannabis market (*The Independent*, 'Decriminalise Personal Drug Use to Free up Prison Space, Say Lib Dems', 18 March 2017). The Green Party tend to advocate a reduction in the use of the criminal law and punishment, arguing that restorative justice (see **1.3.4.5**) provides the best hope for dealing with the causes and consequences of offending behaviour (Green Party (2015) *Crime and Justice*: https://policy.greenparty.org.uk/cj.html).

One example of the impact of shifting political priorities and philosophies even within a government is the criminalisation of cannabis possession. Cannabis is a controlled drug under s. 2 of the Misuse of Drugs Act 1971 and possession of it is an offence under s. 5 of that Act. There are three categories or classes of drugs (A, B, and C), the category determining the maximum penalty that can be imposed (detailed in sch. 4 to the Act: seven years' imprisonment for class A, five years' for class B, and two years' for class C). Under Tony Blair's Government, cannabis was reclassified from a class B to a class C drug. When Gordon Brown was Prime Minister, his personal views on 'soft' drugs led to reclassification of cannabis from class C to a class B, thus increasing the maximum penalty that courts could impose (*The Telegraph*, 'Gordon Brown's Tough Stance on Cannabis', 12 April 2008).

The political contexts to criminal law are important. While there are debates amongst moral philosophers about the appropriate aims and limits of the substantive criminal law, and while those do feed into the actual content of laws, ultimately the legislature decides on what is criminalised and that means the dominant political party can bring to bear its own stance on the law's aims and limits.

Students of the criminal law sometimes expect it to be a closed system of internally coherent, logical, and principled laws that governments have implemented after careful consideration of all the consequences of criminalisation, paying close attention to empirical research evidence and philosophical debate. Frequently it is not. As you read about criminal law in the subsequent chapters, be alert to the political background to statutes and the arguments that might have taken place in Parliament to mould the legislation's final wording. At the same time, do not fall into the trap of blithely assuming that 'political' means 'incoherent' and 'unprincipled'. A richer appreciation of the substantive criminal law comes from teasing out the conflicting approaches to the uses of criminal law. It would be far too simplistic to say that the criminal law is just an incoherent mess of assorted laws. A more sophisticated approach is to acknowledge that substantive criminal law has built up over centuries and is the product of a host of motivations, rationales, and philosophies, sometimes hastily considered, at other times grounded in empirical research and moral philosophy.

1.3.2 Social control and social morality

The criminal law is a series of prohibitions backed up with the threat of punishment. The criminal law represents the rules of social control within a society. But how are the rules determined? Is there an essential criterion which determines which behaviour merits criminal sanction? The Wolfenden Committee, *Report of the Committee on Homosexual Offences and Prostitution* (Cmnd 247, 1957) stated (at paras 13 and 14) that the functions of the criminal law are:

> to preserve public order and decency, to protect the citizen from what is offensive or injurious and to provide sufficient safeguards against exploitation or corruption of others, particularly those who are specially vulnerable because they are young, weak in body or mind or inexperienced or in a state of special physical, official or economic dependence. It is not . . . the function of the law to intervene in the private lives of citizens, or to seek to enforce any particular pattern of behaviour, further than is necessary to carry out the purposes we have outlined.

To this extent the criminal law is a reflection of corporate or societal morality. The wrongdoing which the criminal law seeks to punish is that which threatens the fundamental values upon which a society is founded. While it is harmful to the individual to be robbed or assaulted, it is also harmful as such behaviour threatens the security and well-being of society as a whole. The criminal sanction operates then as a form of social control both punishing the offender and reasserting society's mores.

1.3.3 **What conduct should be classified as criminal?**

Why is particular conduct prohibited by the criminal law? What is the social morality which the criminal law reflects? Is the fact that certain conduct is regarded as
immoral by the majority of citizens a sufficient justification, in itself, for making
that conduct punishable by law?

To determine what is immoral is far from straightforward. Ideas of what is
immoral vary from one society to another and from one generation to another. In
any society, however, there is a common core of morality which reflects standards
of behaviour to which the majority of citizens in that society conform, deviations
from which will provoke censure. Many of these rules of morality will be enforced
by the criminal law, such as prohibitions on murder, violence to the person, sexual
assaults, and theft. As Gross states (at p. 13):

> It seems obvious that those crimes of violence, theft and destruction that stand as para-
> digms of crime and comprise the core of any penal code are also moral wrongs. Everyone
> has a right to be free of such harm inflicted by others, and when murder, rape, arson,
> assault or [theft] is committed there is also a moral wrong since a moral duty to refrain
> from doing harm to others has been breached. The right to be free of such harm does not
> have its origin in law but in a general consensus on the rights enjoyed by any member of
> society, or even by any person, no matter how he lives. This consensus is a more funda-
> mental element of society even than the law, and for that reason the violation of such a
> right is a moral wrong and not simply a legal wrong.

Not all rules of social morality, however, are subject to enforcement by the criminal
law. Adultery may be regarded by many as immoral but it is not a crime. Lying may
be immoral but it is not necessarily a crime (see **Chapter 13**). Similarly, many prohibitions of the criminal law are morally neutral. There is no rule of social morality
which dictates that the speed limit for vehicles in built-up areas should be 30 mph,
nor does social morality dictate that seatbelts should be worn in vehicles or that
persons under 18 should not be served alcohol in licensed premises. These laws may
be justified on the basis that they improve safety for, or prevent harm to, citizens.
They may be matters on which there is a fair degree of social consensus but this is
not due to any common perception of morality.

Legal philosophers have long disputed what the proper sphere of the criminal law
should be. The nineteenth-century philosopher J. S. Mill in his essay *On Liberty*
expressed the view that the only legitimate purpose for which legal coercion could be
exercised over any member of a civilised community is to prevent harm to others. The
Wolfenden Committee extended this (see **1.3.2**). By contrast Lord Devlin in *The
Enforcement of Morals* (1965) expressed the view that the primary function of the criminal law was to maintain public morality. In his opinion 'intolerance, indignation and
disgust' were vital to a society and conduct which aroused such feelings amongst
right-thinking members of society deserved suppression by means of the criminal law.

The views expressed by Lord Devlin subsequently seemed to receive approval in
the House of Lords.

> In *Shaw* v *DPP* [1962] AC 220, D was convicted of conspiracy to corrupt public morals
> arising from his publication of the 'Ladies Directory' advertising the names and

addresses of prostitutes, together with photographs and details of the 'services' they were prepared to offer. The House of Lords upheld the conviction, Viscount Simonds stating (at p. 267):

> In the sphere of the criminal law I entertain no doubt that there remains in the courts of law a residual power to enforce the supreme and fundamental purpose of the law, to conserve not only the safety and order but also the moral welfare of the State, and that it is their duty to guard against attacks which may be the more insidious because they are novel and unprepared for.

By contrast, Lord Reid, dissenting, reflected the view of Mill. He was of the opinion that there was 'no such general offence known to the law as conspiracy to corrupt public morals'. Lord Reid went on to state (at p. 275):

> Even if there is still a vestigial power [in the courts to extend the law of conspiracy], it ought not, in my view, to be used unless there appears to be general agreement that the offence to which it is applied ought to be criminal if committed by an individual. Notoriously, there are wide differences of opinion today as to how far the law ought to punish immoral acts which are not done in the face of the public. Some think that the law already goes too far, some that it does not go far enough. Parliament is the proper place, and I am firmly of opinion the only proper place, to settle that. When there is sufficient support from public opinion, Parliament does not hesitate to intervene. Where Parliament fears to tread it is not for the courts to rush in.

It is rare for such a stark division to occur in the House of Lords as a result of philosophical differences of opinion regarding the criminal law's functions. While Mill's and Devlin's views are prescriptive it is clear that neither accurately describes the actual province of the criminal law. In reality the justifications for the creation of particular offences may differ. Some offences enforce morality, others are there to protect individuals from harm, and others do both. Indeed defining 'harm' is as difficult a task as defining 'morality'. Should harm be limited to physical harm to others or should the law also adopt a paternalistic approach to protect the individual from harming himself? (All these issues surfaced in the House of Lords' decision in *Brown* [1993] 2 WLR 556 concerning sado-masochism; see **10.7.2**.) Attempting suicide used to be a crime (until the Suicide Act 1961). Now, possessing prohibited drugs, riding a motor cycle without a helmet, or driving a car without wearing a seatbelt are offences. Only the perpetrator and victim will suffer from these activities. Looked at more widely, however, it may be argued that society may also suffer the cost of medical treatment and social security payments to persons maimed or debilitated by, or orphaned or widowed as a result of, these activities. The definition of 'harm' may be widened in another way to include offence to one's sensibilities and psychological harm. Offences under the Obscene Publications Acts 1959 and 1964, or offences such as brothel-keeping (under ss 33 and 33A of the Sexual Offences Act 1956) may be regarded as causing harm in this sense apart from offending against morality.

What is clear from this brief examination is that the decision to criminalise or decriminalise particular activities, whether by judicial decision or legislation, is far from straightforward. A range of considerations may be relevant to that decision, for example, morality, economics, ethics, politics, and philosophy. Changes in morality may lead to changes in the law, for example, s. 1 of the Sexual Offences Act 1967 or the Abortion Act 1967. As views change perhaps other offences will be removed from the criminal calendar; many would argue for the legalisation of voluntary euthanasia or the possession of cannabis.

The decision to use the criminal law to proscribe particular conduct or activities requires a balancing of moral considerations and concepts of harm as well as an assessment of the extent to which the State has a legitimate interest in controlling the acts which an individual does in private which cause harm to no one else. Even if conduct is considered immoral and harmful this will not necessarily justify criminalisation. Other considerations may be relevant such as whether the law would be enforceable and whether a criminal sanction is necessary or appropriate to achieve the end in view. For example, one social problem and public health issue is the spread of sexually transmitted infections (STIs) such as chlamydia, gonorrhoea, and HIV. Sexual promiscuity may be part of the problem's causes. Greater sexual fidelity may reduce the spread of STIs and the harm to individuals and society. Some writers argue that the criminal law can and should play a central role in preventing and responding to the problem by punishing those who are blameworthy for transmitting STIs (for example, G. Mawhinney, 'To Be Ill or Kill: the Criminality of Contagion' (2013) 77(3) J Crim L 202–14). However, criminalising promiscuous sexual behaviour would be impossible to enforce without gross invasion of privacy; it may also be argued that the State has no legitimate interest in seeking to control private consensual sexual activity (see further *Brown* at **10.7.2**). Criminalisation is also not the only possible solution to the problem; greater education about contraception may be sufficient to reduce the spread of STIs. Moral considerations alone are not a sufficient reason for extending the reach of the criminal law. The evidence of the past 40 years also suggests that the view that it is the function of the criminal law to enforce morality is one which is in decline.

It is not possible therefore to present an equation which provides the answer to whether or not such behaviour should be classified as criminal. Many factors of varying weight and relevance have to be weighed in the balance. Furthermore the answer may vary over time as public perceptions of the role of the criminal law, the role of the State, the rights of the citizen, and social morality change.

1.3.4 Criminal law and punishment

Infringing the criminal law exposes the offender to the likelihood of punishment of some sort. What are the purposes of punishment?

1.3.4.1 Retribution

A major purpose which punishment serves is retribution. Under retributive theories, punishment is an end in itself. We do not need to look at the consequences of punishment to know whether punishment is worthwhile or meaningful. There is an intuitive connection between wrongdoing and State punishment. Punishment is meted out to the offender because that is what he deserves for his infraction of the criminal law. This was expressed by J. F. Stephen, *A History of the Criminal Law of England* (1883) (at pp. 81, 82):

> [T]he infliction of punishment by law gives definite expression and a solemn ratification and justification to the hatred which is excited by the commission of the offence, and which constitutes the moral or popular as distinguished from the conscientious sanction of that part of morality which is also sanctioned by the criminal law. The criminal law thus proceeds upon the principle that it is morally right to hate criminals, and it confirms and justifies that sentiment by inflicting upon criminals, punishments which express it.

To some extent, therefore, retribution reflects society's desire for vengeance. When people join together in a society governed by law, they relinquish their own right to retaliate in exchange for the protection which the law offers them. H. Gross gave expression to this view in *A Theory of Criminal Justice* (1979) (at pp. 19–20):

> But society requires that this right [to repay harm with harm] be surrendered by its members, and in exchange undertakes to protect them by laws that can be effective only if violations are punished. The bargain that is struck, then, places a moral obligation on society to punish crime as it places a moral obligation on its members to refrain from breaking the law.

Vengeance or retaliation is only one aspect of retribution. A further element is that of denunciation. The infliction of punishment signals society's disapproval of the criminal's conduct and reaffirms the values the criminal law is designed to uphold. This reflects the more modern view of the appropriate place for retribution in the criminal justice system. In *Sargeant* (1974) 60 Cr App R 74, a case concerning violent crime, Lawton LJ, after rejecting the idea of 'an eye for an eye', gave expression to this view (at p. 77):

> [S]ociety, through the courts, must show its abhorrence of particular types of crime, and the only way in which the courts can show this is by the sentences they pass. The courts do not have to reflect public opinion. On the other hand they must not disregard it. Perhaps the main duty of the court is to lead public opinion. Anyone who surveys the criminal scene at the present time must be alive to the appalling problem of violence. Society, we are satisfied, expects the courts to deal with violence . . . . Those who indulge in the kind of violence with which we are concerned in this case must expect custodial sentences.

The punishment inflicted, however, must not represent a blind act of vindictive retaliation; it must be both reasoned and reasonable. The idea which has gained ascendancy in recent years is that of 'just deserts' based on the philosophical ideas of Kant. A person who commits a crime has gained an unfair advantage over the other members of society. Punishment cancels out that advantage (particularly where the court orders confiscation, restitution, or compensation) while, at the same time, it reaffirms the values of that society by visiting moral disapproval or reprobation on the offender.

The punishment the criminal deserves, of course, must bear some relationship to the harm he has caused. Punishment can only be considered reasonable where the courts respect the concept of proportionality. Proportionality requires that a person receive no more and no less than he deserves for his offence. A justice system based on proportionality will ensure that offences of similar seriousness receive sentences that are broadly similar, so that theft of a chocolate bar from a shop is treated less harshly than sexual assault. Given that we no longer exact literal vengeance (in the talionic sense of an 'eye for an eye'), our modern system of retribution uses a range of common penal currencies to apply across the range of criminal offences, most frequently imprisonment, community sentences, fines, and discharges.

1.3.4.2 Deterrence

A second purpose which punishment can serve is deterrence, whether this be *particular* deterrence (i.e. dissuading the individual criminal from reoffending in the future) or *general* deterrence (i.e. dissuading other possible offenders from offending by the example made of each particular offender).

Deterrence theory rests on key assumptions about human beings, in particular that individuals are rational, carefully weighing the benefits and disadvantages of particular life choices. Jeremy Bentham was a leading proponent of utilitarianism, the theory upon which deterrence rests. He argued that 'pain and pleasure . . . govern us in all we do, all we say, in all we think' (*An Introduction to the Principles of Morals and Legislation* (1907), p. 1). At the extremes, we know that our behaviour will be affected by the prospect of severe punishment. Putting aside concerns about fairness for a moment, we know that people will be affected by the prospect of the death penalty for parking on a double-yellow line or submitting university coursework late. Of course, given that any rational and coherent penal system cannot simply ratchet up the severity of sanctions in this way, deterrence has to work more subtly.

What evidence is there that deterrence 'works' as a strategy? It is difficult to assess the effectiveness of individual deterrence. Some offenders may never offend again even if they are not caught or punished; others may only be deterred where the punishment imposed is so severe that it is out of all proportion to the gravity of the wrongdoing. In relation to general deterrence, courts, in the past, sometimes imposed exemplary sentences to deter others where an offence had become prevalent or was particularly grave (see e.g. *Wilson and Tutt* (1981) 3 Cr App R (S) 102; *Poh and To* [1982] Crim LR 132). While judges may have associated severe sentences with deterrence, the connection was not necessarily valid. In *The Sentence of the Court* (5th edn, 1990) published by the Home Office, it is stated (at para. 3.3):

> The simplest way of evaluating the individual deterrent effect of sentencing is to compare the proportions of offenders undergoing different types of sentence who, when free to do so, continue to commit offences. The almost invariable conclusion of the large amount of research which has been undertaken . . . is that it is hard to show any effect that one type of sentence is more likely than any other to reduce the likelihood of reoffending, which is high for all. Similarly, longer periods of custody or particular institutional regimes do not seem to have a significant effect. Studies comparing the reconviction rates of offenders given community service orders with those given custodial sentences have also shown little difference.

Different sentences therefore have little effect in deterring offenders. *The Sentence of the Court* goes on to state, however (at para. 3.4), that:

> The inference most commonly drawn from research studies is that the probability of arrest and conviction is likely to deter potential offenders whereas the perceived severity of the ensuing penalties has little effect.

Of course, detection and conviction must result in punishment if the rules are not to lose their coercive force. Whether a particular person is susceptible to coercion, however, may depend on other factors. H. Packer, *The Limits of the Criminal Sanction* (1968) observed (at p. 45):

> [T]he deterrent role of the criminal law is effective mainly with those who are subject to the dominant socializing influences of the day . . . . Deterrence does not threaten those whose lot in life is already miserable beyond the point of hope. It does not improve the morals of those whose value systems are closed to further modification, either psychologically . . . or culturally . . .

Thus, the deterrent role of the criminal process is a limited one; those who are set on committing crime may not be deterred by the criminal law. For most members of society, however, the criminal law may serve to educate them on acceptable and unacceptable conduct creating thereby unconscious inhibitions against offending. Gross makes this point (at p. 401):

> The threats are not laid down to deter those tempted to break the rules, but rather to maintain the rules as a set of standards that compel allegiance in spite of violations by those who commit crimes. In short, the rules of conduct laid down in the criminal law are a powerful social force upon which society is dependent for its very existence, and there is punishment for violation of these rules in order to prevent the dissipation of their power that would result if they were violated with impunity.

The most comprehensive research studies suggest there is a weak correlation between the severity of sanctions and crime rates, whereas there is evidence of a strong negative correlation between the *certainty* of sanctions and crime rates (von Hirsch et al., *Criminal Deterrence and Sentence Severity: An Analysis of Recent Research* (1999), p. 49). In other words, there is little evidence that simply increasing the severity of punishment will deter people from offending, but there is evidence that increasing the perception of the likelihood of getting caught will affect people's decisions to offend.

One area where deterrent sentences are used frequently is in respect of jury members who do not follow the oath they have sworn to try the case solely according to the evidence seen and heard in the trial. It is an offence under s. 20A of the Juries Act 1974 (as amended by the Criminal Justice and Courts Act 2015) for a juror to research the case by, for example, asking a question, searching the internet, visiting or inspecting a place or object, conducting an experiment, and asking another person to seek the information. There have been several instances of jury members being imprisoned for accessing the internet during the trial in order to search for information about the defendant, witnesses, or other information concerning the case they are hearing, despite trial judges' strict instructions not to do so (see A.T.H. Smith, 'Repositioning the Law of Contempt: the Criminal Justice and Courts Act 2015' [2015] Crim LR 845–54). In each case, the sentencing judge has stressed the importance of sending out a deterrent message to other jury members that they must not break the law (Law Commission (2013) *Contempt of Court: Juror Misconduct and Internet Publications* http://www.lawcom.gov.uk/project/contempt-of-court-juror-misconduct-and-internet-publications/).

1.3.4.3 Incapacitation

Incapacitation, like deterrence and rehabilitation, is a forward-looking approach to punishment (not in the sense that it is necessarily progressive, but rather that we sentence on the basis of the effects of punishment on future offending behaviour). Retribution is backward-looking; we look backwards to the offender's conduct and punish him for that conduct, in proportion to the seriousness of the offence. We express a fitting amount of disapproval and opprobrium. Incapacitation quite simply focuses on preventing the offender from committing offences in the future.

Incapacitation can mean imprisonment, most obviously. But it can take other forms, such as capital punishment (no longer available in English law); disqualification from driving (under the Road Traffic Offenders Act 1988); and football banning orders (under s. 14A of the Football Supporters Act 1989), which prevent persons convicted of football-related offences from entering football grounds and travelling to football matches outside of the United Kingdom. Each removes the offender's ability to reoffend, permanently or temporarily.

Incapacitation as a form of punishment can be controversial. Section 142 of the Criminal Justice Act 2003 lists 'the protection of the public' as one of the aims of sentencing to which any sentencing court must have regard (see **1.3.4.6**). Imagine that you are a judge or magistrate and the offender before you for sentencing has been found guilty of theft. You have reports from a probation officer that indicate he has a heroin addiction directly linked to the commission of the offence (he stole a smartphone that he hoped to sell quickly in order to buy drugs). The reports also indicate that he has significant issues with anger management and is highly likely to be involved in minor acts of violence, particularly when intoxicated. However, the offence he has committed did not involve violence. If the rationale for punishment that guides you in sentencing is public protection, then you are likely to focus on the future risk he poses. Imprisonment is likely to be an appealingly simple sentence for you to use. For the time that he is imprisoned, he will not be able to offend (at least in public).

However, while incapacitation might be simple in the short term, there are significant issues with both the fairness and effectiveness of incapacitation as a penal theory and practice. Incapacitation can be unfair. The sentence a judge might want to impose to protect the public could be disproportionate to the offence he has committed (in our example, a life sentence will protect the public, but be much longer than is commensurate with the offence, which is theft of a smartphone). Incapacitation might also be ineffective in the long term as it may do little to address the causes of offending behaviour.

The Government introduced controversial sentences of imprisonment for public protection (IPPs) in the Criminal Justice Act 2003, the relevant sections of which came into effect in 2005. These were intended to protect the public from offenders whose offences were not serious enough to warrant life imprisonment but who were thought to be dangerous enough to warrant imprisonment for longer than their offence(s) alone deserved. An IPP is an indeterminate sentence. A person serving one will only be released if he can show the Parole Board that it is no longer necessary for the protection of the public that he be detained (under the Crime (Sentences) Act 1997). The courts imposed thousands of IPPs, as the original legislation required them to impose an IPP if the offender had committed one of a broad range of specified offences and the court considered that there was 'a significant risk to members of the public of serious harm occasioned by the commission by him of further specified offences' (J. Jacobson and M. Hough, *Unjust Deserts: Imprisonment for Public Protection* (2010) Prison Reform Trust, http://www.prisonreformtrust.org.uk/uploads/documents/unjustdesertsfinal.pdf).

Controversies with IPPs illustrate broader problems with incapacitation as a penal strategy. First, predicting likely future behaviour is very difficult. There is evidence that courts tend to over-predict the level of danger that offenders pose (Jacobson and Hough, p. 3), meaning that more offenders received IPPs than were likely actually to commit further specified offences. Secondly, the burden is on the offender to show the Parole Board that it is no longer necessary for the protection of the public that he be detained. That can be very difficult to demonstrate, given that prisons are limited in the number and type of rehabilitative and educational schemes offenders can access to address their offending behaviour. When IPPs were introduced such schemes and programmes were not widely available so offenders with short minimum periods often reached the end of those periods before they could gain access to the relevant rehabilitative programmes. In addition, the practice of moving prisoners within the penal system (usually because of overcrowding) often means prisoners cannot complete these programmes before being moved. Rehabilitative programmes are also expensive to provide and since the 2008 financial crisis, government cutbacks to public services, including prisons, have meant there is less money available to direct towards those whom the public quite often regard as undeserving (Jacobson and Hough, p. 19).

Following the Legal Aid, Sentencing and Punishment of Offenders Act 2012, courts can no longer impose new IPPs although many offenders remain in prison on IPPs, with little prospect of release. Many offenders have served terms of imprisonment significantly longer than their original offences deserved (e.g. BBC News Online, 'The prisoner "trapped" 10 years into a 10-month jail sentence', 30 May 2016). In this sense, incapacitation can mean sentences that are disproportionate to the offence(s) committed.

Incapacitation can be an appealing short-term solution that masks more complex problems within our criminal justice system. Many of those in prison, and a significant number serving IPPs, have mental disorders, personality disorders, and/or are on psychiatric medication. There are significantly higher rates of mental health problems amongst prisoners than the general population ('The Bradley Report', *Lord Bradley's Review of People with Mental Health Problems or Learning Disabilities in the Criminal Justice System* (2009) p. 8). There are also very low levels of literacy amongst prisoners, a problem exacerbated by the difficulties of providing educational services to prisoners in a time of public sector 'austerity' (Criminal Justice Joint Inspection (2015), *A Joint Inspection of the Treatment of Offenders with Learning Disabilities Within the Criminal Justice System*, http://www.justiceinspectorates.gov.uk/cjji/inspections/learningdisabilitiesphase2/).

1.3.4.4 **Rehabilitation**

The pre-1960s penal debate was premised upon the idea of rehabilitation. Proba-tion was introduced as a disposal following conviction to give effect to this reha-bilitative ideal. The idea of rehabilitation even found expression in the Prison Rules 1964 which stated that 'the purpose of the training and treatment of con-victed prisoners shall be to encourage and assist them to lead a good and useful life'. The idea of rehabilitation also underpins parole, which was introduced by the Criminal Justice Act 1967. So far as prison is concerned this ideal has largely been abandoned as the problems of overcrowding and underfunding have taken their toll, making the most immediate concern of prison governors that of containment.

In the 1970s there was been a movement away from rehabilitation as an objective of punishment. Studies on both sides of the Atlantic revealed that the recidivism rate varies little between offenders who received retributive sentences and those who received rehabilitative sentences (see e.g. S. R. Brody, *The Effectiveness of Sen-tencing* (Home Office Research Study No. 35, 1976)). Similarly, rehabilitation as a basis for sentencing offenders led to disparity in punishment as the sentencer was looking to the needs of the offender rather than the offence committed as the start-ing point in determining the appropriate sentence.

During the 1980s and early 1990s there was a growing interest on the part of the Home Office in community sentences as these may be as effective as prison, in terms both of their retributive and deterrent value, and incur a lower financial and social cost as the prisoner can serve his sentence (e.g. community service) in the community. Interest in such punishments has revived as recent governments have called for a 'rehabilitation revolution' in penal policy (Ministry of Justice (2013), *Transforming Rehabilitation: A Revolution in the Way We Manage Offenders*, https://consult.justice.gov.uk/digital-communications/transforming-rehabilitation/ supporting_documents/transformingrehabilitation.pdf). The Government has reduced the overall budget of the Prison Service and sought to reduce the number of offenders sentenced to imprisonment. There is much research evidence that reveals the nature and extent of criminogenic factors (such as the links between drugs and acquisitive crime, and between alcohol and violent crime) (Ministry of Justice (2013), *The Factors Associated with Proven Re-offending Following Release from Prison*, https://www.gov.uk/government/uploads/system/uploads/attachment_ data/file/491119/re-offending-release-waves-1-3-spcr-findings.pdf). There is also emerging evidence on the types of intervention that are most effective in helping offenders move away from criminality (Ministry of Justice (2013), *Transforming Rehabilitation: A Summary of Evidence on Reducing Reoffending*, https://www.gov.uk/ government/uploads/system/uploads/attachment_data/file/243718/evidence-reduce-reoffending.pdf).

1.3.4.5 **Reparation and restorative justice**

Since the 1980s, another set of approaches to dealing with offenders has grown in practical and academic importance, all falling under the umbrella term 'restor-ative justice' (RJ). Marshall defined RJ as 'a process whereby parties with a stake in a specific offence collectively resolve how to deal with the aftermath of the offence and its implications for the future' (T. Marshall, *Restorative Justice: An Overview* (1999) Home Office Research Development & Statistics Directorate,

London, p. 5). Daniel Van Ness states its principal objective is the 'restoration into safe communities of victims and offenders who have resolved their conflicts' (D. Van Ness, 'New Wines and Old Wineskins: Four Challenges of Restorative Justice' (1993) 4 *Criminal Law Forum* 251, 257). RJ's proponents argue that victims and community members can and should have an active role in criminal justice and the resolution of conflicts. RJ promotes an alternative approach to the concept of crime; it requires seeing crime not as an abstract offence against the State, but rather as harmful conduct causing injury, distress, and suffering, and as a symptom of a deeper community or social malaise (I. Edwards, 'Restorative Justice, Sentencing and the Court of Appeal' [2006] Crim LR 110–23, 113). In contrast to the traditional criminal justice system (which RJ advocates say deals merely with crime's symptoms), RJ seeks to deal with both the causes *and* the symptoms.

In practice, RJ can mean a range of things, from the offender literally repairing the damage he has caused (e.g. by cleaning graffiti from the victim's property), to restorative meetings between victim and offender in which the victim can express to the offender how they have suffered and the offender has an opportunity to explain and apologise. RJ theory posits that victim satisfaction with the process will be boosted, their emotional distress lessened, and offenders will have a chance to make amends for the harms they have caused and be reintegrated into the community. Restorative justice has grown in importance in recent years, particularly in pre-trial schemes that divert offenders from the criminal justice system such as 'conditional cautions' (CPS (2013), *The Director's Guidance on Adult Conditional Cautions*, https://www.cps.gov.uk/publications/directors_guidance/adult_conditional_cautions.html).

1.3.4.6 The current sentencing framework

Until 1991 the sentencing system in England and Wales lacked a coherent structure. Retribution, deterrence, incapacitation, and rehabilitation were all advocated by courts and governments as the aims of sentencing, without there being any explanation of how these aims were to be reconciled or of which was to take priority if they came into conflict (see e.g. *Sargeant* (1974) 60 Cr App R 74). In the late 1980s the Government began to consider the sentencing system and the relative merits of the various objectives that may be achieved through punishment. The Government's approach was set out in the White Paper, *Crime, Justice and Protecting the Public* (Cm 965, 1990). It was recognised that rehabilitation, while it may be sought, may not always be achieved and cannot be used as a justification for imprisonment (see paras 2.6 and 2.7). Deterrence, while it may have immediate appeal, probably operates only with those who are law-abiding in the first place. The White Paper stated (at para. 2.8):

> But much crime is committed on impulse, given the opportunity presented by an open window or unlocked door, and it is committed by offenders who live from moment to moment; their crimes are as impulsive as the rest of their feckless, sad, or pathetic lives. It is unrealistic to construct sentencing arrangements on the assumption that most offenders will weigh up the possibilities in advance and base their conduct on rational calculation. Often they do not.

The approach the Government opted for, therefore, was one based on the idea of retribution. The White Paper stated (at para. 2.9):

> The Government's proposals therefore emphasise the objectives which sentencing is most likely to meet successfully in whole or in part. The first objective for all sentences is denunciation of and retribution for the crime. Depending on the offence and the offender, the sentence may also aim to achieve public protection, reparation and reform of the offender, preferably in the community. This approach points to sentencing policies which are more firmly based on the seriousness of the offence, and just deserts for the offender.

In 1991 the Criminal Justice Act was passed reflecting in its provisions, to a large extent, the views expressed in the White Paper. Its sentencing provisions were subsequently consolidated with other sentencing legislation in the Powers of Criminal Courts (Sentencing) Act 2000. The emphasis on retribution was apparent in that the concept of proportionality was made a central principle of sentencing.

Since 2000 there have been several major pieces of legislation dealing with sentencing, making for immense complexity when it comes to trying to determine whether a provision is in force, has been amended, or repealed and in trying to determine what sentence is actually available for any particular offence. (It should be borne in mind that while prosecution and conviction may occur many years after an offence was committed the court is limited to applying the law that was in force at the time of the offence.) However, the Criminal Justice Act 2003 (CJA 2003) provides a smorgasbord in s. 142, which sets out the purposes of sentencing as follows:

> (1) Any court dealing with an offender in respect of his offence must have regard to the following:
>   (a) the punishment of offenders,
>   (b) the reduction of crime (including its reduction by deterrence),
>   (c) the reform and rehabilitation of offenders,
>   (d) the protection of the public, and
>   (e) the making of reparation by offenders to persons affected by their offences.

The sentencing framework is based on threshold tests for imposing custodial and community sentences. Section 152(2) of the CJA 2003 provides:

> The court must not pass a custodial sentence unless it is of the opinion that the offence, or the combination of the offence and one or more offences associated with it, was so serious that neither a fine alone nor a community sentence can be justified for the offence.

Section 153(2) requires that where a fixed-term custodial sentence is passed it should be for 'the shortest term that is commensurate with the seriousness of the offence'.

The threshold for community sentences is set out in s. 148(1) of the CJA 2003:

> A court must not pass a community sentence on an offender unless it is of the opinion that the offence, or the combination of the offence and one or more offences associated with it, was serious enough to warrant such a sentence.

By s. 148(2) when imposing a community sentence, the court must ensure that the restriction on liberty placed on the offender is commensurate with the seriousness of the offence. Prison, accordingly, is to be reserved as a punishment for the most serious offences, but even if the custody threshold is satisfied, personal mitigation factors may come into play and dictate that a fine or community penalty is more appropriate. Section 166 provides that courts can take into account any 'such matters as they consider relevant in mitigation of sentence'. This preserves the discretion of judges and magistrates to take account of factors such as poor mental or physical health, age, remorse, and so on when deciding what type of sentence to impose and how onerous it should be.

The *seriousness* of the offence is central to assessing both what type of sentence is appropriate (custodial, community, financial) and the length or burden of the sentence (e.g. how many years' imprisonment, how many hours of unpaid work, how much of a fine: under s. 164, the amount of a fine that the court imposes must reflect the seriousness of the offence and take into account the offender's financial circumstances). Sentencers must thus start by considering the seriousness of the offence. Section 143(1) of the 2003 Act states that '[i]n considering the seriousness of any offence, the court must consider the offender's culpability in committing the offence and any harm which the offence caused, was intended to cause or might forseeably have caused'.

Section 143(2) is of considerable importance. It states that when considering how serious the offender's offence is, the court *must* treat as an aggravating factor any recent and relevant previous convictions that the offender has. If the offence was committed on bail, the court must treat that as an aggravating factor (s. 143(3)).

The 2003 Act, by s. 167, also created the Sentencing Guidelines Council (SGC) to give guidance to the courts on sentencing. The Coroners and Justice Act 2009 replaced the SGC with the Sentencing Council (SC). The SGC was, and the SC is, responsible for issuing general guidance on sentencing and guidelines for specific offences (see http://www.sentencingcouncil.org.uk). Under s. 125(1) of the Coroners and Justice Act 2009, sentencers must follow any relevant sentencing guidelines unless it would be contrary to the interests of justice to do so. There is now an extensive list of sentencing guidelines covering most of the main offence categories, including theft, fraud, robbery, sexual offences, assaults, drugs offences, manslaughter, intimidatory offences, and offensive weapons.

In its *Overarching Principles: Seriousness* Guideline (2004), the SGC provided guidance on how a sentencer should approach an individual case when choosing from the smorgasbord of purposes:

1.3 The sentencer must start by considering the *seriousness* of the offence, the assessment of which will:
- determine which of the sentencing thresholds has been crossed;
- indicate whether a custodial, community or other sentence is most appropriate;
- be the key factor in deciding the length of a custodial sentence, the onerousness of requirements to be incorporated in a community sentence and the amount of any fine imposed.

1.4 A court is required to pass a sentence that is commensurate with the seriousness of the offence. The *seriousness* of an offence is determined by two main parameters: the *culpability* of the offender and the *harm* caused or risked being caused by the offence.

The guidance goes on, at 1.6 and 1.7, to set out the hierarchy of the levels of criminal culpability as intention to cause harm, recklessness as to causing harm, knowledge by a defendant of the risks his actions entail, and negligence. 'Harm' itself may be harm to individuals such as 'physical injury, sexual violation, financial loss, damage to health or psychological distress' (1.9). Where no harm has arisen from the offence, for example where the conviction is for conspiracy or attempt, the court will assess the relative dangerousness of the offender's conduct considering 'the likelihood of harm occurring and the gravity of the harm that could have resulted' (1.11). Community harm may include 'economic loss, harm to public health, or interference with the administration of justice' (1.12).

The guidance recognises that assessing seriousness is a difficult task, particularly so where there is an imbalance between culpability and harm (1.15) as sometimes the harm that results may be greater than that intended (1.16; see e.g. **9.3.3.1**, 'Constructive manslaughter') or the culpability may be higher than the harm resulting from the offence (1.16; see e.g. **Chapter 8**, 'Inchoate offences'). In fixing the level of culpability courts also have to factor in motive, whether the offence was planned or spontaneous and whether the offender was in a position of trust (1.17).

Particular offences have sentencing guidelines that include lists of the aggravating and mitigating factors relevant to those offences. Offence guidelines provide sentence ranges and starting points which relate to offence seriousness and which the sentencer will use as a baseline against which to factor in particular aggravating and mitigating factors.

Sentencing is, accordingly, an extremely complex task with courts having to evaluate and balance so many different factors when sentencing an offender for a particular offence. It is unsurprising that courts make errors and that many appeals against sentence are pursued each year. In the year October 2016 to September 2017 the Court of Appeal dealt with 2,659 applications to appeal sentence (The Court of Appeal (Criminal Division), *Annual Report 2016–2017*, p. 24). These complexities, however, elude politicians, commentators, and tabloid journalists when they raise a hue and cry over the latest unduly lenient sentence that provokes their ire. Inevitably, calls for further legislation and demands for greater consistency in sentencing ensue without any recognition of the fact that every offence and every offender is different and that very different sentences for two offenders convicted of the same offence may be both justifiable and consistent.

One area that particularly mystifies members of the public is why offenders receive discounts for pleading guilty. Under s. 144 of the Criminal Justice Act 2003, if the offender has pleaded guilty, the sentencing court must take into account the stage in the proceedings at which he indicated he would plead guilty and the circumstances in which he gave that indication. The current sentencing guideline for guilty pleas states that the defendant is entitled to a one third discount if his guilty plea is indicated at the first stage of proceedings (normally the first hearing at which a plea or indication of plea is sought and recorded by the court), with a sliding scale of reduction in the discount for pleading guilty to one tenth if the guilty plea is entered on the first day of trial (Sentencing Council, *Reduction in Sentence for a Guilty Plea Definitive Guideline*, 2017, p. 5). The reduction can be decreased further, even to zero, if the guilty plea is indicated during the course of the trial. There is a separate scale of reductions for guilty pleas in murder cases, with a maximum possible reduction of one sixth and never more than five years (p. 8).

English law provides such discounts to encourage early guilty pleas, which have several benefits. In particular, victims and witnesses will be spared the ordeal of having to go to court and give evidence and there will be cost savings for the police, the Crown Prosecution Service, and Her Majesty's Courts and Tribunals Service. Such cost savings could be argued to benefit witnesses and victims in allowing time and resources to be concentrated on investigating and prosecuting other cases. Having a guideline on the appropriate reduction for a guilty plea promotes consistency and allows defence lawyers to give accurate advice to defendants.

As you learn about the substantive criminal law, remember that it would be highly misleading to say that breaching the law always or even usually results in imprisonment. Imprisonment is one of a range of sentences that judges and magistrates can impose and is used in only a small percentage of cases in England and Wales. Statistics show that the most common sentence given is actually a fine, accounting for 75 per cent of all sentences in 2017 (Ministry of Justice (2018), *Criminal Justice Statistics Quarterly, England and Wales, December 2017*, p. 23). Fines have been consistently the most common sentence in the last decade. Community orders were imposed on 8 per cent of offenders in 2017. Approximately 4 per cent received a suspended sentence of imprisonment. Immediate custody was imposed on 7 per cent of all adult offenders sentenced in 2017, of which 16 per cent were for one month or less.

The use of non-custodial sentences needs to be seen in the context of the financial pressures on the Government. Imprisonment is expensive. The average annual cost per prisoner in 2014/15 was £35,371 (Ministry of Justice (2017), *Costs Per Place and Costs Per Prisoner By Individual Prison*, p. 3). As we saw at **1.3.1**, in 1990 the Government described imprisonment as 'an expensive way of making bad people worse'. Research suggests that there is a high recidivism rate for offenders who receive short custodial sentences compared to similarly situated offenders who receive community sentences or suspended sentences of imprisonment for similar offences (Ministry of Justice (2015), *The Impact of Short Custodial Sentences, Community Orders and Suspended Sentence Orders on Re-offending*, pp. 1–3). Short-term custody (less than 12 months in prison, without supervision on release) was consistently associated with higher rates of proven reoffending than community orders and suspended sentence orders. There is evidence that particular requirements imposed as part of community orders and suspended sentence orders have great benefits in terms of reducing reoffending compared to short custodial sentences. At the start of 2019, the Government announced it was considering abolishing sentences of imprisonment of less than six months, the Prisons Minister stating that they are 'long enough to damage you and not long enough to heal you' ('Ministers consider ending jail terms of six months or less' BBC News Online, 12 January 2019, https://www.bbc.co.uk/news/uk-46847162).

1.4 Substantive criminal law and the criminal process

While this book is focused on the substantive criminal law, appreciating some procedural aspects of the criminal process will help us understand the substantive criminal law in the context of the criminal justice system as a whole.

1.4.1 **Classifying offences**

There are thousands of criminal offences, the vast majority being of statutory creation and of a regulatory nature. Our concern is generally with the major offences (e.g. murder, manslaughter, rape, assault, theft, robbery, burglary, criminal damage, deception) and the general principles underlying criminal liability. While most offences are now of statutory creation, the criminal law originally was laid down in judges' decisions. Some offences, such as murder and manslaughter, are still common law offences lacking a statutory definition.

At common law, crimes were classified generally as either felonies or misdemeanours. Subsequently this classification was adopted by Parliament when it came to create offences by legislation. The principal felonies were homicide, rape, theft, burglary, robbery, and arson. A misdemeanour was any offence that was not a felony. Felonies were more serious than misdemeanours. The classification had important consequences in terms of the power of arrest and the penalties available on conviction. There was a general power of arrest without warrant in respect of felonies but not in respect of misdemeanours. On conviction for a felony the felon was liable to forfeiture of his land and goods (abolished by the Forfeiture Act 1870). Gradually the distinctions between felonies and misdemeanours were eroded by legislation. Finally, in the Criminal Justice Act 1967, all distinctions between felonies and misdemeanours were abolished.

1.4.2 **Mode of trial**

A second classification of offences relates to mode of trial, with a distinction between **summary** and **indictable** offences. Summary offences are less serious than indictable offences and are tried before a magistrates' court. Indictable offences are more serious and are tried in the Crown Court before a judge and jury. Many offences are *triable either way* (see s. 17 of and sch. 1 to the Magistrates' Courts Act 1980 (MCA 1980)). Theft is one such offence; the maximum penalty available on trial on indictment is seven years' imprisonment whereas the maximum sentence which a magistrates' court may impose is generally six months' imprisonment (see s. 31 of the 1980 Act; but should s. 154 of the Criminal Justice Act 2003 ever come into force the maximum in respect of any one offence will be 12 months).

The magistrates make the allocation decision whether an offence should be tried summarily or on indictment where it is triable either way having regard to the representations made by the prosecutor and the accused and all the case's circumstances (see s. 19 of the 1980 Act). The magistrates' court must also follow the Sentencing Council's definitive *Allocation Guideline* (2015), which states that either-way offences should be tried summarily unless the outcome would clearly be a sentence in excess of the court's powers for the offence(s) concerned after taking into account personal mitigation and any potential reduction for a guilty plea. The guideline also states that either-way offences should be tried in the Crown Court if they are of unusual legal, procedural, or factual complexity.

For some offences, the value of sums involved determines the venue of the trial. For offences of criminal damage, if the value of the alleged damage is less than £5,000 then the case will be tried summarily (MCA 1980, s. 22). This has led on occasion to the unusual situation where defendants have argued that the damage they are alleged to have committed is particularly costly and valued at more than £5,000 so that they can secure trial by jury. This has arisen in some cases involving environmental protesters who have campaigned against the development of genetically modified crops by damaging or destroying them (e.g. *R (Abbott)* v *Colchester Magistrates' Court* [2001] EWHC Admin 136). They have sought trial by jury so that they plead 'lawful excuse' and appeal to the jury's sympathies (see **Chapter 15**).

If the court decides to proceed summarily they must ask the defendant whether he consents to be so tried, or whether he wishes to assert his right to trial by jury (see s. 20 of the 1980 Act as amended by sch. 3, para. 6 of the Criminal Justice Act 2003). The right to trial by jury, which dominates public perceptions of the criminal trial, is thus rooted in the mode of trial decision.

Why might defendants choose trial by jury over trial in the magistrates' courts? It is possible that some defendants perceive that there is a higher conviction rate in the magistrates' court than the Crown Court and that their chances of acquittal are greater if they elect trial by jury. Black and minority ethnic defendants in particular might perceive that trial by jury will be fairer, particularly if they think that they are unlikely to get a fair hearing in the magistrates' court (S. Cammiss (2004), *Determining Mode of Trial: An Analysis of Decision Making in Magistrates' Courts*). The right to elect trial by jury for either-way offences has been controversial in recent years, particularly as trial in the Crown Court is more expensive than trial in the magistrates' court. The National Audit Office estimates that if all of the 61,473 'either-way' cases heard in the Crown Court in 2014–15 had been held in the magistrates' court, court running costs would have been reduced by £45.1 million (National Audit Office (2016), *Efficiency in the Criminal Justice System*, HC 852, https://www.nao.org.uk/wp-content/uploads/2016/03/Efficiency-in-the-criminal-justice-system.pdf, p. 23). Successive governments have thus tried to restrict this right. First, they have attempted (unsuccessfully) to remove entirely the right of defendants to elect trial by jury and make the allocation decision solely one for the magistrates (e.g. the Labour Government introduced the Criminal Justice (Mode of Trial) Bills in 1999/2000 to effect such a change, but met with fierce resistance in Parliament from those who defended the right to elect). Secondly, they have reclassified triable-either-way offences as summary-only, which has the effect of restricting the number of cases being heard in the Crown Court (e.g. common assault was reclassified as a summary-only offence by s. 39 of the Criminal Justice Act 1988).

1.4.3 Substantive criminal law and the decision to prosecute

The substantive criminal law's definition and scope are also crucial to the work of the Crown Prosecution Service (CPS), the statutory body responsible under the Prosecution of Offences Act 1985 for prosecuting the vast majority of criminal offences in England and Wales (there are other bodies with responsibility for particular areas of criminality, such as the Serious Fraud Office and the Revenue and Customs Prosecution Office). The CPS must decide what offence(s) to charge a suspect with. The case-file from the police might suggest a range of possible offences with which the suspect could be charged. Under the *Code for Crown Prosecutors*, the CPS must decide two things: whether prosecution is in the public interest and whether there is sufficient evidence for a realistic prospect of conviction (CPS, 2013). For example, imagine that a person driving a car has injured a pedestrian after driving in a way that falls below the standard of a normal driver. The CPS will have to decide what offence, if any, he has committed. Is this a case of careless and inconsiderate driving under s. 3 of the Road Traffic Act 1988 or dangerous driving under s. 2 of that Act? The person might be guilty of causing serious injury by dangerous driving under s. 1A of that Act if the injury amounts to 'grievous bodily harm'. If the injuries are not serious enough to be so described, a separate charge under s. 47 or s. 20 of the Offences Against the Person Act 1861 might be appropriate (CPS Road Traffic Offences—*Guidance on Charging Offences Arising from Driving Incidents* http://www.cps.gov.uk/legal/p_to_r/road_traffic_offences_guidance_on_prosecuting_cases_of_bad_driving/).

The CPS's policies are of great significance in providing guidance to prosecutors for the real-life application of complex or controversial areas of law. For example, a person commits an offence under s. 2 of the Suicide Act 1961 if he or she does an act capable of encouraging or assisting the suicide or attempted suicide of another person, and that act was intended to encourage or assist suicide or an attempt at suicide. The consent of the Director of Public Prosecutions (DPP) is required before an individual may be prosecuted. There have been several cases in which individuals who have wanted to commit suicide but been physically unable to do so have sought to challenge the legality of that offence and clarify its parameters. The House of Lords in *R (on the application of Purdy)* v *Director of Public Prosecutions* reported at [2009] UKHL 45 required the DPP 'to clarify what his position is as to the factors that he regards as relevant for and against prosecution' (para. 55) in cases of encouraging and assisting suicide. In response, the CPS published guidance on how prosecutors should apply the two-stage test in these difficult cases, including identifying 16 factors that may weigh in favour of prosecution being in the public interest and six factors that tend against prosecution. The policy does not change the law but does provide more detail than the CPS's generic Code and enables us to understand how these cases will be dealt with in real life.

An important, informal part of the criminal process is 'charge-bargaining' (or 'plea-bargaining'). The offence with which the suspect is charged might not be the offence to which the offender ultimately pleads guilty or of which he is found guilty. The CPS can alter charges or terminate proceedings altogether. *The Code for Crown Prosecutors* states that prosecutors should select charges that reflect the seriousness and extent of the offending supported by the evidence and give the court adequate powers to sentence and impose appropriate post-conviction orders (para. 6.1). The Code also says that prosecutors should 'never go ahead with more charges than are necessary just to encourage a defendant to plead guilty to a few. In the same way, they should never go ahead with a more serious charge just to encourage a defendant to plead guilty to a less serious one' (para. 6.3). However, the Code later states that:

9.2 Prosecutors should only accept the defendant's plea if they think the court is able to pass a sentence that matches the seriousness of the offending, particularly where there are aggravating features. Prosecutors must never accept a guilty plea just because it is convenient.

9.3 In considering whether the pleas offered are acceptable, prosecutors should ensure that the interests and, where possible, the views of the victim, or in appropriate cases the views of the victim's family, are taken into account when deciding whether it is in the public interest to accept the plea. However, the decision rests with the prosecutor.

It is possible then that the CPS will decide to accept a guilty plea to a lesser offence than that with which the suspect was originally charged (e.g. malicious wounding under s. 20 of the Offences Against the Person Act 1861 instead of wounding with intent to cause grievous bodily harm under s. 18).

1.4.4 Burden and standard of proof

In criminal cases the burden of proof is on the prosecution; it is for the prosecution to prove the charge against the accused, which may also involve disproving any defence the accused raises. The prosecution will seek to prove its case by calling evidence such as that from witnesses to the alleged offence, forensic evidence, evidence of incriminating items found in the accused's possession, a confession he may have made to the police, and circumstantial evidence—for example, his presence at the scene of the crime before or shortly after it was committed. If the prosecution fail to establish a prima facie case that the accused committed the alleged offence, the judge will, at the conclusion of the prosecution case, direct the jury to acquit the accused. If a prima facie case is made out, the trial will continue and the accused may call witnesses, present evidence, and testify himself if he so desires. At the conclusion of all the evidence the prosecution and defence will make their closing submissions and the judge will sum up to the jury, whose task is then to reach a verdict. The jury are only entitled to convict the accused if the prosecution has discharged the burden of proof and satisfied them beyond reasonable doubt of the accused's guilt. If the jury are left with a reasonable doubt as to his guilt they must acquit; they may not be satisfied that he is innocent, but if they are not sure of his guilt the case against him has not been proved.

This rule was expressed clearly in the House of Lords in *Woolmington* v *DPP* [1935] AC 462.

> D was charged with the murder of his wife who had left him. His defence was that he had gone to his wife taking the gun with him to show her and tell her that he was going to commit suicide, and in showing it to her it had gone off accidentally. The judge directed the jury that once the prosecution proved that D killed the deceased, it was for D to show that the killing was not murder. The House of Lords held that this was a misdirection. The accused in a criminal trial is presumed innocent until proved guilty. It was not enough to show that D had done the act, it had also to be proved that he did so with the necessary criminal intent. It was for the prosecution to prove this rather than for the defence to disprove it. Viscount Sankey LC stated (at pp. 481–2):

> > Throughout the web of the English criminal law one golden thread is always to be seen, that it is the duty of the prosecution to prove the prisoner's guilt . . . . If, at the end of and on the whole of the case, there is a reasonable doubt, created by the evidence given by either the prosecution or the prisoner, as to whether the prisoner killed the deceased with a malicious intention, the prosecution has not made out the case and the prisoner is entitled to an acquittal. No matter what the charge or where the trial, the principle that the prosecution must prove the guilt of the prisoner is part of the common law of England and no attempt to whittle it down can be entertained.

While the overall burden of proof is upon the prosecution, the accused may have either an evidential burden or a burden of proof in respect of any defence he may seek to raise. If the accused's defence is anything more than a simple denial that he committed the alleged offence, he will bear an evidential burden to make this a live issue in the trial. The prosecution cannot be expected to anticipate all the possible defences an accused might raise. Accordingly, the burden on them to negate the accused's defence only arises when the accused has raised that defence. In *Woolmington* the accused's defence was accident; it was incumbent upon him to tender some evidence to this effect, either by testifying himself or calling other witnesses or by cross-examination of prosecution witnesses. Once he had raised this issue the prosecution was obliged to disprove it if they were to secure a conviction. Similarly, if the accused wishes to raise other defences such as self-defence, or duress, or automatism, he must discharge this evidential burden.

In some exceptional cases, however, a burden of proof is cast upon the accused in respect of certain defences he may wish to raise. The only such exception at common law is that of insanity. If D wishes to plead that he was insane at the time he committed the offence with which he is charged, he bears the burden of proving insanity. Other exceptions have been created by statute—for example, diminished responsibility (s. 2(2) of the Homicide Act 1957) or 'lawful authority or reasonable excuse' for the possession of an offensive weapon in a public place (s. 1(1) of the Prevention of Crime Act 1953). Where a burden of proof is cast upon the accused he is not required to prove his defence beyond reasonable doubt, but rather to the civil standard of proof; that is, he must prove his defence on a balance of probabilities (see *Carr-Briant* [1943] KB 607, 610).

In respect of some sexual offences, the Sexual Offences Act 2003 (s. 75) states that the jury can presume that the complainant did not consent and that the defendant did not reasonably believe that the complainant consented if the prosecution can prove that one of six circumstances existed. If they can, the defendant bears the burden of adducing sufficient evidence to 'raise an issue' as to whether the complainant consented or the defendant reasonably believed she did. This is known as a rebuttal presumption, meaning that the defendant has to rebut the presumption in order for the issue to be live at trial. The Act also states that in two circumstances there will be a *conclusive* presumption that the complainant did not consent and that the defendant did not believe that the complainant consented (see **Chapter 8**). The defendant will not be able to rebut the presumption.

1.4.5 **The functions of judge and jury**

The judge is in overall control of the proceedings. He will decide all legal questions which may arise—for example, whether a particular piece of evidence is admissible, whether a particular witness may be compelled to testify, and whether the prosecution has raised a prima facie case against the accused. At the end of the prosecution case, the defence may submit that there is 'no case to answer' and the judge should allow that submission and stop the trial when there is no evidence upon which, if the jury accepted the evidence adduced by the prosecution, a reasonable jury, properly directed, could convict (*R v Galbraith* [1981] 1 WLR 1039). At the end of the case he will sum up to the jury. This will usually involve a summary of the evidence which each side has tendered and may involve, in addition, pointing out inconsistencies in the evidence or omissions, or points where both sides are not in dispute, thereby highlighting the key issues which will have to be settled by the jury. The judge will also direct the jury on the law. He will instruct them on the necessary requirements of the offence which the prosecution must prove and the requirements of any defence the accused has raised which they must disprove or which he must prove. The jury's task then will be to determine what the facts were and apply the law to these facts to see whether all the requirements of the offence have been proved and the requirements of any defence negated by the prosecution. If the jury are satisfied beyond reasonable doubt that all these requirements have been proved or negated they will convict. If, however, the jury have a doubt as to any requirement of the offence which may not have been proved, or a requirement of the defence which may not have been negated, or, if it is a case where the defence have a burden of proof, they are satisfied that the defence have discharged that burden, they must acquit. Following the House of Lords' judgment in *R* v *Wang* [2005] UKHL 9, there are no circumstances in which a judge is entitled to direct a jury to return a verdict of guilty.

One problem which has arisen in recent years is the tendency of judges to avoid their responsibility to declare and explain the law to the jury. In specifying the requirements of a particular offence, it is the responsibility of the judge to explain to the jury what particular words mean. For example, the offence of burglary is committed, inter alia, where the accused enters a building as a trespasser, and steals therein (see s. 9(1)(b) of the Theft Act 1968). It is not sufficient for the judge blandly to state to the jury that the prosecution must prove (i) that the accused entered, (ii) that what he entered was a building, (iii) that he was a trespasser, and (iv) that he stole therein. The jury may not know what constitutes 'trespass' or what constitutes 'stealing'. Further elucidation of these concepts is therefore required by the judge if the jury are to be equipped to perform their task of applying the law to the facts as they find them. In recent years, however, judges have taken a relaxed view of their own responsibilities. Where a statute uses 'an ordinary word' they have been content to leave it to juries to decide upon the meaning of that word and then apply it to the facts as they find them. Thus judges have resisted defining words like 'intention' or 'dishonesty', being content to leave it to the juries to determine what they mean. At many points in this book this judicial attitude will be subjected to criticism as it presumes a degree of linguistic ability on the part of jurors which may not actually exist. It also leaves to juries the task of determining what the law is before applying it to the case before them. This harbours the obvious danger of inconsistency between juries and, it is suggested, the even greater danger of injustice to the accused. Where the liberty of the citizen is at stake there is a great need for certainty and clarity in the law. These goals can only be attained when the judges accept their responsibility to declare and explain the law.

After the closing speeches and the trial judge's summing up, the jury retires to consider its verdict. The jury should reach a unanimous verdict of either guilty or not guilty. However, the verdict need not be unanimous if the jury has been deliberating for at least two hours and the judge considers the jury has had such time as is reasonable having regard to the nature and complexity of the case (Juries Act 1974, s. 17).

The jury as an institution has been subject to criticism in recent years in light of the cost of jury trials, the legal and factual complexity of some cases (especially serious fraud trials), allegations of some jurors' exhibiting racist or sexist attitudes, and concerns about jurors' ability to try a case solely according to the evidence they have seen or heard in court and not by reference to what they have read on the internet. A major research study in 2010 by Cheryl Thomas, *Are Juries Fair?*, examined the fairness of the jury decision-making process, including the impact of race on jurors' verdicts, improper behaviour by jurors (including accessing the internet), and the extent to which jurors understand judges' legal directions (C. Thomas (2010) *Are Juries Fair?* Ministry of Justice Research Series 1/10). In broad terms, the study found that there was little evidence of racial discrimination and that some jurors did look on the internet for information about their cases, despite the trial judges having told them not to do so. Interestingly, and perhaps worryingly, the study found that while many jurors perceived the judge's directions as easy to understand, only a minority actually understood the directions fully in the legal terms used by the judge. This should alert us to both the importance of clarity in judges' directions and the need to help jurors comprehend their task, including by providing written guidance as appropriate.

1.4.6 The magistrates' courts

As you read about the substantive criminal law, remember that the dominant image we might have of criminal trials as taking place in the Crown Court is far from the day-to-day reality of the English criminal justice system. Most criminal cases are summary offences and thus go no further than the magistrates' courts. Most either-way offences remain in the magistrates' courts. In the 12 months ending March 2018, 1.38 million defendants were proceeded against at magistrates' courts, of which approximately 1.1 million were charged with summary offences (half of which were motoring offences). Approximately 250,000 defendants were prosecuted for triable-either-way offences, of which only about one fifth were committed for trial at the Crown Court (Ministry of Justice, *Criminal Justice Statistics Quarterly: March 2018*, https://www.gov .uk/government/collections/criminal-justice-statistics-quarterly, p. 15).

Bear in mind the practical importance of the role of magistrates as you learn about the substantive criminal law. Magistrates (and district judges (magistrates' courts)) are responsible for fact-finding and applying the law. We will see throughout the book that in English criminal law there are important, ordinary words that jury members must, to some extent, interpret and apply for themselves, using their 'common sense'. For example, if a defendant pleads self-defence, the jury will have to decide whether he used 'reasonable' force to defend himself (s. 3 of the Criminal Law Act 1967). While there is some guidance for jury members that judges can give (see s. 148 of the Legal Aid, Sentencing and Punishment of Offenders Act 2012 (LASPO 2012); **Chapter 6**), ultimately whether the force was 'reasonable' is for the jury to decide. In property offences, the key issue is frequently whether the defendant acted 'dishonestly'. For example, in theft did the defendant appropriate another person's property dishonestly (s. 1 of the Theft Act 1968)? In the Crown Court, the judge will tell the jury to consider whether what the defendant did was dishonest according to the current standards of ordinary decent people, a matter upon which the trial judge should not give further guidance and which the jury can be entrusted to decide (*Ivey* v *Genting Casinos UK Ltd* [2017] UKSC 67; see **Chapter 12**). Jury members are broadly representative of the community. Their names are drawn at random from the electoral register and there are now tightly limited categories of people who will be excused from jury service (see ss 3 and 9 of the Juries Act 1974). One of the main arguments in favour of trial by jury is that the defendant will perceive the jury's verdict as legitimate because it is a decision of his peers. By contrast, a criticism of the magistracy in England and Wales is that it is not representative of the community. Magistrates are significantly older and less ethnically diverse than the population they serve and the defendants who come before them (Transform Justice (2016), *The Role of the Magistrate?*, p. 6, http://www.transformjustice.org.uk). The demographic profile of the magistracy might be significant when we study the substantive criminal law. Magistrates might have particular views of how people *should* behave, views that will feed into their assessments of whether the defendant used 'reasonable' force or acted 'dishonestly'. Given that magistrates deal with most criminal cases, think carefully about how magistrates might interpret and apply key words and phrases in the substantive law.

1.4.7 Criminal appeals

Appeals from the magistrates' courts are governed by ss 108–110 of the MCA 1980. A person convicted by a magistrates' court may appeal to the Crown Court against his sentence if he pleaded guilty, and against the conviction or sentence if he pleaded not guilty. Under s. 111 of the MCA 1980, both the prosecution and defence can appeal 'by way of case stated' on the grounds that the decision was wrong in law or in excess of jurisdiction.

A person convicted in the Crown Court has the right of appeal under s. 1 of the Criminal Appeal Act 1968, but he must obtain the leave of the Court of Appeal or have the trial judge grant a certificate that the case is fit for appeal (s. 1(2)). Section 2 provides that the Court of Appeal must allow an appeal against conviction if they think that the conviction is unsafe; and shall dismiss such an appeal in any other case.

The development of the substantive criminal law by the appellate courts results largely from challenges to trial judges' directions to juries. Most of the cases you will consider are important because the appellate courts have had to decide whether the trial judge correctly directed the jury on the relevant law (or whether the magistrates properly directed themselves). By clarifying what the trial judge *should* have told the jury, the appellate courts establish precedents. This means the trial judge's directions to the jury are very important. Judges now use a *Crown Court Compendium* (Judicial College (2017) https://www.judiciary.gov.uk/publications/crown-court-bench-book-directing-the-jury-2/), which provides a set of specimen directions that they can use to explain clearly to juries what the relevant law is and what they must focus upon in their deliberations (the *Compendium* replaces the earlier *Crown Court Benchbook* (2010)).

As we will see in subsequent chapters, some of the key cases in criminal law involved appeals from people who pleaded guilty. That may seem odd. How can a person appeal when he has admitted his guilt? In some situations, people will plead guilty when the trial judge rules before or during trial on a particular issue of law in a way that makes it difficult or impossible for a defendant to argue that he is not guilty. For example, we will consider in **Chapter 5** a series of important appellate court decisions on **automatism** and **insanity**. In several of these cases, the trial judge ruled that the evidence the defendant wanted to adduce (put before the court) in support of a plea of automatism (which leads to a complete acquittal if successful) was actually evidence that would support a special verdict of not guilty by reason of insanity (which until 1991 led to indefinite detention in a mental hospital; see **Chapter 5**). Thus in some cases defendants changed their plea to guilty to avoid the prospect of indefinite detention and appealed against the judge's ruling on the law, arguing that they should have been able to claim automatism. The appellate courts' rulings thus produced the precedents on automatism and insanity.

You will also encounter the term, 'Attorney General's Reference' in many case names throughout this book. Under s. 36 of the Criminal Justice Act 1972, where a person tried on indictment has been acquitted, the Attorney General may, if he desires the opinion of the Court of Appeal on a point of law which has arisen in the case, refer that point to the Court. The Court shall then consider the point and give its opinion on it. Crucially, the opinion of the Court cannot affect the acquittal in that trial. The Court can then (of its own motion or in pursuance of an application) refer the point to the Supreme Court. The first reference was in 1974 (*Attorney General's Reference (No. 1 of 1974)* [1974] QB 744). In *Attorney General's Reference (No. 1 of 1975)* [1975] QB 773, 778, Lord Widgery CJ said that such references are not confined to cases 'where very heavy questions of law arise . . . On the contrary, we hope to see this procedure used extensively for short but important points which require a quick ruling of this court before a potentially false decision of law has too wide a circulation in the courts.' However, there is no power to refer questions of law that are purely theoretical, however interesting or difficult: *Attorney General's Reference (No. 4 of 1979)* [1981] 1 All ER 1193.

The second main way in which an 'Attorney General's Reference' arises is in respect of sentences. Under s. 36 of the Criminal Justice Act 1988, the Attorney General can apply to the Court of Appeal for leave to challenge sentences for indictable offences and specified either-way offences as being 'unduly lenient'. Following *Attorney General's Reference (No. 4 of 1989)* (1989) 11 Cr App R (S) 517, a sentence is unduly lenient where it 'falls outside the range of sentences which the judge, applying his mind to all the relevant factors, could reasonably consider appropriate'. The court should only grant leave in exceptional circumstances, and not in borderline cases (*Attorney General's Reference (No. 5 of 1989)* (1989) 11 Cr App R (S) 489).

The final aspect of the appeals process to note is the role of the Criminal Cases Review Commission (CCRC), which was established by s. 8 of the Criminal Appeal Act 1995, after a series of high-profile miscarriages of justice, including the cases of the Birmingham Six and Guildford Four. The principal role of the CCRC is to investigate cases where people have been convicted and lost an appeal, but believe they have been wrongly convicted of a criminal offence. The CCRC has the power to investigate cases and refer them back to the Court of Appeal, but only if there is a 'real possibility' that the conviction would not be upheld if the reference were made, and the reason is because of 'an argument, or evidence, not raised in the proceedings which led to it or on any appeal or application for leave to appeal against it' (s. 13(1) of the Criminal Appeal Act 1995). As of November 2018, the CCRC had referred 657 cases to the Court of Appeal, of which 437 appeals were allowed (http://www.ccrc.gov.uk). The CCRC is under significant pressure in terms of resources, with its funding having been cut significantly in recent years, despite the commission receiving a rocketing number of applications (up from 885 in 2003/4 to 1,439 in 2017/18). The CCRC's capacity to identify and rectify miscarriages of justice should concern anyone who wants a justice system that convicts only those who are guilty (*The Guardian* (2018) 'Miscarriage of Justice Body's Funding Cuts Criticised as Workload Grows', 9 September 2018).

1.4.8　The European Convention on Human Rights

The Human Rights Act 1998, which came into force on 2 October 2000, gives effect in English law to the rights guaranteed in the European Convention on Human Rights and Fundamental Freedoms. Where Parliament is considering new legislation, s. 19 of the 1998 Act requires a minister in charge of a bill before Parliament to make a statement of compatibility or, if the bill is not compatible with the Convention, to make a statement to this effect. As a result Parliament must now pay particular regard to the Convention to ensure that new laws do not breach the rights which it guarantees. In addition, the courts in applying all legislation must interpret it, so far as it is possible to do so, in a way which is compatible with the Convention rights (s. 3). If a compatible interpretation is not possible, the court must apply the existing law to the case before it but the High Court and appellate courts may make a declaration of incompatibility (s. 4). Where the common law conflicts with the Convention, courts are likely to override the common law because of the obligation on them, as a public authority, not to act in a way which is incompatible with a Convention right (s. 6). Accordingly, the Convention will have considerable impact on criminal courts particularly on matters relating to criminal procedure, evidence, and sentencing. It may, however, also have relevance in certain areas of the substantive criminal law. In the chapters which follow, reference to the European Convention on Human Rights and cases of the European Court of Human Rights will be made where relevant.

FURTHER READING

A. Ashworth, 'Punishment, Compensation and the State' (1986) 6(1) OJLS 86–122.

A. Ashworth, 'Is the Criminal Law a Lost Cause?' (2000) 116 LQR 223.

J. Feinberg, *Harm to Others: The Moral Limits of the Criminal Law* (Oxford: Oxford University Press, 1984).

D. J. Galligan, 'The Return of Retribution in Penal Theory' in C. F. H. Tapper (ed.), *Crime, Proof and Punishment: Essays in Memory of Rupert Cross* (London: Butterworth, 1981).

A. von Hirsch and J. V. Roberts, 'Legislating Sentencing Principles: The Provisions of the Criminal Justice Act 2003 Relating to Sentencing Purposes and the Role of Previous Convictions' [2004] Crim LR 639.

D. Husak, 'The Criminal Law as Last Resort' (2004) 24(2) OJLS 207–35.

J. Jacobson, G. Hunter, and A. Kirby, *Structured Mayhem: Personal Experiences of the Crown Court*, 2015 (Criminal Justice Alliance http://criminaljusticealliance.org/wp-content/uploads/2015/11/Structured-Mayhem1.pdf).

G. Lamond, 'What Is a Crime?' (2007) 27 OJLS 609.

J. V. Roberts, 'Sentencing Guidelines and Judicial Discretion: Evolution of the Duty of Courts to Comply in England and Wales' (2011) 51(6) Br J Criminol 997–1013.

C. Thomas, *Are Juries Fair?* (2010, Ministry of Justice, Research Series 1/10, https://www.justice.gov.uk/downloads/publications/research-and-analysis/moj-research/are-juries-fair-research.pdf).

D. A. Thomas, 'Form and Function in Criminal Law' in P. R. Glazebrook (ed.), *Reshaping the Criminal Law: Essays in Honour of Glanville Williams* (London: Sweet & Maxwell, 1978).

P. Thornton, 'Trial by Jury: 50 Years of Change' [2004] Crim LR 119–37.

2

Actus reus

2.1 The elements of crime

2.1.1 General

The criminal law does not seek to punish people for their evil thoughts; an accused must be proved to be responsible for conduct or the existence of a state of affairs prohibited by the criminal law before liability may arise. For many summary offences, the prosecution only has to prove that D was responsible for that conduct or that the state of affairs existed. For more serious offences, whether liability arises will depend further on D's state of mind at the time.

 Key Point

> A Latin maxim encapsulates this principle—*actus non facit reum, nisi mens sit rea*—the act itself does not constitute guilt unless done with a guilty mind. The conduct or state of affairs which a particular offence prohibits is called the *actus reus* and the state of mind which D must be proved to have had at the time of the conduct or during the existence of the state of affairs is called the *mens rea*.

The terms *actus reus* and *mens rea* are simply useful labels to be attributed to the constituent parts of any crime being analysed; they do not have any meaning in themselves. They have no greater meaning than, for example, the terms 'obverse' and 'reverse' used when describing coins. Just as the words and designs on coins will vary so too will the *actus reus* and *mens rea* of different crimes.

It is particularly important when analysing the *mens rea* of offences to realise that this term is not prescriptive. In some offences nothing short of intention to bring about the prohibited consequence will suffice (e.g. theft, see **Chapter 12**) whereas in others recklessness will suffice (e.g. assault, see **Chapter 10**). While the Latin maxim *actus non facit reum, nisi mens sit rea* is a useful tool, there are many offences, largely of a minor and regulatory nature, where *mens rea* is not required. These are called strict liability offences and are of statutory creation (see **4.2**). In such cases proof by the prosecution of *mens rea* is not required in respect of at least one element of the *actus reus*.

The use of the Latin terms *actus reus* and *mens rea* has been criticised. In *Miller* [1983] 2 AC 161, 174 Lord Diplock stated that:

> [I]t would . . . be conducive to clarity of analysis of the ingredients of a crime that is created by statute . . . if we were to avoid bad Latin and instead to think and speak . . . about the conduct of D and his state of mind at the time of that conduct, instead of speaking of *actus reus* and *mens rea*.

However, the terms *actus reus* and *mens rea* are so widely used that they will be retained for the purposes of exposition in this book.

While most crimes may be analysed in terms of *actus reus* and *mens rea*, a few crimes exist where these concepts merge. In some offences the *actus reus* may only be proved by proving *mens rea*. For example, s. 1(1) of the Prevention of Crime Act 1953 makes it an offence for any person, without lawful authority or reasonable excuse, to have with him in any public place any offensive weapon. Section 1(4) defines 'offensive weapon' as 'any article made or adapted for use for causing injury to the person, or intended by the person having it with him for such use'. If, for example, D is found carrying a pick-axe handle in a public place, the issue whether this amounts to the *actus reus* of the offence will depend on his intention at the time as this article does not fall into either of the first two categories of articles 'made or adapted for use for causing injury'. If there is no intent to use it to cause injury then there is no offensive weapon and thus no *actus reus*. In some other offences the *actus reus* implies a mental element.

 Example

If D is charged with possession of a controlled drug such as heroin or cannabis contrary to s. 5 of the Misuse of Drugs Act 1971 it is necessary to prove that he knew he possessed the thing which turns out to be the drug even though he does not know its nature (see *DPP* v *Brooks* [1974] AC 862; *Boyesen* [1982] AC 768); it is not possible to possess something if you do not know of its existence and thus in the absence of this mental element of knowledge there can be no *actus reus*.

2.1.2 Defences

So far the suggestion has been that if the prosecution prove the commission of an *actus reus* by D with the necessary *mens rea*, criminal liability will have been established. This ignores the fact that D may be able to rely upon some justification or excuse to avoid criminal liability.

 Question

Do justifications or excuses, more commonly referred to as defences, form part of the definition of a crime or are they outside the definition, operating like a trump card in bridge?

Glanville Williams in *Criminal Law: The General Part* (2nd edn, 1961) expresses the view that all the constituents of a crime are either *actus reus* or *mens rea* stating (at p. 20):

> *Actus reus* includes . . . not merely the whole objective situation that has to be proved by the prosecution, but also the absence of any ground of justification or excuse, whether such justification or excuse be stated in any statute creating the crime or implied by the courts in accordance with general principles.

An alternative view expressed by D. J. Lanham, '*Larsonneur* Revisited' [1976] Crim LR 276, is that a crime is 'made up of three ingredients, *actus reus*, *mens rea* and (a negative element) absence of a valid defence'. Which view is correct is not crucial; it can even be argued that both are partially correct if a distinction is drawn between justifications and excuses. A. T. H. Smith, 'On *Actus Reus* and *Mens Rea*' in P. R. Glazebrook (ed.) *Reshaping the Criminal Law* (1978), states (at p. 99):

> [T]he distinction is that we excuse the actor because he is not sufficiently culpable or at fault, whereas we justify an act because we regard it as the most appropriate course of action in the circumstances, even though it may result in harm that would, in the absence of justification, amount to a crime.

 Example

An example of a justification is self-defence. If D is charged with unlawfully and maliciously wounding V contrary to s. 20 of the Offences Against the Person Act 1861 he may admit that he did wound V and intended to do so, but he would not be convicted if he did so only in response to V's murderous assault upon him. In such circumstances wounding V would not be unlawful as it would be justified by the defence of self-defence. As the wounding was not unlawful it can be said that there was no *actus reus*; similarly as D only intended to wound V in circumstances where this was justified, there was no intention to wound V unlawfully (see further **6.4.2.3**). By contrast, if D wounded V because he was told to do so by X who was holding D's wife hostage, threatening to kill her if he did not obey, D could plead the defence of duress. In this situation, D intended to wound V and did so unlawfully (as he had no justification for so doing) but the defence of duress would operate to excuse him from the consequences of conviction and punishment. There has been an *actus reus* and *mens rea* but the defence of duress is superimposed much as a trump card might be played in bridge (see further **6.2**).

2.2 Defining an *actus reus*

Each crime must be looked at individually to determine what must be proved to establish its *actus reus*. In the case of a common law crime (such as murder) the definition of its *actus reus* is to be found in the decisions of the courts; in the case of a statutory crime (such as theft) the definition of the *actus reus* is to be found in the statute as interpreted judicially in decided cases. Generally, however, it is necessary to know which elements of the definition of an offence comprise the *actus reus*. **The** term *actus reus* has a much wider meaning than the 'act' prohibited by the law which it implies. A useful working definition is that it comprises all the elements of the definition of the offence except those which relate to the mental element (*mens rea*) required on the part of D. The definition of an offence may prohibit acts or omissions (conduct) but it may prohibit these only in particular circumstances. In some cases the definition of the offence may require particular consequences to ensue from the conduct. **A distinction which flows from this is that between 'conduct crimes' and 'result crimes'.** A 'conduct crime' prohibits conduct regardless of consequences whereas a 'result crime' prohibits particular consequences which ensue from conduct on the part of D. In a limited number of cases, offences prohibit particular states of affairs without reference to conduct or its consequences. The ambit of the criminal law may be illustrated by the following examples of offences.

 Example

Perjury is a 'conduct crime' which is committed whenever D makes a statement on oath which he does not believe to be true (s. 1 of the Perjury Act 1911). The offence is committed whether or not the statement is believed as the result of D's prohibited conduct is irrelevant; it is the conduct which is prohibited. The relevant circumstance in the *actus reus* of this offence is that the statement is made on oath. An example of a 'result crime' is murder where it must be proved that D's conduct caused the deceased's death. If the intended result of the death of V does not occur, the law of attempts, under the Criminal Attempts Act 1981, provides for a charge of attempted murder—a 'conduct crime'. An example of a 'state of affairs' offence, where the definition of the *actus reus* is concerned neither with conduct nor its consequences, is being in charge of a motor vehicle on a road or other public place while unfit to drive through drink or drugs contrary to s. 4(2) of the Road Traffic Act 1988. If D is in charge of the vehicle (a state of affairs) it matters not whether he was driving the vehicle, sitting in it, or asleep in it (*DPP* v *Watkins* [1989] QB 821).

2.3 Proving an *actus reus*

If D has the *mens rea* for a particular offence but does not bring about the *actus reus* he is not guilty of committing that offence. This is illustrated by the case of *Deller* (1952) 36 Cr App R 184.

> P was selling a car to D and accepted D's car in part exchange after D represented to him that it was 'free from all encumbrances'. D believed this representation to be false as he had previously executed a document with a finance company which purported to be a hire purchase agreement in respect of the car. If this agreement was valid the car was not free from encumbrances and D had lied to P. If, however, the agreement was in reality a loan on the security of the car it was void as it had not been registered under the Bills of Sale Act 1878 and thus D's representation would, in fact, be true. D was charged with, and convicted of, obtaining P's car by false pretences contrary to s. 32 of the Larceny Act 1916. As the jury found the agreement was a loan on the security of the car, the Court of Criminal Appeal quashed D's conviction as this

agreement was void and thus the car was unencumbered. There were, accordingly, no false pretences because 'it may be quite accidentally and, strange as it may sound, dishonestly, [D] had told the truth' (*per* Hilbery J at p. 191). D clearly intended to make false representations but the representations he made were true; while he had *mens rea* there was no *actus reus*. If such facts were to recur the correct charge would be *attempted* fraud by false representation.

2.4 Conduct must be voluntary

2.4.1 General

 Question

D is driving his car when, without warning, he suffers a heart attack which renders him incapable of controlling the vehicle. D slumps over the steering wheel, his foot depresses the accelerator and the car careers through a red traffic light. The vehicle continues along the road and crashes into the rear of E's car which is stopped at a zebra crossing. E's vehicle is forced on to the crossing where it hits V breaking his leg. If D was charged with failure to stop at a red traffic light, dangerous driving, and criminal damage to E's car, and E was charged with failing to accord precedence to a pedestrian on a zebra crossing and causing V grievous bodily harm, could they be convicted? Have they committed the *actus reus* of any of these offences?

Where the *actus reus* of an offence requires conduct on the part of D, whether an act or omission, liability will only arise where the conduct is willed; it is not sufficient that D by his bodily movements performed the prohibited conduct or brought about the prohibited consequence defined by the *actus reus* of the offence. In *Bratty v AG for Northern Ireland* [1963] AC 386 (at p. 409), Lord Denning stated that the 'requirement that it should be a voluntary act is essential, not only in a murder case, but also in every criminal case'. **In offences requiring *mens rea*, if the conduct is not willed there will also be an absence of *mens rea* on the part of D, but even if the offence is one of strict liability, requiring no proof of *mens rea*, it is still necessary to prove that D's conduct was voluntary.** To convict and impose punishment on an accused who was not responsible for his conduct would be unjust.

In the earlier example, driving through a red traffic light is a strict liability offence. There is no need to prove that D was aware that the light was red and drove through it intentionally. The only matter which the prosecution must prove is that D was driving the vehicle when it went through the red traffic light. However, as D had been incapacitated by the heart attack, there was at the time no voluntary act of driving and thus no *actus reus*. The charge of dangerous driving would similarly fail. The charge of criminal damage would also fail as, although D's car caused damage to E's car when it crashed into it, this was not the result of a voluntary or willed act on the part of D. Had D felt warning pains before the heart attack and continued driving he might be liable, particularly if he had previously had such an attack and recognised the pains as warning symptoms.

In *Kay v Butterworth* (1945) 173 LT 191 (see also *Hill v Baxter* [1958] 1 QB 277), D was driving home after night-shift work when, overcome by sleep, he drove into a party of soldiers. He was convicted of driving without due care and attention and dangerous driving as, realising that he was becoming drowsy, he should have stopped and it was immaterial that he was not conscious of his actions when the accident happened. Humphreys J stated:

> A person, however, who through no fault of his own, becomes unconscious while driving, for example, by being struck by a stone, or by being taken ill, ought not to be liable at criminal law.

In *Bell* [1984] 3 All ER 842, further examples of involuntary conduct for which no criminal liability may arise were given by Goff LJ who stated (at p. 846):

> [A] motorist . . . [who] has been attacked while driving by, for example, a swarm of bees or a malevolent passenger, or because he has been affected by a sudden blinding pain, or because he has become suddenly unconscious by reason of a black-out, or because his vehicle has suffered some failure, for example, through a blow-out or through the brakes failing.

In our example E would be acquitted as his failure to accord precedence to a pedestrian was due to the external application of force on his vehicle which was beyond his control (see *Leicester* v *Pearson* [1952] 2 QB 668). Similarly, there was no voluntary act on E's part which caused V's injury.

In the example of D and E a distinction may be drawn between the causes of their involuntary conduct. E's conduct was caused by the external application of physical force. Another example would be where A is carving the Sunday joint when B seizes his hand holding the knife and thrusts it into C killing him. If A was charged with murder he would be acquitted as there was no voluntary act on his part. In our earlier example D's involuntary conduct was due to his loss of consciousness. Where a person does physical acts while in a state of unconsciousness this is referred to as **automatism**. For example, a person may perform physical acts while concussed or in a state of somnambulism or while suffering a fit or seizure. Automatism will be considered further in **Chapter 5**.

2.4.2 **State of affairs offences**

While most offences require voluntary conduct on the part of D to establish their *actus reus*, there are some offences which prohibit the existence of a state of affairs. An example given earlier is s. 4(2) of the Road Traffic Act 1988, being in charge of a motor vehicle on a road or other public place while unfit to drive through drink or drugs. For as long as D is in charge of the vehicle while unfit the *actus reus* is committed. This is so even though D may not be responsible for his unfitness, as where his lemonade has been laced with alcohol, although this may constitute a special reason for not disqualifying him from driving (see *Shippam* [1971] RTR 209; *Pugsley* v *Hunter* [1973] RTR 284).

While there may be strong public policy reasons for adopting an 'absolute liability' approach to 'situational' road traffic offences because of the obvious dangers involved to members of the public, it is questionable whether this approach should be adopted in other cases of 'state of affairs' offences. Should a person be convicted of a criminal offence, with the attendant stigma and punishment, when they might be in no way morally blameworthy for the prohibited state of affairs existing? The courts, however, have not shown any reluctance to convict people of situational offences where they have not been responsible for bringing about the prohibited state of affairs.

> In *Larsonneur* (1933) 97 JP 206, L, a French citizen was required to leave the United Kingdom. She went to Eire but was deported and brought back to Holyhead by the Irish police who handed her over to British police officers. On a charge under the Aliens Order 1920 that she 'being an alien to whom leave to land in the United Kingdom has been refused, was found in the United Kingdom' L was convicted. The Court of Criminal Appeal upheld her conviction, Hewart CJ referring to the circumstances of compulsion which brought about her return to the United Kingdom as 'perfectly immaterial'.

The Court was totally unconcerned to discover whether L had caused that state of affairs. The suspicion must be that the Court would have upheld her conviction even if a group of kidnappers had removed her from Eire and had brought her to the United Kingdom; a requirement of culpability (i.e. voluntariness) on the part of D leading to the creation of the state of affairs would have been desirable and could easily have been implied by the Court of Criminal Appeal in its construction of the statute.

Larsonneur was not an aberrant decision. The Divisional Court revived the controversy with its decision in *Winzar* v *Chief Constable of Kent, The Times*, 28 March 1983.

> W had been brought to hospital on a stretcher. He was diagnosed as being merely drunk and was asked to leave. When he was later found slumped on a seat in the corridor the police were summoned. They removed him to the road, concluded he was drunk and placed him in their police car. W was charged with being found drunk on the highway contrary to s. 12 of the Licensing Act 1872. The Divisional Court construed the words 'found drunk' to mean 'perceived to be drunk' and upheld his conviction on the basis that, as the purpose of the offence was to deal with the nuisance of public drunkenness, it was sufficient to establish guilt to prove that the person was drunk while in a public place; how he came to be there was irrelevant.

The report does not indicate how W came to be taken to hospital. If he had been found lying in the street originally there might be no cause for complaint. The decision, however, is expressed in broad terms and may be criticised on two bases. First, it is arguable that the officers first perceived W's condition while he was in hospital; by taking him outside to the public highway they had procured the commission of the offence. Secondly, in the absence of express words in the statute dispensing with the need to prove voluntary conduct on the part of D bringing into existence the prohibited state of affairs, the requirement of voluntariness should have been implied on the basis that penal statutes should be construed strictly in favour of D.

An objective requirement that the creation of the state of affairs be reasonably foreseeable at the time D embarked on the course of conduct which ultimately led to that state of affairs would suffice. For example, if D is drinking in a public house it is reasonably foreseeable that he will end up on the public highway either at closing time or if he leaves or is ejected earlier. If, however, he is drinking at home, it is not reasonably foreseeable that this will happen. Thus if Winzar had been at home unconscious from his drinking when a third party summoned the ambulance to take him to hospital, the reasonable foreseeability test would not be satisfied. If, however, he had been drinking in a public house when he collapsed the test would be satisfied, albeit the roundabout way in which he ended up on the highway could not have been foreseen at the time he commenced his drinking.

In the most recent case involving a state of affairs offence, the Court of Appeal has adopted a more enlightened approach than that shown by the courts in *Larsonneur* and *Winzar* where D bears no responsibility for the creation of the state of affairs.

> In *Robinson-Pierre* [2013] EWCA Crim 2396, D was tried for an offence of being the owner of a dog that caused injury while dangerously out of control in a public place (see s. 3(1) and (4) of the Dangerous Dogs Act 1991). The Court of Appeal considered the question of liability on the basis that the dog had been unleashed by a third party and not by any act of D. The Court stated that Parliament **did have the power to create a 'state of affairs' offence** for which D would be liable even though that state of affairs may not have been brought about by any act of D, **provided that the statutory wording made it clear that this was Parliament's intention**. In this case, the statute was not clear as to whether this was Parliament's intention and thus D would not be liable for the act of the third party.

2.5 Omissions

2.5.1 General

 Question

A, knowing that B cannot swim, pushes him into the deep end of the swimming pool intending that he should drown. C, a swimmer using the pool, ignores B's struggles and his cries for help. D, the life-guard employed by the council to rescue anyone in difficulty, ignores B's cries, believing them to be a prank. E, B's father who is swimming in the pool, also ignores B's cries, reckoning that it is time his wimpish son either sinks to oblivion or learns to swim. B drowns. Will A, C, D, and E be liable for unlawful homicide (i.e. either murder or manslaughter depending on their *mens rea*)? A is the only one to have performed a positive act which caused B's death. C, D, and E failed to act to save B but they did not do any positive act to cause his death. If liability is to arise it would depend on there being a duty upon them to act to prevent B's death although they are not responsible for the existence of the life-threatening situation.

Generally the common law was concerned to prohibit particular results from occurring and it punished an accused for causing the prohibited result by his positive acts. Gradually the courts came to recognise limited liability for omissions where a duty to act could be implied, D failed to act, and the prohibited result ensued. Not all offences, however, are capable of commission by omission. It is a question for the courts whether a particular offence is capable of commission by omission (see e.g. *Firth* (1990) 91 Cr App R 217, *Ahmad* (1986) 84 Cr App R 64, **13.3.1**). Some offences cannot be committed by omission, for example, burglary and robbery. In some offences the definition of the *actus reus* may make it clear that it may only be committed by an act.

Murder or manslaughter may be committed by omission. In the earlier example D and E could be found liable for unlawful homicide provided *mens rea* could be established as the courts have recognised a duty to arise under contract (see *Pittwood* (1902) 19 TLR 37, **2.5.2.2.1**) and a duty on the part of parents to care for their children and protect them from physical harm (see *Gibbins and Proctor* (1918) 13 Cr App R 134, **2.5.2.2.2**). A problem in relation to D and E, however, is that they did not actually cause B's death in the sense in which causation is generally understood (see **2.6**). **The courts do not appear to have grappled with the principles of causation specifically in relation to omissions.** The Law Commission in its Draft Criminal Code Bill (Law Com No. 177) specifically addresses this issue in cl. 17(1) which states: 'a person causes a result . . . when . . . (b) he omits to do an act which might prevent its occurrence and which he is under a duty to do according to the law relating to the offence'.

With regard to C, he would not be liable as there is no general duty to be a 'Good Samaritan'. The position of the common law was summarised in *Lord Macaulay's Works* (ed. Lady Trevelyan), vol. VII (1866), p. 497:

> In general . . . the penal law must content itself with keeping men from doing positive harm, and must leave to public opinion, and to the teachers of morality and religion, the offence of furnishing men with motives for doing positive good. It is evident that to attempt to punish men by law for not rendering to others all the service which it is their [moral] duty to render to others would be preposterous. We must grant impunity to the vast majority of those omissions which a benevolent morality would pronounce reprehensible, and must content ourselves with punishing such omissions only when they are distinguished from the rest by some circumstance which marks them out as peculiarly fit objects of penal legislation.

While C's disregard of B's plight and failure to render assistance may be morally reprehensible it falls outside the ambit of the criminal law.

2.5.2 **Classifying omissions**

 Key Point

The analysis of offences into *conduct crimes* and *result crimes* is useful when examining liability for omissions. G. P. Fletcher in *Rethinking Criminal Law* (1978) distinguishes two forms of liability for omissions. The first type he designates 'breach of duty to act', where liability may be imposed for breach of a statutory obligation to act. This relates to conduct crimes where there is no requirement for the occurrence of harm to be proved. The second type of liability which relates to result crimes he designates 'commission by omission', where liability is imposed 'for failing to intervene, when necessary, to prevent the occurrence of a serious harm such as death or the destruction of property' (at p. 421). Fletcher's classification will be used to examine the situations in which the criminal law imposes liability for omissions.

2.5.2.1 **Breach of duty to act**

Various statutes impose duties to act on individuals in specified circumstances. An individual finding himself in the specified circumstances who fails to perform that duty will commit an offence. For example, a motorist who, without reasonable excuse, fails to provide a police officer with a specimen of breath when required to do so under s. 6 of the Road Traffic Act 1988 is guilty of an offence. The penalty for this offence of omission is the same as the offence of commission of which the motorist was suspected. Thus a motorist suspected of driving a vehicle while unfit due to drink or drugs is liable to the same penalty whether he provides the specimen which would establish his guilt or whether he refuses to provide it. A more serious offence relating to non-disclosure of information is created by s. 19 of the Terrorism Act 2000. If information comes to the attention of D in the course of his trade, profession, business, or employment giving rise to a belief or suspicion that another person has committed one of a range of offences under the Act, D commits an offence if he does not disclose his belief or suspicion and the information on which it is based to the police as soon as is reasonably practicable.

The previously discussed examples are all of statutory creation where it is specifically stated that failure to perform the duty imposed by the statute is an offence. In some situations the common law has recognised an offence where a duty imposed by common law or statute has been neglected.

> In *Dytham* [1979] QB 722, D, a police constable, was on duty in uniform near a club when a man was ejected from the club and kicked to death by a 'bouncer'. D took no steps to intervene and when the incident was over he drove off having told a bystander that he was going off duty. D was charged with the common law offence of misconduct whilst acting as an officer of justice, in that he had wilfully and without reasonable excuse or justification neglected to perform his duty to preserve the Queen's Peace and to protect the person of the deceased or arrest his assailants or otherwise bring them to justice. D contended that there was no such offence known to the law and that misconduct required a positive act or an element of corruption but mere non-feasance was not enough. The Court of Appeal, in upholding his conviction, placed reliance on a passage in Stephen's *Digest of Criminal Law* which stated:

>> Every public officer commits a misdemeanour who wilfully neglects to perform any duty which he is bound either by common law or by statute to perform provided that the discharge of such duty is not attended with greater danger than a man of ordinary firmness and activity may be expected to encounter.

Lord Widgery stipulated the requirements of the offence as being wilful neglect not mere inadvertence, and the neglect must be culpable in the sense that it is without reasonable excuse or justification. He stated (at p. 727):

> This ... element of culpability ... is not restricted to corruption or dishonesty but ... must be of such a degree that the misconduct impugned is calculated to injure the public interest so as to call for condemnation and punishment. Whether such a situation is revealed by the evidence is a matter that a jury has to decide.

It is interesting that Dytham was charged with a conduct crime and not the result crime of manslaughter. This is presumably because it was considered that causation could not be established as it would be impossible to prove that V would not have died but for Dytham's failure to perform his duty.

Misconduct in a public office would appear to be an offence applicable to all holders of public office. The nature of the offence will obviously vary depending upon the duties, statutory or common law, placed upon the office holder (see also *AG's Ref (No. 3 of 2003)* [2004] EWCA Crim 868). Another common law offence which may be committed by omission in breach of a duty, in this case a statutory one, is cheating the revenue (see *Mavji* [1987] 1 WLR 1388).

2.5.2.2 Commission by omission

The situations examined so far have involved 'conduct crimes'.

Question

Is it possible to commit a 'result crime' by omitting to act?

Not all omissions will give rise to liability; liability will depend on there being a duty, recognised by the law, to act or intervene in the circumstances. There are several situations in which the law has recognised the existence of such duties. The situations in which a duty may arise are not closed; new situations may give rise to the recognition of a duty.

In *Khan and Khan* [1998] Crim LR 830 two drug dealers appealed convictions for manslaughter arising out of their supply of heroin to the deceased and their failure to summon medical assistance when she went into a coma following her consumption of the drug. In quashing their convictions Swinton Thomas LJ stated:

> To extend the duty to summon medical assistance to a drug dealer who supplies heroin to a person who subsequently dies on the facts of this case would undoubtedly enlarge the class of persons to whom, on previous authority, such a duty may be owed. It may be correct to hold that such a duty does arise . . . Unfortunately, the question as to the existence or otherwise of [such] a duty . . . was not . . . at any time considered by the Judge, and the jury was given no direction in relation to it.

By contrast, in *Evans (Gemma)* [2009] EWCA Crim 650 the Court of Appeal recognised the extension of the duty and upheld a conviction in similar circumstances as the trial judge had correctly identified the duty of care that could have existed, leaving it to the jury to determine whether it did exist on the facts of the case. The judge had directed the jury that if they were satisfied that D had supplied the heroin to V, she having self-injected and died from an overdose with D admitting failing to seek medical assistance when she discovered V's condition, they could convict. The Court of Appeal held that where a person creates, or contributes to the creation of, a state of affairs that he knows or ought reasonably to know has become life-threatening, a consequent duty on him to act by taking reasonable steps to save the other's life would normally arise. The supply of heroin to V represented D's contribution to the creation of the life-threatening situation. This represents an extension of the *Miller* principle (see **2.5.2.2.4**) as the act of supply itself did not create that situation; rather it required V to self-administer the drug in an excessive amount. The Court of Appeal affirmed that whether a situation gave rise to a duty was a question of law for the judge to determine. (See further **9.3.3.2.**)

2.5.2.2.1 *Duty arising out of contract*
Where the failure to fulfil a contractual obligation is likely to endanger lives, the criminal law will impose a duty to act. The duty will be owed not only to other parties to the contract but also to any other person whose life may be endangered.

> In *Pittwood* (1902) 19 TLR 37 D was convicted of gross negligence manslaughter following the death of a road user who was hit by a train on a level crossing. D was employed by the railway company to look after the crossing and ensure that the gate was shut when a train was due to pass. When the collision occurred D was away from his post having left the gate open. His actions were regarded as grossly negligent, and his contention that his contractual obligations gave rise to no duty to the public was dismissed as he was paid to keep the gate shut and protect the public.

2.5.2.2.2 *Duty arising out of relationship*
The existence of close relationships can give rise to a duty to act. It is generally accepted at common law (although there is little direct authority) that parents are under a duty to their children to protect them from physical harm and spouses are under a duty to aid each other (see *Smith* [1979] Crim LR 251, **2.5.2.2.3**). In *Gibbins and Proctor* (1918) 13 Cr App R 134, a man and a woman with whom he was living were convicted of the murder of the man's child, the child having starved to death because they withheld food from her. The man breached the duty parents owe their children. The woman, by taking money to buy food, had assumed a duty towards the child (see **2.5.2.2.3**). Section 1 of the Children and Young Persons Act 1933 includes the offence of wilful neglect and imposes a duty on parents and those who are legally responsible for a child under the age of 16 to provide adequate food, clothing, and medical care for that child. More recently, s. 4 of the Domestic Violence, Crime and Victims Act 2004 makes it an offence to cause or allow a child or vulnerable adult to die or suffer serious physical harm. The offence includes situations where the defendant failed to take reasonable steps to protect the victim from risks that D was or ought to have been aware of.

2.5.2.2.3 *Duty arising from the assumption of care for another*
If a person voluntarily undertakes to care for another person who is unable to care for himself, whether from infancy, mental illness, or other infirmity, a duty will be owed to that person (see *Nicholls* (1874) 13 Cox CC 75). The duty may arise from an express undertaking to care for the other, as in *Nicholls* where a grandmother took into her home her grandchild after the child's mother died, or it may be implied as in *Instan* [1893] 1 QB 450. In the latter case D, who was without independent means, lived with her aunt who became ill and for the last 12 days of her life was unable to care for herself or summon help. D did not give her any food or seek medical assistance but she continued to live with the aunt and eat her food. D

was convicted of manslaughter on the basis that by remaining with the aunt a duty was imposed on her to care for the aunt, which duty she had wilfully and deliberately left unperformed.

The principle in *Instan* was extended by *Stone and Dobinson* [1977] QB 354, so that a duty to care for another may be easily incurred although onerous or difficult to execute.

> S's sister F came to live with him and his mistress D in 1972. F was suffering from anorexia nervosa and, although initially able to look after herself, her condition deteriorated until she was confined to bed by July 1975. S was 67, partially deaf, nearly blind, and had learning disabilities. D was 43 but was described as 'ineffectual and inadequate'. S and D tried to find F's doctor but failed. They took F such little food as she required. D and a neighbour once gave her a bed bath. S and D were unable to use a telephone and no one was informed of F's condition. A neighbour was unsuccessful in getting a local doctor to attend. When F died S and D were convicted of manslaughter and on appeal their convictions were upheld, the Court of Appeal being satisfied that the jury were entitled to find that S and D, by the minimal attention they had given F, had assumed a duty to care for her and had been grossly negligent in the performance of this duty as a result of which F had died.

It is unclear from the judgment whether it would have been held that S and D had incurred a duty to care for F if, when she became infirm and unable to care for herself, they had simply ignored her.

> The principle in *Stone and Dobinson* was followed in *Ruffell* [2003] EWCA Crim 122, where the Court of Appeal upheld the defendant's conviction for manslaughter. On an evening in February V was at D's house at D's invitation and both partook of a mixture of heroin and cocaine. V lapsed into unconsciousness and D engaged in some efforts to revive him—placing him by a window to get some fresh air, splashing water on his face, placing him in a bath, wrapping him in towels, and placing him by a radiator. The following morning D telephoned V's mother informing her that he was sick due to drinking vodka and that he was sitting on D's doorstep. V's mother asked D to take V inside and cover him with a blanket. D agreed to do so but did not, returning to bed to sleep. Three hours later V was found on the path by workmen and neighbours. He was taken to hospital but pronounced dead three hours later. The cause of death was hypothermia and opiate intoxication. The trial judge directed the jury that they could find that D had assumed a duty of care from the fact that V was a guest in D's house and a friend of D, and that D had sought to revive him following his taking of the drugs. If they considered that D had assumed this duty, they were entitled to consider whether putting V outside amounted to a breach of that duty. The jury convicted D and the Court of Appeal upheld the conviction endorsing the trial judge's direction to the jury.

 Question

Can a person under a duty to care for another ever be released from that duty?

An issue which is left unresolved in the case law is whether a person who is under a duty to care for another, whether due to relationship or because the duty is imposed as a result of care rendered to a helpless or infirm person, may be released from that duty by the person to whom it is owed. For example, if the person wishes to die and does not want medical attention, is the 'carer' under a duty to contravene their requests and obtain medical aid?

> In *Smith* [1979] Crim LR 251, S was charged with manslaughter following the death of his wife. She had a marked aversion to doctors and medical treatment and would not allow S to seek medical attention after she had given birth to a still-born child at home. When she finally gave him permission it was too late and she died before the doctor arrived. Medical evidence was such that she could have been saved had medical aid been sought originally. In summing-up to the jury Griffiths J directed them:

> > to balance the weight that it is right to give to his wife's wish to avoid calling a doctor against her capacity to make rational decisions. If she does not appear too ill it may be reasonable to abide by her wishes. On the other hand, if she appeared desperately ill then whatever she may say it may be right to override.

The suggestion seems to be that if a person is capable of making rational decisions he may release a carer from his duty of care. In this case the jury could not agree on the charge of manslaughter and were discharged from giving a verdict. This was only a first-instance decision and it left unresolved the question whether a person may release another from the duty of care in anticipation of that duty arising.

 Question

Could an ageing wife release her husband from his duty of care by telling him that if she fell ill at any time in the future she wanted to be left to die at home without medical attention being called?

The answer to this question was given by the House of Lords in the course of its decision in *Airedale NHS Trust* v *Bland* [1993] 2 WLR 316. An application was made by the Trust for a declaration whether it was lawful for doctors to withdraw life-supporting medical treatment, including artificial feeding through a nasogastric tube, from a patient in one of its hospitals who was in a persistent vegetative state (PVS) with no prospect of recovery or improvement, when it was known that the discontinuance of the treatment would cause his death within a matter of weeks. (Mr Bland was one of the victims of the 1989 Hillsborough Stadium disaster.) The House of Lords held that the treatment could be removed and a doctor would not be acting unlawfully in so doing (see further *R (Burke)* v *GMC* [2004] EWHC 1879 (Admin)).

Lord Goff of Chieveley, giving the leading judgment, stated several principles which apply in the treatment of patients. First, there was **no absolute rule that a patient's life had to be prolonged regardless of the circumstances**. While the fundamental principle was the sanctity of human life, this principle was not absolute. His Lordship was recognising that respect for human dignity demands that the quality of the life in question must be considered. Secondly, **the principle of self-determination required that respect be given to the expressed wishes of the patient**. Thus, if an adult of sound mind refused treatment the doctors responsible for his care had to give effect to his wishes. If the patient was incapable of communicating, an earlier expression of refusal of consent to treatment in certain circumstances would be effective. **Where, however, the patient was both incapable of communicating and had given no earlier indication of his wishes, there was no absolute obligation upon the doctor to prolong his life regardless of the circumstances. The question was what was in the best interests of the patient.** Where a patient is incapable of giving consent, treatment may be provided if it is in his best interests (see *re F (Mental Patient: Sterilisation)* [1990] 2 AC 1, **10.8**). Likewise it may be discontinued if this is in his best interests. His Lordship considered that the question should be carefully formulated as it was not whether it was in the patient's best interests that treatment should be ended but rather whether it was in his best interests that treatment which had the effect of artificially prolonging his life should be continued. Such treatment would not be appropriate where it had no therapeutic purpose, which would be the case where it was futile because the patient was unconscious and had no prospect of any improvement in his condition.

Thirdly, **where such conditions pertained, the treatment being futile, there was no duty on a doctor to continue life-supporting treatment as it was not in the best interests of his patient**. Accordingly, although the discontinuance of treatment would amount to an omission, it would not be unlawful as it would not be in breach of duty to the patient. Similar principles applied with regard to the decision whether to put a patient on life-supporting treatment in the first place. Finally, Lord Goff emphasised that doctors in deciding whether to initiate or discontinue life-support treatment for a patient had to act in accordance with a responsible and competent body of relevant professional opinion on the principles set down in *Bolam* v *Friern Hospital Management Committee* [1957] 1 WLR 582. In *Airedale NHS Trust* v *Bland* guidance was to be found in a 'Discussion Paper on Treatment of Patients in Persistent Vegetative State' issued in September 1992 by the Medical Ethics Committee of the British Medical Association which provided four safeguards which should be observed before discontinuing life-support for such patients:

(1) Every effort should be made at rehabilitation for at least six months after injury.

(2) The diagnosis of irreversible PVS should not be considered confirmed until at least 12 months after the injury.

(3) The diagnosis should be agreed by at least two other independent doctors.

(4) Generally, the wishes of the patient's immediate family would be given great weight.

In all cases where it is decided to end life-support treatment it is good practice to seek a declaration from the High Court as to the lawfulness of any proposed course of action but this is not a legal requirement (see *R (Burke)* v *GMC* [2006] QB 273).

2.5.2.2.4 *Duty arising from creation of a dangerous situation*

Where a person inadvertently and without the appropriate *mens rea* does an act which starts a chain of events which, if uninterrupted, will result in harm to another or his property (or any other interest protected by the criminal law), that person, on becoming aware that he was the cause, is under a duty to take such steps as lie within his power to prevent or minimise the risk of harm. If, before the harm occurs, he realises what he has done and with appropriate *mens rea* he fails to take such steps, he will be criminally liable. The authority for this principle is *Miller* [1983] 2 AC 161.

> D, a vagrant who was squatting in a house, awoke to find that a cigarette he had been smoking had set fire to the mattress on which he was lying. He did not attempt to extinguish the fire but moved to another room. The house caught fire. D was convicted of arson contrary to s. 1(1) and (3) of the Criminal Damage Act 1971. The House of Lords dismissed his appeal against conviction holding that when D became aware of what he had done in setting the mattress on fire he was under a duty to take such steps as were within his power to prevent or minimise the damage to the property at risk. Lord Diplock stated (at p. 181):

> > I see no rational ground for excluding from conduct capable of giving rise to criminal liability, conduct which consists of failing to take measures that lie within one's power to counteract a danger that one has oneself created, if at the time of such conduct one's state of mind is such as constitutes a necessary ingredient of the offence.

The steps which an accused is required to take to counteract the danger he has caused are such as are reasonable in the circumstances. Clearly he would not be expected to attempt to put out a raging inferno; all that might be required is a telephone call summoning the fire brigade. In the case of a minor fire he might reasonably be required to extinguish it himself if all that would be required was a bucket of water or that he stamp on it with his shoe. The jury will have to decide what D could reasonably have been expected to do. That means that the nature of the duty is somewhat unclear and lacks the certainty that should underpin the criminal law. However, it is inherent in liability for omissions that the tests jurors have to apply will inevitably require them to judge what a person *should* have done.

In *DPP* v *Santana-Bermudez* [2003] EWHC Admin 2908, the Administrative Court applied the *Miller* principle in unusual circumstances.

> V, a police officer, sought to carry out a lawful search of D and asked him to turn out his pockets, the contents of which included some syringes. She then asked him if he was sure that he had no more needles. He lied to her and her finger was pierced by a hypodermic needle when she commenced a search of his pockets. The Administrative Court held that where someone by act or word or a combination thereof created a danger and thereby exposed another to a reasonably foreseeable risk of injury which materialised, this could amount to the *actus reus* of assault occasioning actual bodily harm.

In this situation it was clearly D's duty to tell the truth. Whether a conviction would ensue would depend upon proof of intention or recklessness.

The existence of this duty to act arises from the creation by D of the dangerous situation. Their Lordships in *Miller* spoke in terms of a physical act on the part of D setting the train of events in motion. They did not address the question whether an initial omission which set in motion a train of events which placed a person or property in peril might found liability.

 Question

D parks his car on a hill and omits to apply the handbrake. He is walking up the path to his house when he remembers this and turns to see his car start to roll down the hill towards children playing in the street. D realises the danger they are in but he hates children and decides to do nothing either to try to stop his car or warn the children of the danger. V, one of the children, is hit by his car sustaining a broken leg. If D is charged with causing grievous bodily harm with intent contrary to s. 18 of the Offences Against the Person Act 1861 would he be liable? There was no physical act on the part of D which caused the injury but rather an omission, i.e. his failure to apply the handbrake. Should the principle of *Miller* be extended?

2.6 Causation

2.6.1 General

Where an accused is charged with a result crime, it is necessary for the prosecution to prove that his acts or omissions caused the prohibited consequence. In murder or manslaughter, for example, it is necessary to prove that D, by his acts or omissions, caused the death of V. Similarly, in criminal damage, it is necessary to prove that D's acts or omissions caused damage to, or destruction of, property belonging to another. If the death, damage, or destruction occurred because of some other cause then the offence has not been committed even though all the other elements of the *actus reus* are present and D had the necessary *mens rea*. D, however, may be guilty of some other offence such as attempt (see *White*, **2.6.2**). In the case of result crimes for which liability is strict (see **4.2**) causation may be established even though D did not intend or have knowledge of the harm or was not negligent thereto (see *Southern Water Authority* v *Pegrum and Pegrum* [1989] Crim LR 442; *National Rivers Authority* v *Yorkshire Water Services* [1994] Crim LR 451; *Environment Agency* v *Empress Car Co. (Abertillery)* [1999] 2 AC 22).

The issue of causation is for the jury or magistrates to decide upon. The cases which have given rise to problems have usually involved homicide. But, even in homicide cases, causation rarely becomes an issue, as how V died is usually not in dispute. Where there is a dispute it is the duty of the trial judge to direct the jury on the legal principles relating to causation and for the jury, applying those principles, to decide if the causal link between D's conduct and the prohibited consequence has been established. Usually it will be sufficient to direct the jury 'simply that in law D's act need not be the sole cause, or even the main cause, of V's death, it being enough that his act [or omission] contributed significantly to that result' (*Pagett* (1983) 76 Cr App R 279, *per* Robert Goff LJ). Occasionally, when a particular problem relating to causation arises, such as whether the act of a third party has broken the chain of causation, it is (*per* Robert Goff LJ at p. 290):

> for the judge to direct the jury . . . in the most simple terms, in accordance with the legal principles which they have to apply. It would then fall to the jury to decide the relevant factual issues which, identified with reference to those legal principles, will lead to the conclusion whether or not the prosecution have established the guilt of the accused of the crime of which he is charged.

In simplifying causation for the jury, the judge may refer to the two principles of causation, namely that an accused can only be convicted if they are satisfied that his conduct was both a *factual cause* and a *legal cause* of V's death. The discussion will centre on homicide but the principles are equally applicable to other offences where causation may be in issue.

2.6.2 Factual causation

D's conduct must be a *sine qua non* of the prohibited consequence; i.e. it must be established that the consequence would not have occurred as and when it did *but for* D's conduct. This is sometimes referred to as the **'but for'** test.

> In *White* [1910] 2 KB 124 D put cyanide into his mother's drink with intent to kill her. Later his mother was found dead with the glass containing the poisoned drink beside her three parts full. Medical evidence established that she had died of heart failure and not from poisoning. D was acquitted of murder as he had not caused her death and thus there was no *actus reus*. He was, however, convicted of attempted murder.

The fact that factual causation is established, however, does not mean that legal causation can be established.

 Example

A shows B a job advertisement. B applies for the job and C, the employer, invites her for interview. On her way to the interview B is attacked by D while walking through a park and killed. But for A showing B the advertisement she would not have applied for the job and but for C inviting her for interview she would not have been in the park and been killed as and when she was. No one would argue, however, that A's and C's acts should be regarded as legal causes of B's death. It is D's acts which are the legal cause of B's death.

2.6.3 Legal causation

 Key Point

Not all 'but for' causes are legal causes of an event. Legal causation is closely connected to ideas of responsibility and culpability.

Glanville Williams in *Textbook of Criminal Law* (2nd edn, 1983) states (at p. 381):

> When one has settled the question of but-for causation, the further test to be applied to the but-for cause in order to qualify it for legal recognition is not a test of causation but a moral reaction. The question is whether the result can fairly be said to be imputable to the defendant. . . . If the term 'cause' must be used, it can best be distinguished in this meaning as the 'imputable' or 'responsible' or 'blamable' cause, to indicate the value-judgment involved.

The discussion which follows will examine the conditions for the attribution of legal causation.

2.6.3.1 Consequence must be attributable to a culpable act

If the culpable act D performed did not contribute to the consequence legal causation will not be established. Thus although D may have been grossly negligent in performing an act he will not be held responsible for a prohibited consequence which would have occurred whether or not he was negligent. This is illustrated by the case of *Dalloway* (1847) 2 Cox 273.

> D was driving a horse and cart without holding the reins which were lying loose on the horse's back. A child ran in front of the cart and was killed. Erle J directed the jury that if the driver could have saved the child by using the reins they should convict him of manslaughter, but if they thought he could not have saved the child by pulling the reins they must acquit him. The jury acquitted him presumably satisfied that the child's death could not have been avoided and thus the child's death was not attributable to D's negligence. But for the cart being on the road the child would not have died, but driving a cart on the road is not itself a culpable act.

The principle in *Dalloway* would similarly apply on a charge of causing death by dangerous driving if the death would have occurred regardless of the manner of D's driving.

The principle in *Dalloway* appeared to have been overlooked by the Court of Appeal when it considered a new offence created by s. 3ZB of the Road Traffic Act 1988 (which was added by s. 21(1) of the Road Safety Act 2006). This created the offence of causing death by driving a motor vehicle when driving without an appropriate licence or when uninsured. The offence carries a penalty of up to two years' imprisonment. In *Williams* [2010] EWCA Crim 2552, the Court of Appeal held that the offence could be committed without proof of any fault or other blameworthy conduct on the part of D in relation to his driving, the only issue being whether he had been driving without a licence or insurance or while disqualified and that death had been caused.

> D had been driving without a licence or insurance when V stepped out in front of his vehicle without looking; it was accepted that there was nothing that D could have done to have avoided the fatal collision. Obviously 'but for' D's vehicle being on the road the collision would not have happened as and when it did; but the Court did not pay attention to the issue of legal causation which would have resulted in the inevitable conclusion that it was V's own actions which had caused his death rather than any culpable act on the part of D.

The decision in *Williams* was followed by the Court of Appeal in *Hughes* [2011] EWCA Crim 1508.

D was driving a campervan on a main road in good conditions. He was driving fault-lessly when V, driving a car, veered across the road and collided with him. D and his family survived the collision but V died. V had been driving a long distance following a series of 12-hour night shifts and was driving under the influence of heroin; his driving prior to the collision had been erratic. D, however, had no insurance and only a provisional driving licence. Although his driving was faultless and he could not have avoided the collision he was prosecuted for the s. 3ZB offence. At his trial it was sub-mitted on D's behalf that he could not be convicted as he had not caused the death of V. The Recorder of Newcastle ruled in his favour on this point but the Crown appealed this ruling and the Court of Appeal, considering itself bound by the decision in *Williams*, held that the prosecution did not have to prove any element of fault on the part of D, it being sufficient that he had merely been involved in the collision as this amounted in law to his causing the death. D appealed to the Supreme Court which unanimously allowed the appeal ([2013] UKSC 56).

The Supreme Court acknowledged that the decision of the Court of Appeal would render D guilty despite bearing no fault for the collision. The Supreme Court recognised that while the offences of driving when uninsured, disqualified, or unlicensed are offences of strict liability, it would be novel for the aggravated offence of causing death under s. 3ZB to be regarded also as one of strict liability. The Court stated (at para. 17):

> It is certainly true that an uninsured person ought not to be driving at all, . . . but . . . [t]o say that he is responsible because he ought not to have been on the road is to confuse criminal responsibility for the serious offence of being uninsured with criminal responsi-bility for the infinitely more serious offence of killing another person. The criminal law is well used to offences of which there are aggravated forms carrying additional punish-ment where greater harm has been done. . . . But ordinarily, the greater punishment is linked to additional harm which is caused by a *culpable act* on the part of the defendant. In the case of section 3ZB, it is not. [Emphasis added]

The Supreme Court considered that had Parliament wished to impose absolute liabil-ity upon a driver for a death which resulted from an accident where he was driving when uninsured, disqualified, or unlicensed, it could have done so in terms which left no room for doubt. Section 3ZB, however, used the words 'causes . . . death . . . by driving' which the Supreme Court concluded imported the concept of causation. Once this is accepted, a 'but for' cause cannot be considered sufficient to establish causation, the Supreme Court highlighting the established distinction in case law 'between conduct which sets the stage for an occurrence and conduct which on a common sense view is regarded as instrumental in bringing about the occurrence' (at para. 23). The Supreme Court took the view that while D's driving created the oppor-tunity for his car to be run into by V, 'what brought about [V's] death was his own dangerous driving under the influence of drugs'. The Court went on (at para. 25):

> It was a matter of the merest chance that what he hit when he veered onto the wrong side of the road for the last of several times was the oncoming vehicle which Mr Hughes was driving. He might just as easily have gone off the road and hit a tree, in which case nobody would suggest that his death was caused by the planting of the tree, although that too would have been a sine qua non.

The Supreme Court emphasised that s. 3ZB was a penal provision of considerable severity as it created an offence of homicide, and thus is of the greatest gravity, conviction for which would leave the defendant at risk of imprisonment for a substantial term and with a lifelong conviction for homicide which would require disclosure in multiple situations. **The Court emphasised that penal statutes should be construed with a degree of strictness in favour of D** (see **4.2.3**). **Unambiguous language would be necessary to exclude the normal approach to causation.** In the absence of such, the principles of causation would be applied and thus to prove the s. 3ZB offence the prosecution would have to show that D had 'done something other than simply putting his vehicle on the road so that it is there to be struck' (at para. 28). It follows from the expression 'causes . . . death . . . by driving' that if D is to be liable to conviction for the s. 3ZB offence there must be some act or omission in the control of the car that involves some element of fault, 'something in the manner of his driving which is open to proper criticism . . . which contributed in some more than minimal way to the death' (at para. 32). The Supreme Court went on to try to identify what situations might fall within this construction of the s. 3ZB offence, recognising that many cases of driving would amount to careless or inconsiderate driving and fall under s. 2B of the 1988 Act (see **9.3.5.1**) and that the circumstances in which a prosecution for the s. 3ZB offence would be brought would be fairly rare.

In *Taylor* [2016] UKSC 5, the Supreme Court applied its approach in *Hughes* [2013] UKSC 56 to the offence of aggravated vehicle-taking under s. 12A(2)(b) of the Theft Act 1968 (which requires the prosecution to prove that the vehicle was unlawfully taken and, owing to the driving of the vehicle, an accident occurred by which injury was caused to any person). D was charged with, inter alia, aggravated vehicle-taking involving a fatal accident but without fault in the manner of his driving. The Supreme Court followed *Hughes* and stated that 'the driving cannot be said to have caused the accident if it merely explained how the vehicle came to be in the place where the accident occurred' (at para. 29). It is implicit in the words 'owing to the driving of the vehicle' that there must be some element of fault which contributes in some more than minimal way to the injury. (See further **12.4.2**.)

2.6.3.2 The culpable act must be a more than minimal cause of the consequence

In homicide D's act may be considered a cause of death if it has accelerated V's death. It is no answer to a charge of murder or manslaughter to say that V was dying from a fatal disease or injury and would have died within a short time had D not hastened his death (see *Dyson* [1908] 2 KB 454). If, however, D's act produces only a very trivial acceleration of the death of V, it may be ignored under the *de minimis* principle (see *Hennigan* [1971] 3 All ER 133 and *Cato* [1976] 1 WLR 110). On occasions judges have stated that D's act must be a 'substantial' cause of V's death. This would tend to state the principle too favourably for D (see *Malcherek and Steel* [1981] 1 WLR 690). In *Pagett*, Robert Goff LJ stated that '[D's] act need not be the sole cause, or even the main cause, of the victim's death, it being enough that his act contributed significantly to that result'. Whatever the terminology used the idea which is sought to be communicated to the jury is that **D's contribution to the death of V must be more than minimal.** The test is far from scientific as what is sought from the jury is not an exact measurement but, to use Williams' term, a 'moral reaction'; is the death of V morally attributable to D? This is, perhaps, what Devlin J had in mind when he directed the jury in *Adams* [1957] Crim LR 365.

Dr Adams was charged with murder of one of his patients by means of administering pain-relieving drugs. Devlin J directed the jury that it did not matter that the patient's death was inevitable and that her days were numbered:

> If her life were cut short by weeks or months it was just as much murder as if it was cut short by years. The law knows no special defence [by which doctors might be justified in administering drugs which would shorten life in cases of severe pain,] but that did not mean that a doctor who was aiding the sick and dying had to calculate in minutes, or even in hours, and perhaps not in days or weeks, the effect upon a patient's life of the medicines which he administers or else be in peril of a charge of murder. If the first purpose of medicine, the restoration of health, can no longer be achieved there is still much for a doctor to do, and he is entitled to do all that is proper and necessary to relieve pain and suffering, even if the measures he takes may incidentally shorten life . . . The law is the same for all, and what I have said to you rests simply upon this: no act is murder which does not cause death. 'Cause' means nothing philosophical or technical or scientific. It means what you twelve men and women sitting as a jury in the jury box would regard in a common-sense way as the cause.

In such circumstances a jury would presumably not find causation, as their moral reaction would be that the doctor was seeking to relieve pain and only incidentally accelerated the patient's death. If, however, the pain-relieving drugs were administered not by a doctor but by the sole beneficiary under her will, and were administered to hasten the inheritance, one could assume that a jury would exhibit a different moral reaction and would find causation to be established.

2.6.3.3 The culpable act need not be the sole cause

D's act need be neither the sole nor the main cause of the prohibited consequence. Other causes contributing to the consequence may be the acts of others or even of the deceased himself. The onus on the prosecution is to establish beyond reasonable doubt that D's acts were a significant cause of the prohibited result. There is no onus on the prosecution to establish that any supervening act was not a significant cause of the result (*R* v *Mellor* [1996] 2 Cr App R 245). In the directions to the jury, the trial judge must keep the jury focused on deciding the extent of D's responsibility for the result.

2.6.3.3.1 *The actions of third parties*

> In *Benge* (1865) 4 F & F 504, the actions of third parties contributed significantly to the deaths. D, the foreman of a track-laying crew, misread the railway timetable so that the track was up at a time when a train was due. D placed a signalman with a flag 540 yards up the line although the company regulations specified 1,000 yards. The engine-driver was not keeping a good look-out and several deaths resulted from the ensuing accident. D argued that if the signalman had gone the correct distance and the driver had kept a proper look-out there would not have been an accident. D was convicted of manslaughter after Pigott B directed the jury that if D's conduct mainly or substantially caused the accident it mattered not that it might have been avoided if the others had not been negligent.

The facts of cases need not be as unusual as *Benge*. For example, if A and B both attack C, A stabbing him in the lung and B stabbing him in the abdomen, both would be liable for homicide if he dies as a result of the combined effect of the wounds even though neither wound was, of itself, mortal. There are other circumstances, however, where a subsequent act may supersede an antecedent act which otherwise would have caused death. For example, A poisons B with a slow-acting poison. Before it takes effect C decapitates B with an axe. In this situation C's act is the sole cause of B's death. A, however, could be charged with attempted murder (see e.g. *Rafferty* [2007] EWCA Crim 1846).

2.6.3.3.2 *The actions of the victim*

The deceased by his negligence may contribute to his own death. For example, if D is driving in excess of the speed limit when V, who is blind, walks across the road and is hit by D killing him, it matters not that V's negligence contributed to his death if D could have avoided hitting him had he been observing the speed limit (see *Longbottom* (1849) 3 Cox CC 439).

   Where V brings about his own injuries or death this may be legally attributable to D where he has caused V reasonably to apprehend violence to himself and he has died in seeking to escape. In such a situation D will only be found to have caused V's injuries or death where V's response to D's violence or threat of violence was 'within the range of responses which might be expected from a victim placed in the situation which he was' (*Williams* [1992] 2 All ER 183, 191, *per* Stuart-Smith LJ). V's response must be 'proportionate to the threat, that is to say that it was within the ambit of reasonableness and not so daft as to make it his own voluntary act which amounted to a *novus actus interveniens* and consequently broke the chain of causation' (*Williams* [1992] 2 All ER 183, 191, *per* Stuart-Smith LJ; see also *Lewis* [2010] EWCA Crim 151). In deciding whether V's response was reasonably foreseeable the jury should bear in mind 'any particular characteristic of the victim and the fact that in the agony of the moment he may act without thought and deliberation' (*Williams* [1992] 2 All ER 183, 191, *per* Stuart-Smith LJ). (See also *Roberts* (1971) 56 Cr App R 95; *Mackie* (1973) 57 Cr App R 453; *DPP* v *Daley* [1979] 2 WLR 239; *Hayward* (1908) 21 Cox CC 692.)

> In *Marjoram* [2000] Crim LR 372, D, who was 16, was part of a group of young people who went to V's room in a hostel in order to confront V. D broke open the door, finding V on the window ledge. V then jumped or fell to the ground two stories beneath. D was convicted of inflicting grievous bodily harm contrary to s. 20 of the Offences Against the Person Act 1861. He argued on appeal that for the purposes of the question whether a reasonable person could have foreseen V's attempt to escape as a possible consequence of D's assault, the reasonable person should be the same age and sex as D. The Court of Appeal ruled that as the issue concerned the effect of D's conduct on V's mind, the test had to be objective to avoid the absurdity where there were two defendants of one being held not to have caused the injury because he had not foreseen V's flight, and the other being held to have caused it because he had foreseen V's flight.
>
>   In *Roberts*, *Williams*, and *Marjoram*, each victim acted on the spur of the moment to escape an immediate threat to her personal safety. The legal position is somewhat less clear when the victim's actions are not an immediate response to an imminent threat. For example, can D be said in law to have caused V's suicide if D has bullied V or subjected V to psychological abuse? In **2.6.3.4** and the **Law in Context feature**, we will explore that in more detail.

2.6.3.4 D must take his victim as he finds him

D cannot complain if V is particularly susceptible to physical injury as where, for example, he suffers from brittle bones or haemophilia; if death ensues from an injury which would not have been fatal in a person of sound health it will still be attributable to D. In *Martin* (1832) 5 C & P 128 Parke J stated (at p. 130):

> It is said that the deceased was in a bad state of health; but that is perfectly immaterial, as, if the prisoner was so unfortunate as to accelerate her death, he must answer for it.

The principle that D must take his victim as he finds him is not limited to consequences flowing from pre-existing medical or physiological conditions; it has been extended to cover V's mental condition or religious beliefs.

> In *Blaue* [1975] 1 WLR 1411, D stabbed V, the wound penetrating her lung. At hospital V was told that a blood transfusion and surgery were necessary to save her life. V died after refusing a blood transfusion as it was contrary to her beliefs as a Jehovah's Witness. Medical evidence indicated that V would not have died if she had accepted the transfusion. On appeal from his conviction for manslaughter, D argued that V's refusal of a transfusion was unreasonable and broke the chain of causation. The Court of Appeal rejected this argument in categorical terms. Lawton LJ stated (at p. 1415):

> > It has long been the policy of the law that those who use violence on other people must take their victims as they find them. This in our judgment means the whole man, not just the physical man. It does not lie in the mouth of the assailant to say that the victim's religious beliefs which inhibited him from accepting certain kinds of treatment were unreasonable. The question for decision is what caused her death. The answer is the stab wound. The fact that the victim refused to stop this end coming about did not break the causal connection between the act and death.

Had the Court of Appeal adopted the 'reasonable foresight' test used in the 'flight' cases discussed at **2.6.3.3.2** there would have been no need for a value judgement to be made on the reasonableness of the victim's religious beliefs; the only issue would be whether such refusal of treatment was reasonably foreseeable. This is the position in the law of tort. Lawton LJ distinguished between crime and tort stating that 'the criminal law is concerned with the maintenance of law and order and the protection of the public generally'. Glanville Williams, in a casenote in (1976) 35 *Cambridge Law Journal* 15, observes that this argument ignores the fact that Blaue was in any event punishable severely for wounding with intent. The need to protect the public could be reflected in the sentence for such an offence just as much as in the sentence for manslaughter. In such a circumstance the label under which punishment is imposed would appear to be purely symbolic. Symbolism, however, may sometimes serve a purpose. Had V been unable to obtain medical assistance it would have been unarguable that the wound caused her death. Why should Blaue be allowed to avoid a conviction for manslaughter because of V's choice not to accept medical treatment? V's omission did nothing to interrupt the chain of causation flowing from Blaue's initiating act.

Question

Could taking his victim as he finds him include holding D liable where V commits suicide following D's attack on him?

Where V commits suicide following D's attack on him, this will break the chain of causation if it is done for a reason other than the attack on him. In *Dear* [1996] Crim LR 595, the Court of Appeal accepted that if V had reopened wounds inflicted on him by D because of shame over an alleged sexual assault by V on D's daughter (which was the background to D's attack on him) rather than because of the fact of the attack (which was serious and had disfigured him), this would break the chain of causation. As the evidence to this effect was described as 'tenuous' and had been put before the jury with an adequate direction, the Court saw no grounds for overturning D's conviction for murder. The Court emphasised that death resulted from bleeding from an artery which D had severed and thus, whether or not V had reopened the wound, D's 'conduct made an operative and significant contribution to the death'. The Court, however, did not address the question whether, if the victim commits suicide because of an attack by D, it must be proved that such suicide was a reasonably foreseeable consequence of D's acts before causation can be established. In *R v D* [2006] EWCA 1139, [2006] Crim LR 923, the Court of Appeal, in quashing a conviction for manslaughter, *obiter* left open the possibility of such a conviction where it was triggered by a physical assault which represented the culmination of a course of abusive conduct, and the final assault played a significant part in causing V to commit suicide where V was someone with a fragile and vulnerable personality. The Court of Appeal left many questions unanswered in this case. The physical assault had not left any wound which could constitute an operating cause at the time of death.

The Court of Appeal in *R v Wallace (Berlinah)* [2018] EWCA Crim 690 has gone some way towards clarifying the impact of a victim's suicide on the defendant's liability.

> In a jealous rage, BW threw sulphuric acid at or upon V with intent to burn, maim, disfigure, or disable him or to do some grievous bodily harm to him. There was no dispute that she had thrown the acid over V and that he sustained truly dreadful injuries as a result. V was terribly disfigured, completely paralysed, and in a permanent state of unbearable physical and psychological pain that his doctors could not ameliorate (para. 3). With assistance, V travelled to Belgium where he chose to be voluntarily euthanised by a lethal injection lawfully administered to him by doctors in a hospital, in accordance with Belgian law which permits voluntary euthanasia. BW was charged with V's murder and with applying a corrosive substance with intent, contrary to s. 29 of the Offences Against the Person Act 1861.

Did V's choice to be euthanised and the doctors' actions in giving effect to that decision break the chain of causation and mean BW could not be guilty of murder? The prosecution's case was that BW intended to cause him really serious harm and had caused his death; her actions were a substantial and operating cause of V's death. The defence submitted that there was no case to answer. Whilst the defendant's actions may properly be seen as the factual cause of death ('but for' her actions, he would not have wanted to have a lethal injection), V's choice to die combined with the actions of the Belgian doctors who ended his life constituted an intervening cause breaking the chain of causation. The defence also submitted that if V had been given a lethal injection in England or Wales, that doctor would face a murder charge and such an unlawful act would be bound to constitute an independent, intervening act.

The trial judge acceded to the defence request that there was no case to answer. She said:

> It seems to me that if one is to accord proper respect to the decision and actions of persons with free will acting autonomously (whether as a victim or third-party intervener) then the legal result of their free and voluntary choice and/or positive act to end their own or another's life must as I see it be to break with what had gone before, disconnecting both the choice to die and the death itself from the circumstances generating the occasion for it. When [V] made the brave, desperate, profoundly sad decision that his life with such appalling disability was so burdensome that he preferred to leave it, and when the doctors opened the door for him to go and ushered him through, his choice and their actions each disconnected his death, in law, from the culpable activity which had caused his dreadful injuries. In my view, a jury properly directed, could reach no other conclusion and for that reason I have decided that the case of murder must be withdrawn from them.

The prosecution successfully appealed against that ruling. The Court of Appeal held that the murder charge should not have been withdrawn from the jury. Lady Justice Sharp held:

> The intervening acts of [V] and the doctors were not, on these facts, random extraneous events, or acts unconnected with the fault element of the defendant's conduct. They were very closely, indeed inextricably, bound up with it . . . Looked at in this way, [V's] death, his requests to the doctors, and the act of euthanasia itself carried out in accordance with his wishes, were not discrete acts or events independent of the defendant's conduct, nor were they voluntary, if by this is meant they were the product of the sort of free and unfettered volition presupposed by the novus actus rule. Instead they were a direct response to the inflicted injuries and to the circumstances created by them for which the defendant was responsible. If the question is then asked whether, on a common sense view, the defendant's conduct merely set the stage for [V's] death, or was instrumental in bringing it about, we consider the jury could properly answer that question in the prosecution's favour. (at paras 60–61)

In response to the argument that the doctors' acts in bringing about V's death constituted a *novus actus interveniens*, the Court held that those acts were not sensibly divisible from V's choice. V's near-total paralysis meant that suicide was not an option. The Court of Appeal was very clear that V's death at the hands of Belgian doctors, rather than by his own hands, made no difference to the legal outcome: 'It would seem an odd result, if a defendant who paralysed one victim but not another in identical circumstances (so the second could take their own life, but the first could only do so through the intervention of a third party) would be legally responsible for the death of the second victim but not the first' (at para. 85).

The Court of Appeal ordered a retrial. While not being prescriptive about the precise wording that the trial judge should use, the Court said that the following direction to the jury would be appropriate (in addition to directions on the *mens rea* for murder):

> In order to convict the defendant on count 1 you must be sure that the defendant's unlawful act of throwing acid over [V] caused his death. This is a question of fact that you should answer using your collective common sense. It is common ground that but for the injuries caused by the acid attack, [V] would not have undergone voluntary euthanasia. If you are sure this is the case, go on to ask yourself:
>
> (a) Are you sure that the defendant's unlawful act of throwing acid over [V] was a significant and operating cause of death? The injuries do not need to be the only cause of death but they must play more than a minimal part in causing [V's] death. Consider all the circumstances, including the nature and extent of [V's] injuries, the passage of time, intervening events, the involvement of the doctors in carrying out the voluntary euthanasia at [V's] request, what [V] was told and what he said.
>
>   If your answer is yes, proceed to question . . . (b). If you are not sure, your verdict on count 1 will be not guilty.
>
> (b) Are you sure that at the time of the acid attack it was reasonably foreseeable that the defendant would commit suicide as a result of his injuries? In answering this question consider all the circumstances, including the nature of the attack, what the defendant did and said at the time and whether or not [V's] decision to undergo voluntary euthanasia fell within the range of responses which might have been expected from a victim in his situation. If your answer is yes, your verdict on count 1 will be guilty. If your answer is no, your verdict on count 1 will be not guilty.

At her retrial, Wallace was found not guilty of murder but guilty of applying a corrosive substance with intent. Note that the Court of Appeal did not say that BW had caused his death; rather, they held that it was at least arguable and should have been left to the jury to decide on the particular facts of the case. Whether the defendant has caused a particular result remains a question of fact for the jury.

The significance of this case is discussed in more detail in the **Law in Context feature**.

2.6.3.5 Intervening events and acts

Between the initial act or omission of D which sets in motion the train of events which result in the prohibited consequence occurring, other events or acts may intervene. The question will arise whether such an event or act amounts to a *novus actus interveniens*—that is, a new act which intervenes to break the chain of causation. **The general principle is that an intervention by a third party will constitute a *novus actus* where it is 'free, deliberate and informed'** (*Pagett* (1983) 76 Cr App R 279, 288, *per* Sir Robert Goff LJ, quoting Hart and Honoré, *Causation in the Law* (1959); see also *Latif* [1996] 1 WLR 104, 115, *per* Lord Steyn). A natural event will do so where it is not reasonably foreseeable. There are several situations in which it may be argued that the chain of causation has been broken.

2.6.3.5.1 *Medical treatment*

> **? Question**
>
> Where D inflicts an injury upon V which requires medical treatment, is he to be held liable if that treatment is improper or negligent? While it may be foreseeable that V will require medical treatment, is it foreseeable that he might receive improper or negligent treatment?

In *Jordan* (1956) 40 Cr App R 152, D stabbed V who was taken to hospital and the wound was stitched. Eight days later V died. D was convicted of murder. On appeal fresh evidence was called which disclosed that at the time of death the wound was healed but D had died as a result of (1) a Terramycin injection to prevent infection, administered after V had shown intolerance to a previous injection, and (2) the intravenous introduction of large quantities of liquid which had caused V's lungs to become waterlogged. The treatment was described as 'palpably wrong' and the Court of Appeal quashed the conviction as, if the jury had heard this evidence, they 'would have felt precluded from saying that they were satisfied that death was caused by the stab wound'. The problem with the judgment is that no clear principle was stated for determining when the chain of causation might be broken by medical treatment. Hallett J stated (at p. 157):

> We are disposed to accept it as the law that death resulting from any normal treatment employed to deal with a felonious injury may be regarded as caused by the felonious injury but we do not think it necessary . . . to formulate . . . the correct test which ought to be laid down with regard to what is necessary to be proved in order to establish causal connection between the death and the felonious injury. It is sufficient to point out here that this was not normal treatment.

Treatment which is 'not normal', however, is not necessarily 'palpably wrong'.

In *Smith* [1959] 2 QB 35, D, a soldier, stabbed V twice with a bayonet in a barrack-room fight. Another soldier carrying V to the medical reception station dropped him twice. The medical staff were under pressure as others had been injured in the fight. They did not realise that one of V's wounds had pierced a lung and caused a haemorrhage and gave V treatment which, in light of this information, was described at D's trial as 'thoroughly bad and might well have affected his chances of recovery'. V died and D was convicted of murder. On appeal D's counsel sought to argue that the treatment he received was abnormal and that, if the treatment impeded the chance of V recovering, the death did not result from the wound. The appeal was dismissed, Lord Parker CJ stating (at pp. 42, 43):

> [I]f at the time of death the original wound is still an operating cause and a substantial cause, then the death can properly be said to be the result of the wound, albeit that some other cause of death is also operating. Only if it can be said that the original wounding is merely the setting in which another cause operates can it be said that the death did not result from the wound. Putting it in another way, only if the second cause is so overwhelming as to make the original wound merely part of the history can it be said that the death does not flow from the wound.

Where the medical treatment is negligent but the wound is still operating, it would seem that both the perpetrator of the wound and the doctor treating it could be said to have caused the death. In such a situation, however, there would be little likelihood of a prosecution for manslaughter being brought against the doctor. Where, however, the wound has healed and negligent treatment independently causes death a prosecution of the doctor may ensue.

It is arguable that had the jury been in full possession of the facts in *Jordan* they legitimately could have found that the wound was simply the setting in which the palpably wrong treatment operated to cause death. An analogous example might be where a doctor administers a drug to V mistaking him for another patient and V dies as a result.

In *Cheshire* [1991] 3 All ER 670, **the Court of Appeal shifted the point of focus away from the question whether the original wound was still an operating cause at the time of death to whether death was attributable to the acts of D.**

> D shot V in the leg and abdomen. Respiratory problems ensued necessitating a tracheotomy. V suffered further respiratory problems and infections culminating in his death two months after the shooting due to cardio-respiratory arrest. This occurred because V's windpipe had become obstructed due to narrowing where the tracheotomy had been performed. The medical staff failed to diagnose and treat this rare complication. Although the gunshot wounds were healed at the time of death, the Court of Appeal upheld D's conviction for murder on the basis that the respiratory complications were a direct consequence of D's *acts* which, despite medical negligence, remained a significant cause of V's death.

This is undoubtedly correct as the failure of diagnosis did not cause V to die but simply hindered measures being taken which might have kept him alive. There are similarities with *Smith* who also suffered the misfortune of misdiagnosis. The Court of Appeal was of the opinion that only in the most extraordinary and unusual case would medical treatment break the chain of causation as 'treatment which falls short of the standard expected of the competent medical practitioner is unfortunately only too frequent in human experience for it to be considered abnormal in the sense of extraordinary' (*per* Beldam LJ, at p. 675). By 'extraordinary' it appears his Lordship meant 'unforeseeable'. His Lordship went on to suggest the terms in which a jury should be directed where they have to consider whether negligent medical treatment, rather than the injuries inflicted by D, were the cause of V's death (at p. 677):

> [I]t is sufficient for the judge to tell the jury that they must be satisfied that the Crown have proved that the acts of D caused the death of the deceased, adding that D's acts need not be the sole cause or even the main cause of death, it being sufficient that his acts contributed significantly to that result. Even though negligence in the treatment of the victim was the immediate cause of his death, the jury should not regard it as excluding the responsibility of D unless the negligent treatment was so independent of his acts, and in itself so potent in causing death, that they regard the contribution made by his acts as insignificant.

> **Question**
>
> How likely is it that negligent medical treatment will break the chain of causation?

It is submitted that only in rare cases where positive treatment is given, either in terms of surgical operation or medicinal prescription, will medical negligence supervene to become an independent cause of death rendering D's acts 'insignificant'. Examples might be where poison is administered in mistake for a drug, or a drug is administered in an excessive quantity resulting in an overdose, or medical staff continue to administer a drug to which V has displayed intolerance and V dies as a result, or an unnecessary operation is performed in the course of which V dies. If, however, due to misdiagnosis treatment which would have been effectual if administered is not given and V dies, the death can still be linked directly to D's original act as in *Smith* and *Cheshire*. The situation is no different from that where D refuses medical treatment (see **2.6.3.5.2**) or where medical treatment is not available. If there is negligence in the treatment of V, for example, a doctor operating to save his life makes a mistake and V dies during the operation, D's acts will remain a cause of death as such an eventuality is not so extraordinary as to be unforeseeable; the operation was a direct result of D wounding V and thus was not independent of D's acts. The crucial issue is whether D's acts contributed significantly to the victim's death and, if they did, it matters not whether the medical treatment was incompetent or mistaken (see *Mellor* [1996] 2 Cr App R 245).

> **Question**
>
> What happens if D's act causes serious injuries to V such that he is only kept alive by a life-support machine and this is ultimately switched off?

A problem which has arisen due to advances in medical technology is that of a victim who has suffered serious injuries whose life is sustained by a life-support machine. If the machine is switched off by the doctors treating V, who is responsible for the death? This issue arose in two appeals heard together by the Court of Appeal: *Malcherek and Steel* [1981] 1 WLR 690. Both appellants had caused serious injuries to their victims whose lives were sustained by life-support machines. When the doctors treating the victims concluded, after extensive tests, that they were 'brain dead', they switched off the machines, whereupon the victims ceased breathing, their hearts ceased beating, and their blood ceased circulating and 'conventional death' occurred. The Court of Appeal upheld the convictions for murder, Lord Lane CJ stating (at p. 696):

> There is no evidence in the present case here that at the time of conventional death, after the life-support machinery was disconnected, the original wound or injury was other than a continuing, operating and indeed substantial cause of the death of the victim.

While it was immaterial whether the doctors' actions were also causes of death, the Court of Appeal did state *obiter* that they regarded such a suggestion by counsel for the appellants as 'bizarre'. This is undoubtedly correct as when the doctors switched off the machines they merely ceased artificially to sustain lives which had been effectively ended by the initial injuries.

Malcherek and Steel dealt with switching off life-support machines where the victims are already 'brain dead'. It is assumed that the same principles apply where life-supporting treatment is removed from a patient in a PVS (see *Airedale NHS Trust v Bland*, **2.5.2.2.3**). In deciding that case the House of Lords were not addressing the issue of causation, but in the course of his speech Lord Goff stated that **in discontinuing life-supporting treatment a doctor is 'simply allowing the patient to die in the sense that he [is] desisting from taking a step which might prevent his patient from dying as a result of his pre-existing condition'**. If V is in a PVS as a result of D's act, his death after discontinuance of life-supporting treatment would also be caused by D's act.

2.6.3.5.2 *Neglect by the victim*

 Question

What happens if V mistreats or neglects to treat injuries D caused him and he dies?

If V mistreats or neglects to treat injuries perpetrated by D, this will not prevent legal attribution of responsibility to D where death results. In *Holland* (1841) 2 Mood & R 351, D cut V severely on the finger. The wound became infected and V ignored medical advice that he should have the finger amputated or his life might be endangered. The wound caused lock-jaw and V died. Maule J directed the jury that it made no difference whether the wound was instantly mortal, or whether it became so by reason of V not having adopted the best mode of treatment as 'the real question is, whether in the end the wound inflicted by the prisoner was the cause of death'. The jury convicted D of murder. Medical science has advanced greatly and a refusal of treatment today in such a case might be regarded as unreasonable. However, the Court of Appeal in *Blaue* established that the reasonableness of V's conduct is not a relevant issue when considering causation (see *Blaue*, **2.6.3.4**). In *Dear* [1996] Crim LR 595 (**2.6.3.4**) Rose LJ stated:

> It would not, in our judgment, be helpful to juries if the law required them . . . to decide causation in a case such as the present by embarking on an analysis of whether a victim had treated himself with mere negligence or gross neglect, the latter breaking but the former not breaking the chain of causation between the defendant's wrongful act and V's death.

It would seem that D also has to accept his victim's phobias, irrationality, or stupidity. These matters, however, would be pertinent when sentencing an accused convicted of manslaughter where the death could easily have been avoided had the deceased not mistreated or neglected to treat the injury. On a murder conviction the trial judge must impose a sentence of life imprisonment but the matters might be relevant when setting the minimum period that D must serve before he can be considered for release by the Parole Board (see **9.2**).

2.6.3.5.3 *Naturally occurring events*

If D renders V unconscious and leaves him lying on a beach with an incoming tide, V's drowning will be attributable to D. In such a situation, while the original injury did not, of itself, cause death, this will not avail D as the event was objectively foreseeable as likely to occur in the normal course of events. By contrast, if D renders V unconscious and leaves him in a building and thereafter the building collapses in an earthquake, V's death will not be attributable to D as V was not left in a position of obvious danger and such an event would not be expected to occur in the normal course of events.

2.6.3.5.4 *Intervention by a third party*

The acts of a third party may intervene to break the chain of causation, as where, for example, the injured victim dies when the ambulance in which he is being taken to hospital crashes, or, while in hospital he is attacked and killed by an insane patient who has escaped from the psychiatric ward. Where the act of the third party is a reasonable act of self-defence in response to the act of D, or a reasonable act done in the execution of a duty to prevent crime or arrest an offender, this will not break the chain of causation (*Pagett* (1983) 76 Cr App R 279). In *Pagett* D fired a shotgun at police officers attempting to arrest him while holding V against her will and using her body as a shield. The officers returned fire and killed V. D was convicted of manslaughter and his conviction upheld by the Court of Appeal. The same principle would apply if the police had returned fire hitting a bystander.

There used to be two problematic cases in this area of third-party interventions. In *Environment Agency* v *Empress Car Co. (Abertillery)* [1999] 2 AC 22, D Co. had on its land a diesel tank which had an outlet pipe connected to it which led to a drum. The outlet pipe was controlled by a tap which was not locked. An unknown person opened the tap resulting in the contents of the tank draining into the drum, overflowing and polluting a river. D Co. was charged with causing polluting matter to enter controlled waters contrary to s. 85(1) of the Water Resources Act 1991. D Co. denied causing pollution but was convicted. The House of Lords dismissed D Co.'s appeal. Incredibly the leading judgment by Lord Hoffmann **drew no distinction between deliberate acts of third parties and interventions of nature stating that**:

> The true common sense distinction is, in my view, between acts and events which, although not necessarily foreseeable in the particular case, are in the generality a normal and familiar fact of life, and acts or events which are abnormal and extraordinary . . . . There is nothing unusual about people putting unlawful substances into the sewage system and the same, regrettably, is true about ordinary vandalism. So when these things happen, one does not say: that was an extraordinary coincidence, which negatived the causal connection between the original act of accumulating the polluting substance and its escape. In the context of section 85(1), the defendant's accumulation has still caused the pollution.

There was something almost perverse about this reasoning which concluded that D should be responsible for a result which he did not cause simply because the act of vandalism by which it was caused was not so extraordinary as to be unforeseeable.

There is a major difference between a natural event and the action of a third party: the act of the third party is 'free, deliberate and informed'. In the instant case it was also malicious. In such a case D's liability ends up depending on the choices and actions of others rather than his own choices and actions. In *Kennedy (No. 2)* [2007] UKHL 38 the House of Lords confined the authority of *Empress* to strict liability pollution offences overruling a number of Court of Appeal decisions which purported to apply *Empress* to manslaughter (see later and see further *L* [2008] EWCA Crim 1970 and **Chapter 9**).

The second problem case was that of *Kennedy* [1999] Crim LR 65. D supplied a heroin-filled syringe to V who paid him and injected it and subsequently died. D was convicted of manslaughter. The Court of Appeal placed considerable emphasis on the fact that D's supply of the syringe amounted to encouragement to V to inject himself. A person who encourages another to commit an offence may be liable as an accessory to that offence because of the encouragement offered, not because the encouragement causes the relevant consequence—it is the principal who causes it. In the instant case, however, V, being the deceased, could not be the principal to manslaughter, only D could be that, but V's injection of himself with heroin was the immediate cause of his death (cf. *Dalby*, 9.3.3.1.1). As in the *Empress* case D merely produced the setting in which a third party's free, deliberate, and informed act intervened. D did not force, induce, or deceive V into injecting himself; his appeal should have been allowed.

In *Dias* [2001] EWCA Crim 2986, on facts similar to *Kennedy*, the Court of Appeal quashed the conviction of D for manslaughter as self-injection by V was not unlawful and thus there was no offence which D could have encouraged. The Court, however, left unresolved whether a conviction for constructive manslaughter could have been upheld had the case been presented to the jury on the basis of unlawfully causing a noxious thing to be administered to V. The Court expressed the view that V's self-injection 'might well have been seen as an intervening act' which would probably have broken the chain of causation between the supply of the heroin to V and his death. The Court, however, considered that this issue should have been left to the jury to determine. Unfortunately it did not enlarge on the circumstances in which self-injection would not have the effect of breaking the chain of causation. Most commentators believed that this should only arise where D forces V to inject himself or deceives V as to the nature of the substance in the syringe or V, by reason of his age or mental condition, is unable to understand what he is doing.

 Question

Have the courts sorted out the confusion in subsequent cases?

Since the decision in *Dias* the Court of Appeal had several opportunities to provide clarification but on each occasion it either avoided the issue or further added to the confusion (*Richards* [2002] EWCA Crim 3175, *Rogers* [2003] EWCA 945, *Kennedy* [2005] EWCA Crim 685). *Kennedy* was appealed to the House of Lords when the Court of Appeal certified the following question of general public importance:

When is it appropriate to find someone guilty of manslaughter where that person has been involved in the supply of a class A controlled drug, which is then freely and voluntarily self-administered by the person to whom it was supplied, and the administration of the drug then causes his death?

In *Kennedy (No. 2)* [2007] UKHL 38, their Lordships answered the question with a unanimous and resounding 'Never'. The House of Lords reasserted the principle that the criminal law assumes the existence of free will. Lord Bingham of Cornhill stated (at para. 14):

> The law recognises certain exceptions, in the case of the young, those who for any reason are not fully responsible for their actions, and the vulnerable, and it acknowledges situations of duress and necessity, as also of deception and mistake. But, generally speaking, informed adults of sound mind are treated as autonomous beings able to make their own decisions how they will act, and none of the exceptions is relied on as possibly applicable in this case. Thus D is not to be treated as causing V to act in a certain way if V makes a voluntary and informed decision to act in that way rather than another. There are many classic statements to this effect. In his article *'Finis for Novus Actus?'* (1989) 48(3) CLJ 391, 392, Professor Glanville Williams wrote:
>
> > 'I may suggest reasons to you for doing something; I may urge you to do it, tell you it will pay you to do it, tell you it is your duty to do it. My efforts may perhaps make it very much more likely that you will do it. But they do not cause you to do it, in the sense in which one causes a kettle of water to boil by putting it on the stove. Your volitional act is regarded (within the doctrine of responsibility) as setting a new "chain of causation" going, irrespective of what has happened before.'
>
> In chapter XII of *Causation in the Law*, 2nd edn (1985), p 326, Hart and Honoré wrote:
>
> > 'The free, deliberate, and informed intervention of a second person, who intends to exploit the situation created by the first, but is not acting in concert with him, is normally held to relieve the first actor of criminal responsibility.'
>
> This statement was cited by the House with approval in *R v Latif* [1996] 1 WLR 104, 115. The principle is fundamental and not controversial.

The House of Lords affirmed the doctrine of *novus actus interveniens* and its importance in maintaining the essential division between principals and accessories. The mess made by the Court of Appeal in its series of misguided decisions over a period of nine years was thus cleared up. What is disappointing is that it took so long for the fundamental errors made by the Court of Appeal to be recognised and remedied. It must be an issue of concern that the defendants in numerous cases were convicted of manslaughter, and that they were sentenced to lengthy terms of imprisonment when they were guilty of no homicide offence, all because senior appellate judges lacked understanding of the doctrine of causation.

 Question

But is there not a possible problem remaining with the conviction of Evans for gross negligence manslaughter?

An issue arising from the decision in *Evans (Gemma)* [2009] EWCA Crim 650 (see **2.5.2.2**) is whether the Court of Appeal adequately considered the principles of causation before affirming the conviction for gross negligence manslaughter. D's liability arose from her failure to take reasonable steps to save V's life following her overdosing on the heroin D had supplied, which supply created, or contributed to the creation of, the state of affairs which became life-threatening. It may be argued that it was not the supply which created the dangerous situation; rather it was V's voluntary act of self-injection which occurred after the act of supply and before the danger arose. The Court of Appeal briefly adverted to *Kennedy (No. 2)*, but did not examine the principles of causation in any detail concentrating rather on other gross negligence manslaughter cases. If the point at which the duty arose was only when the life-threatening situation had developed and D became aware of it, it may be that V's prior act of taking the heroin did not break the chain of causation. If, however, the focus is placed on the initiating act which contributed to the creation of the dangerous situation, namely the supply of the heroin, as being the point when the duty arose, then V's act of taking the heroin could break the chain of causation. As D's duty requires awareness of the existence of the dangerous situation, it is submitted that the chain of causation between the duty arising and the death occurring was not broken by any act of V as her self-administration preceded this point.

2.7 Coincidence of *actus reus* and *mens rea*

Question

If D commits the *actus reus* of an offence requiring proof of *mens rea*, at what point in time must he have had the requisite *mens rea*?

Where an offence requires *mens rea* the prosecution must prove that D had *mens rea* at the time he did the act which caused the *actus reus* (*Jakeman* (1982) 76 Cr App R 223).

> In *Jakeman* D had booked two cases containing cannabis onto a flight from Accra to Rome and from there to London. The flight was diverted from Rome to Paris. D had repented of her intention to import the cannabis into England and did not claim her cases in Paris. Officials in Paris, however, sent the cases to London where the cannabis was discovered. D was charged with being knowingly concerned in the importation of cannabis. The Court rejected her defence that she had repented of her criminal intent at the time the cannabis entered England. They stated that what mattered was her 'state of mind at the time the relevant acts are done'. In this case the relevant act was booking her luggage to London, at which time she intended it to arrive in London, and it was immaterial that innocent agents at a Paris airport subsequently became instrumental in it being sent to London.

Question

What happens if the *actus reus* is established by means of a continuing act?

Where an *actus reus* may be brought about by a continuing act, it is sufficient that D had *mens rea* during its continuance albeit that he did not have *mens rea* at its inception (*Fagan* v *Metropolitan Police Commissioner* [1969] 1 QB 439).

> In *Fagan* D accidentally drove his car onto a policeman's foot. The officer asked him to move but he delayed doing so. D was convicted of assaulting the constable in the execution of his duty. It was clear that at the time of driving onto the officer's foot D did not have the necessary *mens rea* for the offence. The Divisional Court, however, held that the assault involved a battery (unlawful application of force to another person) and that this battery continued after the car came to rest, and thus there was a continuing act of assault for which D had the necessary *mens rea* at some time during its continuance.

The Divisional Court also stated that **if an act is complete, even though results continue to flow from it, the subsequent inception of *mens rea* cannot convert it into an offence.** For example, if D accidentally runs over V in his car and V sustains injuries from which he dies some time later, D's desire that V die, formed after the accident, will not convert V's death into murder. The act which caused death was complete prior to the formation of D's desire, even though the results of the act continued to flow up to the point of V's death.

If the facts of *Fagan* were to recur D could now be convicted under the 'duty' principle in *Miller* (see **2.5.2.2.4**). The 'continuing act' principle remained relevant in some circumstances. In *Kaitamaki* [1985] AC 147 (see further *Cooper and Schaub* [1994] Crim LR 531), the Privy Council affirmed the decision of the New Zealand Court of Appeal that, for the purposes of rape, sexual intercourse is a continuing act. Thus, if D penetrated V with consent (or believing he had consent), and then declined to withdraw on consent being revoked (or on realising that V did not consent), he was guilty of rape as he had formed the *mens rea* for the offence during the continuance of the *actus reus*. The Sexual Offences Act 2003 has affirmed this approach, providing in s. 79(2): 'Penetration is a continuing act from entry to withdrawal.'

Where D's continuing act amounts to the *actus reus* of an offence and at some point D had the necessary intent for the offence, a subsequent change of heart on D's part will not cancel out his prior intent (see *Styles* [2015] EWCA Crim 1619).

> In *Styles* D was charged with possessing a shotgun with intent to commit an indictable offence contrary to s. 18(1) of the Firearms Act 1968. D had a gun in his possession when making a journey to a location where it was alleged he was going to kill V. Following a question from the jury whether a change of mind could cancel a prior intent, the issue arose whether D could be convicted if he had the relevant intent to kill at some point during the journey or whether he had to have the intent during the entirety of the journey. The trial judge directed the jury that it was enough that he had the relevant intent at any stage within the timeframe of the indictment—a change of mind did not cancel a prior intent. The Court of Appeal upheld the conviction.

Question

What happens if there are several acts which combine to bring about a consequence and D had *mens rea* only part of the time during which those acts were committed?

The cases examined so far have involved one act to which *mens rea* may be linked. In several cases the problem has arisen of a consequence ensuing from a combination of several acts but *mens rea* did not exist for the commission of each act. Is it sufficient that D had *mens rea* at some stage during the course of events?

> In *Thabo Meli* [1954] 1 WLR 228, the appellants struck V over the head with intent to kill him. V's body was rolled over a cliff to make his death appear to be an accident. In fact V died from exposure and not from the initial blow to the head. The appellants had *mens rea* when they struck V, but V died from the act of disposal when they did not have *mens rea* as they believed they were disposing of a corpse. The appellants were undoubtedly guilty of attempted murder but the Privy Council upheld the convictions for murder because, as they stated (at p. 230), it was:

> > impossible to divide up what was really one series of acts in this way. There is no doubt that D set out to do all these acts in order to achieve their plan and as parts of their plan; and it is too refined a ground of judgment to say that, because they were under a mis-apprehension at one stage and thought that their guilty purpose had been achieved before in fact it was achieved, therefore they are to escape the penalties of the law.

In framing the decision in this way the Privy Council appear to have delivered a policy decision as there was no *mens rea* when the act immediately causing the death was performed. The fact that all the acts were performed in pursuance of an antecedent plan, and death ensued from the execution of that plan, appeared to be crucial to the decision of the Privy Council. In *Church* [1966] 1 QB 59, the Court of Appeal extended the *Thabo Meli* 'series of acts' doctrine to a case of manslaughter where there was no antecedent plan. In the course of a fight with V, D struck and attempted to strangle her. She fell unconscious and D, believing her to be dead, threw her into a river where she drowned. The Court of Criminal Appeal was of the opinion that it was sufficient for a conviction if the conduct constituted 'a series of acts which culminated in her death'. The Court stated *obiter* that the jury could have convicted of murder 'if they regarded the appellant's behaviour from the moment he first struck her to the moment when he threw her into the river as a series of acts designed to cause death or grievous bodily harm'. As the act of disposal is for the purpose of disposing of a body, it being D's belief that death had occurred already, it is difficult to see how the series of acts could be described as being 'designed to cause death'. The act which caused death was designed to dispose of a corpse! The principle the Court was endeavouring to state has been clarified by another case.

In *Le Brun* [1991] 4 All ER 673, there was neither an antecedent plan nor did D believe that he was dealing with a corpse as he attempted to drag the unconscious body of his wife away from the place where he had assaulted her following an argument in the course of which she had refused to go home. In moving his wife she slipped from his grasp and hit her head on the pavement causing a fractured skull from which she died. D was convicted of manslaughter following a direction to the jury by the trial judge that they could convict of murder or manslaughter, depending on the intention with which the original blow was struck, if D had 'accidentally dropped V causing her death whilst either: (a) attempting to move her to her home against her wishes . . ., and/or (b) attempting to dispose of her body or otherwise cover up the previous assault'. The Court of Appeal upheld D's conviction for manslaughter applying *Church*, Lord Lane CJ stating (at pp. 678, 679):

> It seems to us that where the unlawful application of force and the eventual act causing death are parts of the same sequence of events, the same transaction, the fact that there is an appreciable interval of time between the two does not serve to exonerate the defendant from liability. That is certainly so where the appellant's subsequent actions which caused death, after the initial unlawful blow, are designed to conceal his commission of the original unlawful assault. . . . In short, in circumstances such as the present, . . . the act which causes death and the necessary mental state to constitute manslaughter need not coincide in point of time.

Accordingly, the 'transaction' principle applies not only where D is disposing of what he believes to be a corpse but also when he is attempting to move V to a place contrary to her will or where D is attempting to cover up his original crime. The Court of Appeal did not expressly declare that the **'transaction' principle** is equally applicable to murder, but presumably it is.

An alternative approach to this problem is to express it as an issue of causation. If, for example, D by an assault (for which he has *mens rea*) renders V unconscious leaving him on a beach with an incoming tide and V drowns, D will be guilty at least of manslaughter as V's death was reasonably foreseeable. Why should it make any difference if D, believing V to be dead as a result of his assault on him, throws V into the water where he drowns? It is equally foreseeable by the reasonable person that V might not be dead and thus may die from drowning. D's second culpable act cannot be regarded as a *novus actus interveniens* as it is all part of the same transaction or series of acts (see Smith and Hogan, *Criminal Law* (13th edn, 2011) at p. 140). The Court of Appeal in *Le Brun* accepted that the problem could also be expressed as one of causation. However, the Court continued to focus on the later act which immediately caused death rather than regarding the original act, which was done with *mens rea*, as a cause of death. If the original act, performed with *mens rea*, is seen as a cause of death, with everything subsequent being regarded as an unbroken chain of causation, there is no problem of a lack of coincidence between *actus reus* and *mens rea*; there is no need to rely on a 'transaction principle'. **It is arguable that the transaction principle has arisen because the courts have failed to recognise that the *actus reus* of an offence comprises conduct, circumstances, and consequences.** They have treated the act which immediately led to death as the *actus reus* when it could equally be seen as the consequence flowing from the original conduct. In the South African case of *S v Masilela* [1968] (2) SA 558, Ogilvie Thompson JA came closest to this position when he described D's earlier acts of strangulation as 'a direct and contributory cause' of V's later death which resulted from carbon monoxide poisoning when D set fire to his house believing him to be dead; had V not been unconscious he could have escaped from the house.

? Question

What happens if it is not possible to determine which of D's acts caused V's death?

In *Thabo Meli*, *Church*, and *Le Brun* it was clear that death ensued from the second act. Where it is not possible to determine which of the two acts caused death, D may be convicted only if the prosecution prove that he acted with *mens rea* on both occasions (*AG's Reference (No. 4 of 1980)* [1981] 1 WLR 705). The facts of *AG's Reference* were that D had slapped V on the face causing her to fall down a flight of stairs and bang her head. D dragged her upstairs by a rope tied around her neck, placed her in the bath, and drained off her blood before cutting up her body and disposing of the pieces. It was impossible to determine the cause of death. The Court of Appeal held that it is not necessary to prove which act caused death but the jury could only convict of manslaughter if they were satisfied *both* (i) that the fall downstairs was the result of an intentional act by D which was unlawful and dangerous (i.e. 'unlawful act' manslaughter), and (ii) that the act of cutting V's throat was an act of gross criminal negligence (i.e. gross negligence manslaughter). The same principle would apply on a charge of murder provided D had the requisite *mens rea* when he performed each act. For example, D hits V over the head intending to kill him but believing that V is not dead he slits his throat to complete the job before disposing of the body in an incinerator. In this example D has the necessary *mens rea* for murder when he hits V and when he slits his throat. The problem, however, with the principle in *AG's Reference* is that it is too favourable to D as the jury must acquit if they are not satisfied that each act was performed with *mens rea*. It is submitted that if it is proved that D had the relevant *mens rea* when he performed the first act, he should be guilty of homicide, as either this act caused death and thus there is no problem or, if the second act caused death, a conviction can be supported on the basis of the transaction principle or on the basis of causation, as the first act was a contributory cause of death.

␣ The law in context

Legal causation and liability for causing another's suicide

The law on the circumstances in which a person will be criminally liable for causing another's suicide is unclear. There have been several cases where some have argued that a particular person *should* be charged for causing another person to commit suicide. For example, several young people have committed suicide after experiencing 'cyberbullying' and blackmail (e.g. BBC News Online, 'Amanda Todd cyber-bully case: Dutchman to be extradited to Canada', 28 June 2016). Several women's suicides appear to be linked to their being sexually assaulted or subject to controlling behaviour (BBC News Online, 'Michael Brewer: Victim "Killed Herself" During Trial' 8 February 2013, https://www.bbc.co.uk/news/uk-40758095). In one case, a coroner held that 'cowboy builders' unlawfully killed an elderly man who hanged himself

→

→

because of distress at being cheated by them into paying £4,000 for minor building work (*The Times*, 14 June 1996). In 2017, Nicholas Allen pleaded guilty at Stafford Crown Court to manslaughter on the basis that he had caused his former partner's suicide by subjecting her to a sustained campaign of stalking, harassment, and intimidation (CPS 'Man Jailed for Manslaughter after Stalking his Former Partner' 28 July 2017, https://www.cps.gov.uk/west-midlands/news/man-jailed-manslaughter-after-stalking-his-former-partner). Could the perpetrators of the bullying, sexual assault, or fraud be said legally to have caused the person's death? How far does and should the law go to criminalise those who may have caused another's suicide? Our concern here is with issues of causation and not with questions about the scope of the Suicide Act 1961, under which it is a specific offence intentionally to encourage or assist the suicide or attempted suicide of another person.

Suicide and responsibility

These are, at a philosophical and policy level, fundamental questions about responsibility. Those of you who have seen or read JB Priestley's *An Inspector Calls* will recall that the play's central theme is responsibility: who was responsible for the death of Eva Smith, the young woman who was mistreated by each member of the Birling family and other acquaintances? As Inspector Goole says to the characters, 'Each of you helped to kill her.'

Legal causation concerns attribution of responsibility and appellate judgments express decisions about moral considerations. If an individual has free will, that person is solely responsible for committing suicide. His decision is freely taken and absolves others' from moral and legal responsibility. This approach is evident in *Kennedy (No. 2)*, in which the House of Lords held that it is never appropriate to find a defendant guilty of manslaughter when the person to whom he has supplied a Class A drug makes a free, deliberate, and informed decision to self-administer that drug, resulting in death. A more deterministic resolution of the metaphysical problem of causation might have maintained a causal link between supplier and 'consumer'. Those who favour more social notions of responsibility, in which we can properly be held accountable for the consequences of our actions that ripple out from their immediate effects, would argue that while a person might not hang the noose or hand the suicidal victim a gun, he might still fairly be said to be to blame in a looser sense. However, as we saw in **Chapter 1**, the rule of law requires certainty and clarity.

Suicide and the different strands of causation law

We have seen that the defendant's culpable act need not be the sole or main cause, it being enough that the defendant's acts contributed significantly to the result (*R v Pagett* [1983] Crim LR 393). English law thus recognises that there could be multiple causes of a person's suicide. However, there are several strands to English law on causation that pull in different directions in terms of deciding whether a person can be said to have caused another to commit suicide. The 'thin skull' rule (*R v Blaue* [1975] 1 WLR 1411) states that D must take his victim as he finds him, meaning there is no barrier to a manslaughter prosecution where D has committed a dangerous, unlawful act (such as assault or rape) that has resulted in V's suicide, even if the suicide was an unusual or unforeseeable reaction. However, in a line of cases concerning the victim's behaviour, the courts have stated that the chain of causation will be broken if the victim's response was not reasonably foreseeable (*R v Roberts* (1971) 56 Cr App R 95). The jury must decide that question. Jurors are likely to have different views about whether a particular person's suicide was reasonably foreseeable. As we saw earlier, in the leading case of *R v Dear* [1996] Crim LR 595, the Court of Appeal stressed that the test is whether D's conduct made 'an operative and significant contribution to the death'. The Court stressed (in

→

→

apparent exasperation at abstruse metaphysical questions) that that question 'is necessarily answered, not by philosophical analysis, but by common sense' according to the case's particular circumstances.

The reference to 'common sense' presupposes a degree of consensus about when we bear responsibility for our actions' consequences but, as we see from *An Inspector Calls*, there are many perspectives on how 'significant' a contribution our actions are to other people's decisions. A central theme of the play is how age, class, and gender affect attitudes to responsibility. In some situations there will be clarity. For example, in the American case of *People* v *Lewis* (1899) 57 P. 470, V was dying painfully from a gunshot wound from D and committed suicide by cutting his throat. Most people would agree that in those circumstances, D's actions had significantly contributed to V's death. However, in the circumstances of a sexual assault victim who commits suicide partly as a result of the psychological distress and partly as a result of a depressive personality, the application of 'common sense' is unlikely to yield a simple jury verdict on the question of whether the sexual assault 'contributed significantly' to her death.

R v Wallace (2018): Clarifying the law?

As outlined at **2.6.3.4**, the Court of Appeal in *R* v *Wallace (Berlinah)* [2018] EWCA Crim 690 held that it was open to the jury, when considering a murder charge, to conclude that the victim's decision to end his life following D's acid attack on him causing horrific injuries could not be described as 'voluntary' in the sense of being the product of free and unfettered volition. The defence had contended that V's decision to apply for euthanasia was a 'voluntary' act breaking the chain of causation. The Court distinguished *Kennedy*, saying that the jury might conclude on the very special facts of the case that there was nothing that could decently be described as voluntary either in the suffering or in the victim's decision to end his life, given the truly terrible situation he was in (at para. 76). This was a 'response by a victim to (extreme) circumstances created by a defendant's unlawful act, which were persisting and which had put the victim into a position where he made a "choice" that he would never otherwise have had to make or would have made (not therefore, as we have said, the sort of free and unfettered volition presupposed by the novus actus rule)' (at para. 76). It did not follow from the finding that his decision to be euthanised was voluntary (as required by Belgian law before doctors will be permitted to administer life-ending drugs) that it was voluntary for the principles of English law on causation.

Wallace clarifies that prosecutions for murder or manslaughter are possible when D's acts have contributed to V's suicide. What is less clear are the circumstances in which a person will be guilty. Wallace was acquitted at her re-trial. We do not know why the jury concluded that she was not guilty of murder. However, the Court of Appeal stressed that trial judges need to invite juries to use their 'common sense' and made reference to the test of reasonable foreseeability: at the time of the acid attack was it reasonably foreseeable that the victim would commit suicide as a result of his injuries? (at para. 86). The jury would have considered all the circumstances, including the nature of the attack, what the defendant did and said at the time, and whether V's decision to undergo voluntary euthanasia fell within the range of responses which might have been expected of a victim in his situation. That might have led them to conclude that deciding to die was an extreme reaction to his injuries, even taking into account their horrific nature.

What might that mean for other cases in which the victim has committed suicide? In some cases we would expect all juries to conclude that D caused V's suicide. Few people would deny that those who jumped to their deaths from the Twin Towers on 9/11 to avoid being burned alive had been caused to do so by the actions of those who flew the planes into the buildings. Wallace's responsibility for V's death seemed to be clear, in that V's death was a direct response to D's acid attack, a connection that was not blurred by any pre-existing suicidal tendency or

→

→

by any other physical or mental condition he may have had before the injuries were inflicted (*per* Sharp LJ at para. 53). Yet inviting the jury to consider whether his death was reasonably foreseeable seems to have led them to conclude that V had other options and his decision was a result of 'free and unfettered volition'.

The type of cases in which uncertainties about liability are most likely to arise is domestic abuse-related suicide. The Court of Appeal in *Dhaliwal* [2006] 2 Cr App R 24 clarified that, as a matter of law, prosecution for manslaughter is not excluded where unlawful conduct caused recognisable psychiatric illness with resulting suicide. In *Dhaliwal*, the CPS tried unsuccessfully to bring a charge of unlawful act manslaughter against Gurjit Dhaliwal's abusive partner, founded upon a long history of psychological abuse which caused her to take her own life. The prosecution failed because the Court took the view that there was no basis for arguing that emotional distress short of being a recognised psychiatric illness constituted 'bodily harm'. Vanessa E. Munro and Ruth Aitkin suggest that the Court of Appeal in *Wallace* has signalled the *potential* for prosecutions in such cases, particularly as the Court re-affirmed the context-specific and fluid nature of causation (Vanessa E. Munro and Ruth Aitken [2018] Crim LR 732–41, 740). However, they highlight the potential problems with these cases:

> In many domestic abuse situations that involve more 'mundane' acts of violence and/or controlling behaviour, it may not be possible to attach the victim's desire for death to any one, isolated incident in this way, let alone to one so dramatic [as Wallace's attack on her former partner]. Moreover . . . there may be pre-existing vulnerabilities and conditions (often caused or aggravated by that history of abuse) that complicate the experiential narrative. (at p. 740)

Asking the jury to use its 'common sense' and to consider what might be a reasonably foreseeable response to ongoing domestic abuse could encourage jurors to decide cases based on their misunderstanding of the psychological effects of domestic abuse and to base their verdicts on perhaps the oldest, overly-simplistic trope in popular discussions of abuse: 'why didn't she just leave him?' *Wallace* signals that prosecutions for causing suicide are possible, but leaves many questions unanswered about how far liability will really extend.

Reforming the law

Would the law be any clearer under the Draft Criminal Code's general clause on causation? Clause 17(1) states that a person causes a result when he 'does an act which makes a more than negligible contribution to its occurrence or omits to do an act which might prevent its occurrence and which he is under a duty to do according to the law relating to the offence'. Clause 17(2) states that the chain of causation will be broken 'if an act or event occurs which is the immediate and sufficient cause of the result, which he did not foresee, and which could not in the circumstances reasonably have been foreseen'.

The clause adopts the *Roberts* test of reasonable foreseeability but adds a subjective gloss (that D did not *actually* foresee it). This seems to limit dramatically the criminal liability of a person who assaulted, raped, or defrauded the person who then committed suicide. The jury would have to assess whether the victim's response could reasonably have been foreseen *and* if the defendant actually foresaw the result (the victim's suicide). The clause focuses on the defendant's subjective awareness of the specific result rather than his subjective awareness of the possibility of the result. Proving beyond reasonable doubt that D foresaw the particular result would be difficult, meaning only the most culpable offenders, those who foresaw suicide as a result of their actions, would be deemed to have caused it.

Current English law seems broader than that but the somewhat vague tests from *Dear* and *Roberts* that were endorsed by the Court of Appeal in *Wallace*, combined with the continued application of the thin skull rule from *Blaue*, mean it remains unclear when precisely a person will be criminally responsible for another's suicide.

Key Points

- Proof that an accused is **responsible for conduct or the existence of a state of affairs** is essential before he will be criminally liable.

- **Conduct must be voluntary**: if an accused's actions are involuntary and he is not to blame for his actions being involuntary then no liability arises.

- Some offences require proof that a prohibited **state of affairs** existed. The appellate courts have taken a 'hard line' in holding defendants criminally liable for causing a state of affairs even when they are not blameworthy, although *Robinson-Pierre* (2013) suggests a somewhat softer approach.

- While the general principle of English law is that we are not liable for failing to act, there are several recognised categories of **liability for omissions** in English law. D will be criminally liable when he has breached: a duty to act, a duty arising out of contract, a duty arising out of close relationships or the assumption of care for another, or a duty arising from the creation of a dangerous situation.

- For result crimes, the prosecution must prove that D was the **factual and legal cause** of the prohibited result. Causation is a **question of fact** for the jury or magistrates. In most cases, causation is not an issue.

  - Factual causation means that **but for** D's conduct, the result would not have occurred.

  - Legal causation is closely connected to ideas of responsibility and culpability.

    - The consequence must be **attributable to a culpable act** on D's part and that act must be a **more than minimal cause** of the consequence. In most cases, the trial judge need simply tell the jury to consider whether D made a **significant contribution** to the prohibited result.

    - D's culpable act need not be the sole cause of the result. D will still be liable despite the actions of third parties and/or the actions of the victim that have contributed towards causing the prohibited result if D has contributed significantly to the outcome.

    - D must 'take his victim as he finds him'.

    - Intervening events and acts, such as medical treatment, naturally occurring events, and the victim mistreating or neglecting his own injuries can break the 'chain of causation'.

    - The free, deliberate, and informed intervention of a second person that leads to the prohibited result will normally relieve D of criminal responsibility.

- *Actus reus* and *mens rea* must **coincide in time**. The *actus reus* can be a **continuing act**.

FURTHER READING

L. Alexander, 'Criminal Liability for Omissions: an Inventory of Issues' in S. Shute and A. P. Simester (eds), *Criminal Law Theory: Doctrines of the General Part* (Oxford: Oxford University Press, 2002).

A. Ashworth, 'The Scope of Criminal Liability for Omissions' (1989) 105 LQR 424.

A. Ashworth, 'A New Generation of Omissions Offences?' [2018] Crim LR 354–64.

H. Gross, 'A Note on Omissions' (1984) 4 LS 308.

B. Hogan, 'Omissions and the Duty Myth' in P. Smith (ed.), *Criminal Law: Essays in Honour of J. C. Smith* (London: Butterworth, 1987).

A. C. E. Lynch, 'The Mental Element in the *Actus Reus*' (1982) 98 LQR 109.

V. E. Munro and R. Aitken, 'Adding Insult to Injury? The Criminal Law's Response to Domestic Abuse-Related Suicide in England and Wales' [2018] Crim LR 732–41.

M. Nkrumah, '*R* v *Kennedy* Revisited' (2008) 72 JCL 117.

A. Norrie, 'A Critique of Criminal Causation' (1991) 54 MLR 685.

J. E. Stannard, 'Medical Treatment and the Chain of Causation' (1993) 57 JCL 88.

G. Williams, 'Criminal Omissions—the Conventional View' (1991) 107 LQR 86.

3

Mens rea

3.1 Introduction

Where a person has performed acts or brought about consequences which constitute the *actus reus* of an offence he will generally be found guilty of the offence only if he had the necessary *mens rea* at the time he acted. The exceptions to this are offences of strict liability and offences which may be committed negligently—for example, careless driving. ***Mens rea* refers to the mental element necessary for a particular crime.** This may differ from one crime to another and the definition of each crime must be examined to determine what state of mind is required. Words used in offences to convey a requirement of *mens rea* are, for example, intention, recklessness, maliciousness, wilfulness, or knowledge (together with their adjectival and adverbial variants).

> Offences may have more than one mens rea requirement. For example, fraud by false representation is an offence under s. 2 of the Fraud Act 2006. A person commits an offence if he **dishonestly** makes a false representation and **intends** by that false representation to make a gain for himself or another or to cause loss to another or to expose another to a risk of loss. Section 2(2) provides that a representation is false if it is untrue or misleading and D **knows** that it is, or might be, untrue or misleading.
>
> The prosecution must thus prove beyond reasonable doubt that D had the requisite **intention** and that he had the requisite **knowledge**. The term 'dishonestly' seems also to require proof that D had a particular state of mind but, as we will explore in detail in **Chapter 12**, that is not necessarily so.

Offences which require *mens rea* are generally regarded as being more serious than those which may be committed negligently or for which liability is strict. The term imports a notion of culpability or moral blameworthiness on the part of the offender. For most of the twentieth century, scholars understood *mens rea* to require an advertent state of mind, meaning that the defendant was aware of at least the possibility that a result might occur or that a state of affairs might exist. Those offences which could be committed negligently, or for which liability was strict, imposed liability on the person who may have done the prohibited act or caused the prohibited consequence inadvertently, without being aware of the possibility that a result might occur or that a state of affairs might exist. Towards the end of that century, however, the dividing line between *mens rea* and negligence became blurred as judges struggled to define the meaning of *mens rea* words, particularly **intention** and **recklessness**, creating uncertainty and confusion. This was particularly unsatisfactory in the light of the stigma and punishment for the individual which attend conviction for a criminal offence. Key functions of the criminal law are to label conduct appropriately and punish in proportion to the blame that the defendant deserves for his conduct. It was also unacceptable in a country which purports to adhere to the principles deriving from the idea of the rule of law. J. Raz in 'The Rule of Law and its Virtue' (1977) 93 LQR 195, at pp. 198, 199 states:

> The law must be open and adequately publicised. If it is to guide people they must be able to find out what it is. For the same reason its meaning must be clear. An ambiguous, vague, obscure or imprecise law is likely to mislead or confuse at least some of those who desire to be guided by it.

The advent of the twenty-first century has witnessed a significant shift as the House of Lords has reconsidered the meaning of recklessness in *G* [2003] UKHL 50 and has confronted and dealt with most, if not all, of these criticisms. The House of Lords also brought some much-needed clarity to the meaning of intention in *Woollin* [1998] 3 WLR 382, although some confusion remains.

3.2 **Intention**

In many offences the *mens rea* required is that of intention to cause the prohibited result. Murder is committed when a person unlawfully kills and intends to kill or cause really serious harm (see **Chapter 9**). A person commits **a serious non-fatal** offence (punishable with up to life imprisonment) under s. 18 of the Offences Against the Person Act 1861 if he unlawfully wounds or causes really serious harm and intends, inter alia, to cause really serious harm. Theft is committed when a person dishonestly appropriates property belonging to another with the intention of permanently depriving the other of that property (see **Chapter 12**). Intention is one of the most blameworthy states of mind: we usually have no hesitation in condemning a person who wants to cause serious harm or who takes property and does not want its owner to get their property back. For such offences, it is not enough to show that the person was aware of a possibility that serious harm might occur or that the property owner might not get their property back. In those situations the person is **reckless about the result** rather than acting with **intention to bring about the result. Such people might also deserve blame and condemnation but generally we would accept they are not as blameworthy as those who act with intent.**

3.2.1 **What might intention mean?**

Intention is a word in ordinary use. Its meaning, however, is not clear. When dissenting in *Caldwell* [1982] AC 341, Lord Edmund Davies stated (at p. 357):

> The law in action compiles its own dictionary. In time, what was originally the common coinage of speech acquires a different value in the pocket of the lawyer than when in the layman's purse.

It is important, therefore, that technical words, such as 'intention', should be clearly defined. Unfortunately, however, to use Glanville Williams' words, 'judges decline to define [intention], and they appear to adjust it from one case to another' (see Williams, 'Oblique Intention' [1987] CLJ 417). The *Concise Oxford Dictionary* defines 'intend' as 'have as one's purpose' and 'intention' as 'intending, one's purpose . . . object . . . ultimate aim'. As used in the criminal law, *intention* does not appear to have such a clear or restricted meaning. There are basically four possible states of mind which may be encompassed within the term 'intention'.

 Example

Let us assume that D has insured V's life. He decides to kill V in order to obtain the insurance money. D's *desire* is to kill V and his *motive* is to obtain the money. The following four examples of D killing V illustrate the four states of mind which may constitute intention.

(i) D shoots at V in order to kill him. In this situation V's death is both desired and intended by D. The consequence of V's death may be said to be D's purpose, aim, or objective. This variety of intention we can call *direct intention*. D may realise that his chances of hitting V are slim because of the distance or his poor ability with a gun, but this does not affect his intention which is to kill V.

(ii) D sees V standing behind a window and shoots at V in order to kill him, realising that to do so the bullet must first break the window. In this situation it may be said that D intends also to break the window as this is a necessary precondition to killing V. This may be described as *oblique intention*; breaking the window is D's subsidiary aim or secondary purpose which must be achieved if he is to achieve his ultimate aim or primary purpose. Glanville Williams in 'Oblique Intention', states (at p. 421):

> **Direct intention** is where the consequence is what you are aiming at. **Oblique intention** is something you see clearly, but out of the corner of your eye. The consequence is (figuratively speaking) not in the straight line of your purpose, but a side effect that you accept as an inevitable or 'certain' accompaniment of your direct intent (desire-intent). There are twin consequences of the act, x and y; the doer wants x, and is prepared to accept its unwanted twin y. Oblique intent is, in other words, a kind of knowledge or realization. . . . Certainty in human affairs means certainty as a matter of common sense—certainty apart from unforeseen events or remote possibilities. Realisation of practical certainty is something higher in the scale than appreciation of high probability. [Emphasis added]

> While there may be a remote possibility that the window may blow open before the bullet passes through it, it is clear at the time D squeezes the trigger that breaking the window is a practical or moral certainty.

→

> →
>
> (iii) D places a bomb under V's seat timed to kill him in mid-flight as he co-pilots a plane over the Atlantic. In this situation D does not desire to kill the crew or passengers on the plane and their deaths are not a precondition to killing V. In the normal course of events, however, their deaths will ensue as the inevitable *by-product* of D's achievement of his primary purpose; they are an inseparable consequence of that end. Again it may be said that at the time of planting the bomb the deaths of the crew and passengers were morally certain if D achieved his primary purpose. Thus, this situation may be regarded as another example of oblique intention.
>
> (iv) D shoots at V, while he is driving a bus, in order to kill him. D foresees that it is highly probable that the passengers on the bus will also be injured or killed. In this situation D does not desire to kill or injure the passengers; their injuries or deaths are not inevitable although highly likely. Does foresight that a consequence is highly probable amount to intention to bring that consequence about or does it only constitute recklessness?

There is much judicial and academic discussion about whether a consequence can be intended if it is not desired. In the examples here at (ii) and (iii) it may be argued that as D's desire was to kill V the consequences of breaking the window or killing the crew and passengers were undesired. A. Norrie, 'Oblique Intention and Legal Politics' [1989] Crim LR 793, argues that secondary consequences flowing from D's primary purpose may also be regarded as desired. As D seeks to bring about the primary purpose in a known set of circumstances, secondary consequences which D obliquely intends may be regarded as desired in a broader sense in that they are part and parcel of the package of circumstances within which D chooses to operate.

The precise meaning of intention matters. It determines who falls within which offence category, if any. In turn, that affects the label and sentence that a person receives. This is particularly important in homicide. D will be guilty of murder if he has intended to kill or cause really serious harm, whereas D may be guilty of manslaughter with a less blameworthy state of mind, such as being reckless as to whether serious harm might result. A conviction for the former carries with it the stigma of the label 'murderer' and a mandatory life sentence, whereas for manslaughter the trial judge has discretion in sentencing (see **Chapter 9**). As you read the following sections, bear in mind that the appellate courts' complex and sometimes contradictory approaches to defining intention (an apparently simple word) are not mere judicial semantics or pedantry but decisions of practical importance in establishing the boundaries of some of the most serious offences.

3.2.2 What should intention mean?

The Law Commission in its Draft Criminal Code (Law Com No. 177) gave the following definition of intention to cause results:

> a person acts—
>
> . . .
>
> (b) 'intentionally' with respect to—
>
> . . .
>
>   (ii) a result when he acts either in order to bring it about or being aware that it will occur in the ordinary course of events . . .

In its commentary on the Code the Law Commission stated (at para. 8.14):

> Acting in order to bring about a result is, as it were, the standard case of 'intending' to cause a result. But we are satisfied that a definition of 'intention' for criminal law purposes must refer . . . to 'the means as well as the end and the inseparable consequences of the end as well as the means'. Where a person acts in order to achieve a particular purpose, knowing that this cannot be done without causing another result, he must be held to intend to cause that other result. The other result may be a precondition . . . or it may be a necessary concomitant of the first result . . . . The result will occur, and D knows that it will occur, 'in the ordinary course of events . . . unless something supervenes to prevent it'. It is, and he knows it is, 'a virtual certainty'. We have adopted the phrase, 'in the ordinary course of events' to ensure that 'intention' covers the case of a person who knows that the achievement of his purpose will necessarily cause the result in question, in the absence of some wholly improbable supervening event.

The Law Commission, accordingly, defined *intention* to include the types of situation given in examples (i), (ii), and (iii) listed earlier. It went on to reject (iv) as a situation involving intention stating (at para. 8.15):

> A person's awareness of any degree of probability (short of virtual certainty) that a particular result will follow from his acts ought not, we believe, to be classed as an 'intention' to cause that result for criminal law purposes.

The Law Commission's definition of intention was adopted in the House of Lords, *Report of the Select Committee on Murder and Life Imprisonment* (Session 1988–89, HL Paper 78). Professor J. C. Smith, however, was of the opinion that the definition could be improved to avoid possible difficulties (see 'A Note on Intention' [1990] Crim LR 85). The most significant difficulty which he considered might arise relates to the type of situation given earlier in example (iii). If the bomber knows that bombs of the type he is using have, for example, a 50 per cent failure rate, Smith stated (at p. 86):

> It may be argued that the defendant does not . . . intend the death of the crew because he is not virtually certain etc., that they will die—he is not aware that it will happen 'in the ordinary course of events', because there is a 50 per cent chance that it will not happen at all.

In *Legislating the Criminal Code: Offences Against the Person and General Principles* (Law Com No. 218) the Law Commission accepted Smith's argument (see paras 7.6–7.14) and proposed the following definition of intention in the Criminal Law Bill appended to the Report:

> 1 . . . . a person acts
>
>   (a) 'intentionally' with respect to a result when—
>
>   (i) it is his purpose to cause it, or
>   (ii) although it is not his purpose to cause it, he knows that it would occur in the ordinary course of events if he were to succeed in his purpose of causing some other result; . . .

The important point to note about the Law Commission's definition is that it both accepts that *intention* should have a meaning wider than in situations like example (i) earlier but that it should not be so wide as to encompass foresight of probability in situations like example (iv) as this is the domain of recklessness.

3.2.3 How have the courts defined intention?

In trials for offences requiring proof of intent, the trial judge must direct the jury as to the meaning of intention. In *Moloney* [1985] 1 AC 905 the House of Lords held that in most cases, the trial judge should 'avoid any elaboration or paraphrase of what is meant by intent, and leave it to the jury's good sense to decide whether D acted with the necessary intent' (at p. 926). Lord Bridge called this 'the golden rule'. A trial judge may find it necessary to explain to the jury that there is a difference between intention and motive, but beyond that the jury will ordinarily be left to use their 'good sense'.

Trial judges face a more difficult task in cases where there is evidence that D might not have wanted to bring about the prohibited result but did foresee a possibility (perhaps a very high degree of probability) that the result might occur. These cases have caused the appellate courts much difficulty.

3.2.3.1 Why is defining intention difficult?

It is difficult to glean from judicial statements a clear definition of intention. **Most of the problems stem from judges being neither clear nor precise in their use of language. Their judgments consequently contain inconsistencies, contradictions, and ambiguities**. There are several reasons for this.

Some of the cases in which the meaning of intention has been considered have involved emotive factual situations which appear to have coloured judicial pronouncements (see e.g. *Steane* [1947] KB 997). The most important cases before the House of Lords have involved murder where their Lordships had to decide what the *mens rea* for murder is (see *Hyam* [1975] AC 55; *Moloney* [1985] 1 AC 905; *Hancock and Shankland* [1986] 1 AC 455). The meaning of intention was thus subsumed within the discussion of the *mens rea* for murder and coloured by considerations of the type of conduct which should be caught by the definition of murder. Their Lordships concluded in *Moloney* that the *mens rea* for murder was intention to kill or intention to cause grievous bodily harm. Having given this definition of the *mens rea* of murder their Lordships considered certain examples of egregious and reprehensible conduct resulting in death. They concluded that such conduct merited conviction for murder although, unrecognised by them, it did not fall within any of the three situations given earlier in examples (i)–(iii) which exemplify the meaning of intention. Their Lordships, in effect, confused policy with principle, stretching the definition of intention to encompass states of mind that are more accurately labelled as 'reckless'. One cannot ignore, however, the pronouncements of the House of Lords and the Court of Appeal. Accordingly, an attempt must be made to make some sense of the cases.

A further problem in some of the cases dealing with intention is judicial confusion of substantive law with the law of evidence. The substantive law lays down the facts which must be proved if D is to be convicted of a particular offence. For example, if D is charged with murder one of the facts which must be proved is that he intended to kill or to cause grievous bodily harm to the deceased. The law of evidence lays down rules relating to the evidence which may be admitted at trial to prove the existence of this fact. The state of a person's mind, however, is not an easy fact to prove unless D provides an admissible confession in which he states what his intention or foresight was. Imagine you are a prosecuting barrister in a murder trial and D has not confessed and has chosen not to give evidence. Your task is to make the jury sure beyond reasonable doubt that D did intend to kill or cause really serious harm. In the absence of such a confession the jury (or magistrates for those offences triable summarily that require proof of intent) are left to use their collective common sense to draw inferences from the circumstances and the natural and probable consequences of D's conduct in those circumstances. This is provided for specifically by s. 8 of the Criminal Justice Act 1967:

> A court or jury in determining whether a person has committed an offence,—
>
> (a) shall not be bound in law to infer that he intended or foresaw a result of his actions by reason only of its being a natural and probable consequence of those actions; but
>
> (b) shall decide whether he did intend or foresee that result by reference to all the evidence, drawing such inferences from the evidence as appear proper in the circumstances.

 Example

D is charged with murder having pushed V over a 50-metre-high cliff on to rocks below where he died. At his trial, D claims he did not intend to kill or seriously injure V but that he only wished to frighten him to teach him a lesson. If the jury disbelieve D (which they undoubtedly would), they can convict him of murder only if they are satisfied beyond reasonable doubt that D intended to kill V or to cause him serious injury. They would be entitled to use their common sense to determine what a person of normal intellect would have foreseen as the outcome of such conduct. The inevitable consequence of such conduct is at least serious injury. They would then be entitled to infer that D is a person of normal intellect and, in the absence of any other credible explanation, that he had such foresight and that his purpose in pushing B over the cliff must have been seriously to injure or kill him.

Of course, there are many situations where consequences are merely probable or even possible rather than inevitable. This does not preclude the jury from inferring that D intended to bring about the probable or possible consequence.

 Example

D is 800 metres from V and fires a rifle at him which results in V being grazed by the bullet. D is charged with attempted murder for which the requisite *mens rea* is intent to kill. D pleads 'Not Guilty' and declines to give evidence having also remained silent when questioned by the police. In the circumstances described, death was not inevitable or even probable. It was, however, possible. In the absence of any credible explanation as to why D fired at V, the jury would be entitled to draw such inferences as are appropriate. One reason for firing the rifle

➡

> →
>
> could have been to kill V. If the jury are satisfied by the evidence (which in this case includes testimony from witnesses who overheard an argument between D and V in which D threatened to kill V) that the only proper inference to draw is that D's purpose was to kill V, they may convict. If the chances of killing V decrease with distance there will come a point where D is too far away for death to be a realistic possibility. In the absence of any other evidence from which an inference of intention could be drawn, an inference of intention to kill would not be proper as the act of shooting in such circumstances does not point (with the degree of sureness required to satisfy the burden of proof) to the conclusion that D's aim or purpose was to kill V.

The appropriateness of drawing inferences also may vary depending on other evidence which is available, for example, evidence relating to the intelligence of D may be pertinent to the question whether D foresaw any particular risk which his actions involved. **But where inferences are drawn, what should not be variable is the meaning of 'intention' for the purpose of determining whether the conclusion to which the evidence points amounts to 'intention'. Intention must mean 'aim' or 'purpose'.** There has been some confusion in the cases regarding the conclusion at which a jury may arrive where they have drawn inferences from the evidence as to the defendant's state of mind (see *Moloney, Hancock and Shankland,* and *Woollin,* **3.2.3.3** and **3.2.3.4**). In particular where D's aim or purpose has not been to bring about the consequence which resulted from his acts, it would be inappropriate to permit a jury to conclude that he intended that consequence where the only appropriate inference from the evidence was that he foresaw it as possible or probable. Such a state of mind amounts to recklessness but not to intention. The cases which follow, however, have sometimes confused the two concepts.

3.2.3.2 *Mohan* (1976): Approaching a clear definition

The cases are in agreement that intention covers situation (i) in **3.2.1** where D does an act with the aim or purpose of causing a particular result. The problem centres on situations (ii) and (iii)—that is, whether oblique intention will suffice where the definition of the *mens rea* element of an offence requires intention to cause a particular result. In *Mohan* [1976] QB 1 **the Court of Appeal defined intention as 'a decision to bring about, in so far as it lies within D's power [the prohibited consequence], no matter whether D desired that consequence of his act or not'.** James LJ also stated (at p. 11):

> [E]vidence of knowledge of likely consequences, or from which knowledge of likely consequences can be inferred, is evidence by which intent may be established but it is not . . . to be equated with intent. If the jury find such knowledge established, they may, and using common sense, they probably will find intent proved, but it is not the case that they must do so.

In this case D was charged with attempting to cause grievous bodily harm with intent having driven a car at a policeman who was blocking his path as he endeavoured to escape. The definition of intention which the Court of Appeal gave clearly included the type of situation given in example (ii) earlier; D may not have desired to injure the policeman as an end in itself but he was prepared to do so as a precondition to escaping which was his ultimate aim or purpose. The Court also excluded situation (iv) from the definition of intention. This followed dicta in *Hyam* [1975] AC 55. In that case Lord Hailsham stated (at p. 65):

> I do not believe that knowledge or any degree of foresight is enough. Knowledge or foresight is at best material which entitles or compels a jury to draw the necessary inference as to intention.

Lord Hailsham made it clear later in his judgment (at pp. 73, 74) that **intention was to be distinguished from desire and foresight of probable consequences**. He clearly included within his definition of intention, however, both types of situation given in examples (ii) and (iii) stating that intention includes 'the means as well as the end and the inseparable consequences of the end as well as the means'. Thus he went on to state:

> [A] man may desire to blow up an aircraft in flight in order to obtain insurance moneys. But if any passengers are killed he is guilty of murder, as their death will be a moral certainty if he carries out his intention. There is no difference between blowing up the aircraft and intending the death of some or all of the passengers.

After *Mohan* and Lord Hailsham's speech in *Hyam* one would have thought that the meaning of intention was clear. Situations of the type exemplified in (i), (ii), and (iii) in **3.2.1** constituted intention and situation (iv) did not. Evidence that a consequence was foreseeable as highly probable was simply circumstantial evidence which might persuade the jury to draw the inference that D intended the consequence. But the question always is 'what was D's subjective state of mind?' If the jury are not satisfied that D actually foresaw the consequence as a moral certainty in situations like (ii) and (iii) the inference of intention would not be appropriate. If the consequence was D's aim or purpose it does not matter that he only foresaw a possibility of achieving it. This distinction between what intention is and how it may be proved is consistent with s. 8 of the Criminal Justice Act 1967 (see **3.2.3.1**).

3.2.3.3 *Moloney* (1985): Intention and foresight of consequences

In the 1980s the House of Lords had two further attempts at defining intention, both of which were in the context of appeals from convictions for murder. The problem with *Hyam* was that while Lord Hailsham was clear regarding the meaning of intention, there was uncertainty regarding the actual *mens rea* of murder. The other four Law Lords appeared to accept that foresight by D of a high probability of death or serious bodily harm resulting from his conduct would suffice to constitute the *mens rea* of murder. In *Moloney* the House of Lords declared that the *mens rea* for murder is intention to kill or to cause grievous bodily harm, nothing else will suffice. The issue to be clarified was the meaning of intention.

In *Moloney* M was charged with murder. The appellant's account of the incident was that he had been drinking with his stepfather when the stepfather challenged him to a competition to see who could load, draw, and fire a shotgun in the shortest time. In doing so the appellant shot his stepfather, killing him. The issue was essentially a factual one; there was a dispute between the prosecution and the defence as to whether the appellant knew the gun was pointing at the deceased when he fired it. M claimed that he had not aimed the gun and that he had no idea that in firing it he would injure his stepfather. The issue for the jury should have been a simple one as stated by Lord Bridge (at p. 917):

> If they were sure that, at the moment of pulling the trigger . . . the appellant realised that the gun was pointing straight at his stepfather's head, they were bound to convict him of murder. If, on the other hand, they thought it might be true that, in the appellant's drunken condition and in the context of this ridiculous challenge, it never entered the appellant's head when he pulled the trigger that the gun was pointing at his father, he should have been acquitted of murder and convicted of manslaughter.

Either the appellant had the direct intent of killing or seriously injuring his stepfather or he had not. Unfortunately the trial judge confused the issue by directing the jury that 'a man intends the consequence of his voluntary act (a) when he desires it to happen, whether or not he foresees that it probably will happen and (b) when he foresees that it will probably happen, whether he desires it or not'. The equation of intention with foresight of probability rendered an appeal inevitable. M argued that the direction might have led the jury to conclude that they could convict if M was reckless as to whether he might cause serious injury. In the House of Lords Lord Bridge considered the direction on 'foresight of consequences' to be an example of an irrelevant direction which would only confuse a jury. If when the appellant fired the gun he knew that it was pointing at his stepfather's head, the inference was inescapable 'using words in their ordinary, everyday meaning, that he intended to kill his stepfather'.

Lord Bridge went on to consider the correct direction for all crimes, including murder, where a specific intent is required. (An offence of specific intent is one which requires intention to be proved; recklessness will not suffice as an alternative state of mind.) Lord Bridge considered that **'the golden rule' is to 'avoid any elaboration or paraphrase of what is meant by intent, and leave it to the jury's good sense to decide whether D acted with the necessary intent'** (at p. 926), although an explanation that intention is something quite different from motive or desire is frequently necessary. Further explanation or elaboration should only be given where necessary to avoid misunderstanding in the light of the facts and the way the case has been presented to the jury in evidence and argument (see further *Fallon* [1994] Crim LR 519). While Lord Bridge did not express himself particularly clearly at this point, it seems he was referring to cases where the evidence suggests that D's ultimate aim or purpose was to bring about something other than the prohibited consequence which he had caused—that is, cases where D had an oblique intent. In such cases, Lord Bridge stated, **foresight of a high degree of probability is not equivalent to intention** but 'as an element bearing on the issue of intention . . . belongs, not to the substantive law, but to the law of evidence'. **When elaboration is required, two questions should be put to the jury** (at p. 929):

First, was death or really serious injury in a murder case (or whatever relevant consequence must be proved to have been intended in any other case) a natural consequence of the defendant's voluntary act? Secondly, did the defendant foresee that consequence as being a natural consequence of his act? The jury should then be told that if they answer yes to both questions it is a proper inference for them to draw that he intended that consequence.

Question

In *Hyam*, Lord Hailsham referred to a result being 'certain' whereas in *Moloney* Lord Bridge used the phrase 'natural consequences'. Does 'natural' mean something different to 'certain'?

The term 'natural consequence' is ambiguous. Something may be natural, in the sense of being causally connected to the original act, but it is not necessarily a certain consequence. The example often given is that conception may be a natural consequence of sexual intercourse but it is by no means certain. Lord Bridge appears to have meant to convey, however, the idea that the consequence must have been foreseen as certain. Earlier in his speech he stated (at p. 929):

[Natural] conveys the idea that in the ordinary course of events a certain act will lead to a certain consequence unless something unexpected supervenes to prevent it.

He also stated (at p. 925) that the probability of the consequence taken to have been foreseen must be little short of overwhelming before it will suffice to establish the necessary intent. Such a probability, however, would appear to be indistinguishable from a consequence which is certain unless prevented by some unexpected supervening event. Lord Bridge then illustrated his point by the following example of a person who has an ultimate aim or purpose whose achievement will necessarily involve another consequence (at p. 926):

A man, who, at a London airport, boards a plane which he knows to be bound for Manchester, clearly intends to travel to Manchester, even though Manchester is the last place he wants to be and his motive for boarding the plane is simply to escape pursuit. The possibility that the plane may have engine trouble and be diverted to Luton does not affect the matter. By boarding the Manchester plane, the man conclusively demonstrates his intention to go there, because it is a moral certainty that that is where he will arrive.

In this example, Lord Bridge states that boarding the plane 'demonstrates . . . intention'; he does not state that this is evidence from which intention is to be inferred. In other parts of his speech, and particularly when he framed his two-part test, Lord Bridge did speak in terms of drawing inferences. It is his test which has subsequently been taken to have conveyed his meaning.

Inferring intention from foresight, rather than treating a particular degree of foresight as intention, can create confusion. In a case where the prohibited consequence was not D's aim or purpose, nor desired by him as an end in itself or means to an end, the task for the prosecution would be to prove what he foresaw. For example, imagine a person pours petrol through the letter-box of another person's house, sets the petrol alight and in the ensuing fire the other person dies. D claims that his purpose was to terrify the other person and that he did not intend to kill or cause him serious harm. In the absence of an admission by D that he intended to kill or cause serious harm, the jury would be left to infer this from the evidence. In our example, that other evidence includes eyewitness testimony from someone who saw D waiting for V to return home before starting the fire and evidence that D knew V's house had no means of escape other than the door through which the petrol was poured. If the jury are satisfied that D foresaw death or serious injury as morally certain at the time he acted it would be correct to say he intended that result in the 'oblique' sense of the word—no further *inferring* should be required. Doubtless juries would use their common sense and equate foresight of a consequence as morally certain with intention but it would have been much more helpful if Lord Bridge had said so clearly.

3.2.3.4 *Hancock and Shankland* (1986): Intention, foresight, and probability

A mere nine months later the House of Lords was considering the meaning of Lord Bridge's judgment in *Hancock and Shankland* [1986] 1 AC 455. The phrase 'natural consequence' had created judicial confusion. This is another example of a case where the only issue was one of fact but the matter was complicated by the trial judge's direction to the jury.

> The accused were miners on strike. They pushed a block of concrete and a concrete post from a bridge over a three-lane highway on which a miner was being taken to work by taxi. The block hit the taxi killing the driver. The accused were charged with murder, the prosecution alleging that they intended to kill or cause serious injury. The accuseds' case was that their intention was only to block the road and frighten the miner as they believed the block was positioned over the middle lane when the taxi was in the nearside lane.

The issue for the jury should have been to determine which version of the facts was to be believed. If the accused were to be believed then a conviction for manslaughter would follow as there clearly was no intention to kill or cause serious injury. If, on the other hand, they disbelieved the accused and the prosecution satisfied them beyond reasonable doubt that the accused knew the block was positioned above the lane along which the taxi was driving, the inference that they intended to kill or cause serious injury would have been inescapable as one could imagine no other reason for dropping the block. **The only issue in fact was what was their aim or purpose?** If it was to kill or cause serious injury it would not matter whether they only foresaw a slight chance of success.

Unfortunately the judge complicated matters by directing the jury in accordance with Lord Bridge's judgment in *Moloney* relating to foresight of consequences. He told the jury, 'You . . . may find it helpful to ask: Was death or serious injury a natural consequence of what was done? Did a defendant foresee that consequence as a natural consequence?' He did not explain that 'natural consequence' did not simply mean causally connected and thus the appeal was based on the ambiguity of this phrase. The Court of Appeal quashed the convictions for murder and the House of Lords affirmed this on the basis that the phrase 'natural consequence' required amplification. Lord Scarman stated (at p. 473):

[Lord Bridge] omitted any reference in his guidelines to probability. He did so because he included probability in the meaning which he attributed to 'natural' . . . . [T]he probability of a consequence is a factor of sufficient importance to be drawn specifically to the attention of the jury and to be explained. In a murder case where it is necessary to direct a jury on the issue of intent by reference to foresight of consequences the probability of death or serious injury resulting from the act done may be critically important. Its importance will depend on the degree of probability: if the likelihood that death or serious injury will result is high, the probability of that result may . . . be seen as overwhelming evidence of the existence of the intent to kill or injure . . . . In my judgment, therefore, the *Moloney* guidelines as they stand are unsafe and misleading. They require a reference to probability. They also require an explanation that the greater the probability of a consequence the more likely it is that the consequence was foreseen and that if that consequence was foreseen the greater the probability is that that consequence was also intended.

The suggestion that the *Moloney* guidelines were 'unsafe and misleading' is important. Without some reference to the defendant's foresight of the prohibited result's probability, juries might think they simply have to decide whether D has caused the result (in the sense that they might think the result was a natural consequence of D's acts). A direction in terms of foresight of consequences should only be appropriate where the consequence which occurred was not D's direct aim or purpose. Lord Scarman's judgment served to dilute the meaning Lord Bridge intended to convey. A jury, directed in accordance with Lord Scarman's dicta, could infer intention from foresight of *high probability* whereas Lord Bridge would only permit a jury to draw such an inference where the consequence was foreseen as a *moral certainty*. Lord Scarman's **direction gave little indication of the precise degree of probability of the result occurring that D must have foreseen. Without precise guidance, different juries may arrive at different verdicts depending on whether they feel D's conduct should be condemned as murder.**

3.2.3.5 *Nedrick* (1986): The 'virtual certainty' test
The conflict between *Moloney* and *Hancock and Shankland* led the Court of Appeal to seek to restore some order to the confusion in *Nedrick* [1986] 1 WLR 1025.

In *Nedrick* D had a grudge against V. With the intention of frightening V, he poured paraffin through her letter box and on to the front door of her house and ignited it. A child died in the ensuing fire and D was charged with murder. The trial judge directed the jury that D is guilty if 'he knew that it was highly probable that the act would result in serious bodily injury to somebody inside the house, even though he did not desire it . . .'. D was convicted of murder . On appeal he argued that the trial judge's direction had equated foresight of the consequence with intention to cause that consequence. The Court of Appeal quashed the conviction, substituting a conviction for manslaughter. Lord Lane CJ stated two questions which might be helpful to a jury when determining whether D had the necessary intent (at p. 1028):

(1) How probable was the consequence which resulted from the defendant's voluntary act?
(2) Did he foresee that consequence?

Lord Lane CJ went on to explain that if D did not appreciate that death or serious harm was likely to result from his act, he did not intend to bring it about. If he did appreciate the risk but thought that it was only slight, then a jury might easily conclude that he did not intend to bring about the result. Lord Lane CJ continued (at p. 1028):

> On the other hand, if the jury are satisfied that at the material time the defendant recognised that death or serious harm would be virtually certain (barring some unforeseen intervention) to result from his voluntary act, then that is a fact from which they may find it easy to infer that he intended to kill or do serious bodily harm, even though he may not have had any desire to achieve that result . . . . Where the charge is murder and **in the rare cases where the simple direction is not enough, the jury should be directed that they are not entitled to infer the necessary intention unless they feel sure that death or serious bodily harm was a virtual certainty (barring some unforeseen intervention) as a result of the defendant's actions and that the defendant appreciated that such was the case.**
>
> Where a man realises that it is for all practical purposes inevitable that his actions will result in death or serious harm, the inference may be irresistible that he intended that result, however little he may have desired or wished it to happen. The decision is one for the jury to be reached upon a consideration of all the evidence. [Emphasis added]

Lord Lane CJ endorsed the view that it is only in cases where a consequence is foreseen as virtually certain that intention may be inferred. He expressly stated that on a murder charge if a simple direction would not suffice, the jury should be directed that they are not entitled to infer intention unless satisfied that death or serious bodily harm was virtually certain to result from D's acts and D foresaw this.

3.2.3.6 The current law on the meaning of intention: *Woollin* (1997)

The Court of Appeal in *Nedrick* brought clarity to the meaning of intention by clarifying that nothing less than foresight on D's part that the prohibited result was a virtual certainty would suffice. However, an issue arose from Lord Lane's use of the word 'infer'. He stated that the jury could infer intention from foresight of virtual certainty. Did that mean that foresight of a consequence as a virtual certainty was the same as intention as a matter of substantive law or merely evidence from which the jury could decide that D intended the consequence?

The leading case is now *R v Woollin* [1998] 3 WLR 382, a House of Lords, decision.

> Woollin threw his three-month-old son four or five feet across a room in the direction of his pram causing him a fractured skull from which he died. He was charged with his son's murder and argued that he had not intended to cause his baby serious harm. The prosecution accepted that it had not been D's aim or purpose to kill or seriously injure his child. The case, accordingly, was not one where the simple direction on intention could suffice. The trial judge directed the jury that they could infer that D intended to cause serious harm if they were satisfied that, in throwing his son, he appreciated that there was a substantial risk of causing serious injury. D was convicted and contended on appeal that the judge had enlarged the mental element of murder to an unacceptable extent by using the phrase 'substantial risk'. The Court of Appeal dismissed that ground of appeal but the House of Lords unanimously rejected the decision of the Court of Appeal, quashed the conviction for murder, and substituted a conviction for manslaughter.

Lord Steyn, giving the leading judgment, affirmed that the case had been one requiring the *Nedrick* direction relating to virtual certainty. He stated (at p. 392):

> By using the phrase 'substantial *risk*' the judge blurred the line between intention and recklessness, and hence between murder and manslaughter. The misdirection enlarged the scope of the mental element required for murder. It was a material misdirection.

Lord Steyn also took the opportunity to clarify the *Nedrick* direction and the effect of a jury finding that a defendant foresaw death or serious injury as a virtual certainty. Juries must consider all the evidence to determine what state of mind the defendant had when he acted. How that state of mind should be characterised in law is a matter of definition. Lord Steyn moved from treating the *Nedrick* direction as one relating purely to evidential matters to one relating to definition. He stated **first** (at p. 390) **that the 'effect of the critical direction is that a result foreseen as virtually certain is an intended result'** and, **secondly,** *Nedrick* **'stated what state of mind (in the absence of a purpose to kill or cause serious harm) is sufficient for murder'**. It seems clear from this that in Lord Steyn's view, where a jury is satisfied beyond reasonable doubt on the evidence that D foresaw death or serious injury as virtually certain to result from his actions, this amounts to an intention to bring about that consequence and thus satisfies the *mens rea* requirement for murder; no further step of drawing inferences from such a finding is required. This would seem to lay to rest the fiction that foresight of a virtually certain result is simply evidence from which the jury may infer intention.

Lord Steyn went on to reformulate the *Nedrick* direction and to abbreviate it to two crucial questions. The reformulation involved substituting for the word 'infer' the word 'find' so that the direction reads:

> Where the charge is murder and in the rare cases where the simple direction is not enough, the jury should be directed that they are not entitled to find the necessary intention unless they feel sure that death or serious bodily harm was a virtual certainty (barring some unforeseen intervention) as a result of the defendant's action and that the defendant appreciated that such was the case.

The only other statement a judge might choose to make is one reminding the jury that their decision must be made upon consideration of all of the evidence in the case. This is uncontroversial as this is the duty of the jury in any case whether the issue is one of intention or some other matter.

3.2.3.7 **Controversies and issues that remain after *Woollin***

Undoubtedly the House of Lords could have been clearer in their decision. **There are three particular problems which may arise. First, the *Nedrick* direction is framed in the negative.** A better reworking of it would have been to state that if the jury are sure that D foresaw death or serious bodily harm as a virtual certainty (barring some unforeseen intervention) as a result of his action, this amounts to an intention to bring about that result. This would have been in line with Lord Steyn's dictum that 'a result foreseen as virtually certain is an intended result' and would have made clear that there is no discretion on the part of the jury once it has found that D foresaw death or serious bodily harm as a virtual certainty. When a trial judge adopted this approach, the Court of Appeal was presented with the opportunity to provide the necessary clarification. In *Matthews and Alleyne* [2003] EWCA Crim 192, however, they concluded that **'the law has not yet reached a *definition* of intent in murder in terms of appreciation of a virtual certainty'** (para. 43), retreating from the ground to which Lord Steyn had laid claim. Rix LJ went on to state (at paras 43 and 45):

> [W]e do not regard *Woollin* as yet reaching or laying down a substantive rule of law. On the contrary, it is clear from the discussion in *Woollin* as a whole that *Nedrick* was derived from the existing law . . . and that the critical direction in *Nedrick* was approved, subject to the change of one word . . . .
>
> [W]e think that, once what is required is an appreciation of virtual certainty of death, and not some lesser foresight of merely probable consequences, there is very little to choose between a rule of evidence and one of substantive law. It is probably this thought that led Lord Steyn to say that a result foreseen as virtually certain is an intended result.

So Lord Steyn, according to the Court of Appeal, has not provided a definition of intention. Foresight of death as a virtual certainty remains evidence from which intention (in the sense of aim, objective, or purpose) may be found. We are no closer to knowing what the elusive state of mind is that a jury has to find in order to conclude that D had the requisite intention. Perhaps it is simply a moral reaction providing the jury with sufficient leeway to decide, in an appropriate case, not to convict despite a conclusion that D foresaw death as a virtual certainty (see **3.2.3.5**). In *Matthews and Alleyne*, where the defendants had killed the victim by throwing him from a bridge into a river 25 feet below, knowing that he could not swim, the Court of Appeal did not consider there could be any moral leeway once the jury concluded the appellants had foreseen death as a virtual certainty, Rix LJ stating (at para. 46):

> If the jury were sure that the appellants appreciated the virtual certainty of [V's] death and also that they then had no intention of saving him from such death, it is impossible to see how the jury could not have found that the appellants intended [V] to die.

A further issue is that the test requires death or serious bodily harm to be a virtual certainty before consideration is given to D's appreciation of such. The issue should not be whether the result was a virtual certainty but rather whether when he acted D foresaw it to be such. D's culpability lies in acting with that degree of foresight. How should a jury determine a case where they conclude that D acted with a primary purpose having foreseen that if he achieved that purpose a secondary consequence (V's death) would be a virtual certainty, although the jury (with the benefit of hindsight) take the view that the secondary consequence was not, in fact, virtually certain to ensue from the achievement of D's primary purpose? Again, Lord Steyn's statement that 'a result foreseen as virtually certain is an intended result' suggests that the jury should find that D intended that result whereas a reworked *Nedrick* direction (making it clear that foreseeing death or serious bodily harm as a virtual certainty (barring some unforeseen intervention) as a result of his action amounts to intending to bring about that result) would suggest a finding of intention could not be made in these circumstances.

A final problem is the meaning of 'virtual certainty'. It is clear that Lord Steyn considered it to mean something which is as certain as things can be in this life as he described the test (at p. 391) as:

> very similar to the threshold of being aware 'that it *will* occur in the ordinary course of events' in the Law Commission's draft Criminal Code . . . .

This led him to conclude, differently from Lord Bridge in *Moloney*, that:

> It may exclude a conviction for murder in the often cited terrorist example where a member of the bomb disposal team is killed. In such a case it may realistically be said that the terrorist did not foresee the killing of a member of the bomb disposal team as a virtual certainty. That may be a consequence of not framing the principle in terms of risk-taking . . . . [But] I am satisfied that the *Nedrick* test, which was squarely based on the decision of the House in *Moloney*, is pitched at the right level of foresight.

Thus foresight of probability (of whatever degree) is not enough. A trial judge could not be faulted if, to avoid any confusion on the part of the jury, he sought to make it clear to them that foresight of a consequence as being highly probable does not equate to foresight of a virtual certainty.

While Lord Steyn specifically limited his comments to the crime of murder, it would be highly undesirable if courts were to adopt a different approach to the meaning of intention in other offences.

3.2.3.8 Good motives and oblique intent

An issue left unresolved in *Woollin* is whether a good motive may be a reason for a jury not finding intention where D acted realising that if he achieved his primary purpose the consequence prohibited by the offence (death in the case of murder) was virtually certain to ensue. Motive may, exceptionally, be made an element of an offence. For example, the Crime and Disorder Act 1998 provides for an enhanced penalty where certain offences are racially or religiously aggravated, such as assaults, criminal damage, or public order offences. An offence is racially or religiously aggravated where it 'is motivated (wholly or partly) by hostility towards members of a racial or religious group, based on their membership of that group' (see s. 28(1)(b)). But generally motive is irrelevant to liability, even where that motive may be good (see e.g. *Smith* [1960] 2 QB 423; *Chandler* v *DPP* [1964] AC 763). That a good motive does not absolve a person from criminal liability was affirmed by the Privy Council in *Yip Chiu-Cheung* v *R* [1994] 3 WLR 514 (see **8.3.3.3.2**) where it was held that an undercover officer who agreed with others (in this case the appellant) to carry out a crime intending that crime to be committed (albeit so that he could obtain evidence to convict those others), had the *mens rea* for conspiracy. Similarly the House of Lords held in *Latif* [1996] 1 All ER 353 that a customs officer who brought heroin to England as part of an operation designed to catch a major trafficker (the appellant), had the necessary intention to evade the prohibition on the importation of heroin and, if charged, would have been guilty of an offence contrary to s. 50(3) of the Customs and Excise Management Act 1979.

In both *Yip Chiu-Cheung* and *Latif* the statements concerning motive and intention came in the context of appeals by appellants for whom there might be little moral sympathy. The problem which remains, however, is those actors for whom there would be considerable moral sympathy but whose conduct may appear to fall within the strict letter of the law. For example, a doctor treating a terminally ill patient may use an analgesic to relieve pain knowing that a point will come when the increased doses necessary to relieve the pain will kill the patient. There are two antagonistic tensions at play: first, the logic of the *Nedrick/Woollin* test for oblique intention if applied without moderation could catch those whose motive for pursuing their primary purpose (pain relief in this example) is morally inconsistent with the *mens rea* for the offence, the *actus reus* of which was the side effect of achieving their primary purpose (cf. *Adams*, **2.6.3.2**); and secondly, the reluctance of judges expressly to frame a defence (whether based in justification or excuse) to cover those who act from a good motive. This problem is set in even starker contrast when the virtually certain side effect of D achieving his morally commendable primary purpose is death, as in the pain relief case, and thus, prima facie, could amount to murder, whereas the accepted *mens rea* for murder does not cover, for example, the terrorist bomber who is reckless towards the bomb disposal team but does not foresee death as a virtual certainty.

If a prosecution for murder is brought against a doctor whose patient has died as a result of treatment prescribed by the doctor, how should the trial judge direct the jury? First, the trial judge could adopt a *Gillick* approach (*Gillick* v *West Norfolk and Wisbech AHA* [1986] AC 112) and direct the jury that 'the bona fide exercise by a doctor of his clinical judgement [is a] complete negation of the [*mens rea* for murder]', i.e. there is no intention to kill. Secondly, (and perhaps operating in tandem with the first approach) he could direct the jury on intention without making any reference to the *Nedrick* direction on the basis that Lord Steyn recognised that the decision whether to give this direction is one for the trial judge to make on the basis of the circumstances of the case. Thirdly, and in contrast to the first two approaches, the trial judge could give the *Nedrick* direction but, in doing so, may emphasise the fact that whether the jury 'find' intention is entirely a matter for them and leave it to the jury to arrive at a decision based on their own view of the morality of the situation. Finally a judge may direct a jury that a finding of foresight of death as a virtual certainty is intention. In this latter situation, the doctor would be forced to rely on the somewhat ill-defined defence of necessity to avoid conviction (see **6.3**).

In two cases the trial judges have adopted a similar approach. In *Cox*, Winchester Crown Court, 18 September 1992, 12 BMLR 38, D, a consultant rheumatologist, was charged with attempted murder of V, a patient who was terminally ill and in extreme pain. A short time before V's death D had administered an injection of potassium chloride in a quantity which could have no therapeutic purpose. The charge was attempted murder as V had been cremated and thus the actual cause of death could not be established. In directing the jury Ognall J adopted the *Gillick* position stating:

If a doctor genuinely believes that a certain course is beneficial to his patient, either therapeutically or analgesically, then even though he recognises that that course carries with it a risk to life, he is fully entitled, nonetheless, to pursue it. If in those circumstances the patient dies, nobody could possibly suggest that in that situation the doctor was guilty of murder or attempted murder.

The problem in the instant case, however, was that the drug used had no therapeutic qualities and thus D's primary purpose may have been to kill rather than to alleviate pain. In directing the jury on this point Ognall J directed them that if D's primary purpose was to bring V's life to an end he was guilty of attempted murder. He also made it clear that if D's primary purpose was to kill V, his motive for doing so could afford him no defence. The jury convicted.

> In *Moor*, Newcastle Crown Court, 11 May 1999, D, a GP, was charged with murdering V, a patient whom he believed to be terminally ill and in pain from cancer, by administering diamorphine to him. In directing the jury on the question of *mens rea*, Hooper J adopted a two-stage approach. First, unless the prosecution satisfied them that the purpose of the injection of diamorphine was not to give treatment which D believed to be proper treatment to relieve pain and suffering, they should acquit. If, however, they were so satisfied, secondly, they had to consider whether D's intention in giving the injection was to kill. The jury acquitted.

The approach in *Moor* is consistent with that in *Cox*: if D's purpose is proper medical treatment (pain relief would be such) his purpose is not to kill and he should be acquitted (even though he realises that death is a virtually certain consequence of the treatment). If, however, his purpose is not proper medical treatment, the question for the jury is whether his intention was to kill. By adopting this approach (the *Gillick* approach) these two trial judges have avoided giving the *Nedrick* direction. In effect a good motive is operating to negate findings of oblique intent.

> The problem of killing in order to save life arose in unusual and traumatic circumstances in the case of *Re A (Children) (Conjoined Twins: Medical Treatment) (No. 1)* [2000] 4 All ER 961, involving the twins Jodie and Mary. The court had to consider whether it would be lawful for doctors to perform an operation to separate the twins the effect of which would be the inevitable death of Mary. The twins shared a common aorta which enabled Jodie's heart to pump the blood she oxygenated through Mary's body, as Mary's heart and lungs were deficient and incapable of sustaining her life. Mary's brain was also not fully developed. If an operation to separate them were not performed, both twins were expected to die within six months due to the strain being placed on Jodie's heart. If separated, the prospects for Jodie's survival were good albeit that she would suffer some disabilities and require further surgery. Mary was incapable of independent existence.
>
> The Court of Appeal was faced with three problems: **first, what was in the best interests of the children; secondly, if those interests were in conflict, could that conflict be resolved so as to allow one to prevail; and, thirdly, if the prevailing interest was in favour of the operation, could the operation be performed lawfully**. The first two questions raised family law issues, the third related to the criminal law. Ward LJ, with whom Brooke LJ agreed, concluded that while it was in Jodie's best interests for the operation to take place, this was not in Mary's best interests as it would mean her death. He stated that 'each life has inherent value in itself and the right to life, being universal, is equal for all of us'. Where the best interests of the children were in conflict, the court's task was to balance the welfare of each child against the other to find the 'least detrimental alternative'. This balancing exercise would not involve valuing each life but rather the 'worthwhileness' of the proposed treatment. For Mary the treatment was not worthwhile as she had always been

'designated for death' due to her disabilities. She was only alive because she was sucking 'the lifeblood out of Jodie' and by so doing would ultimately kill her. Only the doctors could save Jodie whereas Mary was beyond help. In those circumstances the balance weighed heavily in Jodie's favour, Ward LJ stating:

> The best interests of the twins is to give the chance of life to the child whose actual bodily condition is capable of accepting the chance to her advantage even if that has to be at the cost of the sacrifice of the life which is so unnaturally supported.

Turning to the criminal law there were two main issues: **first, whether the operation to separate the twins would involve the intentional killing of Mary; and, secondly, if so whether this could be justified**. Both Ward LJ and Brooke LJ concluded that the doctors performing the operation would, following the decision of the House of Lords in *Woollin* [1998] 3 WLR 382, intend to kill Mary, however much they might not desire that result, as they would recognise her death as being the virtually certain consequence of their acts. (By contrast Walker LJ adopted the approach in *Gillick*.) The dilemma for the doctors, however, was not just a moral or social one but also a legal one as the failure to operate could amount to a breach of their duty to act in Jodie's best interests. This raised the crucial question in the case, originally framed by Lord Mackay in *Howe* [1987] 1 AC 417 (see **6.2.7**) **whether 'the law should recognise in any individual in any circumstances, however extreme, the right to choose that one innocent person should be killed rather than another'?** As the doctors' duties to Jodie and Mary were in conflict Ward LJ concluded that **'the law must allow an escape through choosing the lesser of two evils'** in which case, the operation being justified, would involve no unlawful act. Furthermore, as the reality of the situation was that Mary was slowly killing Jodie (even though this unique situation could not be classed as unlawful), the doctors were entitled to come to Jodie's defence to remove the threat of fatal harm Mary presented. This is, **in effect, a defence of necessity**; Brooke LJ expressly framed his solution in terms of a defence of necessity (see further **6.3.3**). Walker LJ was also prepared, if necessary, to extend the defence of necessity to cover the instant case.

A problem which remained was the Human Rights Act 1998 and Art. 2 of the European Convention. The Court of Appeal was satisfied that the operation would not constitute a breach. Ward LJ took the view that with the rights of each child being in conflict and a solution being required, it was inconceivable that the court in Strasbourg would arrive at a different conclusion from the Court of Appeal. Brooke and Walker LJJ took the view that Art. 2(1), which protects individuals from being 'intentionally' deprived of life, was not infringed as 'intentionally' in this context had to be given its natural and ordinary meaning and thus applied 'only to cases where the purpose of the prohibited action is to cause death'. Thus, as the doctors' purpose would be to save the life of Jodie rather than to cause the death of Mary, the operation would not constitute a violation of Art. 2.

3.2.4 Basic, specific, and ulterior intent

Judges have compounded the uncertainty regarding the meaning of the word 'intention' by their use of the word 'intent' in differing contexts. When reading judgments you will encounter the terms 'basic intent', 'specific intent', and 'ulterior intent'. The meaning of these terms is important.

Key Point

The term 'basic intent' is used to describe offences for which the mental element required is intention, knowledge, or recklessness.

The phrase 'basic *mens rea*' would probably be more accurate as one of the ideas which the term seeks to convey is that the offence may be committed recklessly, in that there is no requirement that intention be proved.

The phrase 'basic intent' should be contrasted with both the phrases 'specific intent' and 'ulterior intent'. In *DPP* v *Morgan* [1976] AC 182, Lord Simon said that crimes of basic intent meant 'those crimes whose definition expresses (or, more often implies) a *mens rea* which does not go beyond the *actus reus*'. Here Lord Simon was drawing a distinction between crimes of 'basic intent' and crimes of 'ulterior intent'.

Key Point

A crime of 'ulterior intent' is one where the definition of the *mens rea* requires proof of an intention to bring about a consequence beyond the actual *actus reus* of the offence.

This is best explained by examples. Burglary may be committed where a person enters a building as a trespasser with the intention of stealing, causing grievous bodily harm, or causing criminal damage. The *actus reus* is complete as soon as D enters the building as a trespasser, he need not go on to commit one of these further offences. The *mens rea* required is, first, that D knows he is a trespasser or is reckless as to this fact and, secondly, that he intends to commit one of the three further offences. This latter element of the *mens rea* is the 'ulterior intent' as **it is a requirement beyond the *actus reus*** which is satisfied by proof that D has entered as a trespasser. Other offences of 'ulterior intent' are, for example, wounding with intent to cause grievous bodily harm, wounding with intent to resist or prevent the lawful apprehension of any person, and assault with intent to rob.

Key Point

The term 'specific intent' encompasses both crimes of 'ulterior intent' and other offences in respect of which D may plead that he lacked *mens rea* due to his intoxication at the time he committed the *actus reus*.

If an offence is one of 'basic intent' D may not plead intoxication. Offences of 'basic intent' may be committed recklessly or with intent where the intent relates only to the act done (i.e. a conduct crime) and not to its consequences (see further *Heard* [2007] EWCA Crim 125, **5.5.3**) whereas offences which the courts have classified as ones of 'specific intent' are either offences of 'ulterior intent' or offences for which proof of intention alone is required and the intention relates to the consequences as an aspect of the *actus reus*, for example, murder.

3.3 Knowledge

Where an act, omission, state of affairs, or event is unlawful where certain circumstances exist, and the offence is one requiring *mens rea*, knowledge of those circumstances on the part of D will establish *mens rea*. Many statutory offences impose this *mens rea* requirement by using the word 'knowing' or 'knowingly'. But, even where this word is not used, the courts have shown a willingness to imply it into statutory offences (see *Sweet* v *Parsley* [1970] AC 132). In *Roper* v *Taylor's Central Garages* [1951] 2 TLR 284, Devlin J stated that 'knowingly' only says expressly what is normally implied. Of course, the use of the word expressly in a statutory provision avoids all doubt. Often the word 'knowing' is used with the word 'believing' following as an alternative. In *Sherif and others* [2008] EWCA Crim 2653, the defendants were charged, inter alia, with offences contrary to s. 38B of the Terrorism Act 2000, of having information which they knew or believed might be of material assistance in preventing the commission by another of an act of terrorism. The 'others' were the men who bombed the London Underground and a bus on 21 July 2005. The Court of Appeal approved a direction from the trial judge that:

> Knowledge involves having seen, heard or experienced something yourself. Belief involves reaching a conclusion based on credible evidence, often from a number of sources.

The Court also confirmed that the test of knowledge or belief is a subjective one— whether D himself knew or believed a particular circumstance to exist. In addition, of course, that belief has to be correct as a person cannot 'know' something if, in fact, it is something else (see *Montila* [2004] UKHL 50, [27]).

 Key Point

This was confirmed in *Saik* [2006] UKHL 18 where their Lordships held that 'knowledge means true belief' (at para. 26). Thus D must believe, subjectively, that a particular circumstance exists (e.g. that goods are stolen, for the purposes of handling stolen goods) and that circumstance must, objectively, exist, i.e. the goods must be stolen.

In *Roper* Devlin J stated that there were three degrees of knowledge. The first is '**actual knowledge**', where D knows for a fact that the relevant circumstance exists. Actual knowledge is the equivalent of intention in that if D acts knowing the circumstance to exist he may be said to have acted intentionally in respect of it. Under s. 67 of the Sexual Offences Act 2003 the offence of voyeurism is committed where D, for the purpose of obtaining sexual gratification, observes V doing a private act (e.g. taking a shower), and he knows that V does not consent to being observed for his sexual gratification. The requirement here seems to be for actual knowledge. This is surprising in the context of this statute where for many more serious offences, such as rape, the absence of a reasonable belief in consent is sufficient to establish liability. One might have expected that absence of reasonable belief in consent would have been more appropriate in this offence where generally D will not know V and thus it will be impossible to prove actual knowledge on D's part of V's lack of consent.

The second degree of knowledge, according to Devlin J, is **'wilful blindness'** which is equivalent to subjective recklessness (discussed at **3.4.2.1**). Where knowledge or belief is required proof of wilful blindness may provide the evidential basis for the tribunal of fact (magistrates or jury) to conclude that the defendant had the necessary knowledge or belief (see *Westminster City Council* v *Croyalgrange Ltd* [1986] 2 All ER 353). In this case the defendant company was convicted of knowingly permitting the use of premises as a sex establishment without a licence. Lord Bridge stated (at p. 359):

> [I]t is always open to the tribunal of fact, when knowledge on the part of a defendant is required to be proved, to base a finding of knowledge on evidence that the defendant had deliberately shut his eyes to the obvious or refrained from inquiry because he suspected the truth but did not want to have his suspicion confirmed.

In *Sherif and others* the Court of Appeal confirmed this approach approving a direction to the jury where the judge indicated that:

> [I]t was not sufficient for the prosecution to establish that a defendant had closed his eyes, but that the jury was entitled to conclude, if satisfied that he had deliberately closed his eyes to the obvious because he did not wish to be told the truth, that that fact was capable of being evidence to support a conclusion that that defendant either knew or believed the fact in question.

In cases of handling stolen goods, however, where the *mens rea* requirement is that D did so knowing or believing the goods to be stolen, the courts have held that wilful blindness is not sufficient (see **14.5**).

The third degree of knowledge, according to Devlin J, is **'constructive knowledge'** which is really a species of negligence and rarely suffices to establish criminal liability. Phrases such as 'reasonable cause to believe', 'reason to believe', or 'reason to suspect' in the definitions of offences import this degree of knowledge. Liability is, in effect, incurred where D would know if he made the enquiries which a reasonable and prudent person would make or applied his mind to the situation in the way in which a reasonable person would have done. This variety of knowledge was adopted in ss 1 and 4 of the Protection from Harassment Act 1997 (see **4.1.3**). In *Flintshire County Council* v *Reynolds* [2006] EWHC 195 (Admin) the respondent had been charged under s. 112 of the Social Security Administration Act 1992 with knowingly producing information which she knew to be false in a document particular for the purpose of obtaining a benefit. On a case stated, following her acquittal at the magistrates' court, the Divisional Court held that constructive knowledge is not enough to demonstrate that something has been done knowingly in the context of a criminal statute.

The amount of knowledge required to establish guilt need extend no further than the circumstance which the definition of the offence prescribes. For example, it is sufficient for a conviction for handling stolen goods that D knew the goods to be stolen although he was ignorant or mistaken as to the nature of the goods (*McCullum* (1973) 57 Cr App R 645). Where the offence involved is being knowingly concerned in the fraudulent evasion of a prohibition on the importation of various types of goods contrary to s. 170(2) of the Customs and Excise (Management) Act 1979, different penalties apply depending on the nature of the goods. However, a mistake as to the nature of the goods will not prevent D being convicted of a more serious offence than that which he believed he was committing.

> In *Ellis, Street and Smith* (1986) 84 Cr App R 235, the accused knew they were importing prohibited goods concealed in secret compartments in cars. They believed the goods were pornographic materials when they were, in fact, cannabis, a Class B controlled drug. The maximum penalty for importing Class B controlled drugs is 14 years' imprisonment whereas the maximum for importing pornographic goods is two years. The Court of Appeal held, however, that knowledge that the goods being imported were prohibited was all that was required.

This contravenes the principle in *Courtie* [1984] AC 463 that the imposition of separate penalties in a statutory provision creates separate offences. Under the *Courtie* principle, importing pornographic goods is a separate offence from importing controlled drugs. The courts, however, are prepared to accept the *mens rea* of a lesser offence to establish guilt of a greater offence even though the greater offence may have been one which D would never have contemplated committing. The potential for injustice is considerable when it is realised that the maximum penalty for importing Class A controlled drugs, such as heroin or cocaine, is life imprisonment.

Where the *mens rea* requirement is knowledge, it must be proved that D had the requisite knowledge at the time of committing the offence. If D previously knew the prescribed fact but has forgotten it at the time he acted, this will not suffice (see *Russell* (1984) 81 Cr App R 315).

3.4 Recklessness

3.4.1 What might recklessness mean?

For some offences, such as murder or an attempt, only intention suffices to establish criminal liability. But for many crimes the *mens rea* required is intention or recklessness. Recklessness provides the baseline for liability in most offences and thus it is important to define clearly the parameters of this concept so that it is distinguishable from negligence which generally (subject to a few statutory exceptions and 'gross negligence manslaughter') does not suffice for criminal liability. A person may be reckless as to a consequence or as to a circumstance. **The notion that recklessness conveys is that of taking an unjustifiable risk.** This is reflected in the Draft Criminal Code where the Law Commission defines the term in cl. 18 as follows:

> a person acts—
> . . .
> (c) 'recklessly' with respect to—
>   (i) a circumstance when he is aware of a risk that it exists or will exist;
>   (ii) a result when he is aware of a risk that it will occur; and it is, in the circumstances known to him, unreasonable to take the risk.

Not all risk-taking is unreasonable; circumstances may exist which justify taking a risk. Whether taking a risk is justifiable depends on a balancing of the social utility or value of the activity involved against the probability and gravity of harm which might be caused. The Law Commission stated in its *Working Paper on the Mental Element in Crime* (Law Com No. 31 at p. 53):

> The operation of public transport, for example, is inevitably accompanied by risks of accident beyond the control of the operator, yet it is socially necessary that these risks be taken. Dangerous surgical operations must be carried out in the interests of the life and health of the patient, yet the taking of these risks is socially justifiable.

The tribunal of fact performs this balancing task using the objective test of whether a reasonable and prudent man would have taken the risk in the circumstances. Thus, if an act has no social utility but involves a slight possibility of the risk of harm, this would suffice to render the taking of that risk a reckless act.

 Question

If the tribunal of fact concludes that D has taken an unreasonable risk, is this sufficient to establish criminal liability? Or is awareness of the risk on the part of D necessary before criminal liability may be imposed? To put this another way, is it necessary for D to have foreseen the risk at the time he acted or is it sufficient that a reasonably prudent person would have foreseen the risk?

In most cases D is a reasonable person and will have foreseen what other reasonable persons would have foreseen. In some cases, however, D, because of mental disorder, may be incapable of foreseeing what reasonable people would have foreseen. In such a case is D to be found criminally liable for this failure or should criminal liability be limited to those who are, in some way, culpable because they are responsible actors? There are potential dangers of injustice if the meaning of recklessness is too broad and loose, extending to those who are not properly blameworthy and who do not deserve the serious labels and punishments that accompany criminal offences.

The views of the courts on this matter have changed over the years. The change was prophesied by Glanville Williams in *Criminal Law: The General Part*, para. 24, who identified the potential for the concept of recklessness to merge with that of carelessness due to three factors: first, 'the etymology of the word'; secondly, 'the constant pressure to extend the reach of the criminal law on account of the supposed policy of the individual case'; and thirdly, the need for a formula to be used to instruct juries because of the difficulty of proving recklessness. This third factor can cause a shift of emphasis from asking the jury 'to consider whether the defendant *must* have foreseen the consequence' to asking them 'whether the defendant *ought* as a reasonable man to have foreseen it'.

3.4.2 How have the courts defined recklessness?

3.4.2.1 Subjective recklessness

The courts originally gave recklessness a *subjective* meaning. **Thus an accused would be found to be reckless only where he had recognised the possibility of the prohibited consequence occurring (or the particular circumstance existing) and he had carried on regardless.** The leading authority on subjective recklessness is *Cunningham* [1957] 2 QB 396; as a result, this concept of recklessness is often referred to as '*Cunningham* recklessness'. In *Cunningham*:

> D removed a gas meter from an unoccupied house so that he could steal the money it contained. He left behind the fractured pipe from which gas was escaping. The gas seeped into the neighbouring house and P inhaled it. D was convicted of maliciously administering a noxious thing so as to endanger life contrary to s. 23 of the Offences Against the Person Act 1861. D's conviction was quashed as the judge had instructed the jury that 'maliciously' meant 'wickedly'. The Court of Criminal Appeal approved of the definition propounded by C. S. Kenny in *Outlines of Criminal Law* (1902) which stated:

> > In any statutory definition of a crime, 'malice' must be taken not in the old vague sense of wickedness in general but as requiring either (i) an actual intention to do the particular *kind* of harm that in fact was done or (ii) recklessness as to whether such harm should occur or not (i.e. **D has foreseen that the particular kind of harm might be done, and yet has gone on to take the risk of it**). It is neither limited to, nor does it indeed require, any ill-will towards the person injured.
> > The issue which had not been clearly left to the jury was whether D had actually foreseen that removal of the gas meter might cause injury to someone but nevertheless had gone on to remove it. [Emphasis added]

In more recent statutory provisions the word 'maliciously' is not used; Parliament uses the words 'intentionally' or 'recklessly' expressly. In its Report, *The Mental Element in Crime* (Law Com No. 89), the Law Commission attributed this subjective meaning to recklessness. The Criminal Damage Act 1971 resulted from the work of the Law Commission who in its Report, *Offences of Damage to Property* (Law Com No. 29), approved the *Cunningham* definition of recklessness. Section 1 of the Act makes it an offence for a person to destroy or damage property belonging to another intentionally or recklessly. Several cases arose in the 1970s concerning the meaning of the word 'reckless' in this section (see *Briggs* [1977] 1 WLR 605; *Parker* [1977] 1 WLR 600; *Stephenson* [1979] 1 QB 695). In all of these cases the Court of Appeal confirmed that the test was subjective—it had to be proved that D recognised the risk even though, perhaps because of bad temper, he had suppressed it or driven it out.

> In *Stephenson* D suffered from schizophrenia. He had crept into a hollow in a large straw stack and lit a fire to keep warm. The stack caught fire. The trial judge directed the jury that they could find D guilty if they were satisfied he had closed his mind to the obvious fact of risk from his act and that schizophrenia might be a reason which made a person close his mind to the obvious fact of risk. In effect he was directing the jury that if a reasonable prudent person would have recognised the risk as obvious

they should convict D. The Court of Appeal quashed the conviction, Geoffrey Lane LJ stating (at p. 703):

> A man is reckless when he carries out the deliberate act appreciating that there is a risk that damage to property may result from his act. It is however not the taking of every risk which could properly be classed as reckless. The risk must be one which it is in all the circumstances unreasonable for him to take . . . . We wish to make it clear that the test remains subjective, that the knowledge or appreciation of risk of some damage must have entered the defendant's mind even though he may have suppressed it or driven it out . . . . The schizophrenia was on the evidence something which might have prevented the idea of danger entering the appellant's mind at all. If that was the truth of the matter, then the appellant was entitled to be acquitted. That was something which was never left clearly to the jury to decide.

3.4.2.2 *Caldwell* recklessness—an objective interlude

Unfortunately what seemed clear to the Court of Appeal was far from clear to the House of Lords. **Recklessness received radical redefinition in the 1980s in *Caldwell* [1982] AC 341.**

> In *Caldwell* D got drunk and set fire to a hotel in pursuit of a grievance he had against the owner. There were guests in the hotel at the time but the fire was discovered and extinguished before any serious damage was done. D was indicted on two counts of arson. He pleaded guilty to the first count of intentionally or recklessly damaging property belonging to another contrary to s. 1(1) of the Criminal Damage Act 1971 but pleaded not guilty to the second count of damaging property with intent to endanger life or being reckless whether life would be endangered contrary to s. 1(2) of the 1971 Act. He claimed that he was so drunk at the time that the thought that he might be endangering life had never crossed his mind. The trial judge directed the jury that drunkenness was not a defence to this charge and he was convicted. The House of Lords affirmed that where the prosecution indict D on the basis that he was reckless whether life was endangered, drunkenness is not a defence as this is an offence of 'basic intent' (see **5.5** for a discussion on intoxication).

This should have been enough to dispose of the case. Their Lordships, however, took the opportunity to redefine recklessness. Lord Diplock, with whom Lords Keith of Kinkel and Roskill agreed, delivered the judgment of the majority. He stated his test of recklessness as follows (at p. 354):

> In my opinion, a person charged with an offence under s. 1(1) of the 1971 Act is 'reckless as to whether or not property would be destroyed or damaged' if (1) he does an act which in fact creates an obvious risk that property will be destroyed or damaged and (2) when he does the act he either has not given any thought to the possibility of there being any such risk or has recognised that there was some risk involved and has none the less gone on to do it.

Lord Diplock considered that the two states of mind in his test, of foresight of risk and failure to give thought to the possibility of there being any such risk, were equally blameworthy. This, to say the least, is highly questionable as the person who deliberately takes a risk would appear to be much more culpable than the one who does not recognise the risk.

 Question

If an accused were to be convicted for failing to give thought to an obvious risk, an important issue to be decided would be to whom the risk had to be obvious; was it the reasonably prudent person or D himself had he bothered to consider the matter?

In *Lawrence* [1982] AC 510, Lord Diplock stated (at p. 526):

> Recklessness on the part of the doer of an act does presuppose that there is something in the circumstances that would have drawn the attention of an ordinary prudent individual to the possibility that his act was capable of causing the kind of serious harmful consequences that the section which creates the offence was intended to prevent . . .

This view was reluctantly accepted by the Divisional Court as the correct one in *Elliott* v C [1983] 1 WLR 939.

> D, who had been out all night without sleep, entered a garden shed where she found white spirit which she poured onto an old carpet and lit to keep warm. The fire spread to the shed which was destroyed. D was 14 years old and had learning difficulties. The magistrates acquitted her, finding that she had given no thought to the risk of the shed being destroyed, but that even if she had given thought to the matter the risk would not have been obvious to her. The Divisional Court ruled that it was only necessary for the risk to have been obvious to the reasonably prudent person.

In *Stephen (Malcolm R)* (1984) 79 Cr App R 334, it was argued that the reasonably prudent person should at least be of the same age and sex as D and bear such of his characteristics as would have affected his ability to appreciate the risk involved in his conduct. The Court of Appeal rejected this argument and confirmed that the risk needed only to have been obvious to the reasonably prudent person who was a person of mature years and understanding. Thus the individual was to be judged against a standard which he may have been constitutionally incapable of attaining.

After 22 years of confusion and injustice the issue of the meaning of recklessness returned to the House of Lords in G [2003] UKHL 50, where their Lordships overruled their decision in *Caldwell* as 'offensive to principle and apt to cause injustice' accepting that 'the need to correct it was compelling'.

> In G [2003] UKHL 50, two boys aged 11 and 12 entered the back yard of a shop and set fire to some newspapers they found there, throwing the papers under a large plastic wheelie-bin. The boys left, after which the bin caught fire, in turn setting another bin on fire, and the fire spread eventually causing £1 million worth of damage to the shop. The boys were charged with arson contrary to s. 1(1) and (3) of the

Criminal Damage Act 1971. Their defence was that they had expected the paper fires to extinguish themselves. It was accepted that neither boy appreciated that there was any risk of the fire spreading in the way it had. The trial judge directed the jury in accordance with *Caldwell* that if the defendants had created a risk of the building being damaged by fire that would have been obvious to the ordinary reasonable adult bystander, they should convict them if either they had given no thought to the possibility of there being such a risk, or, having recognised that there was some risk involved they had nonetheless gone on and done the act. The jury had difficulty reaching a verdict and asked the judge why they should consider the test as perceived by a reasonable person. The trial judge expressed regret at the law he had to apply and counselled them that even if they found the law harsh, they had to apply it as it was. The jury convicted the boys and the Court of Appeal dismissed their appeal. The point of law of general public importance certified for consideration by the House of Lords was:

> Can a defendant properly be convicted under section 1 of the Criminal Damage Act 1971 on the basis that he was reckless as to whether property was destroyed or damaged when he gave no thought to the risk but, by reason of his age and/or personal characteristics the risk would not have been obvious to him, even if he had thought about it?

Their Lordships effectively answered the certified question in the negative but went further. Lord Bingham, with whom the other four Law Lords expressed their agreement, stated (at para. 41):

> I would answer the certified question obliquely, basing myself on clause 18(c) of the Criminal Code Bill annexed by the Law Commission to its Report 'A Criminal Code for England and Wales Volume 1: Report and Draft Criminal Code Bill' (Law Com No. 177, April 1989):
> 'A person acts recklessly within the meaning of section 1 of the Criminal Damage Act 1971 with respect to—
>
> (i)   a circumstance when he is aware of a risk that it exists or will exist;
>
> (ii) a result when he is aware of a risk that it will occur; and it is, in the circumstances known to him, unreasonable to take the risk.'

There were several reasons for Lord Bingham's decision. His Lordship was of the view that **it could not be supposed that by 'reckless' Parliament, in legislating the Criminal Damage Act 1971, had meant anything different to the Law Commission in its Report** (Law Com No. 29) and its Working Paper No. 23 which had preceded it, wherein it was plain that in replacing the word 'maliciously' in the previous legislation with the word 'reckless' the intention was to retain the meaning of that word as defined in *Cunningham*. The decision of the majority in *Caldwell* was a misconstruction of the Act and amounted to a 'demonstrable error', or, as Lord Steyn put it, '*Caldwell* adopted an interpretation of section 1 which was **"beyond the range of feasible meanings"**.' This being so, Lord Bingham identified four reasons why the decision in *Caldwell* should be overruled despite its longevity and approval in other cases.

First, conviction for serious crime required not simply proof of causation by the defendant of the injurious result but also proof that when he so acted the defendant's state of mind was culpable. His Lordship stated (at para. 32):

> [I]t is not clearly blameworthy to do something involving a risk of injury to another if (for reasons other than self-induced intoxication: *DPP* v *Majewski* [1977] AC 443) one genuinely does not perceive the risk. Such a person may fairly be accused of stupidity or lack of imagination, but neither of those failings should expose him to conviction for serious crime or the risk of punishment.

Secondly, Lord Bingham considered that the *Caldwell* direction could lead to obvious unfairness as the instant case demonstrated. His Lordship stated (at para. 33):

> It is neither moral nor just to convict a defendant (least of all a child) on the strength of what someone else would have apprehended if the defendant himself had no such apprehension.

Thirdly, his Lordship was influenced by the reasoned and outspoken criticism of *Caldwell* expressed by leading academics, practitioners, and judges (including Lords Edmund-Davies and Wilberforce who dissented in *Caldwell*).

Finally, the majority's interpretation of 'recklessly' in s. 1 of the 1971 Act was a misinterpretation which was 'offensive to principle and . . . apt to cause injustice'. His Lordship rejected the suggestion of a simple modification of the *Caldwell* direction for the benefit of children as such would continue to offend the principle that conviction should depend upon proving a culpable state of mind.

A further reason to support their Lordships' conclusion was expressed by Lord Steyn who recognised the general trend towards a subjective approach to liability, in respect of which s. 8 of the Criminal Justice Act 1967 (see **3.2.3.1**) was of central importance. This subjective approach was supported by a number of their Lordships' earlier decisions: *Morgan* [1976] AC 182 (see **3.6.1.1.1**); *Beckford* [1988] AC 130 (see **3.6.1.1.2**); *B (A Minor)* v *DPP* [2000] 2 AC 428 (see **3.6.1.1.3** and **4.2**); and *K* [2002] 1 AC 462 (see **4.2**).

While the decision of their Lordships is confined to the meaning of the word 'reckless' in the Criminal Damage Act 1971, it is difficult to see how the objective test could be revived in the context of any other statutory offence without Parliament expressly legislating for that interpretation. This is confirmed by the decision of the Court of Appeal in *AG's Reference (No. 3 of 2003)* [2004] EWCA Crim 868, where the Court applied the subjective definition of recklessness to the offence of misfeasance in public office further intimating that it applies generally in the criminal law. The Court considered how the House of Lords had interpreted 'wilful neglect' in the case of *Sheppard* [1981] AC 394 (see **3.5**), taking the view that a subjective test was required whereby it was necessary for D to have a subjective awareness of the duty to act or a subjective recklessness as to the existence of the duty.

3.5 **Wilfulness**

The term 'wilfully' is often used in statutes. The cases are inconsistent regarding the question whether or not this imports a requirement of *mens rea*. In *Arrowsmith* v *Jenkins* [1963] 2 QB 561, on a charge of wilful obstruction of the highway contrary to s. 121(1) of the Highways Act 1959, the Divisional Court held that it was sufficient that D by an exercise of free will did an act which caused an obstruction. This seemed to import nothing more than a requirement of voluntariness. As such the word 'wilfully' is effectively otiose as the requirement of voluntariness is implied by the general principles of the criminal law. There is, however, a notable number of similar decisions relating to other statutory offences (see e.g. *Maidstone Borough Council* v *Mortimer* [1980] 3 All ER 552; *Hudson* v *MacRae* (1863) 4 B & S 585; *Cotterill* v *Penn* [1936] 1 KB 53).

By contrast, in the earlier case of *Eaton* v *Cobb* [1950] 1 All ER 1016, the Divisional Court held that the word 'wilfully' imported a requirement of *mens rea*. Humphreys J stated (at p. 1017):

> In my view 'wilfully obstruct' in a statute which makes such obstruction a criminal offence means wilfully to obstruct . . . the test . . . is whether or not the obstruction was intentional.

In this case D had opened his car door in the path of a cyclist after having checked his mirror and seeing the road apparently clear. The Divisional Court took the view that while he wilfully opened the door he did not 'wilfully obstruct' the highway as there was no intention so to do. This decision is similar to those of the offence of wilfully obstructing a police constable in the execution of his duty contrary to s. 51(3) of the Police Act 1964. In *Lewis* v *Cox* [1985] QB 509, Webster J stated (at p. 516):

> [T]he simple facts which the court has to find are whether the defendant's conduct in fact prevented the police from carrying out their duty, or made it more difficult for them to do so, and whether the defendant intended that conduct to prevent the police from carrying out their duty or to make it more difficult to do so.

In this case D had twice opened the rear door of a police van with the object of discovering from his friend who had been arrested where he was being taken. While D's ultimate aim may not have been obstruction, this was, in fact, a necessary precondition to the achievement of his ultimate aim. As he knew the van would be prevented from driving away by his opening of the door, he therefore intended the obstruction.

In *Sheppard* [1981] AC 394, the House of Lords imported a *mens rea* requirement into the offence of wilful neglect of a child contrary to s. 1 of the Children and Young Persons Act 1933. Section 1 provides:

> (1) If any person who has attained the age of sixteen years and has the custody, charge, or care of any child or young person under that age, wilfully assaults, ill-treats, neglects, abandons, or exposes him . . . in a manner likely to cause him unnecessary suffering or injury to health . . . that person shall be guilty of a misdemeanor . . .

The case arose from the failure of parents to procure medical aid for their child who died from malnutrition and hypothermia. In relation to the four positive acts which the section proscribes ('neglect' being a failure to act), Lord Diplock expressed the view that the word 'wilfully' imported *mens rea*. If the word was to be understood as simply requiring a voluntary act, this was not its natural meaning and it would be otiose. Regarding neglect, which in this case involved the failure to provide medical aid, Lord Diplock stated (at pp. 404, 405):

> Such a failure . . . could not be properly described as 'wilful' unless the parent *either* (1) had directed his mind to the question whether there was some risk . . . that the child's health might suffer unless he were examined by a doctor and provided with such curative treatment as the examination might reveal as necessary, and had made a conscious decision, for whatever reason, to refrain from arranging for such medical examination, *or* (2) had so refrained because he did not care whether the child might be in need of medical treatment or not.

While part (2) appears to suggest *Caldwell* recklessness, in *AG's Reference (No. 3 of 2003)* [2004] EWCA Crim 868, the Court of Appeal concluded that the test was one of subjective recklessness as Lord Diplock intended to exclude from liability those parents who, through lack of intelligence or ignorance, are genuinely unaware of the threat to their child's health (see also *Turbill* [2014] EWCA Crim 1422). Following the decisions in *Sheppard* and *AG's Reference (No. 3 of 2003)* earlier cases which suggest that the word 'wilfully' simply imports the requirement for a voluntary act, rather than subjective *mens rea*, must be of doubtful authority.

3.6 Mistake

? Question

If D makes a mistake will this affect his criminal liability?

The answer to this question will depend on the nature of the mistake D makes. D's mistake may be such as to negate his *mens rea* in respect of a circumstance which is part of the *actus reus* of the offence.

ℰ Example

D is charged with the theft of an umbrella which he took from an umbrella stand in a restaurant. If D believed the umbrella was his own there would be no dishonesty (i.e. *mens rea*) in respect of the appropriation of 'property belonging to another' (i.e. a circumstance in the *actus reus*—see s. 1 of the Theft Act 1968). If, however, *mens rea* is not required in respect of a particular circumstance, a mistake in respect of it may be of no relevance.

A mistake may also be made with regard to circumstances which justify or excuse the commission of an offence such as pleas of self-defence or duress (for example, a person might mistakenly believe that she is going to be physically attacked by another person and needs to use force to defend herself).

An issue which has been problematical for many years is whether a mistake must be a reasonable one (i.e. such as a reasonable person might have made in the circumstances) before it will relieve D of liability. Needless to say judicial pronouncements on this issue have been contradictory.

Mistakes may be divided into two categories, namely *relevant* mistakes and *irrelevant* mistakes. Most uncertainty and inconsistency have arisen in respect of relevant mistakes.

3.6.1 Relevant mistakes

A mistake may be relevant where it relates to either a definitional element of the offence or an excusatory claim (e.g. duress). The definitional elements of the offence are the *actus reus* and justificatory claims such as self-defence. The latter may be viewed as part of the *actus reus* (see **2.1.2**). At one time, only mistakes which were reasonable could operate to negate liability. In *DPP v Morgan* [1976] AC 182, the House of Lords removed this requirement in certain circumstances so that an honest mistake could suffice. Consequently relevant mistakes have to be divided into those relating to definitional elements of the offence and those relating to non-definitional elements.

3.6.1.1 Mistake as to a definitional element of the offence
There are three categories of mistake as to a definitional element of an offence.

3.6.1.1.1 *Mistake negating* mens rea
Where an offence is one requiring *mens rea* D must have *mens rea* in relation to every element of the *actus reus*.

Key Point

If D's mistake is to operate to negate his liability it must relate to the existence of an element of the *actus reus*; it is not sufficient that his mistake is as to some quality of an element of the *actus reus*.

For example, D steals a Jaguar belonging to V believing it to be green. The car is red but D is colour-blind. His mistake is one of quality and will not affect his liability. He intended to appropriate property belonging to another and he did so. In *McCullum* (1973) 57 Cr App R 645, it was held that it was sufficient for a conviction for handling stolen goods that D knew the goods were stolen albeit that he was ignorant or mistaken as to the nature of the goods. Similarly, in *Ellis, Street and Smith* (1986) 84 Cr App R 235 (see **3.3**), it was sufficient that D knew the goods they were importing were prohibited goods, albeit they thought they were importing pornography rather than drugs. These examples should be contrasted with the example in **3.6** of taking the wrong umbrella, where the mistake relates to the existence of an element of the *actus reus*. If D believes that the property he is taking is his own he is not acting dishonestly as he does not believe he is appropriating property belonging to another; his mistake negates his *mens rea* (see further discussion of s. 2 of the Theft Act 1968, **12.2.2.1**). The result would be the same if D had destroyed the umbrella believing it was his own and had been charged with criminal damage contrary to s. 1(1) of the Criminal Damage Act 1971 (see *Smith (David)* [1974] QB 354).

Formerly a mistake as to the existence of a definitional element would only operate to negate D's *mens rea* where the mistake was a reasonable one. The House of Lords considered this issue in *DPP v Morgan* [1976] AC 182.

> This was a case involving rape where the appellants claimed that they believed the victim was consenting when she was not. The trial judge had directed the jury that they should acquit only if they were satisfied that the appellants' mistake as to the victim's consent was reasonable. The House of Lords held this was a misdirection as the only requirement was that the belief in consent be an honest one. Lord Hailsham stated (at p. 214):

>> Once one has accepted . . . that the prohibited act in rape is non-consensual sexual intercourse, and that the guilty state of mind is an intention to commit it, it seems to me to follow as a matter of inexorable logic that there is no room either for a 'defence' of honest belief or mistake, or of a defence of honest and reasonable belief or mistake. Either the prosecution proves that D had the requisite intent, or it does not. In the former case it succeeds, and in the latter it fails.

Thus **an honest belief in consent negates *mens rea***; a 'defence' of mistake is, in reality, a denial that the prosecution has proved its case. Of course, the more reasonable the mistake is, the more likely it is that D will be believed. Lord Hailsham recognised this when he went on to state (at p. 214):

> Since honest belief clearly negatives intent, the reasonableness or otherwise of that belief can only be evidence for or against the view that the belief and therefore the intent was actually held . . .

 Question

Does the principle in *Morgan* apply generally to all offences requiring *mens rea* or only to the offence of rape?

In *Phekoo* [1981] 1 WLR 1117, the Court of Appeal confined the decision to the offence of rape holding that mistakes as to definitional elements in other offences had to be reasonable if they were to negative *mens rea*. In *Kimber* [1983] 1 WLR 1118, the Court of Appeal held that the same inexorable logic which spawned the decision in *Morgan* also dictated that on a charge of indecent assault *mens rea* would be negatived by an honest belief in the victim's consent. This same logic dictates the

same result in all offences requiring *mens rea*. That this is correct has been confirmed by the House of Lords in *B (A Minor)* v *DPP* [2000] 2 WLR 452 (see **3.6.1.1.3**).
Where a particular offence requires only negligence in respect of an element of
the *actus reus*, then the mistake must be a reasonable one if it is to negative
negligence (see 3.6.1.1.3). If strict liability applies to an element of the *actus*
***reus* a mistake, reasonable or not, will be irrelevant (see 4.2).**

While the principle in *Morgan*, that an honest mistake in respect of a definitional
element negates *mens rea*, has become of general application, the law relating to
consent in respect of sexual offences has been changed when the Sexual Offences
Act 2003 came into effect. For offences committed after May 2004 belief in consent,
to be effective, must be reasonable. (For further discussion of consent in respect of
sexual offences see **Chapter 11**.)

3.6.1.1.2 *Mistake as to a justificatory claim*

 Question

D hits V in the belief that V was about to attack him when, in fact, V was simply performing an
April Fools' Day prank. Will D's plea of self-defence succeed to negate his liability where it is an
honestly held belief or must the belief be a reasonable one?

In *Albert* v *Lavin* [1982] AC 546, the Divisional Court held that an accused could rely
on his mistaken belief only when pleading self-defence where that belief was based
on reasonable grounds. This raises the question whether a justification is something
separate from the definitional elements of an offence (see **2.1**). If it is there might be
some reason in principle for requiring such mistakes to be reasonable. If, however,
the absence of a justificatory claim is part of the definitional elements of the offence
the inexorable logic of *Morgan* would seem to apply. In *Kimber*, Lawton LJ disagreed
with the reasoning in *Albert* v *Lavin*. When the issue arose directly in *Williams (Gladstone)* (1984) 78 Cr App R 276, the Court of Appeal departed from *Albert* v *Lavin*.

> D was convicted of assault occasioning actual bodily harm. D had witnessed what he
> believed to be an assault by M on N. D intervened and punched M. D claimed he
> honestly believed that N was being unlawfully assaulted by M and that he was trying
> to rescue N. In fact M was acting lawfully, seeking to arrest N for a robbery he had
> seen him commit. The jury were directed that D's mistake would be relevant if it was
> honest and based on reasonable grounds. The Court of Appeal quashed D's convic-
> tion. The Court defined 'assault' as 'an act by which the defendant, intentionally or
> recklessly, applies unlawful force to the complainant'. Thus the force must be unlaw-
> ful and D must intend to apply unlawful force to the victim.

Lord Lane CJ stated that the mental element cannot be substantiated 'by simply
showing an intent to apply force and no more'. He was of opinion that there are
three situations where the use of force is lawful. First, in limited circumstances the
victim may consent to the force (but see now *Brown*, **10.7**); secondly, where the
defendant is acting in self-defence; and thirdly, where the defendant is using reasonable force in the prevention of crime or to arrest offenders under s. 3 of the

Criminal Law Act 1967. If D makes a mistake he is to be judged against the facts as he believed them to be. The Court stated (at p. 281):

> [T]he jury should be directed first of all that the prosecution have the burden or duty of proving the unlawfulness of the defendant's actions; secondly, if the defendant may have been labouring under a mistake as to the facts, he must be judged according to his mistaken view of the facts; thirdly, that is so whether the mistake was, on an objective view, a reasonable mistake or not.

In *Beckford* v *R* [1988] AC 130, the Privy Council approved the decision in *Williams* as correctly stating the law. Lord Griffiths stated (at p. 144):

> If then a genuine belief, albeit without reasonable grounds, is a defence to rape because it negatives the necessary intention, so also must a genuine belief in facts which if true would justify self-defence be a defence to a crime of personal violence because the belief negates the intent to act unlawfully.

The element of unlawfulness is thus part of the definitional elements of the offence and requires *mens rea* to be proved in respect of it. If D mistakenly believes he is acting in self-defence he does not intend to act unlawfully (see further *Blackburn* v *Bowering* [1994] 3 All ER 380; *Faraj* [2007] EWCA Crim 1033). Section 76(4) of the Criminal Justice and Immigration Act 2008 provides that if the defendant claims to have held a particular belief as regards the existence of any circumstances '(a) the reasonableness or otherwise of that belief is relevant to the question whether D genuinely held it; but (b) if it is determined that D did genuinely hold it, D is entitled to rely on it for the purposes of subsection (3), whether or not— (i) it was mistaken, or (ii) (if it was mistaken) the mistake was a reasonable one to have made.' Note however that s. 76(5) states that s. 74 'does not enable D to rely on any mistaken belief attributable to intoxication that was voluntarily induced'. We will look at the effects of mistaken beliefs that arise as a result of intoxication at **5.5**.

Some statutory offences prohibit conduct where it is done 'without lawful excuse' (see e.g. ss 1(1), 2, and 3 of the Criminal Damage Act 1971). In these offences the absence of lawful excuse is one of the definitional elements of the offence which the prosecution must prove. Section 5(3) expressly declares that it is sufficient that a belief in one of the circumstances which would constitute a lawful excuse is honest; there is no requirement that the belief be based on reasonable grounds (for a full discussion of s. 5 of the Criminal Damage Act 1971, see **15.2.2.2**).

3.6.1.1.3 *The problem of* Tolson
The offence of bigamy under s. 57 of the Offences Against the Person Act 1861 is committed where a person 'being married, shall marry any other person during the life of the former husband or wife'. A proviso to the section provides that it shall not extend to second marriages where the first marriage has been dissolved or annulled, or where the husband or wife has been continually absent from the person who is remarrying for seven years, and has not been known by that person to be living within that time.

In *Tolson* (1889) 23 QBD 168, a wife remarried five years after last seeing her husband whom she believed to have been lost at sea. She was charged with bigamy when it was discovered that he was still alive. She did not come within the proviso. Stephen J directed the jury that an honest belief on reasonable grounds that the husband of the prisoner was dead was not a defence to a charge of bigamy. The jury convicted her but in response to a question put to them by the judge said that they found that she believed on reasonable grounds and in good faith that he was dead. The Court for Crown Cases Reserved quashed her conviction.

In *Gould* [1968] 2 QB 65, it was held that a reasonable belief that the first marriage had been dissolved was a defence. In *Morgan* the decision in *Tolson* was approved along with other bigamy cases which followed it (see *King* [1964] 1 QB 285 and *Gould*). Lord Fraser stated that 'bigamy does not involve any intention except the intention to go through a marriage ceremony'. It is a general principle that *mens rea* is required as to all the elements of the *actus reus* of an offence unless these are excluded expressly or by necessary implication. The approval of *Tolson* in *Morgan* can only be explained on the basis that *mens rea* was not required as to the element of 'being married', negligence being sufficient. If this is correct, there is nothing to distinguish the state of mind of the bigamist from that of every other person who marries. As bigamy is a serious offence it is disappointing that the House of Lords did not take the opportunity to disapprove of *Tolson* as the requirement of *mens rea* should not lightly be set aside. In a recent family law case, *Azizi* v *Aghaty* [2017] 1 FLR 351, the High Court confirmed that the *Tolson* principle remains good law. An honest and reasonable belief by the defendant in a fact which, if true, would make his second marriage lawful is a good defence.

Their Lordships confronted the problem again in *B (A Minor)* v *DPP* [2000] 2 WLR 452 (see **4.2.3.2**). The requirement that a mistaken belief had to be based on reasonable grounds was described by Lord Nicholls (at pp. 457, 458) as a 'relic from the days before a defendant could give evidence in his own defence' which explained why juries would judge a defendant's state of mind 'by the conduct to be expected of a reasonable person'. In *Sweet* v *Parsley* [1970] AC 132 (see **4.2.3.1**) Lord Diplock had stated that (at p. 163):

> [A] general principle of construction of any enactment, which creates a criminal offence, [is] that, even where the words used to describe the prohibited conduct would not in any other context connote the necessity for any particular mental element, they are nevertheless to be read as subject to the implication that a necessary element in the offence is the absence of a belief, held honestly and upon reasonable grounds, in the existence of facts which, if true, would make the act innocent.

Lord Nicholls concluded that this presumption required modification to reflect the current state of the criminal law on mistakes of fact by omitting the reference to reasonable grounds. He did not, however, pass any comment to resolve the status of *Tolson* which remains an aberrant decision limited to bigamy and awaits a suitable opportunity for their Lordships to overrule it. The House of Lords did not take the opportunity offered in *R* v *K* [2001] UKHL 41, [2001] 3 WLR 471 (see **4.2.3.1**) to resolve the uncertainty surrounding the status of *Tolson* but, by confirming that the presumption of *mens rea* is to apply unless excluded expressly or by necessary implication, it must be taken to have implicitly overruled *Tolson* such that if similar circumstances were to arise in the future an honest belief in the death of a spouse should be sufficient to defeat a charge of bigamy.

3.6.1.2 Mistake as to a non-definitional element

Where an accused seeks to rely on an excusatory defence (see **6.1**) his plea involves an admission that he performed the *actus reus* of the offence with the requisite *mens rea*. If the defence is successful D is excused the normal consequences of conviction and sentencing which would otherwise ensue. If an accused makes a mistake in respect of an element of an excusatory defence, such as duress, the issue arises whether such a mistake must be a reasonable one. In *Graham* (1982) 74 Cr App R 235, Lord Lane CJ made it clear that an accused may only rely on the defence of duress where his belief that he would be killed or seriously injured if he did not commit the offence was a reasonable one. In *Howe* [1987] 1 AC 417, the House of Lords endorsed this view without further consideration. Subsequent cases have confirmed that in duress or duress of circumstances **D's belief in the threat which compels him to act must be reasonable** (see e.g. *Abdul-Hussain et al.* [1999] Crim LR 570; *Cairns* [1999] 2 Cr App R 137; *Safi* [2003] EWCA Crim 1809). The House of Lords, in *Hasan* [2005] UKHL 22, has confirmed the objective nature of the test (see further **6.2.3.2**). Lord Bingham of Cornhill, whose reasoning was approved by Lords Steyn, Rodger, and Brown, stated (at para. 23):

> But the words used in *Graham* and approved in *Howe* were 'he reasonably believed'. It is, of course, essential that the defendant should genuinely, i.e. actually, believe in the efficacy of the threat by which he claims to have been compelled. But there is no warrant for relaxing the requirement that the belief must be reasonable as well as genuine.

This different treatment of mistakes, dependent on whether they relate to matters of justification or of excuse, has the potential for further anomalous consequences.

 Example

In 'Necessity, Duress and Self-defence' [1989] Crim LR 611, Professor Elliott gives the example of a motorist, D, who honestly but unreasonably believes he is being attacked by V. If D drives away in a dangerous fashion and is charged with dangerous driving, he would not succeed if he raised a plea of duress of circumstances (see **6.3**) because of his unreasonable mistake. By contrast, if he drove his car at V, on a charge of dangerous driving he could raise the defence of self-defence.

The Law Commission in its Draft Criminal Code proposed to deal with this anomaly by cl. 41, which provides that 'a person who acts in the belief that a circumstance exists has any defence that he would have if the circumstance existed'; there is no requirement that the belief be reasonable.

3.6.2 Irrelevant mistakes

3.6.2.1 Mistake and offences of strict liability

An offence is one of strict liability where *mens rea* is not required in respect of an element of the *actus reus*; *mens rea* may be required in respect of other elements of the offence. If D makes a mistake in respect of an element for which liability is strict his mistake is irrelevant as his state of mind need not be established in respect of that element in order to determine guilt (see **Chapter 4**). If the mistake is in respect of an element for which *mens rea* is required, the mistake will operate in the normal way as regards liability (see *Blackburn* v *Bowering* [1994] 3 All ER 380). In *Prince* (1875) LR 2 CCR 154, D was convicted of an offence under s. 55 of the Offences Against the Person Act 1861 (since repealed). Under the 1861 provision it was an offence unlawfully to take an unmarried girl under the age of 16 out of the possession of her father against his will. D was convicted although he had reasonable grounds to believe the girl was over 16. The Court of Crown Cases Reserved affirmed his conviction holding that the offence was one of strict liability in respect of the circumstance of the girl's age. As knowledge of the girl's age was not required, a mistake thereto was irrelevant (on age-related offences and strict liability see *B (A Minor)* v *DPP* [2000] 2 AC 428, **4.2.3.1**). Lord Bramwell stated, however, that had D mistakenly believed the girl's father had consented to her being taken, or if he believed she was not in anyone's possession, care, or charge, his conviction would have been quashed as an intention to take the girl out of her father's possession against his will had to be proved.

 Question

Can a person be convicted even if he does not know the law or is mistaken about it?

In *Howells* [1977] QB 614, D was convicted of possession of a revolver without a firearm certificate, contrary to s. 1 of the Firearms Act 1968. D thought the gun was an antique which would have been covered by an exception under s. 58(2); in fact it was a modern replica, possession of which was unlawful without a certificate. His appeal against conviction was dismissed by the Court of Appeal on the ground that 'to allow a defence of honest and reasonable belief that the firearm was an antique and therefore excluded would be likely to defeat the clear intention of the Act'.

In Australia and Canada there is a defence of honest and reasonable belief which may be raised to a charge of a strict liability offence. In *Proudman* v *Dayman* (1943) 67 CLR 536 (an Australian case), Dixon J stated (at p. 540):

> As a general rule an honest and reasonable belief in a state of facts which, if they existed, would make the defendant's act innocent affords an excuse for doing what would otherwise be an offence.

The legislature may expressly exclude this defence in any statutory offence, in which case the offence is one of absolute liability. L. H. Leigh, *Strict and Vicarious Liability* (1982) at pp. 58–61 points out that there are dicta in *Sweet* v *Parsley* [1970]

AC 132 and *Morgan* which could be built upon to give recognition to such a defence in England and Wales but so far no court has sought to do so.

3.6.2.2 Ignorance of the law

As a general rule, ignorance of, or a mistake as to, the law is irrelevant as the citizen is presumed to know the law of the land. This presumption is applied even if it was impossible for D to know the law. In *Bailey* (1800) Russ & Ry 1, D was a sailor who, before the end of a voyage, committed an act which constituted an offence under a statute which had been passed after the voyage had commenced. Being at sea, D could not have known of the statute's existence. D was convicted but the judges recommended a pardon. The prosecution have to prove only that an accused brought about the *actus reus* of the offence with which he is charged with the requisite *mens rea*; they do not have to prove that he knew that what he was doing was contrary to the law. For example, if D comes from a country where anal intercourse with a boy under the age of 16 is not an offence and in this country has anal intercourse with a man who is under 16 in the belief that it is not an offence here, this does not negate his liability as he intentionally did the act which constituted the *actus reus* of the offence (see *Esop* (1836) 7 C & P 456).

> In *Lee, The Times*, 24 October 2001, D was charged with assault with intent to resist lawful arrest contrary to s. 38 of the Offences against the Person Act 1861. D had been driving his car when he was stopped by police officers for a roadside safety check. On smelling alcohol on D's breath one of the officers asked him to perform a breathalyser test. The officer concluded that the test was positive and told D that he was under arrest. D disputed the test and punched both officers. At his trial D claimed that he believed the arrest to be unlawful and thus had no intention to resist lawful arrest. In upholding his conviction the Court of Appeal held his mistake was one of law as to the authority of the officer to arrest him as compared to one of fact, for example whether the person seeking to arrest him was a police officer (cf. *Brightling* [1991] Crim LR 364; *Blackburn v Bowering* [1994] 3 All ER 380). Relying on *Bentley* (1850) 4 Cox CC 406 the Court took the view that the lawfulness of the arrest was a question of law, not one of fact, and it depended on the officer's belief, not D's belief.

The *mens rea* for the offence was an intention to resist arrest and knowledge that the person he assaulted was a person seeking to arrest him. Thus D's belief that he had not committed an offence was irrelevant.

There is an exception to the general rule stated earlier. In some cases D's mistake as to the civil law may negate his *mens rea* in respect of an element of the *actus reus* of the offence with which he is charged.

> In *Smith (David)* [1974] QB 354, D was charged with criminal damage to fixtures in a flat of which he was the tenant. D had installed the fixtures to cover wiring he had installed for his stereo equipment. When he was given notice to quit, D damaged the fixtures in removing the wiring. He claimed he believed he was damaging his own property as he had installed it. D's mistake was as to the civil law; in fact, fixtures become the property of the landlord. D's conviction was quashed as he did not intend to damage 'property belonging to another'.

If D had removed the fixtures and taken them with him when he left he would not have been liable for theft as s. 2(1)(a) of the Theft Act 1968 specifically deals with mistakes as to the civil law. It provides that an appropriation of property is not to be regarded as dishonest if the appropriator believed that he had in law the right to deprive the other of it.

In each case it is crucial to determine the *mens rea* required by the offence. If *mens rea* is not required as to the element of the *actus reus* in respect of which D is mistaken, his mistake will be irrelevant. If, however, negligence is required as to that element, D's mistake will negate his liability if it was a reasonable one. In the case of bigamy an accused will not be liable if he reasonably, but mistakenly, believed that his first marriage had been dissolved (a mistake of civil law) at the time he entered into the second marriage (see *Gould* [1968] 2 QB 65).

3.6.2.3 Transferred malice

 Question

D wishes to kill X. He sees a person whom he believes to be X and shoots at him, killing him. In fact he has killed V, X's twin brother. Can D avoid a conviction for murder because his mistake brought about an unintended result?

D will be liable as he intended to kill another person unlawfully and he killed the person at whom he was aiming. His mistake is as to a matter which the law treats as irrelevant, namely the identity of the victim. Likewise if D intends to burn down 10 Downing Street, but in the dark he mistakenly sets fire to No. 11, he will be guilty of arson as he has, without lawful excuse, intentionally damaged property belonging to another.

 Question

Would it make any difference if D had shot at X but at the moment D pulled the trigger X had bent over and the bullet had hit and killed V who was behind him?

In this situation D has not killed the person at whom he was aiming but he has caused the *actus reus* of murder and he did intend to kill.

In *Latimer* (1886) 17 QBD 359, D's conviction for unlawfully and maliciously wounding V was upheld, although D had aimed the offending blow with his belt at X and it had glanced off striking V and causing a severe wound. The Court applied the doctrine of 'transferred malice' Lord Coleridge CJ stating (at p. 361):

It is common knowledge that a man who has an unlawful and malicious intent against another, and, in attempting to carry it out, injures a third person, is guilty of what the law deems malice against the person injured, because the offender is doing an unlawful act, and has that which the judges call general malice, and that is enough.

If, in *Latimer*, the belt had glanced off X and the buckle had connected with a valuable vase, breaking it, D would have brought about a different *actus reus* to that intended, namely criminal damage. In such a case if D was charged with criminal damage his intention to injure X could not be combined with this *actus reus* to support a conviction as the *actus reus* he has caused and *mens rea* he had relate to different offences (see *Pembliton* (1874) LR 2 CCR 119). Of course, if it could be proved that D had foreseen this risk and gone on to take it, D could be convicted of criminal damage on the basis of recklessness. He might also be charged with attempting to wound X. Andrew Ashworth makes the point that in virtually all cases of transferred malice D could have been convicted of attempt and thus there is no need for the doctrine (see 'Transferred Malice and Punishment for Unforeseen Consequences' in P. Glazebrook (ed.), *Reshaping the Criminal Law* (1978)). Professor Ashworth argues that charging attempt would be an improvement as then D would be prosecuted for the intended harm rather than the accidental result. The Law Commission in its Draft Criminal Code, however, opted to retain the doctrine of transferred fault (see also Law Com No. 218, paras 42.1–42.6). In its *Commentary on Draft Criminal Code Bill* (Law Com No. 177) it states its primary reason for this as follows (at para. 8.57):

> Where a person intends to affect one person or thing (X) and actually affects another (V), he may be charged with an offence of attempt in relation to X; or it may be possible to satisfy a court or jury, without resort to the doctrine, that he was reckless with respect to V. But an attempt charge may be impossible (where it is not known until trial that the defendant claims to have had X and not V in contemplation); or inappropriate (as not describing the harm done adequately for labelling or sentencing purposes). Moreover, recklessness with respect to V may be insufficient to establish the offence or incapable of being proved.

In *AG's Reference (No. 3 of 1994)* [1996] 2 WLR 412, the doctrine of transferred malice was affirmed and applied in a novel way by the Court of Appeal.

> D stabbed his pregnant girlfriend in the abdomen. No injury to the foetus was detected. The child was born prematurely and died subsequently due to complications arising from her premature birth. D was charged with murder. The trial judge directed an acquittal on the ground that no conviction for either murder or manslaughter was possible in law. Before the Court of Appeal three arguments were raised. Relying on Glanville Williams, *Criminal Law: The General Part* (paras 44 and 48) it was argued, first, that an 'unexpected difference of mode [by which the relevant consequence occurs should] be regarded as severing the chain of causation if it is sufficiently far removed from the intended mode' and, secondly, that the doctrine of transferred malice 'should be limited to cases where the consequence was brought about by negligence in relation to the actual victim'. The Court of Appeal considered that it was neither right nor necessary 'to reintroduce any question of causation at the stage when *mens rea* falls to be considered' and that there was no justification for the proposed imposition of a requirement of negligence toward the intended victim. A further argument that malice could not be transferred to a person who was not in being at the time of the act causing death was also rejected. The Court of Appeal concluded that malice could be transferred in this situation. Lord Taylor CJ stated earlier in his judgment:

> In the eyes of the law the foetus is taken to be a part of the mother until it has an existence independent of the mother. Thus an intention to cause serious bodily injury to the foetus is an intention to cause serious bodily injury to a part of the mother just as an intention to injure her arm or her leg would be so viewed. Thus consideration of whether a charge of murder can arise where the focus of the defendant's intention is exclusively the foetus falls to be considered under the head of transferred malice, as is the case where the intention is focused exclusively or partially upon the mother herself.

On further appeal to the House of Lords [1997] 3 WLR 421, their Lordships held that D could be convicted of manslaughter but not of murder. An intention to harm the mother could not be equivalent to intent to harm the foetus or the child it would become, since they were two distinct organisms living symbiotically. There was no basis for extending the doctrine of transferred malice to a case where there had been no intention to injure the foetus. The *mens rea* for murder was not, therefore, present. Without further explanation, Lord Mustill referred to the doctrine of transferred malice as a 'fiction' which lacked a 'sound intellectual basis'. When the doctrine is applied in the context of murder where D aimed to kill X but missed and killed V, there is no fiction involved where he is charged with the murder of V and it is proved that he had the intention to kill a person. The law would be deficient if it did not protect the public generally in circumstances such as these. Their Lordships, however, had no difficulty in concluding that D could be guilty of manslaughter resulting from an unlawful and dangerous act. It was unnecessary for the act to have been directed against the person who died as a result of it or for D to have known that his act was likely to injure that person. It was sufficient to prove that D intentionally stabbed the mother, that the act caused the death, and that reasonable people would have appreciated the risk that some harm would result to *a person*, not necessarily the foetus or person it would become. There was an argument that a foetus should not be regarded as being a potential victim of manslaughter. This was firmly rejected, Lord Hope of Craighead stating (at p. 443):

> For the foetus, life lies in the future, not the past. It is not sensible to say that it cannot ever be harmed, or that nothing can be done to it which can ever be dangerous. Once it is born it is exposed, like all other living persons, to the risk of injury. It may also carry with it the effects of things done to it before birth which, after birth, may prove to be harmful. It would seem not to be unreasonable therefore, on public policy grounds, to regard the child in this case, when she became a living person, as within the scope of the *mens rea* which B had when he stabbed her mother before she was born.

If the doctrine of transferred malice could not be applied to the foetus for the purposes of a conviction for murder, how could a conviction for manslaughter (which is also homicide) be possible? If a manslaughter verdict is possible, why not a murder verdict given that in the instant case D had the necessary *mens rea* for murder and his act caused the death of a person, the *actus reus* of murder? Their Lordships do not answer this question. Indeed, they do not appear to recognise that there is something incongruous about the decision they gave. The only consolation is that the facts are so unusual that it is unlikely that this decision will be the source of injustice in the future.

AG's Reference (No. 3 of 1994) was distinguished in *CP (A Child)* v *Criminal Injuries Compensation Authority* [2014] EWCA Civ 1554, a case involving a mother's excessive drinking during pregnancy causing foetal alcohol spectrum disorder to the foetus. The Court of Appeal ruled that a foetus was not a 'person' for the purposes of the offence of administering poison contrary to s. 23 of the Offences against the Person Act 1861 (see further **10.5.1**).

If D shoots at X because he believes that X is about to shoot him but he misses and kills V, D could plead self-defence if charged with V's murder. If he was justified in shooting X (this depends on using only such force as was reasonable in the circumstances), and thus did not intend *unlawfully* to kill another person, he cannot be convicted of murdering V as there is no *mens rea* to transfer. Where, however, X and D engage in a gunfight in the course of which X shoots at D, misses and kills V, neither X nor D having a justification for their actions, both would be guilty of murder by means of the doctrine of transferred malice, X as the principal and D as an accessory (see *Gnango* [2011] UKSC 59, **7.1.2.1**).

 The law in context

Law reform and conflicting approaches to mens rea for serious offences: an example

Debates about criminal law reform often reflect deeper philosophical debates about the appropriate moral basis for criminal liability. Many scholars and judges consider subjectivism to be the only principled basis on which to impose criminal liability for serious offences. Subjectivist theory is rooted in the principle of individual autonomy: moral blame, and therefore criminal liability, arises only when a person can be said to have chosen to behave in a particular way or to cause (or risk causing) particular consequences. A defendant should thus be judged according to what he believed he was doing or risking (J. Horder, *Ashworth's Principles of Criminal Law* (8th edn, 2016) p. 174). As Ashworth puts it in *Positive Obligations in Criminal Law* (2013, p. 133):

> Underpinning the subjectivist doctrines is a notion of autonomy based on the capacity to reason and to exercise will power. The argument is that, if a legal system is to claim moral authority over its subjects and to respect their autonomy, it should adhere to rule-of-law principles in its criminal law, by ensuring fair warning, maximum certainty of definition, subjective requirements for criminal liability, and so on.

However, subjectivism is not without its critics. While few scholars now support the type of objective approach adopted in *Caldwell*, some argue that punishment for culpable inadvertence (where the defendant did not appreciate the consequences of his actions or appreciate that a particular circumstance existed) *can* be justified for serious offences. In a critique of the Lords' decision in *R* v *G*, Amirthalingam argued that 'blind adherence to subjectivism' results in a disparity between the legal requirement of *mens rea* and the community's sense of moral wrong (K. Amirthalingam, '*Caldwell* Recklessness is Dead, Long Live Mens Rea's Fecklessness' (2004) MLR 491–500, 492). He argues that:

> The blameworthiness of an accused is not determined merely by inquiring whether there existed a 'subjective' mens rea; it requires an additional crucial step of asking whether the 'mens was rea'. This inquiry involves an 'objective' element and

→

→

includes inadvertence within mens rea . . . One cannot determine blameworthiness or culpability without reference to some external standard. This calls for a
degree of objective evaluation, which is shunned by the subjectivists. (p. 495)

H. L. A. Hart argued that we can blame a person when 'he could have thought about what he
was doing' with just as much confidence as we can blame someone for intentional wrongdoing when 'he could have done otherwise', assuming he has the normal physical and mental
capacities for doing what the law requires and abstaining from what it forbids (H. L. A. Hart,
Punishment and Responsibility (1968) p. 151). Those who favour *constructive liability* argue that
once a person has crossed the 'moral threshold' of committing a criminal offence, one can
legitimately be punished for the consequences that follow, even if one did not foresee them
(J. Horder, 'A Critique of the Correspondence Principle in Criminal Law' [1995] Crim LR 759–
70). In some situations then it is arguable that a person may deserve punishment for failing to
advert to the consequences of their actions or whether particular circumstances existed.

This tension between subjectivism and objective approaches runs through debates about
criminal law reform, as we will see throughout the book. The debates are particularly acute
when the issue is whether a person is criminally liable for the unintended consequences of
their actions. For example, a person who throws a single punch and causes another person's
death is currently liable for unlawful act manslaughter, as he has committed an unlawful act
that caused death and reasonable people would appreciate the unlawful act carried the risk of
some harm (see **Chapter 9**). For this serious offence, English law adopts an objective approach
to liability: the defendant does not need to be aware even of the risk of any harm resulting
from his action, as long as other people would have appreciated the risk of some harm resulting (*DPP* v *Newbury* [1977] AC 500). English law is very strict in this respect, adhering to a
constructive, objective approach to liability rather than subjectivism. This is largely for policy
reasons: the law's harshness arguably acts as a deterrent and communicates through the
offence label the state's disapproval of minor criminal acts that *could* cause serious harm.

The Law Commission has tended to adhere to subjectivist approaches in its recommendations for law reform. In its Consultation Paper on *Involuntary Manslaughter* (1996) the Law
Commission advocated a subjective approach to liability for 'one-punch killers' saying that it is
wrong in principle for the law to 'hold a person responsible for causing a result that he did not
intend or foresee, and which would not even have been *foreseeable* by a reasonable person
observing his conduct' (Law Commission (1996) *Involuntary Manslaughter* (Law Com No. 347:
HMSO, London, para. 3.6)). The Commission argued that unlawful act manslaughter is unprincipled because 'it requires only that a foreseeable risk of causing *some* harm should have been
inherent in the accused's conduct, whereas he is convicted of actually causing death, and . . .
punished for doing so' (para. 3.6). The Commission recommended that unlawful act manslaughter be abolished in its present form and that such a 'one-punch killer' should only be
convicted of manslaughter if he was *aware of a risk that his conduct will cause death or serious
injury* and it was unreasonable for him to take that risk having regard to the circumstances as
he knows or believes them to be.

This subjective approach met with a distinctly cool reception from the Government, which
emphasised the need for an *objective* approach to liability, which (the Government argued)
would be more likely to deter and bolster public confidence in criminal justice by demonstrating to victims' families that the law focused on their relative's death rather than the defendant's state of mind (Home Office (2000) *Reforming the Law on Involuntary Manslaughter: The
Government's Proposals* (HMSO, London) p. 10). The Government told the Law Commission
to rethink its proposals, instructing them that intentional or reckless criminal behaviour which
results in death should attract 'an appropriate charge' and that 'anyone who embarks on a

→

→

course of illegal violence has to accept the consequences of his act, even if the final consequences are unforeseeable' (p. 10). The Commission's most recent proposals seek to steer something of a middle course between subjectivism and constructive liability. The Commission recommends in its latest proposals that a 'one-punch killer' should only be guilty of manslaughter if he killed through a criminal act and *intended to cause injury* or was *subjectively aware that the act involved a serious risk of causing injury*. The second limb of that test preserves a subjective approach while the first limb adopts a somewhat objective, constructive approach in that a person could be liable for a homicide offence when they intended something much less serious than the harm that resulted.

While scholars might tend to favour subjectivism as the principled basis for criminal liability, the Government has advocated objective approaches for some serious offences to capture those who are arguably culpably inadvertent. Seen in the context of political imperatives to be 'tough on crime' and to be on the side of crime victims and their families, objectivism has an appeal that subjectivism lacks. It gives more weight to the consequences of D's actions when apportioning blame, unlike subjectivism's focus on D's foresight and culpability. We will see this tension between subjectivist and objectivist approaches throughout the book, in the context of a range of important offences, in particular murder, manslaughter, rape (and other sexual offences), theft, and non-fatal offences against the person.

 Key Points

- *Mens rea* is one of the fundamental building blocks of criminal liability, particularly for serious offences.

- There are a range of *mens rea* terms: intention, recklessness, knowledge, and wilfulness.

- Intention has been a difficult term for the courts to interpret.

  - In most cases where intention is an issue, the 'golden rule' is that a trial judge should avoid elaboration of its meaning and leave it to the jury's good sense to decide whether D acted with the necessary intent (*Moloney* (1985)). An explanation that intention is distinct from motive or desire will frequently be needed.

  - The leading case is *R v Woollin* (1997), in which the House of Lords clarified how juries should be directed on its meaning where a fuller direction is needed. The Lords held that juries in murder cases should be directed 'that they are not entitled to find the necessary intention unless they feel sure that death or serious bodily harm was a virtual certainty (barring some unforeseen intervention) as a result of the defendant's actions and that the defendant appreciated that such was the case'.

- The courts have delineated three types of intent:

  - ulterior intent (where the definition of the offence requires proof of an intention to bring about a consequence beyond the offence's *actus reus*);

  - specific intent (which encompasses offences of ulterior intent and other offences in respect of which D may plead that he lacked *mens rea* due to his intoxication at the time he committed the *actus reus*); and

  - basic intent (which describes offences for which the mental element is intention, knowledge, or recklessness).

- Knowledge means true belief: D must believe that a particular circumstance exists.

→

➡

- Recklessness has a subjective meaning, following *R* v *G* (2003). A person acts recklessly with respect to a circumstance when he is aware of a risk that it exists or will exist and with respect to a result when he is aware of a risk that it will occur, and it is in the circumstances known to him unreasonable to take the risk.

- A person acts 'wilfully' when he does or fails to do something (such as failing to provide adequate medical treatment for a child) deliberately or not caring whether that something may be needed (*Sheppard* (1981)).

- A mistake may negate liability where D has a genuine, honest belief about the existence of an element of the *actus reus*, unless the particular offence requires only negligence in respect of an element in the actus reus, in which case the mistake must be a reasonable one to negative negligence (*B* v *DPP* [2000] 2 AC 428).

- If D pleads self-defence, he is entitled to be judged on the facts as he honestly believed them to be even if he is mistaken, unless that mistaken belief arises from intoxication, in which case he will be judged on the circumstances as they were.

- If D pleads duress and claims to have had an honest but mistaken belief that he would be killed or seriously injured if he did not commit the alleged crime, he may only rely on the defence if his mistaken belief was a reasonable one.

- Ignorance of, or a mistake as to, the law is irrelevant.

- The doctrine of transferred malice means that if D acts with *mens rea* towards a person (e.g. D shoots a gun intending to kill A), that *mens rea* will transfer if D actually hurts or kills another person (e.g. A ducks and B dies).

FURTHER READING

J. Chalmers and F. Laverick, 'Fair Labelling in Criminal Law' (2008) 71 MLR 217.

R. A. Duff, 'The Politics of Intention: A Response to Norrie' [1990] Crim LR 637.

E. Griew, 'States of Mind, Presumptions and Inferences' in P. Smith (ed.), *Criminal Law: Essays in Honour of J. C. Smith* (London: Butterworth, 1987).

J. Horder, 'Transferred Malice and the Remoteness of Unexpected Outcomes from Intentions' [2006] Crim LR 383.

D. Kimel, 'Inadvertent Recklessness in the Criminal Law' (2004) 120 LQR 548.

A. Norrie, 'Oblique Intention and Legal Politics' [1989] Crim LR 793; 'Intention: More Loose Talk' [1990] Crim LR 642.

A. Pedain, 'Intention and the Terrorist Example' [2003] Crim LR 579.

A. P. Simester, 'Moral Certainty and the Boundaries of Intention' (1996) 16 OJLS 445.

A. T. H. Smith, 'Error and Mistake of Law in Anglo-American Criminal Law' (1985) 14 Anglo-Am LR 3.

G. Williams, 'Convictions and Fair Labelling' [1983] CLJ 85.

G. Williams, 'Oblique Intention' [1987] CLJ 417.

G. Williams, 'The *Mens Rea* for Murder: Leave it Alone' (1989) 105 LQR 387.

4

....

Negligence and strict liability

4.1 Negligence

4.1.1 The meaning of negligence

Mens rea, **as it has been traditionally understood, requires an advertent state of mind on the part of D.** Intention and recklessness are states of mind falling within the compass of *mens rea*. **Negligence has not been accepted by scholars as a *mens rea* term as it does not require advertence on the part of D to a particular risk.** Negligence is, however, a type of legal fault as it sets an objective standard to which a person's behaviour must conform. The standard set is that of the reasonable (or prudent) person. Thus if a reasonable person would have recognised the risk of a consequence occurring or a circumstance existing in the situation in which D acted (or omitted to act), D will be liable whether or not he gave any thought to the possibility of there being a risk involved in his conduct.

The *Caldwell* recklessness test overlapped to some degree with negligence as, under *Caldwell*, D could be liable where he failed to give thought to an obvious risk. Negligence, however, covers an area which *Caldwell* did not cover. If a person gives thought to a risk but concludes that there is no risk or that it is negligible he could not be liable under *Caldwell*. The concept of negligence, however, includes the person who has given thought to the possibility of the risk existing and unreasonably concluded that it does not exist. Negligence also covers the person who recognises the risk but takes steps which he believes would eliminate it, if the steps he takes fall below the standard of conduct to be expected from the reasonable person.

4.1.2 Arguments for and against negligence as a basis for criminal liability

Basing liability on negligence may be justified because people can properly be blamed for failing to do or consider things that ordinary people would have done or considered. Carelessness and thoughtlessness are concepts with which we are familiar in everyday life. The careless person may not be as blameworthy as the person who intentionally causes a result or who is aware of the result's possibility when he acts, but that does not mean that he deserves no blame. Someone who behaves in a way that reasonable people would not may be risking significant harm to others or to property and negligence enables the legal system to censure those people for their behaviour. For example, negligence must underpin road traffic offences such as driving without due care and attention, for the sake of safety and to ensure that common standards of behaviour are clearly established and punished if breached. Negligence also helps to make our criminal justice system efficient and effective. It is easier to prove that a person did not do what a reasonable person would have done than it is to prove that he subjectively intended, foresaw, or knew about results or states of affairs. In turn, the ease of proving negligence may deter people, who will know that they will not be able to defend themselves by saying 'I did not appreciate what the results of my actions might be or what state of affairs existed.'

There are strong arguments of principle against imposing criminal liability for being negligent. While negligence is a fundamental concept at the heart of civil liability in tort law, criminal law is not concerned with payment of damages; the state imposes punishment and stigma that should be applied only to those individuals who truly deserve them. A person who acts carelessly or without thought might deserve some blame, but we tend not to say that those people are the ***most* blameworthy people deserving the most serious state intervention, punishment. It is particularly harsh to label merely careless people with the stigmatising label of 'criminal' for doing or failing to do something that they lacked the capacity to appreciate might be harmful. Imposing criminal liability on the basis of negligence may lead to the punishment and stigmatising of those who, because of their personal characteristics such as age or mental disorders, were not able to appreciate what ordinary, reasonable people could.**

4.1.3 Criminal liability for negligence

Traditionally the common law did not impose liability for negligence with the exception of manslaughter where 'gross' negligence is a ground of liability (see **9.3.3.2**). There are few crimes where negligence is the sole basis of liability. The most notable example is s. 3 of the Road Traffic Act 1988 (as substituted by s. 2 of the Road Traffic Act 1991), under which it is an offence to drive a motor vehicle on a road without due care and attention or without reasonable consideration for other persons using the road. This offence is generally referred to as careless driving. In *McCrone* v *Riding* [1938] 1 All ER 157, Lord Hewart CJ stated the standard of driving which is required as follows (at p. 158):

> That standard is an objective standard, impersonal and universal, fixed in relation to the safety of other users of the highway. It is in no way related to the degree of proficiency or degree of experience to be attained by the individual driver.

This standard applies to all drivers, even the inexperienced learner driver. **The standard set is that of the reasonably prudent and skilful driver.** If D drives in a way in which such a reasonable driver would not have driven, he will be liable.

Negligence as to the existence of a circumstance is sometimes sufficient to establish liability. This is sometimes referred to as 'constructive knowledge' (see **3.3**).

For example, under s. 25 of the Firearms Act 1968 it is an offence 'for a person to sell or transfer any firearm or ammunition to . . . another person whom he knows or has reasonable cause for believing to be drunk or of unsound mind'. Constructive knowledge is a basis of liability for the two offences created by the Protection from Harassment Act 1997 to deal with the problem of harassment. The Protection of Freedoms Act 2012, by s. 111, created two new offences of stalking by inserting two sections, ss 2A and 4A, into the 1997 Act. A person may be convicted of the summary offence, under s. 2, of pursuing a course of conduct, as defined in s. 1, which amounts to harassment of another if he knows or *ought to know* that it amounts to harassment; or the indictable offence, under s. 4, of engaging in a course of conduct which causes another to fear, on at least two occasions, that violence will be used against him, if he knows or *ought to know* that his course of conduct will cause the other so to fear. The justification for the imposition of liability based on constructive knowledge is the difficulty which might exist of proving *mens rea* on the part of those who engage in harassment or stalking who often suffer from mental or personality disorders (see further Allen, 'Look Who's Stalking: Seeking a Solution to the Problem of Stalking' [1996] 4 Web JCLI).

In the Sexual Offences Act 2003 there are a number of offences intended to protect children from sexual harm, abuse, and exploitation. For serious offences such as rape of a child under 13, assault by penetration of a child under 13, sexual assault of a child under 13, and causing or inciting a child under 13 to engage in sexual activity, a child under 13 is considered incapable of consenting (ss. 5, 6, 7, and 8 respectively). It is Parliament's intention that liability in respect of the circumstance of the child's age should be strict and it should not be a defence that the defendant believed the child to be over 13. For other offences, such as sexual activity with a child and causing or inciting a child to engage in sexual activity (ss. 9 and 10 respectively) the defendant will not be guilty where the child is over 13 but under 16 and he reasonably believes that the child is 16 or over. In G [2006] EWCA Crim 821 (affirmed by the House of Lords [2008] UKHL 37), the Court of Appeal found that the need for a mental element in respect of age for the s. 5 offence was negatived by necessary implication arising from the contrast between, for instance, the s. 9 offence with its reference to reasonable belief that the child was over 16, and the absence of any such reference in relation to children under 13. It is clear that for these offences liability is strict where the child is under 13 but negligence is required where the child is 13 or over.

Although liability is rarely imposed for negligence there are two other ways in which negligence may become relevant. In some strict liability offences statute may provide that it is a defence for D to prove that he was not negligent. For example, under the Trade Descriptions Act 1968, which creates a number of offences which require no proof of *mens rea* or negligence by the prosecution, s. 24(1) provides that it is a defence for the person charged to prove:

(a) that the commission of the offence was due to a mistake or to reliance on information supplied to him or to the act or default of another person, an accident or some other cause beyond his control; and

(b) that he took all reasonable precautions and exercised all due diligence to avoid the commission of such an offence by himself or any person under his control.

The second way in which negligence may be relevant is the converse of the first; negligence in respect of a subsidiary element of the *actus reus* of the offence with which he is charged may deprive D of a defence which would otherwise have been available to him. For example, bigamy is an offence where negligence in respect of the subsidiary element of 'being married' is sufficient. Thus if an accused goes through a second ceremony of marriage having made an unreasonable mistake that his former marriage has been annulled or dissolved or that his spouse is dead, he will be guilty of bigamy (see *King* [1964] 1 QB 285).

4.1.4 Does the reasonable person share any of D's characteristics?

While the standard against which D's conduct is measured is objective, that of the reasonable person, the question arises whether there are situations in which a subjective element may be imported into negligence so that the reasonable person shares any physical or mental limitations from which D might suffer. It is clear that if D had some special knowledge which the ordinary person would not possess, the standard against which he will be judged is that of the reasonable person possessing that special knowledge (see *Lamb* [1967] 2 QB 981).

The Misuse of Drugs Act 1971 contains various offences relating to the production, cultivation, possession, and supply of drugs. Section 28 provides a defence in relation to some of these offences:

> (2) . . . it shall be a defence for the accused to prove that he neither knew of nor suspected nor had reason to suspect the existence of some fact alleged by the prosecution which it is necessary for the prosecution to prove if he is to be convicted of the offence charged.

In *Young* [1984] 1 WLR 654, D sought to rely on his intoxication as his reason for not suspecting that he was in possession of a controlled drug. The Courts-Martial Appeal Court held that this would not avail him as a defence based on the ground of 'no reason to suspect' involved the concept of objective rationality. There are many statutory defences based on 'reasonable cause' or 'reasonable grounds' to believe (see e.g. s. 1(5) of the Official Secrets Act 1989) and these have been interpreted as imposing an objective test of whether the reasonable person would have held the requisite belief (see *McArdle* v *Egan* (1933) 150 LT 412). It would appear that if there was an objective reason to suspect, it will not avail D that persons suffering from his mental or physical incapacities would not have been aware of it.

In the Sexual Offences Act 2003, however, the offences of rape, assault by penetration, sexual assault, and causing sexual activity without consent are offences which may be committed where the defendant 'does not reasonably believe that B consents'. Whether a belief is reasonable is to be determined having regard to all the circumstances, including any steps the defendant has taken to ascertain whether the complainant consents. This is not, strictly speaking, an offence of pure negligence as the standard is not that of the 'reasonable person' (a standard to which a particular defendant might not be able to attain, where e.g. he had learning difficulties or suffered from a mental disorder) but rather what is reasonable in all the circumstances (a test which is flexible enough to take into account the particular characteristics of the defendant) (see **11.2.2.3.2**).

4.2 **Strict liability**

4.2.1 **The meaning of strict liability**

> **Key Point**
>
> If *mens rea* or negligence need not be proved in respect of one or more elements of the *actus reus* of an offence, that offence is one of strict liability.

This must be contrasted with absolute liability. If an offence is one of absolute liability even the absence of voluntariness on D's part will not avail him. Very few offences involve absolute liability (see *Larsonneur* and *Winzar* v *Chief Constable of Kent*, **2.4.2**). **If an offence is one of strict liability the prosecution must prove the** *actus reus* **was committed by D; this involves establishing that D's conduct was voluntary.**

While an accused may not be found guilty of a strict liability offence where his conduct was involuntary, just as he could not be convicted of an offence requiring *mens rea* or negligence, he may be convicted even though he caused the prohibited consequence inadvertently and in a totally blameless way.

> **Example**
>
> D, a butcher, asked a vet to examine a carcass to check that it was fit for human consumption, and, on receiving the vet's assurance that it was fit, he offered it for sale. D was convicted of the offence of exposing unsound meat for sale because the meat turned out to be unfit for human consumption, the vet having negligently performed his examination (see *Callow* v *Tillstone* (1900) 83 LT 411).
>
> D had exercised due care and taken reasonable steps to avoid committing the offence; his conduct was quite blameless. The offence, however, was one of strict liability as neither *mens rea* nor negligence were required in respect of the unsoundness of the meat. Short of not selling meat at all, there was no way for D to avoid liability.

Similarly, if D is charged with driving a motor vehicle on a road either while unfit through drink contrary to s. 4 of the Road Traffic Act 1988, or with a level of alcohol in his blood, breath, or urine above prescribed limits contrary to s. 5, he will be convicted even though he was unaware of his condition and not responsible for it, as where it is due to his soft drink being surreptitiously laced with alcohol. The courts have held that these road traffic offences are strict liability offences which impose liability on the blamelessly inadvertent driver in the previously mentioned situation, although the court when sentencing may treat the 'laced drink' as a special reason for refraining from disqualifying the driver under s. 34(1) of the Road Traffic Offenders Act 1988 (see *Shippam* [1971] RTR 209).

It should be noted that while liability may be strict in respect of one element of the *actus reus, mens rea* **or negligence may be required in respect of other elements.**

In *Prince* (1875) LR 2 CCR 154, D was convicted of taking an unmarried girl under the age of 16 out of the possession of her father against his will, contrary to s. 55 of the Offences Against the Person Act 1861. D believed on reasonable grounds that the girl was 18 but he knew she was in the custody of her father. D was convicted as knowledge that the girl was under 16 was not required.

By contrast, in *Hibbert* (1869) LR 1 CCR 184, D met a girl of 14 in the street and took her to another place where they had sexual intercourse. D was acquitted of the s. 55 offence as it was not proved that he knew the girl to be in the custody of her father; *mens rea* was required as to this element.

Section 55 of the Offences Against the Person Act 1861 was replaced by s. 20 of the Sexual Offences Act 1956. Whether this was a strict liability offence was left in some doubt following the decision of the House of Lords in *B (A Minor)* v *DPP* [2000] 2 WLR 452 (see **4.2.3.2**) where their Lordships cast doubt on the reasoning of the Court in *Prince* in concluding that liability was strict in respect of the *actus reus* element of age. Their Lordships did not overrule *Prince*, however, as the correct construction of s. 20 was not an issue before them. The s. 20 offence has been repealed by the Sexual Offences Act 2003.

4.2.2 The origins of strict liability

It is a presumption of the common law that *mens rea* is required to be proved to establish guilt of a criminal offence. Strict liability invariably arises in respect of offences created by statute. The precursors to offences of strict liability are to be found in some eighteenth-century regulatory statutes relating to the adulteration of foodstuffs and tobacco, which created defences for merchants and others charged with such offences to prove that the adulteration took place without their knowledge and despite the exercise of due diligence to prevent it (see further L. H. Leigh, *Strict and Vicarious Liability* (1982)). In the nineteenth century there was an increase in regulatory legislation concerned with food and drugs, health, liquor, factories, pollution, and other public welfare matters. Faced with this welter of legislation and the difficulties of enforcement, the courts dispensed with the requirement of *mens rea* in many cases where there were no express words in the statute requiring proof of *mens rea*. This development could be justified on several grounds. First, earlier regulatory legislation requiring proof of *mens rea* made convictions difficult to secure. Secondly, later legislation either did not use words, such as 'maliciously', 'intentionally', 'knowingly', 'wilfully', or 'permitting', which would impose a requirement of *mens rea*, or these words were used in some sections of Acts and not in others. Thirdly, most of this regulatory legislation could be regarded as creating offences *mala prohibita* rather than *mala in se*. **Offences such as murder, rape, and theft are *mala in se* because they are inherently immoral. Regulatory offences generally do not involve inherently immoral activities. Conduct becomes criminal simply because it is prohibited.** For example, many strict liability offences relate to driving vehicles and the safety and construction of vehicles. There is nothing inherently immoral in driving at 71 mph as opposed to 69 mph. Driving at 71 mph is an offence, however, because Parliament has decided that, in the interests of safety, a line has to be drawn somewhere between acceptable speed and unacceptable speed. Regulatory offences are created by Parliament for the better running of society and the penalty is imposed to encourage observance of the law. Those who break such laws, however, may not really be thought of as criminals in popular understanding.

Question

Is strict liability confined to regulatory offences?

Strict liability has not been confined to regulatory offences (see *Prince*, **4.2.1**) and, indeed, it was not a necessary consequence of the difficulty of proving such offences. The legislation could have been interpreted to involve a reversal of the burden of proof so that D would be convicted unless he proved that he had not been at fault, i.e. a 'no negligence' or 'due diligence' defence could have been implied. While not going this far, courts in recent years have sought to reaffirm the presumption of *mens rea* and are, perhaps, less willing to find that an offence is one of strict liability.

4.2.3 Identifying offences of strict liability

Question

How do courts decide when construing a statute whether or not the offence it creates is one of strict liability?

If Parliament did its job properly there should never be any room for doubt whether or not an offence is one of strict liability. If *mens rea* is required this could be expressly stated by using one of the long list of words (e.g. intentionally, knowingly, wilfully, permitting, etc.) which impose this requirement. Alternatively, if the offence is intended to be one of strict liability, this could be expressly stated as was the case with ss 1 and 2 of the Contempt of Court Act 1981 which expressly stated that strict liability applied to certain offences under the Act. Unfortunately, many statutory provisions remain silent and the courts are left to statutory interpretation whereby they seek to discover the intention of Parliament. Certain factors or considerations assist the courts in this quest.

4.2.3.1 The presumption of *mens rea*

Key Point

The absence of express words imposing a requirement of proving *mens rea* is not conclusive that the offence is one of strict liability.

In the earlier part of the last century judges were, perhaps, more easily persuaded that strict liability was intended in such circumstances. In 1969, however, the House of Lords, in its decision in *Sweet* v *Parsley* [1970] AC 132, reaffirmed the presumption of *mens rea*. If it is clearly expressed that an offence is to be one of strict liability, the courts would carry out the will of Parliament. This first point was recently reiterated by the Supreme Court in *Lane and Letts* [2018] UKSC 36 by Lord Hughes (at para. 9):

> Whilst the [presumption as to mens rea] is of great importance in the approach to the construction of criminal statutes, it remains a principle of statutory construction. Its importance lies in ensuring that a need for mens rea is not inadvertently, silently, or ambiguously removed from the ingredients of a statutory offence. But it is not a power in the court to substitute for the plain words used by Parliament a different provision, on the grounds that it would, if itself drafting the definition of the offence, have done so differently by providing for an element, or a greater element, of mens rea. The principle of Parliamentary sovereignty demands no less. Lord Reid [in *Sweet* v *Parsley*] was at pains to observe that the presumption applies where the statute is silent as to mens rea, and that the first duty of the court is to consider the words of the statute.

Where, however, the statute is silent, Lord Reid stated the position as follows (at p. 148):

> In such cases there has for centuries been a presumption that Parliament did not intend to make criminals of persons who were in no way blameworthy in what they did. That means that whenever a section is silent as to *mens rea* there is a presumption that, in order to give effect to the will of Parliament, we must read in words appropriate to require *mens rea* . . . . In the absence of a clear indication in the Act that an offence is intended to be an absolute offence, it is necessary to go outside the Act and examine all relevant circumstances in order to establish that this must have been the intention of Parliament. I say 'must have been' because it is a universal principle that if a penal provision is reasonably capable of two interpretations, that interpretation which is most favourable to the accused must be adopted.

Lord Pearce outlined the matters which the court would examine to determine whether Parliament's intention had been to impose strict liability (at p. 156):

> But the nature of the crime, the punishment, the absence of social obloquy, the particular mischief and the field of activity in which it occurs, and the wording of the particular section and its context, may show that Parliament intended that the act should be prevented by punishment regardless of intent or knowledge.

In the case before them the House of Lords [in *Sweet* v *Parsley*] concluded that the offence was not one of strict liability. Miss Sweet had been convicted of being concerned in the management of premises which were used for the purpose of smoking cannabis contrary to s. 5(b) of the Dangerous Drugs Act 1965. Miss Sweet had let rooms in a farmhouse to students. She had retained a bedroom for her own use on the occasions when she visited the property, but she resided elsewhere. The House of Lords held that knowledge that the premises were being used for the prohibited purpose was required. Section 8 of the Misuse of Drugs Act 1971, which replaced the 1965 Act, avoids ambiguity by expressly imposing the requirement of knowledge.

The Privy Council, in *Gammon (Hong Kong) Ltd* v *AG of Hong Kong* [1985] AC 1, reaffirmed the presumption of *mens rea*. Lord Scarman indicated in his speech the matters which a court should consider to determine whether that presumption had been rebutted by a particular statutory provision. He stated (at p. 14):

> In their Lordships' opinion, the law . . . may be stated in the following propositions . . . :
>
> (1) there is a presumption of law that *mens rea* is required before a person can be held guilty of a criminal offence;
>
> (2) the presumption is particularly strong where the offence is 'truly criminal' in character;
>
> (3) the presumption applies to statutory offences, and can be displaced only if it is clearly or by necessary implication the effect of the statute;
>
> (4) the only situation in which the presumption can be displaced is where the statute is concerned with an issue of social concern; public safety is such an issue;
>
> (5) even where a statute is concerned with such an issue, the presumption of *mens rea* stands unless it can also be shown that the creation of strict liability will be effective to promote the objects of the statute by encouraging greater vigilance to prevent the commission of the prohibited act.

In *B (A Minor)* v *DPP* [2000] 2 WLR 452 the House of Lords reaffirmed the common law presumption that *mens rea* would be required to be proved unless Parliament has indicated the contrary intention either expressly or by necessary implication. Lord Steyn saw this presumption in constitutional terms as an aspect of the principle of legality, quoting with approval Lord Hoffmann's dictum in *R* v *Secretary of State for the Home Department, ex parte Simms* [1999] 3 WLR 328 at p. 341:

> But the principle of legality means that Parliament must squarely confront what it is doing and accept the political cost. Fundamental rights cannot be overridden by general or ambiguous words. This is because there is too great a risk that the full implications of their unqualified meaning may have passed unnoticed in the democratic process. In the absence of express language or necessary implication to the contrary, the courts therefore presume that even the most general words were intended to be subject to the basic rights of the individual.

Raising the presumption of *mens rea* to the level of a constitutional principle has the impact that the presumption is greatly strengthened and thus will be less easy to rebut. This position was affirmed by the House of Lords in *R* v *K* [2001] UKHL 41, [2001] 3 WLR 471, in a case involving an alleged indecent assault by a man aged 26 on a 14-year-old girl contrary to s. 14 of the Sexual Offences Act 1956 (now replaced by s. 3 of the Sexual Offences Act 2003; see **11.4**). The appellant claimed he believed the girl to be over the age of 16 at the time of the consensual sexual intimacy between them. In quashing the appellant's conviction the House of Lords concluded that the language of s. 14 did not, as a matter of necessary implication, exclude the presumption of *mens rea*. Indeed, reading the presumption into the section avoided absurdity and anomaly. Lord Steyn confirmed (at para. 32) that **the applicability of** the presumption was not dependent on there being an ambiguity in the text of the statute. Rather the presumption applies unless there is express language to the contrary or it is ruled out by necessary implication—that is, 'an implication which is compellingly clear' (*B (A Minor)* v *DPP* [2000] 2 WLR 452, 464, *per* Lord Nicholls of Birkenhead; see also *M and B* [2009] EWCA 2615).

The result of their Lordships' decisions in *B* and *K* is that the presumption of *mens rea* has greater force than previously. In the realm of age-related sex offences, however, the impact of *B* and *K* is much more limited as the Sexual Offences Act 2003 has created a raft of age-related offences where liability is strict (see **11.6**). Likewise if on analysis the court concludes that the offence is a regulatory one the force of the presumption of *mens rea* does not appear to be that great, as a series of Court of Appeal decisions indicate (see *Doring* [2002] Crim LR 817; *Muhamad* [2003] EWCA Crim 1852; *Matudi* [2004] EWCA Crim 697).

In the four sections which follow, the factors which courts consider in deciding whether the presumption of *mens rea* has been rebutted will be examined. While a consideration of one factor may point to rebuttal of the presumption, consideration of the others may point to the presumption being upheld. The decision in respect of each particular offence may involve a balancing of competing factors.

4.2.3.2 The statutory context

? Question

If the section of an Act which creates an offence does not contain any of the usual *mens rea* words such as 'intentionally', 'knowingly', or 'recklessly', is that not the best indication that Parliament intended the offence to be one of strict liability?

If words which impose the requirement of *mens rea* are present in the section under consideration, there is no room for confusion as the intention of Parliament will have been clearly expressed. The absence of such words, however, is not conclusive that *mens rea* is not required as it is in this circumstance that the presumption of *mens rea* operates. Assistance may be sought from other sections in the statute. If *mens rea* words are used in other sections but not in the section under consideration, this may suggest that Parliament intended this section to create a strict liability offence. The perceived purpose of the provision may be of importance in arriving at a conclusion.

> In *Cundy* v *Le Cocq* (1884) 13 QBD 207, D, a publican, was convicted of selling intoxicating liquor to a person who was drunk contrary to s. 13 of the Licensing Act 1872. D did not know the person was drunk nor was there any evidence that D was negligent. D's conviction was upheld, however, by the Divisional Court which examined other sections of the Act and found that they contained the word 'knowingly' which s. 13 did not contain. Its view that the offence was one which did not require *mens rea* was confirmed by its examination of the purpose of the Act which it concluded was 'for the repression of drunkenness' and it was therefore right to place upon the publican the responsibility of determining whether his customer was sober and thus remove from him the temptation to sell liquor without regard to the sobriety of the customer.

The statutory context may extend to other statutes.

> In *B (A Minor)* v *DPP* [2000] 2 WLR 452, B, aged 15, sat next to a girl aged 13 on a bus and asked her several times to perform oral sex with him which she refused to do. He was charged with inciting a girl under the age of 14 to commit an act of gross indecency with him, contrary to s. 1(1) of the Indecency with Children Act 1960 (since replaced by ss 8 and 10 of the Sexual Offences Act 2003). B honestly believed the girl was over 14 but when the justices ruled that this was no defence to the charge he changed his plea to guilty. On a case stated by the justices, the Divisional Court of the Queen's Bench Division dismissed B's appeal. The Divisional Court certified, inter alia, that the following point of law of general public importance was involved in its decision: 'Is a defendant entitled to be acquitted of the offence of inciting a child aged under 14 to commit an act of gross indecency … if he may hold an honest belief that the child in question was aged 14 years or over?' The House of Lords said yes and considered other sexual offences under the Sexual Offences Act 1956 involving an age element. Lord Nicholls of Birkenhead stated (at p. 460):

> If the interpretation of section 1 of the Act of 1960 is to be gleaned from the contents of another statute, that other statute must give compelling guidance. The Act of 1956 as a whole falls short of this standard. So do the two sections, sections 14 and 15, which were the genesis of section 1 of the Act of 1960.

Other factors, such as the seriousness and breadth of the offence, also pointed against the presumption being rebutted.

4.2.3.3 The social context

Examining the statutory context of an offence may not be sufficient to resolve the question whether the presumption of *mens rea* has been rebutted; in such circumstances the social context of the offence is highly relevant. In *Gammon* (see **4.2.3.1**) Lord Scarman stated that the presumption of *mens rea* was particularly strong where an offence was 'truly criminal' but this presumption could be displaced where the offence related to an issue of social concern. This seems to be suggesting that some offences are more 'criminal' than others and that offences relating to issues of social concern are not truly criminal. This raises the problem of how one is to distinguish a 'real crime' from a 'quasi-crime'. The distinction seems to be between offences which involve infractions of the moral code and those offences of a regulatory nature which involve a breach of the law but to which no social stigma attaches—that is, those offences 'which are not criminal in any real sense but are acts which in the public interest are prohibited under a penalty' (*per* Wright J, in *Sherras* v *De Rutzen* [1895] 1 QB 918, 922). The problem with this dichotomy is that public morality changes from one generation to the next. For example, offences relating to pollution may have been regarded as purely regulatory and not truly criminal when enacted. Now, we are likely to regard those guilty of pollution as being criminals because of increased public awareness of environmental issues and the serious and long-term harm which may result from pollution. The distinction that should be made is perhaps between regulatory offences and other offences as some regulatory offences may involve moral stigma.

Question

How do the courts distinguish between 'real' and 'quasi-'crimes?

In deciding if an offence is 'quasi-criminal' the courts pay attention to two particular factors. First, they consider whether the offence is one of general application to all members of the public or applies to a specific class of persons who are engaged in a particular activity, trade, or profession such as selling food, drugs, liquor, or engaging in industrial activities. If the offence is of the latter type the courts will more readily hold it to be one of strict liability. In *Sweet* v *Parsley* [1970] AC 132, Lord Diplock stated (at p. 163):

> Where penal provisions are of general application to the conduct of ordinary citizens in the course of their everyday life, the presumption is that the standard of care required of them in informing themselves of facts which would make their conduct unlawful is that of the familiar common law duty of care. But where the subject-matter of a statute is the regulation of a particular activity involving potential danger to public health, safety or morals, in which citizens have a choice whether they participate or not, the court may feel driven to infer an intention of Parliament to impose, by penal sanctions, a higher duty of care on those who choose to participate and to place on them an obligation to take whatever measures may be necessary to prevent the prohibited act, without regard to those considerations of cost or business practicability which play a part in the determination of what would be required of them in order to fulfil the ordinary common law duty of care.

This may help to explain the House of Lords' decision in *Pharmaceutical Society of Great Britain* v *Storkwain Ltd* [1986] 1 WLR 903.

> In *Pharmaceutical Society of Great Britain* v *Storkwain Ltd* (1986) the defendants were retail chemists. The prosecution alleged that they unlawfully sold certain medications which were controlled substances, meaning sales would only be lawful if they were in accordance with a prescription issued by an appropriate practitioner. The prescriptions presented by customers for the particular medications were forgeries. At their trial for offences under ss 58(2) and 67(2) of the Medicines Act 1968, the stipendiary magistrate dismissed the informations holding that the presumption of *mens rea* applied and that the defendants had believed in good faith and on reasonable grounds that the prescriptions were valid.
>
> The Divisional Court allowed the prosecutor's appeal and the House of Lords dismissed the defendants' appeal. On its true construction s. 58(2)(a) of the Medicines Act 1968 created an offence of strict liability. Accordingly, the fact that the defendants supplied prescription-only drugs in accordance with a forged prescription and without fault on their part, afforded no defence to an information laid under that subsection since the prosecution did not have to prove *mens rea*. Lord Goff held that other offences in the 1968 Act explicitly required proof of *mens rea*, indicating that s. 58 did not. The prohibition was specific to pharmacists and D had chosen to engage in that profession. Lord Goff adopted as his own the words of Farquharson J in the Divisional Court:
>
> [I]t is perfectly obvious that pharmacists are in a position to put illicit drugs and perhaps other medicines on the market. Happily this rarely happens but it does from time to time. It can therefore be readily understood that Parliament would find it necessary to impose a heavier liability on those who are in such a position, and make them more strictly accountable for any breaches of the Act.

It could be argued, however, that Parliament must be presumed to be legislating within the context of what is practicable in the real world. Pharmacists could only avoid dispensing drugs on a forged prescription if they checked every prescription with the doctor who appeared to have written it; such a practice could hardly be considered practicable. The imposition of strict liability thus appears to be harsh and unnecessary. The purpose of the legislation, to encourage pharmacists to take care when dispensing drugs, could have been achieved by the imposition of a requirement that the prosecution must prove negligence.

The courts also consider the social danger which the offence is aimed at preventing. The greater the social danger the more likely it is that the presumption of *mens rea* will be found to be rebutted. Consequently many strict liability offences relate to the control of pollution, drugs, driving, the regulation of industrial activities, and hygiene and safety in respect of the production and sale of food.

Many motoring offences impose strict liability. Motoring is an activity in which citizens generally engage and thus motoring offences might be expected to require proof of *mens rea* or negligence. However, as the potential danger to the public is grave, courts have found the presumption of *mens rea* to have been rebutted. For example, it is an offence to cause or permit another person to use a motor vehicle without insurance (ss. 143(1) and (2) of the Road Traffic Act 1988). The courts have repeatedly held that the prosecution are not obliged to prove that D knew that the other person did not have valid insurance; the offence does not require *mens rea* in that respect (see *Tapsell* v *Maslen* [1967] Crim LR 53; *Baugh* v *Crago* [1975] RTR 453; *Ferrymaster Ltd* v *Adams* [1980] RTR 139; *Lloyd-Wolper* v *Moore* [2004] EWCA Civ 766).

In the field of pollution strict liability is imposed. In *Alphacell Ltd* v *Woodward* [1972] AC 824, the House of Lords held D company guilty of causing polluted matter to enter a river, contrary to s. 2(1)(a) of the Rivers (Prevention of Pollution) Act 1951 although there was no evidence that the company knew of the pollution or that they had been negligent. Lord Salmon stated (at p. 848):

> It is of the utmost public importance that rivers should not be polluted. The risk of pollution . . . is very great. The offences created by the Act of 1951 seem to me to be prototypes of offences which 'are not criminal in any real sense, but are acts which in the public interest are prohibited under a penalty.' . . . I can see no valid reason for reading the word 'intentionally', 'knowingly' or 'negligently' into section 2(1)(a) . . . . This may be regarded as a not unfair hazard of carrying on a business which may cause pollution on the banks of a river. If . . . it were held . . . that no conviction could be obtained . . . unless the prosecution could discharge the often impossible onus of proving that the pollution was caused intentionally or negligently, a great deal of pollution would go unpunished and undeterred . . . .

The House of Lords was influenced by the devastating effects pollution can have, the assumption of responsibility by voluntarily choosing to conduct a business which may cause pollution, and the need to deter others from causing pollution by encouraging greater vigilance. Similar considerations influenced the Privy Council in *Gammon Ltd* v *AG of Hong Kong* [1985] AC 1. The appellants, who were respectively the registered contractor, the project manager, and the site agent for building works, were charged with deviating in a material way from work shown on an approved plan contrary to the Hong Kong Building Ordinance. Part of a temporary support system on the building site had collapsed. The issue to be decided was whether the appellants had to know that their deviation was *material* or whether liability was strict in relation to this element of the offence. The Privy Council held that the offence was one of strict liability. They were influenced by the threat to public safety which would arise from material deviations from plans, the need to deter the incompetent from engaging in building work, and the need to encourage greater vigilance on the part of those who do engage in such work.

4.2.3.4 The severity of the punishment

 Question

Does a heavy maximum sentence guarantee that the offence will not be found to be one of strict liability?

The decisions of the courts in this area vary considerably. On the one hand the provision of a low maximum punishment by Parliament may indicate that the offence is one which is not truly criminal, thereby giving support to a finding of strict liability. The assumption is that a high maximum penalty indicates that the offence is truly criminal and that an accused should only be convicted where he is shown to be blameworthy. On the other hand, however, the provision of a severe punishment, such as prison, may lend support to the contention that the offence deals with a matter of grave social danger for which strict liability is appropriate.

In the *Storkwain* case the House of Lords were not persuaded by the argument that Parliament could not have intended to impose strict liability for an offence which carried a maximum sentence of two years' imprisonment as the other factors which they considered pointed to strict liability. In *Gammon* the Privy Council considered that the maximum penalty of a fine of $250,000 and imprisonment for three years indicated the 'seriousness with which the legislature viewed the offences'. While this was a 'formidable' argument against strict liability, viewed in light of the ordinance as a whole their Lordships concluded (at p. 17) that:

> [T]here is nothing inconsistent with the purpose of the ordinance in imposing severe penalties for offences of strict liability. The legislature could reasonably have intended severity to be a significant deterrent, bearing in mind the risks to public safety arising from some contraventions of the ordinance.

Similarly, in *Howells* [1977] QB 614, on a charge of possession of a firearm without a firearm certificate contrary to s. 1(1)(a) of the Firearms Act 1968, the Court of Appeal concluded that the fact that the maximum penalty was five years' imprisonment did not preclude the imposition of strict liability. The Court found that other factors such as the wording of the Act and the danger to the community resulting from possession of lethal firearms outweighed this factor.

By contrast, in *B (A Minor)* v *DPP* (see **4.2.3.2**) the House of Lords took the view that the more serious the offence the less likely it was that the presumption of *mens rea* would be rebutted. Lord Nicholls of Birkenhead stated:

The more serious the offence, the greater is the weight to be attached to the presumption, because the more severe is the punishment and the graver the stigma which accompany a conviction.

In the instant case the maximum penalty was 10 years' imprisonment and, in addition, the notification requirements under Part I of the Sex Offenders Act 1997 applied indicating an offence of truly criminal character to which considerable stigma is attached (the notification requirements, now under Part 2 of the Sexual Offences Act 2003, oblige an offender to notify the police of personal details, such as changes of address, for a specified period). A further concern was the breadth of the offence as, according to Lord Nicholls, an act of gross indecency 'can embrace conduct ranging from predatory approaches by a much older paedophile to consensual sexual experimentation between precocious teenagers of whom the offender may be the younger of the two'. Lord Steyn pointed out that as the offence covers incitement to an act of gross indecency, verbal sexual overtures between teenagers where one was under the age of 14 would also be covered (as in the instant case). (For a discussion of age-related offences under the Sexual Offences Act 2003 see **11.6**.)

4.2.3.5 Promoting the enforcement of the law

The fact that a statute deals with an issue of social concern is not sufficient to displace the presumption of *mens rea* unless strict liability will be effective in encouraging vigilance and observance of the law. In *Reynolds* v *G. H. Austin & Sons Ltd* [1951] 2 KB 135, the defendant company was charged with a contravention of the Road Traffic Acts. The company was a private hire coach company who had contracted to take members of a women's guild on an outing. The organiser of the outing advertised to the general public that there were spare tickets available. The company did not have a public service licence and performed the contract unaware that the trip had been advertised to the public. The Divisional Court held that the offence was not one of strict liability. Devlin J stated (at pp. 149, 150):

> [I]f a man is punished because of an act done by another, whom he cannot reasonably be expected to influence or control, the law is engaged, not in punishing thoughtlessness or inefficiency, and thereby promoting the welfare of the community, but in pouncing on the most convenient victim . . . [W]here the punishment of an individual will not promote the observance of the law either by that individual or by others whose conduct he may reasonably be expected to influence then, in the absence of clear and express words, such punishment is not intended.

In *Lim Chin Aik* v *The Queen* [1963] AC 160, the Privy Council quashed the appellant's conviction, under s. 6(2) of the Immigration Ordinance 1952 of the State of Singapore, for remaining in Singapore (after having entered) when he had been prohibited from entering by an order made by the Minister under s. 9. The Privy Council stated that it was not enough to label the statute as one dealing with a grave social evil and infer that strict liability is intended. It was important also to enquire whether strict liability would assist in the enforcement of the regulations. In the instant case the imposition of strict liability would simply serve to convict a 'luckless victim' as the prohibition had not been published or made known to the appellant. Thus strict liability will not be imposed where D either has no means of knowing the law or of taking action to ensure observance of the law (cf. *R (Grundy & Co. Excavators Ltd and Parry)* v *Halton Division Magistrates' Court* [2003] EWHC 272 (Admin)).

4.2.4 Justifications for strict liability

The two justifications generally given for the creation of strict liability offences are that **they encourage greater safety and improved standards of prevention, thereby offering the public better protection from the risks inherent in particular activities**, and that **they relieve the prosecution of the difficult task of proving *mens rea*, thereby increasing both administrative efficiency and the deterrent effect of conviction.**

 Question

Is strict liability necessary for the protection of the public and the enforcement of particular laws?

A facile answer would be, 'Yes, it must be because Parliament has enacted so many offences which impose strict liability.' The fact that Parliament has created so many strict liability offences, however, does not establish the necessity of their existence. Strict liability offences are only necessary if there is no other means of achieving the ends of protecting the public and enforcing the law.

Baroness Wootton argued ardently in favour of the extension of strict liability to cover all crimes in *Crime and the Criminal Law* (2nd edn, 1981). She stated (at p. 46):

> If ... the primary function of the courts is conceived as the prevention of forbidden acts, there is little cause to be disturbed by the multiplication of offences of strict liability. If the law says that certain things are not to be done, it is illogical to confine this prohibition to occasions on which they are done from malice aforethought; for at least the material consequences of an action, and the reasons for prohibiting it are the same whether it is the result of sinister malicious plotting, of negligence or of sheer accident.

This begs the very important question of **what is a forbidden act?** In murder the forbidden act is causing the death of another person. A surgeon who performs an operation on a patient could be found to have committed the forbidden act if his patient dies under anaesthetic even though the chances of success of the operation were low but the risk was taken as, without the operation, the patient would have died in a few weeks or months. To find such a surgeon guilty of murder would be ludicrous and would involve divorcing the law from the social and moral context in which it operates, not to mention deterring all other surgeons from performing operations involving any risk of death. Such an approach, far from protecting the public, would end up leaving them more at risk. What the law seeks to prevent is forbidden acts in the circumstances where the perpetrator of the act is morally culpable. Baroness Wootton would seek to distinguish the culpable from the blameless by leaving it to the judge to mete out an appropriate sentence. Such an approach, however, does not overcome the stigma attached to criminal conviction. Nor does it make for efficiency as the courts would be cluttered with prosecutions of blameless individuals who would ultimately be dealt with by means of an absolute discharge. It is not possible to protect people from all harm; the law's role, however, is to seek to protect them from the intentional or reckless infliction of harm and, in some circumstances, from the negligent infliction of harm. If harm could not have been prevented by the exercise of reasonable care, the prosecution of the blamelessly inadvertent will not prevent the occurrence of such harm in the future.

In the area of regulatory offences the social context is important. We need people to engage in industrial processes, to make and sell food, to dispense drugs, to drive motor vehicles. There may be risks involved in all these activities meriting the exercise of care on the part of those engaging in them. The law should encourage such care but not be so harsh as to discourage people from embarking upon these enterprises in the first place. Thus the blamelessly inadvertent pharmacist should not be punished for dispensing drugs on a forged prescription if he was exercising the degree of care to be expected of pharmacists consistent with considerations of economics and practicability. Similarly, the butcher selling meat should take reasonable precautions to avoid selling meat which is unfit. Punishing him where, despite such precautions, he has sold unfit meat serves no purpose unless it is to discourage the sale of meat altogether (see *Callow* v *Tillstone*, **4.2.1**). Alternatively, if the butcher is forced to employ an analyst to test every carcass this would raise his costs to the extent that meat would become too expensive for many people to afford, which in turn would have detrimental effects on the ordinary consumer, the farmer, and all those involved in processing and selling meat. It is also highly questionable whether strict liability leads to a higher standard of care. In *R* v *City of Saulte Ste Marie* (1978) 85 DLR (3d) 161, before the Supreme Court of Canada, Dickson J stated (at p. 171):

> There is no evidence that a higher standard of care results from absolute liability. If a person is already taking every reasonable precautionary measure, is he likely to take additional measures, knowing that however much care he takes, it will not serve as a defence in the event of breach? If he has exercised care and skill, will conviction have a deterrent effect upon him or others?

By contrast, in *Alphacell*, Lord Salmon took the view that strict liability would encourage those who might be potential polluters 'not only to take reasonable steps to prevent pollution but to do everything possible to ensure that they do not cause it'. This may reflect a degree of commercial naivety on the part of Lord Salmon. If expenditure of thousands of pounds for preventive measures will not ultimately prevent the risk of pollution, the factory owner may prefer to save his money, keep his unit costs down, retain his competitiveness, increase his profits, and run the risk of being caught and fined several hundred pounds should his operations cause pollution at a time when an inspector is around.

 Question

Does strict liability deter, prevent crime, and ensure efficient law enforcement?

Clearly the prosecution's task is facilitated as, in strict liability offences, it is only necessary to prove that the *actus reus* was committed and there is no need to prove the more difficult issue of *mens rea*. Indeed, if the prosecution seeks to lead evidence that the defendant had *mens rea* or was negligent, this evidence must be excluded as it is irrelevant to the issues which they must prove to establish guilt of the offence charged (see *Sandhu* [1997] Crim LR 288). In the many regulatory offences that exist this makes enforcement easier; a pollution inspector need only prove that D's factory is discharging effluent into the river, or a health inspector need only prove that meat sold was unfit. No enquiry need be made to discover if D knew that he was causing pollution or selling unfit meat.

This, however, ignores a problem. How is a sentencer to sentence someone convicted of a strict liability offence if he does not know whether he committed the offence intentionally, recklessly, negligently, or inadvertently despite the most stringent precautions? The person who intentionally causes pollution deserves a very much heavier sentence than the one who has exercised reasonable care. Indeed, the sentencing guidelines for offences under the Environmental Protection Act 1990 state that the judge or magistrates' task at sentencing is to determine what category of seriousness the offence falls into, taking into account the offender's culpability as well as the harm caused (Sentencing Council, *Environmental Offences: Definitive Guideline* (2014) p. 15). There are four categories of culpability in the sentencing guidelines: deliberate, reckless, negligent, and low or no culpability. The category of culpability determines, in combination with the harm that D caused or risked, the likely sentence; the guideline indicates a range from custody for deliberate pollution to a fine for acts that were genuinely accidental. As the prosecution at trial only have to establish that pollution was caused by D, the facts which would disclose the level of D's culpability would not be proved in the trial. This may necessitate a further post-conviction hearing to determine the factual basis of the offence (see *Newton* (1982) 4 Cr App R (S) 388).

This may cancel out any efficiency benefits deriving from dispensing with the proof of *mens rea* for the purposes of conviction. It may also be difficult to establish the factual basis of the offence as the investigating official may not have inquired into, or obtained evidence relating to, the culpability of D as this was not necessary for the purposes of obtaining a conviction. If he does make such inquiries and acquire evidence he is performing the same task as an officer investigating a crime requiring proof of *mens rea* and this will defeat any claim of administrative efficiency. In addition, if there is any doubt as to the factual basis of the offence, this must be resolved in favour of D as the normal burden of proof applies (see *Newton* and *Gortat and Pirog* [1973] Crim LR 648). If efficiency is to be obtained and no evidence of culpability sought, all offenders will appear the same and thus will be treated as if they had been blamelessly inadvertent; i.e. culpability is reduced to the level of the lowest common denominator. If this occurs, sentences will not serve to deter the culpable. In addition, if a result arises from blameless inadvertence and could not, by the exercise of reasonable care, have been avoided, the imposition of a penalty will not prevent future infractions unless the offender desists entirely from the activity involved. If penalties which truly reflect the offender's culpability can only be determined by thorough investigation and proof to the same standard required for conviction, there would seem to be little reason for having strict liability offences.

If regulatory offences are seeking to encourage the exercise of reasonable care, strict liability would not appear to be necessary. If a person has exercised reasonable care and the forbidden harm still occurs, punishing him will not make the incidence of that harm any less likely in the future. The punishment appears unjust and serves no purpose. If punishment is not inflicted, as where an absolute discharge is given because D is blameless, the whole process of prosecution and trial appears pointless and militates against efficiency in respect of other cases relating to blameworthy offenders. The conclusion thus seems to be that strict liability achieves nothing which could not be achieved by means of a requirement of negligence. It may be that considerations of administrative efficiency might dictate that on proof of the *actus reus* a presumption of negligence is raised, subject to rebuttal by proof on the balance of probabilities by D that he was not negligent. This is not unacceptable as if D has been exercising reasonable care in respect of a particular activity in which he is engaged he should be able to prove this by evidence of the production system, supervision, checks, safety precautions, etc. involved.

4.2.5 Defences to strict liability

In some jurisdictions the courts have developed a defence to offences of strict liability. The High Court of Australia in *Proudman* v *Dayman* (1943) 67 CLR 536, and the Supreme Court of Canada in *R* v *City of Saulte Ste Marie* developed a general due diligence (or 'no-negligence') defence to strict liability offences which places the burden of proof on D. In the latter case Dickson J stated (at p. 181):

> The correct approach . . . is to relieve the Crown of the burden of proving *mens rea*, having regard to . . . the virtual impossibility in most regulatory cases of proving wrongful intention. In a normal case, the accused alone will have knowledge of what he has done to avoid the breach and it is not improper to expect him to come forward with the evidence of due diligence . . . . This involves consideration of what a reasonable man would have done in the circumstances. The defence will be available if the accused reasonably believed in a mistaken set of facts which, if true, would render the act or omission innocent, or if he took all reasonable steps to avoid the particular event.

The courts in England and Wales have not yet been prepared to import a common law 'due diligence' defence for strict liability offences. Parliament, however, has sought to mitigate the worst effects of strict liability by including defences in some statutes. Due diligence defences have been provided in, for example, s. 67 of the Offices, Shops and Railway Premises Act 1963; s. 24(1) of the Trade Descriptions Act 1968; s. 34 of the Weights and Measures Act 1985; and s. 28 of the Misuse of Drugs Act 1971. In some statutes the due diligence defence has been combined with a 'third-party' defence requiring D to prove both that he exercised due diligence and that the offence was due to the act or default of a third party (see e.g. s. 21(2) of the Food Safety Act 1990). If successful such a defence leaves the third party liable to conviction on the basis of strict liability. If, for example, a shopkeeper was charged with an offence under s. 8 of the Food Safety Act 1990 based on his sale of a bottle of ginger ale to a customer which, when opened, was found to contain the decomposed remains of a snail, the shopkeeper might avoid conviction if he proved that he had exercised all due diligence and that the contravention was due to the act or default of the manufacturer. If the bottle was made of dark glass there would be nothing that the shopkeeper could do to check the contents other than open it and pour them out; this would not be reasonable. But if the bottle was made of clear glass, and the snail was visible, the shopkeeper would fail in his defence as, although not responsible for the contamination, he could have discovered it by a cursory inspection. If the third party responsible for the contravention is not identifiable, the third-party defence is not available.

4.2.6 Strict liability and the ECHR

Article 6(2) of the European Convention on Human Rights provides that 'everyone charged with a criminal offence shall be presumed innocent until proved guilty according to law'. It has been argued that strict liability offences contravene this presumption as on proof of the act or conduct guilt is presumed. In *Salabiaku* v *France* (1998) EHRR 379, the European Court of Human Rights held that there was no contravention as:

> [i]n principle the contracting States may, under certain conditions, penalise a simple or objective fact as such irrespective of whether it results from criminal intent or from negligence.

In essence the Art. 6(2) right is concerned with ensuring a fair trial in procedural terms and is not concerned with the fairness of the substantive law. This was affirmed by the Divisional Court in *Barnfather* v *Islington London Borough Council* [2003] EWHC 418 (Admin). However, in *Salabiaku* the European Court stated, somewhat obscurely, that 'presumptions of fact or law' in criminal proceedings should be confined within 'reasonable limits'. Reliance was sought to be placed on this proposition in *G* [2008] UKHL 37 where the appellant had been convicted of rape contrary to s. 5 of the Sexual Offences Act 2003 which is a strict liability offence where the complainant is under 13. The appellant (who was aged 15) pleaded guilty on the basis that he believed she was 15 and the intercourse was consensual (albeit that a child under 13 cannot consent to penetrative sex). The House of Lords unanimously held that strict liability did not violate Art. 6(1) or (2). The Art. 6(1) guarantee of a fair trial and the Art. 6(2) presumption of innocence had no bearing on the substantive law enacted by signatory States. Lord Hope of Craighead sought to explain *Salabiaku* on the basis that the contracting States are free to apply the criminal law to any act, so long as it is not one which is carried out in the exercise of one of the rights protected under the Convention. Thus, even if legislation creating a criminal offence might breach other Convention rights, it will not render the trial under which it is enforced unfair.

On the second question before the House—whether it is 'compatible with a child's rights under article 8 . . . to convict him of rape . . . in circumstances where . . . his offence fell properly within the ambit of s.13'—Lord Hope and Lord Carswell dissented. They were of opinion that a conviction for rape was disproportionate and incompatible with Art. 8 as the act fell within the less serious offence of sexual activity with a child under ss 9 and 13 of the Sexual Offences Act 2003 which was more than adequate to protect the rights of the girl. The majority disagreed taking the view that Art. 8 was not engaged and upheld the conviction. They further stated that even if Art. 8 was engaged, the prosecution was 'both rational and proportionate in pursuit of the legitimate aims of the protection of health and morals and of the rights and freedoms of others' (Baroness Hale at para. 55).

In *G* v *UK* [2011] ECHR 1308, the European Court of Human Rights, considering G's conviction for rape of a child under 13, did not consider that the absence of a defence based on reasonable belief that the complainant was aged 13 or over gave rise to any issue under Art. 6 as it was not the court's role to dictate the content of domestic criminal law. By a majority the Court also held that while the applicant's Art. 8(1) right to respect for private life was engaged, the margin of appreciation allowed to Member States, while narrow where matters of intimacy were involved, nonetheless did provide for conviction for this offence as there was under Art. 8(2) a powerful countervailing public interest in the legitimate aim of protecting young and vulnerable children from premature sexual activity, exploitation, and abuse. The Court did not, however, consider whether prosecuting for this offence rather than the lesser alternative offence under ss 9 and 13 of the Sexual Offences Act 2003 was 'necessary in a democratic society'. G was, after all, himself under 16 and the maximum sentence under s. 5 is life imprisonment (as compared to five years for the alternative); furthermore there was no evidence to suggest that the complainant was specifically exploited and abused.

 The law in context

A strict liability case study: section 53A of the Sexual Offences Act 2003

Section 53A of the Sexual Offences Act 2003 (introduced by s. 14 of the Policing and Crime Act 2009) provides a controversial example of the use of strict liability. Under s. 53A(1) it is an offence for a person (A) to pay for 'sexual services' of a 'prostitute' (B) if a third person (C) has engaged in 'exploitative conduct of a kind likely to induce or encourage B to provide the sexual services' for which A has paid or promised payment. The offence is punishable with a level 3 fine (up to £1,000).

The offence was intended to curb demand for prostitution by deterring and punishing men from using women trafficked into the United Kingdom or otherwise exploited. Putting aside the arguments about criminalising acts associated with prostitution (see **Chapter 1**), the offence's most interesting aspect is s. 53A(2)(b), which states that it is 'irrelevant whether A is, or ought to be, aware that C has engaged in exploitative conduct'. The offence is thus one of strict liability: the prosecution need not prove that A knew or suspected that B was forced, threatened, coerced, or deceived into providing sexual services. All the prosecution need prove is that A actually made or offered payment to B and that C in fact engaged in the specified exploitative conduct. If both facts can be proved, A is guilty.

Why make this offence one of strict liability?

From the Government's perspective, making this offence one of strict liability addresses the sexual exploitation of trafficked women through demand reduction, deterring those who create the demand (Home Office (2004), *Paying the Price: A Consultation Paper on Prostitution*, para. 1.7). The 2009 Act's Explanatory Notes make clear that the section's aim is to reduce demand for prostitution and shift the focus of enforcement from those working as prostitutes

→

→

to those paying for sex. The message to men is clear: do not pay for sexual services, because if you do you are risking punishment and a criminal record. Lord Brett, the Government's Minister in the House of Lords during the bill's passage, said:

> This is simply another weapon in the armoury and not an attempt to reduce our endeavours to ensure that the horrible trafficking of women for sex is brought to a halt as soon as possible. This is very much part of a general response to the problem of trafficking. Taking steps to tackle the demand for trafficking for sexual exploitation was one of the actions recommended in the UK Action Plan on Tackling Human Trafficking. It was also a requirement imposed by Article 6 of the Council of Europe Convention on Action against Trafficking in Human Beings, which the UK has now ratified … [T]his offence is one part of a comprehensive approach to trafficking … To tackle demand, it [is] necessary to criminalise those who contribute to the demand for trafficking and other forms of sexual exploitation by paying for sex with those who are subject to exploitation and to deter those who pay for sex in such circumstances. (Hansard, HL Vol. 712, col. 250 (1 July 2009))

During the bill's parliamentary passage, several amendments were proposed that would have included a *mens rea* requirement, that A must know or be reckless as to whether B is subject to exploitation (see Kingston and Thomas, 'The Police, Sex Work, and Section 14 of the Policing and Crime Act 2009' (2014) *Howard Journal of Criminal Justice* 255–69). The Government's response was that strict liability is the:

> most effective way of ensuring that those who pay for sex consider the circumstances of the prostitute . . . . It places the risk on the sex buyer of paying for sex with someone who is being controlled for gain . . . . The aim . . . is to shift the emphasis and to . . . take greater action against those who contribute to the demand for prostitution . . . . By removing strict liability, the amendments would significantly weaken the offence. (5 February 2009, HC Hansard, col. 257)

Several MPs noted that requiring the prosecution to prove 'knowledge' or 'recklessness' in the law would make the law more complicated and difficult to enforce. The prosecution would find it very difficult to prove that A was aware of the possibility that B was subject to exploitation, given that the offence will have been committed in private and a defendant could easily argue, 'I didn't know she was being exploited.' The exploited women would be expected to give testimony in court, a significant burden for women who are already vulnerable. Strict liability means court time (and money) can be saved, encouraging men to plead guilty rather than contest a charge, when they realise the prosecution need not prove that D knew, or was aware of the possibility, that B was being exploited.

Does strict liability make the offence unfair and over-inclusive?

However, concerns have been expressed about the use of strict liability for this type of offence. The campaign group Liberty criticised the offence for being 'drafted extremely broadly' and based on a 'rushed and ill-thought out policy' (2009, *Briefing on the Second Reading on the Coroners and Justice Bill*, pp. 7–8:https://www.liberty-human-rights.org.uk/sites/default/files/coroners-and-justice-second-reading-briefing.pdf). There is little scope for challenging the offence under Art. 6(2) of the European Convention (given the clarity of the legislation and appellate decisions holding that strict liability for other offences under the Sexual Offences Act 2003 does not contravene the European Convention (see **4.2.6**)). However, the offence is

→

→

arguably a disproportionate response to the social problem it purports to tackle. A criticism of the offence, which applies to the general use of strict liability, is that it widens the net of criminal liability, including people who are not blameworthy and/or deserving of the criminal sanction. The criminal law's communicative function, by which society condemns seriously blameworthy conduct, is impaired when liability is imposed in the absence of fault (J. Horder, *Ashworth's Principles of Criminal Law* (2016), p. 181). The Bar Council argued the offence is wrong in principle because a man 'may be guilty in circumstances where he could have no idea at the time that he was committing the offence' (quoted in Kingston and Thomas (2014), p. 259). There is no defence of mistake or due diligence: it will not avail a man to show he took all reasonable precautions to ensure the woman whose sexual services he bought was not being exploited.

Does making this offence one of strict liability mean it is effective?

Others challenged the likely efficacy of the offence. For example, Evan Harris MP argued that the maximum punishment for the offence would not be tough enough actually to deter men. A principal argument for strict liability is that the law's clarity should deter and ensure compliance (assuming men know about the law). However, from a utilitarian perspective, the limited sanction available might not deter if the benefits to the 'punter' of running the risk of detection outweigh the likely sanction. Research suggests that there have been hardly any prosecutions for the new offence. Kingston and Thomas found that most police forces (81 per cent) have not used it, suggesting that the section does not address the problem of exploitation it purports to. There is little evidence that it has deterred men or reduced the prevalence of prostitution arising from trafficked women. Also, clients who have done their 'due diligence' and purchase services from women they genuinely and reasonably believe are not being exploited by a third party may be deterred from reporting exploitation of women because they fear arrest. Using strict liability can be part of a strategy for tackling a social problem but its fairness and efficacy remain controversial.

 Key Points

- Some offences impose liability for negligence, meaning they set an objective standard to which D's actions must conform. The standard is that of a reasonable or prudent person.

- If *mens rea* or negligence need not be proved in respect of one or more elements of the *actus reus* of an offence, that offence is one of strict liability.

- The absence of express words imposing a requirement of proving *mens rea* is not conclusive that the offence is one of strict liability. There is a presumption that when a statute is silent as to *mens rea*, the offence requires proof of *mens rea* before D can be guilty.

- That presumption can be rebutted where:
  - the statute clearly or by necessary implication indicates that proof of *mens rea* is not required;
  - the offence is not 'truly criminal' in character;
  - the offence does not carry a severe punishment. The more serious the offence is, the more likely the courts are to hold that the presumption applies; or
  - the statute is concerned with an issue of broad social concern.

- In English law there is no general 'due diligence' defence to offences of strict liability.

FURTHER READING

Georgetown Law School, 'Symposium on Crime Without Fault' (2018) 12(3) *Criminal Law and Philosophy* 363–538.

B. Jackson, '*Storkwain*: A Case Study in Strict Liability and Self-regulation' [1991] Crim LR 892.

L. H. Leigh, *Strict and Vicarious Liability* (London: Sweet & Maxwell, 1982).

C. Manchester, 'Knowledge, Due Diligence and Strict Liability in Regulatory Offences' [2006] Crim LR 213.

I. Paulus, 'Strict Liability: Its Place in Public Welfare Offences' (1978) 20 Crim LQ 445.

G. Richardson, 'Strict Liability for Regulatory Crime: The Empirical Research' [1987] Crim LR 295.

J. C. Smith, 'Responsibility in Criminal Law' in P. Bean and D. Whynes (eds), *Barbara Wootton, Essays in Her Honour* (London: Tavistock, 1986), 141.

M. Smith and A. Pearson, 'The Value of Strict Liability' [1969] Crim LR 5.

5

....

Capacity and incapacitating conditions

5.1 **Introduction**

A person should only be held criminally liable where he has the capacity to understand his actions, in the sense of being able to understand the nature of those actions and the circumstances in which they occur, and to recognise the consequences which may flow from them. Also, a person should only be held criminally liable where, understanding his actions, he has the capacity to control them. Moral culpability should not attach to the person who at the time he acted (or omitted to act) was unable to understand what he was doing and/or unable to control what he was doing, as such a person is not a responsible actor and therefore is not deserving of blame or punishment. The criminal law has recognised this requirement of rational capacity by excepting persons who lack rational capacity from liability in certain circumstances. According to N. L. A. Barlow, 'Drug Intoxication and the Principle of *Capacitas Rationalis*' (1984) 100 LQR 639 (at p. 647), the principle or presumption of rational capacity operates as '**a precondition to punishment; as a standard, a criterion, for determining eligibility for and immunity from punishment**'. In this chapter the issues of infancy, insanity, automatism, and intoxication will be examined. These conditions are often said to give rise to defences. They will be examined in this chapter, however, rather than **Chapter 6**, as they specifically relate to the issue of whether D had rational capacity at the time of his act. In the case of defences such as duress or self-defence, there is no question of D's rational capacity being in doubt; implicit in these defences is the idea that D did exercise rational judgement and chose to act as he did but his claim is that his acts were either justified or excusable because of the circumstances in which he found himself.

5.2 **Age and criminal responsibility**

For the purposes of criminal procedure, sentencing, and criminal liability there are various terms applied to different age groups. A *child* is a person aged 10 years or more but under 14 years of age. A *young person* is aged 14 years or more but under

17 years of age. A *young offender* is aged 14 years or more but under 21 years. The procedures before the courts and the sentences available on conviction will vary according to the age of the offender. But before issues of sentencing arise the issue of criminal liability has to be considered. **It is an irrebuttable presumption of the criminal law that a child under 10 years of age at the time an alleged offence was committed cannot be found guilty of that offence** (see s. 50 of the Children and Young Persons Act 1933, as amended). A child under 10 is said to be *doli incapax*—that is, incapable of crime. This presumption derives from a recognition of the immaturity of children who will not have a fully developed understanding of what is right and wrong nor the ability to appreciate the consequences of their acts fully. If a child is charged with an offence and it is established that he was under 10 years of age at the time the alleged offence was committed, the case against him will be dismissed without any inquiry whether he understood what he was doing. The local authority, however, may commence proceedings under s. 31 of the Children Act 1989 for an order placing the child in the care of a local authority or putting him under the supervision of a local authority. In such proceedings the child's welfare is the paramount consideration of the court (s. 1(1) of the Children Act 1989) and, under s. 31(2), an order may only be made if the court is satisfied:

(a) that the child concerned is suffering, or is likely to suffer, significant harm; and

(b) that harm, or the likelihood of harm, is attributable to—

   (i) the care given to the child, or likely to be given to him if the order were not made, not being what it would be reasonable to expect a parent to give to him; or

   (ii) the child's being beyond parental control.

The Crime and Disorder Act 1998 provides further powers to deal with children under 10 who have committed acts which, in the case of those over 10, could have constituted criminal offences, or who have behaved in a manner that caused or was likely to cause harassment, alarm, or distress to one or more persons not of the same household as himself. Under s. 11 a local authority may apply to a family court for a 'child safety order' to be made placing the child under the supervision of a social worker or a member of the youth offending team, for a period of up to 12 months.

A consequence of the *doli incapax* principle is that not only is the child not guilty of the crime, but the child has not committed a crime. But, if the offence was instigated by another person, that person, rather than being a secondary party, becomes the principal acting through an innocent agent; he commits the crime (for example, a parent telling his six-year old son to steal some items from a supermarket). Where the offence is one such as rape, which cannot be committed through an innocent agent, the secondary party may be convicted where he or she has procured the *actus reus* with the requisite *mens rea* (see further *DPP v K and B* [1997] 1 Cr App R 36, **7.1.3.3**). The absence of a crime may also negate the criminal liability of others. For example, in *Walters v Lunt* [1951] 2 All ER 645, a mother and father were acquitted of the charge of receiving from their son a child's tricycle knowing it to be stolen. As the son was seven years of age he could not steal and thus the tricycle was not stolen. Had the parents instigated the taking of the tricycle by their son they would have stolen it through an innocent agent.

Where a child was 10 years of age or over and under the age of 14 at the time of the alleged offence, there used to be a rebuttable presumption at common law that the child was *doli incapax*. The presumption could be rebutted by proof that the child knew the act he was doing was seriously wrong; this was something additional to the *mens rea* for the offence.

In *C (A Minor) v DPP* [1995] 3 WLR 888 the Divisional Court expressed the view that the presumption did a serious disservice to the law and ruled that it was no longer part of the law of England. C appealed to the House of Lords. The point of law certified for their Lordships' consideration was:

> Whether there continues to be a presumption that a child between the ages of 10 and 14 is *doli incapax* and if so, whether that presumption can only be rebutted by clear positive evidence that he knew that his act was seriously wrong, such evidence not consisting merely in the evidence of the acts amounting to the offence itself.

Their Lordships allowed the appeal answering both questions in the affirmative, considering that any change in the law was a matter within the exclusive remit of Parliament. In a Home Office consultation paper, *Tackling Youth Crime*, September 1997, the Labour Government argued that the presumption was archaic, illogical, and unfair and stood in the way of intervening at an early stage to seek to rehabilitate young offenders and prevent future offending. This begs the question as to whether criminal prosecution, conviction, and sentencing of young offenders can be rehabilitative. The consultation paper was followed by a White Paper ominously titled, *No More Excuses—A New Approach to Tackling Youth Crime in England and Wales* (Cm 3809) where the Government indicated its intention to abolish the presumption rejecting an alternative solution which was to reverse the presumption. The rebuttable presumption of *doli incapax* in respect of children aged over 10 was duly abolished by s. 34 of the Crime and Disorder Act 1998. To all intents and purposes all children over the age of 10 are assumed to have reached the same level of moral culpability as adults.

There was some doubt whether s. 34 merely abolished the presumption of *doli incapax* but left the possibility of a child defendant raising a defence to the effect that he did not know that what he was doing was seriously wrong. In *T* [2008] EWCA Crim 815 the Court of Appeal decided that no defence of *doli incapax* survived the enactment of s. 34. The Court took the view that by the time s. 34 was enacted, whatever the position may have been historically, the presumption was coterminous with the concept (defence) of *doli incapax* such that when Parliament abolished the presumption it also abolished the defence. When this decision was appealed further to the House of Lords in *JTB* [2009] UKHL 20, it was confirmed. The upshot of this is that where a child between the ages of 10 and 14 is prosecuted no issue as to his comprehension of the wrongness of his act may arise. However, this does not prevent such a child seeking to rely on his age as a factor relevant to *mens rea* (e.g. whether he foresaw the consequences of his acts even though those consequences might have been obvious to an adult) or to defences (e.g. the reasonableness of his acts under the defence of duress).

Boys under the age of 14 used to be irrebuttably presumed to be incapable of sexual intercourse and thus could not be convicted as perpetrators of rape (*Groombridge*

(1836) 7 C & P 582), offences involving sexual intercourse (*Waite* [1892] 2 QB 600), or buggery whether as agent or as patient (*Tatam* (1921) 15 Cr App R 132). This presumption was abolished by s. 1 of the Sexual Offences Act 1993.

5.3 Insanity

5.3.1 Introduction

The defence of insanity is concerned with D's mental state at the time when the alleged offence was committed. D's mental state may be relevant at two other times. **First, in a criminal trial it is relevant at the time he is arraigned and called to plead to the charge against him.** Under ss 4 and 4A of the Criminal Procedure (Insanity) Act 1964 (as substituted by s. 2 of the Criminal Procedure (Insanity and Unfitness to Plead) Act 1991 and amended by s. 22 of the Domestic Violence, Crime and Victims Act 2004) an accused may be found 'unfit to plead' where it is established that because of his mental condition he is unable to understand the charge and the difference between a plea of guilty and a plea of not guilty, to challenge jurors, to instruct counsel, and to follow the proceedings (*Robertson* [1968] 3 All ER 557).

The issue of D's fitness to plead is determined by the judge as soon as it arises (s. 4(3) of the Criminal Procedure (Insanity) Act 1964). If the judge considers it expedient to do so, having regard to the supposed disability and where it is in D's interests, he may postpone consideration of the issue up to the time of the opening of the case for the defence (s. 4(2)). This is appropriate where the prosecution case appears weak as they may not be able to establish a prima facie case to answer; the judge will then direct the jury to acquit.

An accused may not be found unfit to plead except on the written or oral evidence of two or more registered medical practitioners, at least one of whom is approved for the purposes of s. 12 of the Mental Health Act 1983 by the Secretary of State as having special experience in the diagnosis or treatment of mental disorder. If D is found unfit to plead the trial must not proceed. A jury will then determine on the basis of evidence (if any) already adduced or on evidence adduced by the prosecution and/or a person appointed by the court under s. 4A of the 1964 Act to put the case for the defence (i.e. defence counsel), whether D did the act or made the omission constituting the *actus reus* of the offence charged against him (s. 4(2)). If the issue of unfitness to plead arose on the arraignment and the judge ruled that D was unfit to plead, a jury will be empanelled to determine whether D did the act or made the omission. If the issue of unfitness arose later in the course of the trial (or was postponed by the trial judge), the jury by whom D was being tried will determine this issue (s. 4A(5)). If not satisfied that D did the act or made the omission, the jury should acquit of the count in question (s. 4A(4)). If the jury are satisfied D did the act or made the omission, the judge decides on the correct disposal. He may make an order for admission to a hospital approved by the Secretary of State (with or without an order restricting D's discharge), a supervision order, or an absolute discharge (s. 5(2) of the 1964 Act; s. 24 of the Domestic Violence, Crime and Victims Act 2004 substituted a new s. 5 into the 1964 Act). If the sentence for the offence is fixed by law (i.e. murder), and D has a mental disorder requiring specialist treatment under the Mental Health Act 1983, the court must order detention in hospital with restriction on discharge without limit of time (s. 5(3)). The Home Office Circular (24/2005) explained the effect of the new s. 5 thus (at para. 12):

> [T]he court is only obliged to make a hospital order with a restriction order on a charge of murder if the conditions for making a hospital order are met. If the conditions are not met, for example if the reason for the finding of unfitness to plead related to a physical disorder, the court's options are limited to a supervision order or absolute discharge.

The second time when the mental condition of D will be relevant is when he has been convicted. His mental condition will be relevant to the question of the appropriate sentence to be imposed (see further M. Wasik, *A Practical Approach to Sentencing* (5th edn, 2014)). Section 166(1) of the Criminal Justice Act 2003 gives courts a general power to mitigate the offender's sentence and s. 166(5) states that when sentencing a mentally disordered offender the court does not have to impose a sentence of imprisonment merely because the offence is so serious that a custodial sentence would normally be the only justifiable sentence. Other than in cases of murder, courts retain the power to deal with mentally disordered offenders in the manner they consider most appropriate in all the circumstances. Courts are also obliged to consider, before imposing a custodial sentence, any information relating to the mentally disordered offender's mental condition and the likely effect on that condition of imprisonment and on any treatment that may be available for it (s. 157(3)).

If an accused is found to have been insane at the time the *actus reus* was committed the verdict the jury return is 'not guilty by reason of insanity' (s. 2(1) of the Trial of Lunatics Act 1883). This is referred to as the 'special verdict'. Prior to 1991 on such a verdict being returned the judge had to order D to be detained in a hospital to be selected by the Home Secretary (s. 5(1) of and sch. 1 to the Criminal Procedure (Insanity) Act 1964). The fact that the consequence of a special verdict was automatic committal to a mental hospital was one of the deterrents against pleading insanity or, in some cases, from running a line of defence which might have been interpreted by the court as an insanity defence (see *Sullivan* and *Hennessy*, **5.3.5.1**). The prospect of indefinite detention in a mental hospital led some defendants to plead guilty and cast themselves upon the mercy of the judge when sentencing them, rather than rely on a defence which was technically available to them. The Criminal Procedure (Insanity and Unfitness to Plead) Act 1991 gives much greater discretion in disposing of an accused on a special verdict being returned. The court has the same powers of disposal as are available where an accused is found unfit to plead (see earlier).

 Key Point

While much ink is expended in textbooks and academic journals seeking to explain, analyse, and rationalise the defence of insanity, it is, in practice, a rarely used defence. Part of the reason for its infrequent use is that many of those accused of murder, who in the past might have raised the defence of insanity, now raise the defence of diminished responsibility under s. 2 of the Homicide Act 1957 (see **9.3.2.1**).

A study of the operation of the defence by R. D. Mackay, 'Fact and Fiction about the Insanity Defence' [1990] Crim LR 247, reveals that in the 14 years from 1975 to 1988 there were only 49 verdicts of 'not guilty by reason of insanity'. Of these verdicts 14 were returned in murder cases, 23 in cases of non-fatal assaults, and the remainder were returned in a variety of cases involving arson, robbery, burglary, deception, and reckless driving.

In a further study covering the five years immediately following the coming into force of the Criminal Procedure (Insanity and Unfitness to Plead) Act 1991 there were 44 findings of 'not guilty by reason of insanity' (see R. D. Mackay and G. Kearns, 'More Fact(s) about the Insanity Defence' [1999] Crim LR 714, 716). The authors speculate that the reason for this increase is that 'the new legislation has started to become more widely known by lawyers and psychiatrists as it has permeated the body of medico-legal knowledge. This in turn may have led to an appreciation that the 1991 Act has removed the more glaring disincentives inherent within the 1964 Act of running a defence of [not guilty by reason of insanity].' The vast majority of offences in respect of which the special verdict was returned were offences of violence. In 17 cases the disposal was as it would have been prior to the passage of the 1991 Act; a restriction order without limit of time. However, in 23 cases a community-based disposal was utilised. The authors speculate that this fact will, itself, stimulate greater use of the insanity defence. The fact remains, however, that the 1991 Act has not removed the stigmatising label of 'insane' which may still deter some defendants from raising the insanity defence. In addition, the Act did not address the problem of the legal definition of insanity which remains grossly outdated and fails to recognise developments in medical knowledge.

A further study by R. D. Mackay, B. J. Mitchell, and L. Howe for the years 1997–2001 ('Yet More Facts about the Insanity Defence' [2006] Crim LR 399) records a continued but gradual increase in the use of the insanity defence with offences against the person being the most represented and only a small number of cases of murder. The most frequent diagnosis is that of schizophrenia. The majority of those found not guilty by reason of insanity receive supervision orders. Mackay's most recent research covers the years 2002–2011 (R. D. Mackay 'Ten More Years of the Insanity Defence' [2012] Crim LR 946–54). It found a gradual increase in the number of special verdicts returned each year, suggesting that the legislative changes enacted by the 1991 and 2004 Acts are having an ongoing effect. The study also found an increase in the percentage of hospital-based disposals.

5.3.2 The rationale for a defence of insanity

 Key Point

There are five different ways in which a person's mental condition may affect his responsibility for his conduct.

1. D may perform a prohibited act in a state of impaired consciousness due to some mental condition or internal cause. In such a condition his act is involuntary and he is referred to as an automaton.
2. D may be conscious and perform willed bodily movements which constitute the *actus reus* of an offence but due to his mental condition he may not know or understand what he is doing.

→

> 3. D may be conscious and able to comprehend what he is doing but due to his mental condition be unaware that it is wrong.
>
> 4. D may know what he is doing and that it is wrong but due to his mental condition he may not be able to control what he is doing.
>
> 5. D may know what he is doing and that it is wrong but due to a delusional state he may believe that his act is appropriate.
>
> In each of these cases it could be said that D is not a responsible actor at the time of his act as he is not totally in touch with reality. The capacity for rational judgement has been impaired. As such punishment may not be appropriate. However, if he continues to be a danger to the community, it may be necessary for the community to be protected from him.

These five states of impairment vary in their impact on the definitional elements of the offence. In the first state there is no *actus reus* as the act was not voluntary and, necessarily, if it was not voluntary there was no *mens rea* either. In the second state there is an *actus reus* but no *mens rea*. In the third, fourth, and fifth states there is an *actus reus* and *mens rea* but serious doubts arise with regard to the rational capacity, and thus responsibility, of the actor.

While it was stated earlier that the criminal law had recognised the principle of rational capacity by exempting persons from criminal liability who lack it, the recognition of this principle has been almost accidental rather than designed. This becomes evident from a study of the operation of the defence of insanity. The effect of this defence is that in certain circumstances individuals who lacked rational capacity at the time of the commission of the alleged offence are excused from criminal liability; **the defence covers the first three conditions outlined earlier**. The defence has developed, however, in the absence of a clearly articulated theoretical foundation and in isolation from modern medical opinion. As a result **the defence is deficient** for being over-inclusive and under-inclusive. It does not cover a particular type of individual who clearly lacks rational capacity, namely those who fall within the fourth and fifth situations outlined earlier. **In other circumstances, the defence of insanity is unjust as it brings within its ambit individuals who, in any other context, would not be considered insane**—for example, the epileptic (*Sullivan*) or the diabetic (*Hennessy*) or the sleep-walker (*Burgess* [1991] 2 QB 92), who technically fall within the first situation outlined earlier. This problem highlights the difficulty in delineating the dividing line between automatism and insanity, or, as it is often termed non-insane automatism and insane automatism. Not all individuals who are reduced to an automatous condition are insane; some are insane, some are clearly sane, and others fall in between because their condition technically fits the criminal law's definition of insanity but does not correspond to any medical definition of insanity. Indeed, psychiatrists no longer talk of insanity but prefer to use terms such as mental illness or mental disorder.

While the Criminal Procedure (Insanity and Unfitness to Plead) Act 1991 has addressed the problem of the injustice of the automatic disposal to a mental hospital, it has not addressed the problem of the definition of insanity and the tendency of the defence to cover inappropriate conditions while failing to cover other conditions where rational capacity is absent. There are other problems with the defence in respect of the way in which it conflicts with other general principles of criminal liability which will be dealt with later.

5.3.3 The M'Naghten Rules

Key Point

The law relating to the defence of insanity is to be found in the rules set out in *M'Naghten* (1843) 10 Cl & F 200, which delineate the circumstances in which D will be held not to have been legally responsible for his conduct. These rules are not concerned with medical definitions of insanity, and, indeed, these may bear little resemblance to the clinical definition.

The origin of the M'Naghten Rules is interesting. Daniel M'Naghten was found to be insane and acquitted on a charge of murdering Sir Robert Peel's private secretary, it being his intention to kill Peel. He was committed to hospital but there was a public outcry at the perceived leniency of the verdict. The matter was debated in the House of Lords, where it was decided to seek the opinion of the judges on the legal principles relating to insanity. The joint answer given by 14 judges is not technically binding as a precedent as it is only an opinion rather than a judgment upon a case before a court. The rules, however, have been treated as authoritative ever since.

The principles stated by the judges are as follows:

(1) Everyone is presumed sane and to possess a sufficient degree of reason to be responsible for their crimes until the contrary is proved.

(2) To establish a defence of insanity it must be clearly proved that at the time of committing the act, D was labouring under such a defect of reason, from disease of the mind, as (a) not to know the nature and quality of the act he was doing; or (b) if he did know it, not to know he was doing what was wrong.

5.3.4 Procedural matters

Question

Who bears the burden of proving insanity?

The first principle stated earlier refers to the presumption of sanity. **If D is to raise the defence of insanity the burden of proving it is upon him.** Generally it is for the prosecution to prove the guilt of D beyond reasonable doubt and to disprove any defence he may raise. In the case of insanity it is not sufficient for D to raise the defence; he bears a burden of proving it. He is not required to prove it beyond reasonable doubt but need only do so on a balance of probabilities.

This raises a problem: **if D is claiming that he did not know what he was doing,** relying on ground 2(a) (see **5.3.5.3**), **he is being asked to prove on the balance of probabilities something the contrary of which the prosecution have not proved.** If the prosecution prove beyond reasonable doubt that he knew what he was doing, that would be an end to the matter. But if they fail to prove this it seems superfluous, and indeed illogical, to require D to prove the contrary on a balance of probabilities. The courts, however, have not recognised this problem although Glanville Williams did in *Criminal Law: The General Part* (2nd edn, 1961), para. 165, where he argued that on ground 2(a) it should only be necessary for D to introduce evidence of insanity which raises a reasonable doubt whether he had the necessary *mens rea*. Further support for this argument is gained by the fact that if D's defence is one of automatism due to some cause other than a disease of the mind, the burden of proof remains on the prosecution and D need only raise a doubt to succeed. In *AG's Reference (No. 3 of 1998)* [1999] 3 WLR 1194, the Court of Appeal confirmed that where the issue of insanity is raised during a trial, the prosecution are relieved of the duty of proving *mens rea* as s. 2(1) of the Trial of Lunatics Act 1883 only requires it to be proved that D 'did the act or made the omission charged'. The Court did not address the problem of the burden of proof on D.

? Question

Does raising a defence such as automatism or diminished responsibility harbour risks for a defendant?

While an accused may decide expressly not to raise the defence of insanity, the nature of his defence may, in effect, amount to an insanity defence as where, for example, he claims he was acting as an automaton or lacked *mens rea* and medical evidence points to this being due to a disease of the mind giving rise to a defect of reason of the appropriate kind outlined in the second principle stated earlier. In the past it was obviously in D's interests to claim that he was an automaton or lacked *mens rea* without expressly claiming he was insane, as he would hope simply to be acquitted without suffering committal to a mental hospital which was the automatic consequence of a special verdict being returned.

✓ Key Point

Whether a defence amounts to one of insanity is a question of law to be decided by the judge on the basis of the medical evidence (see *Dickie* [1984] 3 All ER 173). In exceptional circumstances a judge may raise the issue of insanity and leave it to the jury providing there is evidence embracing all the relevant considerations in the M'Naghten Rules (see *Thomas* [1995] Crim LR 314). If the judge concludes that the medical evidence supports a defence of insanity he should leave it to the jury to decide if D was insane.

In several of the cases discussed later the trial judge ruled that D's defence of automatism was, in effect, one of insanity as the medical evidence of his mental condition established that it was due to a disease of the mind. In the past in such cases the result was often that D changed his plea to guilty to avoid the consequences of the special verdict. It is also open to the prosecution to raise the issue of insanity. In *Bratty v AG for Northern Ireland* [1963] AC 386, Lord Denning stated (at p. 411):

> When it is asserted that the accused did an involuntary act in a state of automatism, the defence necessarily puts in issue the state of mind of the accused man: and thereupon it is open to the prosecution to show what his true state of mind was. The old notion that only the defence can raise a defence of insanity is now gone. The prosecution are entitled to raise it and it is their duty to do so rather than allow a dangerous person to be at large.

Where the defence raise a plea of diminished responsibility in response to a charge of murder (see **9.3.2.1**), it is open to the prosecution to rebut this by adducing or eliciting evidence of insanity (see s. 6 of the Criminal Procedure (Insanity) Act 1964). In such circumstances the burden of proving insanity will be on the prosecution (see *Bastian* [1958] 1 WLR 413).

The ultimate question whether D was insane is for the jury to determine; although the medical evidence will be crucial to their decision, it is not for doctors to decide the issue but for the jury to decide it on the basis of their evidence. However, **the jury must act on the evidence tendered**; if this all points to D being insane but the jury convict, such a conviction may be overturned on appeal on the ground that no reasonable jury could have reached such a verdict (*Matheson* (1958) 42 Cr App R 145). But if there is other evidence to the contrary, a jury verdict will not be overturned simply because the medical evidence supported the defence (see *Rivett* (1950) 34 Cr App R 87; *Latham* [1965] Crim LR 434).

5.3.5 The constituents of the defence

 Key Point

There are three conditions to be satisfied in any case where a defence of insanity is raised:

1. that D was suffering from a disease of the mind;
2. that this gave rise to a defect of reason; and
3. that as a result he either did not know the nature and quality of his act or he did not know that what he was doing was wrong.

These will be examined in turn.

5.3.5.1 Disease of the mind

 Question

Is this phrase one that doctors use?

Disease of the mind is a legal term and not a medical term. The law is concerned with the question whether D is to be held legally responsible for his acts. This depends on his mental state and its cause complying with legally defined criteria. The issue for the court is whether D had a defect of reason arising from a disease of the mind. The problem, however, is that psychiatrists prefer to use terms such as psychoneurosis and psychosis rather than disease of the mind. The former comprises anxiety states, obsessional states, and hysteria; these conditions would not generally meet the criteria for insanity. Most psychoses, on the other hand, satisfy the legal criteria of insanity. Psychoses may be divided into two categories: organic or functional. Organic psychoses are due to a physical cause such as poisoning of the brain by alcohol or drugs; infections such as syphilis; degeneration of the brain due to poor blood supply or tumours; or brain diseases, including senile dementia, atherosclerosis, and chorea. Functional psychoses include conditions such as schizophrenia, paranoia, psychopathic personality traits, and manic depression. There are other conditions which may cause a malfunctioning of the mind which, while they may have an organic cause, are not neuroses or psychoses—for example, epilepsy or hyperglycaemia arising from diabetes. **The problem for the medical witness is whether he should speak the language of the psychiatrist or convert these terms into what he believes they equate to in the legal terminology.** The issue is in relation to the medical evidence regarding the effects of such a disease on D's mental faculties, as the jury ultimately have to decide if the other criteria of the defence of insanity have been satisfied. If the psychiatrist seeks to translate medical terms into legal terms there is a danger that he will subvert the role of the jury by answering questions which are for their consideration, whereas, if he does not and simply confines himself to the role of the expert witness giving evidence for the jury's evaluation, there is a danger that he will mystify the jury.

This does not answer the question, however, of **what constitutes a disease of the mind**.

> In *Kemp* [1957] 1 QB 399, it was argued that 'disease of the mind' meant that there had to be an organic disease of the brain which had caused degeneration of the brain. D was charged with causing grievous bodily harm having made a motiveless attack on his wife with a hammer. He suffered from arteriosclerosis which affected the flow of blood in his brain and had caused a temporary loss of consciousness during which the attack was made. He did not suffer from mental disorder nor had his brain degenerated. Devlin J rejected the arguments of the defence that this was simply a case of automatism and ruled that the defence being raised was one of insanity, stating (at p. 407):
>
>> The law is not concerned with the brain but with the mind, in the sense that 'mind' is ordinarily used, the mental faculties of reason, memory and understanding. If one read for 'disease of the mind' 'disease of the brain', it would follow that in many cases pleas of insanity would not be established because it could not be proved that the brain had been affected in any way, either by degeneration of the cells or in any other way. In my judgment the condition of the brain is irrelevant and so is the question whether the condition of the mind is curable or incurable, transitory or permanent.

Devlin J went on to explain that the words 'disease of the mind' were included in the M'Naghten Rules to limit the words 'defect of reason' which were not intended to apply to defects of reason 'caused simply by brutish stupidity without rational power'. This sought to distinguish the untrained mind from the diseased mind.

In *Bratty* Devlin J's dicta in *Kemp* received the approval of Lord Denning in the House of Lords who added a further gloss, stating (at p. 412):

> [A]ny mental disorder which has manifested itself in violence and is prone to recur is a disease of the mind. At any rate it is the sort of disease for which a person should be detained in hospital rather than be given an unqualified acquittal.

This represents a particularly ill-considered dictum. Diseases of the mind may manifest themselves in other ways which do not involve violence—for example, pyromania or kleptomania. In addition there are conditions which manifest themselves in violence which do not fall within the definition of disease of the mind as the case of *Quick* [1973] QB 910 discloses.

> D was a diabetic who committed an assault when suffering from hypoglycaemia (a deficiency of blood sugar caused by taking insulin and failing to eat) causing D to be unaware of what he was doing. The trial judge ruled that his defence of automatism amounted to a plea of insanity, whereupon he pleaded guilty rather than face the prospect of the jury returning the special verdict and being sent to a secure psychiatric hospital. The Court of Appeal quashed his conviction ruling that the cause of his condition was not his diabetes but his use of insulin which was an external factor and his defence of automatism should have been left to the jury. Lawton LJ interpreted the phrase 'disease of the mind' to mean a 'malfunctioning of the mind caused by disease' whereas a 'malfunctioning of the mind of transitory effect caused by some external factor such as violence, drugs including anaesthetics, alcohol and hypnotic influences cannot fairly be said to be due to disease'.

The use of the criterion of internal/external causes to distinguish insanity from automatism is fatuous. Hypoglycaemic coma may be caused by overproduction of insulin by the pancreas. As this is an internal cause, it would be classed as a disease and result in a finding of insanity should the sufferer commit an offence while in hypoglycaemic coma due to an overactive pancreas. Is the person suffering from an overactive pancreas more deserving of the label 'criminally insane' than the diabetic who does not control his food and insulin intake? The current state of the law suggests an affirmative answer. To say that the law is an ass is to engage in understatement.

In *Sullivan* [1984] AC 156 the House of Lords had to grapple with the problem of the dividing line between insanity and automatism.

> D pleaded guilty to assault occasioning actual bodily harm after the trial judge ruled that his defence of automatism to a charge of inflicting grievous bodily harm was really a defence of insanity. D, who had attacked a friend, kicking him about the head and body, claimed the attack was committed during an epileptic seizure and he was not aware of doing it. Lord Diplock expressed his approval of Devlin J's dictum in *Kemp* and went on to state (at p. 172):

> > If the effect of a disease is to impair [the faculties of reason, memory, and understanding] so severely as to have either of the consequences referred to in the latter part of the Rules, it matters not whether the aetiology of the impairment is organic, as in epilepsy, or functional, or whether the impairment itself is permanent or is transient and intermittent, provided that it subsisted at the time of the commission of the act.

Lord Diplock did state that automatism would be available as a defence where temporary impairment resulted from an external physical factor although he did not consider it necessary to examine in detail the possible causes of automatism.

Although Sullivan's attack on his friend appeared to be purposive, despite his being unconscious, a result of the decision in the case is that an epileptic who involuntarily connects with someone while his arms and legs are thrashing about in the course of a seizure is insane for the purposes of criminal liability whereas a diabetic in hypoglycaemic coma, caused by a low blood-sugar level, is not. By contrast, however, a diabetic in hyperglycaemic coma, caused by a high blood-sugar level, is insane. This is the conclusion of the Court of Appeal in *Hennessy* [1989] 2 All ER 9.

> D, a diabetic, was charged with taking a conveyance without authority and driving whilst disqualified. He raised the defence of automatism claiming that due to stress, anxiety, and depression he had failed to take his insulin which resulted in hypergly-caemic coma. The trial judge ruled that this was in reality a defence of insanity as the condition was due to the disease of diabetes. D changed his plea to guilty and appealed. The Court of Appeal took the view that in *Sullivan* Lord Diplock had sought to distinguish between external factors giving rise to a malfunction of the mind and inherent causes giving rise to such a malfunction. The Court upheld the trial judge's ruling that diabetes constituted a disease of the mind as it was an inherent defect. Counsel for D argued further that the stress, anxiety, and depression from which he was suffering were external factors. The Court held, however, that while they may be the result of the operation of external factors (*per* Lord Lane CJ, at p. 14):

> > they are not separately or together external factors of the kind capable in law of causing or contributing to a state of automatism. They constitute a state of mind which is prone to recur. They lack the feature of novelty or accident, which is the basis of the distinction drawn by Lord Diplock in *R v Sullivan*.

In *Quick* Lawton LJ had said that **'the law should not give the words "defect of reason from disease of the mind" a meaning which would be regarded with incredulity outside the court'**. It is difficult to imagine that the ordinary person would not regard these decisions with incredulity.

 Question

Is it desirable that epileptics face the prospect of being labelled criminally insane if they are unfortunate enough to suffer a seizure during the course of which they thrash around and involuntarily hit or kick a third party?

Society may require protection from epileptics who, in the course of an epileptic seizure, engage in purposive conduct of a violent or dangerous nature (as appeared to be the case in *Bratty*) but no such distinction has been drawn by the courts.

 Question

Is the distinction between a diabetic in hyperglycaemic coma and one in hypoglycaemic coma so marked in its dangers, consequences, and risk of recurrence that the former should be found insane while the latter goes free?

In the cases of *Quick* and *Hennessy* the conduct involved appeared to be purposive rather than convulsive but the outcome in each case differed. The fact that the judges in *Quick, Sullivan,* and *Hennessy* accepted guilty pleas from the defendants tends to indicate dissatisfaction with the operation of the insanity defence.

Judicial dissatisfaction spilled over into open rebellion in Kingston Crown Court on 10 September 1990 (see *The Independent*, 11 September 1990). In the case of *McFarlane* Judge Bertram Wakely gave a direction to the jury in open and express defiance of the decision of the House of Lords in *Sullivan*. D was charged with inflicting actual bodily harm on a policeman during a search of her home for allegedly stolen property. D had suffered from epilepsy for 14 years. The defence case was that she struck the officer during an epileptic fit brought on by the strain of a dawn raid by several officers. Rather than directing the jury on the special verdict, Judge Wakely directed them that if they believed that D might have been having an epileptic fit they should return a verdict of not guilty. The jury acquitted D. While Judge Wakely may not have applied the law (as authoritatively declared in *Sullivan*) his judgment was an application of the spirit of Lawton LJ's dictum in *Quick*. One can only hope that one day both law and spirit will be in step! (See further the examples of *Bilton* and *Davies* and compare with *Lowe*, all referred to by R. D. Mackay and B. J. Mitchell in 'Sleepwalking, Automatism and Insanity' [2006] Crim LR 901.)

 Question

R. D. Mackay and M. Reuber, 'Epilepsy and the Defence of Insanity—Time for Change?' [2007] Crim LR 782, point out that it is well known that flashing lights and flash photography may trigger epileptic seizures, sometimes even in people who would not otherwise have seizures. If Sullivan's seizure had been triggered by flashing lights, would this have been an 'external factor' meriting an acquittal on the basis of non-insane automatism?

It had been hoped that reform of the insanity defence might be prompted by the enactment of the Human Rights Act 1998. Article 5 of the European Convention on Human Rights provides:

1. Everyone has the right to liberty and security of person. No one shall be deprived of his liberty save in the following cases and in accordance with a procedure prescribed by law;

    . . .

    (e) the lawful detention . . . of persons of unsound mind . . .

In the leading case before the European Court of Human Rights, *Winterwerp* v *Netherlands* (1979) 2 EHRR 387, the Court stated (at para. 39):

In the Court's opinion, except in emergency cases, the individual concerned should not be deprived of his liberty unless he has been reliably shown to be of 'unsound mind'. The very nature of what has to be established before the competent national authority—that is, a true mental disorder—calls for objective medical expertise. Further, the mental disorder must be of a kind or degree warranting compulsory confinement. What is more, the validity of the continued confinement depends upon the persistence of such a disorder.

It is doubtful whether conditions such as diabetes, epilepsy, or somnambulism would be classified by objective medical experts as mental disorders. Certainly they would not fall within the definition of 'mental disorder' in s. 1 of the Mental Health Act 1983 (as amended) which governs the conditions for civil commitment to a mental hospital (until 2007 the definition referred to 'mental illness, arrested or incomplete development of mind, psychopathic disorder and any other disorder or disability of mind', but s. 1(2) of the Mental Health Act 2007 amended s. 1 of the 1983 Act so that mental disorder now means 'any disorder or disability of the mind').

Imagine that D, a diabetic in hyperglycaemic coma, kills someone and is charged with murder. D's plea of automatism is rejected and the prosecution prove insanity, the jury return the special verdict and the judge commits D to a secure mental hospital with a restriction order. D appeals against the special verdict and the hospital committal claiming that they are incompatible with Art. 5. Detention of such a person who is not of 'unsound mind' would be a breach of Art. 5. This is what prompted the substitution of a new s. 5 into the Criminal Procedure (Insanity) Act 1964 by s. 24 of the Domestic Violence, Crime and Victims Act 2004. D now would not receive a hospital order with a restriction order under the Mental Health Act 1983 as he does not have a mental disorder of a nature of degree which makes it appropriate for him to be detained in a hospital for medical treatment. But, however much one might consider that a diabetic, epileptic, or sleep-walker should not be labelled insane, no change has been made in the test for insanity. The change effected by the 2004 Act, accordingly, is only a half-measure as the incongruities of the insanity defence remain unaddressed.

5.3.5.2 Defect of reason

If the defence of insanity is to succeed, the disease of the mind must give rise to a defect of reason. This appears to mean that **the powers of reasoning must be impaired**. If D simply fails, because of confusion or absent-mindedness, to use the powers of reasoning which he has, this will not bring him within the M'Naghten Rules.

> In *Clarke* [1972] 1 All ER 219, D was charged with the theft of items from a supermarket. Her defence was that she had no intention of stealing but had absent-mindedly placed the items in her shopping basket. She called medical evidence to establish that her absent-mindedness was due to a combination of depression and diabetes. The trial judge ruled that this was a defence of insanity, whereupon she pleaded guilty and appealed. The Court of Appeal quashed the conviction as D was not someone deprived of her powers of reasoning but simply someone who was momentarily absent-minded or confused who thus lacked the necessary *mens rea* for the offence.

If D's defect of reason is to be effective in establishing the defence of insanity, it must affect his legal responsibility for his conduct in one of the two ways specified in the M'Naghten Rules. Thus he must prove that either he did not know the nature and quality of his act or, if he did know this, he did not know that what he was doing was wrong.

5.3.5.3 The cognitive tests

The final aspect *part of the M'Naghten Rules concerns cognition and there are two limbs to this part of the Rules*. **A person will only be deemed legally insane with the**

Rules if at the time of the act either he did not know the nature and quality of his act or he did not know that the act was legally wrong.

It might be thought that a person who is legally insane will necessarily lack *mens rea* for the particular offence and that that is the basis for the special verdict. Indeed, until 2018 the courts had held that insanity at the time of the commission of the alleged offence is merely a particular situation where the *mens rea* is lacking (*DPP* v *Harper* [1997] 1 WLR 1406 and *R* v *Horseferry Road Magistrates' Court, ex p. K* [1996] 2 Cr App R 574). That was important because it led the courts to hold that the defence was only available to a defendant if he was charged with an offence requiring a mental element (and was therefore not available to a person charged with an offence of strict liability, such as driving with excess alcohol). However, in *Loake* v *CPS* [2018] 1 Cr App R 16, the Divisional Court held that that was an over-simplification of the basis of the insanity defence. Irwin LJ and Knowles J said:

> In virtually every case where the defendant proves that he did not know the nature and quality of his act at the time he performed it, then he will not be criminally responsible irrespective of the first limb of the M'Naghten test, because he will lack the mens rea for the alleged offence. The woman who squeezes her husband's throat believing she is strangling a deadly snake does not have the mens rea for murder, because she lacks the necessary intention to kill or cause really serious harm . . . To that extent, insanity as it operates in that context adds little, in the sense that the defendant would fall to be acquitted of murder in any event by reason of lack of mens rea (although the effect of the special verdict might be that the disposal is different).
>
> It is not correct, however, simply to regard insanity reductively, as operating simply on the basis that someone who is suffering from a disease of the mind will always lack mens rea for the offence.
>
> It is possible for someone to have the full mens rea for a criminal offence whilst at the same time, because of a defence of reason arising from a disease of the mind, not know what he is doing is wrong. (paras 39–41)

In *Loake*, the issue was whether the defence of insanity was available on a charge under s. 2 of the Protection from Harassment Act 1997, an offence whose mental element is that a person 'ought to know' that his conduct amounts to harassment. The court held that the defence was of general application and was not precluded by this objective test.

5.3.5.3.1 *Nature and quality of the act*

In *Codere* (1916) 12 Cr App R 21, it was argued that the word 'nature' referred to the physical character of the act whereas the word 'quality' referred to its moral character. The Court of Criminal Appeal rejected this contention holding that 'nature and quality' referred only to the physical character of the act. Thus it is necessary for D to prove that he did not know what he was doing, or did not appreciate the consequences of his act, or did not appreciate the circumstances in which he was acting. **In all of these situations D would lack *mens rea* but, because his defect of reason is due to a disease of the mind, he is liable to the special verdict rather than simple acquittal.** This limb of the defence will cover the automaton who does an act in a state of impaired consciousness (e.g. *Sullivan* and *Hennessy*). It will also cover the person who acts under a delusion—for example, D believes he is chopping down a tree when, in fact, it is a person. Similarly it covers the person who cuts off a sleeper's head because 'it would be great fun to see him looking for it when he woke up' (see J. F. Stephen, *History of the Criminal Law*, vol. II (1883), p. 166); such a person does not understand the consequences of his acts. By contrast if D, suffering from a pathological fear of women, kills V because he believes V is a woman, but V is, in fact, a man in drag, his mistake is immaterial and will not avail him as it does not affect his knowledge that he is killing another person.

Following *Loake* (2018), it does not follow that a person who satisfies the mental element for an offence will necessarily know the nature and quality of their act; presence of *mens rea* does not preclude reliance on the defence. The Divisional Court gave the example of a person suffering from severe dementia who is unable to recall events beyond a few minutes and who repeatedly telephones another person believing they are doing so for the first time. Such a person would not know the nature of their actions as they would not know the sustained nature of the calls. However, if charged under s. 2 of the Protection from Harassment Act 1997, they would satisfy the entirely objective mental element for that offence, namely that he 'ought to know' that the conduct amounts to harassment. As in *Loake*, the person could plead insanity on the basis that they did not know the nature or quality of their actions as a result of a disease of the mind that caused a defect of reason.

5.3.5.3.2 *Knowledge that the act is wrong*

 Key Point

Under this limb of the Rules there is an implicit admission by D that he had the *mens rea* for the offence but that he was not a responsible actor as he did not know that what he was doing was wrong.

The law in relation to this limb of the defence is not particularly clear. There are two possibilities: (1) that D must prove that he did not know that the act was contrary to the law; or (2) that D must prove that he did not know that the act was wrong according to the standard adopted by reasonable people. In *M'Naghten* the suggestion was that if D knew the act was wrong, in the sense of being one which he knew he ought not to do, this would be fatal to his defence whether or not he knew the actual law prohibiting it as 'the law is administered upon the principle that everyone must be taken conclusively to know it, without proof that he does know it'. This view was reinforced by *Codere* where the Court stated that 'the standard to be applied is whether according to the ordinary standard adopted by reasonable men the act was right or wrong'. Thus it appeared that the defence of insanity would fail if D knew either that his act was prohibited by the law or that it was regarded as wrong by reasonable people.

Doubt was cast on this proposition by the case of *Windle* [1952] 2 QB 826.

D killed his wife by giving her a fatal dose of aspirin. The wife was certifiably insane and had spoken of committing suicide on many occasions. On giving himself up to the police D said, 'I suppose they will hang me for this.' At his trial for murder, medical evidence was given that D suffered from a form of communicated insanity called *folie à deux*, although the experts on both sides agreed he knew that he was doing an act prohibited by the law. Devlin J withdrew the defence of insanity from the jury and D was convicted. The Court of Criminal Appeal upheld the conviction, Lord Goddard CJ stating *obiter* (at pp. 833, 834):

> Courts of law can only distinguish between that which is in accordance with law and that which is contrary to law . . . . The law cannot embark on the question, and it would be an unfortunate thing if it were left to juries to consider whether some particular act was morally right or wrong. The test must be whether it is contrary to law . . . [I]n the M'Naghten Rules 'wrong' means contrary to law and not 'wrong' according to the opinion of one man or of a number of people on the question of whether a particular act might or might not be justified.

This judgment appears to widen the defence as an accused who knew his act was morally wrong may still raise the defence if his contention is that because of his defect of reason he did not know it was legally wrong to do what he did. *Windle* was confirmed by the Court of Appeal in *Johnson* [2007] EWCA Crim 1978 where it was held that knowledge of illegality was the sole criterion of what was wrong.

As the Divisional Court made clear in *Loake*, it is possible for a person to have the *mens rea* for a criminal offence while at the same time, because of a defect of reason arising from a disease of the mind, not know what he is doing is wrong (see para. 41). The Divisional Court gave the following example:

> If a man intentionally kills his wife because of his deluded belief that he is under threat from a representative of Satan and has received a divine order to slay, and that it is lawful to comply with divine orders, then he possesses the mens rea for murder but is not guilty of murder because he does not know that what he is doing is unlawful. (at para. 41)

This limb of the M'Naghten Rules has been criticised. Glanville Williams, *Textbook of Criminal Law* (2nd edn, 1983) at p. 645, argued that 'unless very benevolently interpreted it adds almost nothing to the other questions'. The Butler Committee, *Report of the Committee on Mentally Abnormal Offenders* (Cmnd 6244, 1975) stated (at p. 218):

> Knowledge of the law is hardly an appropriate test on which to base ascription of responsibility to the mentally disordered. It is a very narrow ground of exemption since even persons who are grossly disturbed generally know that murder and arson are crimes.

This would suggest that this limb of the defence, if applied strictly, will be of little use. Almost half of the special verdicts returned in Mackay's 1990 study (see **5.3.1**) were based on this ground. His study also revealed that trial courts are effectively ignoring the dicta in the appellate cases and special verdicts are being returned in cases where D knew his act to be legally wrong but did it because of delusions which caused him to believe it to be morally right!

Mackay concluded (at p. 251):

> In many of these cases there seems to have been little attempt made to distinguish between lack of knowledge of legal wrong . . . and unawareness of moral wrong. Indeed, the general impression gained from reading the documentation in these cases was that the wrongness issue was being treated in a liberal fashion by all concerned, rather than in the strict manner regularly depicted by legal commentators.

The later research by Mackay and Kearns in 1999 confirms that this continues to be the case where the 'wrongness' limb was used in 25 out of the 44 cases studied. They state (at p. 723):

> [T]he overwhelming impression is that the question the majority of psychiatrists are addressing is: if the delusion that the defendant was experiencing at the time of the offence was in fact reality, then would the defendant's actions be morally justified?—rather than the narrow cognitive test of legal wrongness required by the M'Naghten Rules . . . . In so doing, it may be argued that psychiatrists in many respects are adopting a common sense or folk psychology approach and that the courts by accepting this interpretation are, in reality, expanding the scope of the M'Naghten Rules.

(See also R. D. Mackay, B. J. Mitchell, and L. Howe, 'Yet More Facts about the Insanity Defence' [2006] Crim LR 399.) One can only state again that it would be desirable for the law, practice, and theory to be in harmony.

5.3.5.4 Insane delusions and irresistible impulses

Although the jury acquitted M'Naghten, under the test the judges propounded he would have been convicted. He was suffering from paranoia which gave rise to a morbid delusion that he was being persecuted by 'Tories'. This delusion did not prevent him from knowing that he was killing another person and from knowing that it was wrong. It is an arguable point, however, whether he was a responsible actor deserving of punishment.

The judges dealt expressly with the issue of delusions stating:

> [I]f [D] labours under [a] partial delusion only, and is not in other respects insane, we think he must be considered in the same situation as to responsibility as if the facts with respect to which the delusion exists were real. For example, if under the influence of his delusion he supposes another man to be in the act of attempting to take away his life, and he kills that man, as he supposes, in self-defence, he would be exempt from punishment. If his delusion was that the deceased had inflicted a serious injury to his character and fortune, and he killed him in revenge for such supposed injury, he would be liable to punishment.

This does not really add anything to the Rules as this situation is already covered by the test relating to the nature and quality of the act. In the example of self-defence D did not appreciate the circumstances in which he was acting and thus did not know the nature and quality of his act. In the second example D knows that he is killing a person and there is nothing to suggest that he did not know that this was wrong. The problem is that there are delusions which may call into question the responsibility of D for his acts but which do not fall within the Rules. For example, there are many cases where D kills his victim because he believes that the victim is possessed by the devil, or because he is in a paranoid state believing that the victim is persecuting him or plotting his death. In all these cases D would not fall within the Rules if he knows he is killing another person and that killing is wrong. His delusional state, however, would suggest that he is not a responsible actor deserving of punishment even though society deserves to be protected from him. These cases point to a deficiency of the Rules. In practice, however, this deficiency appears to be overlooked as Mackay (1990) cites examples of cases where the special verdict has been returned although the Rules do not appear to have been satisfied.

If D understands what he is doing and knows that it is wrong, the fact that he could not resist the impulse to do it will be of no avail. The Privy Council in *Sodeman* [1936] 2 All ER 1138 ruled that the defence could not be founded on uncontrollable impulse (see also *Kopsch* (1925) 19 Cr App R 50). However, medical evidence that in a particular case irresistible impulse was a symptom of the disease from which an accused was suffering, affecting his ability to know the nature and quality of his act or its wrongness, could be left to the jury (see *AG for South Australia* v *Brown* [1960] AC 432). Thus irresistible impulse on its own will not found a defence, but it may be used to support the claim that D either did not know what he was doing or that it was wrong, where there is medical evidence to that effect. Irresistible impulse is relevant, however, to support a defence of diminished responsibility.

5.3.6 **Proposals for reform**

 Key Point

The M'Naghten Rules have been the subject of persistent criticism by lawyers and doctors on several grounds.

1. They do not reflect current psychiatric thinking on mental disorder—the language used is that of lawyers and has little congruence to the language of psychiatry.

2. The Rules lead to absurd distinctions (such as those between diabetics suffering from hypo-glycaemia and those suffering from hyperglycaemia) which do not reflect any substantial difference in the responsibility of such persons for their acts.

3. The Rules cover persons who normally would not be liable to civil committal to hospital under the Mental Health Act 1983, such as diabetics, epileptics, and sleep-walkers, while failing to cover others who are covered by that Act such as the defendant in *Windle*, those suffering from insane delusions which do not prevent them from knowing what they are doing, and those subject to uncontrollable impulses.

These criticisms have led to various calls for reform. The most significant report was that of the Butler Committee (Cmnd 6244, 1975). The Butler proposals formed the basis for the mental disorder provisions in the Law Commission's Draft Criminal Code. The Draft Code abandoned the language of the M'Naghten Rules and used terms such as 'mental disorder', 'severe mental illness', and 'severe mental handicap' which reflect medical terminology. The latest Law Commission proposals are in its discussion paper, *Criminal Liability: Insanity and Automatism* (July 2013). The Law Commission's research and the responses to its *Scoping Paper* indicate that while there are problems with the insanity defence both legal and medical practitioners manage to work around these. The Law Commission states (at para. 1.8):

> We are convinced, on the basis of our research to date, the vast wealth of academic liter-ature and the reform proposals made by others, that there are significant problems with the law when examined from a theoretical perspective. There is, however, less evidence that the defences cause significant difficulties in practice and a dearth of published research into the operation of the defences.

The respondents had more concerns about the law and procedures relating to unfitness to plead resulting in the Law Commission prioritising this area for its short-term focus. The rationale for concentrating reform efforts on this area is that if procedure were reformed, fewer mentally disordered offenders would be found fit to plead and would not have to utilise the insanity defence. In addition, the political reality is that legislation to reform the insanity defence is unlikely to be forthcoming where there is little practical need for it. Notwithstanding this, the Law Commission makes proposals for reshaping insanity and automatism. It proposes that people should be exempted from criminal responsibility where they totally lack capacity because of a recognised medical condition, such that they could not have avoided committing the crime they are charged with. The defence would be capable of applying to physical, psychological, or psychiatric conditions including epilepsy, schizophrenia, dementia, bipolar disorder, a condition leading to a stroke, obstructive sleep apnoea, and clinical depression. The defence would not be available, however, where the lack of capacity arises from fault on the part of D, such as voluntary intoxication. But if intoxication resulting in total lack of capacity arose from alcohol dependence syndrome, D could rely on this as it is a medical condition. The new defence would be referred to as 'not criminally responsible by reason of a recognised medical condition'. The capacities that would have to be affected would be the capacity:

(i)   to make a judgment rationally about relevant conduct or circumstances,

(ii) to understand that you are doing something wrong, or

(iii) to control physical acts in relation to relevant conduct or circumstances.

The Law Commission recommends that the burden of proof should change with D only being required to satisfy an *evidential* burden to produce evidence from two expert witnesses relating to the elements of the defence, it then being for the prosecution to disprove the defence.

Alongside this defence would be a reformed defence of automatism which would be available where D has a total loss of capacity to control his actions, for which he is not culpably responsible and which is not caused by a recognised medical condition. This would cover something like a reflex action whereas incapacity arising from diabetes, epilepsy, or a sleep disorder would fall under the defence of 'not criminally responsible by reason of a recognised medical condition'.

The Law Commission considers that its proposals have the virtues of providing 'fairer treatment for mentally disordered offenders, avoiding the stigmatising label of insanity', and providing flexibility to accommodate developing medical knowledge.

5.4 **Automatism**

5.4.1 **Defining automatism**

It was stated at **2.4.1** that where the *actus reus* of an offence requires conduct on the part of D, whether an act or omission, liability will only arise where the conduct is willed. **Where a person acts while in a state of unconsciousness or impaired consciousness this is referred to as automatism.** In such a condition the movements of a person's body or limbs are involuntary (see *Watmore* v *Jenkins* [1962] 2

QB 572). In *Bratty v AG for Northern Ireland* [1963] AC 386, 409, Lord Denning defined an involuntary act or automatism as:

> an act which is done by the muscles without any control by the mind, such as a spasm, a reflex action or a convulsion; or an act done by a person who is not conscious of what he is doing, such as an act done whilst suffering from concussion or whilst sleep-walking.

What is required is that D's mind is not controlling his limbs at all; it is not sufficient that D's mind is acting imperfectly if he is still reacting to stimuli and controlling his limbs in a purposive way (see *Broome v Perkins* [1987] Crim LR 271; *Roberts v Ramsbottom* [1980] 1 All ER 7; *AG's Reference (No. 2 of 1992)* (1993) 97 Cr App R 429). Even a trance-like state will be insufficient if D is still performing some purposive acts.

> In *Isitt* (1978) 67 Cr App R 44, D was involved in a road accident and it appeared that he was drunk. He returned to his van and drove off at speed with a police car in pursuit. D evaded the pursuing vehicle and a police road block, finally coming to a halt when he drove up a cul-de-sac only to run off through fields. When finally interviewed at home he claimed he could not remember the incident and, at his trial for dangerous driving, he called psychiatric evidence that the original accident had caused hysterical fugue leading to memory loss. It was claimed that his subconscious mind had taken over so that he did not appreciate what he was doing when he was driving, and although he knew he was trying to get away from the scene of an accident, he was totally unaware of legal restrictions and moral concern. He was convicted and the Court of Appeal dismissed his appeal, Lawton LJ stating (at p. 48):

> > It is a matter of human experience that the mind does not always operate in top gear.
> > There may be some difficulty in functioning. If the difficulty does not amount in law to either insanity or automatism, is the accused entitled to say 'I am not guilty because my mind was not working in top gear'? In our judgment he is not . . . .
> > In our judgment on the psychiatrist's evidence, it is clear that he was accepting that the appellant's mind was working to some extent. The driving was purposeful driving, which was to get away from the scene of the accident. It may well be that, because of panic or stress or alcohol, the appellant's mind was shut to the moral inhibitions which control the lives of most of us. But the fact that his moral inhibitions were not working properly, in our judgment, does not mean that the mind was not working at all.

It is an essential requirement of criminal liability that D's acts or omissions which constitute the *actus reus* of the offence were voluntary (see *Bratty, per* Lord Denning at p. 409). Thus, **if the prosecution cannot prove beyond reasonable doubt that D's conduct was voluntary, he will be acquitted.**

 Key Point

Mental capacity, however, is presumed and the prosecution will only be required to negative an assertion of automatism where the defence have laid a proper evidential foundation for that assertion (*Bratty*). D's own evidence will rarely be sufficient and should be supported by medical evidence which points to the cause of the mental incapacity (*Bratty*). Where the cause of the automatism is a disease of the mind within the M'Naghten Rules, the acquittal will take the form of the special verdict of not guilty by reason of insanity resulting in committal to a mental hospital.

It is therefore crucial to determine which causes of automatism will lead to an out-right acquittal and which will lead to a finding of insanity.

5.4.2 **The causes of automatism**

The distinction between automatism due to a disease of the mind and that due to other causes is a very important one.

> In *Bratty*, D was charged with murder having strangled a girl. He raised three defences: automatism, lack of intent for murder, and insanity. The medical evidence pointed to the attack occurring in the course of a psychomotor epileptic seizure. In such a condition the sufferer may perform complicated acts of a purposive, as opposed to convulsive, kind while in an unconscious or somnambulist state. The trial judge ruled that the defence case was one of insanity as the medical evidence pointed to D's automatous condition being due to a disease of the mind, and refused to leave the other two defences to the jury. The jury rejected the defence of insanity and convicted. This conviction was upheld by both the Court of Appeal and the House of Lords. Lord Denning accepted that the 'major mental diseases, which doctors call psychoses . . . are clearly diseases of the mind'. To these he added 'any mental disorder which has manifested itself in violence and is prone to recur'.

This hardly provided a useful guide for distinguishing automatism from insanity. **The distinction which emerges from subsequent cases centres on classifying causes as being either internal or external.** In *Quick* [1973] QB 910, Lawton LJ, seeking to define 'disease of the mind' stated (at p. 922):

> [T]he fundamental concept is a malfunctioning of the mind caused by disease. A malfunctioning of the mind of transitory effect caused by the application to the body of some external factor such as violence, drugs including anaesthetics, alcohol and hypnotic influences cannot fairly be said to be due to disease.

In *Sullivan* Lord Diplock implicitly accepted the distinction between internal and external causes. A verdict of not guilty would thus be acceptable in 'cases where temporary impairment . . . results from some external physical factor such as a blow on the head causing concussion or the administration of an anaesthetic for therapeutic purposes'. It would appear, therefore, that **automatism will not result in a finding of insanity where the cause is external and physical such as concussion resulting from a blow to the head, or impaired consciousness resulting from the administration of drugs (e.g. insulin leading to hypoglycaemia) or anaesthetics.** Stress, anxiety, or depression which lead to impaired consciousness are not themselves external physical factors (see *Hennessy* [1989] 2 All ER 9), but where they are due to an external physical factor and they lead to impaired consciousness, automatism may be successfully pleaded (see *R* v *T* [1990] Crim LR 256).

> In *R* v *T*, D was charged with robbery and causing actual bodily harm. In her defence she claimed she was acting as an automaton as a result of being raped three days prior to the alleged offences. Medical evidence supported her claim of being raped and a psychiatrist diagnosed that she was suffering from post-traumatic stress

disorder which brought about a dissociative state such that the offences had been committed during a psychogenic fugue and she was not acting with a conscious mind or will. Southan J, at Snaresbrook Crown Court, held that the issue of automatism should be allowed to go to the jury as the rape was an external factor and post-traumatic stress was not a disease of the mind.

In *Rabey* (1977) 37 CCC (2d) 461, where D sought to plead automatism based on a dissociative state caused by the psychological blow of rejection by a girl with whom he had become infatuated, the Supreme Court of Canada held that 'the ordinary stresses and disappointments of life which are the common lot of mankind do not constitute an external cause'. The Court was of the opinion that the impact of this ordinary event on D was primarily due to his psychological or emotional make-up.

Rape can hardly be considered one of the 'ordinary stresses or disappointments of life'. In *R v T* Southan J considered that 'such an incident could have an appalling effect on any young woman, however well-balanced normally'. The case is consequently easily distinguishable from *Rabey*.

In *Roach* [2001] EWCA Crim 2698 the Court of Appeal highlighted the importance of taking into account the causative factors resulting in a state of automatism.

> D suffered from an underlying condition which could have led to a state of insane automatism. There was evidence, however, that external factors, namely the combination of alcohol and prescribed drugs, may have rendered D an automaton when he committed the offence. In quashing his conviction because of a misdirection by the trial judge, Potter LJ stated (at para. 28) that:

> [T]he legal definition of automatism allows for the fact that, if external factors are operative upon an underlying condition which would not otherwise produce a state of automatism, then a defence of (non-insane) automatism should be left to the jury.

While the distinction between internal and external causes may appear conceptually simple it has not always been strictly applied. The condition which causes a problem for the courts is that of somnambulism. There are numerous examples of people engaging in purposive conduct while apparently asleep who, when awake, either remember nothing at all or recall the events as a dream. If D performs an act while asleep the cause for such unconscious conduct would appear to be internal. If, in response to a charge, he pleaded automatism based on somnambulism, the outcome should be a ruling that this was a defence of insanity. However, there are cases where such pleas have been accepted as simple automatism, as in *Lillienfield, The Times*, 17 October 1985. In this case, the Crown Court treated as automatism the actions of D who, in a state of somnambulism, had stabbed a friend 20 times. In *Bratty* Lord Denning blithely placed acts done while sleep-walking in the same category as those done while concussed. He cited with approval the dictum of Stephen J in *Tolson* (1889) 23 QBD 168, 187:

> Can anyone doubt that a man who, though he might be perfectly sane, committed what would otherwise be a crime in a state of somnambulism, would be entitled to be acquitted? And why is this? Simply because he would not know what he was doing.

The fatal flaw in this line of reasoning, however, is the assumption that because, in common parlance, such a person would not be described as insane, the law will treat him similarly. The same questions asked by Stephen J could be asked in respect of the diabetic in a hyperglycaemic coma (*Hennessy*) and the epileptic (*Sullivan*); the law, however, regards these people as insane and the case of the sleep-walker is indistinguishable. The Court of Appeal came to this conclusion in *Burgess* [1991] 2 QB 92. D pleaded automatism due to sleep-walking in response to a charge of wounding with intent. The trial judge ruled that this was a case of insane automatism. On appeal against the jury's finding that D was not guilty by reason of insanity, the Court of Appeal upheld the trial judge's ruling; D's automatism was due to an internal cause. (See further the examples of *Bilton* and *Davies* and compare with *Lowe*: all referred to by R. D. Mackay and B. J. Mitchell in 'Sleepwalking, Automatism and Insanity' [2006] Crim LR 901.)

On 15 October 2008 Harry Cohen MP introduced a Private Members' Bill, the Rape (Defences) Bill, to amend the Sexual Offences Act 2003 to prohibit the defence of sleep-walking or non-insane automatism in proceedings relating to rape. Several cases which received media coverage prompted this move as it appeared that defendants, mostly following heavy drinking, raised sleep-walking in their defence to charges of rape and received acquittals without any ruling such as that made in *Burgess* being given by the trial judges. If alcohol induced the sleep-walking this could render it self-induced (see **5.4.3**) and, if it did not, it would arise from an internal cause and be a case of insane automatism. The bill was not enacted, but it is clear that the issue of sleep-walking as a defence, and how it relates to that of insane automatism, requires clarification. The CPS has taken the step of responding to recent media reports of such cases by reminding prosecutors that '[i]t is essential that this defence is robustly challenged' and drawing attention to the persuasive authority of *Finegan* v *Heywood*, *The Times*, 10 May 2000, in which the Scottish High Court of Justiciary held that the defence of automatism is not available where deliberate and self-induced intoxication has induced parasomnia (https://www.cps.gov.uk/legal-guidance/defences-sleepwalking-defence-sexual-offence-cases).

5.4.3 Self-induced automatism

Automatism is self-induced where it results from something which D has done or failed to do. The most frequent example of self-induced automatism is intoxication arising from the voluntary ingestion of alcohol or proscribed drugs. The effect of intoxication on criminal liability is discussed in detail later (see **5.5**). For present purposes it is sufficient to state that **where D's state of impaired consciousness is due to self-induced intoxication by drink or drugs this will not avail him if the crime with which he is charged is one of 'basic intent', although it may negative *mens rea* for a crime of 'specific intent'** (evidence of intoxication may help D to create a doubt as to whether he had formed the intent necessary to be convicted of the offence) (see **5.5.3**). **Where automatism is due to some cause other than intoxication by alcohol or proscribed drugs, D cannot be convicted of an offence of specific intent and it may provide a defence to crimes of basic intent** (*Bailey* [1983] 1 WLR 760).

In *Bailey*, D raised automatism as his defence to charges under ss 18 and 20 of the Offences Against the Person Act 1861 of unlawful wounding and wounding with intent. D was a diabetic and claimed he had failed to take sufficient food after taking insulin which caused a hypoglycaemic coma in the course of which he committed the offence. The jury convicted D of the s. 18 offence on the direction from the recorder that self-induced automatism was no defence to offences of specific or basic intent. The Court of Appeal ruled that the recorder's direction was clearly wrong in respect of the s. 18 offence which was one of specific intent. They also held that self-induced automatism, other than due to intoxication by alcohol or drugs, may provide a defence to crimes of basic intent. Griffiths LJ stated (at p. 765):

> The question in each case will be whether the prosecution have proved the necessary element of recklessness. In cases of assault, if the accused knows that his actions or inaction are likely to make him aggressive, unpredictable or uncontrolled with the result that he may cause some injury to others and he persists in the action or takes no remedial action when he knows it is required, it will be open to the jury to find that he was reckless.

The Court based its ruling on the view that there was an absence of common knowledge amongst diabetics of the possible effects of failure to take food after insulin, whereas it is common knowledge that those who become intoxicated by alcohol or drugs may become aggressive or do dangerous or unpredictable things. If, however, a diabetic did appreciate the risk of becoming aggressive, unpredictable, or uncontrollable due to a failure to take food after taking insulin and he deliberately ran that risk, this would amount to recklessness and lead to liability for any offence of basic intent which he committed in that state.

5.5 Intoxication

5.5.1 Intoxication and responsibility

Intoxication may result from the consumption of alcohol or other drugs. As alcohol is the most widely available intoxicant it is not surprising that most cases in which the issue arises relate to alcohol-induced intoxication. The principles which apply, however, are the same whether it is alcohol, amphetamines, barbiturates, hallucinogens, or other drugs which cause the intoxication. In an intoxicated state a person's mental powers of perception, reasoning, self-control, judgement, and ability to foresee consequences may all be impaired as well as his physical reactions and coordination. In some circumstances, intoxication is the essence of a criminal offence as where, for example, D is found drunk in a public place, or is under the influence of drink or drugs when in charge of a motor vehicle in a public place. Other offences may be committed by D when intoxicated, in which case it is important to determine whether his intoxication is relevant to his criminal liability.

 Question

Is an accused to be acquitted of a criminal offence because he was, due to his voluntary intoxication, deprived of the capacity to control his conduct or to formulate the *mens rea* required for the offence?

A person who is insane or an automaton will be acquitted because he bears no responsibility for his condition and is not, therefore, responsible for, or culpable in respect of, acts he performed in that condition. By contrast, a voluntarily intoxicated person is responsible for his own impaired condition. If the criminal law treats intoxicated offenders differently from those suffering from other incapacitating conditions this may be justifiable on that basis. If the intoxicated offender is convicted of offences he committed whilst in that condition, conviction and punishment may deter him in future from becoming intoxicated and, hopefully, from reoffending. As we will see, deterrence underpins the law on the relevance of intoxication on criminal liability.

5.5.2 The effect of voluntary intoxication on criminal liability

Intoxication is not a defence which may be pleaded in answer to a charge; it does not operate to excuse D's conduct. It is no excuse for D to say that had he been sober he would never have done as he did (see *DPP v Majewski* [1977] AC 443), nor may he raise a plea of automatism based on voluntary intoxication (see *Lipman* [1970] 1 QB 152). **The only relevance of intoxication is in respect of the question whether D had the *mens rea* required for the offence;** he may not have formed the *mens rea* because of his intoxication or he may have acted under a drunken mistake which negates his *mens rea*. If he did form the necessary *mens rea*, however, it matters not that he was intoxicated at the time or that he had done something which he would not have done if sober (*Bowden* [1993] Crim LR 380). If the offence is one of negligence or strict liability intoxication will be irrelevant to D's liability. **Where the offence is one requiring *mens rea*, however, voluntary intoxication is only relevant if the offence is one of 'specific intent' as opposed to one of 'basic intent'.**

5.5.3 Offences of specific and basic intent

 Key Point

> The law relating to intoxication is essentially the result of policy decisions by the courts. On occasion, however, judges engaged in the pretence that their decisions were, in fact, dictated by principle. Upon closer scrutiny the principles proved to be flawed, thereby creating doubt and confusion. The flaws were not obvious when the principles were first articulated but became so as the doctrine of *mens rea* developed in a way which meant that it no longer fitted neatly alongside the principles relating to intoxication. Further developments in both areas have resulted in clarification of the principles although they still do not fit neatly side by side.

The early authorities treated drunkenness as an aggravating factor but during the nineteenth century the rigidity of this rule was gradually relaxed in a piecemeal fashion. The authorities were considered in *DPP v Beard* [1920] AC 479, where the term 'specific intent' was first coined by Lord Birkenhead.

> D raped a girl and, while doing so, suffocated her. The House of Lords restored a conviction for murder on the basis of the 'felony murder rule' (which has since been abolished by s. 1 of the Homicide Act 1957). This rule stated that where a person killed in the course of committing a felony D would be convicted of murder without

any need to prove malice aforethought. As it was not contested that Beard intended to rape his victim and death ensued from this, his drunkenness was irrelevant as it did not affect his formation of the *mens rea* for rape. In the course of his speech Lord Birkenhead, after examining the authorities, stated (at p. 499):

> [T]hese decisions establish that where a specific intent is an essential element in the offence, evidence of a state of drunkenness rendering the accused incapable of forming such an intent should be taken into consideration in order to determine whether he had in fact formed the intent necessary to constitute the particular crime.

It is far from clear what Lord Birkenhead meant by the word 'specific'; most probably he meant nothing more than the *mens rea* required by the particular crime in question. This view finds support in statements Lord Birkenhead made later in his speech to the effect that the general principle was that 'a person cannot be convicted of a crime unless the *mens* was *rea*' and thus 'drunkenness rendering a person incapable of the intent, would be an answer'.

Subsequent cases, however, have placed the dicta of Lord Birkenhead in a different light. It is now clear that evidence of drunkenness is relevant for the purpose of considering whether or not D had the necessary intent; **it is not necessary that he be rendered incapable of forming the intent by his drunkenness** (see *Pordage* [1975] Crim LR 575; *Sheehan and Moore* (1974) 60 Cr App R 308). This is also consistent with the effect of s. 8 of the Criminal Justice Act 1967 (see **3.2.3.1**). But this principle has been limited in its ambit by judges who seized on the term 'specific intent' and gave it a specialised meaning which Lord Birkenhead probably never intended. They considered that it would be undesirable if those who reduced themselves into an aggressive, dangerous, or unpredictable condition escaped all criminal liability; if they did they would be undeterred from reducing themselves into that condition in the future. Thus after *Beard* judges started to speak of offences of 'specific intent' to which intoxication could be pleaded and those of 'basic intent' to which the question of intoxication was irrelevant. Lord Birkenhead had never mentioned the term 'basic intent' and thus had not sought to create any such distinction between offences. He had specifically referred to unlawful homicide stating that if intoxication rendered D incapable of forming the intent to kill or to do grievous bodily harm, he would not be guilty of murder but would be guilty of manslaughter. Lord Birkenhead was not sure what the justification for this was; perhaps principle or perhaps the policy that persons who killed when drunk deserved to be punished for their drunkenness. As the principles relating to 'unlawful act manslaughter' were far from clear at this stage his confusion was understandable; he did not say, however, that manslaughter was an offence of basic intent.

The leading case is now *DPP* v *Majewski* [1977] AC 443.

> D was intoxicated as a result of taking barbiturates, amphetamines, and alcohol. In this condition he struck a police officer and was charged with assault occasioning actual bodily harm and assaulting a police officer in the execution of his duty. He sought to rely on his intoxication to establish that he was so intoxicated that he did not form the appropriate *mens rea*. The House of Lords held that intoxication was only relevant where the offence charged was one of specific intent, but where, as in

the case of assault, the offence was one of basic intent intoxication substituted for *mens rea*. Thus an accused may be convicted of a basic intent offence even though, as a result of his voluntary intoxication, he did not have the *mens rea* normally required to be proved, and even if his intoxication rendered him an automaton. Elwyn Jones LC described this as a substantive rule of the common law unaffected by s. 8 of the Criminal Justice Act 1967. He explained how intoxication operated in an offence of basic intent as follows (at pp. 474, 475):

> If a man of his own volition takes a substance which causes him to cast off the restraints of reason and conscience, no wrong is done to him by holding him answerable criminally for any injury he may do while in that condition. His course of conduct in reducing himself by drugs and drink to that condition in my view supplies the evidence of *mens rea*, of guilty mind certainly sufficient for crimes of basic intent. It is a reckless course of conduct and recklessness is enough to constitute the necessary *mens rea* in assault cases.

As a statement of principle, this is open to criticism on three grounds. First, a presumption of recklessness conflicts with s. 8 of the Criminal Justice Act 1967, which requires a jury to examine all the evidence before deciding whether D did foresee the result which his conduct brought about. Secondly, if becoming intoxicated is reckless, this recklessness arises at a time prior to the commission of the *actus reus* of the offence and thus there is no coincidence of *actus reus* and *mens rea*. Thirdly, recklessness involves a recognition of the risk which eventuates in the commission of the *actus reus*. At the time D becomes intoxicated it is only general or unspecified risks which may exist; there was no suggestion that when Majewski became intoxicated he foresaw the actual risk which eventuated. Thus the recklessness arising from intoxication relates to a time prior to the commission of the *actus reus* and a risk of an unspecified nature unconnected to any specific *actus reus*.

If intoxication is to give rise to this irrebuttable presumption of recklessness which will provide the *mens rea* element for offences of basic intent, it can only be supported as a decision based on policy considerations; it is not one which is derived from the principles of the criminal law. Lord Salmon was prepared to admit this as he stated that the decision was not one which could be supported by logic but was one which accorded with 'justice, ethics, and common sense' as it sought to preserve individual liberty, an important aspect of which is the protection of citizens against physical violence.

 Question

How are crimes of basic intent distinguished from crimes of specific intent?

Unfortunately, the basis for distinguishing them is not entirely clear. One suggestion was that crimes of specific intent were those of ulterior intent (see **3.2.4**). Lord Simon recognised a problem with this as murder, an offence universally accepted as being one of specific intent, was not one of ulterior intent. He suggested that the crucial factor is that 'the *mens rea* in a crime of specific intent requires proof of a purposive element'. This suggestion, however, is equally flawed as the *mens rea* of murder does not necessarily involve a purpose equivalent to the result caused—for example, where D intends to cause grievous bodily harm but his victim dies. In Lord Elwyn Jones' view, the crucial factor in offences of assault, dictating that they were offences of basic intent, was that they could be committed recklessly. Thus, following *Majewski*, there was considerable doubt in relation to the factor which distinguished offences of specific intent from those of basic intent. The only way to be sure was to await a judicial decision in respect of each offence to discover into which category an offence was to be placed.

In *Caldwell* [1982] AC 341, Lord Diplock stated that *Majewski* is authority for the proposition that **'self-induced intoxication is no defence to a crime in which recklessness is enough to constitute the necessary *mens rea*'** (see also *Hardie* [1985] 1 WLR 64). This dictum in itself, however, does not precisely determine whether an offence is one of specific intent; rather it indicates that offences which may be committed recklessly are not. In *Heard* [2007] EWCA Crim 125, the Court of Appeal addressed the point.

> D was heavily intoxicated. He exposed his penis and rubbed it against the thigh of a police officer who arrested him for sexual assault contrary to s. 3(1) of the Sexual Offences Act 2003. At his trial D claimed to have no recollection of the event owing to his intoxication. He further sought to plead in his defence that his voluntary intoxication was a complete defence as it prevented him from having the intent to touch the officer which had to be proved under s. 3(1). The trial judge ruled that the s. 3(1) offence was one of basic intent and that consequently voluntary intoxication was not a defence. The Court of Appeal held first that the fact that he was disinhibited and did something he would not have done when sober, and the fact he could not recall the incident, did not lead to the conclusion that the touching was not intentional. A drunken intent was still an intent. If it could be said that the mind of the person charged with sexual assault had gone with his deliberate physical act of touching, the intoxication was irrelevant. Secondly, and *obiter*, they were satisfied that the fact that the offence could not be committed recklessly did not conclude the question whether this was an offence of specific intent. Crimes of specific intent are those where the offence requires proof of purpose or consequence, which includes crimes of ulterior intent. Sexual assault required no more than proof of a basic intent with the result that voluntary intoxication could not be relied upon to negate that intent.

The Court of Appeal placed reliance on Lord Simon in *DPP* v *Majewski* who drew a distinction between '**(i) intention as applied to acts considered in relation to their purposes and (ii) intention as applied to acts apart from their purposes'**. It would appear that **evidence of voluntary intoxication is only relevant and admissible where the offence is one of 'ulterior' intent** (e.g. burglary, see **14.2**) **or where the required intention relates to a prohibited consequence** (e.g. murder, see **9.2**). If the requirement of intention relates only to the performance of the prohibited act, in this case touching, then the offence remains one of basic intent for the purposes of intoxication. Thus basic intent is not limited to those offences where recklessness suffices. The Court, however, recognised that **there is no universally logical test for distinguishing between crimes in which voluntary intoxication can be advanced as a defence and those where it cannot**; there is a large element of policy and categorisation will be conducted on an offence-by-offence basis.

It follows that if the word 'intention' appears in the definition of an offence, it is necessary carefully to determine what needs to be 'intended' as, notwithstanding the appearance of the word 'intention', the offence may be one of basic intent. If the required intention relates to a prohibited consequence or if the required intention is 'ulterior' then the offence would appear to be one of 'specific intent'. If, however, the word 'intention' relates only to the performance of the prohibited act itself then the offence is one of basic intent. Proof in the instant case that the touching was voluntary (i.e. deliberate as opposed to accidental) was sufficient to establish liability. The offence of attempt falls within specific intent as although this is a conduct crime (the intended substantive offence not having been committed) the more than merely preparatory act is carried out purposively—i.e. with the purpose of committing the substantive offence. It is probable also that if *Heard* is followed, criminal damage/arson being reckless whether life is endangered will be categorised as an offence of specific intent as the state of mind goes to an ulterior or purposive element of the offence.

The approach adopted by the Court of Appeal in *Heard* is very much rooted in policy considerations. Prior to the enactment of the Sexual Offences Act 2003 the offence of indecent assault, which could be committed recklessly, was one of basic intent. The replacement offence of sexual assault under s. 3 of the 2003 Act requires proof of intentional touching. If the previous understanding of *Majewski* had been applied, this would be an offence of specific intent. As many sexual assaults are committed by persons who have consumed drink or drugs, such a change would have presented the possibility of intoxication being raised as a defence in many such cases. The Court of Appeal's reinterpretation of *Majewski* closes off that avenue of defence.

 Question

If D successfully pleads intoxication in respect of an offence requiring specific intent, will he thereby avoid criminal liability for his actions?

In cases of offences against the person where D successfully pleads intoxication in respect of an offence of specific intent, he will not avoid criminal liability as generally there will be an alternative offence of basic intent of which he may be convicted.

For example, if he is charged with murder, he may be convicted of manslaughter; if he is charged with wounding with intent to cause grievous bodily harm contrary to s. 18 of the Offences Against the Person Act 1861, he may be convicted of malicious wounding contrary to s. 20. If, however, he is charged with a property offence of specific intent (e.g. theft), there will generally be no alternative basic intent offence with which he may be charged. In some cases of burglary (which when charged under s. 9(1)(a) of the Theft Act 1968 is an offence of specific intent) D may have committed criminal damage (an offence of basic intent) to gain entry to the premises but many burglaries do not involve any damage.

The effect of the rules relating to voluntary intoxication is that if D is charged with an offence of basic intent a plea of intoxication will be fatal as it will relieve the prosecution of the duty of proving *mens rea*. It is still unclear whether the prosecution may seek to prove D's intoxication at the outset. There is nothing in the speeches in *Majewski* which would rule this out; as their Lordships treated intoxication as the equivalent of *mens rea* it could be argued that they implicitly accepted the propriety of the prosecution proving it. There is no reason of policy to object to this; if the reason for the intoxication rule is the desire to protect the public, that protection would be effectuated by permitting the prosecution to prove intoxication.

5.5.4 Degree of intoxication and jury direction

? Question

To rely on intoxication in his defence, must D be incapable of forming the requisite intent for the crime?

When intoxication is raised in defence to a crime of specific intent the question in issue is not whether the defendant was *incapable* of forming the intent, but whether, even if still capable, he did form that intent (see *Pordage* [1975] Crim LR 575; *Garlick* [1981] Crim LR 178). The burden of proof remains on the prosecution to prove beyond reasonable doubt that, regardless of the alleged intoxication, D formed the requisite intent (see *Sheehan and Moore* (1974) 60 Cr App R 308; *Pordage* [1975] Crim LR 575). In *Sheehan and Moore* the Court of Appeal made it clear that a direction based on *Beard* was not appropriate and was inconsistent with s. 8 of the Criminal Justice Act 1967 (see **3.2.3.1**). Geoffrey Lane LJ stated (at p. 312):

> [I]n cases where drunkenness and its possible effect on the defendant's *mens rea* is an issue, we think that the proper direction to a jury is, first, to warn them that the mere fact that the defendant's mind was affected by drink so that he acted in a way in which he would not have done had he been sober does not assist him at all, provided that the necessary intention was there. A drunken intent is nevertheless an intent . . . The jury should . . . be instructed to have regard to all the evidence, including that relating to drink, to draw such inferences as they think proper from the evidence, and on that basis to ask themselves whether they feel sure that at the material time the defendant had the requisite intent.

Where on a charge of an offence of specific intent evidence of intoxication emerges during the trial which might lead a reasonable jury to conclude that there is a reasonable possibility that D did not form the intent, whether or not D expressly raises it, the judge is under an obligation to direct the jury on this matter as intent is an essential element of the offence which the Crown has to prove (see *Bennett* [1995] Crim LR 877; *Brown and Stratton* [1998] Crim LR 485; cf. *Groark* [1999] Crim LR 669).

Two cases have undermined the clarity of this position (the Court of Appeal in *McKnight, The Times*, 5 May 2000 and the Privy Council in *Sooklal* v *The State of Trinidad and Tobago* [1999] 1 WLR 2011). The Court of Appeal and Privy Council in those cases asserted that evidence of intoxication must be to the effect that it rendered D *incapable* of forming the requisite intent rather than being relevant to the question of whether D actually *had* the requisite intent at the time of the alleged act form the requisite intent. It is submitted that the earlier decisions of the Court of Appeal are correct in principle and the decision in *McKnight* and the Privy Council decision in *Sooklal* are in error. If there is any evidence that D may not have formed the necessary intent due to intoxication this should be left to the jury as it relates to the crucial issue which the prosecution are under a burden to prove beyond reasonable doubt, namely *mens rea*.

5.5.5 The problem of Dutch courage

 Question

If D, having decided to commit a particular offence of specific intent, takes drink or drugs to give himself the courage to do so, may he rely on his intoxication at the time he committed the offence to establish that he did not have the *mens rea* required?

In *AG for Northern Ireland* v *Gallagher* [1963] AC 349, D decided to kill his wife and bought a knife and a bottle of whiskey. He drank the whiskey and killed his wife. He sought to argue in the alternative that he either was insane at the time he killed her or he was so drunk that he was incapable of forming the intent to do so. He was convicted of murder. In the House of Lords Lord Denning stated (at p. 382):

> If a man, whilst sane and sober, forms an intention to kill and makes preparation for it, knowing it is a wrong thing to do, and then gets himself drunk so as to give himself Dutch courage to do the killing, and whilst drunk carries out his intention, he cannot rely on this self-induced drunkenness as a defence to a charge of murder, nor even as reducing it to manslaughter. He cannot say that he got himself into such a stupid state that he was incapable of an intent to kill. . . . The wickedness of his mind before he got drunk is enough to condemn him, coupled with the act which he intended to do and did do.

While this may conflict with the requirement of contemporaneity between *actus reus* and *mens rea*, it is an exception justifiable on grounds of policy. As Smith and Hogan argue (*Criminal Law* (13th edn, 2011), at p. 326), if D had used an innocent agent to commit the murder he would have been liable and thus D in his responsible state should be liable for the acts he intended should be done in his irresponsible state.

5.5.6 Intoxication and defences

 Question

When people are intoxicated they may misunderstand or misperceive things and then react in this light. Does this mean they could rely on their drunken mistakes to raise a defence which would not have been available to them if they had been sober?

5.5.6.1 **Duress**

If an accused is relying on a defence of duress and claims that he made a mistake because of his intoxicated condition so that, for example, he believed he was under threat when in fact there was no threat, his drunken mistake will not avail him as it will necessarily be unreasonable (see **6.2.3**).

5.5.6.2 **Loss of control**

For the provocation defence, D could not rely on his intoxication as a reason for his loss of self-control; he was expected to exercise the self-control of a sober and reasonable person (see *Newell* (1980) 71 Cr App R 331). Under the defence of loss of self-control, intoxication is also irrelevant along with all other circumstances whose only effect is to reduce D's capacity for tolerance or self-restraint (see s. 54(3) of the Coroners and Justice Act 2009; **9.3.2.2.3**). This does not mean that D cannot plead loss of self-control if he was intoxicated at the time of the killing. It means that if a sober individual in the defendant's circumstances, with a 'normal degree of tolerance and self-restraint' (see s. 54(1)(c)) would not have behaved in the same way as the defendant when confronted by the relevant qualifying trigger, the defence will fail. However, if a defendant with a severe problem with alcohol or drugs had been mercilessly taunted about the condition, to the extent that it constituted a qualifying trigger, the alcohol or drug problem would then form part of the circumstances for consideration: *R v Asmelash* [2013] EWCA Crim 157.

5.5.6.3 **Self-defence**

Where a defence is one of justification, such as self-defence, a mistaken belief in respect of the circumstances upon which the defence is founded will not ordinarily deprive D of the right to rely on that defence provided the belief was honestly held; there is no requirement that it also be reasonable (see *Williams (Gladstone)* (1984) 78 Cr App R 276; Criminal Justice and Immigration Act 2008, s. 76(4); **3.6.1.1.2**). The effect of mistake in such a case is to negate the *mens rea* for the offence as the definition of the offence (whether it be murder, malicious wounding, assault, etc.) requires that the act be done *unlawfully*; if D believes he is acting in self-defence he does not intend to act *unlawfully*.

 Example

D, genuinely believing that V is about to kill him, defends himself from the anticipated attack and kills V. D should not be guilty of murder as he did not intend unlawfully to kill V or cause him grievous bodily harm.

If D's mistake was a drunken one, one would expect that he should still be able to rely upon it as the offence of murder is one requiring a specific intent.

In *O'Grady* [1987] 3 WLR 321, however, the Court of Appeal took a different view. Lord Lane CJ considered that in such cases there was no difference between offences of basic intent and those of specific intent. Contradicting his own judgment in *Williams* (although he did not appear to realise this), he stated that the issue of mistake should be considered separately from that of intent. This is, to say the least, a novel idea; it is also fatuous as if a person is mistaken he does not have the requisite intent, mistake and intent being simply two sides of the same coin. In Lord Lane's view, however, where the jury are satisfied that the defendant was mistaken in his belief that any force, or the force which he in fact used, was necessary to defend himself and are further satisfied that the mistake was caused by voluntarily induced intoxication, the defence must fail. The anomalous result of this decision, however, is that if D, when drunk, shoots at what he believes to be a stag but it turns out to be a person, he may plead intoxication in response to a charge of murder as this will be relevant in considering whether he had the specific intent to kill or seriously injure a person whereas, if D, when drunk, mistakenly believes that V is about to kill him and he shoots and kills V, he will be found guilty of murder.

O'Grady was followed by the Court of Appeal in *O'Connor* [1991] Crim LR 135, where the Court held that intoxication was irrelevant to the question whether D believed he was acting in self-defence. The conviction for murder was quashed, however, as the trial judge had not directed the jury to take account of D's intoxication when considering whether he had formed the specific intent to cause grievous bodily harm. What better illustration of the illogicality of the *O'Grady* decision could there be? A jury might be forgiven for thinking that a trial judge had taken leave of his senses following a direction that they must ignore D's intoxication when considering whether he believed he was acting in self-defence, but that his intoxication must be taken into account in deciding whether he intended to kill or cause grievous bodily harm. In *Hatton* [2005] EWCA Crim 2951, the Court of Appeal confirmed that the conclusion in *O'Grady* was a general one and it is not open to a defendant to rely on a mistake induced by voluntary intoxication as a basis for raising self-defence whether the charge was murder or manslaughter.

While Lord Lane's judgment in *O'Grady* is unsupportable in terms of principle it was, in fact, a policy decision. Lord Lane considered that where V has, through no fault of his own, been injured or killed because of a drunken mistake, '[r]eason recoils from the conclusion that in such circumstances a defendant is entitled to leave the Court without a stain on his character'. In fact, a defendant would not leave the court without a conviction as he could be convicted of an offence of basic intent. In *O'Grady* D was convicted of manslaughter at first instance. In such circumstances a manslaughter verdict could be returned either because manslaughter is an offence of basic intent and thus intoxication supplies the *mens rea* for unlawful act manslaughter, or on the basis that D's mistake was grossly negligent, thereby founding a charge of gross negligence manslaughter.

Confusion in this area is compounded by the Court of Appeal decision in *Richardson and Irwin* [1999] 1 Cr App R 392.

> D and E as a drunken prank seized V, their friend whom they claimed they believed was consenting, and held him over a balcony. V fell sustaining several broken bones and D and E were charged with unlawfully and maliciously inflicting GBH contrary to s. 20 of the Offences Against the Person Act 1861. Unbelievably the Court of Appeal held that D's and E's convictions should be quashed as the trial judge should have directed the jury that, when considering the question of consent, they should have taken account of evidence that the defendants' minds were affected by alcohol.

Section 20 is an offence of basic intent and one would have expected the Court to rule that intoxication is irrelevant on such a charge. This decision, however, gives rise to the strange anomaly that D's intoxication relieves the prosecution of the need to prove foresight of some harm but does not relieve them of the need to prove absence of a belief in consent. This decision is consistent with the questionable authority of *Aitken* [1992] 1 WLR 1006 (see **10.3.2**) but the Court of Appeal did not consider the cases of *O'Grady* [1987] 3 WLR 321 or *O'Connor* [1991] Crim LR 135. The authority of *Richardson and Irwin*, accordingly, must be open to doubt. It is certainly difficult to find any policy reason to support the decision, particularly when one considers that, had D and E not been drunk, they would not have made the mistake regarding V's consent and most probably would not have engaged in such dangerous horseplay.

Section 76 of the Criminal Justice and Immigration Act 2008 re-states the common law principles on self-defence. Section 76(5) states that D is not able to rely on any mistaken belief attributable to intoxication that was voluntarily induced. In *Taj (Simon)* [2018] EWCA Crim 1743, the Court of Appeal was confronted with the issue of mistaken self-defence where D's mistake was caused by drug-induced psychosis. D was suffering from a drug- or alcohol-induced psychotic disorder at the time of the offence but he was not intoxicated at that time and there was no evidence of him having recently consumed alcohol or drugs. Taj attacked an electrician whose van had broken down, mistakenly believing (and having no reasonable grounds for believing) that the man was involved in terrorist activity. He was charged with attempted murder and the trial judge withdrew the issue of self-defence as D was suffering from a direct reaction to the voluntary taking of intoxicants consumed in the weeks preceding the incident. Giving the judgment in the Court of Appeal, Sir Brian Leveson P held the trial judge had been right to withdraw self-defence, stating (at para. 56):

> *DPP v Majewski* focused on crime committed while specifically under the influence of drugs or alcohol. Having said that, however, it is difficult to see why the language (and the policy identified) is not equally apposite to **the immediate and proximate consequences of such misuse**. That is not to say that long standing mental illness which might at some stage have been triggered by misuse of drugs or alcohol would be covered. The point is that a defendant who is suffering the immediate effects of alcohol or drugs in the system is, in truth, not in a different position to a defendant who has triggered or precipitated an immediate psychotic illness as a consequence of **proximate ingestion** of or drugs in the system whether or not they remain present at the time of the offence.' [Emphasis added]

The Court noted that medical science has advanced such that the longer term consequences of abusing alcohol or drugs are better understood. In the present case, D's paranoia that led to the mistaken belief that the victim was a terrorist was a direct result of D's drinking and drug-taking in previous days and weeks. The words 'attributable to intoxication' in s. 76(5) are broad enough to encompass a mistaken state of mind that results from being drunk or intoxicated at the time and:

> a mistaken state of mind immediately and proximately consequent upon earlier drink or drug-taking, so that even though the person concerned is not drunk or intoxicated at the time, the short-term effects can be shown to have triggered subsequent episodes of e.g. paranoia. (para. 57)

While this broad reading of s. 76(5) is defensible on grounds of both policy and simple statutory interpretation, it might effectively deny the opportunity of pleading self-defence to those defendants who are more properly viewed as suffering from mental disorder rather blameworthy under the deterrence-based intoxication rules. This approach was evident in *Harris* [2013] EWCA Crim 223. D was charged with the aggravated form of arson, in that he started a fire being reckless as to whether the life of another would thereby be endangered. He argued that he had not given any thought to the risk arising from starting a fire because of a mental disorder, alcoholic psychosis, that was caused by sudden cessation of a prolonged period of heavy drinking. At the time of starting the fire, D was not intoxicated. The trial judge ruled that this was a case of voluntary intoxication but in quashing his conviction, Lord Hughes CJ said:

> [T]here is scope for the argument that an illness caused by his own fault ought as a matter of policy to be treated in the same way as is drunkenness at the time of the offence. This would, however, represent a significant extension of *DPP* v *Majewski* . . . But in the present state of the law, *Majewski* applies to offences committed by persons who are then voluntarily intoxicated but not to those who are suffering mental illness. This defendant was, it is clear, suffering from a condition of mental illness when he set fire to his own house.

In *Taj*, the Court of Appeal distinguished *Harris* on the ground that Taj's paranoia was the direct and proximate result of his immediately prior *consumption* of drink and drugs, rather than being a result of the cessation of such consumption. Lord Leveson saw the Court's decision in *Taj* as a simple 'application of *Majewski*, rather than an extension of that decision, or at the highest, a most incremental extension' (para. 57).

5.5.6.4 Criminal damage and lawful excuse

To add further to the confusion in the area of intoxication and defences, the courts apply different principles to specific statutory defences which provide that a particular belief provides a defence to the charge.

> In *Jaggard* v *Dickinson* [1980] 3 All ER 716, D went to a house which she believed belonged to E. She believed, correctly, that E would not object to her breaking into his house. D was drunk, however, and had gone to the wrong house. D was convicted of criminal damage and appealed, contending that, despite her intoxication, she was entitled to rely on the defence of lawful excuse in s. 5(2) and (3) of the Criminal Damage Act 1971. This provides that a person has a lawful excuse if he believes that the person entitled to consent to the damage would have done so had he known of the circumstances, and that it is 'immaterial whether a belief is justified or not if it is honestly held'. As criminal damage is an offence of basic intent D could not have relied on her intoxication to negative her *mens rea*. The Divisional Court, however, held that she could rely on her intoxication as Parliament had 'specifically required the Court to consider the defendant's actual state of belief, not the state of belief which ought to have existed'. The Court considered a belief may be honestly held whether it stems from intoxication, stupidity, forgetfulness, or inattention. Thus D's intoxication was relevant to the defence of lawful excuse for 'it helped to explain what would otherwise have been inexplicable, and hence lent colour to her evidence about the state of her belief'.

The anomalous result of this decision is that if D damages A's property believing, because of a drunken mistake, that it is his own, he will be guilty of criminal damage as this is an offence of basic intent and his drunkenness will substitute for *mens rea*, whereas, if he damages A's property believing, because of a drunken mistake, that it is B's and that B would consent to him doing so, he will have a defence.

In *Magee v CPS* [2014] EWHC 4089 (Admin), D, who was intoxicated, failed to stop after an accident. D was convicted of failing to report an accident, contrary to s. 170(4) of the Road Traffic Act 1988 despite contending that because of her intoxication she did not realise an accident had occurred. D appealed her conviction to the Divisional Court where Elias J highlighted the doubt whether *Jaggard* is still good law. Elias J confined the application of *Jaggard* to the defence under s. 5 of the Criminal Damage Act 1971 whereas for the s. 170(4) offence, he stated (at para 35):

> [T]he onus is on the defendant to negate the natural inference that once the accident has occurred she will have been aware of it. It seems to me that there is no reason why the common law should be construed so as to allow her to pray in aid her own state of drunkenness as the reason for the mistake, and there is every reason of policy why it should not be extended in that way.

5.5.6.5 Intoxication causing insanity

If D's drinking or drug-taking produces a disease of the mind, such as delirium tremens, he may be found insane under the M'Naghten Rules. In *Davis* (1881) 14 Cox CC 563, D raised the defence of insanity based on delirium tremens arising from a history of excessive drinking, although he was sober at the time of the offence. In directing the jury Stephen J stated (at p. 564):

> [D]runkenness is one thing and diseases to which drunkenness leads are different things; and if a man by drunkenness brings on a state of disease which causes such a degree of madness, even for a time, which would have relieved him from responsibility if it had been caused in any other way, then he would not be criminally responsible.

This direction was approved in *Beard* and *Gallagher*. In *Gallagher* there was evidence that D was suffering from psychopathy. The effect of this disease of the mind was to weaken the sufferer's powers of self-control, and this would be aggravated by drink. An impairment of the power of self-control does not fall within the M'Naghten Rules although it is relevant to a defence of diminished responsibility (see *Byrne*, **9.3.2.1**). The House of Lords made it clear that if D's disease of the mind did not bring him within the M'Naghten Rules, this defect could not be rectified by taking into account the aggravating effect of alcohol. It is necessary for the alcohol to cause the disease of the mind and for this to result in the accused either not knowing what he is doing or not knowing that it is wrong.

In *Coley* [2013] EWCA Crim 223, the Court of Appeal had to consider the borderline between insanity and voluntary intoxication.

> D, having taken strong cannabis and possibly suffering a psychotic episode, entered V's house wearing a balaclava and wielding a knife and caused terrible injuries to V. D claimed to have 'blacked out' and there was some suggestion that he may have been

acting out a scenario from a computer game. D sought to plead insanity but the trial judge refused to leave this defence (or the issue of automatism) to the jury, ruling that it was a case of voluntary intoxication; any possible mental abnormality arose from an external cause and was self-induced. On appeal by D the Court of Appeal addressed the issues of insanity and automatism. On the former Hughes LJ stated (at para. 18):

> The precise line between the law of voluntary intoxication and the law of insanity may . . . be difficult to identify in some borderline cases. But the present case falls comfortably on the side of the line covered by voluntary intoxication. . . . If the doctors were right about his state of mind, his mind was to an extent detached from reality by the direct and acute effects on it of the ingestion of cannabis. Every intoxicated person has his mind affected, and to an extent disordered, by the direct and acute effects of the ingestion of intoxicants; all intoxication operates through the brain. Not infrequently it would be perfectly legitimate to say of a very drunken man that his mind had become detached from reality by the intoxication. . . . In order to engage the law of insanity, it is not enough that there is an effect on the mind, or, in the language of the *M'Naghten* rules, a 'defect of reason'. There must also be what the law classifies as a disease of the mind. Direct acute effects on the mind of intoxicants, voluntarily taken, are not so classified. . . . [The appellant's counsel's] superficially simple argument amounts to treating every 'defect of reason' as a 'disease of the mind', but that is not the law.

If D had suffered a 'defect of reason' it arose from his voluntary intoxication. He had rendered himself an automaton; his position was covered by *Quick* [1973] QB 910, the defence of automatism not being available where D has induced his involuntary behaviour by his own fault. The decision by the judge, not to leave automatism to the jury in order to avoid unnecessary complication, was not in error as the jury had to be satisfied that D had formed an intention to kill (and thus that he had acted voluntarily) before they could return a verdict of guilty of attempted murder. The medical witnesses, although hypothesising that D had acted during a psychotic episode and had been affected by delusions or hallucinations, indicated that he would still have been capable of complex organised behaviour—in this case deciding to dress, arm himself with a knife, find the keys to V's house, and let himself in. The Court was satisfied that this was not capable of being described as involuntary action; and whether or not he was acting under a delusion or some other psychotic detachment from reality, the medical evidence indicated he was conscious and in voluntary control of his limbs. The fact that his actions might be irrational was of no relevance as any irrationality was due to his own fault.

5.5.6.6 Intoxication and diminished responsibility

If D pleads diminished responsibility based on an abnormality of mental functioning (see **9.3.2.1.3**) due to some cause other than intoxication, the jury must ignore the effects of D's intoxication when seeking to decide whether the abnormality of mental functioning substantially impaired his ability to understand the nature of his conduct, to form a rational judgement, or to exercise self-control. Alcohol dependency syndrome may amount to an abnormality of mental functioning arising from a medical condition if it substantially impairs D's ability to do one of those three things. For detailed discussion of the relevance of intoxication for the diminished responsibility defence, see **9.3.2.1.4**.

5.5.7 Involuntary intoxication

? Question

What happens when D becomes intoxicated involuntarily?

Involuntary intoxication may arise in three different ways. It may arise where D is drugged by others or his drink is laced with alcohol. Secondly, it may arise from him taking drugs which have been medically prescribed, provided he has taken these drugs in accordance with the instructions. In both these cases he may, in his defence, rely on his intoxication to negative *mens rea* whether the offence be one of specific or basic intent. **If however, D is proved to have formed the requisite *mens rea* for the offence, he will be convicted and the issue of involuntary intoxication will be a mitigating factor in relation to his sentence** (see *Kingston* (1994) 99 Cr App R 286). It is no defence to plead that he would never have committed the offence when sober if he nonetheless formed the requisite *mens rea* in his intoxicated state (see *Davies* [1983] Crim LR 741). If D knows he is drinking alcohol but is mistaken as to its strength, this does not render his intoxication involuntary (see *Allen* [1988] Crim LR 698).

The third situation where intoxication may be treated as involuntary is where D takes a non-dangerous drug, provided he was not reckless in taking the drug.

> In *Hardie* [1985] 1 WLR 64, D was charged with criminal damage with intent to endanger life or being reckless whether life was endangered contrary to s. 1(2) of the Criminal Damage Act 1971. He claimed he did not have the requisite *mens rea* due to intoxication arising from taking Valium tablets given to him by another person, who told him that they would do him no harm. On D's appeal against conviction the Court of Appeal held that *Majewski* did not apply. Unlike alcohol and other dangerous drugs which are liable to cause unpredictability or aggressiveness and thus give rise to the conclusive presumption of recklessness, it was not generally known that taking Valium 'would be liable to render a person aggressive or incapable of appreciating risks or have other side effects such that its self-administration would itself have an element of recklessness'. The correct direction to the jury would have been 'that if they came to the conclusion that, as a result of the Valium, the appellant was, at the time, unable to appreciate the risks to property and persons from his actions they should then consider whether the taking of the Valium was itself reckless'.

The Court derived support from *Bailey* (see **5.4.3**). The test of recklessness would thus appear to require subjective awareness, at the time of taking the drug, of the risk of becoming unpredictable, dangerous, aggressive, or incapable of appreciating risks to others; there is no need to prove foresight of the particular risk which eventuates. The Court did say, however, that the taking of a soporific or sedative drug would not be an answer to a charge of, for example, reckless driving (and, presumably, dangerous driving contrary to s. 2 of the Road Traffic Act 1988).

5.5.8 Proposals for reform

The Butler Committee (Cmnd 6244, 1975) proposed the creation of a new offence of dangerous intoxication. Where an accused was acquitted of a 'dangerous offence' because he lacked the requisite *mens rea* due to voluntary intoxication, a jury would be able to convict him of dangerous intoxication. This alternative offence would be available where D was charged with any offence involving injury to the person or death or consisting of a sexual attack on another, or involving the destruction of, or causing damage to, property so as to endanger life. The maximum sentence on such a conviction would be one year's imprisonment on a first offence and three years for a subsequent offence. The problem with such a conviction, however, is that it does not distinguish between the types of dangerous offences which D may have committed. A minority of the Criminal Law Revision Committee in its Fourteenth Report, *Offences Against the Person*, proposed a modification of the Butler Committee proposal. They proposed that the jury should return a special verdict that D had done the act alleged in a state of intoxication—in effect, 'Guilty but intoxicated'. The court would have the same sentencing powers as are available on conviction for the alleged offence but would be able to reflect the culpability of D in the sentence it pronounces. This verdict would also reflect the actual harm done by D.

The Law Commission in its Consultation Paper No. 127, *Intoxication and Criminal Liability* (HMSO, 1993) recommended the abolition of the *Majewski* rule and the creation of a new offence of criminal intoxication. In its final Report, *Legislating the Criminal Code: Intoxication and Criminal Liability* (Law Com No. 229 (HMSO, 1995)), the Law Commission retreated from this position following the consultation process in which the majority of the judges of the Queen's Bench Division opposed the proposal expressing the view that abolition of the *Majewski* rule would be perceived by the public as unacceptable (para. 1.27) and they, along with others, asserted that the present law did not, in fact, present difficulties to juries and that it worked fairly and without any undue difficulty (para. 1.28). The Law Commission, accordingly, recommended codifying the common law with minor modifications. The draft bill which accompanied the report was, however, unnecessarily complex and thus could hardly be promoted as an improvement on the existing state of the law. The Government duly rejected it in its Consultation Paper, *Violence: Reforming the Offences Against the Person Act 1861* (February 1998 (see **10.10**)).

In 2009, the Law Commission returned to the subject of intoxication in *Intoxication and Criminal Liability* (Law Com No. 314, Cm 7526) which again sought to codify the main principles of the common law but in a more straightforward way. Essentially the Law Commission proposed the retention of the distinction between specific and basic intent offences but it changed the terminology. Where D is voluntarily intoxicated when he commits the external elements of an offence, his intoxication may be relevant to his liability depending upon whether or not the offence is one requiring a fault element greater than subjective recklessness. Five subjective fault elements were specified which the prosecution would have to prove regardless of D's state of intoxication.

These are:

- intention as to a consequence
- knowledge as to something
- belief as to something (where the belief is equivalent to knowledge as to something)
- fraud
- dishonesty.

Under the proposals, for offences for which a lesser fault element is required, D's intoxication at the material time will mean that he will be treated as having been aware of anything of which he would have been aware but for his intoxication. Thus proof of intoxication at the material time substitutes for proof of *mens rea*— that is, the fault element. This is justified on the basis that by becoming voluntarily intoxicated D has made himself dangerous in disregard of public safety, which is:

> morally equivalent to having the fault element of recklessness as to others' safety. Consequently D is to be regarded as having acted with a sufficient fault element to warrant a conviction for the offence. (para. 2.45)

The Commission proposed no change to the common law as regards drunken mistakes and defences. Likewise no change was proposed in respect of involuntary intoxication. The Report did venture into new territory, however, in seeking to place on a statutory basis the law where D is a secondary party, or involved in a joint enterprise, or where he is charged with an offence of encouraging or assisting another person to commit a crime. Here the recommendations descend into complexity with the prospect that the criticisms of the Law Commission's previous Report could apply equally here. Indeed, the Government rejected the proposals, on the basis that they were scarcely more intelligible than the current law and might make it more complex (see Rebecca Williams, 'Voluntary Intoxication—a Lost Cause?' (2013) 129 LQR 264–89).

 The law in context

Mental health and criminal justice

Defendants and offenders with mental disorders pose a challenge for the criminal justice system. As Webb and Harris put it, they are 'categorically awkward; being neither exclusively ill nor uncomplicatedly bad such defendants and offenders totter between two not always compatible discourses of state intervention' (*The Oxford Handbook of Criminology* (2007), p. 496). On one hand, the allegation of an offence having been committed requires proper investigation and eventual sanctioning, to reflect the harm caused to the victim and promote public confidence in the criminal process. On the other, mental disorder might mean that the defendant has little or no culpability. It might also mean that retributive punishment would be meaningless (in that the offender would not understand the State's condemnation) or ineffective (in that rehabilitation and treatment might be the only effective way of preventing reoffending).

Unfortunately there is a lack of information about what actually happens to mentally disordered defendants and offenders as they progress through the criminal process. The Bradley Report (*Review of People with Mental Health Problems or Learning Disabilities in the Criminal Justice System*, 2009, p. 60) noted that there are few reliable research studies that have looked at the prevalence of mental disorders in the criminal justice system. We do know that many mentally disordered defendants come before the courts and most do not fall within the legal definition of insanity. English substantive law treats them the same as those without mental disorder, but in terms of criminal procedure before, during and after the trial, the law does make special provision, as we saw earlier in this chapter.

→

→

Formal government policy has for many years been to divert mentally disordered suspects from the criminal justice system. Home Office Circular 66/90 stresses the desirability of ensuring effective co-operation between agencies so that the best use is made of resources and that mentally disordered persons are not prosecuted where this is not required by the public interest. It is 'desirable that alternatives to prosecution, such as cautioning by the police, and/or admission to hospital, if the person's mental condition requires hospital treatment, or support in the community, should be considered first before deciding that prosecution is necessary' (p. 2). Home Office Circular 12/95 encourages inter-agency working between criminal justice agencies, health services, and social services. In reality though, community mental health services are underfunded, meaning access to them is becoming harder for *non*-offenders, let alone offenders.

At the prosecution stage, Circular 66/90 reminds the CPS that 'careful consideration' should be given to whether prosecution of suspects with mental disorders is in the public interest. Under the Code for Crown Prosecutors (2018: https://www.cps.gov.uk/publication/code-crown-prosecutors), the CPS must 'have regard when considering culpability as to whether the suspect is, or was at the time of the offence, affected by any significant mental or physical ill health or disability as in some circumstances this may mean that it is less likely that a prosecution is required' (para. 4.14). However, the difficulty posed by mentally disordered defendants is evident in that the Code reminds prosecutors they also need to consider 'how serious the offence was, whether the suspect is likely to re-offend and the need to safeguard the public or those providing care to such persons' (para. 4.14).

English law does have special provisions for sentencing mentally disordered offenders. Mental disorder in this context is defined in the Mental Health Act 1983 (as amended) as 'any disorder or disability of the mind' (s. 1). The definition excludes dependence on alcohol or drugs and some types of learning disabilities. This definition is important, as it governs who is affected by the special legal procedures for defendants and offenders with mental disorders. Circular 66/90 states that where prosecution is necessary it is important to find suitable non-penal disposals wherever appropriate. Section 166 of the Criminal Justice Act 2003 states that a court can take into account any such matters as it considers relevant in mitigation of sentence. Section 166(5) reminds sentencers that the threshold test for imposing custody (that the offence is so serious that only such a sentence is warranted) does not oblige them to pass such a custodial sentence on a mentally disordered offender or restrict any such powers to deal with the offender in the way the court considers most appropriate. Section 157 states that in any case where the offender is or appears to be mentally disordered, the court must obtain and consider a medical report before it passes a custodial sentence (other than in murder cases), unless the court is of the opinion that it is unnecessary to obtain one. Section 157(3) requires courts to consider, before passing a custodial sentence on an offender who is or appears to be mentally disordered, 'the likely effect of such a sentence on that condition and on any treatment which may be available for it'.

Courts can impose a mental health treatment requirement as part of a community order (see **Chapter 1**) under s. 177 of the Criminal Justice Act 2003. However, Scott and Moffat found that the use of such requirements is 'startlingly low' and Khanom et al. found that there is 'a striking lack of awareness' of the options available for dealing with MDOs amongst sentencers and other court officials (Scott and Moffat, 'The Mental Health Treatment Requirement: Realising a Better Future' (2012) (Centre for Mental Health/Criminal Justice Alliance) https://www.centreformentalhealth.org.uk/publications/mental-health-treatment-requirement; Khanom et al., 'A Missed Opportunity? Community Sentences and the Mental Health Treatment Requirement' (2009) (London: Sainsbury Centre for Mental Health) http://www.ohrn.nhs.uk/resource/policy/MissedOpportunity.pdf). The prison population has significantly

→

→

higher levels of mental disorder than the general population. The Bradley Report noted that 8 per cent of prisoners suffer from schizophrenia and delusional disorders, compared to 0.5 per cent of the general population; 66 per cent of prisoners have a personality disorder, compared to 5.3 per cent of the general population. The prevalence of psychiatric disorder is even higher among young offenders and juveniles, with 95 per cent suffering from mental disorder, substance misuse problems, or both (The Bradley Report, p. 98). Some argue that this indicates the criminal justice system takes inappropriate account of mental health at the pre-trial and trial stages, that the system is not diverting appropriately, and that prosecutors too readily find that mental disorder is outweighed by other factors in favour of prosecution. Another interpretation is that prosecutors and sentencers have to balance the fact of mental disorder with the seriousness of the offence. In many cases, the offender's mental disorder will be incidental to the offence (e.g. a burglar might coincidentally have severe depression).

The practical reality is that mental health is a pervasive problem for our criminal justice system, from the work of the police on the streets to the overcrowding in our prisons, but despite repeated calls from campaigning groups such as the Howard League for Penal Reform there seems little prospect of a Government moving from a punitive approach to a more rehabilitative one that focuses on treatment and crime prevention before punishment.

 Key Points

AGE

- The age of criminal responsibility in England and Wales is 10.
- The doctrine of *doli incapax* no longer exists.

INSANITY

- Insanity is relevant at the time D is arraigned, as an accused may be found 'unfit to plead' (ss. 4 and 4A of the Criminal Procedure (Insanity) Act 1964).
- A person who is legally insane will receive the special verdict of 'not guilty by reason of insanity' (s. 2 of the Trial of Lunatics Act 1883).
- The tests for insanity were set out in the *M'Naghten Rules* (1843):
  - D was suffering from a disease of the mind, which is a legal not medical term;
  - that gave rise to a defect of reason;
  - as a result, he either did not know the nature and quality of his act or he did not know that what he was doing was wrong.

AUTOMATISM

- Automatism refers to the state of unconsciousness or impaired consciousness in which a person acts involuntarily.
- If the prosecution cannot prove beyond reasonable doubt that D's conduct was voluntary, he will be acquitted.
- It is not sufficient that D's mind was acting imperfectly; what is required is that D's mind is not controlling his limbs at all.

→

→

- The courts have drawn a dividing line between insane automatism (where the cause is internal, such as a disease) and non-insane automatism (where the cause is external to D, such as concussion resulting from a blow to the head).

- Where automatism is self-induced (e.g. through voluntary intoxication), that may negative *mens rea* for crimes of specific intent, but will not avail D if the crime with which he is charged is one of basic intent.

- Self-induced automatism may lead to D's acquittal if the cause is other than intoxication by alcohol or drugs that are known to be dangerous. The test is whether D knew that his actions or inaction were likely to make him aggressive, unpredictable, or uncontrolled (*Bailey* (1983)).

INTOXICATION

- For offences of specific intent, intoxication is relevant to the question of whether D had *mens rea* (*DPP* v *Majewski* (1977)).

- For offences of basic intent, self-induced intoxication is no defence. If D argues at trial that he was so intoxicated he lacked *mens rea*, that admission in itself supplies evidence of *mens rea* (*Caldwell* (1982)).

- A drunken intent is still an intent. There is no separate defence of involuntary intoxication: *Kingston* (1994). Evidence of involuntary intoxication will simply be relevant to the question of whether D had *mens rea*.

FURTHER READING

J. Child, 'Drink, Drugs and Law Reform: A Review of the Law Commission Report No. 314' [2009] Crim LR 488.

S. Gardner, 'The Importance of *Majewski*' [1984] OJLS 279.

M. Gibson, 'Intoxicants and Diminished Responsibility: The Impact of the Coroners and Justice Act 2009' [2011] Crim LR 909.

A. Loughnan, 'Between Fairness and "Dangerousness": Reforming the Law on Unfitness to Plead' [2016] Crim LR 451.

R. D. Mackay, 'Fact and Fiction about the Insanity Defence' [1990] Crim LR 247.

R. D. Mackay, 'Righting the Wrong?—Some Observations on the Second Limb of the M'Naghten Rules' [2009] Crim LR 80.

R. D. Mackay, 'The Coroners and Justice Act 2009—Partial Defences to Murder: (2) The New Diminished Responsibility Plea' [2010] Crim LR 290.

R. D. Mackay, 'Ten More Years of the Insanity Defence' [2012] Crim LR 946.

R. D. Mackay and G. Kearns, 'More Fact(s) about the Insanity Defence' [1999] Crim LR 714.

R. D. Mackay and B. J. Mitchell, 'Sleepwalking, Automatism and Insanity' [2006] Crim LR 901.

R. D. Mackay, B. J. Mitchell, and L. Howe, 'Yet More Facts about the Insanity Defence' [2006] Crim LR 399.

E. Paton, 'Reformulating the Intoxication Rules: The Law Commission's Report' [1995] Crim LR 382.

J. Peay, 'Insanity and Automatism: Questions from and about the Law Commission's Scoping Paper' [2012] Crim LR 927.

J. Rumbold and M. Wasik, 'Diabetic Drivers, Hypoglycaemic Unawareness, and Automatism' [2011] Crim LR 863.

C. Walsh, 'Irrational Presumptions of Rationality and Comprehension' [1998] 3 Web JCLI.

S. White, 'The Criminal Procedure (Insanity and Unfitness to Plead) Act' [1992] Crim LR 4.

W. Wilson et al., 'Violence, Sleepwalking and the Criminal Law: (1) The Medical Aspects' [2005] Crim LR 601.

W. Wilson et al., 'Violence, Sleepwalking and the Criminal Law: (2) The Legal Aspects' [2005] Crim LR 614.

6

General defences

6.1 Introduction

When D is being tried for an offence and the prosecution have sought to prove that he committed the *actus reus* with the requisite *mens rea*, he may respond by giving an explanation—for example, that he acted under an honest mistake or that he brought about the prohibited consequence accidentally. In common parlance such explanations are referred to as defences. This is, however, inaccurate as such explanations are simply assertions that the prosecution have failed to establish an element of the *actus reus* or the *mens rea* of the offence. By contrast, general defences, such as duress, involve D in conceding that he did commit the *actus reus* and that he intended to bring it about but assert that he should be excused for so doing.

 Key Point

Where a defence operates as an excuse D's culpability is negated and he is excused from the normal consequences of conviction and sentencing which would flow from commission of the prohibited act with the requisite *mens rea*. Thus an excuse operates as a shield protecting D from conviction and sentence.

Self-defence and prevention of crime are also usually classified as general defences. If raised successfully such a plea provides a justification for D's use of force.

 Key Point

Where a defence operates as a justification the wrongfulness of D's conduct is negated as his conduct is considered to have been an appropriate course of action in the circumstances in which he found himself. Thus a plea of justification operates to cancel the unlawfulness of D's conduct; there being no unlawful act, there is thus no crime of which to convict him.

Such assertions, accordingly, are not strictly speaking defences but they will be dealt with in this chapter for convenience.

> ### ? Question
>
> Does it matter whether a defence operates as a justification or an excuse?

Whether the defence acts as an excuse or a justification is, from the point of view of D, irrelevant; in either case he is acquitted. It may, however, be important to others that the nature of the defence be determined as it is possible to be convicted of aiding and abetting an accused who is acquitted by reason of an excuse but not one who is acquitted by reason of a justification. In the latter case there is no offence to aid and abet. It is also thought that conduct which is merely excusable may be resisted by a person threatened by it whereas if the conduct is justifiable it is thought that, in some circumstances, it may not be resisted. This is phrased so tentatively because of the complexities which may arise, as the following example illustrates.

> ### 🖉 Example
>
> PC, a plainclothes police officer, has reasonable grounds for suspecting that an offence has been committed and he has reasonable grounds for suspecting that D is guilty of it. He seeks to arrest D as he believes he has reasonable grounds to do so under s. 24(5) of the Police and Criminal Evidence Act 1984. D has not committed any offence and when he sees PC approach him he fears he is about to be assaulted and tries to run off. PC performs a rugby tackle on D, seeking to use reasonable force to arrest an offender under s. 3(1) of the Criminal Law Act 1967. D, believing he is being unlawfully attacked, punches PC breaking his nose. If D is charged with unlawfully and maliciously inflicting grievous bodily harm (GBH) on PC contrary to s. 20 of the Offences Against the Person Act 1861 he could plead self-defence, as he was unaware of PC's identity, but if PC had been in uniform it is thought that he could not resist arrest even though he had not committed any offence.

Classifying defences is important for another reason; it is possible to limit the scope of defences which operate as excuses by confining their operation to certain offences. In effect the courts are saying that certain types of conduct are excusable in some circumstances but other types of conduct are not excusable in any circumstances.

When D pleads one of these general defences there is a burden on him to lay a proper evidential foundation for the defence, making it a fit and proper issue for the jury to consider. In some cases the facts from which the defence might reasonably be inferred may have emerged in the testimony of prosecution witnesses. If not, D must discharge this evidential burden by testifying himself and/or calling witnesses to testify with regard to the defence, thereby making it a live issue in the trial. If this burden is discharged (which is a decision for the judge), the prosecution then have the burden of disproving the defence. If the prosecution fail to discharge this burden by satisfying the jury beyond reasonable doubt that D was not acting, for example, under duress, the jury must acquit him.

The defences considered in this chapter have in common the feature that D claims he acted as he did because of some compelling circumstance which forced him to choose between so acting or some other form of harm occurring.

6.2 Duress

6.2.1 Introduction

 Key Point

When D pleads duress he is claiming that he committed the *actus reus* of the offence with which he is charged, with the relevant *mens rea*, but that he did so because his will had been overborne by the threats of another to inflict harm on himself and/or his family.

Duress does not operate in the way that automatism operates (see **5.4**). Judicial statements to the effect that duress operates to render D's act involuntary are incorrect (see e.g. Widgery LJ in *Hudson and Taylor* [1971] 2 QB 202, 206). The correct explanation of the way in which duress operates was stated by Lord Wilberforce in *DPP for Northern Ireland* v *Lynch* [1975] AC 653, at pp. 679, 680:

> [D]uress . . . is something which is superimposed on the other ingredients which by themselves would make up an offence, i.e. on the act and intention. *Coactus volui* sums up the combination: the victim completes the act and knows that he is doing so; but the addition of the element of duress prevents the law from treating what he has done as a crime.

The defence of duress is a concession to human frailty when faced with the choice of suffering harm or breaking the criminal law; in such a situation there is no real choice. Professor G. P. Fletcher describes this as 'moral involuntariness' (*Rethinking Criminal Law* (1978), p. 803) undeserving of punishment, a view which echoes Lord Morris in *DPP* v *Lynch* (at p. 670):

> [I]t is proper that any rational system of law should take fully into account the standards of honest and reasonable men. By those standards it is fair that actions and reactions may be tested. If then someone is really threatened with death or serious injury unless he does what he is told to do is the law to pay no heed to the miserable, agonising plight of such a person? For the law to understand not only how the timid but also the stalwart may in a moment of crisis behave is not to make the law weak but to make it just. In the calm of the court-room measures of fortitude or of heroic behaviour are surely not to be demanded when they could not in moments for decision reasonably have been expected even of the resolute and the well disposed.

If then it is accepted that there are circumstances in which an accused should be excused from criminal liability because his act was a response to threats made to him, what are those circumstances?

6.2.2 The test for duress

Because the defence of duress is founded on the notion that morally involuntary conduct is not blameworthy, some standard is necessary against which to measure D's conduct. It is not sufficient that he acted because of a threat; if the ordinary person in that situation would have shown greater fortitude and resisted the threat D is morally blameworthy for acceding to the threat. Accordingly, **the test for duress involves both subjective and objective elements**. These were clearly stated by Lord Lane CJ in *Graham* (1982) 74 Cr App R 235, as two questions to be considered by the jury and have since been affirmed by the House of Lords in *Howe* [1987] 1 AC 417:

> (1) Was the defendant, or may he have been, impelled to act as he did because, as a result of what he reasonably believed [the person issuing the threat] had said or done, he had good cause to fear that if he did not so act [that person] would kill him or . . . cause him serious personal injury?
>
> (2) If so, have the prosecution made the jury sure that a sober person of reasonable firmness, sharing the characteristics of the defendant, would not have responded to whatever he reasonably believed [the person making the threat] said or did by [doing as the defendant did]? The fact that a defendant's will to resist has been eroded by the voluntary consumption of drink or drugs or both is not relevant to this test.

The questions are framed so as to **cast the burden of proof on the prosecution** to disprove the defence once it is made a live issue in the trial. Thus, if the jury, while not being convinced that D was threatened and committed the offence charged in response to the threat, feel that he may have been threatened and may have acted as he did in response to the threat, they must give him the benefit of the doubt and pass on to consider the next question. Similarly, if they conclude that a reasonable person might have responded to the threat in the same way as D, the benefit of the doubt again would have to be given to D. It is not for D to prove duress but for the prosecution to disprove it.

There are several points to note about the two tests set out by Lord Lane CJ. The House of Lords provided a detailed analysis of the authorities in *Hasan* [2005] UKHL 22.

6.2.3 The first question: the threat and D's perception of it

The first of the two questions raises two sets of issues. First, what type of threat must exist for the duress defence to succeed? Secondly, is the test a subjective or an objective one: must the threat be real and genuine or will the test be satisfied if D genuinely believes in the threat?

6.2.3.1 The nature of the threat

 Question

How serious must the threat to D be before he can rely on it as a basis for a defence of duress?

For a defence of duress to succeed it is not sufficient for D to claim that his will was overborne by threats. The threats must be of a particular kind if they are to provide the foundation for duress. In *Hudson and Taylor* [1971] 2 QB 202, Lord Widgery CJ stated that **the threats must be of death or serious personal injury** (see also *DPP v Lynch*) however minor the offence D commits might be (see *Eden D.C. v Braid* [1998] COD 259). The Court of Appeal has stated that **the injury anticipated must be physical**—a fear of serious psychological harm will not suffice (see *Baker and Wilkins* [1997] Crim LR 497). It is difficult to explain this limitation, particularly when the House of Lords in *Burstow* [1998] AC 147 confirmed that GBH includes serious psychiatric injury for the purposes of s. 20 of the Offences Against the Person Act 1861 (see **10.3.1**). In *Quayle and others: AG's Reference (No. 2 of 2004)* [2005] EWCA Crim 1415, the Court of Appeal held that a threat of severe pain would not suffice, even if that might lead to psychological injury. The Court appears to have come to this view because of the large element of subjectivity in the assessment of pain where it is not directly associated with any physical injury. While not having to make a final determination on the matter, the Court of Appeal indicated in *Dao and others* [2012] EWCA Crim 1717 that a threat of false imprisonment would not be sufficient on its own to support a defence of duress. **A threat to damage or destroy property is also not sufficient** (*M'Growther* (1746) Fost 13) as 'the law must draw a line somewhere; and, as a result of experience and human valuation, the law draws it between threats to property and threats to the person' (*per* Lord Simon in *Lynch* [1975] AC 653, 687). **Threats to expose sexual immorality will also not suffice** (*Singh* [1973] 1 WLR 1600; *Valderrama-Vega* [1985] Crim LR 220). If D committed the offence of which he stands charged because of some threat less than death or serious personal injury, while this will not excuse him, it may be considered as a factor mitigating sentence. The Court of Appeal reaffirmed these points in *A* [2012] EWCA Crim 434. While also indicating that a threat to cause serious injury would include a threat to rape, Lord Judge CJ stated:

> 64 . . . . Duress cannot and should not be confused with pressure. The circumstances in which different individuals are subject to pressures, or perceive that they are under pressure, are virtually infinite. Such pressures may indeed provide powerful mitigation . . . . Dealing with it very broadly duress involves pressure which arises in extreme circumstances, the threat of death or serious injury, which for the avoidance of any misunderstanding, we have no doubt would also include rape, and which cannot reasonably be evaded.

While the **threats of death or serious injury** must be a *sine qua non* of D's decision to commit the offence (i.e. D would not have committed the offence but for the threats), they **need not be the sole reason for so acting** (*Valderrama-Vega* [1985] Crim LR 220).

> In this case D claimed that he had imported cocaine because of death threats from a Mafia-type organisation. In addition he said he needed the money which he stood to earn as he was under severe financial pressure due to a large debt he owed his bank. Furthermore he had been threatened with the disclosure of his homosexual propensities. The jury had been directed that duress was available as a defence only if D acted

solely because of the death threats; the Court of Appeal held that they should have been left to decide whether D would not have acted as he did but for the death threats.

D may rely on duress even though the threat to kill or injure is made in respect of others. In *Ortiz* (1986) 83 Cr App R 173, the Court of Appeal assumed that a threat to injure D's wife or family could constitute duress (see also *Valderrama-Vega*). This is confirmed by the 'duress of circumstances' case of *Martin* [1989] 1 All ER 652 (see **6.3.2**). In *Hurley and Murray* [1967] VR 526, the Supreme Court of Victoria held that threats to kill or seriously injure D's common law wife could amount to duress. In *Conway* [1988] 3 All ER 1025 (see **6.3.2**) the defence of duress of circumstances was accorded to D where the threat of injury had been made to a passenger in his car. In *Wright* [2000] Crim LR 510, the Court of Appeal approved the Judicial Studies Board specimen direction in which it specifies that **the threat must be directed against D, a member of his immediate family, or a person 'for whose safety the defendant would reasonably regard himself as responsible'** (see also *Hasan* [2005] UKHL 22, where *obiter* the House of Lords approved this at para. 21).

 Question

Is responsibility limited to that arising from relationship or that deriving from the situation in which D finds himself?

In *Abdul-Hussain and others* [1999] Crim LR 570 (see **6.2.5**), Rose LJ, in listing 11 propositions relating to duress and duress of circumstances (see **6.3.2**), stated that '**[i]mminent peril of death or serious injury to the defendant, or those to whom he has responsibility, is an essential element of both types of duress**'. This proposition was reiterated and expanded upon by Lord Woolf CJ in *Shayler* [2001] 1 WLR 2206, where he stated (at para. 49):

> (ii) the evil must be directed towards the defendant or a person or persons for whom he has responsibility or, we would add, persons for whom the situation makes him responsible; . . . . We make the addition to (ii) to cover, by way of example, the situation where the threat is made to set off a bomb unless the defendant performs the unlawful act. The defendant may not have had any previous connection with those who would be injured by the bomb but the threat itself creates the defendant's responsibility for those who will be at risk if he does not give way to the threat.

 Question

To take a duress by threats example, could D, a passer-by, rely on the defence of duress to a charge of aiding or harbouring an escaped prisoner where D did so solely as a result of the prisoner's threats to kill the prison warders whom he was holding at knife-point, if D would not drive the prison van?

It is clear from Lord Woolf CJ's dictum that D would be permitted to rely on the defence of duress in this instance because of the responsibility placed upon him by the situation in which he finds himself. Lord Woolf CJ made it clear later in his judgment that **if an issue arose as to whether 'situational responsibility' actually existed, the matter could be resolved by applying the reasonable person test**. He stated (at para. 63):

> [The defence is to be regarded] as being available when a defendant commits an otherwise criminal act to avoid an imminent peril of danger to life or serious injury to himself or towards somebody for whom he reasonably regards himself as being responsible. That person may not be ascertained and may not be identifiable. However, if it is not possible to name the individuals beforehand, it has at least to be possible to describe the individuals by reference to the action which is threatened would be taken which would make them victims absent avoiding action being taken by the defendant. The defendant has responsibility for them because he is placed in a position where he is required to make a choice whether to take or not to take the action which it is said will avoid them being injured. Thus if the threat is to explode a bomb in a building if the defendant does not accede to what is demanded the defendant owes responsibility to those who would be in the building if the bomb exploded.

An additional requirement concerning the nature of the threat is that there must be a connection between the threat and the offence committed.

 Key Point

Duress by threats may only be relied on as a defence where there is a nexus between the threats made to D and the offence he commits in response to those threats.

In *Cole* [1994] Crim LR 582, D's conviction for robbery was upheld on appeal although he, his girlfriend, and child had been threatened with violence by money lenders if he failed to pay the money he owed them. Simon Brown LJ, relying on dicta in *Hudson and Taylor* [1971] 2 QB 202, *DPP for Northern Ireland* v *Lynch* [1975] AC 653, and *Dawson* [1978] VR 536, stated:

> [I]t is plain that the defence of duress by threats can only apply when the offence charged (the offence which [D] asserts he was constrained to commit) is the very offence which was nominated by the person making the threat, i.e. when [D] was required by the threat to commit the offence charged.

As the money lenders had not nominated any offence as a means by which D should acquire the money to pay them, the defence of duress failed.

It is not clear from *Cole* how specific the instructions from the duressor must be. In Cole's case he robbed a building society. If the money lender had told him to 'steal it or else . . .' would that have been a sufficiently specific nomination of the offence? As robbery involves stealing, presumably it would. But if the money lender had said 'How you choose to get it is up to you; but you had better get it', this, presumably, would not suffice as there is no direction to commit any offence, even though the pressure D is under to get the money is no different. In the latter case D may seek to raise duress of circumstances as his defence (see **6.3.2**), but in such a case the issue of the imminence of the peril facing D will be crucial; as the peril facing Cole would only eventuate later if he failed to pay the money, he could not rely on duress of circumstances.

6.2.3.2 The first question: a subjective or objective standard?

The first question as framed by Lord Lane CJ in *Graham* focuses on the issue of whether D did (or may have done) as he did because of the threats he believed had been made. Although framed as a subjective question, the question also contains two objective elements: first, D's belief can only avail him where it is a reasonable one and second, D must have 'good cause' to fear death or serious personal injury.

In determining the first question in duress it was believed that any condition from which D suffered which may have affected his perception should not be taken into account in determining the reasonableness of his belief. Thus **if D's belief was irrational, he could not rely on it and the defence of duress would fail at this stage without the jury having to proceed to the second question in Lord Lane CJ's test.**

In *Hasan* [2005] UKHL 22, Lord Bingham of Cornhill categorically stated (at para. 23):

> But the words used in *R v Graham* and approved in *R v Howe* were 'he reasonably believed'. It is of course essential that the defendant should genuinely, i.e. actually, believe in the efficacy of the threat by which he claims to have been compelled. But there is no warrant for relaxing the requirement that the belief must be reasonable as well as genuine.

A person who mistakenly believes he is subject to a threat of death or serious injury will therefore only be able to plead duress if he has reasonable grounds for that mistaken belief.

6.2.4 The second question: D's response to the threat

The second question to be considered by the jury is, have the prosecution made them sure that a sober person of reasonable firmness, sharing D's characteristics, would not have responded to whatever he reasonably believed the person making the threat said or did by doing as D did? **This sets a purely objective standard.** Lord Lane in *Graham* stated (at p. 300):

> As a matter of public policy, it seems to us essential to limit the defence of duress by means of an objective criterion formulated in terms of reasonableness . . . . Provocation and duress are analogous. In provocation the words or actions of one person break the self-control of another. In duress the words or actions of one person break the will of another. The law requires a defendant to have the self-control reasonably to be expected of the ordinary citizen in his situation. It should likewise require him to have the steadfastness reasonably to be expected of the ordinary citizen in his situation.

Thus, if an ordinary person sharing the characteristics of D would have resisted the threats, D will be convicted as he is blameworthy for failing to show the degree of fortitude which the criminal law demands of all citizens. If the ordinary person would have responded to the threat in the way D did, D will be acquitted.

Question

What characteristics does the 'sober person of reasonable firmness' have? Which of D's characteristics are attributed to the reasonable person?

There has been uncertainty as to which characteristics of D should be attributed to the reasonable person. Some characteristics, such as age, may be relevant to the degree of fortitude to be expected of D. Characteristics such as physical illness or disability may affect a person's ability to protect themselves or render the threat more grave to them than to a person without that characteristic. Mental characteristics may affect a person's fortitude making that person more timid or pliable.

Key Point

The leading case on the characteristics attributable to the reasonable person within the duress defence is *Bowen* [1996] 2 Cr App R 157.

In *Bowen* the judge refused to allow evidence of D's low IQ and abnormal vulnerability and suggestibility to be presented to the jury. On appeal against this ruling it was also argued that evidence of D's low IQ was relevant to the question whether D had taken reasonable steps to escape from the threat as he had failed to seek police assistance. The Court of Appeal dismissed the appeal and stated the principles which could be derived from the cases. First, 'the mere fact that D is more pliable, vulnerable, timid or susceptible to threats than a normal person' does not amount to a characteristic to attribute to the reasonable person, and psychiatric evidence is not admissible on this matter (see *Horne* [1994] Crim LR 584; *Hurst* [1995] 1 Cr App R 82). Secondly, 'characteristics due to self-induced abuse, such as alcohol, drugs or glue-sniffing' are not relevant (see also *Flatt* [1996] Crim LR 576). Thirdly, any characteristic to be attributed to the reasonable person must be such as makes the defendant less able to resist the threats than persons without that characteristic. Stuart-Smith LJ stated (at p. 166):

> Obvious examples are age, where a young person may well not be so robust as a mature one; possibly sex, though many women would doubtless consider they had as much moral courage to resist pressure as men; pregnancy, where there is added fear for the unborn child; serious physical disability, which may inhibit self-protection; recognised mental illness or psychiatric conditions, such as post traumatic stress disorder leading to learned helplessness.

Stuart-Smith LJ further stated that psychiatric evidence may be admitted to show that D is suffering from some mental illness, mental impairment, or recognised psychiatric condition, provided persons generally suffering from such a condition may be more susceptible to pressure and threats (see also *Walker* [2003] EWCA Crim 1837; *Antar* [2004] EWCA Crim 2708). At what point a low IQ constitutes a 'mental impairment' is not clear, as an IQ of 68 was not regarded as low enough to amount to a characteristic such that it 'makes those who have it less courageous and less able to withstand threats and pressure'. The Court of Appeal, however, largely skipped over the question whether a low IQ might impair a person's ability to recognise or take an avenue of escape which a person of average IQ would have recognised or taken.

The difficulty *Bowen* leaves unresolved is distinguishing cases where timidity or pliability result from a mental illness or psychiatric condition from those where it is simply part of D's character or nature to be such. **Provided the mental characteristic results from a recognised illness or condition it is relevant to the objective question.**

In *Rogers*, unreported, 15 June 1999 (Case No. 99/2314/W4) the Court of Appeal quashed D's conviction, ordering a retrial where evidence of his mental condition came to light when the case was adjourned for reports prior to sentencing. The reports of a consultant psychiatrist and chartered psychologist revealed that he suffered from Asperger's syndrome, a developmental disorder of autistic personality which renders sufferers vulnerable and easily exploited and more susceptible to threats than others not so afflicted. The Court was satisfied that if the trial jury had heard this evidence it might have altered their view of D's plea of duress.

The reference in *Bowen* to post-traumatic stress disorder as an example of a recognised psychiatric condition arises from the earlier case of *Emery* (1993) 14 Cr App R (S) 394.

> D, who claimed to be suffering from 'learned helplessness' (more generally known as 'battered woman syndrome'), had been convicted of cruelty to a child on the basis that she had failed to protect her daughter from the father (her partner) who, over a period of several weeks, had battered the child resulting in her death. The trial judge had admitted evidence from expert medical witnesses which supported D's claim that she was so intimidated by her partner's previous violence to her that she was coerced into taking no steps to obtain help. Lord Taylor CJ, although holding that the medical witnesses had been allowed to go too far, opined that it would have been permissible for them to give an 'account of the causes of the condition of dependent helplessness, the circumstances in which it might arise and what level of abuse would be required to produce it' in order to help explain D's later actions. Such evidence is relevant to the first subjective question whether D may have been acting as she did because she feared that if she did not so act her partner would kill or seriously injure her. Lord Taylor CJ stated (at p. 398):

> The issue the jury had to decide in regard to [D] was, whether or not the prosecution had negatived duress, and therefore the question for the doctors was whether a woman of reasonable firmness with the characteristics of [D], if abused in the manner which she said, would have had her will crushed so that she could not have protected her child.

The history of violence is all part of the duress so that the jury would be asked to envisage its impact on a woman who, prior to the onset of violence, was a person of reasonable firmness. In the instant case the jury rejected the defence of duress. **In each case it will ultimately be for the jury to decide whether an alleged characteristic may have had a bearing on D's response to the threat and what effect such a characteristic might had on a reasonable person similarly positioned.**

If D, because he is intoxicated, mistakenly believes he is being threatened, his mistake will not avail him as such a mistake is necessarily unreasonable. If, rather, he claims that his will to resist was eroded as a result of his intoxication, he will likewise not benefit from this as he is to be judged against the sober person's standard of reasonable firmness. Lord Lane CJ in *Graham* did not advert to the situation where D was involuntarily intoxicated. It is submitted that in such a situation D's case should be considered in the light of his honest beliefs and his response should be measured against the standard of the ordinary person similarly suffering from involuntary intoxication.

6.2.5 Imminence of the threat and opportunities to escape

 Key Point

If D is to succeed in his plea of duress, the threat must have been operative at the time he committed the offence. The issue is not whether the threat could be put into effect immediately if D did not commit the crime but whether the threat was operating on his mind at the time he committed the crime such that he feared death or serious injury would ensue imminently.

In *Hudson and Taylor* [1971] 2 QB 202, Widgery LJ made it clear that what was required was for the offence to be committed under 'immediate and unavoidable pressure' stating (at p. 206):

It is essential to the defence of duress that the threat shall be effective at the moment when the crime is committed. The threat must be a 'present' threat in the sense that it is effective to neutralise the will of D at that time. Hence an accused who joins a rebellion under the compulsion of threats cannot plead duress if he remains with the rebels after the threats have lost their effect and his own will has had a chance to re-assert itself: *Rex v M'Growther* (1746) Fost. 13.

In *Hudson and Taylor* two teenage girls were convicted of perjury having been denied the defence of duress by the recorder as the threat of harm to them could not be put immediately into effect in the courtroom when they were testifying. The girls claimed that they had been threatened with violence by a gang if they did not give false evidence at the trial of one of its members. While testifying the girls had seen one of the gang members in the court. Quashing their convictions Widgery LJ stated (at p. 207):

> When . . . there is no opportunity for delaying tactics, and the person threatened must make up his mind whether he is to commit the criminal act or not, the existence at that moment of threats sufficient to destroy his will ought to provide him with a defence even though the threatened injury may not follow instantly, but after an interval. . . . [T]he threats . . . were likely to be no less compelling, because their execution could not be effected in the court room, if they could be carried out in the streets of Salford the same night.

In *Abdul-Hussain and others* [1999] Crim LR 570, the Court of Appeal followed the approach adopted in *Hudson and Taylor*.

> The appellants raised the defence of duress of circumstances on a charge of hijacking contrary to s. 1(1) of the Aviation Security Act 1982. The appellants were Shiite Muslims from Southern Iraq who had fled to Sudan. They were overstayers in Sudan and feared being arrested and returned to Iraq where they expected to be tortured and executed. To avoid this eventuality they hijacked a plane at Khartoum Airport forcing the pilot to fly to London where they sought political asylum. The trial judge ruled that the defence of duress of circumstances would not be left to the jury as death or injury would not have immediately followed had they not hijacked the plane. The Court of Appeal quashed their convictions as the issue for the jury is whether the threat of imminent death or injury operated on D's mind at the time he committed the crime with which he is charged, so as to overbear his will, there being no need for the execution of that threat to be immediately in prospect. Rose LJ stated:

> [I]f Anne Frank had stolen a car to escape from Amsterdam and been charged with theft, the tenets of English law would not, in our judgment, have denied her a defence of duress of circumstances, on the ground that she should have waited for the Gestapo's knock on the door.

However, in *Hasan* [2005] UKHL 22, Lord Bingham of Cornhill expressed doubts over the decision in *Hudson and Taylor* stating (at paras 27 and 28):

> I can understand that the Court of Appeal . . . had sympathy with the predicament of the young appellants but I cannot, consistently with principle, accept that a witness testifying in the Crown Court at Manchester has no opportunity to avoid complying with a threat incapable of execution then or there . . .
> It should . . . be made clear to juries that if the retribution threatened against [D] or his family or a person for whom he reasonably feels responsible is not such as he reasonably expects to follow **immediately or almost immediately** on his failure to comply with the threat, there may be little if any room for doubt that he could have taken evasive action, whether by going to the police or in some other way, to avoid the crime with which he is charged. [Emphasis added]

This position reflects the excusatory nature of the defence as a concession to human frailty—but a limited one. While D can always avoid committing the crime in question, the issue of concern for D is whether he can avoid the implementation of the threat. When it is directed at his family D may have no confidence that even a police armed response unit could save his family. In weighing these competing factors in the balance, Lord Bingham places priority on the need to prevent crime; D's concern for his family is subsidiary. Its relevance would arise in sentencing when it would be a strong mitigating factor. If D is extremely timorous and fears taking an avenue of escape of which the reasonable person would have availed, he will be denied the defence.

In *Batchelor* [2013] EWCA Crim 2638, the Court of Appeal considered the issue of imminence and immediacy in the context of a series of crimes.

> D appealed his conviction for cheating the public revenue by a series of VAT frauds. D claimed that he committed the offences to raise funds to pay off a debt having been threatened and intimidated by John, the person to whom he was indebted. The trial judge refused to leave duress to the jury because, inter alia, D had ample opportunity over many months to go to the police. The Court of Appeal affirmed this decision stating (at para. 15):

> > The appellant could have gone to the police at any time over a period of two and a half years. Moreover, he was not placed under such fear that he was being forced immediately to pay John. . . . That is not to say, as the judge pointed out in his sentencing remarks, that the appellant may not have been subject to some deeply unpleasant intimidation, but even if his account was true in all the particulars, the appellant could not reasonably believe that the execution of the threat was imminent and immediate. The law requires a certain degree of fortitude to be shown by victims in circumstances such as these.

 Question

Is there any responsibility on D to try to escape the threat?

As duress is an excuse, the fact that there is a threat operating on D's mind will not automatically result in acquittal. The threat and D's response to it must be set in the context of any opportunity of avoiding it whether through escape or seeking official protection. In *Hudson and Taylor* Widgery LJ stated (at p. 207):

> [I]t is always open to the Crown to prove that [D] failed to avail himself of some opportunity which was reasonably open to him to render the threat ineffective, and that upon this being established the threat in question can no longer be relied upon by the defence. In deciding whether such an opportunity was reasonably open to [D] the jury should have regard to his age and circumstances, and to any risks to him which may be involved in the course of action relied upon.

It is not enough that there was, in fact, an opportunity for D to escape the threat; to defeat a claim of duress it is necessary for the prosecution to prove that D both appreciated the opportunity to escape and rejected it, it being one which a reasonable person in a like situation would have taken (see *McDonald* [2003] EWCA Crim 1170).

6.2.6 Duress arising from voluntary association with criminals

Question

Is the defence of duress available to an accused who has voluntarily associated with criminals who use violence, thereby exposing himself to the risk of compulsion?

In *Sharp* [1987] 1 QB 853, D joined a gang which carried out a series of armed robberies of sub-post offices culminating in the murder of a sub-postmaster. He claimed he only took part in this last robbery because a gun had been pointed at his head by another gang member who threatened to blow it off if he did not participate. He was convicted of manslaughter when the trial judge rejected duress as a possible defence. The Court of Appeal, relying on codes in other common law jurisdictions, dicta in *Lynch*, and the decision in *Fitzpatrick* [1977] NI 20, dismissed the appeal. Lord Lane CJ stated (at p. 861):

> [W]here a person has voluntarily, and with knowledge of its nature, joined a criminal organisation or gang which he knew might bring pressure on him to commit an offence and was an active member when he was put under such pressure, he cannot avail himself of the defence of duress.

Thus, as the defence of duress is a concession to human frailty which will be denied where D has failed to avail himself of an opportunity to escape from the duress, so too it is denied to D who freely undertakes the risk of being subjected to duress.

Question

Several questions arise, however, in this situation of voluntary association.

1. Must D be aware of the risk of those with whom he is associating subjecting him to coercion, or is it sufficient that he ought to have been so aware?
2. Must D join the gang or organisation or is it sufficient that he voluntarily associates with them?
3. Must D be aware of simply the risk of coercion or must he be aware of the risk of being coerced into committing offences of the type with which he is being tried?

Initially the answers to these questions deriving from several Court of Appeal cases were not entirely consistent. In *Baker and Ward* [1999] 2 Cr App R 335, the Court opined that voluntary association does not require joining a gang or organisation, it being sufficient that D has involved himself in criminal activities which bring him into contact with other criminals in circumstances where he could be subjected to compulsion; drug-dealing on a scale which is significant could be such a case. The Court also made it clear that when associating with the criminals, D has to be aware of the risk that they might try to coerce him into committing offences '**of the type for which he is being tried**'. By contrast, in *Heath* [2000] Crim LR 109 and *Harmer* [2000] Crim LR 401, the Court upheld convictions holding that it was enough to exclude duress that indebted drug users realised that if they became indebted to their suppliers they might be subjected to violence. The Court appeared to dispense with the requirement that D be aware of the risk of the violence being used to coerce him into committing a crime of the type for which he was being tried. In *Z* [2003] EWCA Crim 12, the Court recognised the conflict between *Heath* and *Harmer*, on the one hand, and *Baker and Ward* on the other. Referring to *Lynch v DPP for Northern Ireland*, *Fitzpatrick*, and *Sharp*, they affirmed that the position as expressed in *Baker and Ward* was the correct one and declined to follow *Heath* and *Harmer*. When *Z* was appealed further to the House of Lords as *Hasan* [2005] UKHL 22 (the House of Lords lifting an anonymity order), their Lordships adopted a contrary position. Lord Bingham of Cornhill stated (at paras 37–38):

> The defendant is seeking to be wholly exonerated from the consequences of a crime deliberately committed. The prosecution must negative his defence of duress, if raised by the evidence, beyond reasonable doubt. The defendant is, *ex hypothesi*, a person who has voluntarily surrendered his will to the domination of another. Nothing should turn on the foresight of the manner in which, in the event, the dominant party chooses to exploit the defendant's subservience. There need not be foresight of coercion to commit crimes, although it is not easy to envisage circumstances in which a party might be coerced to act lawfully. In holding that there must be foresight of coercion to commit crimes of the kind with which the defendant is charged, *R v Baker and Ward* mis-stated the law.
>
> There remains the question . . . whether the defendant's foresight must be judged by a subjective or an objective test . . . . The practical importance of the distinction in this context may not be very great, since if a jury concluded that a person voluntarily associating with known criminals ought reasonably to have foreseen the risk of future coercion they would not, I think, be very likely to accept that he did not in fact do so. But since there is a choice to be made, policy in my view points towards an objective test . . . . The policy of the law must be to discourage association with known criminals, and it should be slow to excuse the criminal conduct of those who do so. If a person voluntarily becomes or remains associated with others engaged in criminal activity in a situation where he knows or ought reasonably to know that he may be subject to compulsion by them or their associates, he cannot rely on the defence of duress to excuse any act which he is thereafter compelled to do by them.

This statement of principle by Lord Bingham is quite sweeping. Effectively D will be denied the defence of duress if he associated with others involved in criminal activity whom he *ought* to have foreseen might subject him to compulsion by threats or violence. (In *Ali* [2008] EWCA Crim 716, the Court of Appeal accepted the very broad nature of this test as including in that case a person who D knew carried a knife and with whom D had been warned against associating.) There is no requirement for foreseeable consequences of the compulsion to be offences of the same type as that charged. The exclusion from reliance on duress, however, is limited to the situation where D remains associated with those who have subjected him to coercion. Presumably D's reasonable attempts to extricate himself from their clutches will restore his entitlement to raise duress as a defence if coercion is subsequently exercised over him.

In her dissenting judgment, Baroness Hale highlighted the potential unfairness of Lord Bingham's approach and expressed her preference for denying the defence of duress only when D foresaw (or should have foreseen) the risk of being subjected to compulsion *to commit criminal offences*. She argued that some abused women might know that they are at risk of violence and compulsion if they stay with their abusive partners but be unable to leave due to physical threats and the cumulative psychological effects of the abuse. Duress should be available to a woman who is then coerced by her abusive partner to commit perjury or shoplift. The majority of their Lordships viewed mitigation in sentencing as an effective way of mitigating the harshness of the law, but Baroness Hale argued that is an unacceptable way of addressing the law's harshness; the law should define what is excusable. The other stringent elements of the law on duress are more than adequate to keep it within bounds in such cases, she argued.

The issue of duress, voluntary association, and abused women is discussed further in the **Law in Context feature**.

6.2.7 Limits to the defence

Because duress is a defence developed by the common law there has been uncertainty about its limits.

 Question

Should a person be required to sacrifice his own life rather than escape by killing another?

This question has been asked and answered differently by the courts over many years. In *DPP for Northern Ireland* v *Lynch* [1975] AC 653, the House of Lords, by a 3:2 majority, held that duress was available to a person charged with aiding and abetting murder.

> D drove a car carrying IRA members on an expedition in which they shot and killed a policeman. D claimed he was not an IRA member and that he believed he would be shot if he did not obey the leader's orders. The trial judge ruled that duress was not available on a charge of aiding and abetting murder. The House of Lords ordered D's retrial in which he pleaded duress but he was obviously disbelieved by the jury as he was convicted.

In *Abbott* v *The Queen* [1977] AC 755, the Privy Council drew a distinction between principals and secondary parties, holding that duress was not available to a principal charged with murder. While there may be a difference in the mode of participation it is difficult to see that there is necessarily any distinction in the degree of culpability between principal and secondary offenders; is the maker of a bomb necessarily less blameworthy than the one who plants it?

The need to draw this distinction between principal and secondary parties charged with murder has been removed by the decision in *Howe* [1987] 1 AC 417 where their Lordships ruled that **duress is not a defence to murder whether as a principal or secondary party** thereby reversing their decision in *Lynch*. Their reasoning at times verge on the fatuous. Lord Hailsham, knowing of many acts of heroism by ordinary people, opined that a law which protected the 'coward and the poltroon' could not be regarded as either 'just or humane'; accordingly the ordinary man, rather than kill another, might be expected to sacrifice his own life. However, there is no general duty to heroism in the criminal law and the standard against which D is generally measured is that of the reasonable man who might be considered neither heroic (or foolhardy) nor cowardly, being a 'sober person of reasonable firmness'. How should one characterise the ordinary man whose family are held hostage under threat of death by terrorists if he does not plant a bomb intended to cause injury? If he resists the threat at the expense of their lives is he a hero? Or if he complies with the threat at the expense of a third party's life is he a poltroon? This scenario, unfortunately, is all too realistic: there were three car-bomb attacks on security forces in Northern Ireland in 1990 where terrorists held families hostage while the husbands were forced to drive the cars containing bombs to police or army installations.

Lords Hailsham, Griffiths, and Mackay expressed the view that to allow duress as a defence to murder would involve overruling *Dudley and Stephens* (1884) 14 QBD 273, which they took to have decided that necessity was not a defence to murder. Lord Griffiths stated that this decision was based on 'the special sanctity that the law attaches to human life and which denies to a man the right to take an innocent life even at the price of his own or another's life'. This ignores the fact that the taking of one life may lead to a net saving of lives. Their Lordships also ignored the fact that *Dudley and Stephens* is a case whose ratio is far from clear (see **6.3.3**).

Lord Griffiths was of the opinion that the defence should not be afforded to a murderer as the 'defence of duress is so easy to raise and may be so difficult for the prosecution to disprove'. If this is so it is an argument for disallowing all defences. It also ignores the fact that in *Graham* the jury convicted where D pleaded duress on a charge of murder and, on the retrial of Lynch for murder, the jury convicted. Further, it contradicts Lord Hailsham who stated that 'juries have been commendably robust' in rejecting the defence where appropriate.

Lords Hailsham and Griffiths expressed the view that the issue of duress in murder would best be dealt with by the executive through the agency of the Parole Board or Royal Pardon. This contrasts with Lord Wilberforce in *Lynch* who stated (at p. 685):

> A law which requires innocent victims of terrorist threats to be tried and convicted as murderers, is an unjust law even if the executive, resisting political pressures, may decide, after all, and within the permissible limits of the prerogative to release them. Moreover, if the defence is excluded in law, much of the evidence which would prove the duress would be inadmissible at the trial, not brought out in court, and not tested by cross-examination.

Lord Bridge considered that it was by legislation alone that the scope of the defence of duress could be defined, while Lord Mackay believed the defence was too uncertain for it to be extended to cover an actual killer. As duress is a common law defence one would have expected their Lordships to accept the responsibility to develop and clarify the common law. Once again Lord Wilberforce recognised this in *Lynch* where he stated (at pp. 684, 685):

> We are here in the domain of the common law: our task is to fit what we can see as principle and authority to the facts before us, and it is no obstacle that these facts are new. The judges have always assumed responsibility for deciding questions of principle relating to criminal liability and guilt, and particularly for setting the standards by which the law expects normal men to act . . . . The House is not inventing a new defence: on the contrary, it would not discharge its judicial duty if it failed to define the law's attitude to this particular defence in particular circumstances.

The rule that duress is not available as a defence to murder is absolute and applies even to a child of the age of criminal responsibility no matter how susceptible he might be to the duress (see *W* [2007] EWCA Crim 1251).

Following the decision in *Howe* there was uncertainty whether duress would be available as a defence on a charge of attempted murder, although Lord Griffiths stated *obiter* that it was not. The issue arose before the House of Lords in *Gotts* [1992] 2 WLR 284.

> D, aged 16, was threatened with death by E, his father, unless he killed his mother who had fled to a women's refuge with the other two children to escape the violence, depravity, and abuse inflicted upon her and the children by E. Subsequently D stabbed his mother but was restrained by bystanders so that, although she sustained serious injuries, she did not die. At his trial the judge ruled that duress was not available on a charge of attempted murder whereupon D pleaded guilty and appealed. The Court of Appeal upheld the trial judge's ruling and the House of Lords, by a 3:2 majority, dismissed D's further appeal. Lord Jauncey of Tullichettle stated (at p. 293):

> It is of course true that withholding the defence in any circumstances will create anomalies but . . . nothing should be done to undermine in any way the highest duty of the law to protect the freedom and lives of those who live under it. I can therefore see no justification in logic, morality or law in affording to an attempted murderer the defence which is withheld from a murderer. The intent required of an attempted murderer is more evil than that required of a murderer and the line which divides the two offences is seldom, if ever, of the deliberate making of the criminal.

The Court of Appeal had been concerned to avoid an anomaly between murder and attempted murder and, in addition, was influenced by the fact that the sentence for attempt was in the discretion of the court. In the instant case the sentence imposed was probation for three years which reflected the mitigating effect duress had in the circumstances. While the Court of Appeal may have been satisfied that no injustice was done to Gotts, they ignored the fact that, had his mother died, a matter totally depending on chance and in no way altering D's culpability, there would have been no discretion in sentencing D as the sentence for murder is life imprisonment for an adult and detention at Her Majesty's pleasure for a juvenile.

If duress is not to be available as a complete defence on a charge of murder perhaps it should be made a partial defence in the way that loss of self-control operates reducing the offence to manslaughter. On a conviction for manslaughter the sentence is in the discretion of the court, thereby providing the judge with the flexibility required so that he can reflect the mitigating nature of the circumstances in the sentence he imposes.

While *Gotts* dealt with the problem of attempted murder, further anomalies remain unresolved. In *Gotts* Lord Lane CJ opined that duress would be available on a charge of conspiracy to murder or incitement to murder as they are one stage further away from the completed offence than is attempt. In *Ness and Awan* [2011] Crim LR 645, McCombe J left the defence of duress to the jury in a case of conspiracy to murder. This approach seems to ignore the fact that for D to be convicted of conspiracy to murder it must be proved he had an intention that V be killed; this is the same *mens rea* that was used by the House of Lords in *Gotts* to justify denying the defence in attempted murder. It also appears that duress may be pleaded as a defence to a charge under s. 18 of the Offences Against the Person Act 1861. Thus D may be acquitted of wounding with intent to cause GBH following a defence of duress, but if V dies subsequently he may be convicted of murder. The *mens rea* of murder is intention to kill or intention to cause serious bodily injury. In both cases D's culpability is the same and the gravity of the threats is no different but the outcome hangs on chance—whether V lives or dies.

 Question

Is the logical conclusion therefore that duress should not be available on a charge under s. 18? Or is it conceivable that the House of Lords were right in *Lynch* but wrong in *Howe*?

In *Gotts* in the Court of Appeal Lord Lane CJ stated, somewhat dismissively, that there would be anomalies wherever the line was drawn. Lord Jauncey, in the House of Lords, was of the same opinion. It is a sad day when the Lord Chief Justice and a Law Lord are not perturbed by anomalies in the criminal law which are the creation of the judges and which are capable of wreaking gross injustices.

The other offence over which there is uncertainty is treason. In *Steane* [1947] KB 997, Lord Goddard CJ took the view that duress was not available on such a charge before doing considerable violence to the definition of intention to permit the quashing of the appellant's conviction. This decision must be considered *per incuriam*; in *Purdy* (1945) 10 JCL 182, Oliver J directed the jury that on a charge of treason based on assisting with German propaganda while a prisoner of war, fear of death would be a defence. In *Lynch* their Lordships cited this case along with *Oldcastle* (1419) 1 Hale PC 50, *M'Growther* (1746) Fost 13, and *Stratton* (1779) 1 Doug KB 239, which all recognised the availability of duress on certain charges of treason but it would not be available as a defence to treason involving the death of the Sovereign (see *Axtell* (1660) Kel 13, cited by Lord Simon at p. 697).

When duress arises in a new situation, the courts adopt the approach articulated by the Court of Appeal in *R* v *Abdul-Hussain* [1999] Crim LR 570 and the proposition that:

> Unless and until Parliament provides otherwise, the defence of duress, whether by threats or from circumstances, is generally available in relation to all substantive crimes, except murder, attempted murder and some forms of treason. (*R* v *Pommell* [1995] 2 Cr App R 607, 615C)

This approach was affirmed by the Court of Appeal in *Shayler* [2001] 1 WLR 2206, when holding that the defence was available to charges under the Official Secrets Act 1989.

6.2.8 Reform

The Law Commission has argued for the reformulation of the test for duress (see Law Com No. 83, para. 228) most recently stating its position in *Legislating the*

Criminal Code: Offences Against the Person and General Principles (Law Com No. 218). Duress is defined in cl. 25(2):

> A person does an act under duress by threats if he does it because he knows or believes—
>
> (a) that a threat has been made to cause death or serious injury to himself or another if the act is not done, and
>
> (b) that the threat will be carried out immediately if he does not do the act or, if not immediately, before he or that other can obtain effective official protection, and
>
> (c) that there is no other way of preventing the threat being carried out, and the threat is one which in all the circumstances (including any of his personal characteristics that affect its gravity) he cannot reasonably be expected to resist.

This makes it clear that with regard to the second question for the jury to consider in duress, the focus should not be on whether a reasonable person would have resisted the threat, but rather on D's ability to resist it. It states at para. 29.14:

> On consultation, there was strong support for our view that the defence should apply where *the particular defendant in question* could not reasonably have been expected to resist the threat. We do not accept the contrary view, for which there was very little support, that the defence should be withheld from the 'objectively weak'. First, such an approach would be ineffectual as a means of law enforcement. If a person is in a condition that makes it unreasonable to expect him to resist, then he will not resist, and the fact that a different person in those circumstances might have resisted will not affect the matter. Second, the purpose of the defence is not to enforce unrealistically high standards of behaviour. Rather, the defence acknowledges that where the defendant could not reasonably have been expected to act otherwise he should not be convicted of a crime.

This approach is consistent with the Law Commission's generally subjectivist position in respect of criminal liability. Those who favour a more objectivist approach support the current position as it sets an objective standard of steadfastness which is considered appropriate in the context of an excusatory defence.

6.3 Necessity

6.3.1 General

The question whether there is a general defence of necessity in English law has long taxed criminal lawyers. Duress relates to the situation where a person commits an offence to avoid the greater evil of death or serious injury to himself or another threatened by a third party. **Necessity relates to the situation where a person commits an offence to avoid the greater evil to himself or another which would ensue from objective dangers arising from the circumstances in which he or that other are placed.** While duress operates as an excuse it was thought that necessity, if it existed as a defence, operated as a justification rendering D's conduct lawful. But is there such a defence?

Early writers on English law such as Bracton, Coke, and Hale all quoted maxims which conceded that necessity might justify conduct which would otherwise be unlawful. In *Moore* v *Hussey* (1609) Hob 96, Hobart J stated: 'All laws admit certain cases of just excuse, when they are offended in the letter, and where the offender is under necessity, either of compulsion or inconvenience.' Examples of necessity given by these writers were: pulling down a house to prevent a fire spreading; a prisoner escaping from a burning jail although statute made prison-breach a felony; jettisoning cargo to save a vessel in a storm (see *Mouse's Case* (1620) 12 Co Rep 63).

In several traffic cases there are *obiter dicta* to the effect that there is a defence of necessity. In *Johnson* v *Phillips* [1976] 1 WLR 65, Wien J stated that a constable would be entitled to direct motorists to disobey traffic regulations if this was reasonably necessary for the protection of life or property. In *Woods* v *Richards* [1977] RTR 201, Eveleigh J stated that the defence of necessity depended on the degree of emergency which existed or the alternative danger to be averted.

Despite these authorities and dicta there was still uncertainty in the law as there were other *obiter dicta* which suggested there was no defence of necessity. In *Buckoke* v *GLC* [1971] Ch 655, Lord Denning stated (at p. 668):

> A driver of a fire engine with ladders approaches the traffic lights. He sees 200 yards down the road a blazing house with a man at an upstairs window in extreme peril. The road is clear in all directions. At that moment the lights turn red. Is the driver to wait for 60 seconds, or more, for the lights to turn to green? If the driver waits for that time, the man's life will be lost. I suggested to both counsel that the driver might be excused in crossing the lights to save the man. He might have the defence of necessity. Both counsel denied it. They would not allow him any defence in law. The circumstances went to mitigation, they said, and did not take away his guilt. If counsel are correct—and I accept that they are—nevertheless such a man should not be prosecuted. He should be congratulated.

It seems strange that the law should operate in a way such as to discourage appropriate conduct; but this it seems to do and little reliance can be placed on the good sense of prosecuting authorities not to prosecute in such circumstances as the following case illustrates.

> In *Kitson* (1955) 39 Cr App R 66, D, who had been drinking and had fallen asleep in a car in which he was the passenger, woke to find the driver gone and the car careering down a hill. He took control of the vehicle and steered it to safety. He was prosecuted and convicted of driving under the influence of drink.

Obviously he should have preferred to die himself or allow the car to kill others rather than take control of it while under the influence of alcohol! Would Lord Denning have congratulated Mr Kitson if he had shown great fortitude and restraint and, rather than be labelled a criminal, he had permitted the car to continue on its course at the expense of the lives of several pedestrians? Presumably he would as in *London Borough of Southwark* v *Williams* [1971] 2 All ER 175 he stated (at p. 179): 'Necessity would open a door which no man could shut . . . . The plea would be an excuse for all sorts of wrongdoing. So the courts must, for the sake of law and order, take a firm stand.'

A counter-argument to this position is that the criminal law should not only be used to discourage inappropriate conduct but should, by means of exceptions to criminal liability, also encourage appropriate conduct.

Statute may effectively incorporate a defence of necessity.

> In *DPP* v *Harris* [1995] 1 Cr App R 170, D, a police officer, was charged with driving without due care and attention, having collided with another vehicle after driving through a red traffic light in pursuit of a vehicle believed to contain armed robbers. Regulation 34(1)(b) of the Traffic Signs Regulations and General Directions 1981 permitted police vehicles to cross traffic lights showing red provided that to do so does not involve the likelihood of danger to the driver of any other vehicle. The Divisional Court took the view that this regulation provided the only defence available to a charge of careless driving in these circumstances and therefore excluded any general defence of necessity.

By contrast, in *Cichon* v *DPP* [1994] Crim LR 918, the Divisional Court held that the offence of allowing a pit bull terrier to be in a public place without being muzzled, contrary to s. 1(2)(d) of the Dangerous Dogs Act 1991, was an absolute offence and Parliament could not have intended any defence of necessity to apply. The owner had removed the dog's muzzle because the dog had kennel cough and he considered it cruel to keep it muzzled while it was coughing. Schiemann J, while being prepared to assume that in some circumstances a defence of necessity could be raised by a defendant, stated:

> The Act does not in terms (and nor in my judgment does the common law) allow the person in control of the dog to make a value judgment as between what is good for the dog and what is good for the rest of mankind. We have here an absolute prohibition and a breach of that prohibition is to be followed by an order for the dog's destruction, however blameless the dog and its owner . . . . No doubt the justification for this hard law was thought to be a desire to protect the public from such dogs . . .

Schiemann J's position, therefore, is to hold that in no circumstances can the anticipated harm to the dog (property) outweigh the potential harm to persons which such an unmuzzled dog might cause. This does leave open the possibility that a defence of necessity might avail where removal of the muzzle is for the purpose of avoiding harm to persons.

 Example

D, while taking his pit bull terrier for a walk, sees E entering a bank armed with a gun. D follows E and observes him threatening the cashier with the gun. D removes the muzzle from the dog which then attacks E, biting the arm which is holding the gun and as a result of which D arrests E. In this case the value judgement would be between harm to the robber and the potential harm to the cashier. It would be difficult to believe that the courts would deny a defence of necessity in these circumstances.

In several twentieth-century cases the defence of necessity was implicitly recognised.

> In *Bourne* [1938] 3 All ER 615, an obstetric surgeon was charged with unlawfully using an instrument with intent to procure a miscarriage, contrary to s. 58 of the Offences Against the Person Act 1861, having performed an abortion on a 14-year-old girl who was the victim of a violent rape. MacNaghten J dealt with the matter from the point of view of the meaning of 'unlawfully' in s. 58, avoiding express mention of necessity. The jury acquitted after being directed that D would not have been acting unlawfully if he acted in good faith to save the girl's life. He stated (at p. 620) that:

> The unborn child in the womb must not be destroyed unless the destruction of that child is for the purpose of preserving the yet more precious life of the mother.

If what was done was not unlawful it was justified; the only justification which covers this choice between evils is necessity. A similar approach was adopted in *Gillick* v *West Norfolk and Wisbech AHA* [1986] AC 112, where the House of Lords stated that a doctor who prescribed contraceptives for a girl under 16 would not be guilty of aiding, abetting, counselling, or procuring the offence of unlawful sexual intercourse committed by her with a man, provided he honestly believed his action to be necessary for the physical, mental, and emotional health of the girl. Lord Scarman stated (at p. 190):

> The bona fide exercise by a doctor of his clinical judgment must be a complete negation of the guilty mind which is an essential ingredient of the criminal offence of aiding and abetting the commission of unlawful sexual intercourse.

The doctor's motive for prescribing contraceptives was, however, irrelevant if he knew that this would have encouraged an underage girl to engage in sexual intercourse (see **3.2.3.8**). Would it not have been more honest for the House of Lords to state openly that necessity would be a defence instead of further confusing intention by declaring that motive may negate guilty mind? (See now s. 73 of the Sexual Offences Act 2003 which expressly legislates that a doctor, in these circumstances, is not guilty of aiding, abetting, or counselling the commission of a sexual offence against the child.)

In *re F (Mental Patient: Sterilisation)* [1990] 2 AC 1, a House of Lords' decision referring to necessity, it was held to be lawful to carry out a sterilisation operation on a mental patient who lacked the capacity to consent as there was a grave risk that she would become pregnant which would have had disastrous psychiatric consequences for her. Lord Brandon of Oakbrook considered that operations on patients incapable of consenting would be lawful provided they were carried out to save life or to ensure improvement or prevent deterioration in the patient's physical or mental health. While Lord Brandon did not expressly mention necessity it is implicit in his speech.

By contrast Lord Goff of Chieveley did mention necessity expressly. He stated that **the common law principle of necessity could justify action which would otherwise be unlawful in three groups of cases: first, cases of public necessity where D interferes with another's property in the public interest** (e.g. destroying his house to prevent the spread of a fire); **secondly, cases of private necessity where D interferes with another's property to save his own person or property from imminent peril** (e.g. where he enters V's land without consent to prevent the spread of fire on to his own land); **and thirdly, 'action taken as a matter of necessity to assist another person without his consent'** (e.g. there is no assault where D seizes V and forcibly drags him from the path of an oncoming vehicle thereby saving him from injury or death). Lord Goff stated that there were many emanations of the third principle and that it was 'concerned not only with the preservation of the life or health of the assisted person, but also with the preservation of his property . . . and even with certain conduct on his behalf in the administration of his affairs'. His Lordship considered that the instant case concerned action taken to preserve the life, health, or well-being of another who is unable to consent to it. In such a situation two conditions must be satisfied to bring the action within the bounds of necessity:

(a) there must be a necessity to act when it is not practicable to communicate with the assisted person, [and]

(b) the action taken must be such as a reasonable person would in all the circumstances take, acting in the best interests of the assisted person.

Lord Goff's three categories are very narrow and appear to be a long way from providing for a general defence of necessity based on a test of balancing harms (i.e. that D commits an offence to avoid a greater evil to himself or another) (see further **6.3.3**).

In *R* v *Bournewood Community and Mental Health NHS Trust* [1998] 3 All ER 289, the defence of necessity was recognised and applied by the House of Lords to justify the informal detention and treatment of a mentally incompetent person who had become a danger to himself. The formal procedures under the Mental Health Act 1983 had not been invoked but the House of Lords held that the common law doctrine of necessity applied, Lord Goff of Chieveley stating (at p. 300):

I have no doubt that all the steps in fact taken . . . were in fact taken in the best interests of Mr L and, in so far as they might otherwise have constituted an invasion of his civil rights, were justified on the basis of the common law doctrine of necessity.

While this case is an example of the defence of necessity being applied, the reasoning of their Lordships does not supply any further explanation of the rationale underpinning the defence nor any further guidance on its ambit and operation.

In *R (Nicklinson)* v *Ministry of Justice* [2012] EWHC 2381 (Admin), the Divisional Court ruled that the defence of necessity would not be available to any person who might assist the claimant, a sufferer of 'locked-in' syndrome, to end his life. This decision was affirmed by the Court of Appeal (see [2013] EWCA Crim 961). The Divisional Court recognised the difference between a doctor not seeking to prolong life and positively acting to end life; the former would not involve any criminal liability as was recognised in *Airedale NHS Trust* v *Bland* (see **2.5.2.2.3**) but extending the law to cover the latter would involve a major change, rather than an incremental development, involving controversial matters of social policy which it was for Parliament to resolve rather than the courts.

6.3.2 **Duress of circumstances: necessity by any other name?**

Perhaps some judicial reluctance to recognise a defence of necessity was due to the general belief that it operated as a justification. In Canada in *Perka et al.* v *The Queen* (1984) 13 DLR (4th) 1, the Supreme Court of Canada held that necessity should be recognised in Canada as an excuse thereby implying 'no vindication of the deeds of the actor'. Thus the defence was seen as a concession to human frailty and was based on 'society's expectation of appropriate and normal resistance to pressure'. In *Lynch* Lord Simon expressed the view that there was no sustainable distinction in principle between necessity and duress, the latter being 'merely a particular application of the doctrine of necessity'.

 Question

Might it be possible, therefore, to incorporate some forms of necessity within an extended defence of duress without opening 'a door which no man could shut'?

This is what appears to have happened almost by sleight of hand in several cases before the Court of Appeal. It is a development which was facilitated by Lord Lane's formulation of the test for duress in *Graham*, which did not require that the person from whom the threat emanated should have specified that D commit a particular crime; the issue is simply whether D may have acted as he did because he feared that if he did not so act he would suffer death or serious injury.

In *Willer* (1986) 83 Cr App R 225, D was charged with reckless driving. To escape a gang of youths who threatened to kill him and his passenger, D drove his car over the pavement and into a shopping precinct. When the assistant recorder ruled that the defence of necessity was not available to him he changed his plea to guilty. The Court of Appeal quashed his conviction. While they appeared to accept that the defence of necessity may have been available, they held that the appropriate defence was one of duress. Watkins LJ stated (at p. 227):

> [T]he assistant recorder upon those facts should have directed that he would leave to the jury the question as to whether or not . . . the appellant was wholly driven by force of circumstance into doing what he did and did not drive the car otherwise than under that form of compulsion, i.e. under duress.

In *Conway* [1988] 3 All ER 1025, D was charged with reckless driving and pleaded necessity, claiming he drove as he did because his passenger feared an attack from two men who were approaching the car. The two men were, in fact, plain-clothes police officers who were approaching the car to arrest the passenger. At trial the judge did not leave the defence of duress of circumstances or necessity to the jury. The Court of Appeal felt constrained to quash the conviction, regarding the decision in *Willer* as binding on it.

The Court of Appeal saw the defence of necessity/duress of circumstances as a 'logical consequence of the existence of the defence of duress as that term is ordinarily understood, i.e. "do this or else"'; thus it would be subject to the same limitations, namely that the harm sought to be avoided must be death or

serious injury. The Court found support for this position in the speech of Lord Hailsham LC in *Howe* [1987] 1 AC 417, where he said (at p. 429):

> Duress is only that species of the genus of necessity which is caused by wrongful threats. I cannot see that there is any way in which a person of ordinary fortitude can be excused from the one type of pressure on his will rather than the other.

In *Martin* [1989] 1 All ER 652, D drove while disqualified from driving after threats from his wife that she would commit suicide if he did not do so. D pleaded guilty to the charge of driving while disqualified when the trial judge ruled that this was an absolute offence to which necessity was not a defence. The Court of Appeal quashed the conviction and Simon Brown J took the opportunity to summarise the principles governing necessity stating (at p. 653):

> [F]irst, English law does, in extreme circumstances, recognise a defence of necessity. Most commonly this defence arises as duress, that is pressure on [D's] will from the wrongful threats or violence of another. Equally however it can arise from objective dangers threatening [D] or others. Arising thus it is conveniently called 'duress of circumstances'.

By formulating the defence of necessity as a form of duress it is clear that English courts regard it as an excuse rather than a justification.

Secondly, Simon Brown J went on to say (at p. 653):

> [T]he defence is available only if, from an objective standpoint, [D] can be said to be acting reasonably and proportionately in order to avoid a threat of death or serious injury.

This acts as a limitation on the circumstances in which necessity may be pleaded. It is not a mere matter of balancing harms so that the defence would be available if the harm committed is less than the harm D feared would otherwise occur. **The defence is only available if the harm D seeks to avoid is that of death or serious injury to himself or another** (see further *Pipe* v *DPP* [2012] EWHC 1821 (Admin)).

Thirdly, Simon Brown J stated (at pp. 653, 654):

> [A]ssuming the defence to be open to [D] on his account of the facts, the issue should be left to the jury, who should be directed to determine these two questions: first, was [D], or may he have been, impelled to act as he did because as a result of what he reasonably believed to be the situation he had good cause to fear that otherwise death or serious physical injury would result; second, if so, would a sober person of reasonable firmness, sharing the characteristics of [D], have responded to that situation by acting as [D] acted? If the answer to both those questions was Yes, then the jury would acquit: the defence of necessity would have been established.

This test is consistent with that stated by Lord Lane CJ in *Graham*, as confirmed by the House of Lords in *Howe*, and it has been further affirmed by the Court of Appeal in *Abdul-Hussain*. In that case the Court drew attention to one issue which may have greater significance in the context of duress of circumstances where the offence committed by D is chosen by him in response to the perceived threat, rather than in duress by threats being specified by the person who is issuing the threats, namely that of proportionality. The jury will have to consider whether the offence which D committed was a reasonable and proportionate response to the threat perceived in the circumstances. This is part of the objective question whether a reasonable person would have done as D did.

The Court of Appeal in *Petgrave* [2019] RTR 6, a case in which the appellant had been convicted of causing serious injury by dangerous driving, confirmed that the tests laid down by Simon Brown J in *Martin* were correct. The Court held that a defendant who wishes to rely on the defence of duress of circumstances cannot put it in issue through his advocate; it must be put in issue by evidence. Once it has become a live issue the *Martin* questions are for the jury to decide; it is not appropriate for the trial judge to treat them as questions on which he can or should rule as a matter of law. Holroyde LJ said:

> The defence of duress of circumstances may in principle be a defence to most crimes (with certain specific exceptions). We accept that it may be a defence to a charge under section 1A of the [Road Traffic Act 1988]. It is a defence by which an accused justifies his commission of what would otherwise be a crime on the ground that he was compelled by force of circumstances to act as he did . . .
>
> The issues for a jury considering the defence of duress of circumstances are those identified by this court in *Martin*. Consideration of the defence therefore requires the jury to reflect upon the accused's reasons for acting as he did, his reasonable belief as to the situation in which he found himself and his good cause to fear death or serious injury, and also to reflect upon whether a sober person of reasonable firmness would have responded in a similar way to the particular situation in which the accused was placed.
>
> We accept that there may be cases in which the evidence adduced as part of the prosecution case provides a basis for a successful submission of no case to answer on the ground that that evidence in itself raised the issue of duress and was such that no reasonable jury, properly directed, could find that the defence had been disproved. But, having regard to the nature of the defence, we think that such cases will be rare. In our judgment, this case is certainly not one of them.

An interesting attempt to plead duress of circumstances was made in *Rodger and Rose* [1998] 1 Cr App R 143, on charges of breaking prison. The appellants claimed they had escaped as they had become suicidal in prison. The trial judge declined to leave the defence to the jury which decision was confirmed by the Court of Appeal. Sir Patrick Russell, having reviewed the decisions in *Willer, Conway, Martin,* and *Pommell* stated:

> All these authorities had one feature in common which is not present in the instant appeals. The feature which was causative of the defendants committing the offence was in all the authorities extraneous to the offender himself. In contrast, in these appeals it was solely the suicidal tendencies, the thought processes and the emotions of the offenders themselves which operated as duress. That factor introduced an entirely subjective element not present in the authorities . . . .
>
> We do not think that such a development of the law would be justified, nor do we think that such an extension would be in the public interest. If allowed it could amount to a licence to commit crime dependent on the personal characteristics and vulnerability of the offender.

In *Quayle and others: AG's Reference (No. 2 of 2004)* [2005] EWCA Crim 1415, the Court of Appeal, approving of *Rodger and Rose*, held that duress of circumstances was not available to several defendants charged with various offences of possession, cultivation, and supply of cannabis which they genuinely and reasonably believed were necessary to avoid pain arising from a medical condition. One of the reasons to support the decision was the absence of an extraneous circumstance capable of objective scrutiny by judge and jury. Following consideration of *Rodger and Rose*, *Abdul-Hussain*, and *Shayler*, the Court stated (at para. 75):

> [T]he requirement of an objectively ascertainable extraneous cause has a considerable, and in our view understandable, basis. It rests on the pragmatic consideration that the defence of necessity, which the Crown would carry the onus to disprove, must be confined within narrowly defined limits or it will become an opportunity for almost untriable and certainly peculiarly difficult issues, not to mention abusive defences.

The requirements of imminence and immediacy apply equally to duress of circumstances. In *Quayle and others: AG's Reference (No. 2 of 2004)* the Court held that the defence could not succeed where 'the defendant was taking a deliberately considered course of conduct over a substantial period of time, involving continuous and regular breaches of the law'. Expanding on this the Court stated (at para. 81):

> Where there is not imminent or immediate threat or peril, but only a general assertion of an internal motivation to engage in prohibited activities in order to prevent or alleviate pain, it is also difficult to identify any extraneous or objective factors by reference to which a jury could be expected to measure whether the motivation was such as to override the defendant's will or to force him to act as he did.

As with the defence of duress, D may only rely on the defence of duress of circumstances so long as the threat continues (see *Pommell* [1995] 2 Cr App R 607). While initial driving with excess alcohol to escape assailants may have been excusable due to duress of circumstances, it would not be necessary for D to continue to drive a further two and a half miles home (see *DPP v Jones* [1990] RTR 34). If D drives off with excess alcohol to escape a threat he will be guilty of the driving offence if the prosecution prove that he continued to drive after the threat had ceased to operate (see *DPP v Bell* [1992] Crim LR 176; *DPP v Mullally* [2006] EWHC 3448 (Admin)).

6.3.3 The limits of duress of circumstances

The defence of necessity recognised as duress of circumstances is subject to the same limitations as the defence of duress (see *Pommell* [1995] 2 Cr App R 607). The positive result of this is that it implies that necessity could be pleaded by a thief if he stole food to save himself from starvation thereby refuting the dictum of Lord Denning in *London Borough of Southwark v Williams* [1971] 2 All ER 175 at 179, that 'if hunger were once allowed to be an excuse for stealing, it would open a door through which all kinds of lawlessness and disorder would pass'. The negative results, however, are that necessity in this form is an excuse and **is not available on a charge of murder or attempted murder**. Things have thus come full circle; in

Howe their Lordships used the case of *Dudley and Stephens* as authority that necessity was not a defence to murder and thus duress should not be a defence to murder. *Howe* was one of the authorities used in *Conway* to develop the defence of duress of circumstances/necessity. The case of *Dudley and Stephens* however is open to several interpretations. In *Lynch* Lord Simon took the ratio to be that there was no defence of necessity known to English law. In *Howe* three of their Lordships interpreted it to mean that necessity was not a defence to murder. The decision in *Dudley and Stephens* could as easily be interpreted as holding there was no necessity to kill in the situation in which the two accused found themselves.

> The defendants were adrift in an open boat with another man and a boy after being shipwrecked. After several days without food and water they decided to kill the boy who was very weak and they fed on his body. Four days later they were rescued. On their trial for murder the jury returned a special verdict finding that the men would have died before rescue had they not eaten the boy who, because of his weak state, would have died sooner, and that there was no reasonable prospect of relief and no appreciable chance of saving life except by killing.

However, there was no greater necessity for killing the boy than any of the three men. Lord Coleridge CJ agreed with this last point. Indeed, as the mariners' peril was due to them being adrift, killing any one of them was not going to assure their rescue and thus it could be argued that there was no necessity to kill anyone. The outcome for the two mariners, however, was that they were convicted of murder but the death sentence was commuted to six months' imprisonment.

As *Dudley and Stephens* is such an unsatisfactory authority it would have been possible and more desirable for their Lordships in *Howe* to ignore it and decide the issue afresh. There are situations in which killing another may be an appropriate action and even commendable but the criminal law discourages such action. Professor J. C. Smith in *Justification and Excuse in the Criminal Law* (1989) gives two illustrations. At the inquest into the deaths arising from the *Herald of Free Enterprise* disaster in Zeebrugge harbour an army corporal gave evidence that he led dozens of people to safety up a rope ladder. On the ladder was a petrified passenger who was refusing to move. When persuasion failed the corporal instructed another passenger below this man to push him off the ladder which he did and he was never seen again. If such a situation were to arise again the criminal law now clearly indicates that a person should die and allow many others to die rather than risk killing the person obstructing their avenue of escape. Should not the criminal law promote the net saving of human life? To quote Professor Smith (at p. 77) 'The law has lost touch with reality if it condemns as murder conduct which right-thinking people regard as praiseworthy.'

The second illustration is related by Joe Simpson in his book *Touching the Void* (1988) (and depicted in the excellent 2003 documentary film of the same name). One climber slipped off a 19,000-foot cliff in the Andes and was left dangling on a rope attached to his partner. When the partner reached the point of exhaustion and realised that his life was in peril he cut the rope. Miraculously the other climber survived as he fell on to a snow-covered ice bridge below. Again, if a climber were to seek guidance from the criminal law before going on an expedition, he would discover that it would direct him in such a situation that he should die along with his partner rather than cut the rope to save himself.

Perhaps the defence of necessity is available to the passengers on the sinking ship and to the climber. While the narrow defence of necessity recognised by Lord Goff in *re F* does not touch on these situations, there are indications in *Re A (Children) (Conjoined Twins: Medical Treatment) (No. 1)* [2000] 4 All ER 961 (see **3.2.3.8**) that necessity may be a broader defence than previously conceded and that it may apply to killing. *Re A* raised the crucial question, originally framed by Lord Mackay in *Howe* [1987] 1 AC 417, whether 'the law should recognise in any individual in any circumstances, however extreme, the right to choose that one innocent person should be killed rather than another'? As the doctors' duties to Jodie and Mary were in conflict, Ward LJ concluded that 'the law must allow an escape through choosing the lesser of two evils', in which case the operation being justified would involve no unlawful act even though it would inevitably result in Mary's death. This was, in effect, a defence of necessity but there was no clear agreement between the three Lord Justices of Appeal on the limits of this defence. The narrowest approach was that of Ward LJ who was concerned to point out the very limited extent to which this decision should be regarded as a precedent, emphasising the uniqueness of the case. He stated (at p. 1018):

> Lest it be thought that this decision could become authority for wider propositions, such as that a doctor, once he has determined that a patient cannot survive, can kill the patient, it is important to restate the unique circumstances for which this case is authority. They are that it must be impossible to preserve the life of X without bringing about the death of Y, that Y by his or her very continued existence will inevitably bring about the death of X within a short period of time, and that X is capable of living an independent life but Y is incapable under any circumstances (including all forms of medical intervention) of viable independent existence.

His judgment offers no hope for the drowning passengers or the tiring climber. Brooke LJ, however, expressly framed the issue in the case as one of necessity adopting the tests for necessity which Sir James Stephen provided in his *Digest of Criminal Law* (1887):

> (i)   the act is needed to avoid inevitable and irreparable evil;
> (ii) no more should be done than is reasonably necessary for the purpose to be achieved;
> (iii) the evil inflicted must not be disproportionate to the evil avoided.

He concluded that as the principles of family law 'point irresistibly to the conclusion that the interests of Jodie must be preferred to the interests of Mary, I consider that all these requirements are satisfied in this case'. This amounts to a general defence of necessity based on a balancing of harms and, as such, would apply to the passengers on the sinking ship and the tiring climber.

Walker LJ had concluded that performing the operation would not involve the commission of the offence of murder in respect of Mary as, applying the principle in *Gillick*, 'the bona fide exercise by a doctor of his clinical judgement [is a] complete negation of the [*mens rea* for murder]' (see **3.2.3.8**). Speaking *obiter*, he stated that he was also prepared, if necessary, to extend the defence of necessity to cover the instant case.

Re A, accordingly, does not finally resolve the question whether there is a general defence of necessity based on a balancing of harms test. Ward LJ's judgment points against this; Brooke LJ's judgment is strongly in favour; and Walker LJ's judgment has *obiter dicta* supportive only of an extension of the defence of necessity to cover the instant case but no more and thus aligns itself more closely to the position of Ward LJ.

When the opportunity arose in *Shayler* [2001] 1 WLR 2206, for the Court of Appeal to indicate whether necessity existed as a defence distinct from duress, it eschewed it, retreating to the comfort zone of duress of circumstances, commending the blurring of lines between the two defences! Duress and necessity are not the same; blurring the distinctions between them can only lead to confusion and injustice. It is to be hoped that when next the Court of Appeal is confronted with this problem it will abandon languor and endeavour to provide a clear and workable statement of the law on necessity. In the post-September 11, 2001 world, such a statement is necessary if, for example, those who might have to deal with a hijacked plane in the air and heading for central London are to know whether the law permits them to shoot it down over the North Sea killing the crew and passengers, this being the only way of avoiding the loss of thousands of lives if the plane is allowed to continue flying to its target.

6.4 Private defence and prevention of crime

6.4.1 General

An accused charged with an offence may seek to plead that he acted as he did to protect himself, or his property, or others from attack, or to prevent crime, or to effect a lawful arrest. In strict terms such pleas are not 'defences' in the sense in which duress is a defence as, if raised successfully, they provide a justification for D's conduct thereby rendering it lawful.

 Example

It is an offence under s. 20 of the Offences Against the Person Act 1861 to wound another person unlawfully and maliciously. If D is charged with this offence but pleads that he inflicted the wound on V who was attacking him with an axe, his use of reasonable force in the circumstances would be justified and thus lawful. As the use of lawful force is not an offence D would be acquitted of the s. 20 offence as an element of the *actus reus* was missing.

Where D pleads one of these justifications the onus is on the prosecution to disprove it beyond reasonable doubt. These principles were stated by Lord Griffiths in *Beckford* v *R* [1988] AC 130, as follows (at p. 144):

> It is because it is an essential element of all crimes of violence that the violence or the threat of violence should be unlawful that self-defence, if raised as an issue in a criminal trial, must be disproved by the prosecution. If the prosecution fail to do so [D] is entitled to be acquitted because the prosecution will have failed to prove an essential element of the crime namely that the violence used by [D] was unlawful.

Self-defence is a justification recognised by the common law. It is a general defence which not only applies to offences of violence but is also available to D where, for example, he threatens to use violence (see *Cousins* [1982] QB 526; *Afzal* [1993] Crim LR 791). It covers not only defence of oneself but also of others (see *Rose* (1884) 15 Cox CC 540; *Duffy* [1967] 1 QB 63); the term private defence is thus more appropriate and less confusing. Private defence overlaps with s. 3 of the Criminal Law Act 1967 which provides:

(1) A person may use such force as is reasonable in the circumstances in the prevention of crime, or in effecting or assisting in the lawful arrest of offenders or suspected offenders or of persons unlawfully at large.

(2) Subsection (1) above shall replace the rules of common law on the question when force used for a purpose mentioned in the subsection is justified by that purpose.

Both the common law and s. 3 impose the same requirement that the force used is such as is reasonable in the circumstances (see *Devlin* v *Armstrong* [1971] NI 13; *McInnes* [1971] 1 WLR 1600). If D uses force to defend himself or another from an unlawful attack by P he will usually also be acting to prevent a crime.

Key Point

Whether D has used reasonable force is a question of fact for the magistrates or jury to decide.

In most cases it will not matter whether the plea is based in private defence or in prevention of crime. But if s. 3 were interpreted as having superseded the common law on private defence, D would be left defenceless where P, in attacking him, is not committing a crime (as where P is under 10 years of age, insane, in a state of automatism, or under a material mistake of fact) and D knows this. In such a case D could not claim to be acting to prevent a crime; he could, however, claim to be defending himself from an unjustified attack and therefore rely on private defence. It appears that the courts accept that private defence and prevention of crime under s. 3(1) coexist as justifications (see *Cousins* [1982] QB 526). Under s. 3(1) 'crime' means an offence under domestic law and does not cover something which is only a crime under international law (see *Jones and others* [2006] UKHL 16).

In one of the worst examples of gesture politics resulting in pointless legislation, the Government, honouring a pledge made by the Secretary of State for Justice to the Labour Party Conference in 2007 to introduce new legislation on the use of force in self-defence and the prevention of crime, enacted s. 76 of the Criminal Justice and Immigration Act 2008 (CJIA). The concern underlying the legislation was that people were reluctant to take action to prevent offences or detain offenders as several who had done so were themselves arrested and prosecuted for using force that they saw as reasonable and necessary. Confusion over the law on self-defence and the use of force in prevention of crime was considered by some in Government and the media to underlie this. Several high-profile instances of householders using force against burglars featured prominently in the popular and political debate. Section 76 was enacted to clarify the operation of the common law on the use of reasonable force in self-defence, in prevention of crime, or in the arrest of offenders (and, by subsequent amendment, it also covers the defence of defence of property).

As initially enacted, the section did not codify all of the law relating to these defences but sought to put into statutory form five principles derived from the case law. To the extent that it simply legislated for what case law had already established, it was pointless. Further, as it did not provide any different answer to the question 'How much force may I use?' than the law already provided, it would not provide any different outcome in situations where 'have-a-go heroes' find themselves arrested and even prosecuted when, for example, they intervene on the street to assist another when attacked. **The question of what is 'reasonable force' is inevitably context-specific and that context includes not only the external circumstances but also D's perception and belief in relation to those circumstances.** Sometimes the only way to determine whether the 'have-a-go hero' was acting reasonably in self-defence or to prevent a crime, rather than unreasonably to exact revenge or as a vigilante, may be to prosecute him for an offence against the person and leave the jury to determine the issue.

The enactment of s. 76 could not stem the problems which arise from context. The use of force by several householders on burglars raised particular problems; not so much to do with self-defence but to do with policing, as the response of the police often appeared heavy-handed and more concerned with the rights of burglars than the fear they might engender in householders awakened late at night to find masked intruders in their home. Following further tabloid newspaper stories and public disquiet, s. 148 of the Legal Aid, Sentencing and Punishment of Offenders Act 2012 amended s. 76, and further amendments to s. 76 were made by the Crime and Courts Act 2013 which provided for a different test to be applied in 'householder' cases. We will examine those cases in **6.4.3.2**.

6.4.1.1 The principles in Section 76

Section 76 only applies where D seeks to raise the common law defences of self-defence or defence of property or the statutory defence under s. 3(1) of the Criminal Law Act and the question arises whether the force used against V was reasonable in the circumstances (s. 76(1) and (2)). The five principles put into statutory form in s. 76 are:

(1) the question whether D's use of force was reasonable in the circumstances is to be decided on the basis of the circumstances D believed to exist (s. 76(3)), even if his belief was mistaken and unreasonable (s. 76(4));

(2) D cannot rely on any mistaken belief attributable to intoxication that was voluntarily induced (s. 76(5));

(3) the degree of force used by D is not to be regarded as having been reasonable in the circumstances as D believed them to be if it was disproportionate in those circumstances (s. 76(6)); in a householder case the test is whether it was 'grossly disproportionate' (s. 76(5A));

(4) in deciding the question in (1) above, a possibility that D could have retreated is to be considered (so far as relevant) as a factor to be taken into account, rather than as giving rise to a duty to retreat (s. 76(6A));

(5) a person acting for a 'legitimate purpose' (i.e. self-defence, defence of property, prevention of crime, or lawful arrest) may not be able to weigh to a nicety the exact measure of any necessary action (s. 76(7)(a)) and evidence of his only having done what he honestly and instinctively thought was necessary for a legitimate purpose constitutes strong evidence that only reasonable action was taken by him for that purpose (s. 76(7)(b)).

The provision provides no guidance on how other problem areas, such as the use of pre-emptive force and unknown circumstances of justification, should be resolved. It also stands in stark contrast to s. 110 of the Serious Organised Crime and Police Act 2005 which limited the powers of a citizen to effect an arrest. That provision seemed to be aimed at discouraging citizens from 'having a go' whereas the rhetoric preceding the enactment of s. 76 appeared to be the opposite. Section 76, accordingly provides little clarification of the law, merely restating in statutory form principles which the case law has long established.

6.4.2 **The necessity of force**

The use of force is not justified if it is not necessary. Whether the use of force was justified is a question of fact for the magistrates or jury to decide. Certain factors will be relevant in considering whether the prosecution have proved beyond reasonable doubt that force was not necessary in the circumstances which existed or which D believed to exist. It is not necessary, however, for there to be an actual attack in progress before D may use force in private defence; it is sufficient if he apprehends an attack and uses force to prevent it. In *Beckford* Lord Griffiths stated (at p. 144): **'a man about to be attacked does not have to wait for his assailant to strike the first blow or fire the first shot; circumstances may justify a pre-emptive strike.'** The danger D apprehends, however, must be sufficiently specific or imminent to justify the actions he takes (see *Devlin* v *Armstrong*), and must be of a nature which could not reasonably be met by more pacific means (*Fegan* [1972] NI 80). Where D's apprehension may justify his response in using force to defend himself, it does not, however, justify him in inciting others to use force. In such circumstances their use of force would be unlawful unless each individually apprehended the unlawful use of violence on himself and acted in response to this apprehension rather than in response to D's incitement (see *Devlin* v *Armstrong*).

6.4.2.1 **Preparing for an attack**

 Question

Where a person apprehends an unlawful attack on himself, may he make preparations to defend himself where those preparations may involve breaches of the criminal law?

This issue arose in *AG's Reference (No. 2 of 1983)* [1984] QB 456.

> D's shop had been attacked and damaged by rioters. Fearing further attacks he made some petrol bombs which he intended to use to protect himself and his property. He was charged with making an explosive substance in such circumstances as to give rise to a reasonable suspicion that he had not made it for a lawful object contrary to s. 4 of the Explosive Substances Act 1883. He pleaded that his lawful object was self-defence and the jury acquitted. The Attorney General referred the case to the Court of Appeal. Lord Lane CJ stated (at p. 470):

The fact that in manufacturing and storing the petrol bombs the respondent committed offences under [the Explosives Act 1875 which prohibits the manufacture and storage of explosives without a licence] did not necessarily involve that when he made them his object in doing so was not lawful. The means by which he sought to fulfil that object were unlawful, but the fact that he could never without committing offences reach the point where he used them in self-defence did not render his object in making them for that purpose unlawful. The object or purpose or end for which the petrol bombs were made was not itself rendered unlawful by the fact that it could not be fulfilled except by unlawful means.

The case is not totally satisfactory as, while it decided in relation to the offence under the 1883 Act that D had made the petrol bombs for a lawful object, it seemed to suggest that he would have been liable for an offence under the 1875 Act. Lord Lane CJ stated (at p. 471):

[A] defendant is not left in the paradoxical position of being able to justify acts carried out in self-defence but not acts immediately preparatory to it. There is no warrant for the submission . . . that acts of self-defence will only avail a defendant when they have been done spontaneously. There is no question of a person in danger of attack 'writing his own immunity' for violent future acts of his . . . . He may still arm himself for his own protection, if the exigency arises, although in so doing he may commit other offences. That he may be guilty of other offences will avoid the risk of anarchy contemplated by the reference.

In relation to a charge under s. 1 of the Prevention of Crime Act 1953 of carrying an offensive weapon in a public place, a person could rely on the defence provided in the section of proving that he had lawful authority or reasonable excuse for carrying it. In *Evans* v *Hughes* [1972] 1 WLR 1452, the Divisional Court stated that only 'an imminent particular threat affecting the particular circumstances in which the weapon was carried' could ground a reasonable excuse. Section 139 of the Criminal Justice Act 1988 creates an additional offence of having an article with a blade or point in a public place without 'good reason or lawful authority'. This is aimed at those in the habit of carrying knives and similar articles.

Professor J. C. Smith criticised the *AG's Reference* decision in *Justification and Excuse in the Criminal Law* (1989) at pp. 122, 123, arguing that, if an act is justifiable because done in self-defence or prevention of crime, this ought to be a sufficient answer to a charge of any crime alleged to be involved in the doing of the act. He provided the following illustration:

If I happen upon a bank robbery and, being shot at by one of the robbers, I pick up the revolver which has been dropped by a wounded policeman and, quite reasonably, fire it in self-defence, I am surely not guilty of an offence under the Firearms Act 1968, s. 1, of being in possession of a firearm without holding a firearm certificate.

As private defence or prevention of crime may only be pleaded in response to offences involving the use of force, the answer to Professor Smith's rhetorical question is that he would be guilty of the offence under s. 1 of the 1968 Act (see Elliott, 'Necessity, Duress and Self-defence' [1989] Crim LR 611, 618), although a charge under s. 1 of the Prevention of Crime Act 1953 could be met by the specific defence provided by that section as interpreted in *Evans* v *Hughes*. Smith and Hogan, in *Criminal Law* (8th edn, 1996), at p. 262, argued that the courts should develop the law so that 'where contravention of *any* law is (i) necessary to enable the right of public or private defence to be exercised, and (ii) reasonable in the circumstances, it ought to be excused'. It is submitted that this is what has partially happened by accident through the development of duress of circumstances. In the robbery example given earlier, on a charge under s. 1 of the Firearms Act 1968, duress of circumstances could be pleaded as an excusatory defence. The issue of imminence of the threat necessary for a successful plea of duress/duress of circumstances obviates the use of the defence by a person who arms himself with a gun because he anticipates that one day he may be attacked; the defence would only be available to the person who arms himself immediately prior to what he believes to be an imminent attack. However, duress/duress of circumstances is only available where D fears death or serious physical injury whereas private defence may be pleaded in justification where a lesser degree of harm is anticipated. Thus Smith and Hogan's plea for further development of the law still requires judicial action if all anomalies are to be removed, particularly as Parliament chose to take no action in s. 76 of the CJIA.

6.4.2.2 Duty to retreat?

Formerly it was believed that the common law imposed a requirement that a person could only plead private defence where he had retreated as far as he could before resorting to the use of force. In *Bird* [1985] 1 WLR 816, the Court of Appeal made it clear that there is no such requirement but rather it is a factor to be considered in deciding whether it was necessary to use force, and whether the force used was reasonable (see s. 76(6A) of the CJIA which gives statutory force to this common law principle). Lord Lane CJ stated (at p. 820) what should have been obvious:

> If the defendant is proved to have been attacking or retaliating or revenging himself, then he was not truly acting in self-defence. Evidence that the defendant tried to retreat or tried to call off the fight may be a cast-iron method of casting doubt on the suggestion that he was the attacker or retaliator or the person trying to revenge himself. But it is not by any means the only method of doing that.

If there were a duty to retreat a person would never be able to use pre-emptive force. Similarly a person is under no duty to refrain from going where he may lawfully go because he knows he is likely to be attacked (see *Field* [1972] Crim LR 435). A distinction must be drawn between the situation where a person acts lawfully but in the realisation that he may be subjected to violence as a result (cf. *Beatty* v *Gillbanks* (1882) 9 QBD 308), and the situation where he deliberately engineers or provokes an attack on himself so that he may respond with force and seek to plead self-defence. In the latter situation the justification of self-defence will not be open to him where V uses only reasonable force to rebuff D's attack (see *Balogun* [1999] 98/6762/X2 and *Browne* [1973] NI 96). But where D starts out as the aggressor, self-defence may be available to him in respect of V's retaliation if V uses violence out of all proportion to that used by D. In such circumstances, D's claim of self-defence will depend on whether he reasonably apprehended that he was in immediate danger from which he had no other means of escape, and whether he used no more force than was necessary (see *Rashford* [2005] EWCA Crim 3377; see also *Keane and McGrath* [2010] EWCA 2514).

6.4.2.3 Mistaken belief in the need to use force

If the prosecution can prove beyond reasonable doubt that there was no necessity to use force this will be an end of the matter, unless D can bring forward some evidence that he was operating under a mistake. First, if D makes a mistake as to the need to use force, the force used is necessarily *objectively* unreasonable, that is, no force being necessary, any force used would be unreasonable.

 Example

V, D's friend, as an April Fools' Day prank disguises himself and pretends to be a robber. D, believing V is a real robber about to rob him, assaults V.

The reasonableness of the force used by D, however, is to be judged in light of the circumstances as he believed them to be (see *Williams* (1984) 78 Cr App R 276; *Beckford* [1988] AC 130, **3.6.1.1.2**; s. 76(3) and (4) of the CJIA). Lord Griffiths stated in *Beckford* (at p. 144) that 'it is an essential element of all crimes of violence that the violence or threat of violence should be unlawful'. In such circumstances, if D uses only such force as was reasonable *in the circumstances as he believed them to be*, the effect of his mistake is that he did not intend to use unlawful force and thus lacked the *mens rea* for any offence of violence against V. Secondly, where D's mistake relates not to the need to use force but to the extent of that necessity, i.e. the gravity of the threat he is facing, the force D uses in response to the perceived threat will, again, be *objectively* unreasonable.

 Example

In a dark alley V confronts D and points a toy pistol at D demanding that he hand over his money or be shot. D, believing the gun to be real, uses his karate skills and aims a fatal blow to V's head.

There was an assault on D which would have justified the use of some force by D to defend himself. The problem is that D anticipated greater danger to himself than existed and used force which may have been appropriate in those anticipated circumstances. Again the reasonableness of the force used by D will be judged according to the circumstances as he believed them to be, not according to the circumstances as they actually were (see *Scarlett* (1994) 98 Cr App R 290 as clarified by *Owino* [1996] 2 Cr App R 128; s. 76(3) and (4) of the CJIA).

In each of these examples it will not matter whether the mistake made is unreasonable (see *Williams*, **3.6.1.1.2**); but obviously the more reasonable the mistake is the more likely it is that the jury will believe D. If, however, D's mistake, whether as to the need to use any force or as to the degree of force necessary, was caused by his voluntary intoxication, the defence will fail (s. 76(5) of the CJIA) whether or not the offence with which he is charged is one of specific or basic intent (see *O'Grady* [1987] 3 WLR 321; *O'Connor* [1991] Crim LR 135, see **5.5.6.3**).

In *Morris* [2013] EWCA Crim 436, the issue arose as to whether D could rely on the defence of prevention of crime where he claimed to have used reasonable force to prevent an ongoing offence albeit that his belief that a crime was being committed was honest but mistaken.

> D, a taxi-driver, thought his passengers were making off without payment and drove his taxi onto the pavement to prevent them getting away, allegedly injuring one of them. D had failed to realise that one of the passengers had remained in the taxi and was ready to pay the fare. D was prosecuted for dangerous driving. An issue arose as to whether D's use of force had to be considered under s. 3 of the Criminal Law Act 1967 as being for the purposes of preventing crime or in effecting the lawful arrest of offenders or suspected offenders. The defence contended that D was acting to prevent crime. The trial judge ruled that the only defence that could be left to the jury was that of effecting a lawful arrest as the offence of making off without payment was complete when the passengers alighted from the taxi and thus there was no offence to prevent. As a lawful arrest required D to have reasonable grounds to believe the passengers had committed an offence, this defence had little prospect of success. D conceded he had not taken the simple step of looking in his rear-view mirror to see if any passengers remained in the vehicle before driving onto the pavement. D was convicted and appealed contending that the jury should have been directed to consider the force D used in the context of his mistaken belief that the passengers were in the act of making off without payment and that he was preventing that crime. The Court of Appeal considered that this defence should have been left to the jury, Leveson LJ stating (at paras 19–20):

> The use of reasonable force in self-defence or in defence of another person is lawful. The essence of these defences is the honestly held belief of the defendant as to the facts (but not the law: see *Jones* [2007] AC 137 . . .). In relation to use of force in the prevention of crime . . . , the defence is afforded by s. 3 of the Criminal Law Act 1967. If honest belief affords a defence under s. 3 in those circumstances, it must equally do so [for] a person who claims to have used reasonable force to prevent the commission of a crime other than a crime of violence against another.
>
> Accordingly, if, as the appellant contended in this case, he honestly believed that the men were making off without payment, he was entitled to use reasonable force in order to prevent the commission of that offence; the jury would thus be required to consider whether driving onto the pavement (howsoever that occurred) was the reasonable exercise of the use of force.

6.4.2.3.1 *Mistake and psychiatric conditions*

 Question

If D suffers from a psychiatric condition which causes him to perceive a greater threat of danger from a situation than others not so affected would, will psychiatric evidence be admissible to assist the jury when considering what D's honest belief might have been?

As the reasonableness of the force D used can only be judged in light of the circumstances as he honestly believed them to be one would think that psychiatric evidence about his condition must be relevant to this issue. However, when the Court of Appeal was confronted with this very situation in the case of *Martin (Anthony)* [2001] EWCA Crim 2245, [2002] 1 Cr App R 27, it ruled that psychiatric evidence relating to D's perception of his circumstances was not admissible. There was medical evidence to the effect that D suffered from a personality disorder which would have caused him to perceive a much greater danger to his physical safety than the average person when he disturbed burglars in his lonely farmhouse and fired at them with his shotgun, killing one and severely wounding the other. The Court of Appeal arrived at its decision on policy grounds, distinguishing self-defence from provocation on the basis that self-defence is both a complete defence and one which applies to all assaults. Neither of these facts seems pertinent to the issue of what D's honest belief was when he fired his shotgun. The Court of Appeal also ignored its own previously declared position in relation to duress (a complete defence to all crimes bar murder and attempted murder) where in *Martin (DP)* [2000] 2 Cr App R 42, treating duress as analogous to self-defence, it held that psychiatric evidence was admissible to explain D's mistaken belief that things said were threatening when they would not have been perceived as such by the average person (see **6.3.2**).

A further reason for the decision supplied by Lord Woolf CJ in *Martin (Anthony)* (at para. 66) was 'the undoubted fact that self-defence is raised in a great many cases resulting from minor assaults and it would be wholly disproportionate to encourage medical disputes in cases of that sort'. Martin, however, stood convicted of murder; it could hardly be considered disproportionate to the gravity of that offence to permit an exploration of medical evidence. Lord Woolf CJ went on to state (*Martin (Anthony)* (at para. 66)):

> Lord Hobhouse . . . in *Smith* [see **9.3.2.2.1**] recognised that in relation to self-defence, too generous an approach as to what is reasonable could result in 'exorbitant defence' . . . .
>
> As a matter of principle we would reject the suggestion that the approach of the majority in *Smith* in relation to provocation should be applied directly to the different issue of self-defence.

With respect, this confuses several issues. The issue in *Smith* related to the objective question on a plea of provocation of whether D exercised the degree of self-control to be expected of the reasonable man; the issue in the current case relates to the subjective question of what was D's honest belief, a matter very different and totally unrelated to any issue before the House of Lords in *Smith*. Secondly, the argument raised on appeal in the instant case was not for a more generous approach to the question of what degree of force might be considered reasonable in response to a particular perceived threat, but rather that relevant evidence as to what was the threat which D perceived should be admitted and then the reasonableness of the force he used in response to that perceived threat be determined in the normal way. But Lord Woolf CJ further confused matters when he stated that evidence that D is suffering from a psychiatric condition might be admitted 'in exceptional cases' where that evidence is 'especially probative'. First, the admissibility of evidence does not depend on whether it is probative but whether it is relevant to an issue in the case. What weight should be attributed to it, i.e. whether it is probative of any particular fact, is a matter for the jury to determine. Secondly, his Lordship did not explain what cases might be considered exceptional nor what he meant by 'especially probative'. If the suggestion is that medical evidence will be admitted only where it relates to a very serious psychiatric condition which greatly impairs D's powers of perception, the Court misunderstands the nature of the defence of self-defence and the effect of mistake on such a plea (see **3.6.1.1.2**). If, as Lord Griffiths stated in *Beckford* v *R* [1988] AC 130 (at p. 144) 'a genuine belief in facts which if true would justify self-defence . . . negates the intent to act unlawfully' the genuineness of that belief does not depend on the seriousness of the psychiatric condition which might have given rise to it. Furthermore, in *Shaw* v *R* [2001] UKPC 26; [2002] 1 Cr App R 10, Lord Bingham of Cornhill, delivering the opinion of the Privy Council, stated (at para. 19) that an essential question for the jury's consideration in a case involving a plea of self-defence is, 'taking the circumstances *and the danger* as the [accused] honestly believed them to be, was the amount of force which he used reasonable?' (emphasis added). This makes it clear that D's honest belief comprises not just his perception of the objective circumstances in which he was placed but also his perception of the danger to which those circumstances gave rise. Lord Woolf's dictum suggests that the danger to which a situation gives rise is something to be assessed objectively rather than from the subjective perspective of D. This runs contrary to every authority in the Court of Appeal and the Privy Council since the Court of Appeal decided *Williams (Gladstone)* (1984) 78 Cr App R 276. Section 76(8) of the CJIA provides that sub-s. (7) (see **6.4.1.1**) 'is not to be read as preventing other matters from being taken into account where they are relevant to deciding' whether D's use of force was reasonable in the circumstances. This would seem to leave the door open to the courts to resile from the position articulated in *Martin (Anthony)* and adopt one consistent with *Martin (DP)* and *Shaw*.

Some of the problems identified above arising from the decision of the Court of Appeal in *Martin (Anthony)* have been addressed in the case of *Press and Thompson* [2013] EWCA Crim 2514.

> P and T were charged with causing V1 GBH with intent contrary to s. 18 of the Offences Against the Person Act 1861 and attempting to cause V2 GBH with intent. V1 and V2 were customers at a burger van who, upon receiving their orders, were attacked by P and T who knocked them to the ground and punched and kicked them. V1 and V2 gave evidence that they had said or done nothing to provoke the attack. P and T gave evidence that V1 and V2 had acted aggressively towards them by words and gestures. At trial T called psychiatric evidence to the effect that following service in Afghanistan he was suffering from PTSD (post-traumatic stress disorder) which could make him hypersensitive to threatening situations and that if he felt threatened he might overreact to protect himself, even if there was no objective reason for him to do so. On T's appeal against his convictions, the Court of Appeal confirmed that his PTSD was relevant to the question whether he held a genuine belief that he was under threat.

This represents a retreat from the position adopted in *Martin* but the Court deftly circumvented this obstacle by treating *Martin* as a case concerned with the objective question of the reasonableness of the force used. As regards the jury assessment of the reasonableness of the force used in the circumstances as T believed them to be, s. 76(7) of the CJIA required the jury to consider whether T 'honestly and instinctively' thought that the force he used was necessary in defence of himself and, ultimately, whether that force was proportionate in the circumstances as he believed them to be (s. 76(6) of the CJIA). However, Pitchford LJ went on to state (at para. 39):

> [A] belief honestly held by the defendant that he did only what was necessary in self-defence is to be treated as 'strong evidence' that the degree of force used was reasonable, but it is not conclusive evidence. The ultimate decision is entirely objective: was the force used proportionate (and therefore reasonable) in the circumstances as the defendant believed them to be? It seems to us that the facts of the present case provide a useful example of circumstances in which the objective test was likely to resolve the ultimate question. Even if [T] genuinely believed himself to be under threat from [V1] and [V2], the jury could assess for themselves from the [evidence including] . . . CCTV film whether [T], even upon his understanding, had gone grossly beyond what was reasonable in the circumstances.

The Court was at pains to emphasise that while the psychiatrist's evidence was to the effect that T's belief that he needed to use force may have been 'deluded', the use of this term was ill-judged as there was no suggestion of a psychotic or other delusion but rather that because of the effects of PTSD he had mistakenly judged the need to use force. The Court was satisfied that the trial judge had correctly directed the jury on the relevance of the evidence of PTSD to the subjective question of whether T had a genuine belief in the need to defend himself and whether he did only what he believed necessary, but ultimately it was for the jury to resolve whether the degree of force was reasonable. The Court did not explore the issues left hanging in *Martin* of what might be 'exceptional cases' or what is meant by 'especially probative', leaving the impression that these dicta have drifted into obscurity and do not present any point of focus for the Court when it now considers self-defence post-CJIA 2008.

Where, however, the belief in the need to use force arises from a delusion, and the issue of insanity arises, the Court of Appeal in the case of *Oye* [2013] EWCA Crim 1725 held that in assessing the reasonableness of force used in self-defence, the jury were to leave out of account an honest and instinctive belief in the necessity to use force which D formed as a result of an insane delusion as to the nature of the threat he faced.

> D was charged with affray following some bizarre and violent behaviour. When in police custody he inflicted serious injury on a police officer and less serious injuries on others before being overpowered and eventually sectioned under the Mental Health Act. At his trial there was unchallenged psychiatric evidence that D was suffering at the time from a psychotic delusion and that he was insane; he regarded the police officers as 'evil spirits' and the injuries were caused to them as he used his 'supernatural powers' to escape from them. The jury convicted and D appealed contending that the judge should have directed a verdict of insanity or, on the basis of concessions made by the prosecution, it had to be accepted that he acted in what he honestly took to be self-defence.

The Court of Appeal rejected the suggestion that D was entitled to rely upon his insane delusion as presenting an honestly held belief in the need to use force in self-defence and also the further suggestion that therefore it must be the case that the force used was reasonable in those circumstances as he believed them to be. The Court relied on strong policy reasons for doing so as the more insanely deluded a person might be in using violence in purported self-defence, the more likely it was that he would be acquitted. The result of this would be that a person in need of protection and hospital treatment or supervision would not get any with the concomitant result that the public would be exposed to the risk of further violence. The Court therefore took the view that whatever the force in the purist (subjectivist) argument, there were strong policy reasons for rejecting the argument put forward on D's behalf. Davis LJ stated (at para. 47):

> An insane person cannot set the standards of reasonableness as to the degree of force used by reference to his own insanity. In truth it makes as little sense to talk of the reasonable lunatic as it did, in the context of cases on provocation, to talk of the reasonable glue-sniffer.

The Court further emphasised that prior to the CJIA 2008 the psychiatric characteristics of an accused could not be taken into consideration on the objective question whether the degree of force used was reasonable in the circumstances. Certainly it is difficult to see how a jury could be asked to consider what degree of force might be proportionate to repel a perceived attack from an 'evil spirit'. But had his insane delusion been of a paranoid nature, for instance that the police officers were mafia assassins who were seeking to kill him, this would have been a mistaken belief that could have formed the basis for consideration of the objective question by the jury. Against such a belief D's use of force might not have been considered disproportionate which could have led to an outright acquittal and the scenario conceived by Davis LJ made a reality.

 Key Point

> Where reliance is placed on a delusion which arises from a psychiatric condition falling within the bounds of the M'Naghten Rules, the court will not countenance a defence of self-defence being raised but reliance may be placed on the defence of insanity.

In the instant case, while the Court of Appeal dismissed the ground of appeal which contended that the trial judge should have directed a special verdict (because, once insanity is raised as a defence, it is a matter for the jury to determine the issue under s. 2(1) of the Trial of Lunatics Act 1883), the Court could not identify any safe or rational basis for the jury having departed from the unchallenged psychiatric evidence and thus quashed the convictions as being unsafe and substituted special verdicts of insanity.

6.4.2.4 Unknown circumstances of justification

While the use of force must have been necessary in the circumstances for D to be able to rely on one of the justifications under consideration, a problem which has arisen is whether D must know or believe that circumstances exist which would justify his use of force even though those circumstances actually do exist. The answer was originally in the affirmative.

> In *Dadson* (1850) 4 Cox CC 358, D, a constable, was on duty watching a copse from which wood had been stolen. P emerged carrying wood which he had stolen. He ran away when D called to him and D shot him so that he could arrest him. D was convicted of shooting at P with intent to cause him GBH. D raised the justification that he was shooting to arrest an escaping felon. Stealing wood was only a felony where the thief had two previous convictions for that offence. In fact P had several such convictions and thus was a felon but D did not know this. D's conviction was upheld as he was not justified in shooting P as the fact that P was committing a felony was not known to him at the time.

When the Criminal Law Act 1967 was passed it was argued by some that s. 2 (now replaced by s. 24 of the Police and Criminal Evidence Act 1984) and s. 3 had the effect of reversing *Dadson*. Thus it was argued that if a person actually had committed an arrestable offence, his arrest would be lawful even though the arresting officer did not know or suspect on reasonable grounds that he had committed that offence. The Law Commission in its reports on *Codification of the Criminal Law* (Law Com Nos. 143 and 177) has recommended that an accused should be able to rely on unknown circumstances of justification in any case where the use of force was necessary and reasonable. Professor Brian Hogan argued strongly against this view in 'The *Dadson* Principle' [1989] Crim LR 679. In *Chapman* (1988) 89 Cr App R 190, the Divisional Court effectively reaffirmed *Dadson* (and thus the principle for which it is authority) pointing out that if a person is unaware of circumstances justifying an arrest he cannot perform a lawful arrest as he will not be able to comply with s. 28(3) of the Police and Criminal Evidence Act 1984 which requires that he inform the suspect of the grounds for the arrest. Thus if the arrest is unlawful any force used to effect it is likewise unlawful.

6.4.3 The reasonableness of the force

Although the prosecution may be unable to prove that D did not honestly believe force to be necessary in the circumstances (as he believed them to be), they may still defeat a plea of private defence if D used more force than was reasonable in the circumstances as he believed them to be, i.e. 'disproportionate' force (see s. 76(6) of the CJIA). **It is for the jury or magistrates to determine what degree of force was reasonable in the circumstances.**

6.4.3.1 Assessing the reasonableness of the force used

Adapting the test laid down by Lord Diplock in *AG for Northern Ireland's Reference (No. 1 of 1975)* [1977] AC 105, 137, the jury, when considering the reasonableness of the force used, should be directed to ask themselves:

> Are we satisfied that no reasonable man (a) with knowledge of the facts as were known to [D] or . . . believed by him to exist (b) in the circumstances and time available to him for reflection (c) could be of the opinion that the prevention of the risk of harm to which others might be exposed if the suspect were allowed to escape [or the defence of himself or others, or the prevention of crime, or the defence of property] justified exposing [D's victim] to the risk of harm to him that might result from the kind of force that [D] contemplated using?

While the jury are carrying out this exercise of balancing harms in the 'calm analytical atmosphere of the court-room . . . with the benefit of hindsight' (*per* Lord Diplock at p. 138) it is important that they seek to place themselves in the position in which D found himself, under all the stresses to which he was exposed and with the time which he had available to him in which to make his decision whether to use force and the degree of force to use. Lord Morris in *Palmer v The Queen* [1971] AC 814, stated (at p. 832):

> There are no prescribed words which must be employed in or adopted in summing up. All that is needed is a clear exposition, in relation to the particular facts of the case, of the conception of necessary self-defence . . . . If there has been an attack so that defence is reasonably necessary it will be recognised that a person defending himself cannot weigh to a nicety the exact measure of his necessary defensive action.

D's own beliefs in the situation are also pertinent to the issue. *Shannon* (1980) 71 Cr App R 192 and *Whyte* [1987] 3 All ER 416, affirmed Lord Morris's view (at p. 832) that:

> If a jury thought that in a moment of unexpected anguish a person attacked had only done what he honestly and instinctively thought was necessary that would be most potent evidence that only reasonable defensive action had been taken. [See s. 76(7)(b) of the CJIA.]

In *Owino* [1996] 2 Cr App R 128, it was argued on appeal, on the basis of a potentially ambiguous dictum in *Scarlett* (1994) 98 Cr App R 290, that, if D uses more force than is reasonable, his belief that the degree of force he is using is reasonable should result in an acquittal as he would not be intending to use unlawful force. If this was so D would be entitled to an acquittal where, for example, he was charged with murder having taken a gun and shot a shoplifter who ran from his shop when D sought to arrest him, D asserting in his defence that he honestly believed that it was reasonable to shoot shoplifters to arrest them. D's mistake, however, in this situation is not one of fact but one of law, i.e. the degree of force which the law permits to be used for the purpose of arresting an offender. Counsel's argument in *Owino* was rejected, Collins J stating (at p. 134):

> What [Beldam LJ] was not saying [in *Scarlett*], in our view (and indeed if he had said it, it would be contrary to authority) was that the belief, however ill-founded, of the defendant that the degree of force he was using was reasonable, will enable him to do what he did. As Kay J indicated in argument, if that argument was correct, then it would justify, for example, the shooting of someone who was merely threatening to throw a punch, on the basis that the defendant honestly believed, although unreasonably and mistakenly, that it was justifiable for him to use that degree of force. That clearly is not, and cannot be, the law.

This position is endorsed by s. 76(7)(b) of the CJIA. D's claim that he did what he honestly and instinctively thought was necessary in the circumstances is 'strong evidence that only reasonable action was taken by D', it is not conclusive; D is still subject to s. 76(6) which stipulates that the force D uses is not to be regarded as reasonable in the circumstances as D believed them to be if it is disproportionate. Determining at what point force becomes disproportionate is for the jury, bearing in mind that D 'may not be able to weigh to a nicety the exact measure of any necessary action' (s. 76(7)(a) of the CJIA).

6.4.3.2 'Householder' cases

Section 43 of the Crime and Courts Act 2013 made further amendments specifically applying to 'householder cases' (s. 76(5A)) where D (not being a trespasser—s. 76(8A)), in, or partly in, a building which is a dwelling uses force against V whom he believes to be in, or entering, the building as a trespasser. 'Householder cases' are distinguished from other cases involving use of force: the degree of force used by D is not to be regarded as having been reasonable in the circumstances as D believed them to be if it was grossly disproportionate in those circumstances.

The intention behind this provision, as set out in the Explanatory Notes to the Act, is 'to give people who defend themselves or others from intruders in their homes greater legal protection' (para. 487). The Explanatory Notes go on to state regarding sub-s. (5A) (at para. 488):

> This provides that in a 'householder case', the level of force used by householders when defending themselves from trespassers (or people they believe to be trespassers) will not be regarded as having been reasonable in the circumstances as they believed them to be if that level of force was grossly disproportionate in those circumstances. In other words, it could be reasonable for householders to use disproportionate force to defend themselves from burglars in their homes.

Many further sub-ss. ((8A)–(8F)) are then required to define what is a 'householder case'. Section 76(8A) limits householder cases to ones where the defence relied on is that of self-defence; it does not apply where the defence relied on is that of defence of property, prevention of crime, or arrest of an offender. If there is uncertainty as to which defence D is relying upon, the jury may have to consider different directions regarding the issue of reasonable force depending on whether the force D used was for the purpose of self-defence or one of the other justificatory defences. The further problem, of course, with this convoluted form of legislative draftsmanship in s. 76 is that the converse of the central proposition in sub-s. (5A) does not necessarily hold true.

 Key Point

> A jury is not bound to conclude that force which is disproportionate, but not grossly so, will be considered to be reasonable force; it is only reasonable force that may be used in self-defence or under s. 3 of the Criminal Law Act 1967.

Grossly disproportionate force has always been unreasonable force; stating that it cannot amount to reasonable force does not provide any greater guidance to jurors or unfortunate householders confronted in the dead of night by an intruder. It may be that Parliament intended some different test to apply, but the agonised language used stops short of stating explicitly that a householder may use disproportionate force (short of being grossly disproportionate force) to defend himself or others from a trespasser within, or partly within, his dwelling, and that such force is not to be regarded as unreasonable. The court have held that s. 76(5A) does not mean that a householder can use any force so long as it is not grossly disproportionate; the question for the jury is always whether the defendant used reasonable force. This interpretation was set out by the Divisional Court in *R (Collins)* v *Secretary of State for Justice* [2016] EWHC 33 Admin. Sir Brian Leveson P explained his reasoning as follows (at paras 23 to 25):

> The effect, and no doubt purpose, of s. 76(5A) is to allow for a discretionary area of judgment in householder cases, with a different emphasis to that which applies in other cases. The obvious example concerns the extent to which it is appropriate to take into account the duty to retreat (which, by s. 76(6A) remains a factor to be taken into account). In a householder case, the failure to do so and, thus, the use of force, may be disproportionate

but still reasonable although in a non-householder case, that would be unreasonable by virtue of s. 76(6). In that regard, it is important to note that Article 8 of the ECHR specifically provides for protection of the home and s. 76(5A) may do little more than provide emphasis to this requirement.

. . .

Admittedly, depending on the meaning attached to the word proportionate, in almost all cases if the degree of force is proportionate it will also be reasonable but that cannot be to equate the two. In the same way that s. 76(5A) is drafted in the negative (allowing but not requiring the fact finder to conclude that force which is disproportionate still has to be reasonable) so s. 76(6) permits a finding that force which is proportionate is not reasonable. Both these provisions underline and acknowledge the critical second limb standard of self defence to be that which is reasonable in the circumstances of the case.

In *Ray (Steven)* [2017] EWCA Crim 1391, a five-member Court of Appeal, presided over by the Lord Chief Justice, held that the Divisional Court's interpretation of s. 76 was correct. Lord Thomas said:

In our view the interpretation placed in *Denby Collins* on the householder's defence under s. 76 of the 2008 Act as amended by the 2013 Act was correct. Once the jury have determined the circumstances as the defendant believed them to be, the issue, under s. 76(3), for the jury is (as it always has been at common law) whether, in those circumstances, the degree of force used was reasonable.

In determining the question of whether the degree of force used is reasonable, in a householder case, the effect of s. 76 (5A) is that the jury must first determine whether it was grossly disproportionate. If it was, the degree of force was not reasonable and the defence of self defence is not made out.

If the degree of force was not grossly disproportionate, then the effect of s. 76(5A) is that the jury must consider whether that degree of force was reasonable taking into account all the circumstances of the case as the defendant believed them to be. The use of disproportionate force which is short of grossly disproportionate is not, on the wording of the section, of itself necessarily the use of reasonable force. The jury are in such a case, where the defendant is a householder, entitled to form the view, taking into account all the other circumstances (as the defendant believed them to be), that the degree of force used was either reasonable or not reasonable.

The terms of the 2013 Act have therefore, in a householder case, slightly refined the common law in that a degree of force used that is disproportionate may nevertheless be reasonable.

In a non-householder case, the degree of force used cannot be regarded as reasonable if it was disproportionate. The amendments to s. 76 put the householder relying on self-defence in a position different from all others relying on the defence. But, Lord Thomas stressed, the difference is 'narrow' and the Court rejected the contention that provided the degree of force used by a householder is not grossly disproportionate then it is necessarily reasonable (at p. 29).

Lord Thomas also provided guidance for trial judges on how they should direct juries in householder cases. He advised that they should avoid presenting jurors with 'esoteric and conceptual distinctions' between what is disproportionate on the one hand and what is unreasonable on the other hand (at p. 33). He said (at p. 34):

> The focus of the jury in the context of a householder case ultimately should be on what is reasonable or unreasonable in the particular circumstances. In the overwhelming majority of cases it therefore should neither be necessary nor helpful in a summing up to use language referring expressly to the contrast between disproportionate and unreasonable force; because once the jury have concluded that the degree of force used was not grossly disproportionate the sole issue is whether the degree of force used was unreasonable in the circumstances. That should be the focus for the jury.

He also recommended that judges give 'some colour' to their directions, for example by highlighting that 'what might be an unreasonable degree of force used when confronting an aggressive individual in a club might not be so when used by a householder confronting an intruder in his own home' and that the use of force that is 'completely over the top, in ordinary language' can never be reasonable (at p. 35).

The size and composition of the Court of Appeal in *Ray* puts beyond doubt the correct interpretation of the 'householder' defence. Several points may be noted however. First, by leaving open the possibility that force that falls short of being grossly disproportionate may be unreasonable, the Court's approach arguably gives little extra protection to those in their homes who confront burglars using proportionate force; the CPS may consider that the public interest in such cases lies in the case being heard before a jury, who will decide whether that proportionate force was nevertheless unreasonable. This is perhaps not what Parliament intended. Secondly, Lord Thomas advised judges to steer juries away from the concept of proportionality once they have decided that the force used was not grossly disproportionate, instead encouraging them to focus on whether the defendant used reasonable force. As Karl Laird notes ([2018] Crim LR 342–4), this seems to go against the historic common law position of determining whether the force used was reasonable by reference to the concepts of necessity and proportionality. The Court appears to be concerned that juries will not be able to cope with these terms, despite them having always been central to determining whether a person acted in self-defence. That in turn raises the question of whether, in non-'householder' cases, juries should be directed to focus solely on the reasonableness of the force the defendant used rather than whether it was necessary and proportionate (Laird, at p. 344).

In determining what constitutes a 'householder case', a 'building' includes a vehicle or vessel (s. 76(8F)) so it would cover D who uses force to repel V seeking to burgle his motorhome or canal boat. A 'dwelling' also covers the situation where D lives in part of a building which is also his place of work and there is internal access between both parts (see s. 76(8B)). For example, a shopkeeper who lives in a flat over his shop may use force to repel a burglar and the degree of force he uses will not be judged against a different standard depending on whether he engages the burglar in his flat, the shop, or the staircase connecting them.

The number of subsections required to define 'householder cases' denotes complexity rather than clarity and will doubtless lead to many problems in practice as judges struggle to provide clear and workable directions to juries.

Example

Section 76(8E) states that the fact that a person has the permission of a trespasser does not prevent that person from being a trespasser for the purposes of s. 76(8A). Can D rely on the householder provisions where he is a lodger in A's house and he uses force to repel V who is seeking to force entry to it, but it transpires that A is, himself, a trespasser? This would mean that D too is a trespasser even though he believed he had lawful permission to be there. Is D's belief that he is not a trespasser a relevant circumstance covered by the provisions on mistake in s. 76(4)? In assessing the reasonableness of the force used by D would the jury be required to consider whether the force used was simply disproportionate or grossly disproportionate in the circumstances as D believed them to be?

6.4.3.3 Excessive force

If the jury conclude that the degree of force which D used in the circumstances as he believed them to be was excessive (whether it be 'disproportionate' which is the standard in most cases, or 'grossly disproportionate' which is the standard in 'householder cases'), i.e. such that no reasonable person, making all due allowance for the pressure under which D was operating, could consider justified, **that use of force will be unlawful.** If D is charged with a non-fatal offence against the person, a distinction may be made between D who mistakenly uses unreasonable force and a similarly situated person who deliberately does so; allowance may be made for the former's incorrect assessment of the appropriate degree of force to use when sentencing him. Where D, however, is charged with murder, no such allowance may be made in choosing the nature of the penalty to impose as the sentence for murder is mandatory life imprisonment. It has been argued that where excessive force is used, and the charge is one of murder, an excusatory defence of excessive force should be recognised which would operate to reduce the conviction to one of manslaughter, thereby giving the court discretion in sentencing D where he makes a mistake as to the degree of force which it would be reasonable to use in the circumstances. In *Palmer* [1971] AC 814, the Privy Council rejected an argument for the recognition of a defence of excessive force and this was affirmed in *AG for Northern Ireland's Reference (No. 1 of 1975)* [1977] AC 105 where Lord Diplock stated (at p. 148):

> If a plea of self-defence is put forward in answer to a charge of murder and fails because excessive force was used though some force was justifiable, as the law now stands [D] cannot be convicted of manslaughter. It may be that a strong case can be made for an alteration of the law to enable a verdict of manslaughter to be returned where the use of some force was justifiable but that is a matter for legislation not for judicial decision.

The Criminal Law Revision Committee (Fourteenth Report, Cmnd 7844, para. 28), the Law Commission (Law Com No. 177, Draft Criminal Code Bill, cl. 59), and the *Report of the Select Committee of the House of Lords on Murder and Life Imprisonment* (HL Paper 78–1, session 1988–9, para. 83) all recommended a qualified defence of excessive force. In *Clegg* [1995] 1 AC 482, the House of Lords revisited the authorities on excessive force and confirmed the existing position but expressed their regret that this was the law; any change in the law, however, was a matter for Parliament to consider. Following this decision the then Home Secretary, Michael Howard, announced a review of the law in this area on 24 January 1995. The *Report of the Inter-departmental Review of the Law on the Use of Lethal Force in Self-defence or the Prevention of Crime* (Home Office, 1996) expressed the view (at para. 83) that a verdict of manslaughter on a charge of murder where excessive force was used 'might assist in a comparatively small number of cases' but did not consider that the availability of such an option:

> would enable the court or jury to achieve a result which would necessarily always be seen as just. More options required finer distinctions and judgements to be made. With more borders between cases, there could be more cases that were seen to fall unfairly on the wrong side of the borderline, this time between acquittal and conviction for manslaughter, and between conviction for murder and manslaughter.

The Report concluded (at para. 84) that a change in this area alone would be difficult to make 'without taking a more fundamental look at the scope and operation of the law on, and the penalty for, murder'.

In *Murder, Manslaughter and Infanticide: Proposals for Reform of the Law* (CP 19/08) the Government accepted the analysis the Law Commission made in its Report *Partial Defences to Murder* (Law Com No. 290) as to the problems with provocation, and subsequently reproduced in its Report *Murder, Manslaughter and Infanticide* (Law Com No. 304). The Government, however, proposed a different approach to reform through the creation of two partial defences to replace provocation, one of which is 'killing in response to a fear of serious violence' (this has been enacted by ss 54–56 of the Coroners and Justice Act 2009—see **9.3.2.2.3**). The defence, however, requires a loss of self-control and thus would not seem to fully address the cases discussed earlier where the problem is not loss of self-control but an error in assessing the degree of force that would be considered reasonable in defending oneself, preventing crime, or arresting an offender. The defence is also limited to circumstances where there is a fear of violence by D and this has to derive from V and be targeted at D or specified others; this would appear to rule out excessive force in arresting an offender.

6.4.4 Extent of the justifications

While the justifications under consideration are generally raised in response to charges of offences against the person, they are not confined to such offences. In *Renouf* [1986] 1 WLR 522, D was charged with reckless driving. He had driven his car in pursuit of another vehicle, the occupants of which had assaulted him and damaged his car. D forced the vehicle off the road and rammed it. He sought to rely on s. 3(1) of the Criminal Law Act 1967 but was convicted when the trial judge ruled that it was incapable of affording a defence to a charge of reckless driving. The Court of Appeal quashed his conviction as the acts alleged to amount to reckless driving constituted the use of force for the purpose of assisting in the lawful arrest of offenders and thus it should have been left to the jury to consider whether it was reasonable (see also *Symonds* [1998] Crim LR 280).

It would appear, however, that these justifications may be pleaded only in relation to offences which are not offences against the person where the circumstances constituting the offence amount to using force. The justifications may not be pleaded in respect of other offences committed incidentally (see **6.4.2.1**). Had Mr Renouf driven recklessly in pursuit of his assailants and then, drawing alongside their vehicle he had pointed a gun at the driver threatening to shoot if he did not stop, he may have been able to plead that he was using reasonable force to arrest an offender had he been charged with assault. By contrast, if he had been charged with driving recklessly he would have failed in a plea of justification in relation to this charge as his reckless driving did not constitute the force in this situation but rather was incidental to his use of force or, as Lawton LJ put it in *Renouf*, it amounted to a reckless act 'antecedent to the use of force'.

6.4.5 Resisting justifiable conduct

In **6.1** the example was given of D seeking to resist his arrest by PC. In the first case, where he did not know that PC was a police officer, D thought he was about to be attacked. In the circumstances as he believed them to be he would have been justified in using force; the only question would be whether the force he used was reasonable (see *Williams* (see **6.4.2.3**); cf. *Kenlin v Gardner* (1967) 2 QB 510). In the second case, where he knew PC was a police officer, and the officer was acting lawfully, he would not be justified in resisting arrest even though he had not committed any crime; if D has made a mistake it is not one of fact but rather one of law relating to the circumstances in which a person may be arrested (cf. *Fennell* [1971] 1 QB 428). If PC, making a lawful arrest, uses more force than is reasonably necessary, D could use force in self-defence as, in this circumstance, the officer would be acting unlawfully in using unjustifiable force. The problematical case would be the situation where PC mistakes D for a dangerous criminal and seeks to use force either to arrest him or to defend himself or others.

 Example

PC sees D walking along the street and hides in a doorway until D walks past and then tackles him from behind seeking to restrain him. In this circumstance the officer is acting lawfully both in seeking to arrest D and with regard to the use of force, provided he honestly believed that force was necessary either to effect an arrest or to defend himself or others and he used no more force than he believed was reasonably necessary. (The amount of force that may be used to effect an arrest may be less than that which may be necessary in self-defence as it is inconceivable that deadly force would be reasonable to effect an arrest whereas it may be reasonable in self-defence.) Is D, however, obliged to submit to the infliction of this force on him? The case law provides no clear answer, but it is submitted that, if D uses force on PC in return, it is arguable that his force is not being used to resist arrest but to resist what he believes to be an unlawful assault. If Williams could use reasonable force to defend someone whom he believed was being assaulted, who was in fact being lawfully arrested, it would be strange if D, believing he was being assaulted, could not use force to defend himself.

6.4.6 **Fatal force and the European Convention on Human Rights**

Article 2 of the European Convention for the Protection of Human Rights and Fundamental Freedoms provides:

> 1 Everyone's right to life shall be protected by law. No one shall be deprived of his life intentionally save in the execution of a sentence of a court following his conviction of a crime for which this penalty is provided by law.
>
> 2 Deprivation of life shall not be regarded as inflicted in contravention of this Article when it results from the use of force which is no more than absolutely necessary:
>
>   (a) in the defence of any person from unlawful violence;
>   (b) in order to effect a lawful arrest or to prevent the escape of a person lawfully detained;
>   (c) in action lawfully taken for the purpose of quelling a riot or insurrection.

The State could be in contravention of Art. 2 where a State official, for example a police officer or a soldier, uses force in circumstances not covered by the exceptions listed in Art. 2(2). These exceptions amount to an exhaustive list and in each case the degree of force permitted to be used must be 'no more than absolutely necessary in the circumstances'. In contrast, s. 3 of the Criminal Law Act 1967 provides for force being used, inter alia, 'in the prevention of crime' and both this provision and the common law on self-defence permit the use of 'such force as is reasonable in the circumstances'. It is this latter test which may have to be reconsidered by domestic courts following the enactment of the Human Rights Act 1998 when considering fatal force used by State officials. The English case law on the use of force does not distinguish between force used by State officials and that used by private individuals.

In *McCann and others* v *United Kingdom* (1996) 21 EHRR 97, the United Kingdom was found to be in breach of Art. 2. Following intelligence information received that a Provisional IRA active service unit was planning a terrorist bomb attack on Gibraltar, SAS soldiers were sent to assist the Gibraltar authorities to arrest them. Three members of the unit were intercepted after they had crossed from Spain into Gibraltar and parked a car. They were shot and killed by the SAS soldiers who believed that they had planted a car bomb which could be detonated by a radio controlled trigger and thus shot them repeatedly to ensure they were unable to trigger the bomb. In fact there was no bomb (although explosives were subsequently discovered in Spain at a property they had rented) nor any radio controlled trigger, nor were they armed. The Court emphasised that Art. 2 was one of the most fundamental provisions in the Convention. They stated that Art. 2(2) did not provide exceptions where it is permissible intentionally to kill but rather instances where it is permissible to use force which may result in the deprivation of life. The crucial point, however, was that the use of force must be no more than 'absolutely necessary' for the achievement of one of the purposes set out in Art. 2(2). This test would be applied strictly and the Court would scrutinise not only the actions of the individuals who use that force but also all the surrounding circumstances including such matters as the planning and control of the operation to see whether it was organised so as 'to minimise, to the greatest extent possible, recourse to lethal force'. On the issue of compatibility of the law on self-defence with Art. 2 the Court concluded (at para. 155) that 'the difference between the two standards is not sufficiently great that a violation of Article 2(1) could be found on this ground alone'. The Court concluded, generally, that in light of the information they had and the instructions they had received, the soldiers did honestly believe, for good reasons, that lethal force was necessary (para. 200). The Court stated (at para. 200):

> It considers that the use of force by agents of the State in pursuit of one of the aims delineated in Article 2(2) of the Convention may be justified under this provision where it is based on an honest belief which is perceived, for good reasons, to be valid at the time but which subsequently turns out to be mistaken. To hold otherwise would be to impose an unrealistic burden on the State and its law-enforcement personnel in the execution of their duty, perhaps to the detriment of their lives and those of others.
>
> It follows that, having regard to the dilemma confronting the authorities in the circumstances of the case, the actions of the soldiers do not, in themselves, give rise to a violation of this provision.

However, the Court went on to conclude that the planning and control of the operation amounted to a breach of Art. 2 as there were errors in the intelligence-gathering and the assumptions made about the attack; insufficient allowance had been made for alternative possibilities; and the training of the soldiers giving rise to immediate reflex actions, which necessarily did not involve assessments of whether less force might be sufficient, 'lacks the degree of caution in the use of firearms to be expected from law enforcement personnel in a democratic society, even when dealing with dangerous terrorists'.

Following *McCann*, argument persisted that the Convention requirement that force be 'absolutely necessary' is arguably more exacting than the domestic test of 'reasonable in the circumstances' and that where the official using force makes a mistake, the beliefs on which the official acted must be based on 'good reason' which again is arguably more exacting than the subjective test of honest belief required by *Gladstone Williams* and *Beckford* and now s. 76 of the CJIA (see **6.4.2.3**). In *R (Bennett)* v *HM Coroner for Inner London* [2006] EWHC Admin 196, Mr Bennett had been shot and killed by a Metropolitan police officer. The Coroner's direction to the jury on self-defence was challenged where she directed them in accordance with English law that they had to determine 'whether the force used was reasonable, having regard to the circumstances which were believed to exist'.

It was claimed that the test of reasonableness did not comply with Art. 2 which it was argued requires that the use of force be 'absolutely necessary'. Collins J, after considering the European case law, concluded (at para. 25):

> [T]he European Court of Human Rights has considered what English law requires for self-defence, and has not suggested that there is any incompatibility with Article 2. In truth, if any officer reasonably decides that he must use lethal force, it will inevitably be because it is absolutely necessary to do so. To kill when it is not absolutely necessary to do so is surely to act unreasonably. Thus, the reasonableness test does not in truth differ from the Article 2 test as applied in *McCann*. There is no support for the submission that the court has with hindsight to decide whether there was in fact absolute necessity. That would be to ignore reality and to produce what the court in *McCann* indicated was an inappropriate fetter upon the actions of the police which would be detrimental not only to their own lives but to the lives of others.

Collins J has squared the circle quite cleverly—the use of fatal force can only be reasonable in all the circumstances where it is absolutely necessary. The court will not make a hindsight assessment whether force was, in fact, absolutely necessary. The police officer on the ground is only able to make his assessment based on his perception of the circumstances that exist. If he is mistaken, fatal force is not actually necessary. But to constrain him by such concerns would, as the European Court recognised in *McCann*, harbour the potential to be to the detriment of his life and others in similar situations. The circumstances, therefore, against which his decision to use fatal force must be assessed are those as he perceived them to be at the time; an honest but mistaken belief, therefore, can provide a 'good reason'. In effect, the European Convention is a document for application in the real world not the perfect world of hindsight.

6.5 Reform

In *Legislating the Criminal Code: Offences Against the Person and General Principles* (Law Com No. 218), the Law Commission includes a draft criminal law bill which seeks, inter alia, to place duress and duress of circumstances on a statutory footing. The main changes which the Law Commission recommends are that the burden of proving the defence should be placed on D on a balance of probabilities, and that the defence should be available in respect of a charge of murder or attempted murder, thereby reversing the House of Lords' decisions in *Howe* and *Gotts*. The change in the burden of proof is presented partly as a trade-off to make the availability of the defence to murder more acceptable (see paras 33.2 and 33.3). In addition, the Law Commission regards the defence of duress by threats as 'wholly exceptional, depending on factors unique to that defence which distinguish it from all others' (para. 33.5) as 'it is much more likely than any other defence to depend on assertions which are peculiarly difficult for the prosecution to investigate or disprove' (para. 33.6). In particular, in duress 'the circumstances on which the defence is founded will characteristically have occurred well before, and quite separately from, the actual commission of the offence' (para. 33.7). This is a very sweeping generalisation. If the problem is the surprise element wrong-footing the prosecution, it could be resolved by requiring the defence to give notice of their intention to rely on the defence of duress.

Problems of proof or disproof arise in relation to all defences whether the defence raised is self-defence or duress. In some cases there may be independent witnesses who can support D's account whereas in others there may not. It is difficult to see how duress requires different treatment or how shifting the burden of proof is any more likely to result in the truth of the claim being established. The Law Commission, however, considers that the plausibility of D's story is important and relevant to the decision (on the reversed burden of proof) 'whether it was more likely than not that what the defendant claimed in fact occurred' (para. 33.10). While plausibility is relevant to the issue of whether or not a story is true it should not be regarded as determinative of that issue as often highly implausible stories are true. On these terms defendants who tell true but implausible stories face the prospect of a miscarriage of justice. The Law Commission, however, supports its proposal further on the basis of the risk that members of a criminal gang may concoct a story which the prosecution would have difficulty in refuting (para. 33.12). There is a risk of concoction in all defences which shifting the burden of proof will not redress but it will make it more difficult for all honest defendants to rely on the defence.

In its 2006 Report, *Murder, Manslaughter and Infanticide* (Law Com No. 304), the Law Commission recommends that:

(1) Duress should be a full defence to first degree murder, second degree murder and attempted murder.

(2) For duress to be a defence to first degree murder, second degree murder and attempted murder, the threat must be one of death or life-threatening harm.

(3) The defendant should bear the legal burden of proving the qualifying conditions of the defence on a balance of probabilities.

At paras 6.43 and 6.44 the Law Commission provides the following explanation for this recommendation:

6.43 The argument that duress should be a full defence to first degree murder has a moral basis. It is that the law should not stigmatise a person who, on the basis of a genuine and reasonably held belief, intentionally killed in fear of death or life-threatening injury in circumstances where a jury is satisfied that an ordinary person of reasonable fortitude might have acted in the same way. If a reasonable person might have acted as D did, then the argument for withholding a complete defence is undermined. In the words of Professor Ormerod, 'if the jury find that the defendant has, within the terms of the defence, acted reasonably, it seems unfair to treat him as a second degree murderer or even a manslaughterer'.

6.44 Further, the option also accords with the way that duress operates as a complete defence in relation to other offences and it is, therefore, conducive to coherence and consistency . . .

The Law Commission, however, reaffirms its commitment to the burden of proof resting upon the defendant where duress is pleaded in respect of murder, adopting the position of Lord Bingham of Cornhill in *Hasan* that duress is 'peculiarly difficult for the prosecution to investigate and disprove beyond reasonable doubt'.

 The law in context

Gender and duress: coerced women and the law

The House of Lords in *Hasan* [2005] UKHL 22 adopted a strict approach to those who voluntarily associate with criminals, withdrawing the duress defence from those who should have known that those with whom they voluntarily associate might subject them to pressure. There are strong policy reasons why English law does not allow duress to operate as a significant mitigating factor. In particular, courts have tended to impose tough deterrent sentences for those caught up in drugs offences to send a strong, clear message to others faced with the decision whether give in to pressure and deter drugs 'barons' from using coerced drugs 'mules' (Baroness Hale, *Hasan*, para. 70).

Some argue that the law is too harsh, particularly as it may leave some women without a defence when they have suffered pressure from abusive partners to commit offences. Some women who have been convicted of smuggling drugs as 'mules' claim to have been coerced into participation by partners threatening harm to their friends or family, or having passports

→

→

or other important documents taken away (in the case of foreign women importing drugs into the United Kingdom). Some writers argue that there are insurmountable legal hurdles facing abused or coerced women who seek to rely on duress (J. Loveless, '*R* v *GAC*: Battered Woman "Syndromization"' [2014] Crim LR 655–67, 656).

Hasan restricts the availability of the defence quite significantly in several ways, each impacting on coerced women. First, the House of Lords emphasised that the apparently subjective strand of the first question in *Graham* is objective in nature ('there is no warrant for relaxing the requirement that the belief [in the threat of death or serious injury] must be reasonable as well as genuine'). A coerced woman will have to show that her belief in the threat from her abusive partner was reasonable, not just genuine.

Secondly, in terms of the second part of the *Graham* tests (would a sober person of reasonable firmness sharing the characteristics of the defendant have responded as D did?), Loveless argues that, following the Court of Appeal decision in *GAC* [2013] EWCA Crim 1472, a coerced, abused woman will need to establish 'learned helplessness' as a precondition to running a duress defence. That might be difficult to prove. It may also not be directly relevant, as the woman might live in a state of persistent fear of violence in which she reasonably believes in the reality of her partner's threats, but does not suffer from a medically recognised psychiatric condition (Loveless, p. 661). The Court of Appeal in *GAC* focused on medical evidence of the appellant's condition to explain her behaviour, which, Loveless argues, wrongly concentrates on her personal inadequacies arising from a medical condition rather than the objective rationality of her actions. Those who are critical of the law's treatment of abused women in the context of defences argue that trials should focus on the reasonableness of an abused woman's actions in the context of her personal experiences, and her experiences as a woman, rather than on her status as a 'battered woman' and her entitlement to claim that she is suffering from 'battered woman syndrome' (this point was made by the Canadian Supreme Court in *Mallott* [1998] 1 SCR 123 in the context of self-defence: see Loveless, p. 655). In *Mallott*, L'Heureux-Dubé, J said (at para. 40):

> It is possible that those women who are unable to fit themselves within the stereotype of a victimized, passive, helpless, dependent, battered woman will not have their claims . . . fairly decided. For instance, women who have demonstrated too much strength or initiative, women of colour, women who are professionals, or women who might have fought back against their abusers on previous occasions, should not be penalized for failing to accord with the stereotypical image of the archetypal battered woman . . . .

Thirdly, the approach of the majority in *Hasan* on the issue of voluntary exposure to the risk of compulsion was to narrow the defence's scope so that serious criminals (drug dealers, terrorists, etc.) cannot plead it successfully, but it is arguably now so tightly drawn as to make unavailable the defence to coerced people who are a long way from being hardened criminals. This was noted by Baroness Hale, one of the Law Lords in *Hasan*, who argued that the approach of the majority was too strict in denying the defence of duress to anyone voluntarily associating with known criminals if 'he had foreseen or ought reasonably to have foreseen the risk of being subjected to any compulsion by threats of violence'. She argued that wording means the defence is denied not only to those 'who choose to become members of illegal organisations, join criminal gangs, or engage with others in drug-related criminality' but also to 'someone who has a quite different reason for becoming associated with the duressor and then finds it difficult to escape', such as 'battered wives' or 'others in close personal or family relationships with their duressors and their associates, such as their mothers, brothers or children' (*Hasan*, para. 78). She argued that the defence should only be denied to a person 'when

→

→

he foresaw (or should have foreseen) the risk of being subjected to compulsion to commit criminal offences', as opposed to the broader exclusionary rule favoured by the majority, stating (at para. 77):

> The battered wife knows that she is exposing herself to a risk of unlawful violence if she stays, but she may have no reason to believe that her husband will eventually use her broken will to force her to commit crimes. For the same reason, I would say that it must be foreseeable that duress will be used to compel the person to commit crimes of some sort. I have no difficulty envisaging circumstances in which a person may be coerced to act lawfully. The battered wife knows very well that she may be compelled to cook the dinner, wash the dishes, iron the shirts and submit to sexual intercourse. That should not deprive her of the defence of duress if she is obliged by the same threats to herself or her children to commit perjury or shoplift for food.

By tightly defining the availability of the duress defence, English law has stated that a woman compelled by an abusive partner to commit offences will have to rely on their circumstances being taken into account through prosecutorial discretion or mitigation in sentencing.

 Key Points

DURESS

– Duress operates as a complete defence and is available to all offences except murder (and possibly treason).

– There are two parts to the tests for duress (*Graham* (1982) and *Howe* (1987)):

   – Was D or may he have been impelled to act as he did because, as a result of what he reasonably believed [the person issuing the threat] had said or done, he had good cause to fear that if he did not so act [that person] would kill him or cause him serious injury?

   – Have the prosecution made the jury sure that a sober person of reasonable firmness, sharing D's characteristics, would not have responded to whatever he reasonably believed [the person making the threat] said or did by [doing as D did]?

– Only a threat or threats of death or serious injury will suffice. The threat(s) need not be the sole cause of D acting. D may rely on duress even though the threat(s) is/are made in respect of others.

– The House of Lords in *Hasan* (2005) held that D must have good cause for believing in the threat; if he mistakenly believes in a threat, duress will only be available if he had reasonable grounds for the mistaken belief.

– The second duress test is an objective assessment of D's response to the threat against the standard of a reasonable person with his characteristics. The leading case on the relevance of particular characteristics is *Bowen* (1996).

– If D voluntarily becomes or remains associated with others engaged in criminal activity in a situation where he knows or ought reasonably to know that he may be subject to compulsion by them or their associates, he cannot rely on duress to excuse any act which he is thereafter compelled to do by them (*Hasan*).

→

→

Necessity/Duress of Circumstances

– Defences of necessity and duress of circumstances have gradually been recognised by the courts, although their extent, and the difference between necessity and duress of circumstances, is somewhat unclear.

– Both necessity and duress of circumstances refer to the situation where a person commits an offence to avoid the harm to himself or another which would ensue from objective dangers arising from the circumstances in which he or that other are placed.

– In *Martin* (1989), the Court of Appeal formulated the tests for duress of circumstances in a similar way to how the Court of Appeal in *Graham* delineated the tests for duress by threats.

– As with duress by threats, duress of circumstances is only available if the harm D seeks to avoid is that of death or serious injury to himself or another, and if the harm is imminent and immediate.

– The defence is available only if, from an objective standpoint, D acted reasonably and proportionately in order to avoid a threat of death or serious injury.

– The defence is not available on a charge of murder or attempted murder.

Private Defence and Prevention of Crime

– Section 3 of the Criminal Law Act 1967 provides that a person may use such force as is reasonable in the circumstances in the prevention of crime or in effecting or assisting in the lawful arrest of offenders or suspected offenders or of persons unlawfully at large.

– Common law recognises a similar defence for citizens.

– Special provision is made for 'householder cases' under s. 43 of the Crime and Courts Act 2013. The level of force in such cases is not to be regarded as having been reasonable in the circumstances as D believed them to be if it is was grossly disproportionate in those circumstances.

– The key case on 'householder cases' is *Ray* (2017), in which the Court of Appeal confirmed the Divisional Court's decision in *Collins* (2016) that the question for the jury remains, 'Did D use reasonable force?' Force may be less than grossly disproportionate but unreasonable.

– Section 76 of the Criminal Justice and Immigration Act 2008 puts into statutory form the principles relating to private defence and the prevention of crime:

  – Whether the use of force was necessary is judged on the facts as D honestly believed them to be;

  – The proportionality of the force used is judged objectively.

– The jury or magistrates decide whether the force used was reasonable.

FURTHER READING

K. J. Arenson, 'The Paradox of Disallowing Duress as a Defence to Murder' (2014) 65 JCL 78.

M. Bohlander, '*In Extremis*—Hijacked Airplanes, "Collateral Damage" and the Limits of the Criminal Law' [2006] Crim LR 579.

A. Buchanan and G. Virgo, 'Duress and Mental Abnormality' [1999] Crim LR 517.

E. Colvin, 'Exculpatory Defences in Criminal Law' (1990) 10 OJLS 381.

D. W. Elliott, 'Necessity, Duress and Self-defence' [1989] Crim LR 611.

S. Gardner, 'Direct Action and the Defence of Necessity' [2005] Crim LR 371.

B. Hogan, 'The *Dadson* Principle' [1989] Crim LR 679.

J. Horder, 'Occupying the Moral High Ground: The Law Commission on Duress' [1994] Crim LR 334.

F. Leverick, 'Is English Self-defence Law Incompatible with Article 2 of the ECHR?' [2002] Crim LR 347.

J. Loveless, 'Domestic Violence, Coercion and Duress' [2010] Crim LR 93.

J. Loveless, 'R v GAC: Battered Woman "Syndromization"' [2014] Crim LR 655.

S. Ost, 'Euthanasia and the Defence of Necessity' [2005] Crim LR 355.

N. M. Padfield, 'Duress, Necessity and the Law Commission' [1992] Crim LR 778.

J. C. Smith, *Justification and Excuse in the Criminal Law* (London: Sweet & Maxwell, 1989).

K. J. M. Smith, 'Duress and Steadfastness: In Pursuit of the Unintelligible' [1999] Crim LR 363.

F. Stark, 'Necessity and *Nicklinson*' [2013] Crim LR 949.

G. Williams, 'The Theory of Excuses' [1982] Crim LR 732.

W. Wilson, 'The Structure of Criminal Defences' [2005] Crim LR 108.

7

....

Parties to crime

7.1 **Accomplices**

7.1.1 **Principals and accessories**

All the parties to a crime are accomplices.

 Example

A decides that he wants V killed. He encourages D to perform the murder. B supplies D with a knife to perform the murder; C supplies A with information regarding V's movements; E drives D and F to V's home and acts as lookout; F assists D to kill V by holding him while D stabs him; and G, V's discontented butler, shouts encouragement at D and F as they attack V. All seven parties are accomplices to the murder of V but only D is the perpetrator of the offence; the others are accessories.

The person who perpetrates the crime is referred to as the principal. A person is the perpetrator if his act is the most immediate cause of the *actus reus* of the offence; in the earlier example D's act is clearly the immediate cause of V's death. Had two people, D and G, stabbed V, they would each be joint principals. In some cases D may be liable as principal even though the *actus reus* was brought about by another. **D will be liable where he has used another person to procure the commission of the offence and that person is not guilty of the offence due to, for example, infancy, lack of *mens rea*, or insanity. Such a person is generally referred to as an 'innocent agent'.** For example, D gives E a parcel telling him it is a birthday present and asks him to deliver it to V. The parcel contains a bomb and V is killed when it explodes. D would be guilty of murder as the principal because E, not knowing the nature of the parcel, lacked *mens rea* and was an innocent agent. Similarly, if D employs E, his eight-year-old son, to climb through windows of houses to steal items, D would be guilty of burglary as principal because E, being an infant, is not criminally liable and is an innocent agent. Problems arise where E is found to be an innocent agent but D is personally incapable of committing the offence as a principal (see **7.1.3**).

Others, not being principals, who participate in the commission of an offence are referred to as accessories or secondary parties and will be liable to conviction if it is proved that they aided, abetted, counselled, or procured the commission of the crime by the principal. The law is to be found in s. 8 of the Accessories and Abettors Act 1861, as amended by the Criminal Law Act 1977:

> Whosoever shall aid, abet, counsel or procure the commission of any indictable offence whether the same be an offence at common law or by virtue of any act passed or to be passed, shall be liable to be tried, indicted and punished as a principal offender.

Section 44 of the Magistrates' Courts Act 1980 contains a similar provision for summary offences.

While the consequence of conviction as a principal or an accessory is the same, it is important in some circumstances to be able to distinguish between them. **The *mens rea* required of the accessory differs from that of a principal and *mens rea* must always be proved even where the principal's offence is one of strict liability.** In some cases an offence may only be committed by persons of a specified class or may not be committed as a principal by persons of a specified class—for example, only a licensee can commit an offence involving a breach of the conditions of the licence (see *Morris* v *Tolman* [1923] 1 KB 166). Where vicarious liability is in issue it is important to identify the principal and the accessory as vicarious liability may only be imposed in respect of the act of a principal (see **7.2**).

The courts have struggled repeatedly to understand the very principles they have declared in respect of principals and accessories. The problem became particularly acute in the context of deaths arising from drug-taking. In their efforts to ensure that drug-suppliers should be held culpable for deaths ensuing from their supply of illicit drugs, the courts distorted the principles of accessorial liability. Where V self-administers an illegal drug as a result of which he dies, he is the immediate cause of his own death, his act being 'free, deliberate and informed'; his act involves the commission of no offence. In *Rogers* [2003] EWCA 945, the Court of Appeal held that D had played a part in the mechanics of the injection of heroin which caused death where he applied the tourniquet to V's arm while V injected himself. By this device the Court concluded that D had committed the *actus reus* of the offence of administering a noxious thing contrary to s. 23 of the Offences Against the Person Act 1861. But how could D be a principal where V's act of self-injection was the most immediate cause of his death? Of course, if the Court had accepted this, then V, as principal, would have been committing no offence as it is a requirement of the s. 23 offence that the noxious thing be administered to another; and if V committed no offence, D could not be convicted as an accessory (see further **2.6.3.5.4**).

In *Kennedy (No. 2)* [2005] EWCA Crim 685, the Court of Appeal added further to the confusion by affirming a conviction for manslaughter where D had supplied the heroin-filled syringe but played no part in its administration by V to himself as a result of which he died. The Court considered that D was acting in concert with V and thus there was no breach in the chain of causation. This reasoning ignored the fact that D and V could not be joint principals as V was not committing any offence. Further, as V was also the immediate cause of the *actus reus* this meant that D could not be a principal. In addition, as V was fully aware of what was going on, he could not be said to be an innocent agent. Nonetheless the Court concluded that D and V were acting in concert in committing the s. 23 offence which formed the unlawful act upon which D's conviction for manslaughter could be founded. These problems were only finally resolved when *Kennedy (No. 2)* [2007] UKHL 38 was decided and overturned Kennedy's conviction for manslaughter; it also declared that the decision in *Rogers* was wrong, reaffirming the principle of *novus actus interveniens* and its intimate connection to the principles underpinning secondary liability (see further **2.6.3.5.4**).

In most cases there will be no problem identifying the principal and the accessory but in some circumstances, while it may be clear that an offence has been committed, and that two or more accomplices were involved, it may be unclear who was the principal and who was the accessory. Thus if A and B were involved in the commission of an offence both may be convicted where it is proved that each of them must have been guilty in one capacity or the other (see *Swindall and Osborne* (1846) 2 Car & Kir 230; *Chan Wing-Siu* v *The Queen* [1985] 1 AC 168). Both may be principals as where, for example, A and B attack V, raining blows on him and he dies (see *Macklin and Murphy's Case* (1838) 2 Lew CC 225), or A and B act in concert to rob a bank, A threatening the staff with a gun while B appropriates the money; provided each had the requisite *mens rea* they could be convicted as principals to murder and robbery.

The cases tend to talk in terms of there being a joint enterprise, or pre-arranged plan or talk of the accused 'acting in concert'. This is not a prerequisite of liability. If A and B independently attack V at the same time and he dies, both may be convicted of murder provided each had the requisite *mens rea* even though there is no pre-arranged plan or agreement between them (see *Mohan* v *R* [1967] 2 AC 187).

> In *Mohan* A and B attacked V with cutlasses killing him. The evidence indicated that only one wound proved fatal but it could not be established who inflicted that wound. A and B appealed against convictions for murder arguing that as there was no pre-arranged plan to attack V the Crown had to show which of them struck the fatal blow. The Privy Council dismissed the appeals on the basis that as A and B were attacking the same man at the same time with similar weapons and with the common intention that he should suffer grievous bodily harm, each of them was present aiding and abetting the other and thus there was no need to prove any pre-arranged plan.

But if the evidence does not establish a common purpose such that each is intending to assist or encourage the other to cause harm (i.e. it only establishes an independent intention to cause harm), neither will be liable for the other's acts. In *Petters and Parfitt* [1995] Crim LR 501, the appellants had been charged with murder and convicted of manslaughter. There was evidence that each had punched the deceased and that one had kicked him causing his death. As the evidence did not establish who had delivered the fatal kick, and the jury had been inadequately directed on the question whether the appellants had been acting independently or whether they had shared a common purpose, the Court of Appeal quashed the convictions.

Where the offence is one of strict liability, and it is unclear which of the accused was the principal, each may be convicted only where the prosecution prove that each had *mens rea*. In *Smith* v *Mellors and Soar* [1987] RTR 210, both M and S were over the blood-alcohol limit when seen running away from a car which had been driven on the road. Driving with a blood-alcohol level above the prescribed limit is a strict liability offence. As it could not be proved who was driving neither could be convicted unless he had the *mens rea* required for conviction as an accessory. Thus the prosecution had to prove that each accused knew that the other had had too much to drink to be fit to drive.

In some cases it may be clear that an offence has been committed and that either A or B committed it, but it is not clear who did it nor is it clear whether the other was an accessory. In such circumstances, if the prosecution cannot bring forward prima facie evidence that each of them is guilty in one capacity or another, the charges against both will be dismissed (see *Uddin* [1998] 2 All ER 744; see also *Banfield* [2013] EWCA Crim 1394). In *Lane and Lane* (1986) 82 Cr App R 5, the evidence showed that the child of the accused had been fatally injured between noon and 8.30 p.m. Each parent had been present for some of the time and absent for some of it but throughout the period the child had always been in the presence of a parent. As it could not be proved who had injured the child nor that each had been involved as principal or accessory, there was no case to answer on the charges of manslaughter against each (see now s. 5 of the Domestic Violence, Crime and Victims Act 2004, **9.3.5.2**). If, however, the prosecution can prove that one of the accused committed the offence and the other aided or abetted him in doing so, then both may be convicted. In such circumstances it does not matter that the principal offender cannot be identified as s. 8 of the Accessories and Abettors Act 1861 states that those who aid, abet, counsel, or procure an offence are 'liable to be indicted, tried and punished as a principal offender' (see *Forman and Ford* [1988] Crim LR 677, **7.1.2.2**).

7.1.2 Aiding, abetting, counselling, or procuring

7.1.2.1 Defining terms

If an accused is charged as an accessory he will be charged with aiding, abetting, counselling, or procuring the particular offence and he is liable to conviction if it is proved that he participated in any one of these four ways (see *Smith, Re* (1858) 3 H & N 227; *Ferguson* v *Weaving* [1951] 1 KB 814). There has been much argument regarding the meaning of each individual term.

'Aiding and abetting' have generally been paired together as if they were synonymous. In *AG's Reference (No. 1 of 1975)* [1975] QB 773, Lord Widgery CJ took the view that each word probably had a different meaning. **'Aiding' suggests helping or assisting** the principal to commit the offence whether before its commission or at the time of its commission. In the scenario given at the beginning of **7.1.1**, B, C, and E all assist D prior to the commission of the murder (see *Thambiah* v *R* [1966] AC 37); F is present assisting him at the time of the offence (see *Clarkson* [1971] 1 WLR 1402), and E also assists at that time by keeping watch (see *Betts and Ridley* (1930) 22 Cr App R 148). **'Abetting' suggests the activity of one who incites, instigates, or encourages** the principal to commit the offence (see *Wilcox* v *Jeffery* [1951] 1 All ER 464). **'Counselling' also suggests advising or encouraging** the commission of the offence. In *National Coal Board* v *Gamble* [1959] 1 QB 11, Devlin J opined that 'abetting' involved presence at the scene of the crime offering encouragement. At common law 'abetting' denoted encouragement at the time of the offence and 'counselling' encouragement given previously. In the scenario in **7.1.1**, A would be liable for counselling the commission of the offence and G for abetting it; F, by his presence and assistance, is also offering encouragement and thus is also an abettor.

In *AG's Reference (No. 1 of 1975)*, Lord Widgery CJ considered that in most cases of aiding, abetting, or counselling the parties would have met and discussed the offence they had in mind. While this may be generally true, it is not a requirement for liability as an accessory. The principal may have met with the accessories separately or there may have been no discussion at all. For example, in the scenario in **7.1.1**, G abetted the offence but he never discussed it or planned it with D or any of the other parties. **What seems to be necessary is some meeting of minds or consensus, namely that the offence committed is the one encouraged and the principal is aware of that encouragement even if he would have committed it without encouragement** (see *Calhaem* [1985] 1 QB 808). The amount of encouragement offered need not be particularly great for liability to arise. In *Gianetto* [1997] 1 Cr App R 1, the Court of Appeal agreed that A could be convicted of murder where, in response to D stating 'I am going to kill your wife', he said 'Oh goody', and D then went ahead and killed A's wife. In the case of aiding, however, there need not be a meeting of minds. For example, in the scenario in **7.1.1**, if H, the maid, restrained W, V's wife, and prevented her from phoning the police or from trying to rescue V, H would have assisted D in committing the offence although D was totally unaware of H's intervention.

An unusual example of aiding and abetting is provided by the case of *Gnango* [2011] UKSC 59.

> G, armed with a gun, was searching for B, who owed him money, at a car park. Upon B appearing he shot at G who took cover behind a car and fired several shots in return. B continued shooting and one of his shots hit V, a passer-by, killing him. The Supreme Court restored G's conviction for murder (which the Court of Appeal had quashed) on the basis that G and B had agreed to shoot and be shot at by the other, each having an intent to kill the other. The intent B had was transferred (see **3.6.2.3**) when B killed V having done so with encouragement from G (through his shooting at B thereby encouraging him to shoot back at G). G, accordingly, had encouraged B's act of murdering V.

It is not necessary to prove any causal link between the assistance or encouragement and the commission of the offence (see *AG's Reference (No. 1 of 1975)*; *Calhaem*; and *Stringer* [2011] EWCA Crim 1396). By contrast 'procuring' involves a different concept altogether. In *AG's Reference (No. 1 of 1975)*, Lord Widgery CJ stated **that procuring required a causal link to be established between what the procurer did and what the principal did. Procuring, Lord Widgery said, means 'to produce by endeavour'** (see also *Luffman* [2008] EWCA Crim 1379).

> The facts of the case giving rise to the Reference were that A surreptitiously added alcohol to D's drink knowing that he would shortly be driving home. D was convicted of the strict liability offence of driving with an excessive quantity of alcohol in his body contrary to s. 6(1) of the Road Traffic Act 1972. A was charged under s. 8 but

acquitted on a ruling of no case to answer. The Court of Appeal held that A's actions amounted to procuring as A had set out to see that a particular state of affairs happened and had taken appropriate steps to produce it. The addition of the alcohol to D's drink was a direct cause of the excess alcohol level in his blood. Thus Lord Widgery stated (at p. 780) that the offence had been procured 'because, unknown to the driver and without his collaboration, he has been put in a position in which in fact he has committed an offence which he never would have committed otherwise'.

The suggestion in *AG's Reference* is that it must be the procurer's purpose to produce the *actus reus*.

In *Millward* [1994] Crim LR 527, M instructed H to drive a tractor and trailer. M knew, but H did not know, that the hitch mechanism was dangerously defective. As H was driving, the trailer became detached causing a fatal accident. H was acquitted of causing death by reckless driving but M was convicted as he had procured the offence.

While it was clear that it was M's purpose to bring about the reckless driving, it was not his purpose to bring about the death. This issue was not discussed in the case. Perhaps the principle is that the purpose requirement is confined to the initiating cause of a consequence. This may be justified on two bases: (1) *mens rea* is not required as to death in the offence of causing death by reckless driving, proof of causation being sufficient, and (2) a secondary party is liable for the unforeseen consequences of an enterprise to the same extent as the principal offender.

7.1.2.2 Presence, activity, and inactivity

Mere presence at the scene of an offence and failure to intervene or prevent it is generally not sufficient to render such a person liable as an accessory, although it may provide evidence (albeit not conclusive) of an intention to encourage the perpetrator (see *Coney* (1882) 8 QBD 534). If a person is to be convicted in such circumstances **it must be proved that there was encouragement in fact and that there was an intention to encourage** (see *Clarkson* [1971] 1 WLR 1402; and *Bland* [1988] Crim LR 41). This may be established by proving that A was present as a result of a prior agreement that the offence be committed (see *Smith* v *Reynolds* [1986] Crim LR 559) or that he did some positive act of assistance or encouragement knowing the circumstances which constitute the offence. It is not necessary to establish that commission of the crime was the accessory's purpose in the latter situation (see *National Coal Board* v *Gamble* [1959] 1 QB 11).

Voluntary presence at the scene of a crime, without more, may amount to actual encouragement.

In *Wilcox* v *Jeffery* [1951] 1 All ER 464, A's presence, as a paying member of the audience at a concert given by D, amounted to aiding and abetting D to contravene the Aliens Order 1920. D had been permitted to enter the United Kingdom only on condition that he take no employment. Further evidence of A's intention to encourage D was derived from A's behaviour in that he had met D at the airport and, after the concert, he wrote and published a laudatory review of the concert in the periodical of which he was the proprietor. In this case there would clearly have been no performance if there had been no audience so the presence of each member of the audience was an encouragement to D to perform.

But presence is not always sufficient to amount to encouragement.

In *Allan* [1965] 1 QB 130, A was present at the scene of an affray. He was totally passive doing nothing to offer encouragement to those involved in the fighting, although he harboured a secret intention to join in if help was needed by the side which he favoured. The Court of Criminal Appeal stated (at p. 138):

> [B]efore a jury can properly convict an accused person of being a principal in the second degree to an affray, they must be convinced by the evidence that, at the very least, he by some means or other encouraged the participants. To hold otherwise would be, in effect, . . . to convict a man on his thoughts, unaccompanied by any physical act other than the fact of his mere presence.

This case is distinguishable from *Wilcox* v *Jeffery* as, without spectators, the affray would still have occurred so mere presence, without more, did not amount to encouragement.

Where A has the right to control the actions of another and deliberately refrains from doing so, his inactivity may amount to actual encouragement. For example, a publican who fails to make his customers leave his premises after closing time may be convicted of aiding and abetting their consumption of alcohol outside hours (*Tuck* v *Robson* [1970] 1 WLR 741). Likewise if the owner of a car is a passenger in it while it is driven dangerously and does nothing to prevent or discourage this, when there was opportunity to intervene, he may be guilty of aiding and abetting the dangerous driving (see *Webster* [2006] EWCA Crim 415). His failure to exercise his right of control is evidence of encouragement (see *Du Cros* v *Lambourne* [1907] 1 KB 40; *Cassady* v *Reg Morris (Transport) Ltd* [1975] RTR 470; *J. F. Alford Transport Ltd and others* [1997] 2 Cr App R 326). Indeed, actual presence is not necessary if it can be proved that A knows of D's illegal activity and deliberately turns a blind eye to it, and D is thereby encouraged to continue this illegal activity, and A knows his inaction is encouraging D so to do (see *J. F. Alford Transport Ltd*).

If A is under a duty to act, his omission to do so may give rise to liability as an accessory just as it may as a principal. While A may not have a right to control D, his omission to fulfil his duty may amount to encouragement of D. For example, if one parent ill-treats his child in the presence of the other parent, the latter's failure to fulfil his or her duty to protect the child may amount to encouragement of the former (see *Russell and Russell* (1987) 85 Cr App R 388). The conclusion of encouragement is not automatic as there may not have been time to intervene or the parent may have been in terror of the other. In *Forman and Ford* [1988] Crim LR 677, a suspect was assaulted while in a cell with two officers. It was not possible to establish which was the assailant and there was no evidence that they were acting in concert. The Court held that both officers could be convicted if the jury are satisfied in respect of each of them that if he himself did not commit the assault he encouraged the other to do so by failing to intervene or report the offence and the other relied on him neither to intervene to prevent nor afterwards to report the offence. In this situation each officer is under a duty to prevent crime and to keep the peace so his inactivity can amount to positive encouragement.

7.1.3 **Proving the principal offence**

Question

Is it possible to convict A as an accessory without convicting D as the principal?

The fact that D has been acquitted in a separate trial does not preclude a court from convicting A as the evidence against D may have been weak. What is necessary is that it be proved beyond reasonable doubt that the principal offence was committed. Several situations may arise.

7.1.3.1 **Absence of an *actus reus***

A person cannot be convicted as an accessory unless there was an *actus reus*.

> In *Thornton* v *Mitchell* [1940] 1 All ER 339, a bus driver reversed his bus relying on signals from his conductor. Two pedestrians behind the bus were hit and injured. The driver was charged with careless driving and the conductor with aiding and abetting that offence. The justices dismissed the charge against the driver as he had done nothing which he should not have done and had not been careless, but they convicted the conductor. The Divisional Court held the conductor could not be convicted as there was no *actus reus* of careless driving. The Court quoted with approval the dictum of Avory J in *Morris* v *Tolman* [1923] 1 KB 166 (at p. 171): 'in order to convict, it would be necessary to show that the respondent was aiding and abetting the principal, but a person cannot aid another in doing something which that other has not done.' As there was no *actus reus* it was not possible to regard the conductor as the principal working through an innocent agent.

This principle was applied in two cases of causing death by dangerous driving (see *Loukes* [1996] Crim LR 341; *Roberts and George* [1997] Crim LR 209). The *actus reus* of this offence involves death being caused by the driving of a vehicle dangerously, which includes situations where 'it would be obvious to a competent and careful driver that driving the vehicle in its current state would be dangerous' (Road Traffic Act 1988, s. 2A). In both cases drivers of tipper trucks were acquitted of the offence, where defects in their vehicles had caused the deaths of other road users, as there was no evidence that the defects were, or would have been, obvious to them. In each case their employers, who had been convicted on the basis of procuring the offences, had their convictions quashed as the acquittals of the drivers meant that in both cases the *actus reus* of the offence had not been established.

7.1.3.2 **Perpetrator exempt from prosecution**

If the perpetrator of the principal offence is, for some special reason, exempt from prosecution, this does not preclude the conviction of another as an accessory for encouraging or assisting the commission of the offence. In *Austin* [1981] 1 All ER 374, the father of a child, assisted by A, snatched the child from the lawful custody of his estranged wife. A was convicted of child stealing contrary to s. 56 of the Offences Against the Person Act 1861 (since repealed). The Court of Appeal held that while the proviso to the section exempted the father from liability to prosecution, he had committed the offence of child stealing. Accordingly, the proviso provided no obstacle to the conviction of A as an accessory to that offence.

7.1.3.3 **Perpetrator not liable to conviction**

Where the principal offence has been committed a person who has encouraged or assisted the principal to commit it will be liable as an accessory even though the offence is one which the accessory could not commit as a principal. Thus a woman may be convicted of rape as an accessory (see *Ram and Ram* (1893) 17 Cox CC 609).

What would happen in such a case, however, if the principal was not liable to conviction because he lacked the requisite *mens rea* or had a defence, but the accomplice had the requisite *mens rea* and did encourage or assist in the commission of the *actus reus*? For example, A, a woman, encourages E to have sexual intercourse with V, against V's will, and she restrains V while E has intercourse. If E successfully raises a plea of insanity, the special verdict of 'not guilty by reason of insanity' will be returned. A could not be convicted as a principal acting through an innocent agent as she is not capable of committing rape as a principal. The law would appear to be deficient if A were to escape criminal liability for rape because of these technicalities.

A possible solution would be to hold that the *actus reus* of rape had been committed in that sexual intercourse occurred to which V did not consent, and that A had aided and abetted the commission of that *actus reus*.

In *Bourne* (1952) 36 Cr App R 125, A forced his wife to commit buggery with a dog. His conviction for aiding and abetting the commission of the offence was upheld on appeal as, although the wife would not have been guilty as principal because of the defence of duress, the *actus reus* of buggery had been committed. It would also have been true to say that the wife had the *mens rea* for the offence as duress acts merely as an excuse which exempts the accused from conviction where she has committed an offence as a result of the threats of another (see **6.2.1**). In *Cogan and Leak* [1976] QB 217, Leak compelled his wife to have sexual intercourse with Cogan. Cogan's conviction was quashed following the House of Lords' decision in *Morgan* (see **3.6.1.1.1**) as his defence of honest belief in Mrs Leak's consent had not been left to the jury. Leak's conviction was upheld as he had procured the commission of the offence. Lawton LJ stated (at p. 223):

> [T]he act of sexual intercourse without the wife's consent was the *actus reus*; it had been procured by Leak who had the appropriate *mens rea*, namely his intention that Cogan should have sexual intercourse with her without her consent . . . it is irrelevant that the man whom Leak had procured to do the physical act himself did not intend to have sexual intercourse with the wife without her consent. Leak was using him as a means to procure a criminal purpose.

This accords with the decision in *Bourne*. **Thus A will be liable as an accessory where he has encouraged, assisted, or procured the commission of an *actus reus* albeit that the perpetrator is not liable as a principal.** The Court of Appeal in *Millward* [1994] Crim LR 527 (see **7.1.2.1**) expressly confirmed this principle and it was applied in *DPP v K and B* [1997] 1 Cr App R 36. In this case the Divisional Court allowed an appeal by the DPP and remitted the case to the magistrate with a

direction to convict the respondents who were girls aged 14 and 11. They had procured a boy, who was never apprehended, to rape a girl, W, whom they had falsely
imprisoned. The evidence established that the boy was over 10 but the prosecution
had been unable to rebut the presumption of *doli incapax* (see **5.2**). The Divisional
Court held that this did not preclude the conviction of the respondents as procurers
as the *actus reus* of rape had been proved and they had 'had the requisite *mens rea*,
namely, the desire that rape should take place and the procuring of it'.

7.1.3.4 Perpetrator and accessory liable but for different offences

The same facts may supply the *actus reus* of several offences. For example,
unlawful homicide includes murder and manslaughter, for which the *actus reus* is
the same, conviction for either depending on the *mens rea* of the accused or the
availability of the mitigating defences of diminished responsibility or loss of control. Accordingly **there is nothing wrong in principle with D being convicted of
murder as a principal and A being convicted of manslaughter as an accessory
if A lacked the *mens rea* for murder.**

 Example

A and D embark on a joint criminal venture to burgle a factory agreeing to knock out V the
watchman with a cosh. D knows that V has an eggshell skull and that such an assault will cause
at least grievous bodily harm (GBH) to him. A is unaware of this and does not contemplate any
injury to V beyond actual bodily harm (ABH). If D coshes V and he dies, D would be liable for
murder as he intended to cause GBH but A would only be liable for manslaughter on the basis
of an unlawful and dangerous act. (See *Yemoh* [2009] EWCA Crim 930; *Carpenter* [2011]
EWCA Crim 2568.)

The converse also applies (and is consistent with the principle in *Bourne*) so that A
may be convicted of the greater offence whereas D is convicted of the lesser as the
actus reus has been committed and the accessory's liability depends on his own *mens
rea*. In *Howe* [1987] 1 AC 417, Lord Mackay (with whom Lords Bridge, Brandon, and
Griffiths agreed) considered the following hypothetical situation (at p. 458):

> A hands a gun to D informing him that it is loaded with blank ammunition only and
> telling him to go and scare X by discharging it. The ammunition is in fact live, as A
> knows, and X is killed. D is convicted only of manslaughter, as he might be on those facts.

Lord Mackay agreed with the Court of Appeal that it would be absurd if A should
thereby escape conviction for murder and that the previous authority of *Richards*
[1974] QB 776 was wrongly decided. He stated (at p. 458):

> [W]here a person has been killed and that result is the result intended by another partic-
> ipant, the mere fact that the actual killer may be convicted only of the reduced charge of
> manslaughter for some reason special to himself does not, in my opinion in any way,
> result in a compulsory reduction for the other participant.

If the perpetrator, D, intentionally kills in pursuance of a joint criminal venture where he and A had agreed only to inflict some minor injury on the victim, the fact that D's act was beyond the common design and uncontemplated by A would absolve A from liability for manslaughter (see **7.1.4.5**).

The examples so far have involved a difference in *mens rea* between A and D. Where murder is charged an accused may be convicted of manslaughter if he successfully raises a defence of diminished responsibility or loss of self-control. Section 2(4) of the Homicide Act 1957 specifically provides that the fact that one party to a killing is not liable to be convicted of murder because of diminished responsibility does not affect the question whether the killing amounted to murder in the case of any other party to it. Section 55(8) of the Coroners and Justice Act 2009 makes similar provision in respect of the defence of loss of self-control.

7.1.4 *Mens rea* of an accessory

The *mens rea* required of an accessory may be simply stated as an **intention to assist or encourage the commission of the principal offence combined with knowledge of the circumstances which constitute the offence.** This statement requires explanation; this will reveal the problems associated with the *mens rea* of accessories.

7.1.4.1 Intention to assist or encourage the principal

Defining the *mens rea* required of accessories has presented major difficulties for the courts. The principal is the one whose act has caused the *actus reus* of the offence and the *mens rea* required of him generally relates to the doing of that act and the bringing about of its causally connected consequences. **As the acts of the accessory do not cause the *actus reus* the *mens rea* required cannot equate exactly to that of the principal.**

 Example

D shoots at V intending to kill him and succeeds. D's *mens rea* directly mirrors the *actus reus* he has brought about. A supplied D with the gun knowing that D wished to kill V, although he hoped D would fail. It can be seen that A's act assists D but the *actus reus* of murder does not directly mirror his state of mind. If A is to be liable for murder it will be because he has intended to assist D knowing that D intends to kill rather than on the basis that he, himself, intended to kill V.

In *National Coal Board v Gamble* [1959] 1 QB 11, the Divisional Court held that intention to assist or encourage had to be proved in addition to knowledge of the circumstances. **The commission of the principal offence may not be the accused's desire, motive, or purpose.** Devlin J stated (at p. 23):

> But an indifference to the result of the crime does not of itself negative abetting. If one man deliberately sells to another a gun to be used for murdering a third, he may be indifferent about whether the third man lives or dies and interested only in the cash profit to be made out of the sale, but he can still be an aider and abettor. To hold otherwise would be to negative the rule that *mens rea* is a matter of intent only and does not depend on desire or motive.

In *NCB* v *Gamble*, A's servant B operated the weigh-bridge at a colliery. B informed D that his lorry was overladen; driving an overladen lorry on the road was an offence. D said that he was prepared to take the risk whereupon B gave him the weigh-bridge ticket and the property in (i.e. ownership of) the coal passed to D. Without this ticket D could not have left the colliery. A was charged with aiding, abetting, counselling, or procuring D's offence of driving an overladen lorry on the road. For the purposes of the appeal it was assumed that B knew he had the right to prevent the lorry leaving the colliery. A, through its servant B, supplied D with an essential item for the commission of the offence, namely the weigh-bridge ticket, and did so knowing the circumstances which would render D's act of driving on the road an offence. A's indifference to this consequence was irrelevant to liability as A, through its servant, had voluntarily done an act which assisted D knowing the circumstances which constituted the offence.

The intention required, therefore, is the voluntary performance of an act with the realisation that this assists or encourages D in his course of conduct (see further *J. F. Alford Transport Ltd and others* [1997] 2 Cr App R 326; see also *Bryce* [2004] EWCA Crim 1231).

A problem with *NCB* v *Gamble* is that it provides the potential for extensive liability for accessories.

 Example

A sees D, a motorist, standing beside a vehicle which has a punctured tyre. He offers to change the tyre. When performing this act of charity he notices that one of the other tyres is partially bald, and therefore illegal. If A completes the task, will he be liable for aiding and abetting D's offence of driving a vehicle on the road with a defective tyre? Or, similarly, if he had noticed that one of the rear light panels was damaged before he changed the wheel, would he be liable for aiding and abetting D's offence of driving with defective lights? If intention does not require proof of a purpose, motive, or desire that the offence be committed, A's voluntary act of assistance with knowledge of the circumstances which constitute the principal offence would seem to be sufficient for liability as an accessory.

While the likelihood of A being prosecuted in this example might seem low, the law's potential breadth means that people such as A are reliant on the CPS deciding that prosecution in such situations is not in the public interest.

7.1.4.2 Knowledge of the circumstances constituting the offence

In *Johnson* v *Youden* [1950] 1 KB 544, Lord Goddard CJ stated (at p. 546):

> Before a person can be convicted of aiding and abetting the commission of an offence he must at least know the essential matters which constitute that offence. He need not actually know that an offence has been committed, because he may not know that the facts constitute an offence and ignorance of the law is not a defence.

The 'essential matters which constitute that offence' refers to the circumstances of the *actus reus*, its consequences (in the case of a result crime), and, in certain circumstances, the *mens rea* of the principal. **A cannot be liable as an accessory if he is unaware of the circumstances which constitute the offence**.

> In *Ferguson* v *Weaving* [1951] 1 KB 814, A, the licensee of a public house, was charged with aiding and abetting customers to commit the offence of consuming intoxicating liquor on licensed premises outside the permitted hours. A did not know that customers were still drinking after closing time. The Divisional Court held she could not be convicted if she did not know that customers were committing the principal offence.

Some matters, however, cannot be known although they may be foreseen, for example, the consequences of the perpetrator's act or his *mens rea*. Thus, **where A gives assistance prior to the commission of the offence, it is more accurate to refer to his 'contemplation' rather than his knowledge**. 'Knowledge' for these purposes includes wilful blindness and subjective recklessness (see *Carter* v *Richardson* [1974] RTR 314; *Blakely* v *DPP* [1991] Crim LR 763) but it does not include constructive knowledge, a species of negligence. In *J. F. Alford Transport Ltd and others* [1997] 2 Cr App R 326, the appellants' convictions for aiding and abetting the making of a false entry on a record sheet (i.e. a tachograph) contrary to s. 99(5) of the Transport Act 1968 were quashed by the Court of Appeal. Nineteen of the company's drivers had pleaded guilty to this offence as principals and the case against the appellants, as managers of a small company, was that they must have known and accepted, if not encouraged, what the drivers had done. Kennedy LJ, giving the judgment of the Court, stated that they accepted that knowledge may be inferred if a defendant shuts his eyes to the obvious, but went on to emphasise that Lord Goddard CJ's dictum in *Johnson* v *Youden* needs to be understood. He placed reliance on Gibbs CJ in the Australian case of *Giorgianni* v *The Queen* (1985) 156 CLR 473 at 483, stating:

> Gibbs CJ accepted that it would be sufficient to infer knowledge if a defendant deliberately refrained from making enquiries the results of which he did not care to have, but, he continued:
>
> > 'The failure to make such enquiries as a reasonable person would have made is not equivalent to knowledge; it is not enough to render a person liable as a secondary party that he ought to have known all the facts and would have done so if he acted with reasonable care and diligence. That is so even when the offence is one of strict liability, so that the actual perpetrator may be convicted in the absence of knowledge.'

As knowledge could not be proved the convictions had to be quashed.

Where the principal offence is one of strict liability, while the principal may be convicted without proof of *mens rea*, **an accessory may be convicted only where *mens rea* is proved**.

> In *Callow* v *Tillstone* (1900) 83 LT 411, A, a veterinary surgeon, was charged with aiding and abetting the exposure for sale by D, a butcher, of unsound meat. A had examined a carcass at D's request and certified it sound. A had performed the

examination negligently and the meat was unsound. D was convicted of the strict liability offence of exposing the meat for sale. A's conviction, however, was quashed as he did not know the meat was unsound.

7.1.4.3 Knowledge of the type of offence

Where A counsels or procures D to commit a particular crime, A necessarily knows the type of offence involved as the commission of the offence is A's purpose. For example, if A writes to D encouraging him to kill V, A will know that if D does so he will commit murder as he will have done so with the necessary *mens rea*.

Where A aids or abets D to commit an offence, commission of that offence may not be A's purpose or object.

> **Example**
>
> A may sell D a gun to make a profit, indifferent to the fact that D intends to use it to kill V. A may not intend for D to kill V, but he gives assistance intentionally knowing that D has the intention to kill. Several problems may arise, however, in cases of aiding and abetting: (i) A may not know the exact details of the crime D has in mind although he knows D intends to kill; (ii) A may not know the exact crime D intends to commit although he knows D is going to commit one of a range of offences; (iii) A knows (or foresees) that if particular circumstances arise D *will* commit a particular offence; and (iv) A knows (or foresees) that if particular circumstances arise D *may* commit a particular crime.

It is crucial, therefore, to determine how precise A's knowledge must be if he is to be convicted as an accessory. This is a question of great practical importance, particularly for people who are involved voluntarily in 'gangs' that participate in criminal activity but who may not know or appreciate what criminal acts members of the gang might be prepared to do.

In *Bainbridge* [1960] 1 QB 129, the Court of Criminal Appeal had to consider situation (i) stated in the previous example.

> A supplied oxygen-cutting equipment to D who used it to break into a bank and steal £18,000. A appealed his conviction claiming that it had to be proved that he knew the precise details of the intended offence. The Court held it was sufficient that A knew the particular type of offence intended which was later committed.

Mere knowledge that the equipment was going to be used for some illegal venture, however, would not be sufficient. In *Bainbridge* the equipment had been used for only one offence. The Court left unresolved the question whether A would have been liable for 'breaking and entering' offences (now burglary) committed on other banks. If A need not know the precise details of the offence the logical answer to this question is that he would be liable for each breaking and entering offence committed by using the equipment he had supplied.

In *Maxwell v DPP for Northern Ireland* (1979) 68 Cr App R 128, the House of Lords approved of, and extended, the principle in *Bainbridge* to cover situation (ii) in the earlier example.

A drove his car guiding members of the UVF (an illegal organisation) in another car to a pub where he knew a terrorist attack was to be carried out whether by guns or bombs or otherwise. The occupants of the other car threw a pipe bomb into the pub. A was charged with (1) doing an act with intent to cause an explosion likely to endanger life or cause serious injury to property and (2) possession of explosive substances with intent to endanger life or cause serious injury to property. A was convicted and his conviction upheld as, although he did not know the precise type of offence that the other UVF members intended to commit, he knew that they intended one of a limited number of serious crimes.

Thus an accessory will be liable where he contemplates the commission of one or more of a range of crimes by the principal and he intentionally lends assistance to the principal who then commits one or more of these offences. Lord Scarman stated (at p. 153): 'An accessory who leaves it to his principal to choose is liable, provided always the choice is made from the range of offences from which the accessory contemplates the choice will be made.' Thus if A gives D a jemmy contemplating only that he will use it to break into houses to steal therein or break open crates to steal their contents, he would be liable for any such offences, but he would not be liable if D used the jemmy to injure a night-watchman who disturbed him as he was attempting to enter the building.

A problem which is unresolved, however, is that burglary is an offence of ulterior intent. The ulterior intent specified under s. 9(2) of the Theft Act 1968 which must be proved for conviction under s. 9(1)(a) is intention to steal, or inflict grievous bodily harm, or cause criminal damage (see **14.2**).

 Question

If D entered a house as a trespasser with the intention of inflicting GBH on the occupant, V, using the jemmy that A provided, could A be convicted as an accessory to burglary?

The answer depends on whether burglary is a 'type' of crime or the different varieties of burglary are different 'types' of crime. It is arguable that D's *mens rea* is one of 'the essential matters which constitute the offence'. If A only contemplated D stealing, D's intention to inflict GBH would appear to render the offence D committed a different type from the offence A contemplated. The contrary argument is that the *actus reus* of burglary is the same regardless of the intent with which it is committed and that A's assistance related to the effecting of the *actus reus*. Perhaps assistance in resolving this conflict may be sought from the cases on deliberate departure by the perpetrator from the joint criminal venture. Breaking into a house with intention to inflict GBH could be considered a substantial variation from the joint criminal venture which envisaged breaking into a house with intent to steal (see **7.1.4.5**). What is not in doubt is that if D does inflict GBH on the occupant, A is not an accessory to the offence of inflicting GBH.

If A and D decide to rob a bank and agree that D will carry a gun to shoot anyone who offers resistance, A will be liable for wounding or murder if D does shoot a bank clerk or customer who resists. This is situation (iii) in the earlier example and A will be liable even though he fervently hoped that no one would resist or if he believed that resistance was only a remote possibility on the basis that 50 robberies had been carried out successfully without any resistance being offered. It matters not that A may have foreseen only a small risk of resistance being offered as he has intentionally participated in an enterprise contemplating wounding or killing if necessary; an intention is no less so because it is conditional on the occurrence of other events (see *Betts and Ridley* (1930) 22 Cr App R 148).

In some cases the agreement between the parties to use force is not express but implied or, as it is referred to in some cases, 'tacit'. If it is a tacit understanding of the parties before the enterprise is embarked upon that violence will be used if certain circumstances arise, A will be liable to the extent of his contemplation. For example, A notices D is carrying a gun, which they had not previously discussed when they agreed to rob an off-licence. A asks D what it is for to which D replies 'Just in case!' If A still goes ahead with the robbery he will be liable to the extent of his intent. If he foresees that D may use the gun with the intent for murder this would amount to powerful evidence that he intended to assist or encourage this offence were D to shoot and kill V who offered resistance (see *Jogee*, **7.1.4.4.2**). If A only contemplated that D would use the gun to frighten but D used it to kill, A will not be liable for homicide (see further **7.1.4.5**).

7.1.4.4 The limits of liability for incidental offences

Situation (iv) in the example above has long presented problems for the courts. In the case law, this situation has been referred to as 'joint enterprise liability'. Generally where two parties, D and A, embark on an agreed criminal venture to commit a particular offence they have a common criminal purpose. If, in the course of that venture, D commits another, incidental, offence the question arises whether A will be liable for this incidental offence as a secondary party. More recently, a new term has been coined, 'parasitic accessory liability', to refer to this situation, This term is more accurate than 'joint enterprise' as the accessory's liability for the incidental offence is parasitic upon his participation in the agreed criminal venture.

While the problem of the limits of the accessory's liability may arise in many contexts, it is most acute where the incidental offence is murder.

 Example

D and A set out to commit a burglary to steal jewellery; they are unexpectedly disturbed by V, the householder, and D draws a knife and kills V. While there may be no problem establishing D's intent to kill, what is it that must be proved in terms of A's contemplation or intention for him to be convicted as a secondary party to murder?

The circumstances in which killings may take place may be even more complicated than this example. Often violence erupts spontaneously and individuals may find themselves embroiled in an affray where punches and kicks are exchanged. If A is assisting D in an altercation with V involving punches and kicks and D produces a knife and stabs V killing him, how is A's criminal liability to be determined? The fact that D may be convicted of murder, where his intention is merely to cause serious injury rather than to kill, further complicates the problem of determining A's liability.

7.1.4.4.1 *Case law before the Supreme Court's decision in* Jogee *(2016)*
In *Anderson and Morris* [1966] 2 QB 110, the appellants were involved in an altercation with V involving punches and kicks when Anderson drew a knife and stabbed V. The trial judge had directed the jury that they could convict Morris of manslaughter if satisfied he had no intent to kill or cause serious bodily harm and no knowledge of Anderson's possession of a knife. Morris was convicted of manslaughter and Anderson of murder. The Court of Appeal quashed Morris's conviction as Anderson's actions were outside the common design. Lord Parker CJ stated (at pp. 118–19):

> [W]here two persons embark on a joint enterprise . . . that includes liability for unusual consequences if they arise from the execution of the agreed joint enterprise but (and this is the crux of the matter) . . . if one of the adventurers goes beyond what has been tacitly agreed as part of the common enterprise, his co-adventurer is not liable for the consequences of that unauthorised act. Finally . . . it is for the jury in every case to decide whether what was done was part of the joint enterprise, or went beyond it and was in fact an act unauthorised by that joint enterprise.

The Court of Appeal adverted to the general principle, derived from *R v Smith (Wesley)* [1963] 1 WLR 1200 and *R v Betty* [1964] 48 Cr App R 6, that a person who took part in an attack resulting in death would be guilty of murder or manslaughter depending on his *mens rea* but would not be liable for homicide where the act which caused death was not just an unusual consequence of the joint criminal venture but an overwhelming supervening event beyond what had been tacitly agreed. In this situation, A has not encouraged or assisted the unlawful and dangerous act performed by D which was the immediate cause of V's death (see further **9.3.3.1**). Where D and A embark on a criminal venture, their individual liability would thus be limited to what they had expressly or tacitly agreed. It would be for the jury to determine what it was that A was intending to assist or encourage D to do; if D's act went beyond the common design, A should not be liable for this independent venture. But, if the commission of the common design resulted in an unusual consequence, both would be liable for this consequence as, for example, where D and A agree to assault V, D punches V, and V falls hitting his skull and dies. Each would be liable for unlawful act manslaughter.

Unfortunately, matters became somewhat complicated following the decision of the Privy Council in *Chan Wing-Siu* [1985] 1 AC 168 which, for 30 years, was the leading case on joint enterprise. (*Chan Wing-Siu* was affirmed by the House of Lords in *Powell and English* [1999] 1 AC 1.) As often happens, however, a misconceived defence argument and ground of appeal can result in a distortion of the law if the court does not identify the misconception but is diverted by it. In this case A, D, and E, armed with knives, went to a flat intending to steal from V, the occupant. V refused to hand over any money whereupon he was stabbed to death. A, D, and E were charged with murder. A claimed he was not involved in the killing as he was restraining V's wife in another room when D and E killed V. A argued at trial, and again on appeal, that it had to be proved that he foresaw that death or GBH would *probably* result from the joint enterprise if a contingency in which a weapon might be used by one of his companions eventuated. The trial judge directed the jury that each party was guilty if proved to have contemplated that a knife *might* be used on the occasion by one of his accomplices with the intention of inflicting serious bodily harm. All three were convicted and ultimately appealed to the Privy Council. Dismissing the appeals, Sir Robin Cooke stated (at p. 175):

> [A] secondary party is criminally liable for acts by the primary offender of a type which the former foresees but does not necessarily intend . . . . [This principle] turns on contemplation or, putting the same idea in other words, authorisation, which may be express but is more usually implied. It meets the case of a crime foreseen as a possible incident of the common unlawful enterprise. The criminal culpability lies in participating in the venture with that foresight.

Unfortunately, the trial judge and appeal courts had misled themselves. The key point is that contemplating something as a possible outcome is not the same as authorising it. **But more importantly, foreseeing a possible outcome is not the same as intending it and encouraging or assisting its commission.** By equating foresight with intent, the Privy Council had greatly expanded the scope of criminal liability of secondary parties.

In a string of cases which followed, the courts focused more and more on foresight and appeared to lose sight of the fact that **the *mens rea* for an accessory is intention** and, in particular, the intention to assist or encourage the commission of the offence the principal ultimately committed. The focus should always have been on what the common design was and whether A intended to assist or encourage D and E to achieve it. In *Powell and English*, Lord Hutton stated (at p. 18):

> [T]here is a strong line of authority that where two parties embark on a joint enterprise to commit a crime, and one party foresees that in the course of the enterprise the other party may carry out, with the requisite *mens rea*, an act constituting another crime, the former is liable for that crime if committed by the latter in the course of the enterprise.

In the three decades since *Chan Wing-Siu* was decided, the incidence of gang violence and the use of guns and knives has increased. There have been many convictions for murder on the basis of parasitic accessory liability and many of those convicted have been juveniles. Campaigns have been conducted to have the law of joint enterprise abolished or, at least, reformed. A major plank in the arguments put forward has been that it is unjust to convict an accessory of murder on the basis of foresight of a possibility that the principal may kill with the intent for murder. It was easier to convict an accessory of murder than the principal, as the principal may only be convicted where it is proved that he had the intent to kill or cause GBH. Arcane and complex arguments were raised in numerous appeals as to what had to be contemplated by A and whether D's actions may have involved a 'fundamental departure' from the common purpose. With each passing year the law became more complicated and the jobs of trial judges in directing juries, and juries in determining their verdicts, more difficult.

Fortunately, the law was clarified in 2016.

7.1.4.4.2 *The Supreme Court's decision in* Jogee *(2016)*
In *Jogee* [2016] UKSC 8 the Supreme Court revisited parasitic accessory liability.

A and D spent the evening drinking and taking drugs, becoming increasingly intoxicated and aggressive. Around midnight they went to N's house but she told them to leave before her boyfriend, V, returned. A and D said they were not scared of him and would sort him out. They left but later D returned and was there when V arrived. N phoned A and told him to fetch D, which he did. Not long afterwards, however, A and D returned to N's house, which D entered and an angry confrontation with V occurred. D seized a knife from the kitchen while A remained outside with a bottle damaging a car. V tried to persuade D to leave. A shouted threats at V of what he would do with the bottle if he could reach him and shouted to D to do something to him. D stabbed V in the throat killing him. Both D and A were convicted of murder. The judge had directed the jury, consistent with *Chan Wing-Siu* and *Powell and English*, that they could convict A if satisfied that he participated in the attack on the deceased, by encouraging D, and realised when doing so that D might use the knife to stab the deceased with intent to cause him really serious harm. A's appeal against conviction was dismissed. A appealed to the Supreme Court.

The Supreme Court engaged in a thorough review of the law on accessorial liability and concluded that the Privy Council and House of Lords in *Chan Wing-Siu* and *Powell and English* took a wrong turning in their reasoning. The Supreme Court observed that had the correct principles been applied the outcomes of the cases might well have been the same as juries, properly directed, could have convicted the defendants of murder. But the courts in both cases had departed from the well-established principle that **the *mens rea* required to convict a secondary party is an intention to assist or encourage the principal to commit the crime**. The courts had wrongly taken the view that the defendants either had to be convicted of murder or acquitted outright without considering that secondary parties could be convicted of manslaughter where the principal was convicted of murder. The Supreme Court examined a line of cases dating back to 1963 (*Smith (Wesley)* [1963]1 WLR 1200; *Betty* (1964) 48 Cr App R 6; *Anderson and Morris* [1966] 2 QB 110; *Reid* (1976) 62 Cr App R 109) which established that even where there was a joint intent to use weapons to overcome resistance or avoid arrest, the participants in a criminal venture might not share an intent to cause death or really serious harm; if the principal caused the death of another with that intent he would be guilty of murder, but another party participating in the venture without that intent would be guilty of manslaughter unless the act which caused death was so removed from what they had agreed as not to be regarded as a consequence of it. Thus a person who takes part in an unlawful attack which results in death would be guilty either of murder or of manslaughter according to whether or not he had the *mens rea* for murder.

In *Anderson and Morris* it was recognised that there were cases where the actual cause of death was not simply an escalation of a fight but an '**overwhelming supervening event**' in which case a secondary party would not be liable where the principal departed completely from what had been tacitly agreed as part of the criminal venture. In such a case, the effect of the overwhelming supervening event is that any assistance or encouragement is spent. But where the secondary party contemplates (as in 'foresees') the possible outcome, this is not to be confused with authorisation as the two are not the same.

The Supreme Court, having recognised that a wrong turning had occurred, reversed the principle established in *Chan Wing-Siu* and affirmed in *Powell and English*. They asserted that **foresight of what might happen is simply evidence from which a jury might infer intention but they need not necessarily do so. Foresight, or contemplation, accordingly is not to be taken as amounting to authorisation. Where the crime D commits is one requiring a particular intent A will be liable as a secondary party if he intentionally assists or encourages D to act with such intent. A conditional intent is sufficient** as, for example, where D and A set out to rob a bank on the understanding that D is armed and will use force if necessary to make good their escape. The Supreme Court explained these principles as follows (at paras 93–94):

> Juries frequently have to decide questions of intent (including conditional intent) by a process of inference from the facts and circumstances proved. The same applies when the question is whether [A], who joined with others in a venture to commit crime [X], shared a common purpose or common intent (the two are the same) which included, if things came to it, the commission of crime [Y], the offence or type of offence with which he is charged, and which was physically committed by D. A time honoured way of inviting a jury to consider such a question is to ask the jury whether they are sure that D's act was within the scope of the joint venture, that is, whether [A] expressly or tacitly agreed to a plan which included D going as far as he did, and committing crime [Y], if the occasion arose.
>
> If the jury is satisfied that there was an agreed common purpose to commit crime [X], and if it is satisfied also that [A] must have foreseen that, in the course of committing crime [X], D might well commit crime [Y], it may in appropriate cases be justified in drawing the conclusion that [A] had the necessary conditional intent that crime [Y] should be committed, if the occasion arose; or in other words that it was within the scope of the plan to which [A] gave his assent and intentional support. But that will be a question of fact for the jury in all the circumstances.

There need be no prior plan; for example, where A sees a fight going on and spontaneously joins in to assist D. The Supreme Court stated (at para. 95):

> In cases where there is a more or less spontaneous outbreak of multi-handed violence, the evidence may be too nebulous for the jury to find that there was some form of agreement, express or tacit. But, as we have said, liability as an aider or abettor does not necessarily depend on there being some form of agreement between the defendants; it depends on proof of intentional assistance or encouragement, conditional or otherwise. If [A] joins with a group which he realises is out to cause serious injury, the jury may well infer that he intended to encourage or assist the deliberate infliction of serious bodily injury and/ or intended that that should happen if necessary. In that case, if D acts with intent to cause serious bodily injury and death results, D and [A] will each be guilty of murder.

The Supreme Court went on to address the problem of homicide where D commits murder but A lacks the intent to be convicted of murder (see paras 96–97):

> If a person is a party to a violent attack on another, without an intent to assist in the causing of death or really serious harm, but the violence escalates and results in death, he will be not guilty of murder but guilty of manslaughter. So also if he participates by

encouragement or assistance in any other unlawful act which all sober and reasonable people would realise carried the risk of some harm (not necessarily serious) to another, and death in fact results . . . . The test is objective. As the Court of Appeal held in *Reid*, if a person goes out with armed companions to cause harm to another, any reasonable person would recognise that there is not only a risk of harm, but a risk of the violence escalating to the point at which serious harm or death may result. Cases in which [A] intends some harm falling short of grievous bodily harm are a fortiori, but manslaughter is not limited to these.

The qualification to this (recognised in *Wesley Smith, Anderson and Morris*, and *Reid*) is that it is possible for death to be caused by some overwhelming supervening act by the perpetrator which nobody in the defendant's shoes could have contemplated might happen and is of such a character as to relegate his acts to history; in that case the defendant will bear no criminal responsibility for the death.

The Supreme Court's decision to depart from the principle in *Chan Wing-Siu* is significant, but only time will tell whether it will have any significant impact on the outcomes of trials. The significance of the decision is that it clarifies the principles of accessorial liability and removes an anomaly. Judges' directions to juries now have to make clear that foresight by A that D might commit a further offence is evidence from which an intent to assist or encourage D to commit that offence may be inferred. Foresight by A that D might commit a further offence is not, in itself, sufficient to convict A.

In *Anwar* [2016] EWCA Crim 551, the Court of Appeal made it clear (at para. 20) that 'the jury will, of course, continue to look at the full picture or factual matrix in order to determine whether the relevant and necessary intent can be inferred'. Obviously, if A has foreseen the possible commission of the further offence and has continued to encourage or assist D in the pursuit of their criminal venture, this will be strong evidence that he also intended to assist or encourage the commission of the further offence. It is difficult to envisage that a jury properly directed would have acquitted Chan Wing-Siu of murder where he was armed with a knife, knew his companions were similarly armed, and he provided assistance by restraining the deceased's wife. As regards Jogee, a retrial was ordered; Jogee was convicted of manslaughter and sentenced to 12 years' imprisonment.

 The law in context

The implications of Jogee *for those convicted under* **Chan Wing-Siu**

There were audible gasps from the Supreme Court's public gallery when Lord Neuberger in *Jogee* announced that the Privy Council had taken a wrong turn in *Chan Wing-Siu* (BBC News Online, 'Joint Enterprise Ruling: A Moment of Genuine Legal History' 18 February 2016, http://www.bbc.co.uk/news/uk-35603309). Some foresaw a rush of applications to the Court of Appeal from people who were convicted under the law as set out in *Chan Wing-Siu*. JENGbA (Joint Enterprise Not Guilty By Association), a group that had campaigned for the law to be changed, hailed the decision as a 'major turning point in British justice' and a significant move away from a 'disproportionate and ill-used doctrine' (*The Guardian*, 'Joint Enterprise Law Wrongly Interpreted for 30 Years, Court Rules' 18 February 2016, https://www.theguardian.com/law/2016/feb/18/joint-enterprise-law-wrongly-interpreted-for-30-years-court-rules).

→

→

What impact will it have on those people who were convicted under the 'foresight' principle in *Chan Wing-Siu*? The Supreme Court was clear that the effect of its decision was 'not to render invalid all convictions which were arrived at over many years by faithfully applying the law as laid down in *Chan Wing-Siu* and in *Powell and English*' (para. 100). The Court held that a conviction that had been arrived at by faithfully applying the law as it stood at the time can only be set aside by seeking exceptional leave to appeal to the Court of Appeal out of time (para. 100). The Court of Appeal has long held that a change to the law that was applied at trial is insufficient to grant such leave (*R v Mitchell* [1977] 1 WLR 753) and will only do so if the defendant can demonstrate substantial injustice.

Some academics and former judges called for the Court of Appeal to deal swiftly with the issue of cases decided under the 'old law' to do justice for those convicted under the old law. Former Lord Justice of Appeal Sir Richard Buxton argued that it would be unacceptable to deny the possibility of correction to persons who were convicted under the old law, particularly when they are serving long sentences of imprisonment and that a 'prudent and just response will be to order a retrial' in those cases where the person has been affected by the injustice of being convicted by a jury that had been directed in accordance with law now recognised by the Supreme Court as incorrect ('Jogee, Upheaval in Secondary Liability for Murder' [2016] Crim LR 324–33, 333). Similarly, Ormerod and Laird argued that if, having regard to the direction given to the jury at trial, the defendant would not (applying the law as stated in *Jogee*) have been convicted of murder or manslaughter then that should surely amount to a substantial injustice justifying the granting of exceptional leave to appeal (D. Ormerod and K. Laird, '*Jogee*: Not the End of a Legal Saga But the Start of One?' [2016] Crim LR 539–52, 550). They argued that, even if the Court could be sure that the defendant would have been convicted of manslaughter, the stigma of the label 'murderer' and the unique sentencing arrangements for murder under the Criminal Justice Act 2003 (see **Chapter 9, Law in Context**) mean there are qualitative and quantitative differences between murder and manslaughter that should be enough to satisfy the Court of Appeal of substantial injustice justifying the grant of exceptional leave to appeal (Ormerod and Laird, p. 551).

However, the Court of Appeal's decision in *R v Johnson and others* [2016] EWCA Crim 1613 sets a high threshold for an appellant to demonstrate that they have suffered 'substantial injustice' (para. 20). The Court said it was not sufficient to have suffered adverse consequences, including the stigma of a murder conviction, to satisfy that test. A change in the law is, in itself, insufficient for leave. The Court explained the basis for its decision (at para. 18):

> The need to establish substantial injustice results from the wider public interest in legal certainty and the finality of decisions made in accordance with the then clearly established law. The requirement takes into account the requirement in a common law system for a court to be able to alter or correct the law upon which a large number of cases have been determined without the consequence that each of those cases can be re-opened.

The Court of Appeal's emphasis on finality and certainty echoes the Supreme Court's view in *Jogee*, when it said that 'alarming consequences' would flow from a general re-opening of old cases on the ground that an appellate court's decision had removed a widely held misconception as to the prior state of the law on which the conviction which it was sought to appeal had been based (para. 100). Within both Courts' judgments, one can read an implicit concern with the administrative and financial cost to the criminal justice system of a dramatic increase in appeals and retrials.

The Court of Appeal in *Johnson* said that its decision 'also takes into account the interests of the victim (or the victim's family), particularly in cases where death has resulted and closure is particularly important' (at para. 18). The reference to victims is striking. The Supreme Court's decision had been met with dismay by some of the families of people killed by people

→

→

convicted under the 'old' law. They argued that if the change led to many retrials, that would be deeply distressing for them having to relive their loved ones' death and undermine the closure that the guilty verdict brought them (BBC News Online, 'Joint Enterprise Ruling "Brings Heartache" for Families' 18 February 2016, http://www.bbc.co.uk/news/uk-35607311). Many of those families thus welcomed the Court of Appeal's decision. However, the Court's judgment provoked angry reactions from the relatives of those imprisoned under the law pre-*Jogee*, some shouting 'No justice, no peace' (BBC News Online, 'Judges Reject Challenge to "Joint Enterprise" Convictions' 31 October 2016, http://www.bbc.co.uk/news/uk-37821764).

The Court explained further that in determining whether the high threshold for demonstrated 'substantial injustice' has been met, it will focus on the strength of the case advanced that the change in the law would, in fact, have made a difference:

If crime A is a crime of violence which the jury concluded must have involved the use of a weapon so that the inference of participation with an intention to cause really serious harm is strong, that is likely to be very difficult. At the other end of the spectrum, if crime A is a different crime, not involving intended violence or use of force, it may well be easier to demonstrate substantial injustice. The court will also have regard to other matters including whether the applicant was guilty of other, though less serious, criminal conduct. It is not, however, in our view, material to consider the length of time that has elapsed. If there was a substantial injustice, it is irrelevant whether that injustice occurred a short time or a long time ago. It is and remains an injustice.

There has not been a flood of post-*Jogee* cases in which the Court of Appeal has overturned convictions. The first and so far only case in which an appellant has been granted exceptional leave to appeal is *R* v *Crilly* [2018] EWCA Crim 168. In that case, the Court of Appeal ordered a retrial in the case of a man who was convicted in 2005 of murder and robbery. The Court of Appeal followed *Johnson* and re-stated the principles to be applied in this area. To qualify for the grant of exceptional leave the applicant had to establish that a substantial injustice would be caused if it was denied. The fact that there had been a change in the law was not in itself sufficient where a person was properly convicted on the law as it stood at the time of trial. The threshold for demonstrating a substantial injustice was a high one. In determining whether that high threshold had been met, the court would have regard to the strength of the case advanced and whether a change in the law would have made a difference. In Crilly's case, he was not accused of intending or foreseeing any violence when they arrived at the scene of the robbery, nor was he accused of inflicting the violence and or intending to cause grievous bodily harm. The facts did not fit easily into the examples given in *Johnson* of the spectrum of offences. However, given that foresight might be evidence of intent but did not equate to intent, the evidence against him was not so strong that it could safely and fairly be inferred that the jury would have found the requisite intent to cause really serious bodily harm. The Court ordered a re-trial and Crilly subsequently pleaded guilty to manslaughter. The case shows that though the 'substantial injustice' threshold is high, it is possible for an appellant to challenge successfully a conviction following *Jogee* (see K. Laird, 'Case Comment on *R v Crilly*' [2018] Crim LR 1009–12).

The practical importance of *Jogee* for future cases is likely to be that in cases of multiple defendants all accused of committing murder, prosecutors will have to be much clearer and more specific about the precise basis on which each defendant is guilty, rather than relying on the *Chan Wing-Siu* test of foresight that some had criticised as too low a threshold and too loose a test (it had acquired the label of a 'lazy law' for police and prosecutors to use easily against gang members: BBC News Online 'Is Joint Enterprise a "Lazy Law"?' 24 April 2013, http://www.bbc.co.uk/news/uk-15299605). However, for some of those convicted in the 30 years between *Chan Wing-Siu* and *Jogee*, what appeared at first to be an opportunity to challenge injustice and fairly label their conduct will actually be of solely academic importance.

7.1.4.5 Liability for acts beyond the common design

 Key Point

Three situations may arise and the liability of an accessory differs between them:

(1) D accidentally commits a different offence in performing the common design or commits the contemplated offence in a different but non-relevant context.
(2) D commits the contemplated offence in unforeseen circumstances.
(3) D deliberately commits an offence outside the scope of the parties' common design.

In situation (1) for example, if A encourages D to assault V and D does so but V dies, both A and D will be liable for manslaughter. Death may have been unforeseen but each party to a joint unlawful enterprise is equally liable for the consequences of acts done in pursuance thereof (see *Baldessare* (1930) 22 Cr App R 70). In *Anderson and Morris* [1966] 2 QB 110, Lord Parker stated the principle as follows (at p. 118):

> [W]here two persons embark on a joint enterprise, each is liable for the acts done in pursuance of that joint enterprise, [and] . . . that includes liability for unusual consequences if they arise from the execution of the agreed joint enterprise.

Similarly the doctrine of transferred malice applies to the liability of accessories. If D, endeavouring to assault V, had accidentally assaulted W, or assaulted W mistaking him for V, both A and D would be liable for the assault; the context of the offence differs from the common design in a non-relevant way (see *Gnango* [2011] UKSC 59, **7.1.2.1**). By contrast, if D had deliberately assaulted W, this would fall within situation (3) and A would not be liable as the execution varies from the common design in a matter of substance. Hawkins stated the principle as follows (2 PC c29, s. 21):

> But if a man command another to commit a felony on a particular person or thing and he do it on another; as to kill A and he kill B or to burn the house of A and he burn the house of B or to steal an ox and he steal a horse; or to steal such an horse and he steal another; or to commit a felony of one kind and he commit another of a quite different nature; as to rob JS of his plate as he is going to market, and he break open his house in the night and there steal the plate; it is said that the commander is not an accessory because the act done varies in substance from that which was commanded.

What amounts to a variation in substance will not always be easy to define. In the examples Hawkins gives the perpetrator departs from the plan in each case in a significant way. An insignificant variation would be the case of robbing JS; if the principal had robbed him on the way back from market the accessory would remain liable for robbery. A variation from the common design, however, will not relieve an accessory of all liability. He may remain liable for incitement or conspiracy or he may be liable for a necessarily included lesser offence. In the example of stealing JS's plate (which falls within situation (3) listed earlier) the accessory would not be liable for burglary but he would be liable for simple theft as the counselled offence was robbery which involves theft and the offence committed was burglary which in this instance also involved theft. Similarly, if A had encouraged D to indecently assault V and D had raped V, A would not be liable for rape but would still be liable for indecent assault as rape necessarily involves indecent assault.

> In *Saunders and Archer* (1573) 2 Plowd 473, S desired to kill his wife and sought the assistance of A who supplied him with poison. S put this poison in an apple and gave it to his wife who ate a little but gave the remainder to their daughter. S watched this without intervening and the daughter died of poisoning. S was held guilty of murder; his failure to intervene amounted to a deliberate variation in substance from the common design and thus A was acquitted.

If S had not been present when the wife gave the apple to the daughter the doctrine of transferred malice would have applied. If the facts of *Saunders and Archer* occurred today, A could be convicted of conspiracy to murder or of aiding, abetting, counselling, or procuring S's attempt to kill his wife (see *Hapgood and Wyatt* (1870) LR 1 CCR 221).

Where the common design involves a conditional intention, the accessory will only be liable where the condition is fulfilled. For example, A and D suspect that V, their accomplice in crimes of robbery, is cheating them out of their fair share of the loot. A suggests to D that he should kill V if this happens again. After V divides the loot fairly following the next robbery D shoots him as D wants a bigger share. A would not be liable as an accessory as the condition had not been fulfilled but he could be liable for conspiracy to kill.

A problem which sometimes arises is that of the contemplated offence being committed by different means. This is situation (2) above involving an unforeseen circumstance. The circumstance may be of no significance and not bear upon the crucial issue which is A's intent. If A contemplates that D might kill V with a gun but nonetheless continues with the enterprise, he cannot hope to evade liability if D kills V with some other weapon. In *English* [1997] 3 WLR 959, Lord Hutton stated (at p. 981):

> [I]f the weapon used by the primary party is different to, but as dangerous as, the weapon which the secondary party contemplated he might use, the secondary party should not escape liability for murder because of the difference in the weapon, for example, if he foresaw that the primary party might use a gun to kill and the latter used a knife to kill, or vice versa.

In the wake of *English* a body of case law, of ever increasing complexity, developed to deal with the issue of 'fundamental departure' as countless appeals were pursued where it was contended that the use of a different weapon by D amounted to a fundamental departure from the common design. The Supreme Court in *Jogee* has consigned this case law to a siding and do not expect it to be revisited. The focus is to be on first the crime A encouraged or assisted rather than the method or weapon by which it was to be committed, and secondly whether or not A had the requisite intent. The Supreme Court stated (at para. 98):

This type of case apart, there will normally be no occasion to consider the concept of 'fundamental departure' as derived from *English*. What matters is whether [A] encouraged or assisted the crime, whether it be murder or some other offence. He need not encourage or assist a particular way of committing it, although he may sometimes do so. In particular, his intention to assist in a crime of violence is not determined only by whether he knows what kind of weapon D1 has in his possession. The tendency which has developed in the application of the rule in *Chan Wing-Siu* to focus on what [A] knew of what weapon D was carrying can and should give way to an examination of whether [A] intended to assist in the crime charged. If that crime is murder, then the question is whether he intended to assist the intentional infliction of grievous bodily harm at least, which question will often, as set out above, be answered by asking simply whether he himself intended grievous bodily harm at least. Very often he may intend to assist in violence using whatever weapon may come to hand. In other cases he may think that D has an iron bar whereas he turns out to have a knife, but the difference may not at all affect his intention to assist, if necessary, in the causing of grievous bodily harm at least. Knowledge or ignorance that weapons generally, or a particular weapon, is carried by D will be evidence going to what the intention of [A] was, and may be irresistible evidence one way or the other, but it is evidence and no more.

Where, however, situation (3) arises D does not merely commit the contemplated offence in circumstances which depart from the common design in an immaterial way but he goes beyond the common design and commits an offence different from that contemplated. This situation seems to arise most often in spontaneous attacks by a group on another or others. The problem for the jury will be to determine what the intentions of the individual assailants were and what possible offences by their fellow assailants they intended to assist or encourage. **The *mens rea* of individuals may diverge even though they agree on the act that will be performed.** For example, in *Gilmour* [2000] 2 Cr App R 407, the Northern Ireland Court of Appeal approved the following hypothetical (originally posed in *Blackstone's Criminal Practice* 1996):

> Suppose [D] and A agree that [D] will post a specific incendiary device to V, A contemplating only superficial injuries to V when he opens it but [D] foreseeing and hoping that the injuries will be serious or fatal. If V is killed as a result, [D] will clearly be guilty of murder, A is clearly not guilty of murder as an accessory but should be guilty of manslaughter because the act done by [D] is precisely what was envisaged. The fact that [D] happens also to have the *mens rea* of murder is irrelevant because it does not change the nature of the act that he does or the manner in which he does it.

Because murder may be committed with an intent to kill or the lesser intent to cause GBH, and GBH covers serious injuries which may not be life threatening as well as those which are, further complications may arise in delineating the ambit of the common design. A good example of the problems that may arise is the case of *Gamble* [1989] NI 268.

> A and B were parties to what they thought was going to be a punishment beating and contemplated that it might involve, at worst, 'knee-capping' V (i.e. shooting V through his knee-caps). The other participants, C and D, however, murdered V in an

attack which involved multiple stab wounds, gunshot wounds, and blows to the head and body. Two of the gunshot wounds would have been fatal had death not been caused by cutting V's throat. Carswell J, sitting without a jury in the Crown Court of Northern Ireland, convicted A and B of wounding with intent to inflict GBH. Counsel for the Crown had argued that as A and B had both intended GBH and that this was sufficient *mens rea* for murder, they should be convicted of murder. In response Carswell J stated (at p. 284):

> Although the rule remains well entrenched that an intention to inflict grievous bodily harm qualifies as the *mens rea* of murder, it is not in my opinion necessary to apply it in such a way as to fix an accessory with liability for a consequence which he did not intend and which stems from an act which he did not have within his contemplation.

In the language of *Jogee* the murder of V was an 'overwhelming supervening act' as clearly there was no evidence from which an intention to encourage or assist C and D in murder could be inferred. As A and B were convicted of wounding with intent, for which the maximum sentence is life imprisonment, there is no substance in the argument that public protection is undermined by the Court's decision. The principle accords respect to the principle of fair labelling.

7.1.5 Withdrawal from the joint enterprise

 Question

If A has encouraged D to commit an offence, or is present assisting D to commit an offence, is it possible for him to escape liability by withdrawing from the enterprise before the offence is committed?

Withdrawal will clearly not affect A's liability for incitement or conspiracy or attempt where the principal has reached the stage of performing a 'more than merely preparatory act' (see **8.4.3**) before A withdraws. Actual withdrawal from the enterprise must be effective if A is to escape liability for the completed offence; a mere change of heart without more is not sufficient (see *Becerra* (1975) 62 Cr App R 212; *Rook* (1993) 97 Cr App R 327). What is required will depend on the assistance or encouragement A has given. If A has counselled D to commit the offence he may withdraw by expressly countermanding or revoking his encouragement (see *Saunders and Archer* (1573) 2 Plowd 473; *Croft* [1944] 1 KB 295) although he may still be liable for incitement. The communication must, where practicable and reasonable, be timely and 'serve unequivocal notice upon the other party to the common unlawful cause that if he proceeds upon it he does so without the further aid and assistance of those who withdraw' (*per* Sloan JA in *Whitehouse* (1941) 1 WWR 112, quoted with approval in *Becerra*).

In *Mitchell* [1999] Crim LR 496, the Court of Appeal ruled that a direction based on *Whitehouse* requiring communication of withdrawal by the accessory to the principal was not necessary when violence was spontaneous rather than pre-planned. A, B, and D had engaged in a fight with U, V, and W, the owner of a restaurant and his two sons after D had assaulted other customers in the restaurant and caused damage to the restaurant. There was some evidence that after leaving V prostrate on the ground having been the recipient of a concerted attack involving beating with a stick, kicking, and stamping on his head, D had returned to administer a further beating to V's head with the stick. The Court of Appeal quashed A and B's convictions for murder and ordered a retrial. If D administered the fatal blows at a time when A and B had desisted from the attack and walked away, their desistance may have been sufficient to constitute withdrawal from the joint enterprise leaving D solely responsible for the murder of V. As this possibility had not been clearly left to the jury the Court of Appeal considered the convictions unsafe. It is submitted that this ruling is too favourable to accessories. A's simple desistance does not in any way countermand the encouragement or assistance he has already rendered to D, nor does it serve any kind of notice on D that the prior encouragement is countermanded. To seek to distinguish pre-planned violence from spontaneous violence will give rise to inane discussions as to the relative meanings of 'spontaneous' and 'pre-planned' which are irrelevant to the question of accessorial liability.

Fortunately the Court of Appeal moved quickly to limit *Mitchell*. In *Robinson*, 3 February 2000 (Case No. 9903443Y3), D and a group of youths had followed V taunting him. The group looked to D for leadership and called on him to hit V. D did so, whereupon the group joined in the attack. D stood back while they did so but when the attack appeared to be going further than he intended, he intervened and the attack ceased. The Court of Appeal followed *Becerra* holding that, in the instant case where violence was not spontaneous, communication of withdrawal was necessary. Furthermore, Otton LJ stated:

> There is a clear line of authority that where a party has given encouragement to others to commit an offence it cannot be withdrawn once the offence has commenced. (See *R v Whitefield* (1983) 79 Cr App R 36; *R v Rook* (1993) 97 Cr App R 327; *R v Pearman* [1996] 1 Cr App R 24.)

His Lordship, who also gave the judgment of the Court in *Mitchell*, quoted from Professor Smith's *Commentary to Mitchell* [1999] Crim LR 496 with approval, and made it clear that *Mitchell* was an exceptional case stating:

> [I]t can only be in exceptional circumstances that a person can withdraw from a crime he has initiated. Similarly in those rare circumstances communication of withdrawal must be given in order to give the principal offenders the opportunity to desist rather than complete the crime. This must be so even in situations of spontaneous violence unless it is not practicable or reasonable so to communicate as in the exceptional circumstances pertaining in *Mitchell* where the accused threw down his weapon and moved away before the final and fatal blows were inflicted.

This appears to be treating *Mitchell* as a very exceptional case and shifting the emphasis away from the spontaneous nature of the violence to the fact that the original violence had clearly ceased and A and B had withdrawn before D returned to inflict further violence. Had the attack been continuing when they withdrew, the suggestion in *Robinson* is that this would not have been effective. The effect of this judgment appears to limit withdrawal where encouragement has been offered to the period prior to the commencement of the offence. If the attack on the victim which D has initiated commences, it will be too late for him to withdraw and avoid liability. Unfortunately, in *O'Flaherty and others* [2004] EWCA Crim 526, the Court of Appeal in *obiter* comments, not having had the benefit of being referred to *Robinson*, expressed approval of the decision in *Mitchell*, that 'while communication of withdrawal is a necessary precondition for disassociation from pre-planned violence it is not necessary when violence is spontaneous'. The Court of Appeal's ability to propagate confusion is depressing.

Where A has supplied the means of committing the crime, a change of heart and quitting of the scene prior to the offence being committed would not be sufficient (*Whitehouse*). In *Becerra*, A, D, and E broke into a house intending to steal. A gave D a knife to use if necessary on anyone interrupting them. When V came downstairs to investigate the noise, A said, 'There's a bloke coming. Let's go', and jumped out of the window. D stabbed V with the knife, killing him. A's conviction for murder was upheld by the Court of Appeal as he had not effectively withdrawn from the joint enterprise. What amounts to effective withdrawal will vary with the circumstances of each case. It was believed that sometimes nothing less than physical intervention would suffice. The Court did not state if this would have been necessary in the instant case; it was sufficient for the purposes of disposing of the appeal to state that what A had done was not enough. The Northern Ireland Court of Appeal adopted a similar approach in *Graham* [1996] NI 157 in upholding A's conviction for murder.

> A had taken a terrorist kidnap victim, V, from a house in which he had hidden following his escape to a house where A knew the kidnappers would be, realising that they would likely kill V. A refused to render any further assistance to the kidnappers and asked them not to harm V. The kidnappers took V to waste ground and shot him in the head. Carswell LJ stated (at p. 169):

>> We consider that at the late stage which the murder plan had reached, and after the appellant had played such a significant part in assisting the killers to accomplish their aim, it could not be a sufficient withdrawal to indicate to them that he no longer supported their enterprise. Something more was required, and the judge was amply justified in holding that what the appellant did was not enough. His pleas were useless and the withholding of co-operation . . . was of minimal effect. We do not find it necessary to attempt to specify what acts would have been required of the appellant in the circumstances. It is sufficient for present purposes for us to say that the steps which he did take cannot be regarded as sufficient for withdrawal.

In *Grundy* [1977] Crim LR 543, A gave burglars information about premises and the habits of the occupants six weeks before the burglary took place. Four weeks later A tried to dissuade them from committing the offence. His conviction was quashed as this evidence of effective withdrawal had not been left to the jury. In *Whitefield* (1983) 79 Cr App R 36, A gave D similar information and agreed to break into the premises with D. Later he withdrew but D went on alone and A took no steps to stop him. The Court of Appeal held that there was evidence that A had served unequivocal notice on D that if he proceeded with the burglary he would do so without A's aid and assistance, and the judge's ruling that this was not enough and that notification of the police or other steps to prevent the burglary was required, was wrong. Both these cases appear to be unduly liberal towards the accessory. The information supplied remained of use to the burglars and was not negated by the suppliers' subsequent efforts to dissuade the burglars. If the appellants in *Grundy* and *Whitefield* had only counselled the commission of burglary without supplying information which assisted the burglars, verbal communication of withdrawal would suffice. Where something more is done, it is submitted that the withdrawal should not be considered effective if the accessory has not notified the police or warned the owners of the premises. The Court of Appeal in *Rook* (1993) 97 Cr App R 327, found it unnecessary, and thus was not prepared, to decide whether, in cases where aid has been given prior to the commission of the crime, steps would be necessary to neutralise such aid for withdrawal to be effective. Unfortunately, in *O'Flaherty and others* [2004] EWCA Crim 526, the Court of Appeal, once again, in *obiter* comments expressed its approval of the decisions in *Grundy* and *Whitefield*. Mantell LJ stated (at para. 60):

> In cases of assistance it has sometimes been suggested that, for there to be an effective withdrawal, reasonable steps must have been taken to prevent the crime. It is clear, however, this is not necessary.

The failure of the Court of Appeal to distinguish between the situation where a person participates only by verbally inciting or encouraging and that where he participates by providing something of continuing use or assistance to the principal (whether it be a weapon or information) is, to say the least, disappointing. In light of the confusion propagated by the Court of Appeal in its various judgments, however, it is not surprising. It is this author's view, as it is of many other commentators, that withdrawal should not, as a matter of principle, be considered effective where it does not neutralise the effect of any assistance already given or, at least, endeavour to do so by taking other reasonable steps.

7.1.6 Victims as accessories

The fact that A is a victim of the offence does not, of itself, prevent him being convicted as an aider and abettor. For example, consent is a limited defence to offences against the person operating only where the action can be positively justified by some public interest. If A is a masochist and he permits D, a sadist, to wound him for his sexual gratification, A would be an aider and abettor to D's offence of unlawful wounding as there is no public interest justifying D's action (see further **10.7**). Similarly, if A permits D to perform an unlawful abortion on her she can be convicted as an aider and abettor to that offence (see *Sockett* (1908) 1 Cr App R 101). Where a statute is designed to protect a certain class of persons, however, a member of that class who is the victim of the offence cannot be convicted as an accessory.

> In *Tyrrell* [1894] 1 QB 710, A, a girl between the ages of 13 and 16, was convicted of aiding and abetting D to have unlawful sexual intercourse with her contrary to s. 5 of the Criminal Law Amendment Act 1885 (see now s. 9 of the Sexual Offences

Act 2003). Her conviction was quashed on appeal, Lord Coleridge CJ stating (at p. 712) that 'it is impossible to say that the Act . . . can have intended that the girls for whose protection it was passed should be punishable under it for the offences committed upon themselves' (see also *Whitehouse* [1977] QB 868).

In *Gnango* [2011] UKSC 59 the Supreme Court made it clear that the victim rule only operates where an offence is created specifically to protect the victim; it does not operate generally where a person happens to be an actual or intended victim of the offence. In this case the fact that G was engaged in a gunfight with B and could have been murdered by him did not serve to shield G from conviction for murder as an accessory when V, a passer-by, was accidentally shot by B who was liable to conviction as principal on the basis of the doctrine of transferred malice (see **3.6.2.3** and **7.1.2.1**).

7.1.7 Entrapment and accessorial liability

Many offences are only detected because of proactive policing—for example, undercover drugs officers infiltrating a smuggling operation or drug-dealing enterprise to obtain evidence against the participants, or an undercover officer or informer infiltrating a gang of robbers to obtain information leading to their apprehension *in flagrante delicto*. Is such an officer ever liable to conviction as an accessory?

> **Key Point**
>
> The situations and persons involved may be divided into four types:
>
> (1) those who merely observe the crime but play no part in the instigation of the offence, namely spies;
> (2) those decoys who accede to the accused's suggestions and thereby help provide the opportunity for the commission of the offence, namely collaborators;
> (3) those decoys who expose the accused to temptation and thereby facilitate the commission of the offence by the accused, namely tempters;
> (4) those decoys who actively entice, encourage, or persuade the accused to commit an offence, which he would not otherwise commit, for the purpose of entrapping him, namely *agents provocateurs*.

The aim of the spy or decoy in all cases is to obtain evidence of the commission of an offence by the accused which will be sufficient for, or necessary to, a prosecution. The propriety of the behaviour of the spy or decoy in so doing varies from one category to another. The courts appear to approve of the behaviour in the first three categories but consider that the behaviour involved in the fourth situation goes too far and involves the *agent provocateur* in complicity in the offence which the accused ultimately commits. In *Mullins* (1848) 3 Cox CC 526, Maule J stated (at p. 531) that a person acting as a spy does not deserve to be blamed 'if he instigates offences no further than by pretending to concur with the perpetrators'. In *Birtles* (1969) 53 Cr App R 469, Lord Parker CJ stated (at p. 473):

> [I]t is vitally important to ensure so far as possible that the informer does not create an offence, that is to say, incite others to commit an offence which those others would not otherwise have committed. It is one thing for the police to make use of information concerning an offence that is already laid on . . . . But it is quite another thing, and something of which this court thoroughly disapproves, to use an informer to encourage another to commit an offence, or indeed an offence of a more serious character, which he would not otherwise commit, still more so if the police themselves take part in carrying it out.

This view has been echoed in subsequent cases such as *McCann* (1971) 56 Cr App R 359; *Mealey and Sheridan* (1975) 60 Cr App R 59; and *McEvilly and Lee* (1973) 60 Cr App R 150.

In *Edwards* [1991] Crim LR 45, undercover officers were introduced to E, a suspected drugs dealer. E agreed to supply them with drugs and agreed a discount on future deals. It was clear that this particular conspiracy to supply drugs to the officers would not have taken place but for the officers' enticement of E. E, however, was prosecuted for conspiracy to supply controlled drugs to persons unknown; the officers' evidence was treated as evidence of this wider, established conspiracy which they clearly had not instigated, and thus they had not acted as *agents provocateurs*.

In *Sang* [1979] 2 All ER 1222, Lord Salmon suggested that police officers and informers involved in improper instances of entrapment should be prosecuted. He stated (at p. 1236):

> I would now refer to what is, I believe, and hope, the unusual case in which a dishonest policeman, anxious to improve his detection record, tries very hard with the help of an *agent provocateur* to induce a young man with no criminal tendencies to commit a serious crime, and ultimately the young man succumbs to the inducement . . . . The policeman and the informer who acted together in inciting him to commit the crime should . . . both be prosecuted and suitably punished.

Lord Diplock also accepted that a police officer or informer would be liable as accessories (at p. 1226). Lord Salmon includes several superfluous requirements such that the police officer be dishonest, the accused be young, and the crime serious. These add nothing to the basic criterion which is that the accused is encouraged to commit an offence which would not otherwise have been committed—that is, to use Lord Parker's words, an offence which was not 'laid on'. The fact that the officer's or informer's motive may have been the detection of crime is irrelevant (see further *Yip Chiu-Cheung* v *R* [1994] 3 WLR 514 and **8.3.3.3**).

In *Smith* [1960] 2 QB 423, D, a private individual seeking to expose corruption in local government, offered a bribe to the mayor of Castleford. D was convicted of corruption contrary to s. 1(2) of the Public Bodies Corrupt Practices Act 1889, the Court of Appeal holding that the purity of his motives provided him with no defence. Where an offence is 'laid on', however, it may be appropriate in some circumstances for a police officer or informer to participate in the offence. In *Birtles* Lord Parker CJ stated (at p. 473):

In such a case the police are clearly entitled, indeed it is their duty, to mitigate the consequences of the proposed offence, for example, to protect the proposed victim, and to that
end it may be perfectly proper for them to encourage the informer to take part in the
offence or indeed for a police officer himself to do so.

If an officer or informer does participate, his behaviour will be lawful. In *Clarke* (1984)
80 Cr App R 344, Macpherson J enlarged upon Lord Parker's dicta stating (at p. 348):

In using the expression 'it may be perfectly proper' the Lord Chief Justice was, in our
judgment, contemplating that in such exceptional cases where an informer (and/or a
policeman) took part in a 'laid on' case there should be no finding that it was unlawful
so to do.

For example, D tells A that he is going to commit a burglary. A is unable to dissuade
him from so doing but agrees to drive D to the scene of the offence. A then telephones the police and D is caught *in flagrante delicto*. The decision in *Clarke* would
suggest that A's assistance was justified. There must be limits to this, however, as
offences involving injury to people or irreparable damage to property should not be
assisted in any way. This limited defence obviously requires considerable clarification by the appellate courts.

Where D commits an offence as a result of improper entrapment this used to be
treated as a mitigating factor to be taken into account in sentencing (see *Sang*, earlier
in this section; *Underhill* (1979) 1 Cr App R (S) 270). In *Sang* the House of Lords
declared that there was no defence of entrapment nor could evidence obtained as a
result of the activities of an *agent provocateur* be excluded by the trial judge in exercise
of his discretion on ground of unfairness as this would let in a defence of entrapment
by the backdoor. Section 78 of the Police and Criminal Evidence Act 1984 reversed
the effect of *Sang* in respect of the discretion to exclude evidence which had been
obtained unfairly. Evidence obtained as a result of entrapment could be excluded
where its admission would have such an adverse effect on the fairness of the proceedings that the court ought not to admit it (see further *Smurthwaite and Gill* (1994) 98
Cr App R 437). Of course, if there is other independent evidence sufficient to prove
the charge against D, exclusion of the evidence of an *agent provocateur* will have little
effect. This problem will largely be obviated by reliance on the doctrine of abuse of
process recognised by the House of Lords in *R v Horseferry Road Magistrates' Court, ex
parte Bennett* [1994] 1 AC 42. In this case their Lordships held that a court has jurisdiction to stay proceedings and order the release of the accused when the court becomes
aware that there has been a serious abuse of power on the part of the executive. To
permit the prosecuting authority to take advantage of such an abuse of power would
be contrary to the rule of law as the State should not be seen to be instigating criminal
offences in order to prosecute them. In *Latif and Shafzad* [1996] 1 WLR 104, the House
of Lords confirmed that this doctrine was applicable in entrapment cases.

In *R v Looseley* and *AG's Reference (No. 3 of 2000)* [2001] UKHL 53, [2002] 1 Cr App
R 29, the circumstances in which entrapment would amount to an abuse of process
were further elucidated. Police conduct would not amount to improper entrapment
where it 'did no more than present the defendant with an unexceptional opportunity

to commit a crime' (*per* Lord Nicholls, para. 23). By contrast there would be a violation of the concept of fairness 'if a defendant were to be convicted and punished for
committing a crime which he only committed because he had been incited, instigated, persuaded, pressurised or wheedled into committing it by a law enforcement
officer' (*per* Lord Bingham of Cornhill, *Nottingham City Council* v *Amin* [2000] 1 Cr
App R 426, 431, cited with approval by Lord Hutton at para. 109). Thus, if the police
do no more than might have been expected from others in the circumstances, there
is no abuse of process.

The courts will engage in a balancing exercise in determining whether in any
particular case the conduct of the police is so seriously improper as to bring the
administration of justice into disrepute. In determining where the balance lies the
court will take account of several factors. First, the nature of the offence may be
relevant as proactive techniques are more appropriate for offences where there is no
victim, such as drug-dealing, or offences where victims are reluctant to report the
offence—for example, corruption. In these cases the secrecy surrounding the activity and the difficulty of detection by conventional means would weigh in favour of
using proactive methods. Secondly, the reason for the particular operation will be
of relevance. Wholesale 'virtue-testing' without good reason would not be acceptable, nor would the conduct of a vendetta against an individual or a group. What is
required is reasonable suspicion either that a particular individual is engaged in
criminal activity or that criminal activity of a particular kind is prevalent in a particular location. In addition the officers carrying out the operation should be duly
authorised to do so in compliance with the *Covert Human Intelligence Sources Code of
Practice* (HO 2014) (pursuant to s. 71(4) of the Regulation of Investigatory Powers
Act 2000). Thirdly, the nature and extent of police participation in the crime is an
important consideration as 'the greater the inducement held out by the police, and
the more forceful or persistent the police overtures, the more readily may a court
conclude that the police overstepped the boundary: their conduct might well have
brought about the commission of a crime by a person who would normally avoid
crime of that kind' (*per* Lord Nicholls, para. 29). A relevant factor may also be the
vulnerability of the defendant. For example, persistent importuning of a drug
addict to supply drugs would overstep the boundary whereas persistent requests of
a suspected drug dealer would not, as drug dealers display a degree of cautious reluctance when approached by a new customer. Thus behaving in the manner of an
ordinary customer of a trade being carried on by the defendant would not normally
transgress the boundary. Finally, the fact that the defendant has a criminal record
will not of itself justify targeting him unless there is evidence to ground reasonable
suspicion that he is currently engaged in criminal activity.

The House of Lords concluded that the position in England and Wales, as it had
developed over recent years, was consistent with the requirements of Art. 6 of the
European Convention on Human Rights as explained in *Teixeira de Castro* v *Portugal*
(1999) 28 EHRR 101.

7.1.8 Reform

In its Report *Participating in Crime* (Law Com No. 305) the Law Commission accepts
that secondary liability for participation in an offence committed by a principal
offender should be retained. It does, however, recommend a series of reforms

designed to make the law more rational and fair. The Report is intended to be read in tandem with its earlier Report *Inchoate Liability for Assisting and Encouraging Crime* (Law Com No. 300) which has resulted in fairly rapid reform by the enactment of ss 44–67 of the Serious Crime Act 2007 (see **8.2**). The Law Commission proposes that D should be liable for aiding and abetting (which will be called under the new scheme 'assisting and encouraging') the commission of an offence by P only if D does his act of assistance or encouragement with the intention that P will thereby commit the offence. Foresight/contemplation will not be enough. Separate provision for joint venture cases is also proposed which will be based on foresight on the part of D of what P might do when, for example, they embark on a joint criminal venture, such as burglary, in the course of which P kills V.

In its Consultation Paper *Murder, Manslaughter and Infanticide: Proposals for Reform of the Law* (CP 19/08) the Government sets out its proposals for reform of the law on complicity in homicide accepting much of the Law Commission's analysis and recommendations. Clauses 1–4 are quoted in the following section. The proposal is to create a new statutory offence of intentionally assisting or encouraging murder (cl. 1) and a statutory offence of murder where P is guilty of manslaughter owing to a lack of *mens rea* and D assisted or encouraged intending P to kill or cause serious injury (cl. 2). The Law Commission's recommendation to retain a broad offence of murder in the context of a joint criminal venture is also adopted (cl. 3). Reform to the 'fundamental difference' principle is also proposed seeking greater flexibility based on whether P's act was within the scope of the joint criminal venture: it would be where the act did not go far beyond that which was planned, agreed to, or foreseen by the secondary party. The fundamental difference principle may only be relied on where D has not foreseen death of V as a possibility, but unlike the current situation, even when successfully raised, it will only result in a reduction of D's liability to manslaughter (cl. 4).

1. Assisting or encouraging the offence of murder

Where a person ('P') has committed the offence of murder, another person ('D') is guilty of the offence if—

(a) D did an act which assisted or encouraged one or more other acts to be done by another person,

(b) P's criminal act was that act or one of those acts, and

(c) D's act was intended to assist or encourage a person to kill, or cause serious injury to, another person.

2. Assisting or encouraging the offence of manslaughter

(1) This section applies where a person ('P') commits the offence of manslaughter in circumstances where P acts without the state of mind required for conviction of the offence of murder.

(2) Another person ('D') is guilty of the offence of murder if—

(a) D did an act which assisted or encouraged one or more other acts to be done by another person,

(b) P's criminal act was that act or one of those acts, and

(c) D's act was intended to assist or encourage a person to kill, or cause serious injury to, another person.

3. Murder in the context of a joint criminal venture

(1) Where—

    (a) two or more persons participate in a joint criminal venture, and

    (b) one of them ('P') commits the offence of murder in the context of the venture, another participant ('D') is guilty of the offence of murder if subsection (2) or (3) applies.

(2) This subsection applies if D foresaw that in the context of the venture a person might be killed by a participant acting with intent to kill, or to cause serious injury to, a person.

(3) This subsection applies if—

    (a) D foresaw that, in the context of the venture, serious injury might be caused to a person by a participant acting with intent to cause such injury, and

    (b) P's criminal act was within the scope of the venture.

(4) P's criminal act was within the scope of the venture if it did not go far beyond that which was planned or agreed to, or which was foreseen, by D.

(5) The existence of a joint criminal venture, and that which was planned, agreed or foreseen as part of such a venture, may be inferred from the conduct of the participants (whether or not there is an express agreement).

(6) D does not escape liability under this section for an offence of murder committed by P at a time when D is a participant merely because D is at that time—

    (a) absent,

    (b) against the venture's being carried out, or

    (c) indifferent as to whether it is carried out.

(7) 'Participant' means a participant in the joint criminal venture.

4. Manslaughter in the context of a joint criminal venture

(1) Where—

    (a) two or more other persons participate in a joint criminal venture, and

    (b) one of them ('P') commits the offence of murder in the context of the venture, another participant ('D') is guilty of the offence of manslaughter if subsection (2) or (3) applies.

(2) This subsection applies if D foresaw that, in the context of the venture, serious injury might be caused to a person by a participant acting with intent to cause such injury.

(3) This subsection applies if—

    (a) D foresaw that in the context of the joint criminal venture harm (other than serious harm), or the fear of harm, might be caused to a person by a participant, and

    (b) a reasonable person in D's position with D's knowledge of the relevant facts would have foreseen an obvious risk of serious injury being caused to a person, or of a person being killed, by a participant in the context of the venture.

(4) The existence of a joint criminal venture may be inferred from the conduct of the participants (whether or not there is an express agreement).

(5) D does not escape liability for manslaughter under this section in relation to an offence of murder committed by P at a time when D is a participant merely because D is at that time—

(a) absent,

(b) against the venture's being carried out, or

(c) indifferent as to whether it is carried out.

(6) 'Participant' means a participant in the joint criminal venture.

7.2 Vicarious liability

In the law of tort an employer is responsible for the torts of his employees acting in the course of their employment. This is known as 'vicarious liability' which is a form of strict liability arising from the employer–employee relationship, without reference to any fault of the employer. There is no such general rule in criminal law; generally if the master is to be liable it will be on the basis of being an accessory under the principles outlined earlier. The principle was stated by Raymond CJ in *Huggins* (1730) 2 Strange 883 (at p. 885):

> It is a point not to be disputed but that in criminal cases the principal is not answerable for the act of the deputy, as he is in civil cases; they must each answer for their own acts and stand or fall by their own behaviour. All the authors that treat of criminal proceedings, proceed on the foundation of this distinction; that to affect the superior by the act of the deputy, there must be command of the superior which is not found in this case.

Huggins was the warden of Fleet prison who was charged with aiding and abetting B, a turnkey, to murder a prisoner who had died as a result of the turnkey's neglect. As this occurred without Huggins's knowledge he was not guilty.

While this is the general rule, it is subject to exceptions. At common law there were two offences for which an employer could be liable for the acts of his employees even if these had not been authorised and he remained ignorant of them, namely **public nuisance** (see *Stephens* (1866) LR 1 QB 702) and **criminal libel** (this was modified by s. 7 of the Libel Act 1843). Occasionally statute expressly imposes vicarious liability. For example, s. 59(1) of the Licensing Act 1964 (now repealed) provided:

> Subject to the provisions of this Act, no person shall, except during the permitted hours—
>
> (a) himself or by his servant or agent sell or supply to any person in licensed premises . . . any intoxicating liquor . . . .

More usually, however, vicarious liability is the result of judicial interpretation of statutory offences of a regulatory nature. Various reasons are put forward to support such interpretations. Imposing liability on the employer for contraventions of legislation by his employees may be a more effective way of encouraging compliance with the legislation; the employer, after all, is the one who has overall control of the business and can regulate the conduct of his employees. It may also be considered unjust to punish an employee for the breach of some regulation as he may not have had the means of detecting the breach or of preventing it. A further justification is that vicarious liability is necessary to make certain provisions effective where some *mens rea* offences may only be committed by persons of a particular status, such as licensees. Such legislation would be rendered useless if the licensee could claim that the act had been performed without his knowledge by his employee; the response of the courts has been to create the 'delegation principle' (see **7.2.2**). While these justifications have some force, they do represent an attempt by the judges to come to the rescue of the legislature as all these problems could have been met by means of better drafting of the legislation.

7.2.1 Vicarious liability by implication

The approach of the courts to statutory interpretation for the purpose of determining whether a provision imposed vicarious liability was stated by Atkin J in *Mousell Bros* v *London and North Western Ry* [1917] 2 KB 836 (at p. 845):

> [W]hile prima facie a principal is not to be made criminally responsible for the acts of his servants, yet the legislature may prohibit an act or enforce a duty in such words as to make the prohibition or the duty absolute; in which case the principal is in fact liable if the act is in fact done by his servants. To ascertain whether a particular Act of Parliament has that effect or not, regard must be had to the words used, the nature of the duty laid down, the person upon whom it is imposed, the person by whom it would in ordinary circumstances be performed, and the person upon whom the penalty is imposed.

In many statutes it is unclear upon whom the duty is imposed; in such cases the courts generally conclude that it is imposed on the employer as he is the one who has control of the enterprise. **Where the performance of the duty requires positive acts the doctrine of vicarious liability is necessary. But where the offence is one of strict liability, consisting of an omission to perform a duty imposed on the employer, he will be personally liable as the perpetrator (without resort to the doctrine of vicarious liability) as, the duty being unfulfilled, the omission is as much his as that of any servant to whom he assigned the task.**

> In *Hodge* v *Higgins* [1980] 2 Lloyd's Rep 589, a vessel was observed in the River Humber at night without a forward light. The master had retired to bed ill leaving the vessel in the charge of the mate. The master was convicted of neglect of duty contrary to s. 27 of the Merchant Shipping Act 1970, which made it an offence for the master of a ship to omit to do anything required to preserve the ship from loss, destruction, or serious damage. The magistrate found, and the Divisional Court upheld his finding, that there was a breach of this duty and the master could not evade his responsibility as the duty was his alone.

Where the offence requires a positive act the courts have to decide if the act of the employee can be attributed to the employer. If it can, without undue strain to the wording of the legislation, and the offence is one of strict liability, the employer will be held to be a joint principal with his employee. Thus words such as 'sell', 'supply', and 'use' have frequently been given this extended meaning.

In *Coppen* v *Moore (No. 2)* [1898] 2 QB 306, D, the owner of several shops, instructed his managers to sell American ham under the description 'breakfast ham'. A shop assistant in one shop, without the knowledge of her manager or D, sold some ham as 'Scotch ham'. It was an offence under s. 2(2) of the Merchandise Marks Act 1887 to sell any goods 'to which any . . . false trade description is applied'. The assistant had done the physical act of selling and committed this offence, but the Divisional Court held that D was also liable as, property in the ham being vested in him, he had in law sold the ham.

Had D not been convicted as a principal by means of the implication of vicarious liability, it would not have been possible to convict him as an accessory due to his lack of knowledge.

Other cases establish that an employer is 'in possession' of goods which his employee possesses (*Melias Ltd* v *Preston* [1957] 2 QB 380), 'uses' a vehicle which his employee uses (*Green* v *Burnett* [1955] 1 QB 78), and 'presents' a play which his employee presents (*Grade* v *DPP* [1942] 2 All ER 118). By contrast, however, only the actual driver of a vehicle can be said to be 'driving' (cf. *Thornton* v *Mitchell* [1940] 1 All ER 339). Likewise, where words which import *mens rea* are used, such as 'knowingly', 'maliciously', 'fraudulently', 'permitting', 'suffering', or 'allowing', the employer can only be liable where he had *mens rea* himself (see *James & Son* v *Smee* [1955] 1 QB 78); his employee's *mens rea* cannot be imputed to him, unless the case falls within the bounds of the 'delegation principle' (see **7.2.2**).

This approach of extending the meaning of words has been used to impose liability not only in the employer/employee situation but also to impose liability on a principal for the act of his agent or independent contractor (see *Quality Dairies (York) Ltd* v *Pedley* [1952] 1 KB 275 and *F. E. Charman Ltd* v *Clow* [1974] 1 WLR 1384), on a partner for the act of his fellow partner (see *Clode* v *Barnes* [1974] 1 All ER 1166), and on a licensee for unlawful sales by the bar staff even though they were not his employees but employees of the owner of the bar (see *Goodfellow* v *Johnson* [1966] 1 QB 83). **The issue is whether there is a sufficient nexus between the parties so that it can be said that the accused had some control over the actions of the other.** A further consideration is whether the imposition of liability would serve to encourage stricter supervision to ensure compliance with regulatory legislation. Ultimately the matter is one for judicial interpretation. The Law Commission, when considering vicarious liability for the acts of independent contractors, stated (Law Com No. 177) at para. 9.49:

> It is one thing to hold that a person carrying on a business of supplying milk or heavy building materials 'uses' a vehicle if he employs an independent contractor to supply those things in the contractor's vehicle. It would be quite another thing to hold that a householder 'uses' the removal van owned by a firm of removers whom he engages to carry his furniture to a new residence.

7.2.2 The delegation principle

Where the offence is not one of strict liability but requires proof of *mens rea* or negligence, the general rule is that an employer cannot be convicted on the basis of vicarious liability without it being proved that he knew what was going on or was negligent. **The delegation principle forms an exception to this rule. Under this** principle the *mens rea* of the employee may be imputed to the employer where it is established that the latter had delegated his responsibilities to the former.

The creation of this principle proved necessary to deal with cases where *mens rea* offences could only be committed by persons of a particular status, such as licensees of licensed premises. If the employee performed the act constituting the *actus reus* of the offence with *mens rea* he could not be convicted as a principal as he was not a person of the requisite status. The licensee, lacking knowledge, could not be a principal and thus the employee could not be convicted as an accessory. The outcome would be that the purpose of the statute in regulating the conditions under which alcohol could be sold would be defeated where the licensee had handed over management responsibilities to his employee.

In *Somerset* v *Hart* (1884) 12 QBD 360, Lord Coleridge CJ suggested that a man could put another in his position so as to represent him for the purpose of knowledge. This was built upon in *Allen* v *Whitehead* [1930] 1 KB 211.

> Under s. 44 of the Metropolitan Police Act 1839 it was an offence for the owner or keeper of a refreshment house knowingly to permit or suffer prostitutes to meet there. D owned a cafe which was run by a manager. The manager knowingly permitted prostitutes to meet there unknown to D. D was convicted as to hold otherwise would be to render the provision nugatory; the manager's knowledge was imputed to him.

In *Linnett* v *Metropolitan Police Commissioner* [1946] KB 290, Lord Goddard CJ indicated the nature of the delegation principle (at p. 294):

> The principle underlying these decisions does not depend upon the legal relationship existing between master and servant or between principal and agent; it depends on the fact that the person who is responsible in law, as for example, a licensee under the Licensing Acts, has chosen to delegate his duties, powers and authority to another.

In this case, accordingly, one of two co-licensees, who was absent, was held liable for the acts of the other who had knowingly permitted disorderly conduct in the licensed premises contrary to s. 44 of the Metropolitan Police Act 1839.

What constitutes delegation is not entirely clear.

> In *Vane* v *Yiannopoullos* [1965] AC 486, D, the licensee of a restaurant was on another floor when a waitress in the restaurant, contrary to instructions, served drinks to two youths who did not order a meal. The magistrate dismissed an information charging him with knowingly selling intoxicating liquor to persons to whom he was not permitted to sell, contrary to s. 22(1)(a) of the Licensing Act 1961. The House of Lords dismissed the prosecutor's appeal.

Lord Evershed stated that delegation required the handing over of all effective management of the premises. Lord Hodson stated that it did not cover cases of partial transfer of authority. Lord Reid did not believe there could be delegation where the licensee remained on the premises. In the course of their speeches some of their Lordships expressed disquiet about the doctrine. Lord Donovan stated that 'if a decision that "knowingly" means "knowingly" will make the provision difficult to enforce, the remedy lies with the legislature'. Lord Reid found difficulty justifying the principle but considered that it was too long-established to overturn it. It appeared, therefore, that what was required was a complete transfer of authority and responsibilities to another person and the absence of the licensee from the premises.

In *Winson* [1969] 1 QB 371, the Court of Appeal confirmed that partial delegation was insufficient to impute knowledge to the licensee (see also *Bradshaw v Ewart-James* [1983] QB 671). In *Howker v Robinson* [1973] 1 QB 178, however, the Divisional Court upheld a conviction of a licensee for selling alcohol to a person under the age of 18 where this had been done by a barman in the lounge while the licensee was in the public bar. The Divisional Court treated the question of delegation as one of fact and accepted the magistrates' finding that there had been delegation. The decision appears unsupportable on two grounds. First, this was not a case of the licensee taking no part in managing the business; if there was any delegation of authority it was only partial. Indeed it is difficult to discover even partial delegation of the licensee's proprietary or managerial functions. Secondly, the justification for the delegation principle is that it is necessary to avoid rendering certain statutory provisions nugatory. In this case, however, a failure to find delegation would not have had this effect as the relevant provision, s. 169(1) of the Licensing Act 1964, specifically prohibited 'the holder of the licence or his servant' from selling alcohol to a person under 18. Thus the barman could have been prosecuted for the offence as liability was not limited to persons with the status of licensees. It is submitted, therefore, that *Howker v Robinson* was wrongly decided.

The Law Commission's Draft Criminal Code (Law Com No. 177) excludes the delegation principle from Code offences (see cl. 29) proposing instead that if Parliament intends vicarious liability to be imposed on the basis of the fault of another it must do so expressly. Clause 29(2) provides that 'a fault element of an offence may be attributed to a person by reason of the fault of another only if the terms of the enactment creating the offence so provide'.

7.2.3 Limitations on vicarious liability

There are three limitations on vicarious liability. **First, vicarious liability can only arise where the person who did the act did so within the scope of his employment or, if not an employee but acting as the accused's agent, within the scope of his authority.** For example, if an employee does an authorised activity in an unauthorised way he remains within the scope of his employment (see *Coppen v Moore (No. 2)*, **7.2.1**). By contrast, if the sales assistant had started to sell stolen goods under a false description the employer would not be liable as he would have been performing a wholly unauthorised activity. Similarly, if an employee uses his employer's vehicle to deliver goods, his use of the vehicle is also his employer's use, but, if he uses it as a get-away vehicle for a robbery, his use, being a wholly unauthorised activity, would not be his employer's use. In *Adams v Camfoni* [1929] 1 KB 95, D was a licensee charged with selling alcohol outside the permitted hours. The sale had been effected by a messenger boy who had no authority to sell liquor or anything else. Accordingly D was acquitted.

Secondly, where the employee's acts amount to the aiding and abetting of an offence, the employer cannot be held vicariously liable for such aiding and abetting on the basis of imputed knowledge, even though the offence was one which he could have personally aided and abetted (see *Ferguson v Weaving*, **7.1.4.2**).

Thirdly, it was held in *Gardner* v *Akeroyd* [1952] 2 QB 743, that **vicarious liability cannot be imposed in respect of an attempt to commit an offence**, even though vicarious liability could have been imposed for the completed offence.

7.2.4 Statutory defences

There is no general defence of due diligence which an employer may plead in respect of an offence committed by his employee for which he is vicariously liable. Some statutes do contain express provision for due diligence defences. For example, section 139 of the Licensing Act 2003 states that it a defence to a charge of carrying on an unauthorised licensable activity (such as selling alcohol outside of the hours permitted by the premise's licence) if (a) his act was due to a mistake, or to reliance on information given to him, or to an act or omission by another person, or to some other cause beyond his control, and (b) he took all reasonable precautions and exercised all due diligence to avoid committing the offence. Other statutes combine the due diligence defence with a 'third-party' defence (see **4.2.5**). Where the offence is a strict liability offence which may only be committed by a person of a particular status, the employee cannot be a principal. If he is not a principal there is no 'third party' whom the employer can bring before the court as the actual offender. A third-party defence can only operate where the offence is one of strict liability and not limited to persons of a particular status, in which case both employer and employee are joint principals.

7.3 **Corporate liability**

A corporation is a legal person and therefore may be criminally liable even though it has no physical existence and cannot act or think except through its directors or employees. A corporation is, for example, a limited company, a public corporation like those formed to run nationalised industries, or a local authority. At common law an unincorporated association is not a legal person and therefore not subject to criminal liability. Section 5 of and sch. 1 to the Interpretation Act 1978 provide that in every Act, unless the contrary intention appears, 'person' includes a body of persons corporate or unincorporate. This definition applies prospectively in respect of unincorporated associations so that these bodies may be criminally liable for offences created after 1 January 1979 (the commencement date for the 1978 Act) where the word 'person' is used in the definition of the offence.

A corporation is vicariously liable for strict liability offences to exactly the same extent as a natural person. A corporation will also be criminally liable for the breach of any statutory duty imposed upon it in a particular capacity such as an occupier or keeper (see *Evans & Co. Ltd* v *LCC* [1914] 3 KB 315). **Its criminal liability extends further than this, however, to cover direct liability for acts performed by natural persons who are identified with it, namely the principle of identification** (see **7.3.1**).

There are **two limitations**, however, to corporate liability identified in *R* v *ICR Haulage Ltd* [1944] KB 551. **First, there are certain offences which, from their**

very nature, cannot be committed by corporations—for example, bigamy, rape, incest, and perjury. In all these cases, if suitable circumstances arose, a corporation could be liable as an accessory. *Obiter dicta* in some old cases suggested that a corporation could not be convicted of an offence of violence. These dicta were followed in *Cory Bros. & Co.* [1927] 1 KB 810 but doubted in *ICR Haulage Ltd* and in *R v HM Coroner for East Kent, ex parte Spooner* (1989) 88 Cr App R 10. In that case, an application for judicial review of the decision of the coroner at the inquest into the deaths resulting from the sinking of the *Herald of Free Enterprise* off Zeebrugge was refused. Bingham LJ, in the Divisional Court, stated *obiter* that a corporation could be convicted of manslaughter on appropriate facts. This was subsequently confirmed by Turner J when P & O European Ferries (Dover) Ltd, two directors, and a senior manager were tried for manslaughter in respect of the deaths resulting from the Zeebrugge disaster (see *R v P & O European Ferries (Dover) Ltd* (1990) 93 Cr App R 72). Turner J held that a company is 'properly indictable for the crime of manslaughter' through 'the controlling mind of one of its agents' who 'does an act which fulfils the prerequisites of the crime of manslaughter'. The prosecution ended in failure, however, when Turner J withdrew from the jury consideration of the charges as there was no evidence that anyone who constituted 'the controlling mind' of the company had the requisite *mens rea* to support a conviction for manslaughter. In 1994, however, OLL Ltd, and its managing director, Peter Kite, were both convicted of manslaughter following the deaths of four teenagers in a canoeing tragedy at an outdoor pursuits centre run by OLL Ltd. The success of this prosecution was probably due to the fact that OLL Ltd was a small company and Peter Kite was aware of the dangers of canoe expeditions in Lyme Bay following a letter from two former instructors at the centre complaining of inadequate safety precautions (see **7.3.3** for discussion of the Corporate Manslaughter and Corporate Homicide Act 2007, which has made prosecutions of corporations for homicide somewhat easier).

Secondly, a corporation will not be convicted of an offence where the only punishment which may be imposed is physical. In *ICR Haulage Ltd*, Stable J stated (at p. 554) that 'the court will not stultify itself by embarking on a trial in which, if a verdict of guilty is returned, no effective order by way of sentence can be made'. Thus a corporation cannot be tried for murder as the only punishment available to the court on conviction is life imprisonment. Where a corporation is convicted of an offence it will be punished by the imposition of a fine and/or compensation order.

7.3.1 The principle of identification

In vicarious liability an employer is held liable for the acts of his employee; in corporate liability a corporation is liable for its own acts. **As a company has no physical existence and cannot think or act, a fiction has to be applied to convert the acts and thoughts of a human person into those of the corporation thereby attributing personality to it.** This fiction is the principle of identification which was explained by Lord Reid in *Tesco Supermarkets Ltd* v *Nattrass* [1972] AC 153 (at p. 170) as follows:

> A living person has a mind which can have knowledge or intention or be negligent and he hands to carry out his intentions. A corporation has none of these: it must act through living persons, though not always one or the same person. Then the person who acts is not speaking or acting for the company. He is speaking as the company and his mind which directs his acts is the mind of the company. There is no question of the company being vicariously liable. He is not acting as a servant, representative, agent or delegate. He is an embodiment of the company, one could say, he hears and speaks through the persona of the company, within his appropriate sphere, and his mind is the mind of the company. If it is a guilty mind then that guilt is the guilt of the company.

It is a question of law for the judge whether a person is to be regarded as the company or simply its employee or agent. The judge when directing the jury must tell them the facts which they must find if a person is to be regarded as having acted as the company. If those facts are proved and the jury are satisfied that that person did the act (or omitted to act) with the requisite *mens rea*, the company can be convicted of the offence. The corporation will only be liable where the person identified with it was acting within the scope of his office; it will not be liable for acts which he did in his personal capacity (see *DPP* v *Kent and Sussex Contractors Ltd* [1944] KB 146). In determining whether a person acted as the company or simply as its servant or agent, a distinction has to be drawn between those who represent the mind of the company and those who represent its hands. In *H. L. Bolton (Engineering) Co. Ltd* v *T. J. Graham & Sons Ltd* [1957] 1 QB 159, Denning LJ stated (at p. 172):

> A company may in many ways be likened to a human body. It has a brain and a nerve centre which controls what it does. It also has hands which hold the tools and act in accordance with directions from the centre. Some of the people in the company are mere servants and agents who are nothing more than hands to do the work and cannot be said to represent the mind or will. Others are directors and managers who represent the directing mind and will of the company, and control what it does. The state of mind of these managers is the state of mind of the company and is treated by the law as such.

The test is whether such persons 'represent the directing mind and will of the company and control what it does' (*per* Lord Reid, *Tesco Supermarkets Ltd* v *Nattrass* [1972] AC 153, 171). This covers directors, the managing director, the company secretary, and other superior officers responsible for managing the affairs of the corporation. If one of these persons delegated some part of his management functions, giving the delegate full discretion to act independently, the delegate would also fall within the class of persons whose acts are those of the corporation (see *Lennard's Carrying Co. Ltd* v *Asiatic Petroleum Co. Ltd* [1915] AC 705 and *Worthy* v *Gordon Plant (Services) Ltd* [1985] CLY 624). Who exactly is covered will vary from case to case but the memorandum and articles of association of the company may provide some guidance.

In the *Tesco* case, the company was charged with an offence under the Trade Descriptions Act 1968 after a 'special offer' poster was displayed in a store for a time when no goods at the special offer price were available. Tesco sought to raise a defence under s. 24(1) of the Act on the grounds that the commission of the offence was due to the act or default of another person, the branch manager of the store, and it had exercised all due diligence to avoid the commission of the offence. The magistrates found that the company had set up a proper system, so it had exercised all due diligence, but they found that the branch manager was not 'another person' as his acts were those of the company. The magistrates convicted the company. On appeal to the House of Lords the conviction was quashed. The House held that the defence was available as the branch manager was 'another person' being the 'hands' and not the 'brains' of the company; there had been no delegation by the board of directors of any of their managerial functions in respect of the affairs of the company to the branch manager. He had to obey general directions from the company and take orders from his regional and district supervisors. Accordingly, his acts or omissions were not those of the company.

The *Tesco* case indicated that the principle of identification operates not only to establish liability but it can excuse liability for certain regulatory offences where a third-party defence is available. As the branch manager did not act as the company, his act was that of a third party. The company, through its superior officers, had established a proper system of supervision and thus had exercised all due diligence (see also *St Regis Paper Co. Ltd* [2011] EWCA Crim 2527).

There are several problems arising from the principle of identification (these have been identified by C. Wells, see 'Further reading'). **First, the larger and more diverse a company is, the more likely it is that it will be able to avoid liability.** Tesco has thousands of branches; a branch manager would have no control over the company's affairs. In a small company the controlling officers are much closer to the action which may involve the commission of offences.

Secondly, the principle in *Tesco* does not fit well with many regulatory offences (including the offence involved in that case) which do not require *mens rea* but for which defences (e.g. due diligence or the third-party defence; see **4.2.5**) exist to mitigate the harshness of strict liability. Should such offences (Wells refers to them as 'hybrid' offences) fall under the identification principle or would they be more appropriately dealt with under the vicarious liability approach? In another case involving Tesco, *Tesco Stores Ltd v Brent LBC* [1993] 2 All ER 718, T was convicted of supplying an '18'-classified video to a person under that age contrary to s. 11(1) of the Video Recordings Act 1984. Under s. 11(1)(b) it was a defence for the accused to prove that he 'neither knew nor had reasonable grounds to believe that the person concerned had not attained that age'. T argued that the directing minds of the company (who would be directors in the London headquarters) had no means of knowing the age of the purchaser. The justices found that the cashier had reasonable grounds to believe that the purchaser was under 18 and convicted T. The Divisional Court dismissed T's appeal holding that it was impracticable to suppose that those who controlled a large company would have knowledge or information about the age of the purchaser, but that as the person who supplied the video was under T's control and she had such knowledge or information, the defence was not available to the company. This effectively meant that the offence was one of vicarious liability (see also *R v British Steel plc* [1995] ICR 587).

Thirdly, the identification principle has also been diluted by the decision of the Privy Council in *Meridian Global Funds Management Asia Ltd v Securities Commission* [1995] 3 All ER 918. In this case the Privy Council attributed knowledge to the company for the purposes of determining their liability for the offence of failing to make a disclosure under the New Zealand Securities Act 1988 where the facts required to be disclosed were known to the senior investment team. This team did not constitute the 'directing mind' of the company. The Privy Council upheld the company's conviction on the basis of its interpretation of the statute, taking into account the statutory language, its contents, and the underlying policy which would be defeated if knowledge on the part of those who constituted the 'directing mind' of the company was required to be proved. This special rule of attribution would apply where a court considers that a statute was intended to apply to companies and application of the identification principle would defeat the purpose of the statute.

The fourth problem is that the company will only be liable if the person identified with it is, himself, individually liable in that he had the *mens rea* for the offence. Where there are several superior officers involved, each may not have the requisite degree of knowledge to constitute the *mens rea* of the offence. In the area of safety, for example, there may be many failures within a corporation at different levels which may coalesce to result in a major disaster resulting in loss of life. Different individuals may know, or do, or fail to do, different things. But, if a company is a legal person, and the knowledge of its officials is its knowledge, can that knowledge be aggregated and, in the aggregate, constitute the *mens rea* for a crime? This particular question has been considered in the context of manslaughter. For a time it was thought that manslaughter was an offence of which a corporation could not be convicted. This view was rejected in *P & O European Ferries Ltd* (1990) 93 Cr App R 72. In *Armstrong* v *Strain* [1952] 1 KB 232, Devlin J stated: 'You cannot add an innocent state of mind to an innocent state of mind and get as a result a dishonest state of mind.' If an offence is one demanding proof of *mens rea* this suggests that it is not possible to aggregate the states of mind of several individuals which individually do not fully satisfy the *mens rea* requirement to conclude that in aggregate they do. Following the decision of the House of Lords in *Seymour* [1983] 2 AC 493, manslaughter demanded proof of recklessness in the *Caldwell/Lawrence* sense (see **3.4.2.2**). In this context the aggregation principle was rejected in *R* v *HM Coroner for East Kent, ex parte Spooner* (1989) 88 Cr App R 10 and *P & O European Ferries Ltd.* Since the decision of the House of Lords in *Adomako* [1995] 1 AC 171 (see **9.3.3.2**), however, manslaughter by gross negligence is not an offence requiring *mens rea*. This being so, is it possible to aggregate the negligence of individuals within a corporation to arrive at a finding of gross negligence on the part of the corporation? In *Kite and OLL Ltd* (Winchester Crown Court, 8 December 1994, unreported) the company was convicted of manslaughter but this followed on the conviction of its managing director, the company being a one-man concern. In *AG's Reference (No. 2 of 1999)* [2000] 1 Cr App R 207, the issue of aggregation was directly addressed. A high-speed train crashed into a freight train at Southall killing seven people and injuring many others. The company operating the high-speed train was indicted for manslaughter but the trial judge ruled that a non-human defendant could only be convicted where guilt of a human being with whom it could be identified was also established. As no such individual was indicted the charges against the company were dismissed. Two questions were referred to the Court of Appeal by the Attorney General:

(a) Can a defendant be properly convicted of manslaughter by gross negligence in the absence of evidence as to that defendant's state of mind?

(b) Can a non-human defendant be convicted of the crime of manslaughter by gross negligence in the absence of evidence establishing the guilt of an identified human individual for the same crime?

The Court of Appeal answered the questions 'Yes' and 'No' respectively, rejecting an argument by the Attorney General that the reasoning in the *Meridian* case should be applied. Relying on *ex parte Spooner* and *P & O European Ferries*, Rose LJ concluded:

> [U]nless an identified individual's conduct, characterisable as gross criminal negligence, can be attributed to the company the company is not . . . liable for manslaughter. Civil negligence rules . . . are not apt to confer criminal liability on a company.

Rose LJ missed the point, however, that the cases on which he relied related to manslaughter when it was considered to be an offence requiring proof of recklessness, whereas following *Adomako* it is an offence of negligence. In addition, in *Adomako* Lord Mackay stated that 'the ordinary principles of the law of negligence apply to ascertain whether or not the defendant has been in breach of a duty of care towards the victim who has died'. Next the jury has to consider causation and then whether the breach was gross enough to constitute a crime. If the operation system was not safe (and there was considerable evidence to this effect as the driver had passed three signals at danger before the crash and both the Automatic Warning System and the Automatic Train Protection System had been switched off), is Rose LJ suggesting that this could not amount to civil negligence unless an actual individual was proved to be negligent? This would, indeed, be novel as negligence is concerned with conduct rather than states of mind. Why should the failures of those in the company concerned with safety not be aggregated to establish negligence overall on the part of the company? While discussions about the liability of a company for manslaughter may no longer excite the same feelings because of the enactment of the Corporate Homicide and Corporate Manslaughter Act 2007 (see **7.3.3.2**) the previously discussed cases remain authorities on the issue of aggregation. Whether the courts will see fit to revisit them in the context of other offences remains to be seen.

So far *Tesco* v *Nattrass* has not been overruled but there clearly are limitations to its applicability such that it would be wrong to treat it as having established an absolute principle. The problem which remains, however, is identifying those circumstances in which the identification principle applies and those in which it does not.

7.3.2 **Liability of officers**

Apart from their liability as perpetrators or accomplices of the offences for which a corporation may be held criminally liable, **the officers of a company may be made liable by statutory provision**. Many statutes, such as the Trade Descriptions Act 1968 (s. 20) and the Gambling Act 2005 (s. 341) contain the following provision or one to the same effect:

> Where an offence under this Act which has been committed by a body corporate is proved to have been committed with the consent or connivance of, or to be attributable to any neglect on the part of, any director, manager, secretary or other similar officer of the body corporate or any person who was purporting to act in any such capacity, he as well as the body corporate shall be guilty of that offence.

While this largely duplicates the liability imposed by the criminal law on perpetrators or accomplices, it does extend it and it may also make the task of the prosecution easier where proving liability under the normal principles would be difficult. 'Consent' and 'connivance' largely overlap with 'aiding, abetting, counselling or procuring', but they may be easier to prove. In particular 'connivance' may be established by proving wilful blindness to the commission of the offence and acquiescence in it (see *Somerset* v *Hart* (1884) 12 QBD 360). The main extension of liability is effected by the words 'attributable to any neglect on the part of' which imposes liability for negligence where the officer has failed to prevent the commission of an offence by the corporation. Section 18 of the Theft Act 1968 contains a similar provision but it omits any reference to 'attributable to any neglect'.

An offence will not be attributable to the neglect of all directors because it is attributable to the neglect of one or of some other official of the company as there is no general duty upon a director to 'supervise his co-directors or to acquaint himself with all the details of the running of the company' (*per* Lord Parker CJ in *Huckerby* v *Elliott* [1970] 1 All ER 189). Lord Parker went on to state (at p. 194):

> [I]t is perfectly proper for a director to leave matters to another director or to an official of the company, and . . . he is under no obligation to test the accuracy of anything that he is told by such person, or even to make certain that he is complying with the law.

Similarly, where an officer of a company has delegated work to his senior staff it is reasonable for him to expect that work to be completed in accordance with the instructions given, so that he will not be guilty of neglect if he does not check such work (see *Lewin* v *Bland* [1985] RTR 171). However, if a director has reason to distrust another director or official or person to whom work has been delegated, or reason to suspect that that person was not carrying out his duty, and he does nothing, this could amount to neglect. In *R* v *McMillan Aviation Ltd* [1981] Crim LR 785, the company was charged with selling goods to which a false trade description had been applied contrary to s. 1 of the Trade Descriptions Act 1968, and a director was charged with the same offence on the basis of attributable neglect. Judge Rubin, in directing the jury in Kingston-upon-Thames Crown Court, stated that he would be liable where it was proved 'that he knew the trade description was false, in which case quite clearly he had a duty to prevent the offence, or that he had reasonable cause to suspect that the company was applying a false trade description, in which case he would have a duty to take steps to see if it was false or not and if he failed to do so he was guilty'.

7.3.3 Reform and the Corporate Manslaughter and Corporate Homicide Act 2007

7.3.3.1 Background

Under the previous law, based on the identification principle, a company could be convicted of manslaughter only where a 'directing mind' of the organisation was also guilty of the offence—that is, some senior individual who embodies the company in his actions and decisions. Where no such senior individual was liable, it was not possible to convict the company even though a series of errors by individuals within the company, when aggregated together, might be sufficient to establish gross breach of duty on the part of the company. In 1996 the Law Commission in its Report *Legislating the Criminal Code: Involuntary Manslaughter* (Law Com No. 237) proposed a new offence of 'corporate killing'. Following this Report the Government published a Consultation Paper, *Reforming the Law on Involuntary Manslaughter: The Government's Proposals* (2000), which endorsed the proposal for a new offence. In March 2005 a draft Corporate Manslaughter Bill (Cm 6497) was published setting out the Government's proposals for reform. The draft bill was subject to pre-legislative scrutiny by the Home Affairs and Work and Pensions Committees whose Report was published in December 2005 (HC 540 I–III). In March 2006 the Government responded in *The Government Reply to the First Joint Report from the Home Affairs and Work and Pensions Committees Session 2005–06 HC 540* (Cm 6755).

The Corporate Manslaughter and Corporate Homicide Act 2007 largely came into force on 6 April 2008. This is a highly technical piece of legislation which will doubtless create numerous practical difficulties and generate considerable appellate work.

7.3.3.2 Corporate Manslaughter and Corporate Homicide Act 2007

The important aspects of the Act are that it dispenses with the need to find a controlling or directing mind that is also personally guilty of manslaughter (the identification principle) and it also greatly reduces the scope for Crown immunity which previously existed. The offence applies (see s. 1(2)) to bodies corporate which covers companies and public bodies such as NHS trusts and local authorities. It also applies to government departments and the police (albeit that certain exclusions apply to public policy decisions, military activities, policing and law enforcement, emergencies, child protection, and probation functions). The offence also applies to a partnership, a trade union, or employers' association, which is an employer.

7.3.3.2.1 *The offence*
The offence is defined in s. 1 as follows:

(1) An organisation to which this section applies is guilty of an offence if the way in which its activities are managed or organised—
   (a) causes a person's death, and
   (b) amounts to a gross breach of a relevant duty of care owed by the organisation to the deceased.

. . .

(3) An organisation is guilty of an offence under this section only if the way in which its activities are managed or organised by its senior management is a substantial element in the breach referred to in subsection (1).

The offence builds on key aspects of the offence of gross negligence manslaughter. The important development, however, is that liability for the offence is dependent upon a finding of gross negligence in the way in which the activities of the organisation are run rather than being contingent upon the guilt of an individual 'directing mind'. The offence is committed where, in particular circumstances, an organisation owes a relevant duty of care and the way in which the activities of the organisation have been managed or organised amounts to a gross breach of that duty and causes a person's death. A substantial element of the gross breach must be the way in which the activities were managed or organised by the senior management. A breach is gross if it falls far below what could reasonably have been expected of the organisation in the circumstances (s. 2(4)(b)). Senior management comprises those who play a significant role in the management of the whole or a substantial part of the organisation's activities. This covers those in the direct chain of management at an operational level and those with strategic or regulatory compliance roles. This approach allows for collective rather than just individual failure to be assessed, unlike the current offence.

7.3.3.2.2 *Relevant duty of care*

Section 2(1) defines the 'relevant duty of care' to mean any of the following duties owed by the organisation under the law of negligence:

(a) a duty owed to its employees or to other persons working for the organisation or performing services for it;

(b) a duty owed as occupier of premises;

(c) a duty owed in connection with—

    (i) the supply by the organisation of goods or services (whether for consideration or not),

    (ii) the carrying on by the organisation of any construction or maintenance operations,

    (iii) the carrying on by the organisation of any other activity on a commercial basis, or

    (iv) the use or keeping by the organisation of any plant, vehicle or other thing;

(d) a duty owed to a person who, by reason of being a person within subsection (2), is someone for whose safety the organisation is responsible.

The duties are fault-based as they must be duties 'under the law of negligence'. Thus the offence does not impose new duties which are not already part of the civil law. The duties which most often lead to prosecutions under the 2007 Act are those of employers and occupiers.

Paragraph (d) relates to persons in custody whether as arrested suspects, prisoners (convicted or on remand), asylum/immigration detainees, and detained mental patients. This was a very contentious amendment to the bill introduced in the Lords by the former Chief Inspector of Prisons, Lord Ramsbotham, because of concerns over deaths in custody. At one point it looked as if the whole bill might fail owing to government objections to this amendment. The compromise negotiated was that the commencement for this part of the Act would require approval of both Houses of Parliament under the affirmative resolution procedure. Section 2(1)(d) came into force on 1 September 2011.

Whether a duty of care is owed in a particular situation is a matter of law for the judge to decide (s. 2(5)). It is then for the jury to determine whether death was caused by a gross breach of duty. The common law rules preventing a duty of care being owed (a) by one person to another because they are both engaged in unlawful conduct, and (b) to a person by reason of his acceptance of a risk of harm, are to be disregarded (s. 2(6)).

7.3.3.2.3 *Gross breach*

Unusually the Act includes fairly detailed provision for the issues which a jury should consider in arriving at the decision whether the death was caused by a gross breach of duty. Section 8 provides:

(1) This section applies where—

  (a) it is established that an organisation owed a relevant duty of care to a person, and

  (b) it falls to the jury to decide whether there was a gross breach of that duty.

(2) The jury must consider whether the evidence shows that the organisation failed to comply with any health and safety legislation that relates to the alleged breach, and if so—

  (a) how serious that failure was;

  (b) how much of a risk of death it posed.

(3) The jury may also—

  (a) consider the extent to which the evidence shows that there were attitudes, policies, systems or accepted practices within the organisation that were likely to have encouraged any such failure as is mentioned in subsection (2), or to have produced tolerance of it;

  (b) have regard to any health and safety guidance that relates to the alleged breach.

(4) This section does not prevent the jury from having regard to any other matters they consider relevant.

Consideration of these matters is obligatory. The task for a jury in any trial for the new offence will not be an easy one; nor will it be easy for the prosecution to jump through all the hoops which the Act sets up in order to reach the point where there could be a reasonable prospect of securing a conviction. It is unlikely that there will be many more prosecutions under the 2007 Act than under the old law. Trials, if they take place, will undoubtedly be lengthy and complex. At the end, if convicted, the only penalty the court will be able to impose is that of a fine (as well as a possible order under s. 9 to take specified steps to remedy the breach and under s. 10 to publicise their conviction). Whether this Act is the remedy sought for the ills of the previous law remains an open question.

 Key Points

ACCESSORIES

– The person who perpetrates the crime is referred to as the principal. A person is the perpetrator if his act is the most immediate cause of the *actus reus* of the offence:

– Others, not being principals, who participate in the commission of an offence are referred to as accessories or secondary parties and will be liable to conviction if it is proved that they aided, abetted, counselled, or procured the commission of the crime by the principal (s. 8 of the Accessories and Abettors Act 1861).

→

➡

- The *mens rea* required of the accessory differs from that of a principal and *mens rea* must always be proved even where the principal's offence is one of strict liability.
- If an accused is charged as an accessory he will be charged with aiding, abetting, counselling, or procuring the particular offence and he is liable to conviction if it is proved that he participated in any one of these four ways.
- The *mens rea* required of an accessory may be simply stated as an intention to assist or encourage the commission of the principal offence combined with knowledge of the circumstances which constitute the offence. The intention required is the voluntary performance of an act with the realisation that this assists or encourages D in his course of conduct.
- A cannot be liable as an accessory if he is unaware of the circumstances which constitute the offence.
- An accessory will be liable where he contemplates the commission of one or more of a range of crimes by the principal and he intentionally lends assistance to the principal who then commits one or more of these offences.
- In *Jogee* (2016), the Supreme Court overturned previous Privy Council and House of Lords, decisions concerning 'parasitic accessory liability'. The Court restated that:
  - The *mens rea* required to convict a secondary party is an intention to assist or encourage the principal to commit the crime.
  - Foresight of what might happen is simply evidence from which a jury might infer intention but they need not necessarily do so. Foresight, or contemplation, accordingly is not to be taken as amounting to authorisation.
  - Where the crime D commits is one requiring a particular intent A will be liable as a secondary party if he intentionally assists or encourages D to act with such intent.

VICARIOUS LIABILTY

- Unlike in tort law, there is no general rule of vicarious liability in English criminal law.
- Sometimes statute imposes vicarious liability. Those statutes may provide for a 'due diligence' defence.
- More usually, however, vicarious liability is the result of judicial interpretation of statutory offences of a regulatory nature.
- Where the performance of the duty requires positive acts the doctrine of vicarious liability is necessary. The courts have to decide if the act of the employee can be attributed to the employer. If it can, without undue strain to the wording of the legislation, and the offence is one of strict liability, the employer will be held to be a joint principal with his employee.
- The issue is whether there is a sufficient nexus between the parties so that it can be said that the accused had some control over the actions of the other.
- The delegation principle forms an exception to this rule. Under this principle the *mens rea* of the employee may be imputed to the employer where it is established that the latter had delegated his responsibilities to the former.
- There are limitations on vicarious liability:
  - First, vicarious liability can only arise where the person who did the act did so within the scope of his employment or, if not an employee but acting as the accused's agent, within the scope of his authority.
  - Secondly, where the employee's acts amount to the aiding and abetting of an offence, the employer cannot be held vicariously liable for such aiding and abetting on the basis of imputed knowledge, even though the offence was one which he could have personally aided and abetted.
  - Third, vicarious liability cannot be imposed in respect of an attempt to commit an offence.

➡

→

CORPORATE LIABILITY

– A corporation is a legal person and therefore may be criminally liable even though it has no physical existence and cannot act or think except through its directors or employees.

– A corporation is vicariously liable for strict liability offences to exactly the same extent as a natural person. A corporation will also be criminally liable for the breach of any statutory duty imposed upon it in a particular capacity such as an occupier.

– The officers of a company may be made liable by statutory provision.

– A company may be directly liable for acts performed by natural persons who are identified with it. As a company has no physical existence and cannot think or act, a fiction, the 'principle of identification', applies to convert the acts and thoughts of a human person into those of the corporation thereby attributing personality to it. The test is whether such persons 'represent the directing mind and will of the company and control what it does'.

– The Corporate Manslaughter and Corporate Homicide Act 2007 extended the law to make somewhat easier prosecutions of organisations for causing death if the way in which the organisation's activities are managed or organised amounts to a gross breach of its duty of care towards the deceased.

FURTHER READING

A. Ashworth, 'Testing Fidelity to Legal Values: Official Involvement and Criminal Justice' (2000) 63 MLR 633.

A. Ashworth, 'Re-drawing the Boundaries of Entrapment' [2002] Crim LR 161.

M. Bohlander, 'The Sexual Offences Act 2003 and the *Tyrrell* Principle—Criminalising the Victims?' [2005] Crim LR 701.

R. Buxton, 'Being an Accessory to One's Own Murder' [2012] Crim LR 275.

R. Buxton, '*Jogee*: Upheaval in Secondary Liability for Murder' [2016] Crim LR 324.

C. M. V. Clarkson, 'Kicking Corporate Bodies and Damning Their Souls' (1996) 59 MLR 557.

C. M. V. Clarkson, 'Corporate Culpability' [1998] 2 Web JCLI.

I. H. Dennis, 'The Mental Element for Accessories' in P. Smith (ed.), *Criminal Law: Essays in Honour of J. C. Smith* (London: Butterworths, 1987).

J. Gobert, 'Corporate Criminality: New Crimes for the Times' [1994] Crim LR 722.

J. Gobert, 'The Corporate Manslaughter and Corporate Homicide Act 2007—Thirteen Years in the Making but Was it Worth the Wait?' (2008) 71 MLR 413.

D. Lanham, 'Accomplices and Withdrawal' (1981) 97 LQR 575.

L. H. Leigh, *Strict and Vicarious Liability* (London: Sweet & Maxwell, 1982).

D. Ormerod and K. Laird, '*Jogee*: Not the End of a Legal Saga But the Start of a New One?' [2016] Crim LR 539.

D. Ormerod and R. Taylor, 'The Corporate Manslaughter and Corporate Homicide Act 2007' [2008] Crim LR 589.

P. J. Pace, 'Delegation—a Doctrine in Search of a Definition' [1982] Crim LR 627.

J. C. Smith, 'Aid, Abet, Counsel and Procure' in P. Glazebrook (ed.), *Reshaping the Criminal Law* (London: Stevens, 1978).

J. C. Smith, 'Criminal Liability of Accessories: Law and Law Reform' (1997) 113 LQR 453.

K. J. M. Smith, 'Withdrawal and Complicity' [2001] Crim LR 769.

C. Wells, *Corporations and Criminal Responsibility* (Oxford: OUP, 2nd edition, 2001).

G. Williams, 'Which of You Did It?' (1989) 52 MLR 179.

G. Williams, 'Victims and Other Exempt Parties in Crime' (1990) 10 LS 245.

8

Inchoate offences

8.1 **Introduction**

A person does not break the criminal law simply by having evil thoughts (*Higgins* (1801) 2 East 5). To plan and scheme in one's mind to commit an offence is not, in itself, unlawful. Where, however, a person takes steps towards effecting that plan to commit a substantive offence, he may in the process commit one of the inchoate crimes of attempt, conspiracy, or encouraging or assisting the commission of an offence. At common law the offence of incitement would have been the third in this list. The Serious Crime Act 2007 abolished the offence of incitement and replaced it with three offences based on encouragement or assistance which came into effect on 1 October 2008.

The law would be seriously deficient as a means of protecting persons or property from harm if it could only intervene after a substantive offence had been committed and the harm done. The inchoate offences permit intervention at an earlier stage before any harm has been done but at a time when D has moved from mere mental planning to the stage of performing overt acts which manifest his intention that a particular substantive offence be committed. 'Inchoate' means 'just begun or undeveloped'. This accurately reflects the nature of these crimes as they are committed when D begins to manifest his criminal intention overtly and at a stage prior to the consummation of that intention in the commission of the substantive offence.

 Example

(i) A bears a grudge against V and decides to set fire to his house; (ii) A tells B of his decision and encourages B to assist him; (iii) B agrees to help and they formulate a plan to effect their purpose; (iv) A and B go to V's house, having first telephoned to check he is not at home, and douse it with paraffin; (v) they set light to the paraffin at different points around the house.

➡

> ➔
>
> At (i) A commits no offence as he is merely thinking evil thoughts. In (ii) his initial recounting of his decision involves no offence but when he encourages B to participate he commits the offence of encouraging the commission of an offence. B commits no offence by listening to A but when he agrees to participate he and A commit the offence of conspiracy (iii). When they set fire to the house (v) they commit the offence of arson. However, at (iv) A and B are guilty of attempted arson.

It is important to note that these inchoate offences are steps on the way to the commission of a substantive offence (but see common law conspiracy, **8.3.4**); they are not crimes existing in the abstract. Thus the indictment would charge A with encouraging B to commit arson, and A and B with conspiracy to commit arson, and attempt to commit arson. An indictment which simply charged D with 'encouragement' or 'conspiracy' or 'attempt' in the abstract would be defective.

Note that a number of the cases in this chapter involve conspiracy, or attempt to commit one of several deception offences, such as obtaining property or services by deception. On 15 January 2007 the Fraud Act 2006 came into force sweeping away a range of offences under the Theft Acts and replacing them with new offences (see further **Chapter 13**).

8.2 Encouraging or assisting offences

In cl. 47 of the Draft Criminal Code (LC 177), which would have codified the existing common law, the Law Commission defined **incitement** as follows:

A person is guilty of incitement to commit an offence or offences if—

(a) he incites another to do or cause to be done an act or acts which, if done, will involve the commission of the offence or offences by the other; and

(b) he intends or believes that the other, if he acts as incited, shall, or will do so with the fault required for the offence or offences.

This would have been a fairly brief and simple definition of the offence of incitement involving little complexity. In its Report, *Inchoate Liability for Assisting and Encouraging Crime* (Law Com No. 300, 2006), the Law Commission proposed the abolition of the common law offence of incitement and its replacement with two new statutory inchoate offences which would prohibit assisting and encouraging crime.

For once the ink had hardly dried on the Law Commission Report when the Government decided to enact legislation based largely upon the Law Commission's recommendations. The Serious Crime Act (SCA) was enacted on 30 October 2007. The SCA does not adopt verbatim the Law Commission draft bill although it does replicate its complexity. Part 1 of the SCA creates Serious Crime Prevention Orders (dubbed super ASBOs) designed to restrict or disrupt those involved in serious crime. Part 2 abolished the common law offence of incitement and replaced it with three new offences. The Act also includes a defence and an exemption from liability.

Key Point

D's liability relates to the (hypothetical) offence he intended or believed would be committed by P. If P commits the offence D will be an accessory to it and additionally liable under the law on secondary liability.

It is unfortunate that this provision has the effect of creating an extensive overlap with the law on secondary participation dealt with in **Chapter 7**. Some of the confusion and overlap might have been mitigated had the Government enacted the Law Commission's recommendations in *Participating in Crime* (Law Com No. 305). The two Reports were meant to form a package for the reform of incitement and secondary liability and would have led to the creation of a total of eight offences. The widening of liability under the offences of encouraging and assisting crime was to be counterbalanced by a narrowing of secondary liability. The piecemeal approach to reform adopted by the Government, however, is hardly desirable and will only lead to confusion in an area of law which is already complicated.

The main provisions of the offences and defences are outlined later. Sections 47 and 65–67 apply to all three offences but will be examined in detail only in relation to the s. 44 offence. When considering the offences under ss 45 and 46, readers should refer back to the analysis under s. 44.

8.2.1 Intentionally encouraging or assisting an offence

Section 44 provides:

(1) A person commits an offence if—

(a) he does an act capable of encouraging or assisting the commission of an offence; and

(b) he intends to encourage or assist its commission.

(2) But he is not to be taken to have intended to encourage or assist the commission of an offence merely because such encouragement or assistance was a foreseeable consequence of his act.

Actus reus	*Mens rea*
Doing an act capable of encouraging or assisting the commission of an offence.	Intention to encourage or assist its commission.

8.2.1.1 *Actus reus*

Whether or not D's act was 'capable' of encouraging or assisting P to commit a crime, is a question of fact. What 'encouraging or assisting' means will be a matter for the jury or magistrates to determine but s. 65(1) makes it clear that encouraging includes threatening or putting pressure on another person to commit an offence. The focus of the offence is on D's act or acts as **the offence is committed when D**

does the relevant act which is capable of encouraging or assisting the commission of an offence with the necessary intent. There is no need for P to be aware of
the encouragement or assistance or to have acted in response to it as liability arises
where D's act is **capable** of encouraging or assisting. This extends the liability
beyond that which the law of incitement covered as that offence required that the
incitement be communicated to someone.

For the purposes of this, and the next two offences, 'act' includes a course of conduct (s. 67). An act 'capable of assisting or encouraging the commission of an
offence' includes 'taking steps to reduce the possibility of criminal proceedings
being brought in respect of that offence' (s. 65(2)(a)) which, although the statute is
silent on the matter, logic dictates must be an act done before the relevant offence
is committed.

 Example

If D being aware that P is going to rob a bank, arranges for a getaway car to be available for
him and lets him know this before D enters the bank, this would be an act capable of encouraging or assisting P in the commission of the robbery. By contrast, if P comes out of the bank
having robbed it, and D assists him at that point in making his getaway by lending him his car,
this act, having occurred after the robbery occurred, is not capable of encouraging or assisting
P in the commission of the robbery.

The 'act' requirement may also be satisfied by D 'failing to take reasonable steps to
discharge a duty' (s. 65(2)(b)). An example given by the Law Commission is that of
a disgruntled security guard, D, who omits to turn on a burglar alarm with the
intention of assisting P to burgle the premises of D's employer. The fact that the
offence requires proof of an ulterior intent means that mere inadvertence—for
example, simply forgetting to switch the alarm on—will not give rise to liability on
the part of D.

D may indirectly encourage or assist the commission of an offence where D
arranges for another, E, to do an act capable of encouraging or assisting P to commit
an offence. If E does so, then D will be treated as having done E's act (s. 66). The
Explanatory Notes give the example of a gang leader D who instructs a member of
his gang E to encourage another person P to kill V.

D may encourage or assist the commission of another inchoate offence, for example D encourages E to solicit P to commit murder (soliciting murder is an offence
under s. 4 of the Offences Against the Person Act 1861). However, the offence of
encouraging or assisting suicide contrary to s. 2(1) of the Suicide Act 1961 is
excluded (see s. 51A of the SCA).

8.2.1.2 *Mens rea*

This is an offence which requires direct intent; oblique intent will not suffice.
Section 44(2) provides that D is not to be taken to have 'intended to encourage or
assist the commission of an offence merely because such encouragement or assistance was a foreseeable consequence of his act'. D's act must be capable of encouraging or assisting the commission of an offence. For example, D's act might be the
supply of a weapon with the intent that P use it to kill or injure another. Alternatively

he might simply offer verbal encouragement to P to commit a particular offence. Under s. 47(5)(a), where the offence D assists or encourages is an offence requiring proof of fault the prosecution must prove that D either:

(i)   intended or believed that P would have the necessary fault, or

(ii) was reckless whether or not P would have the necessary fault, or

(iii) if D were to do the act himself he would have the necessary fault.

Paragraph (iii) is designed to cover the situation where P may lack the requisite *mens rea* for the offence D has assisted or encouraged but D would have had the *mens rea* had he done the act himself. Where this limb is relied upon D is to be assumed to be able to do the relevant act (i.e. there is no defence of impossibility—see s. 47(6)). The Explanatory Notes provide an example of these very particular circumstances which are designed to prevent D from evading liability purely because it is impossible for him/her to commit the offence:

 Example

D (a woman) encourages P to penetrate V with his penis and believes that if P were to do so, it would be without V's consent. P reasonably believes that V does consent so does not have the mental element required for conviction for rape. Therefore, D's fault is determined under s. 47(5)(a)(iii) in that if she were to commit the act, she would do it with the fault required. However it is not possible for a woman to commit the act of penetration with a penis so were it not for this subsection, D would escape liability.

Where the offence D assists or encourages requires proof of particular consequences or circumstances, it must be proved that D either intended or believed that were the act to be done, it would be done in those circumstances or with those consequences, or was reckless thereto (s. 47(5)(b)). The Explanatory Notes to the Act further explain that requiring some degree of belief in relation to the circumstances ensures that D will not be guilty of an offence of encouraging or assisting a strict liability offence unless he believes or is reckless as to whether those circumstances exist. The Explanatory Notes provide the following example (para. 156):

 Example

D asks P to drive him home from the pub as he has had too much to drink. P is insured to drive D's car but unknown to D and P, P was disqualified from driving the day before. P is committing the principal offence of driving whilst disqualified, despite the fact he is not aware that he is disqualified, as this is an offence of strict liability. However it would not be fair to hold D liable in such circumstances.

In respect of consequences, the Explanatory Notes provide the following example (para. 157):

> **Example**
>
> D gives P a baseball bat and intends P to use it to inflict minor bodily harm on V. P however uses the bat to attack V and intentionally kills V. It would not be fair to hold D liable for encouraging and assisting murder, unless he also believes or is reckless as to whether V will be killed.

If D's act is capable of encouraging or assisting the commission of a number of offences, D can be charged with the s. 44 offence in respect of each offence he intends to encourage or assist to be committed (s. 49(2)).

8.2.2 Encouraging or assisting an offence believing it will be committed

Section 45 provides:

> A person commits an offence if—
> (a) he does an act capable of encouraging or assisting the commission of an offence; and
> (b) he believes—
>   (i) that the offence will be committed; and
>   (ii) that his act will encourage or assist its commission.

Actus reus	Mens rea
Doing an act capable of encouraging or assisting the commission of an offence.	Believing: • that the offence will be committed, and • that his act will encourage or assist its commission.

This offence covers the situation where D may not intend that a particular offence be committed but **he believes both that it will be committed and that his act will encourage or assist its commission**. This catches D who supplies a weapon to P believing he is going to use it to commit murder but D is indifferent whether or not P does as his sole concern is to make a profit from the sale.

If D's act is capable of encouraging or assisting the commission of a number of offences, D can be charged with the s. 45 offence in respect of each offence he believes will be encouraged or assisted (s. 49(2)). Thus where D lends P a crowbar believing P will use it to break into houses to steal, D could be liable for each separate burglary P commits.

D will not be liable for the s. 45 offence where he does an act believing it will encourage or assist P to commit another inchoate offence (as listed in sch. 3; see s. 49(4)).

8.2.3 **Encouraging or assisting offences believing one or more will be committed**

Section 46 provides:

> (1) A person commits an offence if—
>
>   (a) he does an act capable of encouraging or assisting the commission of one or more of a number of offences; and
>   (b) he believes—
>
>   (i) that one or more of those offences will be committed (but has no belief as to which); and
>   (ii) that his act will encourage or assist the commission of one or more of them.
>
> (2) It is immaterial for the purposes of subsection 1(b)(ii) whether the person has any belief as to which offence will be encouraged or assisted.

Actus reus	*Mens rea*
Doing an act capable of encouraging or assisting the commission of one or more of a number of offences.	Believing: • one or more of those offences will be committed (but has no belief as to which), and • that his act will encourage or assist the commission of one or more of them.

This offence applies where D may not intend that a particular offence be committed but he believes both that one or more offences **will** be committed and that his act will assist or encourage the commission of one or more of them. It does not matter whether he has any belief as to which offence his act will assist or encourage (s. 46(2)). This offence applies where D provides assistance or encouragement believing that one of a range of offences will be committed—for example, where D drives P to V's house knowing that P is going to wreak revenge on V but not knowing whether he is going to beat up V, kill him, or set fire to his house (cf. *Maxwell v DPP for Northern Ireland*, **7.1.4.3**). The difference, however, from *Maxwell* is that there, a substantive offence is committed and D is charged as an accessory to it whereas for this offence no substantive offence is committed). The focus is upon D's *mens rea*—the offences he believed would be committed (see further *Sadique* [2013] EWCA Crim 1150).

> In *Sadique* D supplied various chemical cutting agents knowing they would assist the recipient drug dealers in supplying Class A or Class B drugs without knowing (and perhaps not wanting to know) which. The Court of Appeal held it is enough that D believes that one of the offences he anticipates might be committed will be committed.

Essentially D is leaving the decision as to which offence to commit to P whom he is assisting or encouraging. D will be liable even though P has no intention to commit any offence, it being sufficient that D **believes** (even though wrongly) that P will commit an offence.

D will not be liable for the s. 46 offence where he does an act believing it will encourage or assist P to commit one or more other inchoate offences (as listed in sch. 3; see s. 49(4)).

8.2.4 Defence of acting reasonably

Section 50 provides:

(1) A person is not guilty of an offence under this Part if he proves—

(a) that he knew certain circumstances existed; and

(b) that it was reasonable for him to act as he did in those circumstances.

(2) A person is not guilty of an offence under this Part if he proves—

(a) that he believed certain circumstances to exist;

(b) that his belief was reasonable; and

(c) that it was reasonable for him to act as he did in the circumstances as he believed them to be.

(3) Factors to be considered in determining whether it was reasonable for a person to act as he did include—

(a) the seriousness of the anticipated offence (or, in the case of an offence under section 46, the offences specified in the indictment);

(b) any purpose for which he claims to have been acting;

(c) any authority by which he claims to have been acting.

Whether D acted reasonably is a question for the magistrates or jury to decide. It is difficult to conceive of circumstances where D charged with the s. 44 offence, which requires intention, could rely on this defence. It is notable that the Explanatory Notes to the Act provide no examples of when the defence could be raised. The Law Commission did not recommend the defence to be available for the s. 44 offence. The Law Commission provided three examples (at para. A.63) of when reliance might be placed on the defence, only one of which merits reproduction, the other two being bizarre:

D, a motorist, changes motorway lanes to allow a following motorist (P) to overtake, even though D knows that P is speeding.

8.2.5 Protective offences: victims not liable

Section 51 provides:

(1) In the case of protective offences, a person does not commit an offence under this Part by reference to such an offence if—

(a) he falls within the protected category; and

(b) he is the person in respect of whom the protective offence was committed or would have been if it had been committed.

(2) 'Protective offence' means an offence that exists (wholly or in part) for the protection of a particular category of persons ('the protected category').

This provision puts on a statutory footing the '*Tyrrell* principle' (see **7.1.6**). The Explanatory Notes provide the following example:

Example

D is a 12-year-old girl and encourages P, a 40-year-old man, to have sex with her. P does not attempt to have sex with D. D cannot be liable of encouraging or assisting child rape despite the fact it is her intent that P have sexual intercourse with a child under 13 (child rape) because she would be considered the 'victim' of that offence had it taken place and the offence of child rape was enacted to protect children under the age of 13.

8.2.6 Jurisdiction

D may be found guilty of an offence under s. 44, 45, or 46 if he anticipates that the conduct he encourages or assists will take place wholly or partly in England and Wales regardless of where D is at the time (s. 52(1)). The Explanatory Notes provide the following example:

Example

D in Belgium sends a number of emails to P in London, encouraging him to plant a bomb on the tube. D can be prosecuted in England and Wales . . . despite the fact he was outside the jurisdiction when he did his act.

The opposite situation, of D being in England and Wales but encouraging or assisting the commission of an offence outside England and Wales, may give rise to liability (see s. 52(2) and sch. 4). There are three situations specified. The first covers offences for which P could be tried in England and Wales (sch. 4, para. 1). For example, D in England, communicates with P who is a British citizen living abroad, encouraging P to kill V living in the same country. Under English law (see s. 9 of the OAPA 1861) murder committed by a British citizen is punishable in English courts wherever it is committed. The second situation applies where D acts wholly or partly in England and Wales and although the offence he encourages or assists might take place outside England and Wales, it is an offence under the law of that place (sch. 4, para. 2). For example, D in England sends an email to P in Spain containing details of how to disarm an alarm system used by a bank in Madrid. D intends to assist P to rob the bank. The third situation arises where D, outside England and Wales, encourages or assists P to commit an offence (also outside England and Wales), but the courts in England and Wales would have jurisdiction if D had himself committed the anticipated offence (sch. 4, para. 3).

The Explanatory Notes give the following example:

Example

D (a British citizen) in Canada sends a parcel of poison to P in France encouraging him to use it to murder V (also in France). It would be possible to try D in England because he is a British citizen and the anticipated principal offence (murder) is one which could be tried in England, Wales, or Northern Ireland as it would be committed by a British citizen.

8.3 **Conspiracy**

8.3.1 **Introduction**

At common law the offence of conspiracy was committed where two or more persons agreed 'to do an unlawful act, or to do a lawful act by unlawful means' (*Mulcahy* (1868) LR 3 HL 306). This definition did not limit liability to agreements to commit crimes but also included agreements to commit some torts, to defraud, to corrupt public morals, or to outrage public decency. In *Kamara* v *DPP* [1974] AC 104, the House of Lords held that an agreement to commit the tort of trespass to land, if accompanied by an intention to inflict more than merely nominal damage, amounted to a criminal conspiracy. The Law Commission (Law Com No. 76, para. 1.113) expressed the view that conspiracy should be confined to agreements to commit criminal offences and it is its aim that legislation should ultimately achieve this result. The Criminal Law Act 1977, which resulted from the work of the Law Commission and created the offence of statutory conspiracy, has only partially achieved this result. Pending a comprehensive review of offences of fraud and of the law relating to obscenity and indecency, s. 5 of the 1977 Act preserved the offence of conspiracy to defraud and, possibly, the offence of conspiracy to corrupt public morals or outrage public decency. Agreements to commit torts, however, are no longer indictable as conspiracy. In its Report, *Fraud* (Law Com No. 276) the Law Commission recommended the abolition of conspiracy to defraud as a separate offence. The Fraud Act 2006, whilst radically altering the law on fraud, did not abolish common law conspiracy to defraud.

8.3.2 **Common elements**

Certain elements are common to both statutory conspiracies and common law conspiracies.

8.3.2.1 **Agreement**

> **Key Point**
>
> The essence of conspiracy is an agreement between two or more persons to effect the particular prohibited purpose. The agreement may be express or implied, but whatever form it takes, the offence of conspiracy is complete as soon as the parties agree. There is no requirement that they begin to put the agreement into effect, nor need all the details of the agreement be settled.

Thus A and B would be guilty of conspiracy to rob where they had agreed to rob a bank even though they had not settled the time or place where the robbery was to take place. While conspiracy is complete as soon as two parties agree to effect an unlawful purpose, the conspiracy will continue to subsist as long as they agree and will only terminate on its completion by performance or by abandonment or frustration (see *DPP* v *Doot* [1973] AC 807). **As conspiracy is a continuing offence, other persons may join an existing conspiracy and become parties to it.** For example, if A approaches C and asks him to join him and B in robbing a bank, when C agrees he becomes guilty of conspiracy to rob. This illustrates a further point that it is not necessary for all the parties to a conspiracy to be in contact with each other. What is necessary is that all the parties to the conspiracy have a common purpose communicated to at least one other party to the conspiracy (see *Ardalan* [1972] 2 All ER 257; *Scott* (1979) 68 Cr App R 164).

8.3.2.2 Parties

While it must be proved that there was an agreement between D and another, that other need not be identified (*Phillips* (1987) 86 Cr App R 18). However, **there must be at least two parties to the agreement**. For example, where the director of a company who is solely responsible for the conduct of the company's business decides to commit an offence in the company's name, he cannot be convicted of conspiring with the company as only one mind was involved albeit that the company has a separate legal personality (see *McDonnell* [1966] 1 QB 233). But where a director conspires in the course of the company's business with other persons or companies, the company may be indicted as a party to that conspiracy (see *R v ICR Haulage Ltd* [1944] KB 551).

Where the only parties to an agreement are husband and wife they cannot be guilty of conspiracy, whether statutory (s. 2(2)(a) of the Criminal Law Act 1977) or common law (*Mawji v R* [1957] AC 126). The same principle now applies to civil partners (following the Civil Partnerships Act 2004) but does not apply to an unmarried couple who live together in a relationship akin to marriage (*R v Suski* [2016] EWCA Crim 24). However, a husband and wife or civil partners can be convicted of conspiracy where a third party is also involved (*Whitehouse* (1852) 6 Cox CC 38; *Chrastny* [1991] 1 WLR 1381), or where the agreement was entered into before they married or entered into a civil partnership (*R v Robinson* (1746) 1 Leach 37).

Where the only other party to an agreement to commit an offence is a child under the age of criminal responsibility, D will not be guilty of conspiracy (s. 2(2)(b)). Where the only other party to an agreement to commit an offence is an intended victim of that offence, D will not be guilty of conspiracy (s. 2(2)(c)). The intended victim of the offence will not be guilty of conspiracy regardless of the number of persons involved in the conspiracy (s. 2(1)). The 1977 Act does not define 'victim'. Smith and Hogan, *Criminal Law* (4th edn) at p. 429 suggested that the meaning of 'victim' is confined to offences which exist for his protection so that he would not be convicted of that offence as an accessory when it is committed by another with his full knowledge and cooperation (see **7.1.6**). This may have been the legislature's intention but it is expressed ambiguously. In *Gnango* [2011] UKSC 59, Lord Phillips adverted, *obiter*, to this issue stating (at para. 49):

> If ['victim'] is given the wide meaning it would seem to produce the surprising result that a conspiracy by two persons that one will commit a terrorist atrocity as a suicide bomber, or to set fire to a house owned by one of them in furtherance of some ulterior motive, would appear not to subject either to criminal liability. There is a case for confining the meaning of 'victim' to persons of a class that the relevant Act is intended to protect . . .

If the issue arises in practice it is a fair assumption that this *obiter dictum* will be followed. There is no common law authority in respect of victims as parties to conspiracies, but the issue is unlikely to arise as it is difficult to imagine an agreement with the proposed victim of a fraud to defraud him. In *Drew* [2000] 1 Cr App R 91, the Court of Appeal stated that it is a misuse of language to describe as a 'victim' a person to whom heroin had been supplied; it is therefore possible to charge such a person with conspiracy along with the supplier of the drugs.

We have seen that where a person cannot commit an offence as a principal this does not prevent him being liable as an accessory (see **7.1.3.3**). His exemption from liability as a principal will likewise not protect him from liability for conspiracy. Thus, for example, a woman may be convicted of conspiracy to rape. Where a person is exempt from liability for an offence, whether as principal or accessory, he will not necessarily be exempt from conviction for conspiracy with another to commit that offence. There is a paucity of authority in this area. The Law Commission recommended that the exemption should extend to liability for conspiracy (see Law Com No. 76, para. 1.56) disapproving of the only authority in favour of liability, *Whitchurch* (1890) 24 QBD 420, where a woman was convicted of conspiring to procure her own abortion though she was not pregnant and could not commit the substantive offence under s. 58 of the Offences Against the Person Act 1861. Parliament did not adopt this recommendation as it was considered that the provision to implement it would unduly complicate the 1977 Act and, in practice, non-pregnant women would not now be prosecuted. It appears that in practice the court will determine the question of liability by considering the purpose of the statute and whether it would be defeated by holding an exempt person liable for conspiracy or whether its purpose requires the extension of the exemption to cover conspiracy.

> In *Burns* (1984) 79 Cr App R 173, the question arose directly. The Court of Appeal upheld the conviction of a father of a child for conspiracy with others to steal the child from the mother, although he was exempt from prosecution for the substantive offence under s. 56 of the Offences Against the Person Act 1861 (s. 56 has since been repealed by the Child Abduction Act 1984). Watkins LJ stated the considerations which influenced the court in its decision as follows (at p. 179):

>> We find [no authority] that leads us to say that it is in any way wrong or unjust for a person who is exempt, in the sense that James Burns was, from prosecution for the substantive offence to be proceeded against for the crime of conspiracy.
>>
>> The dangers of permitting a father of children to collect a posse of men and suddenly launch a siege of the home of his erstwhile wife, to break in and then snatch away sleeping children are surely self-evident. The criminal law does not in our view permit that sort of conduct. When a father who is exempt under s. 56 behaves in that way, it is, in our judgment, not only lawful but right and just that the prosecution should be free to bring a charge of conspiracy against him.

A person who agrees with another who is exempt from prosecution for the substantive offence to commit that offence may be convicted of conspiracy (see *Duguid* (1906) 21 Cox CC 200).

8.3.2.3 Acquittal of the other alleged conspirators

There must be at least two parties to a conspiracy.

 ? Question

If A is charged with conspiracy with B and B is acquitted, can A be convicted?

If other parties, not charged, are alleged to have been involved, the acquittal of B has no consequences for A provided that the prosecution prove that A agreed with at least one other person (see *Anthony* [1965] 2 QB 189). Where A and B are the only alleged conspirators the conviction of one and acquittal of the other need not necessarily involve any inconsistency as the evidence against one may have been much stronger than the evidence against the other; for example, A may have confessed to the conspiracy, such confession being highly probative evidence against A but being of no evidential value against B. If A and B are tried separately the inconsistent verdicts again may be due to the different evidence presented at each trial, or the way in which the case was conducted or simply the different view which different juries take of the witnesses (see *DPP* v *Shannon* [1975] AC 717).

There was some doubt, however, at common law whether a jury trying several conspirators together could convict one and acquit the others, there being no other alleged conspirators. To avoid all doubt s. 5(8) and (9) of the Criminal Law Act 1977 provides:

(8) The fact that the person or persons who, so far as appears from the indictment on which any person has been convicted of conspiracy, were the only other parties to the agreement on which his conviction was based have been acquitted of conspiracy by reference to that agreement (whether after being tried with the person convicted or separately) shall not be a ground for quashing his conviction unless under all the circumstances of the case his conviction is inconsistent with the acquittal of the other person or persons in question.

(9) Any rule of law or practice inconsistent with the provisions of subsection (8) above is hereby abolished.

The effect of this provision is that where all the alleged conspirators are tried together and the evidence against each is of roughly equal weight, the judge should direct the jury that they must either convict all or none, and the judge should make it clear that if they are unsure about the guilt of one of the conspirators, they must acquit all (see *Longman and Cribben* (1980) 72 Cr App R 121; *Testouri* [2003] EWCA Crim 3735). But where the judge considers that the weight of the evidence against each conspirator is markedly different, he must direct them to consider each case separately and that they may convict or acquit as is appropriate according to the evidence (see *Roberts* (1983) 78 Cr App R 41).

8.3.3 Statutory conspiracy

The offence of statutory conspiracy is defined by s. 1(1) and (2) of the Criminal Law Act 1977, as amended by s. 5 of the Criminal Attempts Act 1981, as follows:

(1) Subject to the following provisions of this Part of this Act, if a person agrees with any other person or persons that a course of conduct shall be pursued which, if the agreement is carried out in accordance with their intentions, either—

(a) will necessarily amount to or involve the commission of any offence or offences by one or more parties to the agreement, or

(b) would do so but for the existence of facts which render the commission of the offence or any offences impossible, he is guilty of conspiracy to commit the offence or offences in question.

(2) Where liability for any offence may be incurred without knowledge on the part of the person committing it of any particular fact or circumstance necessary for the commission of the offence, a person shall nevertheless not be guilty of conspiracy to commit that offence by virtue of subsection (1) above unless he and at least one other party to the agreement intend or know that that fact or circumstance shall or will exist at the time when the conduct constituting the offence is to take place.

Actus reus	*Mens rea*
Agreement by two or more persons that a course of conduct shall be pursued which (if carried out in accordance with their intentions) either: • will necessarily amount to or involve the commission of an offence or offences by one or more parties to the agreement, or • would do so but for the fact that commission of the offence or offences is impossible.	• intention that the course of conduct be pursued, and • intention or knowledge that a fact or circumstance necessary for the commission of the offence shall or will exist at the time when the conduct constituting the offence is to take place.

As conspiracy is an offence which centres on the agreement between the parties, which involves a meeting of minds, it is difficult to divide the offence into *actus reus* and *mens rea*. We will, therefore, analyse the separate ingredients contained in s. 1(1) which go to make up the offence.

8.3.3.1 Course of conduct

The essence of conspiracy is that the parties agree upon a course of conduct to be pursued. **For the parties to be liable for conspiracy the agreed course of conduct, if pursued in accordance with their intentions, must necessarily amount to or involve the commission of an offence by one or more of the conspirators.** Where the agreement is to commit a 'result crime' the phrase 'course of conduct' would be meaningless if confined to their actions divorced from the consequences of those actions. For example, if A and B agree to kill V by placing poison in a bottle of milk in his fridge, this will not necessarily result in murder as V may not drink the milk. If the phrase 'course of conduct' covered only the parties' physical acts, A and B would not be guilty of conspiracy to murder. This phrase must therefore include the intended consequences of those actions which, in this case, are the death of V. Thus the course of conduct agreed includes not only the actions intended to be taken but also the consequences of those actions.

If 'course of conduct' includes intended consequences, it is important to determine what consequences the parties intended as their liability will be limited to these. In *Siracusa* (1990) 90 Cr App R 340, O'Connor LJ stated (at p. 350):

> The *mens rea* sufficient to support the commission of a substantive offence will not nec-
> essarily be sufficient to support a charge of conspiracy to commit that offence. An intent
> to cause grievous bodily harm is sufficient to support the charge of murder, but is not
> sufficient to support a charge of conspiracy to murder or of attempt to murder.

In *Siracusa* the accused were charged, inter alia, with conspiracy to import heroin contrary to s. 170(2)(b) of the Customs and Excise Management Act 1979. The jury were directed that if they agreed on a course of conduct to be pursued which, if carried out in accordance with their intentions, would necessarily amount to the offence of being concerned in the fraudulent evasion of the prohibition either on the importation of cannabis or heroin, by one or more of the parties to the agreement, then they were guilty of conspiracy. Case law has established that a person may be convicted of the substantive offence of importing heroin where he believed that cannabis was being imported (see **3.3**). Where conspiracy is charged, however, this will not suffice. O'Connor LJ stated (at p. 350):

> [I]f the prosecution charge a conspiracy to contravene s. 170(2) of the Customs and
> Excise Management Act by the importation of heroin, then the prosecution must prove
> that the agreed course of conduct was the importation of heroin. This is because the
> essence of the crime of conspiracy is the agreement and in simple terms, you do not prove
> an agreement to import heroin by proving an agreement to import cannabis.

The course of conduct agreed also includes any facts or circumstance necessary for the commission of the substantive offence. A person cannot be convicted of conspiracy unless he and at least one other party to the agreement intend or know that such fact or circumstance shall or will exist at the time when the conduct constituting the offence is to take place. This is implicit in s. 1(2) which is not particularly clearly expressed. The substance of this provision is that, where recklessness or negligence suffice with respect to a fact or circumstance of the substantive offence or strict liability applies thereto, a person can be convicted of conspiracy to commit such an offence only where he and another party to the agreement intend that the circumstance shall exist or know that it will exist at the time the offence is to take place. This position has been confirmed by the House of Lords in *Saik* [2006] UKHL 18 after a series of decisions in the Court of Appeal relating to money-laundering offences had held that it was sufficient for the offence of conspiracy to be established that D had the *mens rea* of the substantive offence, which in these cases was satisfied by proof that he suspected, or had reasonable grounds to suspect, that the property was the proceeds of crime; that is, recklessness or negligence sufficed as to the crucial fact or circumstance in the *actus reus* of the substantive offence. Lord Hope of Craighead stated (at para. 58):

> There is no doubt that the requirement [that the defendant and at least one other party to
> the agreement must 'intend or know' that the fact or circumstance 'shall or will exist' at
> the time when the conduct constituting the offence is to take place] was designed to elim-
> inate the risk that someone could be guilty of conspiracy just because he was reckless as to
> the existence or otherwise of the circumstances that would make the conduct criminal.

Question

How can D intend or know that a fact or circumstance will exist?

A problem with s. 1(2), however, is that the words 'intend or know' are not entirely apposite. It is not strictly accurate to state that A intends a fact or circumstance to exist if he has no control over whether or not it exists, nor may it be possible for A, at the time of the agreement, to know that a particular fact or circumstance will exist at some future time. But in examining the constituents of conspiracy an important consideration, which the courts have not always understood or taken into account, is the point in time when the offence of conspiracy is complete. Lord Hope of Craighead highlighted this (at para. 75):

> A conspiracy is complete when the agreement to enter into it is formed, even if nothing is done to implement it. Implementation gives effect to the conspiracy, but it does not alter its essential elements. The statutory language adopts this approach. It assumes that implementation of the agreement lies in the future. The question whether its requirements are fulfilled is directed to the stage when the agreement is formed, not to the stage when it is implemented.

Example

A and B agree to handle particular goods. Several situations may arise:

(i)   they know at the time of their agreement that the goods are stolen; or

(ii) the goods may not yet be stolen but it is their intention that when they are stolen they will handle them; or

(iii) they may not know the provenance of the goods but their agreement is to handle them whether they be stolen goods or goods from a legitimate source.

In situations (i) and (ii) there should generally not be a problem; in (i) A and B know the provenance of the goods at the time they enter into their agreement while in (ii) the purpose of their agreement is to handle stolen goods. In respect of (i) Lord Brown of Eaton-under-Heywood stated (at para. 119):

> But if an agreement is made to handle goods believed to be stolen I for my part would have little difficulty in concluding for the purposes of section 1(2) . . . that the conspirators intended or knew that they would be stolen. Section 1(2) looks to the future so that the putative conspirator's state of mind is in any event better described as belief than as knowledge . . . . One can never be certain that goods that are to come into one's possession at a future time will be stolen but a firm belief can be held and that is sufficient.

In *Saik* the House confirmed that knowledge could not be satisfied by proof only of belief or suspicion. Lord Nicholls of Birkenhead explained (at para. 20):

> Thus on a charge of conspiracy to handle stolen property where the property has not been identified when the agreement is made, the prosecution must prove that the conspirator *intended* that the property which was the subject of the conspiracy *would* be stolen property. [Emphasis added]

Situation (iii), however, is more problematic as it involves conditional intention; A and B have agreed to pursue a course of conduct which, if carried out *in accordance with their intentions*, may, or may not, depending on the provenance of the goods they ultimately handle, involve the commission of the substantive offence of handling. The issue did not strictly arise in *Saik* and the majority did not provide a clear answer. Baroness Hale of Richmond, who dissented, does, however, provide an answer to the conditional intent problem. She uses an example of A and B considering having sex with a woman and agreeing that they will do so *even if* it turns out that she does not consent. Baroness Hale states (at para. 99):

> [I]t is important to distinguish between what happens when the substantive offence is committed—when the men have intercourse with the woman whether or not she consents—and what happens when they agree to do so. When they agree, they have thought about the possibility that she may not consent. They have agreed that they will go ahead *even if at the time when they go ahead they know that she is not consenting*. If so, that will not be recklessness; that will be intent to rape. Hence they are guilty of conspiracy to rape.

How lower courts may resolve the problem of situation (iii) whenever it arises remains to be seen. It is suggested that the approach of Baroness Hale would be consistent with that of the courts in the cases outlined later (see **8.3.3.2**).

If only one of the parties to the agreement has the relevant knowledge or intention there is no conspiracy. For example, if A and B agree to purchase a particular consignment of goods from C, A knowing them to be stolen and B having no such knowledge or belief, neither will be liable for conspiracy to handle stolen goods even though the agreed course of action, if pursued, would necessarily have involved the offence of handling stolen goods by A. Likewise, where the parties differ as to the intended consequences, this will affect their liability for conspiracy. For example, if A and B agree to wound V and A intends that V should die but B only intends that he should sustain grievous bodily harm, there is no conspiracy to kill but there is a conspiracy to cause grievous bodily harm.

8.3.3.2 If the agreement is carried out

Sometimes the agreement the parties make is a conditional one—for example, to beat up V on his way home from the pub if he is alone. Have they agreed on a course of conduct which, if it is carried out in accordance with their intentions, will necessarily amount to or involve the commission of an offence?

> In *Jackson* [1985] Crim LR 444, the appellants' convictions for conspiracy to pervert the course of justice were upheld by the Court of Appeal. They had agreed with W, then on trial for burglary, that if he was convicted they would shoot him in the leg as they considered that the court would then deal with him more leniently. The Court of Appeal held that:

> Planning was taking place for a contingency and if that contingency occurred the conspiracy would necessarily involve the commission of an offence. 'Necessarily' is not to be held to mean that there must inevitably be the carrying out of the offence; it means, if the agreement is carried out in accordance with the plan, there must be the commission of the offence referred to in the conspiracy count.

The object of the agreement was the commission of the offence; if the contingency did not occur no action would be taken. In *O'Hadhmaill* [1996] Crim LR 509, a conviction for conspiracy to cause an explosion was upheld where, during the IRA ceasefire, members of the IRA agreed to make bombs to be used if the ceasefire came to an end. If the ceasefire continued the bombs would not be used. These situations should be contrasted with the situation where the object of the agreement is not the commission of that offence but the attainment of some other object, although the parties may contemplate the commission of an offence to attain that object. The following example was given in *Reed* [1982] Crim LR 819, and approved in *Jackson*:

Example

A and B agree to drive from London to Edinburgh in a time which can be achieved without exceeding the speed limits, but only if the traffic which they encounter is exceptionally light. Their agreement will not necessarily involve the commission of any offence, even if it is carried out in accordance with their intentions, and they do drive from London to Edinburgh within the agreed time. Accordingly the agreement does not constitute the offence of statutory conspiracy or indeed of any offence.

Driving from London to Edinburgh within a particular time was an object which could be attained without the commission of any offence; if the speed limit was broken, this was incidental to the main object of the agreement. In *Reed* the Court of Appeal contrasted the driving example with that of A and B who agree to rob a bank, if when they arrive at the bank it seems safe to do so. 'Their agreement will necessarily involve the commission of the offence of robbery if it is carried out in accordance with their intentions. Accordingly, they are guilty of the statutory offence of conspiracy.' The object of their agreement was robbery; the commission of the offence was not incidental to any other object.

One situation remains.

Question

What if A and B agree to rob the bank and to kill anyone who seeks to prevent their escape. Are they guilty of conspiracy to murder?

The driving example might appear to suggest that they are not, as the main object of their agreement is to rob the bank and this can be attained without necessarily killing anyone. But if this agreement to kill is isolated from the agreement to rob, there is little to distinguish it from *Jackson* as it is an agreement to kill subject to a condition precedent. If no one seeks to prevent their escape the course of conduct will not be pursued, but if anyone does seek to prevent their escape, the agreed course of conduct will necessarily involve the commission of murder. Perhaps the correct approach is to separate the elements of the agreement from each other. The result is two separate agreements to pursue two courses of conduct: first, the agreement to rob the bank, and secondly the agreement, if a particular contingency occurs, to kill. The driving example is not severable in this way; there is one agreement to pursue one course of conduct which may or may not involve the commission of an offence.

8.3.3.3 In accordance with their intentions

At common law the prosecution had to prove not only an agreement to carry out an unlawful purpose but also an intention on the part of any alleged conspirator to carry out the unlawful purpose (see *Thomson* (1965) 50 Cr App R 1). The Law Commission did not recommend any change in the law. In Law Com No. 76, it stated (at para. 7.2):

> A person should be guilty of conspiracy if he agrees with another person that an offence shall be committed. Both must intend that any consequence specified in the definition of the offence will result and both must know of the existence of any state of affairs which it is necessary for them to know in order to be aware that the course of conduct agreed upon will amount to the offence.

The implication of this view was that if A did not intend the substantive offence to be committed he could not be liable for conspiracy, and if there were only two parties to the alleged agreement, the other party likewise could not be guilty of conspiracy.

8.3.3.3.1 *The House of Lords sows confusion*

> In *Anderson* [1986] AC 27, the House of Lords was faced with the problem of an alleged conspirator who claimed he did not intend the substantive offence to be committed. D agreed for a fee to supply diamond wire to cut through prison bars to enable a prisoner to escape. He was convicted of conspiracy to effect the escape of a prisoner and appealed claiming that he intended only to supply the wire, receive his fee, and then go abroad but that he neither intended nor expected the plan to be carried out. Lord Bridge, in a speech with which all the House agreed, stated (at p. 38):

> > I am clearly driven by consideration of the diversity of roles which parties may agree to play in criminal conspiracies to reject any construction of the statutory language which would require the prosecution to prove an intention on the part of each conspirator that the criminal offence or offences which will necessarily be committed by one or more of the conspirators if the agreed course of conduct is fully carried out should in fact be committed.

The House of Lords could have upheld D's conviction on the basis that he had aided and abetted the conspiracy as the others involved clearly had the intention that the substantive offence be committed. Their Lordships chose, however, to uphold his conviction as a principal to the conspiracy. Too great a concern for easing the task of the prosecution has once again led to a distortion of the substantive principles of the criminal law. If it is not necessary to prove an intention on the part of one of the parties to an agreement that the course of conduct be pursued, it would appear to be unnecessary to prove such an intention in relation to any other party. The absurd outcome is that a person may be guilty of conspiracy where no party to the alleged agreement intended the substantive offence to be committed. In such a case there is no agreement to commit a crime, and no statutory conspiracy according to s. 1(1), yet Lord Bridge would permit the conviction for conspiracy of all the parties to this non-existent agreement!

 Question

If a person may be convicted of conspiracy 'irrespective of his intention', what is the *mens rea* of conspiracy?

Lord Bridge's answer to this question was distorted by his concern to render immune from liability 'respectable citizens' who enter into agreements for the purpose of 'exposing and frustrating the criminal purpose of the other parties to the agreement'. His concern would have been unnecessary had he adopted the Law Commission's view, as such a person would not intend the offence to be committed. Lord Bridge's abandonment of the requirement of proof of such an intention prima facie rendered such persons involved in entrapping offenders liable for conspiracy. In order to return them to the realms of innocence Lord Bridge invented a new *mens rea* requirement unsupported by the legislation, the Law Commission, or any common law authority. He stated (at p. 39):

> [T]he necessary *mens rea* of the crime is, in my opinion, established if, and only if, it is shown that the accused when he entered into the agreement, intended to play some part in the agreed course of conduct in furtherance of the criminal purpose which the agreed course of conduct was intended to achieve. Nothing less will suffice; nothing more is required.

This dictum itself contradicts Lord Bridge's earlier dicta as, if the intention of any alleged conspirator is irrelevant, it is impossible to determine the 'criminal purpose which the agreed course of conduct was intended to achieve'. Ignoring this absurdity, this dictum appears to require proof of an intention on the part of an alleged conspirator to play some part in the agreed course of conduct. Anderson's part was to supply the wire and thus their Lordships confirmed his conviction for conspiracy. But it had always been understood that a person could be guilty of conspiracy even though he was to play no active role in the commission of the substantive offence. Lord Bridge's dictum would appear to remove such a person from the realms of liability. For example, A approaches B and asks him to kill C. If B agrees this would have amounted to conspiracy prior to *Anderson*. Now, however, A and B will only be liable for conspiracy to kill where A intended to play some part in the agreed course of conduct, namely the killing of C. Furthermore, far from rendering all persons involved in acceptable entrapment (see **7.1.7**) immune from criminal liability, Lord Bridge's dictum brings some such persons within the realms of criminal liability if they intend to play some part in the agreed course of conduct—such action perhaps being necessary either to maintain their credibility as conspirators or to obtain the evidence necessary for a prosecution. Lord Bridge's good intentions only seem to have served to create more problems than he was seeking to resolve.

8.3.3.3.2 *'Clarifying'* Anderson

In *Siracusa* (1990) 90 Cr App R 340, the Court of Appeal sought to effect a damage limitation exercise by 'clarifying' Lord Bridge's dictum that it must be shown that 'the accused, when he entered into the agreement, intended to play some part in the agreed course of conduct . . .'. O'Connor LJ (a judicial clairvoyant if ever there was one!) stated (at p. 349):

> We think it obvious that Lord Bridge cannot have been intending that the organiser of a crime who recruited others to carry it out would not himself be guilty of conspiracy unless it could be proved that he intended to play some active part himself thereafter.

Thus, in the earlier example where A asks B to kill C, both A and B are, in the opinion of the Court of Appeal, guilty of conspiracy. O'Connor LJ went on to state (at p. 349):

> Participation in a conspiracy is infinitely variable: it can be active or passive. If the majority shareholder and director of a company consents to the company being used for drug smuggling carried out in the company's name by a fellow director and minority shareholder, he is guilty of conspiracy. Consent, that is the agreement or adherence to the agreement, can be inferred if it is proved that he knew what was going on and the intention to participate in the furtherance of the criminal purpose is also established by his failure to stop the unlawful activity. Lord Bridge's dictum does not require anything more.

So 'play some part in' means no more than continuing to concur in the activity of another or failure to stop the unlawful activity. It is hard to believe that this is what Lord Bridge meant. A problem with this interpretation, however, is that it presumes activity on the part of other parties in furtherance of the criminal purpose. It had always been accepted that a conspiracy was complete when the parties agree and there was no requirement of activity in furtherance of the agreement. Doubtless, in many cases, it is only possible to prove the existence of the agreement by inference from the overt acts of the parties, but matters of proof should not be confused with substantive principles. In addition, the real problem with Lord Bridge's speech, that of the abandonment of the requirement that a conspirator intend the substantive offence to be committed, remains.

The authority of *Anderson* has been thrown further into doubt by the Privy Council decision in *Yip Chiu-Cheung* v *R* [1994] 3 WLR 514 which, although not binding on English courts, is highly persuasive particularly as the committee comprised Lords Griffiths, Browne-Wilkinson, Mustill, Jauncey of Tullichettle, and Slynn of Hadley. *Siracusa* was not cited but their Lordships addressed issues raised in *Anderson*.

D had been convicted of conspiracy to traffic in heroin contrary to common law (conspiracy being a common law offence in Hong Kong) and to s. 4 of the Dangerous Drugs Ordinance. The conspiracy concerned an agreement between D and an American undercover drug enforcement agent, E, that he would meet D in Hong Kong where he would receive from him the supply of heroin which E would take to Australia. The Hong Kong authorities were aware of the plan and had agreed not to prevent E from proceeding to Australia as his aim was to identify others in the drugs ring. E, however, missed his flight to Hong Kong and the plan was abandoned. D argued on appeal that E could not be a co-conspirator as he lacked the necessary *mens rea* for conspiracy. The Privy Council distinguished the situation relating to 'respectable citizens' involved in entrapment referred to by Lord Bridge on the basis that a person who enters into an agreement with the purpose of frustrating the crime does not have the *mens rea* to be a conspirator. Lord Griffiths stated (at p. 518):

> The crime of conspiracy requires an agreement between two or more persons to commit an unlawful act with the intention of carrying it out. It is the intention to carry out the crime that constitutes the necessary *mens rea* for the offence.

On this basis, even though E was 'acting courageously and with the best of motives', he intended to commit the offence of drug trafficking. Furthermore, Lord Griffiths added (at p. 518):

> Neither the police, nor customs, nor any other member of the executive have any power to alter the terms of the Ordinance forbidding the export of heroin, and the fact that they may turn a blind eye when the heroin is exported does not prevent it from being a criminal offence.

The fact that E would not be prosecuted does not mean that he would not have committed a crime and thus he had the necessary *mens rea* for conspiracy and therefore was D's co-conspirator.

 Question

Can the reasoning in *Yip Chiu-Cheung* dealing with common law conspiracy be applied to statutory conspiracy?

Although *Yip Chiu-Cheung* concerned common law conspiracy, it is difficult to see any distinction between this and statutory conspiracy. The signs clearly are that if the issue comes before the Supreme Court *Anderson* will not be followed; that much has been hinted at by the Court of Appeal in *King* [2012] EWCA Crim 805. Where there appears to be an agreement between parties to commit an offence but, in fact, none of them intend to carry the agreement out and it is nothing more than a fantasy, there is not a conspiracy; there needs to be some credible evidence of 'executory intent' for the case to be left to the jury (see *Goddard* [2012] EWCA Crim 1756).

8.3.3.4 Necessarily amount to or involve the commission of any offence

 Question

If the course of conduct agreed upon is carried out in accordance with the parties' intentions, will it necessarily amount to or involve the commission of an offence?

If A and B agree upon a course of conduct which they believe will amount to an offence but it is not an offence, their belief will not convert their agreement into the offence of conspiracy. For example, believing that it is illegal to import lace into England, A and B agree to smuggle some into the country. In fact, there is no restriction on the importation of lace, so the agreement, if executed, will not involve the commission of any offence.

The agreement, when executed, must involve one or more of the parties to the agreement in the commission of an offence. Will participation as an aider, abettor, counsellor, or procurer of an offence suffice? In *Hollinshead* [1985] 1 All ER 850, the Court of Appeal held that an agreement to aid and abet an offence was not sufficient; a charge of conspiracy would only be sustainable where the agreement envisaged the commission of the offence as a principal by one or more of the parties. On the appeal hearing of that case, [1985] AC 975, their Lordships did not address this question; they upheld the convictions of the accused for common law conspiracy to defraud and considered it unnecessary to decide whether a statutory conspiracy to aid and abet an offence was possible. The wording of s. 1(1) and the fact that their Lordships did not decide that there was a statutory conspiracy seem to imply that a conspiracy to aid and abet is not possible (see also *Kenning* [2008] EWCA 1534). It should be noted, however, that there are a few statutory offences whose *actus reus* consists of aiding and abetting or procuring something—for example, aiding, abetting, counselling, or procuring another's suicide. In these cases the aider and abettor is the principal so that it is possible to conspire to aid and abet a suicide (see *Reed* [1982] Crim LR 819). In *Dang* [2014] EWCA Crim 348, a conviction for conspiracy 'to be concerned in the production of a controlled drug, namely cannabis, by another in contravention of s. 4(2)(b) of the Misuse of Drugs Act 1971' was upheld where the conspirators agreed to supply hydroponic equipment to assist others to grow cannabis plants. The Court of Appeal confirmed that if the equipment had been used to produce cannabis, the conspirators would by means of their supply (an act of assistance) not merely have been aiders and abettors of the offence of 'being concerned in the production of cannabis' but would have been principals in that offence as providing assistance to those who were to produce the cannabis amounted to 'being concerned in' its production.

8.3.3.5 Impossibility

Section 1(1)(b) (inserted by s. 5 of the Criminal Attempts Act 1981) deals with the problem of impossibility where facts exist which render the commission of the agreed offence impossible. To some extent this provision is unnecessary as the situation is covered by the phrase 'carried out in accordance with their intentions'. For example, A and B agree to kill C by shooting him. Unknown to them he is already dead so commission of the substantive offence of murder is impossible. However, had the agreement been carried out in accordance with their intentions this would necessarily have involved the commission of the offence of murder. The inclusion of s. 1(1)(b), however, is useful as it serves to avoid all doubt.

 Key Point

Thus A and B will be liable for conspiracy in the following circumstances:

(1) They agree to pick V's pocket which, unknown to them, is empty (the offence of theft is impossible in the circumstances).
(2) They agree to break into a safe to steal the contents using a jemmy which, unknown to them, is incapable of effecting their purpose (the offence of theft is impossible because of the inadequacy of the means chosen to commit it).
(3) They agree to have consensual intercourse with V whom they believe to be 15 but who has just celebrated her 16th birthday (the offence of having sexual intercourse with a girl under 16 is impossible as V lacks the necessary quality of being under 16).

These examples illustrate three types of impossibility: impossibility due to the circumstances (often referred to as physical impossibility), impossibility due to inadequacy of means, and impossibility due to the absence of a quality on the part of a person or subject matter (e.g. goods being stolen to support a charge of handling stolen goods) necessary for the commission of the offence (this may also be referred to as legal impossibility). At common law, following the decisions in *Haughton* v *Smith* [1975] AC 476 and *DPP* v *Nock* [1978] AC 979, impossibility was a defence except where it arose from inadequacy of means.

8.3.4 Common law conspiracies

These are limited to conspiracy to defraud and possibly conspiracy to corrupt public morals or outrage public decency.

8.3.4.1 Conspiracy to defraud

Statutory conspiracy involves an agreement to commit an offence. Many frauds are crimes but some are not. Conspiracy to defraud was preserved by s. 5(2) of the Criminal Law Act 1977 to cover those frauds which are not crimes. For some time, however, there was confusion whether a conspiracy to defraud which would involve the commission of an offence could be charged as common law conspiracy. The problem was resolved by s. 12 of the Criminal Justice Act 1987:

(1) If—
    (a) a person agrees with any other person or persons that a course of conduct shall be pursued; and
    (b) that course of conduct will necessarily amount to or involve the commission of any offence or offences by one or more of the parties to the agreement if the agreement is carried out in accordance with their intentions,

the fact that it will do so shall not preclude a charge of conspiracy to defraud being brought against any of them in respect of the agreement.

This provision recognises the overlap between the two forms of conspiracy—they are not mutually exclusive. This leaves prosecutors a choice as to how to charge a particular conspiracy, but this choice should be exercised in accordance with guidance issued by the DPP under s. 10 of the Prosecution of Offences Act 1985, which indicates the circumstances in which a charge of conspiracy to defraud is appropriate. In 2007, the Attorney General's Office published guidance on *The Use of the Common Law Offence of Conspiracy to Defraud* in light of the reforms to property offences effected by the Fraud Act 2006 (https://www.gov.uk/guidance/use-of-the-common-law-offence-of-conspiracy-to-defraud--6). The guidance indicates that prosecutors should first consider whether the behaviour could be prosecuted under statute (either the Fraud Act 2006 or as a statutory conspiracy) and whether the available statutory charges adequately reflect the gravity of the offence. Some types of behaviour may more effectively be prosecuted as conspiracy to defraud (e.g. where there are different types of victims, such as individuals, banks, website administrators, or credit card companies), while other types can only be prosecuted as conspiracy to defraud (e.g. dishonestly infringing another's right, for example the dishonest exploitation of another's patent in the absence of a legal duty to disclose information about its existence).

8.3.4.1.1 *The meaning of 'defraud'*

A conspiracy to defraud **'is an agreement to practise a fraud on somebody'** (*Wai Yu-tsang* v *R* [1991] 4 All ER 664, 671, *per* Lord Goff). There is no need for anyone to be deceived if the course of conduct agreed by the parties is carried out.

> In *Scott* v *Metropolitan Police Commissioner* [1975] AC 819, D was convicted of conspiracy to defraud the copyright owners of films. D agreed with cinema employees to remove films temporarily to copy them without the knowledge or consent of the copyright owners. The copies were to be sold accruing for the conspirators profits which might otherwise have been secured by the copyright owners. Viscount Dilhorne stated (at p. 840):

> > [A]n agreement by two or more by dishonesty to deprive a person of something which is his or to which he is or would or might be entitled and an agreement by two or more to injure some proprietary right of his, suffices to constitute the offence of conspiracy to defraud.

In this case the copyright owners suffered a loss in either of two ways: (i) the sales of the unauthorised copies would affect the sales of legitimate copies of their films; and (ii) under *Reading* v *AG* [1951] AC 507, the accused were bound to account to the copyright owners for any profits they made, which they clearly did not intend to do.

> In *Adams* v *The Queen* [1995] 1 WLR 52, D, a director of EHL, agreed with his five co-defendants, who comprised the investment team, to conduct a series of share transactions through overseas companies and banks thereby making for themselves a profit which they concealed from EHL. The Privy Council upheld D's conviction for conspiracy to defraud. In this case the fraud consisted of the dishonest concealment of information from the company which D was under a duty to disclose to it, namely information concerning the secret profits made. Lord Jauncey of Tullichettle stated (at p. 65):

> Since a company is entitled to recover from directors secret profits made by them at the company's expense, it would follow that any dishonest agreement by directors to impede a company in the exercise of its right of recovery would constitute a conspiracy to defraud.

The victim of the conspiracy to defraud, however, may not suffer economic loss if the agreement is carried out. This will not prevent a conviction for conspiracy to defraud where a deception was involved and the victim was dishonestly deceived into taking an economic risk which he would not otherwise have taken as 'interests which are imperilled are less valuable in terms of money than those same interests when they are secure and protected' (*Allsop* (1976) 64 Cr App R 29, 32, *per* Shaw LJ). In this case the appellant, a sub-broker for a hire purchase company, in collusion with others entered false particulars on application forms in order to induce the company to accept applications which they might otherwise have rejected. The Court of Appeal upheld his conviction for conspiracy to defraud the company. If the creditors fulfilled the terms of the hire purchase agreements the company would suffer no loss but would, in fact, make a profit. The creditors, however, fell into higher risk categories than those with whom the company generally contracted.

Where a person is a public official there may be a conspiracy to defraud where he is dishonestly induced by deception to act contrary to his public duty (*Welham* v *DPP* [1961] AC 103).

In *Wai Yu-tsang* v *R*, the Privy Council affirmed the decisions in *Allsop* and *Welham*.

> D, the chief accountant of a Hong Kong bank, was charged with conspiracy with others to defraud the bank and its shareholders, creditors, and depositors by dishonestly concealing in its accounts the dishonouring of cheques the bank had purchased to the sum of US $124 million. This sum exceeded the assets of the bank and D concealed this fact to prevent a run on the bank. The agreement to conceal this fact amounted to a conspiracy to defraud as it would or might deceive the victims into acting or failing to act so that they suffered economic loss or their economic interests would be put at risk. Delivering the decision of the Board, Lord Goff of Chieveley quoted with approval from Lord Denning's speech in *Welham* (at p. 133):

> The important thing about [the definition of defraud] is that it is not limited to the idea of economic loss, nor to the idea of depriving someone of something of value. It extends generally to the purpose of the fraud and deceit. Put shortly, 'with intent to defraud' means 'with intent to practise a fraud' on someone or other. . . . If anyone may be prejudiced in any way by the fraud, that is enough.

Lord Goff considered that this was confirmed by the cases concerned with persons performing public duties, which were not to be regarded as a special category but rather illustrated the principle that conspiracies to defraud are not restricted to cases of intention to cause the victim economic loss. Thus a person may be defrauded when he is 'prejudiced in any way'. This provides the potential for further widening the ambit of this offence, which already is extremely wide in that it criminalises behaviour which would not be criminal where it is performed by one person, but becomes so when agreed to be performed by two or more persons. It is a very curious law which renders criminal agreements to pursue courses of conduct which Parliament, in the Theft Acts 1968 and 1978, the Forgery and Counterfeiting Act 1981, and the Fraud Act 2006, deliberately chose not to criminalise when performed by an individual.

8.3.4.1.2 *The mens rea of conspiracy to defraud*

The *mens rea* of conspiracy to defraud involves an intention to defraud and dishonesty. The problem which arises is determining what is meant by intention. The dicta in the cases are contradictory and confusing; much of the confusion deriving from the fact that there was equal uncertainty as to the meaning of 'defraud' when many of them were decided. The decision in *Wai Yu-tsang* (see **8.3.4.1.1**) may provide a means of rationalising the decisions. In *Scott* (see **8.3.4.1.1**) Lord Diplock stated that the 'purpose of the conspirators must be to cause the victim economic loss'. In most cases, however, the aim or purpose of the conspirators is to make a profit for themselves; it is rarely their direct purpose to cause a loss to some other person albeit that this might be the inevitable consequence of their agreed course of conduct. Indeed in *Scott* it would appear that the purpose of the conspirators was to make a profit for themselves, the lost profits to the copyright owners of the films being an inevitable consequence of their enterprise. In truth, therefore, they only had an oblique intent in respect of this loss.

In *AG's Reference (No. 1 of 1982)* [1983] QB 751, the Court of Appeal referred to the 'true object of the agreement' as opposed to side-effects or incidental consequences of the conspiracy. In this case loss would have been caused to X Ltd, the makers of whisky, if the defendants' agreement to sell in Lebanon whisky, falsely labelled as made by X Ltd, had been carried out. The Court of Appeal held, however, that this agreement only involved fraud in respect of the Lebanese purchasers who would have been deceived, but would not have involved an agreement to defraud X Ltd as any loss they might have suffered was only incidental to the true object of the agreement. Consequently, the parties could not be charged with conspiracy as it was not the object of the agreement to cause loss to anyone within the jurisdiction.

This decision must be contrasted with *Cooke* [1986] AC 909, where this refined and artificial analysis of 'true object' and 'incidental consequences' was not alluded to by their Lordships. The House upheld the convictions of British Rail stewards for conspiracy to defraud British Rail where they had dishonestly sold to passengers their own food, rather than British Rail food, intending to keep the proceeds. Their object was doubtless to make a profit rather than to cause a loss to British Rail, although this was the inevitable consequence of their actions. Their convictions, therefore, could only be upheld on the basis that they had an oblique intent with respect to causing such loss.

In *Allsop* (see **8.3.4.1.1**), the Court of Appeal opined that it did not matter that D did not desire to cause loss to the company as the deceit he employed deceived the company and imperilled its economic interests. Shaw LJ stated (at p. 32):

> Where a person intends by deceit to induce a course of conduct in another which puts that other's economic interests in jeopardy he is guilty of fraud even though he does not intend or desire that actual loss should ultimately be suffered by that other in this context.

This is in line with the approach of the House of Lords in *Welham* (see **8.3.4.1.1**) which established that 'intent to defraud' should not be given a narrow meaning, involving an intention to cause economic loss to another, but rather meant an intention to practise a fraud on another, or an intention to act to the prejudice of another man's right.

In *Wai Yu-tsang* the Privy Council affirmed *Allsop*, doubted Lord Diplock's dictum in *Scott*, approved *Welham*, and did not refer to either the *AG's Reference (No. 1 of 1982)* or *Cooke*. It would appear, however, that the continuing authority of the *AG's Reference (No. 1 of 1982)* is questionable in light of the decisions in *Cooke* and the instant case. Lord Goff stated (at pp. 671, 672):

> The question whether particular facts reveal a conspiracy to defraud depends upon what the conspirators have dishonestly agreed to do, and in particular whether they have agreed to practise a fraud on somebody. For this purpose it is enough for example that . . . the conspirators have dishonestly agreed to bring about a state of affairs which they realise will or may deceive the victim into so acting, or failing to act, that he will suffer economic loss or his economic interests will be put at risk. It is however important in such a case . . . to distinguish a conspirator's intention (or immediate purpose) dishonestly to bring about such a state of affairs from his motive (or underlying purpose). The latter may be benign to the extent that he does not wish the victim or potential victim to suffer harm; but the mere fact that it is benign will not of itself prevent the agreement from constituting a conspiracy to defraud.

It would appear, therefore, that **an intention to bring about a state of affairs which amounts to defrauding another, whether because he will suffer economic loss, or he is deceived into taking an economic risk, or he is deceived into acting contrary to his public duty, or his rights are placed at risk of prejudice, is sufficient.** The dictum of Lord Goff quoted earlier uses the words 'will or may deceive the victim' suggesting that recklessness is sufficient. This was both unnecessary to the decision before the Privy Council and goes beyond what was decided in *Allsop*.

It must also be proved that D was dishonest. A person is dishonest if he is acting contrary to the standards of honesty of ordinary decent people (*Ivey* v *Genting Casinos (UK) Ltd* [2017] UKSC 67, discussed at **12.2.2.2**; *R* v *Pabon* [2018] EWCA Crim 420).

8.3.4.1.3 *Who is to be the perpetrator of the fraud?*

Statutory conspiracy is only committed where it is intended that at least one of the parties to the agreement perpetrate the offence. It appears, however, that **conspiracy to defraud may be committed even though the fraud is ultimately to be perpetrated by persons who were not parties to the agreement.** This is the purport of the decision in *Hollinshead* [1985] AC 975. Their Lordships upheld convictions for conspiracy to defraud one or more electricity boards where the accused had manufactured and sold to a supposed middleman (in fact a police officer seeking to entrap them) devices designed to alter readings of electricity meters. The fraud on the electricity boards would be perpetrated by the ultimate purchasers of the devices when they used them to alter their meter readings. The course of conduct agreed upon by the accused would not have brought them into contact with the perpetrators of the frauds. Completion of their agreed course of conduct, by selling the devices, did not involve fraud on anyone. Nevertheless, their Lordships held that their purpose was to cause economic loss to the electricity boards. It is clear, however, that their purpose was to make a profit from selling the devices to the middleman; this they would do regardless of what happened to the devices thereafter. Sense may only be made of their Lordships' decision if 'purpose' is interpreted to mean 'intention'. **Conspiracy to defraud, therefore, may be committed where the ultimate fraud is to be perpetrated by a person not a party to the agreement.** In *Hollinshead*, however, it would not be correct to state that it was an inevitable consequence that the electricity boards sustain economic loss (the middleman may not have sold the devices or they may have been destroyed in a fire); it would be more accurate to state that this was virtually certain to result. If the parties to the agreement foresaw this, then it would be open to the jury to infer that they intended that result (see **3.2.3.1**).

8.3.4.2 Conspiracy to corrupt public morals or to outrage public decency

Section 5 of the Criminal Law Act 1977 provides:

(1) Subject to the following provisions of this section, the offence of conspiracy at common law is hereby abolished . . . .

(3) Subsection (1) above shall not affect the offence of conspiracy at common law if and in so far as it may be committed by entering into an agreement to engage in conduct which—

(a) tends to corrupt public morals or outrages public decency; but
(b) would not amount to involve the commission of an offence if carried out by a single person otherwise than in pursuance of an agreement.

Subsection (3) is expressed in very tentative terms for two reasons. First, it was not clear whether there were substantive offences of corrupting public morals or outraging public decency. Secondly, even if there were such offences, para. (b) gives expression to the uncertainty whether corrupting public morals or outraging public decency as the object of a conspiracy perhaps had a wider meaning. If so, action which, if done by a person acting alone, would not constitute either substantive offence might, if agreed to be done by two or more persons, constitute common law conspiracy to corrupt public morals or outrage public decency. The outcome of all this is uncertainty. If the meaning of corrupting public morals or outraging public decency is the same whether charged as substantive offences (if such exist) or as a conspiracy, then conspiracy to corrupt public morals or outrage public decency will be statutory conspiracies if these activities constitute substantive offences. It would obviously have been much more desirable if Parliament had taken the initiative and decided whether corrupting public morals or outraging public decency were substantive offences and, if so, had provided definitions.

 Question

Are there substantive offences of corrupting public morals or outraging public decency and are the definitions of these activities the same whether charged as substantive offences or conspiracy?

In *Shaw* v *DPP* [1962] AC 220, D was convicted of conspiracy to corrupt public morals having published the 'Ladies Directory' advertising the names and addresses of prostitutes, their photographs, and the 'services' they offered. Their Lordships upheld his conviction without deciding whether corrupting public morals was a substantive offence although the Court of Criminal Appeal had held that it was.

In *Knuller* v *DPP* [1973] AC 435, the accused were charged with conspiracy to corrupt public morals and to outrage public decency arising from an agreement to publish, in a magazine called *IT*, advertisements soliciting homosexual acts in private between consenting adults. The conviction for conspiracy to corrupt public morals was upheld.

Lord Simon expressed the view that 'corrupt' was a strong word meaning more than 'lead morally astray', suggesting 'conduct which a jury might find to be destructive of the very fabric of society'. Lord Reid considered that 'corrupt' was synonymous with 'deprave'. The conviction for conspiracy to outrage public decency was quashed as the direction to the jury was defective, although Lords Reid and Diplock thought that this was not an offence known to the law. Lords Simon, Kilbrandon, and Morris held that there was a substantive offence of outraging public decency and thus there could be a conspiracy to do so. The Court of Appeal in *Mayling* [1963] 2 QB 717 had likewise held that it was an offence to outrage public decency. In defining the offence Lord Simon in *Knuller* stated (at pp. 494, 495):

> *R* v *Mayling* shows that the substantive offence (and therefore the conduct the subject of the conspiracy) must be committed in public, in the sense that the circumstances must be such that the alleged outrageously indecent matter could have been seen by more than one person, even though in fact no more than one did see it. If it is capable of being seen by one person only, no offence is committed . . . .
>
> I do not think that it would necessarily negative the offence that the act or exhibit is superficially hid from view, if the public is expressly or impliedly invited to penetrate the cover. Thus, the public touting for an outrageously indecent exhibition in private would not escape . . . Another obvious example is an outrageously indecent exhibit with a cover entitled 'Lift in order to see . . .'. This sort of instance could be applied to a book or newspaper . . . . The conduct must at least in some way be so projected as to have an impact in public.

The jury must also consider whether public decency is outraged by the conduct involved. Lord Simon went on to state (at p. 495):

> It should be emphasised that 'outrage' . . . is a very strong word. 'Outraging public decency' goes considerably beyond offending the susceptibilities of, or even shocking, reasonable people. Moreover the offence is, in my view, concerned with recognised minimum standards of decency, which are likely to vary from time to time. Finally, notwithstanding that 'public' in the offence is used in a locative sense, public decency must be viewed as a whole; and I think the jury should be invited, where appropriate, to remember that they live in a plural society, with a tradition of tolerance towards minorities, and that this atmosphere of toleration is itself part of public decency.

In a series of cases the Court of Appeal confirmed the continued existence of the substantive offence of outraging public decency (see *Gibson* [1990] 2 QB 619; *May* (1989) 91 Cr App R 157; *Lunderbech* [1991] Crim LR 784; *Rowley* [1991] 4 All ER 649; and most recently *Hamilton* [2007] EWCA Crim 2062). It is difficult to envisage conduct which, when done alone, would not amount to the substantive offence of outraging public decency but which, if done in concert, would amount to conspiracy to outrage public decency. It would seem that there is nothing left for the common law offence of conspiracy to cover so that a conspiracy to outrage public decency should be charged as a statutory conspiracy. It is submitted that the same should apply to conspiracy to corrupt public morals albeit the authorities on the existence of the substantive offence are not so clear cut.

One final point relates to the wording of s. 5(3)(b). **If the conduct agreed to be engaged in would 'amount to or involve the commission of an offence', the agreement cannot be charged as common law conspiracy** (if this continues to exist). The word 'offence' in para. (b) is unqualified; it is not confined to the substantive offences of corrupting public morals or outraging public decency.

8.3.4.3 Impossibility in common law conspiracy

The substance of the decision in *DPP v Nock* [1978] AC 979 is that impossibility is generally an answer to a charge of common law conspiracy unless the impossibility arises from the inadequacy of the means to be used to effect the agreed course of conduct. It should be noted, however, that if, at the time of the agreement, the object of the agreement was capable of being achieved, the fact that achievement subsequently becomes impossible due to some supervening event will not provide D with a defence as the offence of conspiracy is complete upon conclusion of an agreement without proof of any further steps to effect it being necessary.

8.4 Attempt

8.4.1 Statutory definition and scope

The common law offence of attempt to commit an indictable offence was abolished by the Criminal Attempts Act 1981 which created a new statutory offence of attempt. The Act was largely the result of the work of the Law Commission (see Law Com No. 102). Section 1(1) of the Act provides:

> If, with intent to commit an offence to which this section applies, a person does an act which is more than merely preparatory to the commission of the offence, he is guilty of attempting to commit the offence.

Actus reus	Mens rea
• doing an act • which is more than merely preparatory to the commission of the intended offence • that offence being an indictable offence triable in England and Wales.	• intent to commit the offence • knowing, or being reckless as to (where recklessness suffices), any material circumstance.

By s. 1(4), liability for attempts is confined to offences which, if completed, would be triable in England and Wales as indictable offences. Thus, generally, there is no liability for an attempt to commit a summary offence. Section 1(4) goes on to exclude from liability attempts to commit the following offences: conspiracy; aiding, abetting, counselling, procuring, or suborning the commission of an offence; and assisting an offender who has committed a relevant offence or compounding a relevant offence contrary to ss 4(1) and 5(1) of the Criminal Law Act 1967.

The definition in s. 1(1) implicitly excludes the possibility of convictions for attempt to commit some other crimes. For example, **the requirement of 'an act' means that a person cannot attempt to commit an offence which can only be committed by an omission. Similarly a person cannot be convicted of an attempt to commit a result crime, such as murder, on the basis solely of an omission where he was under a duty to act.**

Where an offence may not be committed intentionally, for example, involuntary manslaughter, there cannot be an attempt to commit that offence. If D intends to kill he will be liable for attempted murder. It would also appear to be the case that a charge of attempted murder is appropriate even though a verdict of voluntary manslaughter (arising from diminished responsibility, loss of self-control, or suicide pact) could have been returned had the intended victim died (see *Bruzas* [1972] Crim LR 367) or if a verdict of infanticide would have been available (but cf. *Smith* [1983] Crim LR 739).

Section 1(4) also adverts to jurisdictional issues. If D is to be liable for attempt to commit an offence, the offence, if completed, must be one for which he could have been indicted in England and Wales. For example, murder by a British citizen is indictable regardless of where it is committed. Thus if D sends a box of chocolates laced with poison to V who is in France, intending to kill him, D will be liable for attempted murder as soon as the chocolates are posted. If D's intention is only that V be made ill by the chocolates he is not liable for an attempt to administer poison contrary to s. 24 of the Offences Against the Person Act 1861 as such an offence committed abroad is not triable in England. If D is in France and gives the chocolates to V intending to kill him, he could, in theory, be prosecuted in England for attempted murder unless the courts take the view that there is no need for such extraterritorial jurisdiction. If so, they could give a restrictive meaning to the words 'does an act' construing them to require that the acts which constitute the attempt either be done within the jurisdiction or be intended to have some effect within the jurisdiction. If D is outside the jurisdiction when he does the acts which may constitute an attempt, he will be liable to conviction where the acts are designed to have an effect within the jurisdiction (see *DPP* v *Stonehouse* [1978] AC 55). Thus, if D, in France, sends poisoned chocolates to V, in England, intending to make V ill, he will be guilty of an attempt to administer poison (see further **8.5**).

8.4.2 *Mens rea*

The essence of the offence of attempt is intention. While it must be proved that D did an act which was 'more than merely preparatory to the commission of the offence', the acts which may amount to the *actus reus* derive their significance from D's intention. **The acts, in themselves, may appear to be innocent but when added to D's intention they constitute a crime.** For example, if D lights a match beside some curtains in a restaurant this may or may not constitute attempted arson, depending on whether he does so intending to set fire to the curtains or to light a cigarette. Similarly, if D offers V a chocolate this may be an innocent act of generosity or it may constitute attempted murder if D offers it intending to kill V believing, mistakenly, that the chocolate contains poison. In both cases the act of offering the chocolate is exactly the same but it is D's intention which colours the act and converts the second situation into the *actus reus* of attempted murder.

8.4.2.1 Intent as to consequences

It is important to determine what the meaning of 'intent to commit an offence' is in the context of attempt. The Court of Appeal held in *Pearman* (1984) 80 Cr App R 259 that **the word 'intent' in s. 1(1) has the same meaning as at common law**. In *Whybrow* (1951) 35 Cr App R 141, the Court of Appeal held that although on a charge of murder proof of an intention to cause GBH would suffice to establish *mens rea*, **on a charge of attempted murder** 'the intent becomes the principal ingredient of the crime'. Accordingly, it had to be proved that D intended to kill. **Thus where an accused is charged with attempt it must be proved that he had the intention to commit the substantive offence he is alleged to have attempted.** Similarly, if recklessness with regard to causing a consequence will suffice for the substantive offence, only intention to cause that consequence will suffice where attempt is charged (see *O'Toole* [1987] Crim LR 759 where D's conviction for attempted arson was quashed). This is logical as D cannot be said to be trying to bring about a result where that result is not his aim or object but is merely foreseen as a possible consequence of the achievement of his aim or object.

At common law the word 'intent' was defined by the Court of Appeal in *Mohan* [1976] QB 1, 11, as 'a decision to bring about, in so far as it lies within D's power, the commission of the offence which it is alleged D attempted to commit, no matter whether D desired that consequence of his act or not'. This definition encompassed direct intent and oblique intent (see **3.2.1**). In *Pearman* the Court of Appeal approved this definition and explained the meaning of the phrase 'no matter whether D desired that consequence of his act or not' as follows (at p. 263):

> [These words] are probably designed to deal with a case where [D] has, as a primary purpose, some other object, for example, a man who plants a bomb in an aeroplane, which he knows is going to take off, it being his primary intention that he should claim the insurance on the aeroplane when the freight goes down into the sea. The jury would not be put off from saying that he intended to murder the crew simply by saying that he did not want or desire to kill the crew, but that was something that he inevitably intended to do. Similarly, for example, a man who is cornered by the police when he is in a car may have the primary purpose of simply escaping from that situation. If he drives straight at the police officers at high speed, a jury is likely to conclude that he intended to injure a police officer and maybe cause him serious grievous bodily harm.

Some confusion as to the degree of foresight required where oblique intent is involved was caused by the Court of Appeal decision in *Walker and Hayles* (1990) 90 Cr App R 226. W and H threw V from a third-floor balcony after banging his head against a wall, threatening him with a knife, and declaring that they were going to kill him. V survived and W and H were charged with attempted murder. This was not a case involving oblique intent so the only issue should have been as to their intention in throwing him from the balcony: did they intend to kill him? If they intended some lesser degree of harm, this would not suffice for attempted murder. The jury were confused and sought clarification from the judge. Unfortunately the judge directed them in terms of inferring intention from the probability of death ensuing: if the accused knew there was a high probability of death the jury were entitled to infer they intended to kill. The Court of Appeal did not disapprove of using 'high probability' as the measure although they expressed a preference for the phrase 'virtual certainty'. This, however, is not the issue. If direct intention is involved—that is, D has no other aim or purpose in committing the alleged offence than the result involved in that offence—it matters not that achievement of that result is possible, probable, or certain. If achievement of that result is his aim or purpose then he intends it whether or not he is likely to achieve it. For example, D aims a gun at V and fires intending to kill V but misses. D is guilty of attempted murder whether he had a 10 per cent chance of succeeding in his purpose or a 99 per cent chance. If there is doubt as to what D's purpose was (was it only to frighten, to wound, or to kill?) this is a different issue. In this case it may be legitimate to point out that the more probable the result the more likely it is that D intended it, but it must be made clear that this is not conclusive of the matter as all the evidence in the case must be taken into account. It is only where there is evidence that D's aim or purpose was something other than to kill that a direction based on *Nedrick* [1986] 1 WLR 1025 as modified by *Woollin* [1998] 3 WLR 382 (see **3.2.3.6**), should be considered; there did not appear to be any such evidence in *Walker and Hayles*. However, if a jury are satisfied that D's direct intent was to cause GBH they may (but need not necessarily) convict of attempted murder if satisfied that D knew that death was virtually certain to ensue.

 Example

If D throws V off a 100-metre-high cliff (V miraculously surviving by catching hold of a protruding ledge) and claims 'I only wanted to break his legs', a jury should acquit of attempted murder if they believe D. But if they are satisfied that D realised that death was virtually certain to ensue they could infer the intention to kill from that foresight and convict of attempted murder.

The example illustrates the very limited application of the *Nedrick* direction where attempted murder is charged and D claims he only intended to cause GBH.

8.4.2.2 *Mens rea* as to circumstances

The focus so far has been upon consequences; what *mens rea* is required with regard to the material circumstances of the offence? In rape the material circumstance is that V does not consent to penetration of their vagina, anus, or mouth by D's penis (see s. 1 of the Sexual Offences Act 2003).

 Question

If D is charged with attempted rape, having failed to penetrate V, is it sufficient that he intended to penetrate V's vagina, anus, or mouth not reasonably believing that V consented, or must it be proved that he intended non-consensual penetration?

The Law Commission, in its Report (Law Com No. 102, para. 2.15) took the view that intention as to every element of the offence was required, knowledge as to surrounding circumstances equating with intention as to consequences. The Court of Appeal, however, has decided that **if recklessness in respect of a circumstance will suffice for commission of the substantive offence, it will suffice on a charge of attempt to commit that offence.**

> In *Khan* [1990] 2 All ER 783, seven defendants were charged with rape and attempted rape of V, a 16-year-old girl. It appeared that some of the defendants had not succeeded in having intercourse with V. The counts for attempted rape charged the defendants on the basis that they either knew V did not consent or were reckless whether or not she consented. Three defendants were convicted of rape and the other four of attempted rape. Dismissing their appeals against convictions of attempted rape, Russell LJ stated (at p. 788):

>> The only difference between the [offences of rape and attempted rape] is that in rape sexual intercourse takes place whereas in attempted rape it does not, although there has to be some act which is more than preparatory to sexual intercourse. Considered in that way, the intent of the defendant is precisely the same in rape and in attempted rape and the *mens rea* is identical, namely an intention to have intercourse plus a knowledge of or recklessness as to the woman's absence of consent. . . . Recklessness in rape and attempted rape arises not in relation to the physical act of the accused but only in his state of mind when engaged in the activity of having or attempting to have sexual intercourse. . . . The only 'intent' . . . of the rapist is to have sexual intercourse. He commits the offence because of the circumstances in which he manifests that intent, i.e. when the woman is not consenting and he either knows it or could not care less about the absence of consent.

There was no need for the CPS to charge attempted rape in the alternative; had the counts simply alleged attempted rape based upon knowledge, and the defendants had been convicted, they would have had no basis upon which to appeal. In the context of a gang rape it might be considered highly unlikely that any defendant could have successfully raised a doubt that they did not know that V was not consenting. The CPS decision to overplay their hand in charging the counts of attempt in turn led to the Court of Appeal yielding to the temptation to stretch principle to patch up this error rather than quash the convictions of undeserving appellants.

The decision in *Khan* was affirmed by the Court of Appeal in *AG's Reference (No. 3 of 1992)* [1994] 2 All ER 121 where it was held that on a charge of attempted arson contrary to s. 1(2) of the Criminal Damage Act 1971, it was sufficient that D intended to damage the property by fire and was reckless whether life would thereby be endangered. This stretched the realms of liability for attempt further than *Khan* as criminal damage at this time involved *Caldwell* recklessness (see **3.4.2.2**). The Court of Appeal analysed the policy of attempt as requiring the punishment of those who have done their best to supply the element missing from the completed offence. Schiemann J stated (at p. 127):

> If, on a charge of attempting to commit the offence, the prosecution can show not only the state of mind required for the completed offence but also that the defendant intended to supply the missing physical element of the completed offence, that suffices for a conviction . . . . The defendant must intend to damage property, but there is no need for a graver mental state than is required for the full offence.

This dictum is problematic. First, in *Khan*, the recklessness related to a circumstance—the absence of consent on the part of the victim. In aggravated criminal damage, however, the element of endangerment is not a circumstance or state of affairs but part of D's state of mind as to what must be proved as *mens rea* for the substantive offence is intention to endanger life or recklessness thereto. There is no need for actual endangerment to be established (see *Sangha* [1988] 2 All ER 385, **15.3.2**).

Secondly, the dictum presented the possibility of D being guilty of attempting an offence, not only of *Caldwell* recklessness, but also of strict liability where he is neither intentional nor reckless (in either sense) in respect of the circumstance of the *actus reus* to which strict liability attaches. This is an expansion of the law and one, it is submitted, which is undesirable. Thirdly, the 'missing physical element' analysis is, as Professor Simester contends in 'The *Mens Rea* of Criminal Attempts' (2015) 131 LQR 169, 'inconsistent with ordinary language'. He states (at p. 170):

> To 'attempt' to do something is to *try* to do it. If only for the sake of speaking clearly to the citizens it is meant to guide, a law criminalising the 'attempt' to do something should mean what it says, i.e. that trying to do the thing is a crime. Once this is accepted, we can see why the missing element analysis is wrong in principle. Consider the law of rape. Under s.1 of the Sexual Offences Act 2003, it suffices for the full offence that D lacks a reasonable belief about V's consent. Rightly so. But no-one could describe D, however blameworthy he may be, as *trying to rape* someone whom he genuinely yet negligently believes to be consenting to sex. Attempts cannot be made inadvertently. Ordinary language simply does not allow that conclusion. Neither does s. 1(1) of the 1981 Act. And that means the missing element analysis must fail.

In *Pace and Rogers* [2014] EWCA Crim 186, the CPS again overplayed their hand by charging the offence too broadly. The Court of Appeal, however, resisted the temptation to stretch principle, allowed the appeals, and adopted an approach which sought to be true to the wording of the statute.

> The police set up a sting operation to try to gain evidence against the defendants, scrap metal merchants, whom they believed to be dishonest. An undercover police officer presented them with an opportunity to purchase metal which he pretended had been stolen. Under s. 327 of the Proceeds of Crime Act 2002 (POCA) it is an offence to convert or otherwise deal in 'criminal property'. Under s. 340(3) of the POCA property is 'criminal' where (a) it constitutes a person's benefit from criminal conduct *and* (b) the alleged offender knows or suspects that it constitutes or represents such a benefit. As the property was not, in fact, stolen, a prosecution for attempt was brought on the basis that the defendants suspected that the metal was stolen. On appeal from their convictions the Court of Appeal held that for an attempt D must intend all the elements of the *actus reus* of the substantive offence.

This decision, if followed, would amount to a reversal of *Khan*; but in strict precedent terms the Court of Appeal in *Pace* could not overrule the earlier decision in *Khan*. They distinguished it on two bases: first, that it concerned recklessness whereas the case before them concerned suspicion, but that seems to be a distinction without a difference. Secondly, the Court identified that if the defendants in *Khan* had achieved their objective—sexual intercourse with V—they would have committed the substantive offence of rape, whereas it was impossible to commit the substantive offence in the instant case as the scrap metal was not criminal property. The Court accepted, however, that a charge of attempted handling could have been brought by the Crown. For an offence of handling to be proved D must know or believe goods to be stolen. If this state of mind suffices for attempted handling this must be because knowledge or belief (in the sense of settled belief with no significant doubt) are, as regards circumstances, equivalent to intention as regards consequences. The Court arrived at this position by the simple stratagem of applying s. 1(3) of the 1981 Act (see **8.4.4**) where intention is presumed if it would have been found to exist under the facts as D believed them to be. Thus, if D believed the goods to be stolen, when they were not, 'on the facts as he believed them to be', he would, in effect, know them to be stolen. The Court further recognised that suspicion could be used as evidence to prove knowledge, Davis LJ stating (at para 81):

> [A]s observed by Lord Hope in para 62 of his speech in *R. v Saik* . . . , the margin between knowledge and suspicion is perhaps not all that great, at all events where the person has reasonable grounds for his suspicion. Where a defendant can be shown deliberately to have turned a blind eye to the provenance of goods and deliberately to have failed to ask obvious questions, then that can be capable, depending on the circumstances, of providing evidence going to prove knowledge or belief.

Until the Supreme Court resolves the doubts and conflicts left in the wake of these decisions, and assuming that the decision in *Pace* is the preferred one, were the situation in *Khan* to be repeated the CPS could avoid problems by charging attempted rape narrowly on the basis of a belief in the absence of consent. It should also be recognised that in the context of a gang rape participants who failed to have intercourse with the victim could be charged as secondary parties to the offences of those who succeeded. In addition, a failed attempt at rape almost inevitably will involve the commission of a sexual assault.

8.4.2.3 Conditional intent

A final problem to be disposed of is that of conditional intention (cf. **8.3.3.2**). A **person has conditional intent where he intends to commit an offence if a particular condition is satisfied**; for example, D intends to steal from V's car if he finds any items of value in it. There will be an attempted theft where D, with this intent, does an act which is more than merely preparatory to the commission of the offence—for example, opening the car door. Provided the prosecution do not charge D with attempting to steal specific items, there is no obstacle to a conviction. If they specify particular items they would have to prove that D would have stolen these had he discovered them. To avoid such difficulties of proof the prosecution need only charge D with 'attempting to steal from a car'. On such an indictment there is no need to prove that the car contained any items worth stealing, or even any items at all. If the car is completely empty so that theft from it is impossible, this will not prevent a conviction for attempt as the Criminal Attempts Act reversed the decision in *Haughton v Smith* [1975] AC 476 relating to impossible attempts (see **8.4.4**).

8.4.3 *Actus reus*

The *actus reus* of attempt is the doing of 'an act which is more than merely preparatory to the commission of the offence' D intends to commit. This is a question of fact for the jury. Section 4(3) provides:

> Where, in proceedings against a person for an offence under s. 1 above, there is evidence sufficient in law to support a finding that he did an act falling within subsection (1) of that section, the question whether or not his act fell within that subsection is a question of fact.

The trial judge must decide whether there is sufficient evidence to support a finding that D did such an act. If there is not, he will direct an acquittal and, if there is, the jury will be left to decide what acts D did and whether these were more than merely preparatory to the commission of the offence. At some point D's acts will cross over from being **merely preparatory** to being **more than merely preparatory**. The Criminal Attempts Act provides no more guidance than the common law for determining the precise point when an attempt is committed and the trial judge should ordinarily leave that question to the jury, directing them that if they consider that what D did was no more than preparation then they should find him not guilty.

The test generally settled at common law was known as the 'proximity' test formulated in *Eagleton* (1855) 6 Cox CC 559, 571 by Parke B:

> The mere intention to commit a misdemeanour is not criminal. Some act is required and we do not think that all acts towards committing a misdemeanour are indictable. Acts remotely leading towards the commission of the offence are not to be considered as attempts to commit it, but acts immediately connected with it are.

This test was vague, providing no indication when acts passed over from being remote to being immediately connected with the intended offence. But, to some extent, this is inevitable as there is an infinite variety of methods of committing offences and an infinite variety of situations will arise. When examining the common law, the Law Commission recognised this (Law Com No. 102) stating (at para. 2.45):

> [I]n our view there is no magic formula which can now be produced to define what precisely constitutes an attempt . . . . Of the various approaches, only the 'proximity' test has produced results which may be thought broadly acceptable. Its disadvantages are that hitherto it has not worked well in some cases, and that it is imprecise. It shares the latter disadvantage with all other approaches but its flexibility does enable difficult cases to be reconsidered and their authority questioned. Further, where cases are so dependent on what are sometimes fine differences of degree, we think it is eminently appropriate for the question whether the conduct in a particular case amounts to an attempt to be left to the jury.

This led the Law Commission to propose a test which did not differ greatly from the proximity test but which was designed to avoid a problem identified in the proximity test. Proximity suggested that an act had to be immediately connected with the commission of the offence. There was a danger that this would be construed very restrictively limiting liability to situations where D had performed the last act necessary to commit the offence. Thus the Law Commission changed the terminology to indicate that the parameters of attempt were broader than might be suggested by the proximity test. The difference between the tests is essentially one of perspective. The proximity test looked backwards from the commission of the full offence to see if the acts D had performed were close enough to that point. The test in s. 1 looks forwards from the point of preparatory acts to see whether the acts of D have gone beyond the preparatory stage.

From one point of view, all acts, apart from the last one necessary to bring about the commission of the offence, are preparatory acts. The inclusion of the word 'merely', however, suggests a grey area of ill-defined proportions between acts which are purely preparatory and the last act of commission. This grey area covers those acts performed by D when he might be described as being 'on the job' as opposed to preparing for it or, as the Court of Appeal put it in *Gullefer* [1987] Crim LR 195, when D has 'embarked on the crime proper'. This will obviously vary from case to case. An example may help to illustrate the position.

Example

D decides to kill V and with this intention he performs the following acts: (1) he spends several days observing V's movements in order to choose a good place and time for performing the killing; (2) he buys a gun and ammunition; (3) he visits a wood on several occasions for target practice; (4) on the day the offence is to be committed he loads the gun; (5) he drives to the scene of the proposed killing and hides in some bushes awaiting V's arrival; (6) he observes the road watching for V; (7) he sees V and takes aim; (8) he places his finger on the trigger; (9) he squeezes the trigger and fires the gun.

Point (9) is the last act to be performed by D in order to bring about commission of the offence of murder. If a police officer had been observing D, however, could he have intervened at some earlier point to prevent the killing while being sure that D would be convicted of attempted murder? To some extent points (1) to (8) were all acts preparatory to the last act but at some stage D moved from performing *merely preparatory* acts to performing *more than merely preparatory* acts. This would appear to be at some stage after point (4) and before point (9) when he might be described as being 'on the job' or as having 'embarked on the crime proper'. Whether a jury would be prepared to convict of attempted murder (assuming the judge leaves the issue to them) if the officer intervened at point (6) or (7) is highly questionable. Some juries might not even convict where D had reached point (8) if they paid undue attention to the fact that D could still relent and withdraw from committing the offence at that stage. What is clear, however, is that the jury's task does not simply involve applying the declared law to the facts as they find them but, in addition, involves them determining what the law is—that is, defining the meaning of 'more than merely preparatory'. This creates a risk of perverse and inconsistent verdicts.

There have been several decisions of the Court of Appeal which have sought to clarify the new test.

In *Widdowson* (1985) 82 Cr App R 314, D, wishing to obtain a van on hire purchase terms but realising that he would not be accepted as creditworthy, filled in a credit enquiries form in the name of another person and was convicted of attempting to obtain services (the hire purchase of the van) by deception. If the finance company had responded favourably to D's enquiry, it still remained for D to make a formal application for a hire purchase deal. The Court of Appeal quashed the conviction, referring to common law tests which indicated that this would not be considered an attempt. The Court considered that D had not performed every act necessary to achieve the consequence of obtaining services by deception; his acts were not immediately but only remotely connected with the offence alleged to have been attempted; and, using the words of Lord Diplock in *DPP* v *Stonehouse* [1978] AC 55, 68, he had not 'crossed the Rubicon and burned his boats'—that is, he had not reached the point of no return but could still have withdrawn from commission of the offence.

These tests would greatly reduce the ambit of attempt which the Law Commission had hoped to increase.

In *Boyle and Boyle* (1987) 84 Cr App R 270, the appellants were convicted of attempted burglary having been found by a policeman standing by a door, of which the lock and one hinge were broken. The Court of Appeal upheld their convictions being satisfied that the only thing left for them to do to commit the full offence was for one of them to step over the threshold of the property and enter as a trespasser, there being ample evidence of an intention to steal.

The Court also referred to another test which had been approved at common law. This had been propounded in Stephen's *Digest of the Criminal Law* (9th edn, 1950) as follows: 'An attempt to commit a crime is an act done with intent to commit that crime and forming part of a series of acts which would constitute its actual commission, if it were not interrupted.' This is a very vague test as it would appear to encompass all acts of preparation and those which are more than merely preparatory.

In *Jones* [1990] 1 WLR 1057, the Court of Appeal disapproved of the approach to construction of s. 1(1) of the Act which referred to previous conflicting case law. Taylor LJ stated that the correct approach was 'to look first at the natural meaning of the statutory words, not to turn back to earlier case law and seek to fit some previous test to the words of the section'. He cited with approval the judgment of Lord Lane CJ in *Gullefer* [1987] Crim LR 195 (reported also at [1990] 1 WLR 1063) where he stated (at p. 1066):

It seems to us that the words of the Act of 1981 seek to steer a midway course. They do not provide, as they might have done, that the . . . *Eagleton* test is to be followed, or that, as Lord Diplock suggested, the defendant must have reached a point from which it was impossible for him to retreat before the *actus reus* of an attempt is proved. On the other hand, the words give perhaps as clear a guidance as is possible in the circumstances on the point of time at which *Stephen's* 'series of acts' begins. It begins when the merely preparatory acts have come to an end and the defendant embarks upon the crime proper. When that is will depend of course upon the facts in any particular case.

In *Jones* D had been convicted of the attempted murder of F, his former girlfriend's new boyfriend. D bought a gun, shortened the barrel, disguised himself, jumped into the rear seat of F's car as he left his daughter at school, pointed the gun at F and said 'You are not going to like this.' F managed to grab the gun and escape with it from the car. It was not established whether D had his finger on the trigger of the gun when he pointed it at F. The Court of Appeal dismissed D's appeal, Taylor LJ stating (at pp. 1062, 1063):

> Looking at the plain natural meaning of s. 1(1) in the way indicated by the Lord Chief Justice, the question for the judge in the present case was whether there was evidence from which a reasonable jury, properly directed, could conclude that the appellant had done acts which were more than merely preparatory. Clearly his actions in obtaining the gun, in shortening it, in loading it, in putting on his disguise, and in going to the school could only be regarded as preparatory acts. But, in our judgment, once he had got into the car, taken out the loaded gun and pointed it at the victim with the intention of killing him, there was sufficient evidence for the consideration of the jury on the charge of attempted murder. It was a matter for them to decide whether they were sure those acts were more than merely preparatory. In our judgment, therefore, the judge was right to allow the case to go to the jury.

In *Geddes* [1996] Crim LR 894, D's conviction for attempted false imprisonment was quashed. D, equipped with a rucksack in which there was a kitchen knife, rope, and masking tape, had gained access to the boys' lavatory in a school. The Court of Appeal held that while there was no doubting D's intentions, his actions had not advanced sufficiently to merit a finding that he had performed a more than merely preparatory act (see also *Campbell* [1991] Crim LR 268, which was cited with approval). Lord Bingham CJ stated:

> It is, we think, an accurate paraphrase of the statutory test . . . to ask whether the available evidence, if accepted, could show that a defendant has done an act which shows that he has actually tried to commit the offence in question, or whether he has only got ready or put himself in a position or equipped himself to do so.

Professor J. C. Smith in his commentary to *Geddes* observes ([1996] Crim LR at p. 896) that, while D was equipped to perform a kidnapping, there is no offence of going equipped to commit an offence against the person. There is, however, an offence under s. 25 of the Theft Act 1968 of going equipped to commit any burglary or theft which covers conduct which has not advanced beyond the preparatory stages towards commission of a crime. While D need not have performed the last act nor reached the point of no return to be liable for an attempt (see further *AG's Reference (No. 1 of 1992)* [1993] Crim LR 274), the instant case, along with *Jones* and *Campbell*, tends to indicate that everything required to commit the offence must be in place, including the intended victim and that D must have commenced to commit the crime. In *Geddes*, had a child entered the lavatories when D was there and D had approached him, he would then have embarked on the crime proper. In terms of the example given earlier in this section, this suggests that point (7) in that example would have to be reached before the judge would be entitled to leave the case to the jury. If this is so, there may be a need to consider creating an offence similar to s. 25 of the Theft Act 1968 of going equipped to perform a sexual or violent offence against a person.

The facts in *Geddes* might now fall within the offence of trespass with intent to commit a sexual offence contrary to s. 63 of the Sexual Offences Act 2003, provided D's ultimate intent was to commit a sexual offence, he already being a trespasser. This offence would not cover a situation where, although D intended falsely to imprison V, he had no intent to commit a sexual offence. The s. 63 offence would also not cover a situation where, although D has the intent, and is equipped to put that intent into effect, he does not commit a trespass. Of course, if he was arrested attempting to gain access to premises where, if he did so, he would be a trespasser, he could be charged with attempting to commit the s. 63 offence.

While the Court of Appeal's decisions show that a distinction may be drawn between acts which fall within the 'preparation phase' of the intended crime and those which fall within the 'commission phase', it is clear that courts have difficulty in identifying where the line between the two is to be drawn. In *Tosti* [1997] Crim LR 746 Beldam LJ stated that 'there may be actions which are preparatory which are not merely so and which are essentially first steps in the commission of the offence'. The appellants had been convicted of attempted burglary and appealed. Beldam LJ stated:

> The short question for the court today is whether, having carried out a number of merely preparatory acts, that is to say providing themselves with oxyacetylene equipment, having driven to the scene, having concealed the oxyacetylene equipment in a hedge nearby, but having then approached the door of the barn, and bent down to examine how best to go about the job of breaking into the barn, they had committed acts which were preparatory, but not merely so—so that it could be said the acts of preparation amount to acts done in the commission of the offence. Essentially the question is one of degree: how close to, and necessary for, the commission of the offences were the acts which it was proved that they had done?

The Court of Appeal concluded that the judge's decision to leave the case to the jury had been correct. In the instant case the activity of the appellants could be characterised as 'casing the joint'—they had not yet begun to try to force an entry to the premises. If the quashing of the conviction in *Campbell* for attempted robbery was right (where the appellant was arrested outside the door of a post office which he intended to rob in possession of an imitation firearm and a threatening note), it is difficult to see how the instant decision can be correct.

It is doubtful whether the distinction sought to be drawn by the Court of Appeal in *Qadir and Khan*, unreported, 24 July 1997, Case No. 9602311X4, will produce any greater clarity. In this case the appellants had been convicted of being knowingly concerned in the attempted fraudulent evasion of the prohibition on exportation of a controlled drug. Potter LJ emphasised that a judge when ruling whether something was capable of constituting a more than merely preparatory act, should keep in mind the nature of the crime attempted, distinguishing between offences where the focus is upon an act and those where it is upon a transaction. He was of the view that for a crime such as killing or wounding the focus is upon an act at a particular time and acts substantially anterior to the moment of completion of the crime would be merely preparatory. By contrast for an offence of deception or evasion which involves a stratagem carried out over a period of time, as the *actus reus* may take place over an extended period of time, 'the moment of embarkation upon it may be quite remote in time from the point of its anticipated successful outcome'. But as a poisoner may administer poison over a protracted period and a deceiver may practise a deception on the spur of the moment, everything will depend on the individual case!

The only conclusion one can draw from the cases discussed in this section is, perhaps, that courts are becoming more prepared to look further back in time to define the point when mere preparation ceases and commission of the offence begins. But in cases where the act which D has done might be more than merely preparatory to one of several offences the problem which the prosecution will face is proving what his intent was. *Geddes* was considered in *Ferriter* [2012] EWCA Crim 2211.

> D was the last remaining customer in a pub where V was the barmaid. D went behind the bar, wrestled V to the floor and got on top of her and tried repeatedly to pull her trousers down before she broke free. D pleaded guilty to two counts of theft (having stolen money and alcohol after V escaped), but pleaded not guilty to counts of attempted rape or, in the alternative, attempted assault. D was convicted of attempted rape and appealed. On appeal this conviction was quashed and a conviction for sexual assault substituted as the evidence did not support anything more than a conviction for sexual assault.

This was not a case of mere preparation; the jury had ample material on which to conclude that the intention was sexual molestation but, in the absence of an attempt to penetrate V or a confession by D, there was no evidence which could be used to prove intent to commit rape.

One final point to note in respect of the *actus reus* of attempt is that the fact that D is interrupted or desists prior to doing the last act necessary to commit the substantive offence he intended to commit does not prevent his conviction for attempt if he has performed a more than merely preparatory act. Thus there is no defence of withdrawal if the point has been reached where a more than merely preparatory act has been performed.

8.4.4 Impossibility

If D makes a mistake as to the law, believing that it prohibits what he intends to do, he will not be guilty of attempt if he endeavours to carry out his intention. What he is attempting to do is not a crime and the offence of attempt applies only to attempts to commit indictable offences.

 Example

> D comes from a country where adultery is a crime and he believes it is also a crime in England. He attempts to have consensual intercourse with E, a married woman, but fails. Had he succeeded he would have committed no offence; the fact that he fails does not render him liable for attempt as what he attempted to do is not a crime.

Key Point

There are three situations, however, where D may fail to commit an offence because it is impossible to commit it in the circumstances (cf. **8.3.3.5**). For example:

(1) D attempts to steal from V's pocket which, unknown to him, is empty (physical impossibility).

(2) D attempts to break into a safe to steal the contents using a jemmy which, unknown to him, is incapable of effecting his purpose (impossibility arising from inadequacy of means).

(3) D attempts to handle stolen goods but, unknown to him, the goods are not stolen (legal impossibility as the goods lack a quality essential for the commission of the offence).

At common law D would have been convicted of attempt only in the second situation (see *Haughton* v *Smith* [1975] AC 476) as it was considered that in this situation the crime was not really impossible as it could have been committed if D had used different or more adequate means. Thus, in *White* [1910] 2 KB 124, D was convicted of attempted murder where he tried to kill his mother using an insufficient dose of poison. Had he given her sugar, mistaking it for poison, he would not have been convicted as this would have been a case of physical impossibility. The distinctions which the common law made were considered refined and artificial. The Law Commission recommended that the law should be changed (Law Com No. 102, para. 2.96) placing the emphasis on the intention of D provided there was proof of a more than merely preparatory act. This recommendation was put into effect by s. 1(2) and (3) of the Criminal Attempts Act 1981 which provide:

> (2) A person may be guilty of attempting to commit an offence to which this section applies even though the facts are such that the commission of the offence is impossible.
>
> (3) In any case where—
>
>   (a) apart from this subsection a person's intention would not be regarded as having amounted to an intent to commit an offence: but
>
>   (b) if the facts of the case had been as he believed them to be, his intention would be so regarded,
>
> then, for the purposes of subsection (1) above, he shall be regarded as having had an intent to commit that offence.

The purport of s. 1(2) is to render a person liable to conviction regardless of the category of impossibility which prevented commission of the intended substantive offence. Section 1(3) is, essentially, superfluous but it was included as a precaution to deal with the particular situation of legal impossibility. If D intended to handle a particular item, believing it to be stolen, when, in fact, it was not, he might claim that, as he intended to handle only that particular item, he did not intend to handle stolen goods but intended to handle a 'non-stolen item'. Simply to frame the argument exposes its ludicrous nature as D's subjective state of mind was to handle goods he believed to be stolen—that is, an intention to handle stolen goods. The fact that the objective status of the goods was that they were not stolen does not, in any way, impinge upon D's state of mind, just as the fact that a pocket is empty does not alter D's intention to steal from that pocket; if he were to claim that he intended to take nothing as there was nothing to take, he would be laughed out of court. But, to be doubly sure, Parliament enacted s. 1(3) which simply states that if the facts had been as he believed them to be (if the video had been stolen) he shall be regarded as having an intent to commit that offence (handling stolen goods).

But, be prepared for two surprises. In *Anderton* v *Ryan* [1985] AC 560, the House of Lords held that the Act had not affected cases of legal impossibility so that the appellant's conviction for attempting to handle stolen goods was quashed as the item she sought to handle was not stolen, or, as their Lordships put it, her acts **were 'objectively innocent'**. The next surprise is that just over a year later the House of Lords in *Shivpuri* [1987] AC 1 overruled this decision, Lord Bridge declaring (at pp. 21, 22) that:

> [T]he concept of 'objective innocence' is incapable of sensible application in relation to the law of criminal attempts. The reason for this is that any attempt to commit an offence which involves 'an act which is more than merely preparatory to the commission of the offence' but which for any reason fails, so that in the event no offence is committed, must *ex hypothesi*, from the point of view of the criminal law, be 'objectively innocent'. What turns what would otherwise, from the point of view of the criminal law, be an innocent act into a crime is the intent of the actor to commit an offence . . . . A puts his hand into B's pocket. Whether or not there is anything in the pocket capable of being stolen, if A intends to steal his act is a criminal attempt; if he does not so intend his act is innocent . . . . These considerations lead me to the conclusion that the distinction sought to be drawn in *Anderton* v *Ryan* between innocent and guilty acts considered 'objectively' and independently of the state of mind of the actor cannot be sensibly maintained.

As a result, their Lordships dismissed the appellant's appeal from a conviction for attempting to be knowingly concerned in dealing with prohibited drugs. Shivpuri was arrested in possession of a suitcase which he believed contained either heroin or cannabis. He admitted that he intended to receive the drugs and deal in them. In fact the case contained snuff which was not a prohibited drug. Shivpuri had the intention to commit the offence and he had done acts which were more than merely preparatory to the commission of the *intended* offence.

8.5 Jurisdiction

The general rule relating to territorial jurisdiction is that English courts are unable to try persons for offences committed outside England and Wales even if committed by a British citizen (see *Harden* [1963] 1 QB 8). A limited exception to this rule is that a British citizen who commits murder or bigamy abroad may be tried in England and Wales. The jurisdiction of English courts has, however, been extended through legislation and case law. As originally enacted, s. 1(4) of the Criminal Law Act 1977 gave the courts in England and Wales jurisdiction to try conspiracies where the court would have had jurisdiction to try the parties for the substantive offence if they had committed it in accordance with their intentions. Thus if A and B, being British citizens, agree in England to murder V in France, they could be tried in England for conspiracy to murder. If, by contrast, A and B had agreed merely to wound V in France they could not be tried for conspiracy as the English courts have no jurisdiction to try the substantive offence of wounding if committed in France.

Jurisdiction to try conspirators where their agreement is entered into in England and Wales to commit the substantive offence abroad has been extended by legislation. The original extension was introduced by the Sexual Offences (Conspiracy and Incitement) Act 1996 (SO(CAI)A) which created criminal offences to deal with the problem of 'sex tourism' where sexual activity is engaged in abroad with children under the age of 16. The SO(CAI)A adapted the existing offences of conspiracy and incitement to cover conspiracy to commit, or incitement to commit, sexual offences against children where those offences are committed outside the jurisdiction. (References to incitement are now to be treated as references to the offences under ss 44–46 of the Serious Crime Act 2007 (s. 63(1) of the SCA).) The listed offences, which are confined to instances where the victim is under the age of 16, are those contrary to ss 1–12, 14, and 15–26 of the Sexual Offences Act 2003. The agreement or assistance or encouragement to commit such an offence is punishable in England and Wales provided the conduct also amounts to a crime in the country where it was to be committed. The provisions of the SO(CAI)A relating to conspiracy have been repealed by the Criminal Justice (Terrorism and Conspiracy) Act 1998 (CJ(TAC)A) but the provisions relating to encouraging or assisting an offence remain in force. In Part II of the Sex Offenders Act 1997, Parliament extended jurisdiction to cover a range of substantive sexual offences where they were committed against children under 16 outside the jurisdiction by a British citizen or person resident in the United Kingdom. The 1997 Act has been repealed and replaced by s. 72 of the Sexual Offences Act 2003 (see **11.6.2.7**).

The CJ(TAC)A was enacted in the aftermath of the Omagh bombing on 25 August 1998. While the primary focus of the Act was terrorist groups which might undermine the peace process in Northern Ireland, the opportunity was also taken to deal with a long-standing problem of terrorist groups within the United Kingdom who plotted terrorist activities here which were to be carried out abroad. The provisions in the SO(CAI)A relating to conspiracy have effectively been reworked so as to cover all offences. Section 5(1) of the CJ(TAC)A inserts a new s. 1A into the Criminal Law Act 1977 which makes it an offence to conspire within England and Wales to commit an offence outside the United Kingdom. This greatly expands the jurisdiction of English courts as an agreement to commit any offence is covered, not just agreements to commit the sexual offences specified in SO(CAI)A. There are four conditions which must be satisfied. First, that in pursuit of the agreed course of conduct an act or some other event must be intended to take place in a country or territory outside England and Wales (s. 1A(2) as amended by s. 72 of the Coroners and Justice Act 2009). Secondly, that the act or event would constitute an offence in the other country or territory (s. 1A(3)). Thirdly, the agreement to act in that way would be an offence in England and Wales if the act or event were to take place there (s. 1A(4)). Thus the act or event the parties agree to commit or cause to take place must amount to an offence in both England and Wales and the foreign country or territory. Fourthly, there must be some activity by a party to the agreement (or his agent) in England and Wales in relation to the agreement before its formation, or in pursuance of the agreement, or the party became a party to the agreement in England and Wales. Thus, for example, D would be liable to conviction where he agrees with E in England to steal property in France, or where in pursuit of an agreement between himself and E to steal property in France (entered into elsewhere) he comes to England to acquire equipment needed to carry out the theft.

The Criminal Law Act 1977 originally made no provision for the case of an agreement abroad to commit an offence in England. In *DPP* v *Doot* [1973] AC 807, the House of Lords held that such a conspiracy could be prosecuted in England if the parties acted in England in concert and in pursuance of the agreement. Lord Wilberforce was prepared to hold that acts by one conspirator in England should be sufficient to establish liability on the part of all the parties to the agreement. In *Somchai Liangsiriprasert* v *United States* [1990] AC 607, the Privy Council held that in Hong Kong, where the law on conspiracy was the same as the common law in England, an agreement abroad to commit an offence within the jurisdiction was triable as conspiracy even though no overt acts had been performed within the jurisdiction. Lord Griffiths stated (at p. 620):

> But why should an overt act be necessary to found jurisdiction? In the case of conspiracy in England the crime is complete once the agreement is made and no further overt act need be proved as an ingredient of the crime. The only purpose of looking for an overt act in England in the case of a conspiracy entered into abroad can be to establish the link between the conspiracy and England or possibly to show the conspiracy is continuing. But if this can be established by other evidence . . . it defeats the preventative purpose of the crime of conspiracy to have to wait until some overt act is performed in pursuance of the conspiracy . . . . Crime is now established on an international scale and the common law must face this new reality. Their Lordships can find nothing in precedent, comity or good sense that should inhibit the common law from regarding as justiciable in England inchoate crimes committed abroad which are intended to result in the commission of criminal offences in England.

In *Sansom* (1991) 92 Cr App R 115, the Court of Appeal held that the principle enunciated in *Somchai* applied to statutory conspiracies (see also *Naini* [1999] 2 Cr App R 398).

Further provision has been made for the expansion of the territorial jurisdiction of English courts as a response to the growing concern over international crime involving fraud and dishonesty. Part 1 of the Criminal Justice Act 1993 provides courts in England and Wales with jurisdiction over various dishonesty offences and associated inchoate offences related thereto where the offence has an international aspect to it. The jurisdictional provisions apply to 'Group A' and 'Group B' offences which are defined in s. 1. Group A offences include, inter alia, theft, various offences under the Fraud Act 2006 (including fraud and obtaining services dishonestly), blackmail, handling stolen goods, and a range of offences under the Forgery and Counterfeiting Act 1981. Group B offences are encouraging or assisting offences under ss 44–46 of the SCA, conspiracy or attempt to commit a Group A offence, or conspiracy to defraud.

A court in England and Wales has jurisdiction to try a person for a Group A offence where any 'relevant event' occurs in England and Wales. A 'relevant event' is 'any act or omission or other event (including any result of one or more acts or omissions) proof of which is required for conviction of the offence' (s. 2(1)). Thus, for example, if D, in England, by a false representation persuades V to give him property in France, and V does so, D would be guilty of fraud, as a relevant event, the false representation, took place in England (see further s. 4).

By s. 3(2) an accused may be convicted of conspiracy to commit a Group A offence, or conspiracy to defraud, whether or not (a) he became a party to the conspiracy in England and Wales or (b) any act or omission or other event in relation to the conspiracy occurred in England and Wales. What is required is that the substantive Group A offence, if committed, would have involved a 'relevant event' in England and Wales or, in the case of conspiracy to defraud, that the fraud would have been effected in England and Wales. Similarly, on a charge of attempt to commit a Group A offence, D may be guilty of the offence whether or not (a) the attempt was made in England and Wales or (b) it had an effect in England and Wales. For example, D and E in France agree to seek to obtain property from V in England by false representation. If the agreement were to be carried out in accordance with their intentions, a relevant event would take place in England. If D posts the letter containing the false representation in France, an attempt will have occurred even though the letter never arrives at its destination.

Section 5(3) of the 1993 Act gives the courts jurisdiction over conspiracies to defraud where the fraud will take place abroad, provided either (a) a party to the conspiracy (or his agent) did anything in England and Wales in relation to it before its formation, or (b) a party to it became a party in England and Wales (by joining it either in person or through an agent), or (c) a party to it (or his agent) did or omitted anything in England and Wales in pursuance of it. Section 5(2) amends the Criminal Attempts Act 1981 to cover acts done in England and Wales which are more than merely preparatory to the commission of a Group A offence but the offence, if completed, would have occurred in a foreign jurisdiction. Section 5(4) covers encouraging or assisting the commission of Group A offences where the offence encouraged, if committed, would occur in a foreign jurisdiction. In all these cases under s. 5 a person may be convicted only if (1) in the case of conspiracy to defraud 'the agreed course of conduct would at some stage involve (a) an act or omission by one or more of the parties, or (b) the happening of some other event, constituting an offence' in the foreign jurisdiction (see s. 6(1)), or (2) in the case of attempt or encouragement or assistance 'what he had in view would involve the commission of an offence under the law in force where the whole or any part of it was intended to take place' (see s. 6(2)).

 The law in context

Prevention, terrorist offences, and the rule of law

In the wake of terrorist attacks, including the bombings in London on 7 July 2005, the Government has expanded the criminal law to include terrorist-related preparatory conduct. These controversial offences criminalise conduct before it reaches the stage of an attempt or conspiracy and go beyond the standard offences of encouraging or assisting. The Terrorism Act 2006 contains examples of what Ashworth and Zedner, call 'pre-inchoate, facilitative and associative offences' (A. Ashworth and L. Zedner, *Preventive Justice* (2014), p. 180). Under s. 1,

→

→

it is an offence to publish a statement that is likely to be understood as a direct or indirect encouragement or inducement to the commission, preparation, or instigation of acts of terrorism. Section 2 criminalises distribution or circulation of a 'terrorist publication', if the person who distributes or circulates the material is reckless as to whether it provides assistance in the commission of preparation of acts of terrorism. Section 5 makes it an offence for a person 'with the intention of committing acts of terrorism or assisting another to commit such acts' to 'engage in any conduct in preparation for giving effect to his intention'.

There are several justifications for this type of offence, the most obvious of which is crime prevention. The law would 'speak with a strange moral voice' if it only punished terrorists who actually triggered a bomb or fired a gun (R. A. Duff, 'Perversions and Subversions of Criminal Law' in R. A. Duff et al. (eds), *The Boundaries of Criminal Law* (2010), pp. 88–112, 91). The police need powers to intervene early to disrupt would-be terrorists and to curtail the actions of those who support or encourage them. Another justification is retribution. A person's conduct is arguably morally wrong, blameworthy, and deserving of punishment when it involves taking any steps, however small, towards encouraging or inducing others to commit terrorist acts or be involved in any preparatory behaviour.

Is this widening of the 'net' of criminal liability compatible with the rule of law? Arguably, the offences threaten fundamental principles of criminal law: legality, precision, clarity, and maximum certainty. The breadth of the offences is compounded by the far-reaching definition of 'terrorism' in s. 1 of the Terrorism Act 2000 (the Supreme Court in *Gul (Mohammed)* [2013] UKSC 64 expressed concern about the broad definition of 'terrorism'). The pre-inchoate offences can include neutral or normal acts done with a particular intent and thus are in danger of criminalising relatively normal and harmless conduct. They might lead to intrusive enforcement mechanisms intruding into areas of individual liberty, leading to 'the close surveillance of everyday life' (Ashworth and Zedner, p. 109). For example, in 2008 a university student was detained for several days on suspicion of the commission, preparation, or instigation of acts of terrorism because he had downloaded the Al-Qaida training manual from the U.S. Justice Department website in order to research his choice of thesis (D. Anderson, 'Shielding the Compass: How to Fight Terrorism without Defeating the Law' (2013) EHRLR 233–46, 240). In the words of the Independent Reviewer of Terrorism Legislation, the shadow of the precursor offences 'loom[s] over all manner of previously innocent interactions. The effects can, at worst, be horrifying for individuals and demoralising to communities' (Anderson, p. 240). As Ashworth and Zedner note, surveillance and early intervention is likely to be based on stereotypes and to be characterised by discriminatory enforcement (p. 109).

One counter-argument to these concerns is that the proper exercise of prosecutorial discretion acts as a safeguard. However, the Supreme Court in *Gul (Mohammed)* (at para. 36) expressed concern that that argument risks undermining the rule of law. Reliance on prosecutors to avoid injustice through selective prosecution effectively delegates to appointees of the executive (CPS lawyers) the decision whether an activity should be treated as criminal for the purposes of prosecution. Furthermore, such reliance leaves citizens unclear as to whether or not their actions or projected actions are liable to be treated by the prosecuting authorities as criminal, with all the consequences that follow conviction for terrorist-related offences, including severe punishment and stigmatisation.

The Terrorism Acts also grant substantial powers to the police. Under s. 43 police have extended powers to stop and search individuals and under s. 47A of the 2000 Act the police are empowered to stop and search persons in order to prevent acts of terrorism, without reasonable suspicion of their involvement in terrorism, in a specific area for a defined period where the police reasonably suspect an act of terrorism will take place. Under s. 41 and sch. 8 of the 2000 Act, a constable can arrest without a warrant a person

→

→

whom he 'reasonably suspects to be a terrorist' and detain suspects before charge for up to 14 days. Extended powers of this nature and extent represent potentially serious infringements of liberty and have led to numerous charges of incompatibility with the European Convention on Human Rights (e.g. *Gillan* v *United Kingdom* (2010) 50 EHRR 45). The special police powers available under the Terrorism Acts have even been used to stop and question innocent trainspotters (*Daily Telegraph*, 'Trainspotters Being Stopped under Anti-terror Laws', 5 January 2009, http://www.telegraph.co.uk/news/uknews/road-and-rail-transport/4123672/Trainspotters-being-stopped-under-anti-terror-powers.html). The aim of anti-terrorism legislation may be to keep us safe from harm, but it is arguable that the law's legitimate preventative aims have been extended too far and become so disproportionate, excessively broad, and uncertain that our legal system has taken a significant step towards an Orwellian or Kafkaesque police state.

 Key Points

ENCOURAGING OR ASSISTING OFFENCES

– The Serious Crime Act 2007 introduced offences of intentionally encouraging or assisting an offence (s. 44), encouraging or assisting an offence believing it will be committed (s. 45), and encouraging or assisting offences believing one or more will be committed (s. 46).

– Section 50 provides that for each of those offences there is a defence of acting reasonably.

CONSPIRACY

– Section 1 of the Criminal Law Act 1977 defines conspiracy.

– The *actus reus* is agreement by two or more persons that a course of conduct shall be pursued which (if carried out in accordance with their intentions) either:

  – Will necessarily amount to or involve the commission of an offence or offences by one or more parties to the agreement; or

  – Would do so but for the fact that commission of the offence or offences is impossible.

– The *mens rea* is intention that the course of conduct be pursued and intention or knowledge that a fact or circumstance necessary for the commission of the offence shall or will exist at the time when the conduct constituting the offence is to take place.

– There are two common law conspiracies that remain: conspiracy to defraud and conspiracy to corrupt public morals or outrage public decency. A conspiracy to defraud is an agreement to practise a fraud on somebody (*Wai Yu-tsang* (1991)). The *mens rea* involves an intention to defraud and dishonesty.

ATTEMPT

– The law on criminal attempts is set out in s. 1 of the Criminal Attempts Act 1981.

– The *actus reus* is doing an act which is more than merely preparatory to the commission of the intended offence. That is a question of fact for the jury.

– The *mens rea* is intent to commit the offence and knowing or being reckless as to (where recklessness suffices) any material circumstance.

– A person may be guilty of attempting to commit an offence even though the facts are such that the commission of the offence is impossible.

FURTHER READING

D. Bruneau and A. Taylor, 'In Defence of *Pace and Rogers*' [2015] 8 Arch Rev 6.

I. Dennis, 'The Rationale of Criminal Conspiracy' (1977) 93 LQR 39.

I. Dennis, 'The Elements of Attempt' [1980] Crim LR 758.

M. Dyson, 'Scrapping *Khan*?' [2014] Crim LR 445.

P. Mirfield, 'Intention and Criminal Attempts' [2015] Crim LR 142.

A.P. Simester, 'The *Mens Rea* of Criminal Attempts' (2015) 131 LQR 169.

J. C. Smith, 'Conspiracy to Defraud: Some Comments on the Law Commission Report' [1995] Crim LR 209.

K. J. M. Smith, 'Proximity in Attempt: Lord Lane's Midway Course' [1991] Crim LR 576.

F. Stark, 'The *Mens Rea* of a Criminal Attempt' (2014) 3 Arch Rev 7.

G. R. Sullivan, 'Inchoate Liability for Assisting and Encouraging Crime—the Law Commission Report' [2006] Crim LR 1047.

G. Virgo, 'Encouraging or Assisting More Than One Offence' (2012) 2 Arch Rev 6.

M. Wasik, 'Abandoning Criminal Intent' [1980] Crim LR 785.

G. Williams, 'The Lords and Impossible Attempts, or *Quis Custodiet Ipsos Custodes*' (1986) 45 CLJ 33.

9

....

Homicide

9.1 **Introduction**

There are several offences of unlawful homicide: murder, manslaughter, infanticide, and causing death by dangerous driving. There are other offences closely approximating to homicide such as child destruction and abortion. The common element to homicide offences, however, is the *actus reus* which is set out below.

> ### Key Point
>
> The *actus reus* of all homicide offences involves D:
>
> - unlawfully
> - causing death
> - of a human being
> - under the Queen's Peace.

9.1.1 *Actus reus*

Coke described the *actus reus* of homicide as **'Unlawfully killing a reasonable person who is in being and under the King's Peace, the death following within a year and a day'** (Coke, 3 Inst 47). A killing is unlawful where it is not justified (see *Williams* (1984) 78 Cr App R 276; *Beckford* v *R* [1988] AC 130, **3.6.1.1.2**). For example, a killing will not be unlawful if the person who causes death acted in self-defence by using reasonable force.

To be the victim of homicide a person must be 'in being'. A baby still in the womb cannot be the victim of homicide. It is important therefore to determine when a child being born becomes an independent 'person in being'. The problem is not a major one as the last reported case dealing with the matter was *Handley* (1874) 13 Cox CC 79. It appears that the child must be wholly outside the mother (*Poulton* (1832) 5 C & P 329) and be alive having an existence independent of the mother (*Enoch* (1833) 5 C & P 539). It is not necessary for the umbilical cord to have been severed. However, what constitutes an independent existence is problematical. Some cases suggested that the child must have breathed and others added the requirement of having an independent circulation. Medical science now establishes that foetuses have an independent circulation within a couple of months of conception. A further problem is that a child may be born alive but not breathe for several minutes. In *Brain* (1834) 6 C & P 349, Park J stated that breathing was not essential if the child was born alive. Where a child has been poisoned or injured while in the womb, is born alive, but dies thereafter from the poison or injury, this may amount to murder or manslaughter depending on the state of mind of the person who administered the poison or inflicted the injury (see *West* (1848) 2 Car & Kir 784; *Senior* (1832) 1 Mood CC 346). In *AG's Reference (No. 3 of 1994)* [1997] 3 WLR 421, the House of Lords held that for a conviction for murder D must intend for his act to injure or kill the child that the foetus would become. In the absence of such an intention a conviction for unlawful act manslaughter is possible. If his intention relates solely to the mother and the foetus is born alive but dies from injuries sustained in the womb, the doctrine of transferred malice is not applicable (see **3.6.2.3**).

If a person is dead he cannot be the victim of homicide. But what if V's heart has stopped and while a doctor is seeking to resuscitate him D shoots V through the head; can D be convicted of homicide? If the prosecution could not establish that V was alive D could be convicted of attempted murder. In *Malcherek and Steel* [1981] 1 WLR 690, the Court of Appeal adverted to the test of 'brain death'; although they did not have to decide whether this was the legal definition of death they accepted that it was the test which the medical profession used. In *Airedale NHS Trust* v *Bland* there are dicta to the effect that brain-stem death is the legal test of death. If a person is 'brain dead' at the time of D's act, even though being artificially kept alive by mechanical means (perhaps so that vital organs may be used for transplant purposes), it is submitted that he cannot be the victim of homicide.

The phrase **'the King's Peace'** is a strange one as it appears that everyone in the world is under the King's or Queen's Peace, except an enemy alien who is killed in the course of war. If an enemy alien is a prisoner of war he is under the Queen's Peace. Murder and manslaughter are exceptional in that an English court may try a British citizen for these offences if committed in any country (see s. 9 of the Offences Against the Person Act 1861 and s. 3 of the British Nationality Act 1948). If the offence takes place on a British ship or aircraft it can be tried here whether the perpetrator is a British subject or an alien, but English courts have no jurisdiction if the offence occurs on a foreign ship outside territorial waters.

In *Adebolajo* [2014] EWCA Crim 2779, D, who had been convicted of the murder of Fusilier Lee Rigby having attacked him on the streets of Woolwich and attempted to decapitate him, renewed his application for leave to appeal contending that the trial judge was in error in rejecting his submission that he had not killed under 'the Queen's Peace'. He honestly believed he was a soldier fighting a war against the Queen and her forces. The trial judge ruled that the 'Queen's Peace' requirement related to the victim of the offence not the perpetrator and his beliefs. On the renewed application for leave to appeal, Lord Thomas CJ, refusing leave to appeal, stated (at para. 33):

The law is now clear. An offender can generally be tried for murder wherever committed if he is a British subject, or, if not a British subject, the murder was committed within England and Wales. The reference to 'the Queen's peace', . . . went essentially to jurisdiction. Although the Queen's Peace may play some part still in the elements that have to be proved for murder as regards the status of the victim . . ., it can only go to the status of the victim; it has nothing whatsoever to do with the status of the killer. The argument was completely hopeless.

For homicides where the act (or omission) causing death was committed after 17 June 1996, **the rule that death must occur within a year and a day of such act or omission has been abolished**. The rule had become increasingly anachronistic as, with the development of medical knowledge, it is now possible to determine the cause of a person's death even though it may occur a long time after the original injury was inflicted by the defendant. In addition the use of life-support machines in hospitals has meant that patients who might otherwise have died relatively quickly may be kept alive for a considerable length of time in the hope of recovery. In such a case, however, a prosecution for homicide would be precluded if death occurred more than a year and a day after the act which caused it. The Criminal Law Revision Committee's Fourteenth Report on Offences Against the Person (Cmnd 7844, 1980) suggested that 'it would be wrong for a person to remain almost indefinitely at risk for prosecution for murder. A line has to be drawn somewhere and in our opinion the present law operates satisfactorily' (section 39). In *The Year and a Day Rule in Homicide* (Consultation Paper No. 136) the Law Commission reviewed the rule; it recommended its abolition in its Report, *Legislating the Criminal Code: The Year and a Day Rule in Homicide* (Consultation Paper No. 230). Parliament acted promptly in response and passed the Law Reform (Year and a Day Rule) Act 1996. To safeguard against oppressive prosecutions the Attorney General must consent to any prosecution brought more than three years after the original act that caused death or after the perpetrator has already been convicted of an offence committed in circumstances alleged to be connected with the death (see s. 2). In the latter circumstance the offence of which D has previously been convicted will most likely be a non-fatal offence against the person such as wounding or inflicting grievous bodily harm (GBH) but it need not be such; the cause of the deceased's death may have arisen from, for example, the commission of a burglary, criminal damage, or dangerous driving.

9.2 **Murder**

9.2.1 **Definition**

Murder is unlawful homicide committed with 'malice aforethought'.

Actus reus	Mens rea
<ul><li>unlawfully</li><li>causing death</li><li>of a human being</li><li>under the Queen's Peace</li></ul>	With malice aforethought (i.e. intention to kill or cause grievous bodily harm).

The penalty for murder is mandatory life imprisonment (s. 1, Murder (Abolition of Death Penalty) Act 1965). Under the Criminal Justice Act 2003, the trial judge must set a minimum period that the murderer must serve before he can be considered for release by the Parole Board. He must have regard to sch. 21 of the Act, which sets out aggravating and mitigating factors relevant to deciding what that minimum period should be. Once the offender has served the minimum period of imprisonment, the Parole Board will consider whether it is necessary for the protection of the public that the offender continue to be imprisoned. If the Parole Board orders the offender's release, he will be released on licence, which means he can be recalled to prison if he breaches the terms of that licence. For murderers, the licence remains in place for the rest of their lives.

Coke described the *mens rea* required to convict a person for murder as **'malice aforethought'**. If malice aforethought is lacking the unlawful homicide will be manslaughter. It should be noted, however, that 'malice aforethought' is a technical term whose meaning implies neither ill-will nor premeditation. Thus a person who kills out of merciful or compassionate motives to alleviate suffering may, nevertheless, be guilty of murder, just as a person who kills in the 'heat of the moment' without prior planning may be guilty of murder.

> In *Inglis* [2010] EWCA Crim 2637, D killed her son by a heroin injection as he lay in a hospital bed seriously ill. She regarded the act as a mercy killing but the Court of Appeal dismissed her appeal reiterating the position that all 'mercy killings' are unlawful and any change in the law is a matter for Parliament, Lord Judge CJ stating (at para. 37):

> > [W]e must underline that the law of murder does not distinguish between murder committed for malevolent reasons and murder motivated by familial love. Subject to well established partial defences, like provocation or diminished responsibility, mercy killing is murder.

This was not a case of voluntary euthanasia as there was no evidence that the victim requested an assisted suicide; but even if he had, this would also have amounted to unlawful homicide (see also *R (Nicklinson)* v *Ministry of Justice* [2012] EWHC 2381 (Admin)).

It is important, therefore, to determine the meaning of 'malice aforethought'. Prior to 1957 an accused could be convicted of murder where (1) he intended to kill ('express malice'), or (2) he intended to cause GBH ('implied malice'), or (3) he killed in the furtherance of a felony (e.g. rape or robbery) or when resisting or preventing a lawful arrest, even though there was no intent to kill or to cause grievous bodily harm ('constructive malice'). The courts had not been consistent in their use of the terms 'express' or 'implied' malice. Precise definition of 'implied malice' was not necessary as this appeared to overlap with 'constructive malice' as causing GBH was a felony. In 1957 the Homicide Act abolished 'constructive malice'. Section 1 provides:

> (1) Where a person kills another in the course or furtherance of some other offence, the killing shall not amount to murder unless done with the same malice aforethought (express or implied) as is required for a killing to amount to murder when not done in the course or furtherance of another offence.

(2) For the purposes of the foregoing subsection, a killing done in the course or for the purpose of resisting an officer of justice, or of resisting or avoiding or preventing a lawful arrest, or of effecting or assisting an escape or rescue from legal custody, shall be treated as a killing in the course or furtherance of an offence.

The question arose whether, by abolishing 'constructive malice', the Act had abolished liability where D intended to cause GBH but did not intend to kill. As s. 1(1) reserved liability where an accused had 'express malice' or 'implied malice', did 'implied malice' mean something other than an intention to cause GBH? In *Vickers* [1957] 2 QB 664, the Court of Criminal Appeal held that **'implied malice' meant an intention to cause grievous bodily harm**. In *Hyam* [1975] AC 55, the House of Lords failed to arrive at a decision on this issue. In *Cunningham* [1982] AC 566, the House finally decided that an intention to cause GBH was 'implied malice' and was something separate from 'constructive malice'. **The *mens rea* of murder, therefore, is an intention to kill or an intention to cause grievous bodily harm** (as to the meaning of intention see 3.2). In most cases, the trial should not elaborate on the meaning of 'intention' and leave it to the jury's good sense to decide whether D acted with the necessary intent (Moloney [1985] AC 905). In *Woollin* [1999] 1 AC 82, the House of Lords held that in the rare cases where the simple direction is not enough, the jury should be directed that they are not entitled to find the necessary intention, unless they feel sure that death or serious bodily harm was a **virtual certainty** (barring some unforeseen intervention) as a result of the defendant's actions and that the defendant appreciated that such was the case.

'Grievous bodily harm' is a phrase which is to be given its natural meaning (*DPP* v *Smith* [1961] AC 290). In *Smith*, Viscount Kilmuir stated that 'bodily harm' requires no explanation and **'grievous' means 'really serious'**, although a direction to a jury which omitted the word 'really' would not be a misdirection (*Saunders* [1985] Crim LR 230). Thus a person may be convicted of murder even though he did not intend to kill nor even foresee death as a possibility.

 Example

D, a member of a terrorist group, performs a 'knee-capping' on V, a member who has broken the rules of the group. D has performed many such 'knee-cappings' in the past and no victim has ever died and he foresees no risk of V dying. V, however, fears hospitals and does not receive medical treatment and dies from septicaemia caused by the wound. As D intended to cause grievous bodily harm he would be convicted of murder.

In *Rahman* [2008] UKHL 45, Lord Bingham of Cornhill explained the rationale behind the principle of constructive malice (at para. 25):

The rationale of that principle plainly is that if a person unlawfully assaults another with intent to cause him really serious injury, and death results, he should be held criminally responsible for that fatality, even though he did not intend it. If he had not embarked on a course of deliberate violence, the fatality would not have occurred. This rationale may lack logical purity, but it is underpinned by a quality of earthy realism.

9.2.2 **Reform**

A person can thus be guilty of murder when they have unlawfully caused death but did not intend to cause death or even foresee that death might occur. In *AG's Reference (No. 3 of 1994)* [1997] 3 WLR 421, Lord Mustill described 'implied malice' as a 'conspicuous anomaly'. In *Powell (Anthony)* [1999] AC 1 (see **7.1.4.4.1**), Lord Steyn said of the rule (at p. 15) that it turned 'murder into a constructive crime . . . [resulting] in defendants being classified as murderers who are not in truth murderers . . . . It results in the imposition of mandatory life sentences when neither justice nor the needs of society require the classification of the case as murder and the imposition of the mandatory life sentence.' He went on to recommend that 'a killing should be classified as murder if there is an intention to kill or an intention to cause really serious harm coupled with awareness of the risk of death'. Their Lordships accepted, however, that the problem was one which only Parliament could resolve. This issue is one that pervades English criminal law: should a person be guilty of an offence when his *mens rea* does not correspond to the *actus reus*? Those who favour a subjectivist approach to criminal liability tend to argue that he should not, as otherwise he is being punished for an outcome that he did not necessarily foresee and which no other person might have foreseen. Objectivists tend to argue that there is a compelling case for liability: as Lord Bingham explained, the person who intends to cause really serious harm has crossed a moral threshold into the realm of criminality and can properly be held liable for the consequences.

In its Draft Criminal Code (Law Com No. 177), the Law Commission recommended a change in the law. Clause 54 provides:

> (1) A person is guilty of murder if he causes the death of another—
>   (a) intending to cause death; or
>   (b) intending to cause serious personal harm and being aware that he may cause death . . .

The *Report of the Select Committee of the House of Lords on Murder and Life Imprisonment* (HL Paper 78–1, 1989) supported this recommendation, stating (at para. 68):

> A person is not generally liable to conviction for a serious crime where the prohibited result was not only unintended but also unforeseen. This seems to the Committee to be a good rule of moral responsibility which should certainly apply to the most serious crime of all, murder. While the law continues to have two categories of homicide, unforeseen but unlawful killings are properly left to the law of manslaughter.

In 2005 the Home Office announced a review of the law of murder by the Law Commission. The review, however, was to some extent undermined from the outset as the Home Office reaffirmed their commitment to the mandatory life sentence for murder. The Law Commission published a Consultation Paper (No. 177) in December 2005, *A New Homicide Act for England and Wales?* It sought to negotiate the obstacle of the mandatory life sentence by constructing a framework of offences reflecting different degrees of culpability. In its final Report, *Murder, Manslaughter and Infanticide* (Law Com No. 304) the Law Commission retain this framework but with some modification following views expressed in the consultation:

(1) **First degree murder** (mandatory life penalty)

    (a) Killing intentionally.

    (b) Killing where there was an intention to do serious injury, coupled with an awareness of a serious risk of causing death.

(2) **Second degree murder** (discretionary life maximum penalty)

    (a) Killing where the offender intended to do serious injury.

    (b) Killing where the offender intended to cause some injury or a fear or risk of injury, and was aware of a serious risk of causing death.

    (c) Killing in which there is a partial defence to what would otherwise be first degree murder.

(3) **Manslaughter** (discretionary life maximum penalty)

    (a) Killing through gross negligence as to a risk of causing death.

    (b) Killing through a criminal act:

        (i) intended to cause injury; or

        (ii) where there was an awareness that the act involved a serious risk of causing injury.

    (c) Participating in a joint criminal venture in the course of which another participant commits first or second degree murder, in circumstances where it should have been obvious that first or second degree murder might be committed by another participant.

The Government responded to these proposals with its own Consultation Paper, *Murder, Manslaughter and Infanticide: Proposal for Reform of the Law* (CP19/08). The Government rejected the redefinition of the basic offence of murder but proposed to proceed with legislation in the areas of provocation, diminished responsibility, complicity, and infanticide. The Government appeared oblivious to the fact that the Law Commission's proposals in respect of these matters were posited upon its key proposal to reform murder and manslaughter as set out earlier. As one commentator observed, 'The resulting structure, unfortunately, looks rather like a wheel without a hub' (J. R. Spencer, 'Messing Up Murder' (2008) 8 Archbold News 5). The Coroners and Justice Act 2009 duly enacted changes to those four areas without effecting any change to the law of murder (see **9.3**).

9.3 Manslaughter

9.3.1 Introduction

The offence of manslaughter covers several types of unlawful homicides which are not murder. The punishment for this offence is in the discretion of the court and therefore ranges from absolute discharge to life imprisonment, reflecting the immense range of circumstances which may fall within the compass of this offence. In August 2018 the Sentencing Council published definitive sentencing guidelines for manslaughter, which came into force in November 2018. Courts are obliged to follow the guidelines unless to do so would be contrary to the interests of justice (Coroners and Justice Act 2009, s. 125(1)).

The offence of manslaughter may be divided into two generic types: voluntary and involuntary. Voluntary manslaughter is committed where D has **killed with malice aforethought (with the intention to kill or cause GBH),** and thus could be convicted of murder, but there are circumstances present that partially justify or excuse his behaviour, reducing his culpability. Accordingly, where an accused kills while suffering from diminished responsibility, or the killing is done under a loss of self-control or in pursuance of a suicide pact, he will be convicted of manslaughter. Involuntary manslaughter is an unlawful killing committed by an accused who did not have malice aforethought (he did not intend to kill or cause GBH) but who, nevertheless, had a state of mind which the law treats as culpable.

The category of manslaughter is significant for two main reasons. First, the person's conduct will not be labelled as 'murder' or the person as a 'murderer'. The principle of fair labelling requires that the law should attach labels that accurately reflect the nature of D's conduct and the extent of his culpability. Secondly, as the sentence for murder is mandatory life imprisonment, a judge sentencing a person for murder may only reflect the circumstances of the offence and offender in the sentence to a limited extent when setting the minimum period of imprisonment that D must serve. When sentencing for voluntary manslaughter, the judge has greater discretion, even when under an obligation to follow the relevant sentencing guidelines.

9.3.2 Voluntary manslaughter

9.3.2.1 Diminished responsibility

Section 2 of the Homicide Act 1957 created the defence of diminished responsibility. **The defence is not a general defence; it may only be pleaded in defence to a charge of murder.** Its effect, if successfully raised, is in the nature of a partial excuse; D is acquitted of murder but is convicted of manslaughter. On a conviction for manslaughter the judge has discretion when sentencing D whereas, on conviction for murder, the mandatory sentence is life imprisonment. The Sentencing Council's sentencing guidelines for diminished responsibility state the typical sentencing range is from three to 40 years' imprisonment.

The defence has all but replaced the insanity defence on a charge of murder where D was suffering from a mental incapacity. The defence covers all cases which would fall within the M'Naghten Rules and many other conditions which these do not cover. Many guilty pleas to manslaughter on the grounds of diminished responsibility are accepted by the prosecution.

As with insanity, **D bears the burden of proving the defence** (s. 2(2)) on a balance of probabilities (*Dunbar* [1958] 1 QB 1). The Court of Appeal held in *Foye* [2013] EWCA Crim 475 (followed in *Wilcocks* [2016] EWCA Crim 2043) that this is compatible with the presumption of innocence in Art. 6(2) of the ECHR.

Whether a defendant is guilty of murder or manslaughter on the grounds of diminished responsibility is ultimately for the jury to decide. Medical evidence is crucial to the success of the defence (see *Dix* (1981) 74 Cr App R 306) and a jury may not return a verdict of manslaughter on the ground of diminished responsibility unless there is medical evidence supporting the elements of the defence. If the medical evidence supporting a finding of diminished responsibility is uncontradicted, and there is no other evidence that is at least capable of rebutting the defence so that no properly directed jury could fail to find that the defence had discharged the burden on them, a charge of murder should be withdrawn from the jury (see *Matheson* (1958) 42 Cr App R 145; *Bailey* (1978) 66 Cr App R 31; *Golds* [2016] 1 WLR 5231, at [50]). However, as Lord Parker CJ stated in *Byrne* [1960] 2 QB 396, 403, the jury 'are not bound to accept the medical evidence if there is other material before them which, in their good judgment, conflicts with it and outweighs it' (see further *Eifinger* [2001] EWCA Crim 1855). In *Brennan* [2015] 1 WLR 2060, there was undisputed psychiatric evidence; the Court of Appeal held there simply was no basis for a verdict of murder and moreover this was so clear that the judge ought not to have left it open to the jury. In *Golds* [2016] 1 WLR 5231, Lord Hughes JSC considered *Brennan* and stated *per curiam*:

> Certainly a jury is not bound by the expert . . . However, as the Court of Appeal rightly held, if the jury is to be invited to reject the expert opinion, some rational basis for doing so must at least be suggested . . . It is not open to the Crown in this kind of situation simply to invite the jury to convict of murder without suggesting why the expert evidence ought not to be accepted . . . Where . . . in a diminished responsibility trial the medical evidence supports the plea and is uncontradicted, the judge needs to ensure that the Crown explains the basis on which it is inviting the jury to reject that evidence. He needs to ensure that the basis advanced is one which the jury can properly adopt . . . While he needs to make it clear to the jury that, if there is a proper basis for rejecting the expert evidence, the decision is theirs—that trial is by jury and not by expert—it will also ordinarily be wise to advise the jury against attempting to make themselves amateur psychiatrists, and that if there is undisputed expert evidence the jury will probably wish to accept it, unless there is some identified reason for not doing so. To this extent, the approach of the court in *Brennan* is to be endorsed.

Section 2 has been the subject of criticism and there have been various proposals for reform. The Coroners and Justice Act 2009 radically amended s. 2 of the Homicide Act 1957. The amended defence applies to murders committed on or after 4 October 2010. For murders committed prior to that date the original version of the defence applies. In order to understand the new defence we need to understand the original defence and the reform proposals which led to its replacement.

9.3.2.1.1 *The original defence of diminished responsibility*
Section 2 of the Homicide Act 1957 originally provided:

> Where a person kills or is party to the killing of another, he shall not be convicted of murder if he was suffering from such abnormality of mind (whether arising from a condition of arrested or retarded development of mind or any inherent causes or induced by disease or injury) as substantially impaired his mental responsibility for his acts and omissions in doing or being a party to the killing.

It should be noted that the term 'diminished responsibility' was not used in s. 2; it appears in the marginal note. Section 2 is hardly a paradigm of legislative clarity as it appears to conflate two ideas, namely those of impaired capacity and reduced liability. If D was to be convicted only of manslaughter rather than murder it was because his impaired capacity diminished his 'mental responsibility' for his act. The question was a general one, partly an issue of capacity and partly a matter of moral culpability, both including consideration of the extent of any causal link between the condition(s) and the killing (Lord Hughes JSC in *R v Golds* [2016] 1 WLR 5231, at para. 7). The question ultimately resolved itself into a moral one for the jury: whether they thought that D deserved to be convicted of murder or manslaughter. The jury's response, however, could vary greatly depending on the extent of their sympathy for D and the nature of his offence. For example, Peter Sutcliffe (the 'Yorkshire Ripper') was found guilty of murder, despite evidence from four psychiatrists that he was suffering from paranoid schizophrenia at the time of the killings. By contrast the defence has succeeded in cases of severely depressed carers who have acted out of compassion to alleviate their loved ones' suffering by killing them (e.g. 'Stockport Man, 84, Killed Wife with Dementia as "Act of Mercy"' BBC News Online, 22 November 2018, https://www.bbc.co.uk/news/uk-england-manchester-46302864). In its review of homicide law, the Law Commission noted that 'concerns were expressed that [diminished responsibility] is a lottery and that the outcome is more dependent on the persuasiveness of the psychiatrists and the advocates, and the degree of sympathy which the jury has for the defendant, than on any objective criteria.' (Law Commission, *Partial Defences to Murder*, Report LC290, para. 5.49).

A major problem with the defence as originally enacted was the imprecision of the language used which did not readily map onto the language which psychiatrists would use. In *Byrne* Lord Parker CJ defined **'abnormality of mind'** (at p. 403) as:

> a state of mind so different from that of ordinary human beings that the reasonable man would term it abnormal. It appears to us to be wide enough to cover the mind's activities in all its aspects, not only the perception of physical acts and matters, and the ability to form a rational judgment as to whether an act is right or wrong, but also the ability to exercise will-power to control physical acts in accordance with that rational judgment.

The imprecision of the term led to a wide range of conditions forming the basis of diminished responsibility pleas. In *Byrne* sexual psychopathy giving rise to violent perverted sexual desires which Byrne found difficult, if not impossible, to control, amounted to an abnormality of mind. By contrast, in *Seers* (1984) 79 Cr App R 261, D was convicted of the murder of his wife when suffering from chronic reactive depression which constituted an abnormality of mind.

The aetiology of the abnormality of mind was a matter to be determined by medical evidence (*Byrne*). There was little guidance, however, on what was meant by the causes specified in parenthesis. They were meant to rule out emotions such as hatred, rage, or jealousy and external factors such as alcohol or drugs.

The crucial question in a case where diminished responsibility was raised in defence, was whether the abnormality was such as to impair substantially D's mental responsibility for his acts. 'Substantial' meant 'less than total—more than trivial' (see *Lloyd* [1967] 1 QB 175)—a very imprecise test for a jury to apply.

9.3.2.1.2 *Proposals for reform*

The main concerns were the imprecision of the language used in s. 2 and the lack of congruence between that language and the terminology used in psychiatry which then left problems for lay people, namely jurors, to resolve. It is important also to note that as originally enacted **s. 2 did not require proof that the abnormality of mind caused the killing** although in many cases such a causal link was apparent.

In the Consultation Paper, *Murder, Manslaughter and Infanticide: Proposals for Reform of the Law* (CP19/08), the Ministry of Justice accepted the need for a new partial defence of diminished responsibility based on the concept of a 'recognised medical condition'. Rather than providing an explanation for the defendant's behaviour, the Government proposed that the abnormality of mind 'should cause, or be a significant contributory factor in causing, the defendant's conduct'. In 2009 the Government published a summary of the responses to the consultation and outlined its position in *Summary of Responses and Government Position: Response to Consultation CP(R) 19/08*. The amended diminished responsibility defence was duly enacted by s. 52 of the Coroners and Justice Act 2009.

9.3.2.1.3 *The reformed diminished responsibility defence*

Section 52 of the Coroners and Justice Act 2009 replaces s. 2(1) of the Homicide Act 1957 with three new subsections, (1), (1A), and (1B). **The effect of a successful plea of diminished responsibility remains the same, a verdict of manslaughter rather than murder, and the burden remains on the defence to prove the defence on the balance of probabilities.** The aim of the amendments is to modernise the defence so that it better fits with medical practice. The term 'abnormality of mind' has been replaced by **'abnormality of mental functioning'**. The abnormality of mental functioning must arise from **'a recognised medical condition'** rather than the causes specified in parenthesis in the original s. 2. Rather than having to show his mental responsibility was substantially impaired, D will now have to show that his ability to do one or more things—namely **to understand the nature of his conduct, to form a rational judgement, or to exercise self-control**— was substantially impaired. The new defence is more restricted as D has to show, in addition, that his abnormality of mental functioning **caused, or was a significant contributory factor in causing, D's conduct in killing**.

The overlap between insanity and diminished responsibility is now very marked; rather than diminished responsibility being the defence of choice it may be that greater reliance will be placed on the insanity defence. Only time will tell whether this becomes one of the unintended outcomes of the reform.

 The law in context

Children and diminished responsibility

While the new defence reflects some of the proposals made by the Law Commission, the Government remained adamant that developmental immaturity would not be recognised as a ground for raising the defence. The Law Commission had noted that s. 2 does not make specific provision for children who kill, some of whom may lack the capacity for self-control due to psychological problems resulting from abnormal processes of maturation. It recommended the introduction of 'developmental immaturity' as a ground in itself on which a verdict of diminished responsibility could be returned.

However, the Government was insistent that cases of abnormal immaturity on the part of a child would fall within general recognised medical conditions such as learning disabilities and autistic spectrum disorders. This, perhaps, is unduly optimistic and certainly does not address the problem of the 10-year-old who does not have the developmental maturity of an adult

→

> →
>
> when it comes to considering his ability to exercise self-control, nor does it address the problem of the child who, perhaps as the result of extreme neglect and/or abuse, but not suffering any medical condition, simply has missed out on the normal socialising experiences of childhood which teach self-discipline, moral values, and self-control.
>
> The question also arises whether this omission leaves the developmentally immature adult at an advantage over the normal child as a 40-year-old with the mental age of 10 may raise the defence relying on a medical condition to explain his developmental immaturity whereas a normal 10-year-old will be accorded no such opportunity even though the self-control he may be expected to exercise is no different. When exercising their common sense, the jury, comparing the 40-year-old with other normal adults, may conclude that the impairment to his ability to exercise self-control is more than trivial.

Section 52(1) of the Coroners and Justice Act 2009 provides:

> (1)   In section 2 of the Homicide Act 1957 (c. 11) (persons suffering from diminished responsibility), for subsection (1) substitute—
>
> '(1) A person ("D") who kills or is a party to the killing of another is not to be convicted of murder if D was suffering from an abnormality of mental functioning which—
>
> (a) arose from a recognised medical condition,
>
> (b) substantially impaired D's ability to do one or more of the things mentioned in subsection (1A), and
>
> (c) provides an explanation for D's acts and omissions in doing or being a party to the killing.
>
> (1A) Those things are—
>
> (a) to understand the nature of D's conduct;
>
> (b) to form a rational judgment;
>
> (c) to exercise self-control.
>
> (1B) For the purposes of subsection (1)(c), an abnormality of mental functioning provides an explanation for D's conduct if it causes, or is a significant contributory factor in causing, D to carry out that conduct.'

The elements of the defence are examined in the following paragraphs.

(a) *Abnormality of mental functioning* The term 'abnormality of mental functioning' is preferred by psychiatrists over the term 'abnormality of mind'. The hope is both that psychiatrists will be more comfortable with the new terminology and also that conditions put forward by defendants will be tied in more closely to accepted diagnostic criteria thereby discouraging spurious pleas of diminished responsibility. The approach adopted in *Byrne* [1960] QB 396 will still be applicable in that D's mental functioning will be 'abnormal' where it is 'so different from that of an ordinary person that the reasonable [person] would term it abnormal'. The medical expert witnesses should explain the extent to which D's mental functioning deviates from the norm.

(b) *Recognised medical condition* The abnormality of mental functioning has to arise from a recognised medical condition. This term is wider than the three specified causes in the old s. 2. *It includes physical medical conditions as well as psychological and psychiatric conditions.* Thus conditions such as alcohol dependency syndrome, diabetes, and epilepsy which are not mental disorders but which may affect a person's ability to do the things specified in s. 2(1A) are covered. Depressive illnesses will be covered so the defence remains potentially available to victims of prolonged domestic violence or sexual abuse. It is open to question whether some of the more generous examples of accepted pleas under the old law involving mercy killings fall within the amended law; there would have to be clear evidence of a depressive illness having the necessary impact on D's ability to do the specified things in s. 2(1A).

Psychiatrists and psychologists use one of the two internationally accepted classificatory systems when diagnosing mental conditions: either the World Health Organization, International Classification of Diseases (ICD-10) or the American Psychiatric Association, Diagnostic and Statistical Manual of Mental Disorders (DSM-IV). The current terminology in s. 2 means claims of diminished responsibility have to be grounded in valid medical diagnoses under these classificatory systems. While conditions not yet recognised in either classificatory system are not expressly excluded, it will be difficult to raise a defence based on a condition psychiatrists are just beginning to recognise until such condition is included in one of the classificatory systems.

 Question

Is there a danger that pleading diminished responsibility will become too easy if all that D has to do is show he has a 'recognised medical condition'?

This is a potential problem with the amended definition of the defence if the focus is placed on 'recognised medical condition' without paying adequate regard to the additional criteria laid down in the section which have to be satisfied for the defence to succeed. In *Dowds* [2012] EWCA Crim 281, the Court of Appeal faced this problem head-on in the context of a claim that being intoxicated, intoxication being a recognised medical condition, entitled D to rely on the defence.

> D and his partner P were heavy drinkers with a history of violence to each other when drunk. D, having consumed a large quantity of vodka with P, had an argument with her and stabbed her repeatedly. At his trial for murder he sought to raise the defence of diminished responsibility claiming that he could not remember what happened as he was intoxicated and that intoxication was a recognised medical condition. He made no claim to being dependent on alcohol; rather he was electively drunk, his drinking being voluntary. At the trial's outset the judge was invited to rule on whether simple voluntary and temporary drunkenness could found the partial defence of diminished responsibility. He ruled that as a matter of law it could not. On being convicted of murder D appealed. The Court of Appeal referred to the general principle that voluntary intoxication could not provide an excuse. After examining the Law Commission recommendations for reform of diminished responsibility and the Parliamentary history of the new section, the Court concluded that neither could have intended voluntary intoxication to satisfy the criteria for the reformulated defence. Thus, while voluntary intoxication might be a recognised medical condition for psychiatric purposes, it was not one for the purposes of the defence of diminished

responsibility. The fact that psychiatrists or psychologists might be able to identify a condition and describe its causes and consequences does not mean that the condition will automatically have legal significance. Hughes LJ explained (at para. 31):

> The 'imperfect fit' to which the authors of DSM-IV refer is nowhere more clearly demonstrated than in the breadth and kind of conditions which are included in both ICD-10 and DSM-IV. ICD-10 includes, for example, 'unhappiness' (R45.2), 'irritability and anger' (R45.4) 'suspiciousness and marked evasiveness' (R46.5), 'pyromania' (F63.1), 'paedophilia' (F65.4), 'sado-masochism' (F65.5) and 'kleptomania' (F63.2). DSM-IV includes similar conditions and also such as 'exhibitionism' (569) 'sexual sadism' (573) and 'intermittent explosive disorder' (663/667). The last of these is defined as 'discrete episodes of failure to resist aggressive impulses that result in serious assaultive acts or destruction of property, where the degree of aggression is grossly out of proportion to any precipitating psychosocial stressors'. Not all of these are treated by the classification systems as mental disorders, but all are, doubtless, 'recognised medical conditions' in the sense that they are perfectly sensibly included in guides for description of patients by doctors. It follows that a great many conditions thus included for medical purposes raise important additional legal questions when one is seeking to invoke them in a forensic context. 'Intermittent explosive disorder', for example, may well be a medically useful description of something which underlies the vast majority of violent offending, but any suggestion that it could give rise to a defence, whether because it amounted to an impairment of mental functioning or otherwise, would, to say the least, demand extremely careful attention. In other words, the medical classification begs the question whether the condition is simply a description of (often criminal) behaviour, or is capable of forming a defence to an allegation of such.

This is an important decision. While acute intoxication may substantially impair D's capacity, for policy reasons it is not acceptable as a 'recognised medical condition'. Accordingly, the fact that a condition appears in the internationally accepted classifications of diseases (ICD-10 and DSM-IV) is not of itself sufficient to satisfy s. 2(1)(a). However the Court did not provide any criteria for determining which recognised medical conditions would satisfy the statute and which would not. The effect, however, is that the trial judge will rule whether or not the condition D is relying upon for the basis of his diminished responsibility defence is acceptable such that the defence will be left to the jury to determine whether or not the other conditions specified in the statute are met.

(c) *Substantially impaired ability* If D suffers from an abnormality of mental functioning, arising from a recognised medical condition, this may support his claim of diminished responsibility if it substantially impairs his ability to do one or more of the three things listed in s. 2(1A). This contrasts with the previous law which required that D's *mental responsibility* for acting as s/he did was substantially impaired. That test involved a moral question of degree for the jury to determine. The new law contains no reference to 'responsibility' in s. 2 leaving the jury with an apparently factual question rather than a moral one.

Under the previous law, the impairment did not need to be total but it had be more than trivial. It was thought that this approach would carry over to the new defence. As the thing that must be impaired is D's ability to do any, or a combination, of the things listed in s. 2(1A), medical evidence detailing the nature and extent of any such impairment will be quite crucial in enabling the jury to make their assessment of whether that impairment is substantial. In *Golds* [2016] UKSC 61, however, the Supreme Court eschewed limiting the meaning of 'substantial' to 'more than trivial'.

> D, who suffered from schizophrenia, depression, and had auditory hallucinations and paranoid delusions, stopped taking his medication which controlled his condition and, following an argument with his partner, V, stabbed her 22 times as he believed she was a demon. At his trial for murder the three psychiatrists (two for the defence and one for the Crown) were agreed that he was suffering from a significant level of mental illness and that the criteria in s. 2 were satisfied. The plea of guilty to manslaughter was not accepted and the issue went to the jury who convicted D of murder. Counsel for D contended that the judge should direct the jury that his impairment must be treated as 'substantial' if the effect of the abnormality of mental functioning on his ability to do the things specified in s. 2(1A) was 'more than trivial'. The judge refused, leaving the jury to determine for themselves the meaning of 'substantial'. D appealed. The essence of the appeal was that 'substantial' was capable of having two different meanings: either the meaning counsel had argued for at trial or a more stringent meaning to the effect that the abnormality of mental functioning only substantially impairs where, whilst not totally impairing a defendant's ability to do the specified things, it *significantly* or *appreciably* impairs that ability. The Supreme Court dismissed G's appeal and clarified how juries should be directed in murder trials where diminished responsibility is in issue (*per* Lord Hughes JSC, at para. 43):

> (1) Ordinarily in a murder trial where diminished responsibility is in issue the judge need not direct the jury beyond the terms of the statute and should not attempt to define the meaning of 'substantially'. Experience has shown that the issue of its correct interpretation is unlikely to arise in many cases. The jury should normally be given to understand that the expression is an ordinary English word, that it imports a question of degree, and that whether in the case before it the impairment can properly be described as substantial is for it to resolve.
>
> (2) If, however, the jury has been introduced to the question of whether any impairment beyond the merely trivial will suffice, or if it has been introduced to the concept of a spectrum between the greater than trivial and the total, the judge should explain that whilst the impairment must indeed pass the merely trivial before it need be considered, it is not the law that any impairment beyond the trivial will suffice. The judge should likewise make this clear if a risk arises that the jury might misunderstand the import of the expression; whether this risk arises or not is a judgment to be arrived at by the trial judge who is charged with overseeing the dynamics of the trial. Diminished responsibility involves an impairment of one or more of the abilities listed in the statute to an extent which the jury judges to be substantial, and which it is satisfied significantly contributed to his committing the offence. Illustrative expressions of the sense of the word may be employed so long as the jury is given clearly to understand that no single synonym is to be substituted for the statutory word.

Lord Hughes stated that '"substantially impaired" . . . is not synonymous with "anything more than merely trivial impairment"' (at para. 39). This still leaves the jury with responsibility for interpreting that term. There is a clear danger that different juries will have differing understandings of the meaning of 'substantially' and that some might set the standard for impairment at a particularly high level which it would appear that the jury in the instant case had done. The Supreme

Court showed itself alert to this issue though. Lord Hughes noted that 'the understandable itch of the lawyer to re-define needs to be resisted' (at para. 37) and the term can be left to 'the collective good sense' (at para. 40) of the jury in deciding whether the condition in the particular case it is trying reaches the level of substantial impairment.

In *Squelch* [2017] EWCA Crim 204, the trial judge directed the jury that 'substantial' means 'less than total and more than trivial'. The Court of Appeal held that that 'commendably' and 'amply' complies with what Lord Hughes had indicated in giving the judgment in *Golds*.

(d) *Impaired his ability to do one (or more) of three things* For the diminished responsibility defence to succeed, the defendant's abnormality of mental functioning must have substantially impaired his ability to do one of the three things listed in s. 2(1A).

(i) *Ability to understand the nature of D's conduct* This limb may overlap with the first limb of the M'Naghten Rules where the issue is whether D did not know the nature and quality of the act he was doing (see **5.3.3**). However, they differ in that, with the M'Naghten test, the effect of the defect of reason is to rule out *mens rea*, whereas the diminished responsibility defence operates where D has *mens rea* but his understanding is, in some way, impaired. Thus, if D is in a delusional state and stabs V believing V is a three-headed monster, D would not understand the nature and quality of his act such that he would not have the intent to kill another person. His appropriate defence, provided his defect of reason arose from a disease of the mind, would be insanity and not diminished responsibility. By contrast, however, D's appropriate defence would be diminished responsibility if the result of his recognised medical condition is that he does not fully understand cause and effect, and believing that real life is like video games (to which he is addicted) he stabs V in a fit of temper when V attempts to take a game from him, not understanding that real people cannot be revived like the characters in the video game. He has intended serious injury and thus has the *mens rea* for murder. The issue for the jury would be whether there was a more than trivial impairment of his ability to understand the nature of his conduct.

(ii) *Ability to form a rational judgement* Where D's perception of reality is to some extent impaired as a result of his medical condition, this will impact on his ability to form a rational judgement. In *Conroy* [2017] EWCA Crim 81, the Court of Appeal held that in determining whether or not an abnormality of mental functioning had impaired a defendant's ability to form a rational judgement it is not possible neatly to separate D's 'decision-making process' from the ultimate decision D makes:

> There may be cases where an entirely 'irrational' decision may be taken: for example, to kill one's neighbour because of a fixed belief that he is an alien from Mars intent on blowing up innocent people in the village. But that decision and the motivation for it may then be accompanied, in terms of giving effect to the decision, by ostensibly logical and rational decisions with a view to carrying out the intended killing: for example by buying a knife, by waiting for the neighbour to be at home alone and so on. (*per* Davis LJ, para. 30)

As the Court explained, the ability to form a rational judgement imports a consideration of the extent of the abnormality of mental functioning and its impact. That is likely to involve evaluating the abnormality's impact on the person's decision-making generally, but also on the particular decision to kill the victim specifically. Section 2 is not confined to a rational judgement as to whether an act was right or wrong, though that may be an element.

> ### Example
>
> D, after suffering domestic violence for years, develops a severe depressive illness which causes her to believe that the only way to escape her hopeless situation is to kill V, her abusive husband. The issue for the jury would be whether D's illness had impaired, in a more than trivial way, her ability to form a rational judgement. While outside observers might have been able to identify alternative strategies for D, medical evidence as to the effects of the abuse on her psychology and her reasoning abilities will be crucial in providing a basis for the jury's determination.

To an extent, this limb will overlap with the first limb as if D does not fully understand the nature of his own conduct, he will have difficulty in making rational judgements on his own actions. It may be that this limb will provide the basis for future pleas of diminished responsibility in the context of mercy killings if the medical evidence can establish that D suffers from a medical condition (perhaps some form of depression) arising from the demands of continually caring for V in distressing circumstances, such that eventually D's perception of reality becomes distorted and D gives way to V's pleas and kills V.

(iii) *Ability to exercise self-control* Many medical conditions may have effects upon individuals' abilities to control their tempers and to exercise self-restraint. This limb may operate in circumstances where the separate defence of loss of self-control would not succeed because D's loss of self-control is not linked to one of the required qualifying triggers (see **9.3.2.2**).

> ### Example
>
> D, a mentally disordered adult with the intellectual age of an eight-year-old, suffers continual teasing from youths in the neighbourhood. D eventually snaps, losing his self-control, and hits one of the youths with a brick, killing him. The teasing, while unkind, does not come close to constituting 'circumstances of an extremely grave character' such as would be required to raise the defence of loss of self-control (see **9.3.2.2.3**). Medical evidence is presented, however, that D's ability to exercise self-control is not that of a normal adult and the effects of the teasing over a period of time have led to the onset of depression which had a further impairing impact on his ability to exercise self-control. The issue for the jury would be whether or not the impairment of his ability to exercise self-control is substantial.

(e) *The abnormality of mental functioning must provide an explanation for D's conduct in killing* The third requirement of the abnormality of mental functioning, if the defence is to succeed, is that it provides an explanation for D's conduct in killing (or being a party to the killing) (s. 2(1)(c)). Section 2(1B) stipulates that such an explanation is provided where the abnormality of mental functioning 'causes, or is a significant contributory factor in causing, D to carry out that conduct'. Thus there must be a connection between D's abnormality and the killing; it is not enough that D has killed and that he does suffer from an abnormality of mental functioning. The abnormality need not be the sole cause—so other causes, such as provocation, may be at work—but it has to be at least a significant contributory factor such that, without that abnormality, the other cause(s) would not have operated on their own to bring about the killing. Thus, if the abnormality of mental functioning, in the circumstances, made no difference to D's behaviour (i.e. he would have killed as and when he did regardless of his abnormality), the defence will fail.

 Example

D suffers from an abnormality of mental functioning arising from a recognised medical condition (e.g. a brain injury in childhood seriously impairing his mental development) which substantially impairs his ability to exercise self-control such that if annoyed he suffers severe fits of temper in which he becomes violent. If D kills in one such temper fit, he could potentially satisfy the conditions for diminished responsibility if charged with murder. However, if the actual killing committed by D is carried out in a cold and calculated way where D planned it and executed it with his emotions under control, his abnormality of mental functioning would not have caused or been a significant contributory factor in causing him to kill and his plea of diminished responsibility will fail.

Under the previous law D may have succeeded if the jury concluded that morally he should not be held responsible for the killing as no causal connection between the abnormality of mind and the killing was required. This is, perhaps, an extreme example, but others may arise, particularly where D is not the principal but is a participant in a joint enterprise where his abnormality of mental functioning may not play any contributory part in the killing by the principal.

9.3.2.1.4 *Intoxication and diminished responsibility*

A potentially difficult issue arises when a person kills who at the time of the killing claims to have been suffering from an abnormality of mental functioning and to have been intoxicated (whether through alcohol or other drugs) at the time of the killing. The House of Lords in *Dietschmann* [2003] UKHL 10, a decision under the old law, held that the jury's task is to consider whether, notwithstanding the alcohol or drugs he had consumed 'his abnormality of mind substantially impaired his mental responsibility for his acts in doing the killing'. Section 2 does not require the abnormality of mental functioning to be the sole cause of the defendant's acts in doing the killing. The Court of Appeal in *Wood* [2008] EWCA Crim 1305 held that voluntary consumption of alcohol did not constitute an abnormality of the mind (or mental functioning) and that the defence of diminished responsibility is not precluded by the mere fact that a defendant had consumed alcohol voluntarily before committing the fatal act.

In *Stewart (James)* [2009] EWCA Crim 593, the Court of Appeal held that a trial judge structuring a summing-up in relation to a defence of diminished responsibility based on alcohol dependency syndrome should outline the ingredients of the defence, then direct the jury to decide whether the defendant was suffering from an abnormality of mind (now mental functioning) at the time of the killing. It does not necessarily follow from the fact that D suffered from alcohol dependency syndrome that he had established the necessary abnormality. That depended on the jury's findings about the nature and extent of the syndrome and whether, looking at the matter broadly, the defendant's consumption of alcohol before the killing was fairly to be regarded as the involuntary result of an irresistible craving for drink. If the defendant proved the necessary abnormality of mind the next question was whether that was caused by disease or illness, and in the instant class of case the answer to that would normally follow from whatever answer was appropriate to the first question. Finally, assuming that the defendant's alcohol dependency syndrome did constitute an abnormality of mind due to disease or illness that was present at the time of the killing, directions about whether his mental responsibility for what he did was substantially impaired should be addressed in conventional terms.

Most recently, the Court of Appeal in *R v Kay; R v Joyce* [2017] 4 WLR 121 held that the approach in *Stewart* provides a clear and sensible approach. The law does not prevent someone suffering from schizophrenia from relying on diminished responsibility where voluntary intoxication had triggered a psychotic state, but he has to meet the criteria in s. 2(1). He has to establish that his abnormality of mental functioning (in Kay's case a psychotic state) arose from a recognised medical condition that substantially impaired his responsibility. The recognised medical condition might be schizophrenia of such severity that, absent intoxication, it substantially impaired his responsibility; it might be schizophrenia coupled with drink/drugs dependency syndrome which together substantially impaired responsibility. However, if an abnormality of mental functioning arose from voluntary intoxication, and not from a recognised medical condition, an accused could not avail himself of the partial defence.

9.3.2.2 Loss of self-control

Sections 54–55 of the Coroners and Justice Act 2009 introduced the new 'loss of control' partial defence to murder. Section 56 abolishes the defence of provocation with the new defence applying to any murder which occurred on or after 4 October 2010. For murders prior to this date, the defence of provocation continues to apply. For a full exposition of this defence see the online resources.

To help you understand the changes that have been made by ss 54–56, a brief outline of the law of provocation follows.

9.3.2.2.1 *Provocation*

Provocation was only a defence to a charge of murder reducing to manslaughter what, in the absence of provocation, would have been murder. The jury had to convict of manslaughter if they were satisfied both that D killed with the requisite intent and that D may have been provoked. Section 3 of the Homicide Act 1957 provided:

> Where on a charge of murder there is evidence on which the jury can find that the person charged was provoked (whether by things done or by things said or by both together) to lose his self-control, the question whether the provocation was enough to make a reasonable man do as he did shall be left to be determined by the jury; and in determining that question the jury shall take into account everything both done and said according to the effect which, in their opinion, it would have on a reasonable man.

There were two elements to the defence of provocation: **first, the subjective question whether D was provoked to lose his self-control; and, secondly, the objective question whether a reasonable man would have been provoked to lose his self-control and do as he did.**

Loss of self-control did not have to be 'complete' to the extent that D did not know what he was doing; it was sufficient that he may not have been able to restrain himself from doing what he did (*Richens* [1993] Crim LR 384). In *Ibrams* (1981) 74 Cr App R 154 and *Thornton* [1992] 1 All ER 306, the Court of Appeal approved the dictum of Devlin J in *Duffy* [1949] 1 All ER 932, that there must be 'a sudden and temporary loss of self-control, rendering D so subject to passion as to make him or her for the moment not master of his mind'. The fact that D lost his self-control did not mean that his defence of provocation would succeed; the jury had then to consider the objective question. If the jury concluded that the reasonable man might have done as D did, they had to return a verdict of manslaughter. **The purpose of the objective question was to set a standard of self-control against which D's actions are to be measured.**

Two particular problems presented themselves: first, D, due to his characteristics, history, or circumstances, may be particularly sensitive to the alleged provocative words or conduct; and secondly, D, due to his youthfulness or some mental impairment, may not be able to exercise the self-control to be expected of the ordinary adult. At a time before any appellate decisions were made on these issues, Professor Ashworth in 'The Doctrine of Provocation' (1976) 35 CLJ 292, expressed the view (at p. 312) that the defence of provocation was for those who were mentally normal, whereas those suffering from a mental abnormality should rely on the defence of diminished responsibility under s. 2 of the 1957 Act (see **9.3.2.1**). In seeking to apply the objective test, Ashworth concluded (at p. 300) that a distinction had to be drawn between those 'individual peculiarities which bear on the gravity of the provocation [which] should be taken into account, whereas individual peculiarities bearing on D's level of self-control should not'.

In *Camplin* [1978] AC 705, Lord Diplock stated (at p. 717) that the reasonable man is:

> an ordinary person of either sex, not exceptionally excitable or pugnacious, but possessed of such powers of self-control as everyone is entitled to expect that his fellow citizens will exercise in society as it is today.

He accepted (at p. 714) that the reasonable man was the 'embodiment of the standard of self-control required by the criminal law' but, following the 1957 Act, he could be attributed with those characteristics, or placed in those circumstances which would affect the gravity of the taunts or insults directed at D. In addition, age, which may be taken into account in assessing the gravity of the provocation (e.g. a physical threat or assault may be graver due to the less developed physique of a young person), was also relevant when considering powers of self-control as 'to require old heads upon young shoulders is inconsistent with the law's compassion to human infirmity'. **But other factors which might reduce or impair D's powers of self-control were not attributable.** In *Morhall* [1996] AC 90, the House of Lords **emphasised that the reasonable man test represents a standard of self-control.** When directing a jury the judge had to refer them to the hypothetical person:

> having the power of self-control to be expected of an ordinary person of the age and sex of the defendant, but in other respects sharing such of the defendant's characteristics as [the jury] think would affect the gravity of the provocation to him.

Things relevant to the gravity of the provocation should not be confined to characteristics but could include 'the defendant's history or the circumstances in which he was placed at the time', and the characteristics, history, or circumstances did not cease to be relevant because they were discreditable (in Morhall's case the relevant characteristic was his addiction, which formed the focus for taunts). Furthermore, a characteristic could be something temporary or transitory if the subject of taunts or insults.

Despite these clear pronouncements in the House of Lords, the Court of Appeal throughout the 1980s and 1990s continued to intimate that the standard of self-control to be expected of the reasonable person might be modified to take account of the defendant's psychiatric idiosyncrasies. The Privy Council considered those decisions in *Luc Thiet Thuan v R* [1996] 3 WLR 45, concluding that a mental infirmity which impairs an accused's power of self-control was not to be taken into account as it is inconsistent with a person having the power of self-control of an ordinary person who features in the objective test. The mental infirmity of D could be taken into account if it was the subject of taunts by the deceased as this would go to the gravity of the provocation but otherwise it would be irrelevant. Lord Goff reasoned that this position preserved the distinction between diminished responsibility and provocation which it must have been the intention of the legislature in passing the Homicide Act 1957 to maintain.

The House of Lords reconsidered the issue in *Smith (Morgan)* [2000] 3 WLR 654, a case involving an alcoholic suffering from a depressive illness which impaired his ability to exercise self-control, reducing his threshold for erupting with violence. The trial judge accepted the Crown's argument that this evidence was not relevant to the question whether a reasonable man might have lost his self-control. D was convicted of murder and appealed. The Court of Appeal allowed his appeal, substituting a verdict of manslaughter on the ground that his mental impairment was a characteristic to be attributed to the reasonable man not only in assessing the gravity of the provocation but also his reaction to it. The Crown appealed. The Court of Appeal granted leave to appeal and certified the following point of law of general public importance:

> Are characteristics other than age and sex, attributable to the reasonable man, for the purpose of section 3 of the Homicide Act 1957, relevant not only to the gravity of the provocation to him but also to the standard of self-control to be expected?

Unbelievably their Lordships by a majority of three to two answered the question in the affirmative. The majority concluded that Lord Diplock did not intend to draw any distinction between 'characteristics relevant to the gravity of the provocation and characteristics relevant to the power of self-control'. Lord Hoffmann effectively stated that the jury should be trusted to decide what characteristics are relevant:

> The jury must think that the circumstances were such as to make the loss of self-control sufficiently *excusable* to reduce the gravity of the offence from murder to manslaughter. This is entirely a question for the jury.

Following *Smith*, the jury when considering the objective question had to take into account any condition from which D suffered which impaired his ability to exercise self-control. The distinction between diminished responsibility and provocation was left wholly blurred causing considerable confusion. However, in an unprecedented judgment, *AG for Jersey* v *Holley* [2005] UKPC 23, the Privy Council, sitting as a Board made up of nine serving Lords of Appeal in Ordinary, by a majority of six to three followed *Luc Thiet Thuan* and declared that *Morgan Smith* could not be regarded as an accurate statement of English law. The majority held that the s. 3 reference to the 'reasonable man' was intended to refer to the ordinary person—that is, a person of ordinary self-control—and thereby it set an external standard of self-control. Lord Nicholls of Birkenhead, delivering the judgment of the majority, stated (at para. 22):

> Whether the provocative act or words and the defendant's response met the 'ordinary person' standard prescribed by the statute is the question the jury must consider, not the altogether looser question of whether, having regard to all the circumstances, the jury consider the loss of self-control was sufficiently excusable. The statute does not leave each jury free to set whatever standard they consider appropriate in the circumstances by which to judge whether the defendant's conduct is 'excusable'.

The majority recognised that inherent in the use of a uniform standard applicable to all defendants is 'the possibility that an individual defendant may be temperamentally unable to achieve this standard'. While sex and age are relevant to the application of this standard, other abnormalities not found in a person having ordinary powers of self-control, are not. The majority considered that the diminished responsibility defence in s. 2 reflected Parliament's recognition of the potential harshness of s. 3 if it stood alone. A person who claims his mental disorder (for example) caused his behaviour can plead diminished responsibility. It would be wrong for the courts to distort s. 3 to accommodate cases for which Parliament had expressly provided in enacting s. 2.

9.3.2.2.2 *The pressure for reform*
In its Report *Partial Defences to Murder* (Law Com No. 290), published in 2004 before the Privy Council decision in *Holley*, the Law Commission recommended reform of the provocation defence by restoring an objective standard of self-control to recast it in a way consistent with the pre-*Smith (Morgan)* law. If a person suffers from a psychiatric condition affecting their ability to exercise self-control, the Law Commission considered that such should not be taken into account in respect of provocation, being more appropriate for consideration in relation to diminished responsibility (para. 3.130). The Law Commission also recognised that many of the wrong turnings in provocation were well-intentioned responses to the problem of abused women who killed their abusive partners (*Ahluwalia* [1992] 4 All ER 889;

Thornton (Sara) (No.2) [1996] 2 All ER 1023). It explained how its reformed defence would apply in such cases (para. 3.111):

> This is not to deny a defence to an abused person whose temperament may have changed as a result of the provocation [i.e. the history of abuse], for that would be a matter which bore not simply on the defendant's general temperament independent of the provocation but on the effect of the provocation itself. As Lord Millett said in *Smith (Morgan)* about such a case:
>
> 'The question for the jury is whether a woman with normal powers of self-control, subjected to the treatment which the accused received, would or might finally react as she did. . . . It does not involve an inquiry whether the accused was capable of displaying the powers of self-control of an ordinary person, but whether a person with the power of self-control of an ordinary person would or might have reacted in the same way to the cumulative effect of the treatment which she endured.'

A more significant change proposed by the Law Commission related to the subjective test. The Law Commission wished to change the focus of the defence away from the issue of loss of self-control and to provide for the situation where excessive force is used in self-defence which does not provide a defence to murder. In consequence the subjective test was to be significantly reframed so that a defendant would be able to rely on provocation where he acted in response to:

i. gross provocation (meaning words or conduct or a combination of words and conduct) which caused the defendant to have a justifiable sense of being seriously wronged; or

ii. fear of serious violence towards the defendant or another; or

iii. a combination of [(i) and (ii)].

In its Report, *Murder, Manslaughter and Infanticide* (Law Com No. 304), the Law Commission affirmed these recommendations. The Government responded to these proposals with its own Consultation Paper, *Murder, Manslaughter and Infanticide: Proposal for Reform of the Law* (CP19/08). While accepting the Law Commission's analysis of the problems, it proposed a different response, namely to abolish the defence of provocation and replace it with a new partial defence based on a loss of self-control. In January 2009 the Government published a summary of the responses to the consultation and outlined its position in *Summary of Responses and Government Position: Response to Consultation CP(R) 19/08*. The new defence was duly enacted by ss 54–56 of the Coroners and Justice Act 2009.

9.3.2.2.3 *Loss of control*
Section 54(1) sets out the main elements of the defence and provides:

> (1) Where a person ('D') kills or is a party to the killing of another ('V'), D is not to be convicted of murder if—
>   (a) D's acts and omissions in doing or being a party to the killing resulted from D's loss of self-control,
>   (b) the loss of self-control had a qualifying trigger, and
>   (c) a person of D's sex and age, with a normal degree of tolerance and self-restraint and in the circumstances of D, might have reacted in the same or in a similar way to D.

Before examining these elements, it should be noted that **the burden of proof in respect of the defence of loss of control rests on the prosecution** to disprove the defence beyond reasonable doubt (s. 54(5)). This burden arises once 'sufficient evidence is adduced to raise an issue with respect to the defence'. It is for the judge to determine whether or not this evidential threshold has been satisfied which it will be if 'evidence is adduced on which, in the opinion of the trial judge, a jury, properly directed, could reasonably conclude that the defence might apply' (s. 54(6)). If the prosecution do not disprove the defence 'the jury must assume that the defence is satisfied' (s. 54(5)) which means that the judge's determination of whether or not to leave the defence to the jury acquires a degree of significance.

As with provocation there are subjective and objective elements to the defence; s. 54(1)(a) and s. 54(1)(b) represent the subjective elements and s. 54(1)(c) the objective element. In construing the statute, however, courts should treat the old law of provocation as irrelevant as this is a new defence; nor are the Law Commission papers especially helpful (see *Clinton* [2012] EWCA Crim 2).

(a) *Loss of self-control* This term is not defined in the statute but, in *Jewell* [2014] EWCA Crim 414, the Court of Appeal intimated (at para. 23) that it means a loss of the ability to act 'in accordance with considered judgment, or a loss of normal powers of reasoning'. Unlike under provocation, the **loss of self-control need not be sudden** (s. 54(2)). Thus situations, such as in cases of domestic violence, where D's reaction builds up over a period of time are not excluded. However, **the defence may not be relied upon where 'D acted in a considered desire for revenge'** (s. 54(4)); and 'a considered act of revenge, whether performed calmly or in anger, is not a loss of self-control' (*per* Lord Judge CJ, *Clinton* [2012] EWCA Crim 2, para. 128).

It may be difficult to establish that there was a loss of self-control if D has not suddenly reacted by killing V. The longer the delay between the qualifying trigger and the act of killing, the more difficult it will be evidentially to establish actual loss of self-control. Further, how this interacts with s. 54(1)(c) may be problematic; for a person of normal tolerance and self-restraint, a delay between the trigger and the killing may provide a period for cooling off and reflecting on other ways to deal with the situation. Whether these provisions amply accommodate the problems of killings in the context of domestic violence will only be known once the new defence has been in operation for a sufficient period.

(b) *Qualifying trigger* **Loss of self-control may only be relied upon where it is attributable to one or both of the two specified 'qualifying triggers' set out in s. 55:**

> (i) D's fear of serious violence from V against D or another identified person (s. 55(3)); and/or
>
> (ii) a thing or things done or said (or both) which
>
>> (a) constituted circumstances of an extremely grave character, and
>>
>> (b) caused D to have a justifiable sense of being seriously wronged. (s. 55(4))

Before examining these 'triggers' it is important to note that **D cannot rely on either if he has incited the situation to provide himself with an excuse** to use violence in response (see s. 55(6)). Thus if D goes looking for a fight by inciting V or insults V in order to provoke V to insult him, he will be denied the defence. This is perfectly logical as the defence is of an excusatory nature and D's behaviour in such circumstances is hardly to be excused or condoned.

Note also that D may rely on both qualifying triggers.

 Example

D, a victim of repeated incidents of domestic violence, kills her abusive partner, V, having lost self-control both fearing serious violence and also feeling a justifiable sense of being seriously wronged as a result of the abuse to which she has been subjected.

(i) *Fear of serious violence* The first qualifying trigger is **fear of serious violence from V against D or another resulting in D's loss of self-control**. It was perceived that women who killed their abusive partners were ill-served by the defence of provocation because of the requirement for loss of self-control to be sudden and temporary. The new defence imposes no requirement of imminence with regard to the anticipated violence; it is enough that D anticipates an attack, loses her self-control, and kills V. The stereotypical situation intended to be covered would be where V returns home drunk and D, anticipating a further violent and/or sexual attack from V (consistent with his past behaviour) loses her self-control, and while he is dozing on the sofa, stabs him. The trigger would also cover, for example, the situation where V's violence is directed towards the children of the relationship and D kills him to protect them. A general fear for unspecified others will not suffice.

The qualifying trigger may also operate where D, fearing serious violence, loses his self-control, overreacts, and kills V in circumstances where use of a lesser degree of force would have been justifiable and supported a defence of self-defence.

(ii) *Justifiable sense of being seriously wronged* Under provocation anything said or done might amount to provocation whether wrongful or not and whether trivial or serious. The new defence seeks to set a higher threshold before D may rely on things said or done to excuse his loss of self-control. Thus the **things done or said have to amount to 'circumstances of an extremely grave character'**. The issue is not whether D perceives them as such but whether objectively they are such. Where D seeks to rely on things done or said which do not give rise to a fear of serious violence, the focus will generally be on V's behaviour and language (although the statute does not limit the focus to V's words or conduct). Often the situation will be one where insults or taunts are traded by V with D. In the past, under provocation, any evidence of provocative words or conduct had to be left to the jury. Now the provision in s. 54(6) means that the judge will play a crucial role in determining whether a jury, properly directed, could reasonably conclude that the words or conduct constituted circumstances of an extremely grave character. If insufficient evidence is adduced to raise an issue with respect to the defence (meaning evidence on which, in the opinion of the trial judge, a jury, properly directed, could reasonably conclude that the defence might apply), then the defence is unavailable. In *Gurpinar* [2015] EWCA Crim 178, the Court of Appeal stated that the judge's task is to analyse the evidence closely and be satisfied that there was sufficient evidence in respect of each of the three components of the defence; A much more rigorous evaluation of the evidence has to be undertaken before the defence is left to the jury than was required under the law of provocation.

Example

The judicial filter will operate where, for example, V, D's daughter, refuses to enter a marriage arranged for her by D and runs off with her boyfriend, W, whom D does not consider suitable. If D, in the context of so-called 'honour killing' were to kill V or W, it is likely that a judge would not leave the defence of loss of self-control to the jury on the basis that no jury, properly directed, could reasonably conclude that the conduct of V and/or W constituted 'circumstances of an extremely grave character'. The basis for this determination is an objective one taking account of the society in which V and W live, where human rights under the European Convention on Human Rights are enacted into law by the Human Rights Act 1998, and where the rights of V and W to self-determination are valued over and above any interest D might have in the maintenance of family honour.

Even if the threshold of things done or said amounting to circumstances of an extremely grave character is satisfied, D's loss of self-control will not satisfy the subjective limb of the defence unless, in addition, these circumstances caused D to have a justifiable sense of being seriously wronged. **Whether or not D's sense of being seriously wronged is justifiable, is an objective question** to be determined initially by the judge on the basis of whether or not a jury properly directed could reasonably conclude that it was and, if so, the jury will then be left to consider this question. Again, in the context of so-called 'honour killing' D would not get past the judge as any sense of grievance he might have could not be considered justifiable in England and Wales. It is clear from this that loss of self-control as a defence differs significantly from the old defence of provocation which was based on the theory of excuses and tended to tolerate, if not actually indulge, male anger. Conceptually, the idea of justifying homicidal violence is much more difficult to contemplate than the previous approach which simply sought to excuse it.

The upshot of these provisions, accordingly, is that the defence of loss of self-control will be left to juries to consider in a much more limited range of situations than pertained with the defence of provocation. At common law provocation could only be relied on if the deceased used actual violence on the defendant unless one of two exceptions applied, the relevant one here being D discovering V, his wife, in the act of committing adultery. With the passage of s. 3 of the Homicide Act 1957 permitting words alone to constitute provocation, a confession by V to D of her adultery could be sufficient. For many years critics of the defence of provocation used these two examples, along with the problems facing victims of domestic violence in raising the defence, to contend that the defence of provocation was gender-based and favoured men over women. There was little evidence to support the contention that jealous husbands were 'getting away with murder' by successfully raising the defence of provocation (see *Impact Assessment*, pp. 11–12, which accompanied the Government's Consultation Paper), and under the new loss of self-control defence the judge applies the filter to any such pleas having to be satisfied that adultery is both 'extremely grave' and could cause D to have a justifiable sense of being seriously wronged. **Section 55(6)(c) nonetheless expressly provides that 'the fact that a thing done or said constituted sexual infidelity is to be disregarded'.** Thus if V, is caught in the act of adultery by, or confesses adultery to, D, V's partner, D cannot rely on that sexual infidelity to contend that the consequential loss of self-control causing D to kill V, had a qualifying trigger. This has the potential to lead to some hair-splitting on the part of judges and juries.

 Example

In the course of a heated argument V confesses her adultery to D and then taunts D that she had to find someone else to satisfy her as he was always a useless lover and now is impotent. If D loses his self-control and kills V, in deciding if D's loss of self-control was due to a qualifying trigger, the confession of adultery would have to be ignored but the subsequent taunts of being a useless lover and of impotence would have to be taken into account as things said. Whether the taunts would constitute circumstances of an extremely grave character or cause a justifiable sense of being seriously wronged may be open to question when considered in isolation from the confession of adultery.

In the Explanatory Notes accompanying the Coroners and Justice Act 2009, the following example is given of a situation involving sexual infidelity where the defence of loss of self-control might nonetheless still be raised:

[W]here a person discovers their partner sexually abusing their young child (an act that amounts to sexual infidelity) and loses self-control and kills, [the] fact that the partner's act amounted to sexual infidelity must be discounted but that act may still potentially be claimed to amount to the qualifying trigger in section 55(4) on the basis of the other aspects of the case (namely the child abuse).

In *Clinton* [2012] EWCA Crim 2, the Court of Appeal sought to provide clarification regarding the prohibition on having regard to sexual infidelity holding that it applies only where sexual infidelity is the *sole* potential qualifying trigger. In the first example given earlier the sexual infidelity is an essential part of the context in which the loss of self-control occurred and as such would not be excluded in determining whether the other matters were grave and serious enough to constitute a qualifying trigger. In the second example, in reality, it is highly unlikely that a parent discovering the other abusing their child would lose their self-control because of the infidelity rather than because of the commission of an offence against the child.

Perhaps it would have been better to have desisted from enacting s. 55(6)(c) and simply left it to the good sense of judges and of juries to assess sexual infidelity, where relevant, in the context of determining whether it amounts to extremely grave circumstances and whether it could be a justification for D's sense of being seriously wronged. As the *Impact Assessment* did not highlight any real problem with the more broadly based defence of provocation, it could be anticipated that there would not be a problem with the more narrowly based defence of loss of self-control thus making this provision unnecessary. The legislative history of this provision indicates it was reinserted in the bill at a late stage in the parliamentary process suggesting that its enactment was inadequately thought through.

In *Dawes* [2013] EWCA Crim 322, the Court of Appeal considered *Clinton* and emphasised that the new defence is narrower in ambit than the previous defence of provocation under which a judge was bound to leave the defence to the jury if there was any evidence that D was provoked to lose self-control however unmeritorious or trivial the circumstances might have been. The Court took the view that the provisions in s. 55(3), (4), and (5) addressed this problem by limiting the circumstances in which qualifying triggers might arise, Lord Judge CJ stating (at para. 60):

> The result is that some of the more absurd trivia which nevertheless required the judge to leave the provocation defence to the jury will no longer fall within the ambit of the qualifying triggers defined in the new defence. This is unsurprising. For the individual with normal capacity of self-restraint and tolerance, unless the circumstances are extremely grave, normal irritation, and even serious anger do not often cross the threshold into loss of control.

The Court further emphasised that the focus of the new defence is not on D's view of the gravity of the circumstances nor is D's own sense of justification in feeling he had been seriously wronged the test for determining if there was a qualifying trigger. Lord Judge CJ stated (at para. 61):

> The presence, or otherwise, of a qualifying trigger is not defined or decided by the defendant . . . S. 55(3) directly engages the defendant's fear of serious violence . . . . [I]n this type of case s. 55(4) will almost inevitably arise for consideration. Unless the defendant has a sense of being *seriously* wronged s. 55(4) has no application. Even if it does, there are two distinctive further requirements. The circumstances must be *extremely* grave and the defendant's sense of being seriously wronged by them must be *justifiable*. In our judgment these matters require objective assessment by the judge at the end of the evidence and, if the defence is left, by the jury considering their verdict. If it were otherwise it would mean that a qualifying trigger would be present if the defendant were to give an account to the effect that, 'the circumstances were extremely grave to me and caused me to have what I believed was a justifiable sense that I had been seriously wronged'. If so, when it is clear that the availability of a defence based on the loss of control has been significantly narrowed, one would have to question the purpose of s. 55(3), (4) and (5).

(c) *Reaction of person with normal degree of tolerance and self-restraint* If D has killed and sufficient evidence has been adduced to raise the defence of loss of self-control—that is, that D may have lost his self-control and killed, and that loss of self-control may have had a qualifying trigger—he will be entitled to succeed in his defence unless the prosecution disprove that 'a person of D's sex and age, with a normal degree of tolerance and self-restraint and in the circumstances of D, might have reacted in the same or a similar way to D' (s. 54(1)(c)). This is the objective test and has similarities with the test under the Homicide Act 1957 as understood following the decision of the Privy Council in *AG for Jersey* v *Holley* but it is notable that the word 'tolerance' is used in addition to 'self-restraint' indicating that this is something additional to the old concept of self-control. The statute avoids any use of the terms 'reasonable' or 'ordinary' to describe the person against whom D's reaction is to be measured. This person requires some designation, however, for the purposes of exposition, so we will be referring to him/her as the 'normal person'.

The normal person shares D's sex and age. Age clearly may have a relevance to the degree of self-control to be expected of a person; although, perhaps, maturity would be a better factor to consider as people mature at different rates and some never reach full maturity. However, the statute seeks to avoid this kind of complexity and adopts the simple approach of factoring in age and sex (whatever its relevance might be) for the purposes of determining whether the normal person may have reacted as D did. **It is enough that he may have reacted in 'the same or in a similar way to D'.**

In making the assessment of whether the normal person would have reacted in the same or a similar way to D, the normal person will be located in the same circumstances as D. This means that he will have the same history and characteristics as D in so far as these are relevant to the qualifying triggers which prompted the loss of self-control. Thus if D is being taunted about his sexual orientation, the normal person will have the same sexual orientation; if D is placed in fear of serious violence from V, her violent partner, the normal person will have that same history of living in a relationship involving domestic violence.

However, anything in D's circumstances which impairs his capacity to exercise the normal degree of tolerance and self-restraint to be expected of people living in England and Wales today will not be attributed to the normal person (see s. 54(3)). If D has extreme views affecting his tolerance for others whether based on their race, religion, gender, or sexual orientation, those views will not be attributed to the normal person. Similarly if D's capacity for exercising self-restraint is impaired by, for example, mental illness or having had a slower mental development than people of a similar age, these circumstances are not attributed to the normal person. If D's ability to exercise self-control is substantially impaired from other causes, he may be able to rely on the defence of diminished responsibility (see **9.3.2.1**).

In *Rejmanski* [2017] EWCA Crim 2061, the Court of Appeal heard two conjoined appeals, each raising the question of the extent to which a mental disorder (in the two cases, post-traumatic stress disorder (PTSD) and a personality disorder) could be relevant to an assessment of 'the circumstances of the defendant' when considering the partial defence of loss of control. The Court held that the objective test in s. 54(1)(c) is clear and cannot be watered down so as to allow mental disorders to be taken into account by the jury when judging against the standard of a person with a normal degree of tolerance and self-restraint:

> If, and in so far as, a personality disorder reduced the defendant's general capacity for tolerance or self-restraint, that would not be a relevant consideration. Moreover, it would not be a relevant consideration even if the personality disorder was one of the 'circumstances' of the defendant because it was relevant to the gravity of the trigger . . . Expert evidence about the impact of the disorder would be irrelevant and inadmissible on the issue of whether it would have reduced the capacity for tolerance and self-restraint of the hypothetical 'person of D's sex and age, with a normal degree of tolerance and self-restraint'.

The Court did recognise that a mental disorder might be relevant in other ways. As Lady Justice Hallett put it:

> [I]f a mental disorder has a relevance to the defendant's conduct other than a bearing on his general capacity for tolerance or self-restraint, it is not excluded by subsection (3), and the jury will be entitled to take it into account as one of the defendant's circumstances under s. 54(1)(c). However, it is necessary to identify with some care how the mental disorder is said to be relevant as one of the defendant's circumstances. It must not be relied upon to undermine the principle that the conduct of the defendant is to be judged against 'normal' standards, rather than the abnormal standard of an individual defendant.

The Court rejected the view that if a disorder is relevant to, say, the gravity of the qualifying trigger, and evidence of the disorder is admitted in relation to the gravity of the trigger, the jury would also be entitled to take it into account in so far as it bore on the defendant's general capacity for tolerance and self-restraint. The Court was clearly concerned about the objective test in s. 54(1)(c) experiencing the same creeping subjectivisation that the objective test in provocation had endured in the 1990s and in *Smith (Morgan)*. In *Rejmanski*, the Court of Appeal was clear: a disorder may be a relevant circumstance of the defendant, but would not be relevant to the question of the degree of tolerance and self-restraint which would be exercised by the hypothetical person referred to in s. 54(1)(c).

In terms of situations in which a mental disorder might be relevant to the defendant's 'circumstances', the Court cited the example of a personality disorder that caused the defendant to attempt suicide and about which he had been taunted by the deceased. The jury would be entitled to take it into account as one of his circumstances in understanding the effects of the taunts on him, but the jury would have to ask how a person of D's sex and age, with a normal degree of tolerance and self-restraint, might have reacted in D's circumstances, not how a person of D's sex and age with D's personality disorder might have reacted in D's circumstances (see also *Wilcocks* [2016] EWCA Crim 2043).

The Court of Appeal in *Rejmanski* has made it clear that the loss of control defence will not experience the inconsistency which beset the defence of provocation over the past three decades in terms of the relevance of D's characteristics, particularly mental disorders, thus preserving a clear distinction in both theory and practice between the defences of diminished responsibility and loss of control. This reflects the law on provocation as it was understood in *Camplin, Morhall*, and *Luc Thiet Thuan*.

(d) *Loss of control and intoxication* In *Asmelash* [2013] EWCA Crim 157, the issue arose whether D could rely on his intoxication as affecting his capacity for tolerance and self-restraint and have this attributed to the person of D's sex and age under s. 54(1)(c). The Court of Appeal considered the case of *Dowds* [2012] EWCA Crim 281 (see **9.3.2.1.3(b)**), where it had held that a defence of diminished responsibility could not be founded on voluntary intoxication. Parliament had not indicated any dissatisfaction with the established principles of law relating to voluntary intoxication. The Court rejected the contention that the general principles did not apply to the defence of loss of control. If Parliament had intended such a change it would have spelled it out in unequivocal language. No such language had been used. Further, the acceptance of the contention would lead to inconsistency between the two defences of diminished responsibility and loss of control which are often canvassed together before the jury. Lord Judge CJ stated (at para. 24) that:

> [T]he potential for uncertainty and confusion which would follow the necessarily very different directions on the issue of intoxication depending on which partial defence was under consideration, does not bear contemplation.

The Court made clear, however, that the fact that D was intoxicated does not deny him the opportunity of pleading loss of control: it simply means that the defence will be approached without reference to his intoxication. Lord Judge CJ explained the situation, thus (at para. 25):

If a sober individual in the defendant's circumstances, with normal levels of tolerance and self-restraint, might have behaved in the same way as the defendant confronted by the relevant qualifying trigger, he would not be deprived of the loss of control defence, just because he was not sober. And different considerations would arise if, a defendant with a severe problem with alcohol or drugs was mercilessly taunted about the condition, to the extent that it constituted a qualifying trigger, the alcohol or drug problem would then form part of the circumstances for consideration.

9.3.2.3 Suicide pacts

Section 4(1) of the Homicide Act 1957 (as amended by the Suicide Act 1961) provides: 'It shall be manslaughter and shall not be murder for a person acting in pursuance of a suicide pact between him and another to kill the other or be party to the other being killed by a third person'. Section 4(3) defines 'suicide pact' as follows:

> [A] common agreement between two or more persons having for its object the death of all of them, whether or not each is to take his own life, but nothing done by a person who enters into a suicide pact shall be treated as done by him in pursuance of the pact unless it is done while he has the settled intention of dying in pursuance of the pact.

If, for example, D enters into an agreement to kill V and then himself, and having killed V he relents or is prevented from killing himself, he may, on a charge of murder, raise the defence of suicide pact. In this case the burden of proof is upon the defence (s. 4(2)) to prove the facts grounding the defence on the balance of probabilities (*Woolmington* v *DPP* [1935] AC 462).

In its Consultation Paper No. 177, *A New Homicide Act for England and Wales?* published in 2005, the Law Commission recommended the repeal of the defence of suicide pact; deserving cases should be covered by a reformed defence of diminished responsibility. In its Report, *Murder, Manslaughter and Infanticide* (Law Com No. 304), the Law Commission reconsidered this recommendation, now taking the view that the defence should be retained pending a review of the broader question of whether there should be a partial defence of 'mercy' killing.

9.3.3 Involuntary manslaughter

If D did not have the *mens rea* for murder he may be guilty of manslaughter if the killing was unlawful. The label typically given to this branch of homicide is 'involuntary' manslaughter ('involuntary' signifying that D did not intend to kill or cause GBH, rather than indicating that D lacked control over his bodily movements). Involuntary manslaughter is an offence of ill-defined boundaries covering the middle ground between murder and accidental death. Involuntary manslaughter takes two forms. **The first form is constructive manslaughter and the second is gross negligence manslaughter.** Gross negligence manslaughter is sometimes referred to as 'reckless manslaughter'. The two concepts clearly overlap but gross negligence is the broader term covering a greater range of conduct.

Sometimes the facts of a case may fall within the compass of both constructive and gross negligence manslaughter so that a verdict of manslaughter may be available on either of those grounds.

9.3.3.1 **Constructive manslaughter**

Prior to the Homicide Act 1957, the doctrine of constructive malice meant that an accused could be convicted of murder where he killed in the course of committing a felony albeit that he lacked the *mens rea* of murder. A parallel doctrine existed that if an accused killed in the course of doing an unlawful act, which was not a felony, he was guilty of manslaughter. The Homicide Act, by s. 1(1), abolished the doctrine of constructive murder, but constructive manslaughter remains. The term 'constructive manslaughter' refers to the construction or building of liability for a serious offence (manslaughter) from the commission of a less serious offence, such as battery or arson. This is why **the offence is also often referred to as 'unlawful act' manslaughter.** Typically, unlawful act manslaughter will be charged when D has caused another's death by punching him but without intending to cause serious harm, or when a person has committed arson and a person has died in the ensuing fire, but when D did not foresee any serious harm. The fact that death is caused by D's unlawful act, however, is not sufficient to lead to a manslaughter verdict. The term 'unlawful act' is qualified in several ways.

Actus reus	Mens rea
• unlawfully • causing death • of a human being • under the Queen's Peace • by means of a dangerous act which constitutes a crime	with the *mens rea* for the crime which the unlawful and dangerous act constitutes

9.3.3.1.1 *A crime of commission*

In the nineteenth century there was some uncertainty in respect of the nature of the unlawfulness required. In *Fenton* (1830) 1 Lew CC 179, Tindal CJ directed the jury that it was sufficient if D did a wrongful act which was a tort. In *Franklin* (1883) 15 Cox CC 163, Field J doubted *Fenton* finding it abhorrent to construct a crime from a civil wrong. The doubts have since been resolved. In *Andrews v DPP* [1937] AC 576, Lord Atkin confirmed that **something more than negligence (which suffices for civil liability) is required.** In this case D had been driving dangerously when he killed the deceased. Driving is a lawful act which becomes unlawful when performed negligently. Lord Atkin sought to distinguish between acts which become unlawful when performed negligently and acts which are unlawful for some other reason, stating (at p. 585):

> There is an obvious difference in the law of manslaughter between doing an unlawful act and doing a lawful act with a degree of carelessness which the legislature makes criminal. If it were otherwise a man who killed another while driving without due care and attention would *ex necessitate* commit manslaughter.

An act can only be unlawful in these terms, therefore, if it is done with *mens rea* (see *Lamb* [1967] 2 QB 981).

> In *Lamb*, D, in fun, pointed a revolver at a friend. He knew that there were two bullets in the chambers, but neither was opposite the barrel. He did not appreciate that the

cylinder rotated automatically when the trigger was pulled. He pulled the trigger, a bullet was fired and his friend died. D was convicted of manslaughter following a direction from the judge that pointing the revolver and pulling the trigger was an unlawful act even if there was no intent to injure or alarm and that they need not consider whether the pointing of the gun was an assault. (For the definition of assault see **10.1**.) The Court of Appeal quashed the conviction; if there was no assault there was no unlawful act. Sachs J stated (at p. 988):

> [M]ens rea, being now an essential ingredient in manslaughter . . . , . . . could not in the present case be established in relation to the first ground except by proving that element of intent without which there can be no assault.

There was also no *actus reus* of assault in this case as the friend, being a willing participant in the prank, did not apprehend any injury; the *actus reus* of assault is causing the victim to apprehend immediate application of unlawful force to his body.

In *Andrews* [2002] EWCA Crim 3021, the Court of Appeal appears to have ignored this requirement for the basic offence to be one requiring *mens rea* in confirming a conviction where D had injected V with insulin, with V's consent, resulting in V's death. The drug was administered in order to give V a 'rush'. The appeal focused on the issue of consent, the Court of Appeal affirming that consent made no difference to the unlawfulness of D's act. This is consistent with the authorities on consent (see **10.7**). The unlawful act in the immediate case was alleged to have been supplying a prescription-only medicine without a prescription contrary to ss 58 and 67 of the Medicines Act 1968. This is a strict liability offence. It is doubtful whether the Court intended any modification of the principle in *Andrews v DPP* as there was no argument on this point and thus no express statement to that effect. If similar facts arise any such difficulty may be avoided by charging on the basis that the unlawful act was administering a noxious thing contrary to s. 23 of the Offences Against the Person Act 1861 (see **10.5**).

Deaths resulting from the administration of drugs caused difficulties for the Court of Appeal. A problem decision in this area was that of *Cato* [1976] 1 WLR 110, where the Court of Appeal appeared to extend the ambit of unlawful acts.

> D injected V with heroin which V had supplied to D for this purpose. V died from respiratory failure caused by the heroin. D was convicted of manslaughter and of administering a noxious thing so as to endanger life contrary to s. 23 of the Offences Against the Person Act 1861. In upholding the manslaughter conviction, the Court of Appeal stated that, even if they had not upheld the conviction for the s. 23 offence (which they did), they would still have upheld the manslaughter conviction on the basis that by injecting the deceased with heroin which D had unlawfully taken into his possession, he had done an unlawful act.

The problem with this decision was that injecting heroin is not an offence contrary to the Misuse of Drugs Act 1971. Possession of heroin is an offence but V did not die as a result of D's possession of the drug. However, the Court of Appeal elaborated further on the error in *Cato* in *Kennedy* [1999] Crim LR 65, where D supplied a syringe filled with heroin to V who injected it and died. In upholding D's conviction for manslaughter the Court of Appeal did so on the basis either that D was guilty of the s. 23 offence or that the self-injection by V was unlawful and D had assisted and wilfully encouraged this. As to the latter point, D could not be a secondary party to manslaughter, as V's self-injection could not amount to an unlawful act. This position was subsequently adopted by the Court of Appeal in *Dias* [2001] EWCA Crim 2986 (see **2.6.3.5.4**), which doubted whether *Kennedy* could have been decided correctly on this point as it conflicted with *Dalby* [1982] 1 All ER 916. The Court of Appeal concluded that there was no offence of self-injection and thus V was not a principal, with the consequence that D could not be a secondary party. When the Criminal Cases Review Commission referred the case of *Kennedy* back to the Court of Appeal on the basis that there was a real possibility that the Court of Appeal would find the conviction unsafe in light of the doubts expressed in *Dias*, the Court of Appeal upheld the conviction on the basis that D had acted in concert with V to commit the s. 23 offence which amounted to the unlawful act (*Kennedy* [2005] EWCA Crim 685). The Court eschewed any notion that the question of an intervening act on the part of V arose on the basis that D's supply of the heroin-filled syringe to V for immediate use amounted to their acting in concert to commit the s. 23 offence. This was not the last word on the issue, however, as the case went to the House of Lords on the following question of general public importance:

> When is it appropriate to find someone guilty of manslaughter where that person has been involved in the supply of a class A controlled drug, which is then freely and voluntarily self-administered by the person to whom it was supplied, and the administration of the drug then causes his death?

In *Kennedy (No. 2)* [2007] UKHL 38, their Lordships answered the question in one word, 'Never'. They confirmed that **the unlawful act on which a conviction for constructive manslaughter is based must itself be a crime and that act must be a significant cause of death.** Their Lordships recognised that it was the injection which harboured the danger; that act was performed by V as a free, deliberate, and informed act; it was not unlawful for V to do so; and D was not liable as an accessory as V was not the principal; and D's prior acts were nothing more than 'but for' causes (see further **2.6.2**). Their Lordships further indicated that many difficulties would be avoided if the prosecutor clearly specified on the indictment, where constructive manslaughter is charged, the unlawful act on which the count is based.

Of course, **there will be no unlawful act if D had a lawful excuse or justification for doing what he did.**

 Example

> If D punches V in self-defence using reasonable force, but V stumbles and falls on a stone fracturing his skull and dies, D will not be liable for manslaughter as there is no unlawful act (see **6.4.1**). If the force used was excessive and D knew it to be so there would be no justification and the force would be unlawful, providing a foundation for a manslaughter verdict.

Where D has committed an unlawful act of basic intent, the fact that he was intoxicated and lacked *mens rea* will not avail him. In *Lipman* [1970] 1 QB 152, D had killed a person when he was on a hallucinatory trip due to taking LSD. The Court of

Appeal upheld D's conviction for manslaughter. The unlawful act he performed was a battery which was an offence of basic intent and therefore, under *DPP* v *Majewski* [1977] AC 443, his intoxication meant that he had the requisite *mens rea* (see **5.5.3**). If the unlawful act alleged is an offence of specific intent, D may rely on his intoxication as evidence that he lacked *mens rea* (*O'Driscoll* (1977) 65 Cr App R 50), but it is difficult to envisage an offence of specific intent which does not necessarily encompass a lesser offence of basic intent.

Constructive manslaughter requires the commission of an unlawful 'act'. It appears that **an omission will not suffice** (but an omission will suffice for gross negligence manslaughter where there is a duty to act; see **2.5**). In *Lowe* [1973] QB 702, the Court of Appeal quashed D's conviction for manslaughter founded on the offence of wilful neglect of the child so as to cause unnecessary suffering or injury to its health contrary to s. 1(1) of the Children and Young Persons Act 1933. The trial judge had directed the jury that there was no difference between an omission likely to cause harm and an act likely to cause harm. The Court of Appeal, disapproving of *Senior* [1899] 1 QB 283 where, on similar facts, a conviction for manslaughter had been upheld, distinguished between acts and omissions, Phillimore LJ stating (at p. 707):

> [I]f I strike a child in a manner likely to cause harm it is right that if the child dies I may be charged with manslaughter. If, however, I omit to do something with the result that it suffers injury to its health which results in its death, we think that a charge of manslaughter should not be an inevitable consequence even if the omission is deliberate.

Obviously, if the omission was merely negligent, no liability for manslaughter should arise. But there is a great difference between neglect which is due to a lack of thought and that which is wilful, in the sense that there is a deliberate decision not to give food or liquids or to seek medical attention. Such conduct is just as reprehensible as positive acts which are likely to cause harm. *Lowe* is a decision which clearly requires reconsideration.

Whether D has done an unlawful act is a question for the jury to decide; even if all the evidence points to there being an unlawful act, the judge may not decide this issue himself but must leave it to the jury to determine (see *Jennings* [1990] Crim LR 588). If there is no unlawful act, an accused may still be convicted of manslaughter if the judge also directs the jury on gross negligence manslaughter and the requirements of this offence are satisfied (see **9.3.3.2**).

9.3.3.1.2 *The unlawful act must be dangerous*

While it must be established that D had the *mens rea* for the offence which constitutes the unlawful act, this is not sufficient to lead to a conviction for manslaughter. An objective condition must also be satisfied—that is, that the act was dangerous. In *Church* [1966] 1 QB 59, Edmund-Davies LJ explained that **'dangerous' meant that the unlawful act 'must be such as all sober and reasonable people would inevitably recognise must subject the other person to, at least, the risk of some harm resulting therefrom, albeit not serious harm'**. The degree of harm likely to be caused need not be serious, but it must be physical harm rather than a risk of emotional disturbance (*Dawson* (1985) 81 Cr App R 150). However, shock produced by fright may fall within the definition of harm where it produces some physical injury, such as a heart attack.

There is therefore a low threshold for unlawful act manslaughter: if D punches V once and V falls hitting his head on the pavement with a resulting injury that results in death, D will be guilty of manslaughter. That a person can so easily be convicted of the serious offence of manslaughter raises fundamental questions about the scope of criminal law: those who favour a subjectivist approach to liability argue that a person should only be liable for a serious offence when he has foreseen at least some harm from his actions; those who advocate a more objectivist approach suggest that the law's deterrent function is best served by holding those who cross the threshold into criminal behaviour (e.g. by punching another person) liable for the consequences of their actions, even if those consequences were unforeseen by D or unforeseeable to ordinary people in that situation. English law adheres rigidly to the latter approach.

 Questions

Several issues relating to the 'dangerousness' test require clarification:

(a) Must the defendant have any awareness of the danger arising from his unlawful act?

(b) Must the actual form of harm which ensued have been foreseeable by the sober and reasonable person?

(c) Must the act of the defendant be directed at the victim?

Over the years these and a number of other issues have received clarification.

(a) *Must the defendant be aware of the danger arising from his unlawful act?* The courts have stated clearly that dangerousness is to be judged objectively and the prosecution does not have to prove that D was aware of any danger. The leading case is *DPP* v *Newbury* [1977] AC 500.

> In *DPP* v *Newbury*, two boys pushed a paving stone off the parapet of a railway bridge into the path of an oncoming train, hitting the train and killing the guard who was sitting next to the driver. The question for the House of Lords was whether a defendant could be convicted of manslaughter if he did not foresee that his act might cause harm to another. Their Lordships answered the question in the affirmative. Lord Salmon stated (at p. 506):

>> In *Larkin* (1942) 29 Cr App R 18, Humphreys J said, at p. 23: 'Where the act which a person is engaged in performing is unlawful, then if at the same time it is a dangerous act, that is, an act which is likely to injure another person, and quite inadvertently the doer of the act causes the death of that other person by that act, then he is guilty of manslaughter.'
>>
>> I agree entirely . . . that that is an admirably clear statement of the law which has been applied many times. It makes it plain (a) that an accused is guilty of manslaughter if it is proved that he intentionally did an act which was unlawful and dangerous and that that act inadvertently caused death and (b) that it is unnecessary to prove that the accused knew that the act was unlawful or dangerous.

In *JF and NE* [2015] EWCA Crim 351, the Court of Appeal rejected an argument that the objective test as to whether the act was a dangerous one should be adapted to take into account the foreseeability of persons of the appellants' ages and, in the case of one of the appellants, his mental capacity. The law is clear and well-established, and only Parliament can decide whether to change it in the light of the Law Commission's various recommendations. The law is strict; by adhering to an objective approach to dangerousness, any defendant who commits an unlawful act that causes death is potentially liable for the serious offence of manslaughter regardless of the extent to which he appreciated the risks that his acts posed. The offence thus captures a wide range of defendants, from those who appreciate a serious risk of harm from their actions, but lack the appreciation of serious harm as a virtual certainty that is necessary for murder, to those who commit minor criminal acts with no appreciation of any risks flowing from those acts. The threshold is low: the prosecution need prove only that ordinary people would have appreciated the risk of some physical harm.

(b) *Must the actual form of harm which ensued have been foreseeable by the sober and reasonable person?* In *JM and SM* [2012] EWCA Crim 2293, the Court of Appeal held that it is not necessary to prove that sober and reasonable people would have foreseen the particular form of harm which ensued; it is sufficient that they would have foreseen some physical harm.

JM and SM were ejected from a nightclub by the doormen. They returned and began to assault the doormen. In the course of this affray V, an experienced and apparently healthy doorman, went to the assistance of his colleagues. Shortly after the affray had been subdued, V collapsed and died. A post-mortem established that V had been suffering from a renal artery aneurysm; he died from blood loss arising from a rupture to the renal artery. This was highly unlikely to have occurred spontaneously but would have been consequent on shock and a sudden surge in blood pressure due to the release of adrenalin into the circulation during the attack by the defendants and the rupture occurred either while the affray was in progress or in its immediate aftermath. The trial judge ruled that, on this evidence, it would not be open to the jury to convict of manslaughter as they could not be sure that a sober and reasonable person would inevitably recognise the risk that V would die in the way he did as this was a completely different form of harm from the harm recognisable in an affray, such as the danger of being hit or suffering injuries in a fall in the course of dealing with the defendants. On appeal by the prosecution, the Court of Appeal overturned that ruling concluding that there was evidence from which a jury properly directed could conclude that sober and reasonable people observing the affray 'would readily have recognised that all the doormen involved in the effort to control the defendants were at the risk of some harm, and that the fatal injury occurred while it was in progress or in its immediate aftermath while [V] was still subject to its effects'. Lord Judge CJ explained (at para. 20):

In our judgment, certainly since *Church* and *Newbury*, it has never been a requirement that the defendant personally should foresee any specific harm at all, or that the reasonable bystander should recognise the precise form or 'sort' of harm which did ensue. What matters is whether reasonable and sober people would recognise that the unlawful activities of the defendant inevitably subjected the deceased to the risk of some harm resulting from them.

In *Bristow* [2013] EWCA 1540, the defendants sought to steal a vehicle and other property from V's motor repair business which was situated at the end of a single track road. V tried to stop their escape but was knocked down and run over by one of the vehicles they were using and died. It could not be established which vehicle hit V or who was driving it. The Crown contended that from the outset the presence of residential farm buildings along the single track road would have alerted the defendants to the risk of being caught in the act of burglary, which would then result in the need to escape in vehicles along that same single track. In these circumstances a reasonable bystander would recognise the risk of some harm being caused to a person who intervened it being night, dark, the space at the premises being relatively confined with only one escape route, and powerful vehicles involved. On appeal, counsel attempted to argue that no danger in the sense contemplated by *Church* could be said to have arisen until V appeared and a defendant began driving a vehicle. Treacy LJ, emphasising that burglary was a continuing offence, robustly dismissed this submission stating (at paras 34–37):

> This is not a case like *Dawson* or *Watson* where the circumstances demonstrating the risk of harm to the occupier of property did not arise until a point during the burglary or at all. Whilst burglary of itself is not a dangerous crime, a particular burglary may be dangerous because of the circumstances surrounding its commission. We consider that the features identified by the Crown . . . were capable of making this burglary dangerous when coupled with foresight of the risk of intervention to prevent escape.
>
> In those circumstances we consider that the features of this crime were sufficient for the burglary to be capable of being an unlawful act which a reasonable bystander would inevitably realise must subject any person intervening to the risk of some harm resulting . . .
>
> [V] died because the pre-existing risk came to pass when he foreseeably intervened and suffered fatal injury as a result of the appellants seeking to make their escape as part of the burglary . . . . The factual questions for the jury . . . were whether each appellant foresaw the risk of intervention by a third party, and whether the reasonable bystander would consider the venture dangerous in the *Church* sense.
>
> Since the crime to be focused on was the burglary, we reject [counsel's] submission as to the point at which foresight and danger were to be assessed . . . . What needed to be considered was the foresight of the participants as they embarked upon the crime, and what, if anything a reasonable bystander would inevitably have recognised as a risk of physical harm to any person intervening.

(c) *Must the act of the defendant be directed at the victim?* The prosecution does not have to prove that D's acts were directed at the particular victim who died.
In *Goodfellow* (1986) 83 Cr App R 23:

> D was convicted of manslaughter having set fire to the council house in which he lived as he wished to be rehoused. D rescued two of his children but his wife, another child, and another woman died as the fire spread more quickly than he had anticipated. D contended on appeal that his unlawful act was not directed at the victims. The Court of Appeal dismissed the appeal holding that D's act may not have been directed at the victims but it was a direct cause of their deaths and it was, objectively, dangerous.

That the decision in *Goodfellow* is correct is confirmed by the decision in *AG's Reference (No. 3 of 1994)* [1997] 3 WLR 421, in which the appellant had stabbed M, a pregnant woman, which resulted in the premature birth of her child who in turn died some time later due to problems linked to her premature birth. The Court of Appeal affirmed D's conviction for manslaughter. Lord Hope of Craighead stated that **it is enough that the unlawful act creates a risk of harm to someone and there is no need for the unlawful act to be directed at the person who ultimately dies as a result of it.** Lord Hope cited with approval the decision in *Mitchell* [1983] QB 741 where D hit E who was standing in a queue in a post office. E fell against V, an elderly lady, who fell breaking her leg and died thereafter as a result of a pulmonary embolism linked to her fall. Lord Hope also cited with approval *Larkin* and *Newbury* before concluding that D should have been convicted of manslaughter in the instant case. Lord Hope was satisfied that the stabbing of the mother was an unlawful and dangerous act. Lord Hope stated (at p. 446):

> There can be no doubt that all sober and reasonable people would regard that act, within the appropriate meaning of this term, as dangerous. It is plain that it was unlawful as it was done with the intention of causing her injury . . . [A]ll the ingredients necessary for *mens rea* in regard to the crime of manslaughter were established, irrespective of who was the ultimate victim of it. The fact that the child whom the mother was carrying at the time was born alive and then died as a result of the stabbing is all that was needed for the offence of manslaughter when *actus reus* for that crime was completed by the child's death. The question, once all the other elements are satisfied, is simply one of causation. The defendant must accept all the consequences of his act, so long as the jury are satisfied that he did what he did intentionally, that what he did was unlawful and that, applying the correct test, it was also dangerous . . . . In my opinion that is sufficient for the offence of manslaughter.

9.3.3.1.3 *What information is credited to the sober and reasonable person for the purpose of determining whether the unlawful act was dangerous?*

In deciding whether the act was such as all sober and reasonable people would recognise involved the risk of harm, **the sober and reasonable person is credited with the same knowledge as D had at the time of the offence.** In *Dawson* Watkins LJ stated (at p. 157) that the objective test 'can only be undertaken upon the basis of the knowledge gained by the sober and reasonable man as though he were present at the scene of and watched the unlawful act being performed'. It is the responsibility of the judge to inform the jury which facts are relevant for this purpose (*Dawson*).

> In *Dawson*, D and E robbed V's filling station wearing masks and armed with a pickaxe handle and replica gun. Shortly afterwards V died of a heart attack. It was not known to the accused, nor would it have been apparent, that V suffered from heart disease. The convictions for manslaughter were quashed for several reasons, one being that the trial judge had not made it clear that the jury could not take into account the fact that V suffered from heart disease when deciding if the unlawful act was dangerous.

However, **the jury may take into account facts of which D became aware during the course of committing the unlawful act.**

> In *Watson* [1989] 2 All ER 865, D and E threw a brick through the window of V's house and entered it. They confronted V, who was 87, frail, and suffering from a serious heart condition. After abusing V verbally they left and V died 90 minutes later from a

heart attack. Although quashing the convictions for manslaughter on another ground, the Court of Appeal held that the sober and reasonable person could be credited with knowledge of the facts of which the appellants became aware after entering the house, namely the victim's age and frailty. While the offence of burglary was complete upon crossing the threshold, the Court held that the unlawful act comprised the whole of the burglarious intrusion.

The sober and reasonable man will also be aware of the background to the unlawful act which includes preparatory acts done by D as this sets the act in context for the purpose of determining its objective dangerousness.

In *Ball* [1989] Crim LR 730 D loaded a shotgun with two cartridges taken from his pocket which contained live and blank cartridges. He fired the gun at V claiming he only intended to frighten her. The cartridge in the chamber was a live one and V died. On appeal against his conviction for manslaughter it was argued that the objective assessment of the danger of D's act should be based on his mistaken belief that he was firing a blank cartridge and not on the actual fact that he was firing a live cartridge. The Court of Appeal rejected this submission, Lord Lane CJ stating:

> [Once it is] established . . . that the act was both unlawful and that he intended to commit the assaults, the question whether the act is a dangerous one is to be judged not by the appellant's appreciation but by that of the sober and reasonable man, and it is impossible to impute into his appreciation the mistaken belief of the appellant that what he was doing was not dangerous because he thought he had a blank cartridge in the chamber. At that stage the appellant's intention, foresight or knowledge is irrelevant.

9.3.3.2 Gross negligence manslaughter

The second basis on which a person may be convicted of involuntary manslaughter is that of gross negligence. **This head of liability will be relied on where the act of D is not otherwise unlawful or where death results from D's omission to act** (for examples of such duties see **2.5.2.1**). Gross negligence was recognised as the test for manslaughter in *Bateman* (1925) 19 Cr App R 8 and approved by the House of Lords in *Andrews v DPP* [1937] AC 576. In *Bateman* Lord Hewart CJ held that in order to secure a conviction of A for manslaughter the prosecution had to prove that (at p. 11):

> A owed a duty to B to take care, that that duty was not discharged, . . . that the default caused the death of B . . . and that A's negligence amounted to a crime . . . . [I]n order to establish criminal liability the facts must be such that, in the opinion of the jury, the negligence of the accused went beyond a mere matter of compensation between subjects and showed such disregard for the life and safety of others as to amount to a crime against the state and conduct deserving of punishment.

This test required there to be a duty of care owed by D to the victim, breach of which caused the victim's death (see **2.6**) and left it to the jury to determine whether D's negligence was so gross that it demanded punishment as a crime rather than merely the imposition of civil liability and the payment of compensation. It is a very high degree of negligence which has to be established before criminal liability should ensue. This was confirmed by Lord Atkin in *Andrews* where he stated (at p. 583):

> [F]or the purposes of the criminal law there are degrees of negligence: and a very high degree of negligence is required to be proved before the felony is established. Probably of all the epithets that can be applied 'reckless' most nearly covers the case . . . but it is probably not all-embracing, for 'reckless' suggests an indifference to risk whereas the accused may have appreciated the risk and intended to avoid it and yet shown such a high degree of negligence in the means adopted to avoid the risk as would justify a conviction.

For many years the courts used the terms 'recklessness' and 'gross negligence' interchangeably so that it was not clear whether these two concepts were exactly coextensive. Following the House of Lords' decisions in *Caldwell* and *Lawrence* (see **3.4.2.2**) there was a shift in favour of recklessness (see *Seymour* [1983] 2 AC 493). However, in *Adomako* [1995] 1 AC 171, their Lordships reverted to the test of gross negligence as the correct basis upon which to establish liability for manslaughter. In this case the appellant, an anaesthetist, failed to notice for six minutes during an operation that the oxygen supply to the patient had become disconnected from the ventilator. As a result the patient suffered a cardiac arrest and died. The House of Lords affirmed the appellant's conviction. Lord Mackay of Clashfern LC stated (at p. 187) that 'the law as stated in . . . *Seymour* . . . should no longer apply since the underlying statutory provisions on which it rested have now been repealed by the Road Traffic Act 1991'. **His Lordship affirmed the continuing authority of *Andrews* which focused on breach of duty.** He stated (at p. 187):

> The jury will have to consider whether the extent to which the defendant's conduct departed from the proper standard of care incumbent upon him, involving as it must have done a risk of death to the patient, was such that it should be judged criminal . . . . The essence of the matter . . . is whether having regard to the risk of death involved, the conduct of the defendant was so bad in all the circumstances as to amount in their judgment to a criminal act or omission.

 Key Point

Following *Adomako*, therefore, the elements of the offence could be specified as follows:

- D owed V (a human being under the Queen's Peace) a duty of care.
- D breached that duty.
- The breach was grossly negligent thereby rendering it unlawful.
- The breach caused V's death.

9.3.3.2.1 *Duty of care*

Gross negligence manslaughter is the criminal offspring of the civil law of negligence. Duty of care has its ordinary civil law meaning—a person owes a duty of care to another where it is reasonably foreseeable that their acts or omissions will cause harm to another. In most cases of gross negligence manslaughter, the existence of a duty of care will not be contentious: there are a wide range of situations in which the courts will readily accept that D owed a duty of care to V.

In *Singh (Gurphal)* [1999] Crim LR 582, the Court of Appeal held that whether D owed a duty of care was a question of law for the judge to determine. This has been confirmed in subsequent decisions (see *Wacker* [2002] EWCA Crim 1944; *Evans* [2009] EWCA Crim 650). If the facts are in dispute (which will often be the case), it will be for the jury to determine whether, in light of the judge's directions on the law, a duty did exist (see *Willoughby* [2004] EWCA Crim 3365). For example, in the normal doctor/patient situation as pertained in *Adomako* there will not be any dispute over whether or not a duty of care existed; but if, for example, the doctor is on holiday and is asked by V, another holiday-maker, casually over a drink for advice, there could be serious dispute over whether any doctor/patient relationship existed and thus whether any duty of care arose if this turned out to be poor advice and V, acting upon it, died as a result.

The situations in which duties of care may arise are fairly limitless. The courts will apply the ordinary principles of negligence but, necessarily, it may not be entirely clear in advance of a trial what situations are covered by these principles. Further complications arise where omissions are involved as, in addition to the duty of care, there must be a duty to act.

> In *Evans (Gemma)* [2009] EWCA Crim 650 (see **2.6.3.5.4**), D was convicted of manslaughter, along with her mother, T, where she had supplied heroin to her younger step-sister, C, who had taken it and overdosed. D and T kept her under observation overnight but did not seek medical assistance fearing that both they and C would get into trouble. There was no question over the liability of T as her duty of care arose from her parental responsibility for her child (see **2.5.2.2.2**) but D owed no such duty arising out of relationship. The Court of Appeal, however, upheld her conviction on the basis that she was under a duty to take reasonable steps for the safety of C once she realised that the heroin she had supplied her was having a potentially fatal impact on her health. Lord Judge CJ relied on the case of *Miller* [1983] 2 AC 161 HL (see **2.5.2.2.4**) as a basis for the duty to act in the present case which he defined as follows (at para. 31):

> > [W]hen a person has created or contributed to the creation of a state of affairs which he knows, or ought reasonably to know, has become life threatening, a consequent duty on him to act by taking reasonable steps to save the other's life will normally arise.

The duty of care derived from the normal principles of negligence, Lord Judge CJ relying upon their exposition by Lord Scott of Foscote in *Mitchell* v *Glasgow City Council* [2009] 2 WLR 481, at para. 40, where he said:

> If a defendant has played some causative part in the train of events that have led to the risk of injury, a duty to take reasonable steps to avert or lessen the risk may arise.

In D's case, she had played a causative part in the train of events by supplying the heroin; but for this, V could not have self-administered and overdosed. Accordingly, this gave rise to the duty of care and her duty to act arose upon becoming aware of

V's condition. Her failure to take reasonable steps to save V, such as summoning medical assistance, provided the basis upon which the jury could conclude that she had been grossly negligent.

While the civil law of negligence will provide guidance on the recognition of a duty of care, the wider principles of the civil law of negligence are not to be imported into the criminal law. In *Wacker* [2002] EWCA Crim 1944, the defendant sought to place reliance on the principle *ex turpi causa non oritur actio* to argue that, as he had been involved in a criminal enterprise with those who died, there was no duty of care in negligence and thus there could not be any liability for gross negligence manslaughter. In a civil action for negligence *ex turpi causa* would provide a defence to a claim. The issue for the Court of Appeal was whether this principle applied in respect of criminal proceedings.

> D drove his refrigerated lorry, loaded with 60 illegal Chinese immigrants hidden behind a cargo of tomatoes, on to a channel ferry which disembarked at Dover. Customs and Excise officers, doing a spot check on his vehicle, discovered the immigrants, 58 of whom had died of suffocation on the crossing due to an air vent having been sealed by the defendant to reduce the risk of discovery.

The Court of Appeal rejected the argument based on *ex turpi causa* on the basis that the civil law and criminal law served different functions. The criminal law's function was to protect individuals and might step in at the very point where the civil law is powerless to assist. Furthermore, the criminal law will act to prevent serious injury or death even where those subject to the risk of such had consented to it (see *Brown*, **10.7**). On this basis there was no justification in public policy for concluding that the criminal law would not apply where the person responsible for the death and the deceased were involved in some joint criminal venture which involved an element of acceptance of a degree of risk in order to further that venture (see further *Willoughby* [2004] EWCA Crim 3365). D's claim that keeping the vent shut increased the chances of evading detection was an argument which the Court, unsurprisingly, found singularly unattractive (see also *Winter* [2010] EWCA Crim 1474).

9.3.3.2.2 *Grossly negligent breach of duty*

In relation to this variety of manslaughter the central focus is not on D's state of mind but rather on his conduct which fails, to a gross degree, to measure up to an objective standard determined by the jury. The courts will not attempt to specify the degree of negligence required with any greater precision, as they recognise it is not possible to do so. **The reach of the criminal law, therefore, in this area of homicide is left to be determined by the jury who have to assess whether the negligence was gross.** The test laid down in *Adomako* is: **were the accused's acts so bad that in all the circumstances they amounted to a criminal act or omission?** In making this assessment the jury will be asked to consider what a reasonable person of D's age and experience would have foreseen; the issue is not whether D foresaw the particular danger (*S* [2015] EWCA Crim 558).

Of course, if in any case there is proof that D did foresee the serious risk of death and carried on regardless, this would be strong evidence that his conduct was exceptionally bad and meriting a conclusion of gross negligence (see *R (On the application of Rowley)* v *DPP* [2003] EWHC 693 (Admin)).

Question

Negligence presumes that a reasonable person would have foreseen the risk of a particular consequence occurring as a result of the conduct in question. For gross negligence manslaughter, what is the risk which D should have foreseen?

In *Adomako* Lord Mackay referred to 'the risk of death involved'. In *Bateman* the negligence had to display 'a disregard for life and safety' before it could lead to liability. In *Singh (Gurphal)* [1999] Crim LR 582, the Court of Appeal held that on a charge of gross negligence manslaughter **'the circumstances must be such that a reasonably prudent person would have foreseen a serious and obvious risk not merely of injury or even serious injury but of death'**. An obvious risk 'is a present risk which is clear and unambiguous, not one which might become apparent on further investigation' (see *Rudling* [2016] EWCA Crim 741, *per* Sir Brian Leveson P). Thus, in *Rudling*, the failure of a GP to attend a 12-year-old boy who subsequently died from a very rare disease which was not something which any GP could be expected to recognise, could not provide a foundation for a gross negligence manslaughter conviction. At the point where the GP determined that a visit to attend to the patient was not necessary the most that could be concluded was that there might be a risk of serious illness. This was the point where the breach of duty occurred. Sir Brian Leveson P went on to state that 'a mere possibility that an assessment might reveal something life-threatening is not the same as an obvious risk of death'.

The Court of Appeal in *Misra and Srivastava* [2004] EWCA Crim 2375, while holding that the offence of gross negligence manslaughter did not offend the requirement of legal certainty under Art. 7 of the European Convention on Human Rights, confirmed, however, that **only a risk of death will be sufficient to establish the offence; a risk of bodily injury or injury to health was not sufficient**.

In *Rose (Honey)* [2018] QB 328, the Court of Appeal considered whether, in assessing reasonable foreseeability of serious and obvious risk of death in cases of gross negligence manslaughter, it is appropriate to take into account what a reasonable person in the position of the defendant would have known but for his or her breach of duty.

> In February 2012, HR, a registered optometrist, carried out a sight test on V after retinal images had first been taken by an optical consultant/assistant. Following V's examination, HR recorded no issues of concern, said that V did not need glasses and specified the next appointment for 12 months' time. Five months after his sight test, V died. A post-mortem revealed that V had died from an obstruction in his brain, which had been a longstanding chronic problem. A consultant ophthalmologist said that the retinal images taken of the back of V's eyes in February 2012 showed significant congestion of the veins and swelling of the optic nerve. In his opinion, the retinal images taken in February 2012 were abnormal and would ordinarily cause concern to any competent optometrist and give rise to urgent referral to hospital.
>
> HR was charged with gross negligence manslaughter, the prosecution alleging that she had failed properly to examine V's eyes and failed to refer him for the urgent medical treatment he needed.

The trial judge ruled that there was a case to answer. On the issue of foreseeability, he directed the jury to consider whether it was reasonably foreseeable that her breach of her duty of care gave rise to a serious and obvious risk of death and that they should consider this question at the moment that she concluded her examination of V in light of the facts that were known or should have been known to her at that time. On appeal, the appellant submitted that that was a misdirection; failing to examine the back of the eye was admittedly negligent, since this was an essential part of an eye examination, but this was not to the criminal standard, since (given the lack of any symptoms at the time) it was not reasonably foreseeable to a reasonably competent optometrist, that that negligent act of not examining the back of the eyes would carry an obvious and serious risk of death. None of the authorities suggested that, in assessing either the foreseeability of risk or the grossness of the conduct in question, the jury should have been permitted to take into account information which would, could, or should have been available to the defendant following the breach of duty in question.

The Court of Appeal allowed the appeal, holding that a recognisable risk of something serious is not the same as a recognisable risk of death. A mere possibility that an assessment might reveal something life-threatening is not the same as an obvious risk of death: an obvious risk is a clear and unambiguous present risk, not one which might become apparent on further investigation. The President of the Queen's Bench Division, Sir Brian Leveson, stated (at paras 80 and 84):

> The question of available knowledge and risk is always to be judged objectively and prospectively as at the moment of breach, not but for the breach. The question of reasonable foreseeability is evident from the words used, *i.e.* what is reasonably *fore*-seeable at the time of the breach (a prospective view). It is not what would, could or should have been known but for the breach of the identified duty of care, *i.e.* if the breach had not been committed (a retrospective view).
>
> . . .
>
> The Judge appears to have led himself into error by his earlier emphasis on the fact that the question of reasonable foreseeability was an objective, not a subjective, exercise and was not to be decided by reference to 'the actual knowledge of the Defendant at the time of the breach'. In so doing, the Judge appears to have confused or elided two separate matters: (a) the actual knowledge of Ms Rose at the time of the breach and (b) the putative knowledge of the reasonably prudent optometrist in the position of Ms Rose at the time. The two are quite different concepts: the former is subjective; the latter is objective. The test of reasonable foreseeability is, of course, resolutely objective and there is no question of it being decided by reference to the subjective knowledge of the person whose conduct is under scrutiny. The test of reasonable foreseeability simply requires the notional objective exercise of putting a reasonably prudent professional in the shoes of the person whose conduct is under scrutiny and asking whether, at the moment of breach of the duty on which the prosecution rely, that person ought reasonably (*i.e.* objectively) to have foreseen an obvious and serious risk of death.

The Court emphasized the practical importance of its ruling (at para. 94):

> [I]n assessing reasonable foreseeability of serious and obvious risk of death . . . it is not appropriate to take into account what the defendant would have known but for his or her breach of duty. Were the answer otherwise, this would fundamentally undermine the

established legal test of foreseeability in gross negligence manslaughter which requires proof of a 'serious and obvious risk of death' at the time of breach. The implications for medical and other professions would be serious because people would be guilty of gross negligence manslaughter by reason of negligent omissions to carry out routine eye, blood and other tests which in fact would have revealed fatal conditions notwithstanding that the circumstances were such that it was not reasonably foreseeable that failure to carry out such tests would carry an obvious and serious risk of death. For these reasons, this appeal is allowed and the conviction is quashed.

 Key Point

The jury must assess whether the defendant's negligence should be considered gross by considering whether the circumstances are such that a reasonably prudent person would have foreseen a serious and obvious risk of death.

The jury's task is to decide, having regard to the risk of death involved, **whether the accused's acts were so bad in all the circumstances that they amounted to a criminal act or omission** (*per* Lord Mackay in *Adomako*, p. 187). This is a circular test: in deciding whether a crime has been committed, the jury has to decide whether the behaviour amounted to a crime. On the test's circularity, Judge LJ in *Misra* stated (at para. 62):

The decision whether the conduct was criminal is described [in *Adomako*] . . . as 'a' test as to how far the conduct in question must depart from accepted standards to be 'characterised as criminal'. On proper analysis, therefore, the jury is not deciding whether the particular defendant ought to be convicted on some unprincipled basis. The question for the jury is not whether the defendant's negligence was gross, and whether, additionally, it was a crime, but whether his behaviour was grossly negligent and consequently criminal. This is not a question of law, but one of fact, for decision in the individual case.

One view is that no more precise test is possible given the broad range of circumstances in which gross negligence manslaughter can arise. The test is at least simple to put to juries (although whether juries understand the question, and how they negotiate the circularity of the test, are important questions to which we do not have answers). Another view is that Lord Judge's explanation verges on sophistry and fails adequately to address the issues of unpredictability and inconsistency that inevitably follow from entrusting juries with such a loose test. It allows them, indeed encourages them, to convict a person of manslaughter if they think the behaviour was bad enough to deserve the label 'criminal'.

9.3.4 **Reform**

In its Report, *Legislating the Criminal Code: Involuntary Manslaughter* (Law Com No. 237, 1996) the Law Commission identified two major problems relating to the wide range of conduct covered by involuntary manslaughter (at para. 3.1):

[T]he offence encompasses, first, cases involving conduct that falls only just short of murder, where the accused was *aware* of a risk of causing death or serious injury, although he did not *intend* to cause either; second, cases where the accused is a professional person who makes a very serious mistake that results in death; and third, cases where a relatively minor assault ends in death. [Secondly] this leads to problems in sentencing and labelling, including the fundamental problem that many cases currently amounting to unlawful act manslaughter involve only minor fault on the part of the perpetrator, and therefore ought not, perhaps, to be described as manslaughter at all.

The Law Commission specifically highlighted the uncertainty in the current law arising from the terminology used in gross negligence manslaughter, the circular nature of the test the jury are required to apply, and the lack of any clear definition of the extent of liability for omissions. On unlawful act manslaughter it stated (at para. 3.6):

[W]e consider that it is wrong in principle for the law to hold a person responsible for causing a result that he did not intend or foresee, and which would not even have been *foreseeable* by a reasonable person observing his conduct. Unlawful act manslaughter is therefore, we believe, unprincipled because it requires only that a foreseeable risk of causing *some* harm should have been inherent in the accused's conduct, whereas he is convicted of actually causing death, and also to some extent punished for doing so.

The Law Commission in its work has traditionally adopted a subjectivist approach, seeking to impose criminal liability on the basis of three principles (para. 4.5):

The first of these is the 'mens rea principle', which imposes liability only for outcomes which were *intended* or *knowingly risked* by the alleged wrongdoer. The second principle, the 'belief principle', judges a defendant according only to what *she* believed she was doing or risking. Thirdly, according to the 'principle of correspondence', subjectivists insist that the fault element of a crime *correspond* to the conduct element; for example, if the conduct element is 'causing serious injury', the fault element ought to be 'intention or recklessness as to causing serious injury'. This ensures that the defendant is punished only for causing a harm which she *chose* to risk or to bring about.

On this basis the Law Commission recommended the creation of an offence of recklessly causing death for which the maximum penalty should be life imprisonment. Clause 1(1) of the Draft Involuntary Homicide Bill (appended to the Report) defined this offence as follows:

A person who by his conduct causes the death of another is guilty of reckless killing if—

(a) he is aware of a risk that his conduct will cause death or serious injury; and

(b) it is unreasonable for him to take that risk having regard to the circumstances as he knows or believes them to be.

This definition did not strictly comply with the 'correspondence principle' but the Law Commission explained this away on the basis that only a thin line divides behaviour that risks serious injury from that which risks death and it is frequently a matter of chance whether serious injury leads to death. This is consistent with the position regarding the *mens rea* of murder (see **9.2.1**).

In its 1996 Report the Law Commission also recognised that there may be circumstances in which liability based on *inadvertence* may be justified. Such liability should arise where the actor's inadvertence is *culpable*. The Law Commission took the view that culpability depends on two factors: first that the harm to which the actor failed to advert is obviously foreseeable; and secondly, that the actor would have been capable of perceiving the risk had he directed his mind to it. If D is an ordinary person he will be measured against the standard of what would have been reasonably foreseeable by the ordinary person in his situation. But if D is holding himself out as an expert, for example a doctor, the standard will be set higher, namely what would have been obvious to the average doctor in his position (see para. 4.18). In addition, the actor should only be held liable for a death which flows from inadvertent conduct where the conduct inherently involved a risk of death or serious injury. On this basis the Law Commission recommended the abolition of unlawful act manslaughter and the replacement of gross negligence manslaughter with a new offence of killing by gross carelessness.

In May 2000 the Home Office published a Consultation Paper, *Reforming the Law on Involuntary Manslaughter: The Government's Proposals* based on the Law Commission Report No. 237 which the Government largely accepted. The Home Office endorsed the Law Commission's recommendations of an offence of reckless killing, the abolition of unlawful act manslaughter, and its replacement by an offence of killing by gross carelessness but also sought views on whether an additional homicide offence should be created to cover the situation where a death which was unforeseeable occurs and the following requirements apply (para. 2.11):

- a person by his or her conduct causes the death of another;
- he or she intended to [cause some injury] or was reckless as to whether some injury was caused; and
- the conduct causing, or intended to cause, the injury constitutes an offence.

This offence would be slightly narrower than unlawful act manslaughter as at least subjective recklessness as to the risk of some injury is required but liability would still be derived from the consequence of death ensuing. A case such as *Mitchell* [1983] QB 741 (see **9.3.3.1.2**) could still arise. The Home Office provided no justification for basing liability on an accidental outcome rather than intention or foresight.

In its Consultation Paper No. 177, *A New Homicide Act for England and Wales?* published in 2005, the Law Commission revisited its proposals for manslaughter and modified them in light of its recommendation for the creation of two degrees of murder (see **9.2.2**). In its final Report, *Murder, Manslaughter and Infanticide* (Law Com No. 304), the Law Commission recommends an offence of manslaughter that could be committed in three ways:

(1) killing another person through gross negligence ('gross negligence manslaughter'); or
(2) killing another person:
    (a) through the commission of a criminal act intended by the defendant to cause injury, or
    (b) through the commission of a criminal act that the defendant was aware involved a serious risk of causing some injury ('criminal act manslaughter').

The recommendation for gross negligence simply reflects the current position. The recommendation regarding criminal act manslaughter is almost identical to the proposal put forward by the Government for replacing 'unlawful and dangerous act' manslaughter in its Consultation Paper of 2000. In its Consultation Paper No. 177, the Law Commission recommended that the offence of reckless killing, with some modification, be incorporated into the provisional recommendation for 'second degree murder'. In its final Report, *Murder, Manslaughter and Infanticide* (Law Com No. 304), the Law Commission confirmed this recommendation expressing the view that any separate offence of reckless manslaughter to cover foresight of a lesser degree of harm than that required for second degree murder would be very narrow, overlapping with gross negligence manslaughter and would make the law unduly complicated (see **9.2.2**). With regard to gross negligence manslaughter, the Law Commission recommended that the prosecution be required to prove that there was gross negligence as to the risk of causing death, not merely as to causing serious injury. It gave its reasons for this recommendation as follows (para. 3.59):

> Gross negligence manslaughter can be committed even when D was unaware that his or her conduct might cause death, or even injury. This is because negligence, however gross, does not necessarily involve any actual realisation that one is posing a risk of harm: it is a question of how glaringly obvious the risk would have been to a reasonable person. If liability for an offence as serious as manslaughter is to be justified in the absence of an awareness that one is posing a risk, D's negligence must relate to the risk of bringing about the very harm he or she has caused: the risk of causing death. Otherwise, the crime of manslaughter becomes unduly wide and a misleading label for what the offender has done.

The definition they give for this offence is as follows (para. 3.60):

(1) a person by his or her conduct causes the death of another;
(2) a risk that his or her conduct will cause death would be obvious to a reasonable person in his or her position;
(3) he or she is capable of appreciating that risk at the material time; and
(4) his or her conduct falls far below what can reasonably be expected of him or her in the circumstances.

When Parliament enacted the Coroners and Justice Act 2009, no change was made to involuntary manslaughter, the reforms being confined to voluntary manslaughter. It is unlikely that any further reform of homicide will take place in the foreseeable future.

9.3.5 **Other unlawful homicides**

9.3.5.1 **Causing death by dangerous driving**

The Road Traffic Act 1991 abolished the offence of causing death by reckless driving contrary to s. 1 of the Road Traffic Act 1988 (see further S. Cooper, *Blackstone's Guide to the Road Traffic Act 1991* (1991)). By s. 1 of the Act, a new s. 1 was substituted into the 1988 Act which provides that 'a person who causes the death of another person by driving a mechanically propelled vehicle dangerously on a road or other public place is guilty of an offence'. The offence of reckless driving in s. 2 of the 1988 Act was abolished and replaced by a new s. 2 offence of dangerous driving. 'Dangerous driving' is defined in s. 2A to the 1988 Act as follows:

> (1) For the purposes of sections 1 and 2 above a person is to be regarded as driving dangerously if (and, subject to subsection (2) below, only if)—
>
>   (a) the way he drives falls far below what would be expected of a competent and careful driver, and
>
>   (b) it would be obvious to a competent and careful driver that driving in that way would be dangerous.
>
> (2) A person is also to be regarded as driving dangerously for the purposes of sections 1 and 2 above if it would be obvious to a competent and careful driver that driving the vehicle in its current state would be dangerous.
>
> (3) In subsections (1) and (2) above 'dangerous' refers to a danger either of injury to any person or of serious damage to property; and in determining for the purposes of those subsections what would be expected of, or obvious to, a competent and careful driver in a particular case, regard shall be had not only to the circumstances of which he could be expected to be aware, but also to any circumstances shown to have been within the knowledge of the accused.

The Act resulted from the Report of the North Committee set up by the Home Office and the Department of Transport—*Road Traffic Law Review* (1988). The North Committee identified a number of problems with the offences of reckless driving and causing death by reckless driving. The current offences are of an objective nature and require no advertence on the part of a jury to D's state of mind except for 'any circumstances shown to have been within the knowledge of the accused' (s. 2A(3)). He may have recognised that his driving was dangerous or given no thought to the manner of his driving, or have given thought to it and wrongly concluded that it was not dangerous. The focus, rather, is on the quality of D's driving. If a jury decide that D's driving fell far below the objective standard expected of a competent and careful driver under s. 2A(1)(a), they will convict if satisfied that it would be obvious to the competent and careful driver that driving in that way would be dangerous (s. 2A(1)(b)), in that it created a risk 'either of injury to any person or of serious damage to property' (s. 2A(3)).

Section 2A(2) is designed to deal with the situation where D drives a vehicle which is in a dangerous condition. He may drive very carefully but the vehicle itself is dangerous—that is, driving that vehicle on a road in its current state creates a risk either of injury to a person or of serious damage to property. There are two possible problems with this provision. First, if D is a lorry driver and overloads his vehicle or loads it in such a way that the load is unstable, this may not be obvious to the competent and careful driver although obvious to the competent and careful lorry driver. Section 2A(3) provides for this situation in that the competent and careful driver is expected to be aware of 'any circumstances shown to have been within the knowledge of the accused' which would cover any specialist skill or knowledge which D had. Secondly, the facts about the vehicle's condition may indicate that driving it would be dangerous but s. 2A(2) does not impose any requirement that D have knowledge of those facts.

 Question

D leaves his vehicle in a garage to be serviced and an inexperienced mechanic drains the brake fluid and forgets to refill the brake fluid reservoir. If a competent and careful driver knew of the vehicle's 'current state' it would be obvious to him that to drive a vehicle which has no working brakes is dangerous. If D drives the vehicle from the garage and kills V on a zebra crossing when the vehicle fails to stop, would he be liable for causing death by dangerous driving?

The wording of s. 2A(3) suggests that the competent and careful driver is only taken to be aware of circumstances of which he could be expected to be aware. Thus, on those facts, the competent and careful driver would be someone who did not know that the brakes were not working. In *Strong* [1995] Crim LR 428, the Court of Appeal stated that something would be obvious to the competent and careful driver only if it could be 'seen or realised at first glance, evident to him'. If, for example, a fault could only have been discovered by crawling under the vehicle, this would not satisfy the 'obvious' test. If, however, in the above scenario, D on trying the brakes found they did not work but dismissed that from his mind as a fluke, believing that the brakes must be working as the car had just come from the garage, and drove on killing V on a zebra crossing, he would be guilty of the s. 1 offence if the jury concluded that, in such circumstances, it would have been obvious to the competent and careful driver that the vehicle was dangerous. In *Marsh* [2002] EWCA Crim 137, the Court of Appeal stated that the wording in *Strong* should not be taken to prescribe a particular form of words that trial judges must use; 'obvious' is an ordinary English word and judges would be well advised not to attempt to define it further.

A problem which remains following the creation of the s. 1 offence is whether some cases of causing death by dangerous driving may also amount to gross negligence manslaughter. In *Adomako* [1995] 1 AC 171, Lord Mackay LC expressed the view that the use of a manslaughter charge in respect of a road death would be rare. It might be appropriate, however, where the way in which D drove fell so far below what would be expected of a competent and careful driver and it would have been obvious to such a driver that driving in that way created a risk of death. As prosecutors must opt for an offence to charge, and as the maximum sentence for the s. 1 offence is 14 years' imprisonment, it is unlikely that many will be tempted to prosecute for gross negligence manslaughter unless the risk of death was very high (see *Pimm* [1994] RTR 391; *Brown* v *The Queen* [2005] UKPC 18). If there is evidence that a vehicle was used as an instrument to attack or frighten and death occurs as a result, unlawful act manslaughter may be the most appropriate charge (although note that driving carelessly or dangerously does not, in itself, amount to an unlawful act for the purposes of unlawful act manslaughter: *Andrews* v *DPP* [1937] AC 576).

The Road Traffic Act 1991 inserted s. 3A into the 1988 Act, creating the offence of causing death by careless driving when under the influence of drink or drugs to such an extent that the driver is unfit to drive or the proportion of alcohol in his breath, blood, or urine at the time exceeds the prescribed limits. Such a person may be driving a vehicle in a way which is not dangerous, although careless. However, he will be liable to conviction for this offence and on conviction will be liable to imprisonment for up to 10 years.

Section 20(1) of the Road Safety Act 2006 inserted a new s. 2B into the Road Traffic Act 1988 creating a new offence of causing death by careless or inconsiderate driving which is punishable with up to five years' imprisonment. An offence, careless driving, which would not otherwise be punishable by imprisonment, becomes so where death results provided a causal link is proven between the driving and the death. No *mens rea* need be proved as regards the risk of death. The happenstance of death thereby converts a minor crime into a very serious one without there being any concomitant rise in the culpability of the defendant.

9.3.5.2 Causing or allowing the death of a child or vulnerable adult

Where a child or vulnerable adult dies in circumstances where it is clear that the death was non-accidental and caused by a parent or someone else who had care of him, it is often difficult to prove that the death was caused by one or other (or both) parents or carers. The death may have occurred while one of the parents or carers was absent. Alternatively, while it may be possible to prove which parent was responsible for the act which was the immediate cause of death, it may be difficult or impossible to prove whether the other parent was an accomplice in that offence. Section 5 of the Domestic Violence, Crime and Victims Act 2004 creates a specific offence to cover such situations, punishable with a maximum of 14 years' imprisonment. (The Domestic Violence, Crime and Victims (Amendment) Act 2012 extends the reach of s. 5 to cover non-fatal cases where a child or vulnerable adult has suffered serious physical harm, the maximum penalty for this offence being 10 years' imprisonment.) The offence is essentially one of negligence. Section 5 provides:

(1) A person ('D') is guilty of an offence if—

    (a) a child or vulnerable adult ('V') dies or suffers serious physical harm as a result of the unlawful act of a person who—

      (i) was a member of the same household as V, and

      (ii) had frequent contact with him,

    (b) D was such a person at the time of that act;

    (c) at that time there was a significant risk of serious physical harm being caused to V by the unlawful act of such a person; and

    (d) either D was the person whose act caused V's death or serious physical harm or—

      (i) D was, or ought to have been, aware of the risk mentioned in paragraph (c),

      (ii) D failed to take such steps as he could reasonably have been expected to take to protect V from the risk, and

      (iii) the act occurred in circumstances of the kind that D foresaw or ought to have foreseen.

The prosecution does not have to prove which of the alternatives in s. 5(1)(d) applies (s. 5(2)). A person is to be regarded as a 'member of the same household' even if he does not live at the address provided he visits it so often and for such periods of time that it is reasonable to regard him as a member of it. This could cover, for example, a grandparent who looks after a child during the day but does not sleep at the premises. 'Unlawful act' is an act that constitutes an offence (s. 5(5) (a)). For these purposes 'act' includes a course of conduct or an omission (s. 5(6))— for example, failure to feed, or clothe, or seek medical attention for a child. Where D is not the person who performs the unlawful act, he will not escape liability by reason of the fact that the person who did perform it was under 10 years of age or insane (see s. 5(5)(b)). Thus, for example, a parent (D) will be liable where a sibling under the age of 10 does the act which causes V's death and D failed to protect V from the risk, being aware of it. Where D is not the mother or father of V, D may not be charged with this offence if he was under 16 at the time of the act that caused V's death (s. 5(3)(a)). In addition, where the death is the result of a course of conduct and D has failed to take reasonable steps to protect V from the risk arising therefrom, his failure will only count against him from the point he attains the age of 16 (s. 5(3)(b)).

The only circumstances where it would appear to be appropriate to charge D under this section, where D is responsible for the unlawful act that causes V's death, is where D1 and D2 are the parents/carers of V and both are charged under the section it being unclear which of the two is responsible for the unlawful act. In such circumstances D1 and D2 will either each have perpetrated the act or aided and abetted the other to do so or failed to protect V. Where the prosecution can prove that one or other did the unlawful act and that the other failed to take reasonable steps to protect V in circumstances where he either was aware of the risk or ought to have been aware of it, then both should be convicted.

Whether there was a 'significant' risk of serious physical harm is a question of fact for the jury, giving that word its ordinary meaning; the trial judge should not seek to define the word (*Stephens and Mujuru* [2007] EWCA Crim 1249).

Section 5(6) defines 'vulnerable adult' as 'a person aged 16 or over whose ability to protect himself from violence, abuse or neglect is significantly impaired through physical or mental disability or illness, through old age or otherwise'. In *Khan* [2009] EWCA Crim 2, the Court of Appeal considered the breadth of that term.

> V came to England from a rural part of Kashmir to marry her cousin, H. V spoke no English and had no friends in England. V and H lived with their extended family in one house which included H's mother, his sisters D and E, and D's husband, F. V suffered at least three incidents of serious violence at the hands of H, the last of which caused her death. H was convicted of murder. The prosecution case against D, E, and F was that during the three weeks before the final attack on her by H, it must have been apparent to D, E, and F that V had been, and was being, subjected to serious physical violence at the hands of H. The prosecution contended that following the first attack on her three weeks before her death, V thereby became a vulnerable adult. D, E, and F were all convicted of the s. 5(1) offence and appealed. The Court of Appeal dismissed their appeals holding that adults are vulnerable if their ability to protect themselves from violence, abuse, or neglect is significantly impaired, which it was here after the major attack on her three weeks before her death. The vulnerability need

only be temporary as a result of accident, illness, or injury. The Court left open the possibility that even before this V may have been considered vulnerable on the basis of her situation—lonely and friendless in a strange country and totally dependent upon her husband and his family.

What protective steps might be required of a member of the same household depends upon what is reasonable in the circumstances. In *Khan* the Court of Appeal recognised that if another member of the household is subject to the same violence as V, it might not be reasonable to expect that person to have taken any protective steps. In *Uddin* the Court of Appeal held that the words 'or otherwise' in the definition of a 'vulnerable adult' in s. 5(6) bring within the section's protection persons who are vulnerable by reason of causes other than the causes identified in the first two categories (i.e. 'old age' or 'physical or mental disability or illness'). 'Or otherwise' encompasses any cause (other than physical or mental disability or illness or old age) that has the effect on the victim of significantly impairing his ability to protect himself from violence, abuse, or neglect; in principle, there is no limit to the facts and circumstances that might lead to a person finding himself in a state of impaired ability to obtain protection. The third category is not limited to cases of 'utter dependency' (*Uddin* [2017] EWCA Crim 1072).

The Domestic Violence, Crime and Victims (Amendment) Act 2012 extends the reach of s. 5 to cover non-fatal cases where a child or vulnerable adult has suffered serious physical harm, the maximum penalty for this offence being 10 years' imprisonment.

 The law in context

Sentencing for murder and manslaughter

The legal distinction between murder and manslaughter matters in practical terms because there are separate sentencing procedures for each. The death penalty for murder was abolished by s. 1 of the Murder (Abolition of Death Penalty) Act 1965, which states: 'No person shall suffer death for murder, and a person convicted of murder shall be sentenced to imprisonment for life.' However, a murderer will not necessarily spend the rest of his life in prison. Under s. 269(3) of the Criminal Justice Act 2003, the sentencing judge must set a minimum period of years in prison that the offender must serve before the Parole Board can consider his release. That minimum period must be such as the court considers appropriate taking into account the seriousness of the offence, having regard to sch. 21 of the Act.

One common reaction is that 'life should mean life' for murder, as all murders are equally serious. In terms of the minimum period a murderer has to serve, English law states that some murders are more serious than others. Schedule 21 sets out starting points for judges to consider when deciding on the minimum period in the particular case. For example, if the court considers the seriousness of the offence was 'exceptionally high' and the offender was 21 or over at the time, then the appropriate minimum period would be a whole life minimum period, meaning that the person would never be released. Cases that could fall within that category include 'the murder of a child if involving the abduction of the child or sexual or sadistic motivation'. If the court considers the seriousness to be 'particularly high' (e.g. it is a murder that is racially or religiously aggravated or aggravated by sexual orientation) then a

→

→

30-year minimum period would be the appropriate starting point. For murders that do not fall into those higher categories, an appropriate starting point for the minimum period would be 15 years. Note that the minimum periods in sch. 21 are starting points. The judge must set the appropriate period taking into account mitigating and aggravating factors.

The minimum period is the period that the offender must serve before he can be considered for release by the Parole Board. Under s. 28 of the Crime (Sentences) Act 1997, the Parole Board must consider whether it is still 'necessary for the protection of the public that the prisoner shall be confined'. If it is not then the offender is released on licence into the community. This means that the offender is not entirely free: he must comply with the licence conditions and if he breaches them he is liable to be recalled to prison. That licence remains in place for the rest of the person's life and in that sense it is a life sentence, even though the person will not spend the rest of his life in prison.

The legality of a whole life minimum period was challenged in *Vinter and others* [2014] Crim LR 81. The European Court of Human Rights held that for sentences of life imprisonment to be compatible with Art. 3 of the European Convention on Human Rights, there has to be a possibility of review and release. The Court of Appeal's response (*AG's Reference (No. 69 of 2013)* [2014] EWCA Crim 188) was to declare that whole life minimum periods remain lawful because the Secretary of State has the power to release an offender if there are exceptional circumstances justifying his release on compassionate grounds.

By contrast to the special arrangements for sentencing in murder cases, a person convicted of manslaughter will be sentenced under the ordinary principles of sentencing, with the judge having discretion to sentence *up to* life imprisonment. In practice, many people convicted of manslaughter will serve significantly less than that. The Sentencing Council has published a definitive guideline that judges must follow from November 2018 when sentencing for manslaughter: Sentencing Council, *Manslaughter: Definitive Guideline* (2018: https://www.sentencingcouncil.org.uk) For example, someone who is being sentenced for manslaughter on the grounds of loss of control, who killed as a result of very high degree of provocation will, according to the guideline, typically receive a sentence in the range of three to six years (p. 16). The sheer variety of cases in which a person can be guilty of manslaughter on the grounds of diminished responsibility mean that before the establishment of the Sentencing Guidelines Council and the Sentencing Council, courts were reluctant to develop detailed guidelines. The new guidelines indicate a wide offence range of three to 40 years' imprisonment, with the starting point for the particular sentence being determined by the extent to which the offender's responsibility was diminished by the mental disorder and the extent to which the offender's actions or omissions contributed to the seriousness of the mental disorder (e.g. through voluntary abuse of alcohol or drugs). There have been cases in which the offender has received a suspended sentence of imprisonment because of the particular circumstances. For example, an 89-year-old terminally ill man, Phillip Williamson, received a two-year sentence of imprisonment, suspended for two years, for killing his seriously ill wife to save her from further suffering (BBC News Online, 'Man Admits Killing Wife of 60 Years in Lower Earley' 4 August 2016).

Sentencing for unlawful act manslaughter, particularly cases of relatively minor assaults, can be difficult for judges because of the imbalance between the harm the offender has caused (which is obviously great) and the offender's culpability (which can be quite low, for example if the offender has thrown a single punch and the victim has lost his balance and hit his head on a pavement, resulting in death). How have English courts approached these cases? The Court of Appeal's approach in its guideline cases has changed in the last 25 years. In the first significant guideline case (*Coleman* (1992) 95 Cr App R 159) the Court stated that a sentence of 12 months' imprisonment on a guilty plea might well be appropriate to reflect the limited culpability of the offender in a case of a 'one-punch killer'. However, the Court's

→

→

most recent guidance *(AG's Reference (Nos. 60, 62 and 63 of 2009)* [2009] EWCA Crim 2693) reveals a toughened stance. Lord Judge CJ said (at paras 7 and 13):

> *Coleman* was decided at a time when there was less public disquiet about violent behaviour and death in town and city centres and residential streets than there is now . . . *Coleman* provided . . . guidance . . . that is no longer appropriate. What is now required, without of course diminishing the attention to be paid to the actions of the defendant and his intentions at the time, and the true level of his culpability, is that specific attention must now be paid to the consequences of his crime.

This reflects reforms elsewhere in criminal justice and sentencing to increase the rights of crime victims and their families, for example by allowing them to make a Victim Personal Statement (Ministry of Justice, 2013 https://www.gov.uk/government/publications/victim-personal-statement) explaining to the sentencing court how they have been impacted by the offender's behaviour.

For unlawful act manslaughter, the Sentencing Council's 2018 guideline provides for an offence range of between one and 24 years' imprisonment, the court being guided first to an appropriate starting point by the extent of the offender's culpability, from which the judge must balance aggravating and mitigating factors to reach a fair assessment of the offender's overall culpability in the context of the circumstances of the offence.

 Key Points

MURDER

– The *actus reus* of all homicide offences involves D unlawfully causing death of a human being under the Queen's Peace.

– Murder is unlawful homicide committed with 'malice aforethought', which means with the intention to kill or cause GBH *(Vickers)*.

– The golden rule for trial judges is to avoid elaborating on the meaning of 'intention' and leave it to the jury's good sense *(Moloney)*.

– When elaboration is needed, the leading case on the meaning of intention is *Woollin* (1998): a jury should be directed that they are not entitled to find the necessary intent unless they are sure that death or GBH was a virtual certainty, barring some unforeseen intervention, and that D appreciated that.

DIMINISHED RESPONSIBILITY

– Diminished responsibility is a partial defence only to murder.

– The tests for diminished responsibility are set out in s. 2 of the Homicide Act 1957, as amended by the Coroners and Justice Act 2009:

  – D was suffering from an abnormality of mental functioning which arose from a recognised medical condition; and

→

➡

- the abnormality substantially impaired D's ability to do one of three things (understand the nature of his conduct, form a rational judgement, or exercise self-control) and provides an explanation for his acts or omissions.
- Whether impairment is 'substantial' is for the jury to decide, giving that word its ordinary meaning.
- D bears the burden of proving diminished responsibility on the balance of probabilities.

LOSS OF CONTROL

- Loss of control is a partial defence only to murder.
- The legal tests are set out in ss 54 and 55 of the Coroners and Justice Act 2009:
  - Did D's acts or omissions in killing result from his loss of self-control?
  - Did the loss of self-control have a qualifying trigger (a fear of serious violence or a justifiable sense of being seriously wronged)?
  - Might a person of D's sex and age, with a normal degree of tolerance and self-restraint and in D's circumstances, have reacted as D did?
- The burden of proof rests on the prosecution to disprove the defence once sufficient evidence has been adduced by D to make the defence live.
- Sexual infidelity is not, on its own, a qualifying trigger.
- The test in s. 54(1)(c) is objective: D's mental disorder cannot be taken into account by the jury when judging D against the standard of the ordinary person of D's sex and age.

INVOLUNTARY MANSLAUGHTER

- Unlawful act manslaughter is committed when D commits an unlawful act that is objectively dangerous and which causes V's death.
- The test for whether D's act is objectively dangerous is whether sober and reasonable people would have recognised the risk of some harm, albeit not serious harm.
- Gross negligence manslaughter is committed when D owes V a duty of care, he breaches that duty, the breach causes death, and the breach was grossly negligent (*Adomako*).
- The jury decides whether the breach was grossly negligent by considering whether, having regard to the risk of death involved, D's behaviour was so bad that in all the circumstances it amounted to a criminal act or omission.

FURTHER READING

A. Ashworth, 'Reforming the Law of Murder' [1990] Crim LR 75.

A. Ashworth, 'Manslaughter by Omission and the Rule of Law' [2015] Crim LR 563.

C. Elliot, 'Liability for Manslaughter by Omission: Don't Let the Baby Drown!' (2010) 74 JCL 163.

M. Gibson, 'Diminished Responsibility in *Golds* and Beyond: Insights and Implications' [2017] Crim LR 543.

J. Herring and E. Palser, 'The Duty of Care in Gross Negligence Manslaughter' [2007] Crim LR 24.

H. Keating, 'The Law Commission Report on Involuntary Manslaughter: (1) The Restoration of a Serious Crime' [1996] Crim LR 535.

R. McKay, 'The Impairment Factors in the New Diminished Responsibility Plea' [2018] Crim LR 462.

J. Miles, 'The Coroners and Justice Act 2009: A "Dog's Breakfast" of Homicide Reform' (2009) 10 Archbold News 6.

A. Norrie, 'The Coroners and Justice Act 2009—Partial Defences to Murder: (1) Loss of Control' [2010] Crim LR 275.

S. Parsons, 'The Loss of Control Defence – Fit for Purpose?' (2015) 79 JCL 94.

G. Williams, '*Mens Rea* for Murder: Leave it Alone' (1989) 105 LQR 387.

G. Williams, 'Gross Negligence Manslaughter and Duty of Care in "Drugs" Cases: R v Evans' [2009] Crim LR 631.

10

....

Non-fatal offences against the person

In this chapter we consider the main offences involving violence against the person. These are significant in practical terms: the latest statistics from the Crime Survey for England and Wales show that there were an estimated 1.275 million violent offences in the year ending June 2018 (ONS (2018) Crime in England and Wales: year ending June 2018: https://www.ons.gov.uk/peoplepopulationandcommunity/crimeandjustice/bulletins/crimeinenglandandwales/yearendingjune2018#no-change-in-the-most-common-types-of-violent-crime). There is a considerable number of offences in this area, many of which are contained in the Offences Against the Person Act 1861 (hereafter 'the OAPA'), but space dictates that only the most common of these can be examined. From the outset, note that the main piece of legislation covering these offences of great practical importance is more than 150 years old: some of its language is antiquated and there is a lack of principle and coherence running through the main offences.

10.1 **Assault and battery**

Common assault and battery were separate common law crimes. Section 39 of the Criminal Justice Act 1988 stipulates that they are summary offences and specifies the maximum penalty for each is six months' imprisonment. Section 1 of the Assaults on Emergency Workers (Offences) Act 2018, in force from 13 November 2018, provides for a maximum sentence of 12 months' imprisonment where the common assault or battery is committed against an 'emergency worker' (as defined in s. 3) who is acting in the exercise of the functions of such a worker (e.g. a para-medic). It amends s. 39 so that common assault or battery against such a worker will be offences triable either way. The 2018 Act also imposes a duty on sentencing judges and magistrates to treat the fact that the violent offence was committed against an 'emergency worker' as an aggravating factor when considering the seri-ousness of that offence (see s. 2(3) for a complete list of the relevant offences).

It was believed that common assault and battery remained common law crimes. However, in *DPP v Little* [1992] 1 All ER 299, the Divisional Court held that they are, and have been since 1861, statutory offences. Section 47 of the OAPA prescribed the penalty for these offences. This decision is surprising as the definitions of assault and battery are not found in any statute but in the common law. In *Haystead v Chief Constable of Derbyshire* [2000] Crim LR 758, Laws LJ stated that 'in truth, common assault by beating remains a common law offence'. This presents a clear conflict of authority which needs to be resolved.

An indictment charging an indictable offence against the person may include a count of common assault or battery if it is founded on the same facts or evidence as the count charging the indictable offence or is part of a series of offences of the same or similar character as the indictable offence which is also charged (s. 40 of the Criminal Justice Act (CJA) 1988). Thus, if the jury acquit D of the more serious indictable offence, they may still convict of the summary offence.

? Question

Are assault and battery the same offence?

While assault and battery are distinct crimes, judges and statutes often use the term 'assault' or 'common assault' to encompass both these offences (e.g. s. 47 of the OAPA and s. 40(3)(a) of the CJA 1988). In this chapter the term 'assault' will be used in its generic sense to cover both offences. When dealing separately with the offences the terms 'technical assault' and 'battery' will be used. It should be noted that assault and battery are also torts.

10.1.1 Technical assault

A technical assault is committed when D intentionally or recklessly causes the victim to apprehend immediate and unlawful personal violence (see *Fagan v Metropolitan Police Commissioner* [1969] 1 QB 439). This definition was approved by the House of Lords in *Savage and Parmenter* [1991] 1 AC 699, 740.

Actus reus	*Mens rea*
D causes V	D does so
• to apprehend	• intentionally, or
• immediate unlawful personal violence.	• recklessly.

10.1.1.1 *Actus reus*

Question

Does V have to be put in fear?

V must apprehend immediate and unlawful personal violence. The term 'apprehend' is used as it is not necessary for V to be put in fear; **it is sufficient that she anticipates immediate and unlawful personal violence being applied to her by D.** The term 'unlawful personal violence' may be misleading as it is not necessary for V to apprehend a severe attack; the apprehension of any unwanted touching of her by D is sufficient. **Thus all that V need apprehend is a battery**, which was defined by Lord Lane CJ in *Faulkner* v *Talbot* [1981] 3 All ER 468, 471, as '**any intentional touching of another person without the consent of that person and without lawful excuse.** It need not necessarily be hostile, rude, or aggressive . . .'

Personal violence is not unlawful where D is justified in using it (e.g. if D is using reasonable force in self-defence, or to prevent a crime or arrest an offender), or D is engaged in lawful correction (see **10.9**).

Technical assault generally requires some act on the part of D causing V to apprehend immediate unlawful personal violence. For example, where D shakes his fist at V or raises a knife as if to stab V or points a gun at V, there would be a technical assault if V apprehended the immediate application of force on her by D. In the example of the gun, however, there would be no assault if V knew or believed that the gun was not loaded (see *Lamb* [1967] 2 QB 981). There are three issues, however, which need to be considered: first, whether an assault may be committed by omission; secondly, whether an assault may be committed by words; and, thirdly, what does 'immediate' mean?

10.1.1.1.1 *Omissions*

The typical case of technical assault will involve a positive act by D, such as brandishing a knife or waving a fist. In *Fagan* it was stated that **an omission could not constitute an assault.** Fagan accidentally drove onto the foot of a police officer who had instructed him to park his car against the kerb, but then refused to reverse the car off his foot immediately, despite the police officer shouting at him to do so. The Divisional Court upheld Fagan's conviction on the basis that his behaviour constituted a continuing act (cf. *DPP* v *Santana-Bermudez* [2003] EWHC Admin 2908, **2.5.2.2.4**). A failure to desist from a threatening gesture or stance that has been adopted without intent to cause the other person to apprehend violence may therefore constitute a technical assault. For example, D, a burglar, is in V's kitchen holding a knife when V enters, coming face to face with D and the knife. V apprehends immediate unlawful personal violence and D, recognising V's fear, continues to hold the knife in the same position. It is suggested that D has not assaulted V by omission, but rather that by failing to terminate his act of holding the knife in what has become a threatening manner he commits an assault (cf. *Kaitamaki* [1985] AC 147).

10.1.1.1.2 *Words*

While D's actions may amount to a technical assault, the words he speaks at the time may serve to negative this. In *Tuberville* v *Savage* (1669) 1 Mod Rep 3, T placed his hand on his sword and said: 'If it were not assize-time, I would not take such language from you.' 'Assize-time' meant that the judges who travelled around the circuits of England and Wales setting up courts in various places were in the town. The Court held that this was not an assault as his declaration indicated that as the judges were in town he would not use force on S. By contrast, if D puts a gun to V's head and says, 'Be quiet or I'll blow your brains out', this should constitute a technical assault as D's forbearance is conditional on V doing as she is told. In *Read* v *Coker* (1853) 13 CB 850, V sued successfully for assault where D and his servants surrounded him, rolled up their sleeves, and threatened to break his neck if he did not leave the premises.

The authorities, until relatively recently, were somewhat confused on the issue whether words alone could constitute an assault. The matter has now been settled by the House of Lords' decision in *Ireland* [1998] AC 147.

> D had made a series of silent telephone calls to three women as a result of which the women suffered significant psychological symptoms. D was charged with assault occasioning actual bodily harm contrary to s. 47 of the OAPA. His appeal against conviction to the Court of Appeal was dismissed. Swinton Thomas LJ reasoned backwards from the fact that the three victims suffered psychological harm to conclude that there must have been an assault which caused this. He stated ([1997] 1 All ER 112, 115):

>> In our judgment, if the Crown can prove that the victims have sustained actual bodily harm, and that the [appellant] . . . intended the victims to sustain such harm, or [was] reckless as to whether they did sustain such harm, and that harm resulted from an act or acts of the appellant, namely telephone calls followed by silence, it is open to the jury to find that he has committed an assault. As to immediacy, by using the telephone the appellant put himself in immediate contact with the victims, and when the victims lifted the telephone they were placed in immediate fear and suffered the consequences to which we have referred.

The Court of Appeal certified that the decision involved a point of law of general public importance namely: 'Whether the making of a series of silent telephone calls can amount in law to an assault.' In answering this question in the affirmative the House of Lords resolved several issues. Their Lordships affirmed the definition of assault stated earlier (see **10.1.1**) and further resolved that **words may constitute an assault**, Lord Steyn stating (at p. 162):

> The proposition that a gesture may amount to an assault, but that words can never suffice, is unrealistic and indefensible. A thing said is also a thing done. There is no reason why something said should be incapable of causing an apprehension of immediate personal violence, e.g. a man accosting a woman in a dark alley saying, 'Come with me or I will stab you.' I would, therefore, reject the proposition that an assault can never be committed by words.

His Lordship went on to conclude that, depending on the facts, a silent call may also constitute an assault stating (at p. 162):

> [T]here is no reason why a telephone caller who says to a woman in a menacing way 'I will be at your door in a minute or two' may not be guilty of an assault if he causes his victim to apprehend immediate personal violence. Take now the case of the silent caller. He intends by his silence to cause fear and he is so understood. The victim is assailed by uncertainty about his intentions. Fear may dominate her emotions, and it may be the fear that the caller's arrival at her door may be imminent. She may fear the possibility of immediate personal violence. As a matter of law the caller may be guilty of an assault: whether he is or not will depend on the circumstances and in particular on the impact of the caller's potentially menacing call or calls on the victim. Such a prosecution case under section 47 may be fit to leave to the jury. And a trial judge may, depending on the circumstances, put a common sense consideration before the jury, namely what, if not the possibility of imminent personal violence, was the victim terrified about? I conclude that an assault may be committed in the particular factual circumstances which I have envisaged.

The crucial question is whether the silent call has caused the victim to apprehend immediate and **unlawful personal violence. 'Unlawful personal violence' must, however, be understood to mean the application of force to the body of the victim.** There undoubtedly was confusion in the Court of Appeal where Swinton Thomas LJ appeared to accept that the apprehension of further psychological symptoms was equivalent to apprehending immediate unlawful violence. Their Lordships did not grapple with this issue and must be taken to have dismissed it by their affirmation of the definition of assault. They were able to side-step this issue in the context of the appeal before them as the appellant had pleaded guilty at his initial trial, thereby implicitly accepting that the victims had been caused to apprehend immediate unlawful personal violence and that he had the requisite *mens rea*.

10.1.1.1.3 *Immediate unlawful violence*
There is no assault if V does not apprehend immediate unlawful violence. If V apprehends violence at some distant point in the future, this is not sufficient.

 Examples

If D, standing on one side of a deep, fast-flowing river, shakes his fist at V on the other side, there being no means of crossing, the element of immediacy would be lacking. Likewise, if V, departing from a station in a train, sees D on the platform shaking his fist while shouting, 'You're in for a beating when I get my hands on you', there would be no assault as V, while he might fear unlawful personal violence at the hands of D, would fear such occurring at an unspecified future date rather than immediately.

But what does 'immediate' mean? It is important to emphasise that it is not the apprehension which must be immediate. Rather, the apprehension must be that violence is going to ensue immediately. In the Court of Appeal in *Ireland* reliance was placed on *Smith* v *Chief Superintendent of Woking Police Station* (1983) 76 Cr App R 234, where the Divisional Court found that it was open to the magistrates to find that there was an assault where D looked through V's window at 11 p.m. causing her to fear violence from him. The violence, obviously, could not be applied instantaneously but it could follow 'sufficiently immediately for the purposes of the offence' (*per* Kerr LJ at p. 237). In s. 4(1) of the Public Order Act 1986 the phrase 'immediate unlawful violence' is used. Section 4(1) creates the offence of using 'threatening, abusive or insulting words or behaviour . . . with intent to cause a person to believe that immediate unlawful violence will be used against him . . .'. In *R v Horseferry Road Metropolitan Stipendiary Magistrate, ex parte Siadatan* [1991] 1 QB 260, in the Divisional Court, Watkins LJ stated (at p. 269):

> It seems to us that the word 'immediate' does not mean 'instantaneous'; that a relatively short time interval may elapse between the act which is threatening, abusive or insulting and the unlawful violence. 'Immediate' connotes proximity in time and proximity in causation; that it is likely that violence will result within a relatively short period of time and without any other intervening occurrence.

Perhaps the best approximation to 'immediate' is 'imminent'—a word used by Lord Steyn in *Ireland* and which is consistent with the idea that a 'short interval of time' may elapse between the words or acts which constitute the assault and the apprehended violence. This has to be so if it is to be possible to assault via the telephone. In *Ireland* in the Court of Appeal, Swinton Thomas LJ found the New South Wales civil case of *Barton v Armstrong* [1969] 2 NSWR 451 particularly persuasive. In that case Taylor J stated that an assault could occur over the telephone (at p. 455):

> If, when threats . . . are conveyed over the telephone, the recipient has been led to believe that he is being followed, kept under surveillance by persons hired to do him physical harm to the extent of killing him, then why is this not something to put him in fear or apprehension of immediate violence? In the age in which we live threats may be made and communicated by persons remote from the person threatened. Physical violence and death can be produced by acts done at a distance by people who are out of sight and by agents hired for that purpose. I do not think that these, if they result in apprehension of physical violence in the mind of a reasonable person, are outside the protection afforded by the civil and criminal law as to assault.

Whatever the means used to convey the threat, whether it constitutes an assault depends on the victim apprehending immediate unlawful violence. This will be a matter of evidence and a question for the magistrate or jury to determine. If V contemplates anything more than a short interval of time elapsing between the threatening words, acts, or silence on the part of D and the violence ensuing, there will be no assault.

10.1.1.2 *Mens rea*

The *mens rea* of technical assault is an intention to cause the victim to apprehend immediate unlawful personal violence or recklessness as to whether such apprehension is caused (*Venna* [1976] QB 421).

With regard to the meaning of recklessness, in *Spratt* [1990] 1 WLR 1073, the Court of Appeal held that in every offence against the person recklessness was to be given the *Cunningham* meaning, 'in the sense of taking the risk of harm ensuing with foresight that it might happen' (*per* McCowan LJ at p. 1082). The Court of Appeal went on to state that *DPP* v *K (A Minor)* [1990] 1 WLR 1067, in which the Divisional Court held that the *Caldwell* test of recklessness sufficed, had been wrongly decided.

In *Parmenter* (1991) 92 Cr App R 68, the Court of Appeal followed *Spratt*. In the joint hearing of the appeals in *Savage and Parmenter* [1991] 4 All ER 698, the House of Lords was not asked to consider this point but there are dicta in their Lordships' speeches which confirm that advertence to the risk of physical contact is required.

10.1.2 **Battery**

Actus reus	Mens rea
D applies unlawful force to V.	D does so • intentionally, or • recklessly.

The *actus reus* of battery consists of the application of unlawful force by D upon the victim. Often a battery follows from a technical assault, as where V sees D swing his fist at him and then suffers the impact of the blow. It is not necessary, however, for there to be a technical assault for D to be liable for battery. For example, if V is blind or D punches him from behind, D will be guilty of battery even though V has no apprehension of unlawful personal violence. **The slightest touching, if unlawful, is sufficient.** The courts, however, have recognised that ordinary everyday life involves many incidents of contact with other persons which should not be treated as criminal. Drawing a line between acceptable and unacceptable forms of contact is not easy. In *Collins* v *Wilcock* [1984] 3 All ER 374, Robert Goff LJ stated that there was a general exception 'embracing all physical contact which is generally acceptable in the ordinary conduct of daily life'. Whether conduct falls within this exception will depend upon the facts of each particular case, but Robert Goff LJ provided some examples of acceptable conduct (at p. 378):

> So nobody can complain of the jostling which is inevitable from his presence in, for example, a supermarket, an underground station or a busy street; nor can a person who attends a party complain if his hand is seized in friendship, or even if his back is (within reason) slapped . . . . [Also] among such forms of conduct, long held to be acceptable, is touching a person for the purpose of engaging his attention, though of course using no greater degree of physical contact than is reasonably necessary in the circumstances for that purpose.

Thus a police officer may tap a person on the shoulder to gain his attention but he may not restrain the person (*Collins* v *Wilcock*; cf. *Wilson* v *Pringle* [1986] 2 All ER 440).

> In *McMillan* v *CPS* [2008] EWHC 1457 (Admin), A was in a drunken state and was seen by the police shouting, being abusive, and arguing in the garden of her daughter's house. The Divisional Court held that the police officer committed no assault on

A when he took her by the arm to steady her for her own safety and led her (without any resistance) down some steep steps to the street in order to speak to her, as he had been acting within the bounds of what were 'generally acceptable standards of conduct'.

As with technical assault, an omission to act cannot constitute a battery (but cf. *DPP v Santana-Bermudez* [2003] EWHC 2908 (Admin), **2.5.2.2.4**), but if D inadvertently applies force to V and then refuses to withdraw it this may constitute a battery.

> In *Fagan* v *Metropolitan Police Commissioner*, D inadvertently parked his car on a police officer's foot. He refused for some time to reverse off when the officer asked him. He was convicted of assaulting a police officer in the execution of his duty. The Divisional Court held that the battery was a continuing act as force continued to be applied to the officer's foot.

When D formed the *mens rea* after the inception of the *actus reus*, this was superimposed upon the existing act making it into an assault.

 Question

Can D be liable if his initial act does not apply force to V, but D realises that if he does not terminate it, force will be applied to V? For example, D places a pole across a darkened corridor. He hears V running along the corridor and deliberately leaves the pole there realising that V will fall over it, which V does.

If D is not to be convicted of battery it will be on the basis of a very fine distinction which it would be difficult to justify. If D had placed the pole there with the intention of tripping V this has always been assumed to constitute a battery (see *Martin* (1881) 8 QBD 54) (see also *Santana-Bermudez*, **2.5.2.2.4**).

Martin illustrates another principle, namely that **the application of force to V need not be direct**. Although the Court of Appeal in *Martin* overruled the Divisional Court's decision in *DPP* v *K* in respect of *mens rea*, the Court of Appeal did not question its decision with regard to the *actus reus*.

> In *DPP* v *K*, D, a schoolboy, placed acid, which he had removed from the chemistry laboratory, in a hot air drier to conceal it. The next person to use the drier suffered scarring when the machine squirted acid into his face. D was charged with assault occasioning actual bodily harm contrary to s. 47 of the OAPA (see also *Haystead* v *Chief Constable of Derbyshire* [2000] Crim LR 758). Parker LJ stated ([1990] 1 WLR 1067, 1071):
>
> > [I]n my judgment there can be no doubt that if a defendant places acid into a machine with the intent that it shall, when the next user switches the machine on, be ejected onto him and do him harm there is an assault when the harm is done.

In this case, as D was charged with the s. 47 offence, harm had to be proved. There is no need to prove that V suffered harm where the charge is simple battery. Had D simply placed water in the machine, he could have been liable for battery (see *Pursell* v *Horn* (1838) 8 Ad & El 602). Similarly, if D rigs up a 'booby trap' with a bucket of water suspended above a door, he will be liable for battery if the contents spill on to V upon opening the door (see also *Clarence* (1888) 22 QBD 23, 25; but see discussion of *Wilson* at **10.3.1**).

The *mens rea* of battery is intention to apply unlawful force or subjective recklessness as to whether such force might be applied (see *Venna* and **10.1.1.2**).

10.2 Aggravated assaults

There are several offences involving assault which are subject to higher penalties because of the presence of aggravating factors. For each of these offences it must be proved that D committed the *actus reus* of technical assault or battery with the requisite *mens rea* and that the aggravating factor was present. In some offences the aggravating factor is the ulterior intent with which D committed the assault—for example, assault with intent to rob (s. 8(2) of the Theft Act 1968), and assault with intent to resist or prevent the lawful arrest of D or another for any offence (s. 38 of the OAPA; s. 17(1) of and sch. 1 to the Magistrates' Courts Act 1980). In other cases the aggravating factor derives from the circumstances in which the offence is committed—for example, sexual assault (s. 3 of the Sexual Offences Act 2003), and assault on a constable in the execution of his duty (s. 89 of the Police Act 1996).

10.2.1 Racially or religiously aggravated assault

The Crime and Disorder Act 1998 created new offences of racially or religiously aggravated assaults (see s. 29 as amended by s. 39 of the Anti-Terrorism, Crime and Security Act 2001). A racially or religiously aggravated assault is committed where a person commits an offence under s. 20 or s. 47 of the OAPA, or common assault, and either:

(a) at the time of committing the offence, or immediately before or after doing so, the offender demonstrates towards the victim of the offence hostility based on the victim's membership (or presumed membership) of a racial or religious group; or

(b) the offence is motivated (wholly or partly) by hostility towards members of a racial or religious group based on their membership of that group. (s. 28(1))

A 'racial group' means 'a group of persons defined by reference to race, colour, nationality (including citizenship) or ethnic or national origins' (s. 28(4)). A 'religious group' means 'a group of persons defined by reference to religious belief or lack of religious belief' (s. 28(5)).

In the case of assaults based on s. 20 or s. 47 the maximum penalty of five years is increased to seven years and for common assault the maximum penalty is increased from six months to two years. The complexity of this offence is evident from the first reported appeal relating to a prosecution under s. 29, *DPP* v *Pal* [2000] Crim LR 756.

> V, a caretaker at a community centre who was of Asian appearance, sought to eject D, an Asian youth, from the centre. D assaulted him and called him 'white man's arse licker' and a 'brown Englishman'. The justices acquitted, finding that D used the words because he was aggrieved at being asked to leave and thus he was not demonstrating racial hostility. The Divisional Court dismissed the appeal by the prosecution holding that while the words demonstrated hostility towards V's conduct in ejecting him, they did not demonstrate hostility towards V because of his membership of a racial group (Asian).

It seems that D's insults related to what he considered to be V's too close relationship with whites rather than his being an Asian. Thus while the words had a race element within them, this did not fall strictly within the statutory definition of racial aggravation.

The narrow approach adopted by the Divisional Court in *Pal* has not been followed in subsequent cases where the use of racist language has been treated as sufficient to constitute aggravation.

> In *DPP* v *Woods* [2002] EWHC Admin 85, D assaulted V, a doorman, who refused to admit one of D's friends to a club. D also called V a 'black bastard'. The magistrates found that D's hostility arose from his frustration and annoyance and that his frame of mind was such that he would have insulted any doorman by reference to an obvious physical characteristic which he happened to possess. Accordingly they found that the assault was not racially aggravated. On appeal by the prosecution, Maurice Kay J (sitting in the Divisional Court) allowed the appeal, treating the insult as itself 'a demonstration of hostility based on the victim's membership of a racial group' (see also *DPP* v *McFarlane* [2002] EWHC 485 (Admin)).

The Divisional Court appears to be treating the use of racist language as sufficient aggravation although this is not what Parliament stipulated in enacting s. 28.

In *White* [2001] WLR 1352, the Court of Appeal held that a racially aggravated offence could be committed by one member of a racial group against another member of the same racial group. The Court stated that 'a person may show hostility to his own kind whether racial, ethnic or national'. This suggests that an assault at an international sports event accompanied, for example, by the words 'English bastard' would be a racially aggravated assault regardless of the assailant's race or national origins. The Court also went on to hold that the word 'African' described a racial group despite the numerous racial, ethnic, and national groups within the continent of Africa. The Court took the view that, used in England and Wales, the word 'African' denoted someone who was black.

> In *AG's Reference (No. 4 of 2004); R* v *D* [2005] EWCA Crim 889, the Court of Appeal considered the question whether using the term 'immigrant doctor', which indicated that a person was 'non-British' was specific enough to denote membership of a 'racial group'. The Court of Appeal held that whether the use of this term was only an allegation of 'non-Britishness' or amounted to a demonstration of hostility based on the victim's membership of a racial group was a question of fact which was for a jury to determine.

This approach to defining 'racial group' non-inclusively is confirmed by the decision in *Rogers* [2007] UKHL 8.

> The epithet, 'bloody foreigners' was used by D to a group of Spanish women who got in his way as he rode his mobility scooter along the pavement. Their Lordships held that those who were not of British origin constituted a racial group and thus use of the term 'foreigners' fell within s. 28(4) provided that the evidence as a whole proved that D's conduct demonstrated, or was motivated by, hostility to such a group (see also *DPP* v *M* [2004] EWHC 1453 (Admin) see **15.6**).

This seems to imply that everyone who is a different race to D comprises a racial group, albeit that group is multi-racial. This view is supported by their Lordships' reasoning in response to the appellant's argument that a group should be defined by what it is rather than by what it is not. Their Lordships were of the view that the statute intended a broad, non-technical approach to construction. Baroness Hale, delivering the unanimous decision of the House, stated (at paras 12–13):

> The mischiefs attacked by the aggravated versions of these offences are racism and xenophobia. Their essence is the denial of equal respect and dignity to people who are seen as 'other'. This is more deeply hurtful, damaging and disrespectful to the victims than the simple versions of these offences. It is also more damaging to the community as a whole, by denying acceptance to members of certain groups not for their own sake but for the sake of something they can do nothing about. This is just as true if the group is defined exclusively as it is if it is defined inclusively.
>
> The offences do not require particular words to be used. . . . Fine distinctions depending upon the particular words used would bring the law into disrepute.

The way in which the group appears to be defined, therefore, is not according to that group's racial characteristics but according to D's; the reference point is D's race as opposed to V's. Thus, rather than being defined as being of X race, they are defined as being non-X, X being D's race.

 Question

Imagine the scene at a public debate about the United Kingdom's relationship with the European Union if one English advocate of Brexit pokes in the chest an English pro-EU debater and says at the same time, 'European bastard'. If 'African', 'immigrant', and 'foreigner' are treated as referring to a racial group, might 'European bastard' also amount to racial aggravation?

This is a long way from the kinds of racially aggravated assaults Members of Parliament might have had in mind when the legislation was enacted. Now that religious aggravation is included in the offence the ambit of the offence is even greater (see further **15.6**).

Where s. 28(1)(a) is relied upon to establish the element of racial or religious aggravation, the hostility based on the victim's membership of a racial or religious group must be demonstrated at the time of committing the offence or immediately before or after doing so. 'Immediately before or after' was originally tightly limited.

In *Parry* v *DPP* [2004] EWHC 3112 (Admin), the Divisional Court held that a statement made to a police officer 20 minutes after the alleged offence (criminal damage), in which D used racially hostile language in respect of V, was not made immediately after committing the offence. Field LJ stated (at paras 19 and 21):

> These words must be given their plain and ordinary meaning and so construed their effect is to make the subsection strike at words uttered or acts done in the immediate context of the substantive offence. . . . The statement was not made in the immediate context of the substantive offence, but was made by the appellant after he had quit the scene and was sitting in his own house, at least 20 minutes after the door had been damaged.

By contrast, in *Babbs* [2007] EWCA Crim 2737, a conviction was upheld where D had assaulted V having described V and his companions 15 minutes previously as 'fucking foreigners'. D's annoyance arose as both D and V queued at a takeaway. The insulting words were used at the outset and later, when V was served ahead of D, the assault occurred. The judge directed the jury to consider whether the words had been used immediately before the assault. Later in his summing-up he left them with the question whether they were satisfied that immediately before assaulting V D had demonstrated to him a hostility based on his membership of a particular racial group. The only evidence of such hostility, of course, was the words used. However, in a judgment which massages fact and law, Latham LJ held that s. 28(1)(a) is directed not so much to words but to the hostility which is demonstrated towards a victim with the relevant connotation. Latham LJ was of the view that the words used were capable of colouring D's behaviour towards V throughout the subsequent events and that the jury were entitled to conclude that the hostility based upon race had been evinced over a continuing period from the moment the words were first used to the moment when the assault occurred. The problem with this embroidery of the facts is that there was no evidence of continuing hostility being demonstrated; rather the words were uttered, the queuing continued, and 15 minutes later, in response to provocative words ('white trash') and acts (waving his food bag at D) from V, D reacted.

Finally the aggravating factor may be a consequence of the assault such as the occasioning of actual bodily harm (s. 47 of the OAPA). This latter offence will be examined separately later.

 The law in context

Should the definition of 'hate crime' be extended?

Criminological evidence indicates there is a significant amount of 'hate crime' in England and Wales. The latest statistics show a 17 per cent increase in hate crimes recorded by the police in 2017/18 compared to 2016/17 (Home Office, *Hate Crime, England and Wales, 2017/18* (2018) Statistical Bulletin 20/18, p. 7), although some of that increase is attributable to improvements in police recording rather than a real increase in offences. Despite improvements in police recording, a large amount of 'hate crime' goes unpunished. A study published in October 2016 by the European Commission Against Racism and Intolerance found that

→

→

racially motivated or racially aggravated aspects of cases are often filtered out by the police or CPS, or dropped through the process of accepting guilty pleas to lesser, non-aggravated charges (*ECRI Report on the United Kingdom (Fifth Monitoring Cycle)* (2016), p. 9 http://www.coe.int/t/dghl/monitoring/ecri/default_en.asp). Does the law's approach to defining 'hate crime' offences contribute to that process of attrition?

The definition of 'hate crime' agreed by the police, CPS, National Offender Management Service, and other criminal justice agencies does not accord precisely with the legal definitions of relevant offences. The agreed definition states that a hate crime is 'any criminal offence which is perceived, by the victim or any other person, to be motivated by hostility or prejudice towards someone based on a personal characteristic' (Home Office, *Hate Crime, England and Wales, 2017/18* (2018) Statistical Bulletin 20/18, p. 8). The College of Policing's guidance on responding to 'hate crime' states that for recording purposes the victim's perception is the determinative factor in deciding whether an incident is a hate incident, or in recognising the hostility of a hate crime:

> If the victim or another person perceives the crime to have been motivated by hostility or prejudice based on race, religion, sexual orientation, disability or trans-gender identity then the police must record it as such. The victim does not have to justify or provide evidence of their belief, and police officers or staff should not directly challenge this perception. Evidence of the hostility is not required for an incident or crime to be recorded as a hate crime or hate incident. (*Hate Crime Operational Guidance* (2014), p. 5 http://library.college.police.uk/docs/college-of-policing/Hate-Crime-Operational-Guidance.pdf)

However, the legal definitions of the aggravated offences in the Crime and Disorder Act 1998 apply only to situations where a person commits one of a list of offences and, in so doing, demonstrates, or was motivated by *hostility* on the grounds of *race* or *religion*. Evidence of hostility is not needed for the victim's report to be recorded as a 'hate crime', but it is needed for a conviction. The CPS has to be sure there is sufficient evidence to provide a realistic prospect of conviction before bringing the case to court (*Racist and Religious Hate Crime—Prosecution Guidance* (2018) https://www.cps.gov.uk/legal-guidance/racist-and-religious-hate-crime-prosecution-guidance).

In 2014 the Law Commission published its findings into whether hate crime offences should be extended to cover other characteristics, specifically hostility based on sexual orientation, transgender identity, or disability (Law Commission, *Hate Crime: Should the Current Law be Extended?* (2014) Cm 8865, p. 1). The Commission said there were strong arguments for extending the provisions of the Crime and Disorder Act 1998 to include hostility on grounds of sexual orientation, transgender identity, and disability, the main one being that the current law leads to a 'two-tier system' treating differently the statutorily recognised aggravating characteristics. That sends the wrong message about the seriousness with which all hate crime should be viewed (p. 82). The communicative effects of prosecuting offences as aggravated variants were particularly important for some of the Commission's consultees who argued that by labelling appropriately conduct such as violence motivated by homophobia the State could convey strongly its disapproval not just of violence but of hate-based violence against a broader range of minority groups. It might also improve public awareness of hate crime and boost confidence in the criminal justice system.

Extending the offences would also carry practical significance, in the form of higher statutory sentencing maxima and the availability of a challenge to unduly lenient sentences (currently the Attorney General can refer people sentenced for aggravated offences under ss 29–32 of the Crime and Disorder Act 1998 to the Court of Appeal on the grounds that the

→

➡

sentence was 'unduly lenient'). That procedure is not available for offences that are not listed in the Criminal Justice Act 1988 (Reviews of Sentencing) Order 2006. Non-aggravated assaults under s. 47 or s. 20 and non-aggravated criminal damage are not within that Order.

Some of the arguments against extending the current aggravated offences in the Crime and Disorder Act 1998 include the conceptual flaws and evidential problems within the existing aggravated offences (particularly in the test for 'hostility': see **10.2.1**). Far from clarifying and unifying the law, extending offences to include even more characteristics would most likely lead to greater conceptual and legal confusion. Some judges and practitioners who commented on the Law Commission's consultation paper argued that juries can be reluctant to convict defendants for aggravated offences and defendants reluctant to plead guilty to them (p. 120). Other consultees queried whether the current list of offences was sufficient to deal with hostility-based offending involving disability, transphobia, and homophobia. Financial and sexual offences were listed as being more frequent than the offences that currently have aggravated variants under the Crime and Disorder Act 1998 and therefore focusing on extending the latter might be misplaced (p. 122). Another criticism of the proposed extension of aggravated offences was that the list of characteristics that the Law Commission was asked to focus on was somewhat arbitrary: why not extend the offences even further to hostility based on age, gender, homelessness, or belonging to any particular subculture (p. 142)?

The Law Commission's conclusions were twofold. First the enhanced sentencing system for hate crime should be properly applied and its use accurately recorded. Under the Crime and Disorder Act 1998, there are higher maximum sentences than for the base offence (e.g. common assault carries a maximum sentence of six months' imprisonment, while racially or religiously aggravated common assault carries a maximum sentence of two years' imprisonment). For other offences which do not have an aggravated variant, such as theft, the sentencing judge or magistrates must stay within the maximum for that ordinary offence (e.g. seven years for theft). For all offences, under ss 145 and 146 of the Criminal Justice Act 2003, all five of the characteristics under consideration (race, religion, sexuality, transgender identity, and disability) are listed as aggravating factors in sentencing that the court must take into account if the offender demonstrated hostility based on one of them. Some criminal justice stakeholders have expressed concern that enhanced sentencing is not currently used in cases of disability hate crime and homophobic and transphobic hate crime (p. 11) although there is a dearth of empirical evidence relating to sentences passed in cases of transphobic, homophobic, or disability-based hostility (p. 88). The Commission called for the Sentencing Council to publish guidance to courts on how they should sentence hostility-based offending.

Secondly, the Commission called for a further full-scale review of 'hate crimes' to explicate the theoretical underpinnings of such aggravated offences and examine all the available data to establish whether such offences and sentencing provisions should be retained, amended, extended, or repealed; what characteristics need to be protected; and the basis on which characteristics should be selected (p. 13).

In 2019, as part of the Government's Hate Crime Action Plan 2016–2020, the Law Commission started another review into hate crime. This latest review will review the adequacy and parity of protection offered by the law relating to hate crime and to make recommendations for its reform. It will consider whether there should be additional protected characteristics and whether crimes motivated by, or demonstrating, hatred based on sex and gender characteristics, or hatred of older people or other potential protected characteristics should be hate crimes, with reference to underlying principle and the practical implications of changing the law (https://www.lawcom.gov.uk/law-commission-review-into-hate-crime-announced/).

10.2.2 Assault occasioning actual bodily harm

Actus reus	Mens rea
D either: • causes V to apprehend immediate unlawful personal violence; or • applies unlawful force to V; and thereby causes V actual bodily harm.	D intentionally, or recklessly: • causes V's apprehension; or • applies force to V.

An assault occasioning actual bodily harm is an offence triable either summarily or on indictment, the maximum punishment for which is five years' imprisonment.

10.2.2.1 *Actus reus*

The *actus reus* is satisfied by proof of a technical assault or battery which, in addition, has caused actual bodily harm. 'Actual bodily harm' means any hurt or injury calculated to interfere with the health or comfort of the victim (*Miller* [1954] 2 QB 282, 292). **The hurt or injury need not be serious or permanent but must be more than transient and trifling.** The CPS will often have to decide between a charge of common assault or ABH. The CPS Charging Standards for ABH state that a charge of ABH would be appropriate where the seriousness of the offence requires a sentence in excess of the sentencing powers of the magistrates' court (https://www.cps.gov.uk/legal-guidance/offences-against-person-incorporating-charging-standard).

In *R (On the application of T)* v *DPP* [2003] EWHC 266 (Admin), the Administrative Court held that momentary loss of consciousness fell within the meaning of the word 'harm' as it involved 'an injurious impairment to the victim's sensory functions' and it was axiomatic, therefore, that the bodily harm was 'actual'. Harm would not be 'actual' where it was so trivial as to be wholly insignificant. The Court emphasised the point that in *Miller* the Court was excluding only harm which was 'transient *and* trifling' not that which was 'transient *or* trifling'.

In *DPP* v *Smith* [2006] EWHC 94 (Admin), the Divisional Court held that hair was a part of the body and that cutting off a substantial part of it was capable of constituting actual bodily harm; likewise if D put paint or some other unpleasant substance on it which marked or damaged it. While this may undoubtedly be highly distressing for the victim, particularly if not cutting hair has religious significance, it is difficult to see how any hurt or injury or interference with the victim's health or comfort arises. Emotional distress does not in itself amount to actual bodily harm (see *R* v *D* below).

Psychiatric injury is capable of amounting to actual bodily harm but where a prosecution is brought on this basis expert evidence must be brought unless the matter has been admitted by the defence (*Chan-Fook* [1994] Crim LR 432; affirmed in *Ireland* [1998] AC 147). Hysterical and nervous conditions and mere emotions such as fear, distress, or panic do not constitute psychiatric injury. What is required is something that amounts to a recognised psychiatric illness or condition (see *R* v *D* [2006] EWCA Crim 1139).

10.2.2.2 *Mens rea*

There was some doubt about the *mens rea* of the s. 47 offence. It was clear that D had to intend a technical assault or battery or be reckless (in the *Cunningham* sense) whether the victim apprehended or sustained unlawful personal violence (see *Spratt* [1990] 1 WLR 1073). Whether he had to intend in addition to cause actual bodily harm or be reckless thereto was unclear.

> In *Roberts* (1971) 56 Cr App R 95, D ordered V, a passenger in his car, to remove her clothes and he tried to pull off her coat. She jumped out of the moving car and suffered concussion and grazing as a result. The Court of Appeal treated the issue of actual bodily harm as purely one of causation to be determined objectively—that is, 'was it the natural result of what the alleged assailant said and did, in the sense that it was something that could reasonably have been foreseen as a consequence of what he was saying or doing?' (*per* Stephenson LJ).

There was **no need to prove that D intended to cause actual bodily harm or was reckless thereto**. This was confirmed in *Savage* (1990) 91 Cr App R 317. In *Spratt* [1990] 1 WLR 1073, decided by a different panel in the Court of Appeal on the same day as *Savage*, it was held that *mens rea*, amounting to at least subjective recklessness, was required in relation to causing actual bodily harm although this issue was not strictly relevant to the appeal. In neither case was reference made to *Roberts*.

In *Parmenter* (1991) 92 Cr App R 68, the Court of Appeal reviewed both cases and expressed a preference for *Spratt*, interpreting it to have decided as *ratio* that foresight of actual bodily harm is necessary for a conviction for the s. 47 offence, when this was strictly *obiter*. In *Savage and Parmenter* [1991] 4 All ER 698, the House of Lords overruled *Spratt* on this point, reversed *Parmenter*, and held that the statement of principle in *Roberts* was correct.

This is significant. The prosecutor's task is easier following *Savage and Parmenter* than it would have been if the House of Lords had followed *Spratt*. For a conviction under s. 47, the prosecution need prove only that D intentionally or recklessly applied unlawful force to C or intentionally or recklessly caused C to apprehend such force. This means that s. 47 is a constructive crime: liability for the more serious offence is constructed from the *mens rea* for the lesser offence. It would be more onerous for the prosecution to have to prove that D intended or foresaw actual bodily harm, which would mean fewer convictions and arguably undermine the law's deterrent function. However, this also means that a person could be guilty under s. 47 when ABH has resulted from his actions but in circumstances where no reasonable person could foresee that ABH would result. Whether D is liable for the offence under s. 47 or assault/battery may thus depend on chance.

The one remaining absurdity in this area is the sentence for the s. 47 offence. The maximum penalty is five years' imprisonment which is the same as that available for the more serious offence of maliciously inflicting grievous bodily harm contrary to s. 20 of the OAPA. So far Parliament has declined to remove this anomaly.

10.3 Wounding and inflicting grievous bodily harm

Section 20 of the OAPA provides:

> Whosoever shall unlawfully and maliciously wound or inflict any grievous bodily harm upon any other person, either with or without any weapon or instrument, shall be guilty of a misdemeanour, and being convicted thereof shall be liable . . . to imprisonment for not more than five years.

Actus reus	Mens rea
D unlawfully either: • wounds V; or • inflicts grievous bodily harm on V.	D does so maliciously, i.e. intentionally or recklessly.

10.3.1 *Actus reus*

The *actus reus* of this offence consists of unlawful wounding or the unlawful infliction of grievous bodily harm. (For the meaning of 'unlawful' see **10.1.1**.) To constitute a wound the continuity of the whole skin must be broken (*Moriarty v Brookes* (1834) 6 C & P 684). There need be no profusion of blood; one drop would be sufficient. However, a scratch which does not break the inner skin is not a wound (*McLoughlin* (1838) 8 C & P 635), nor is an internal rupture of blood vessels (*C (A Minor) v Eisenhower* [1984] QB 331) but a rupture of the inner skin of the cheek or of the urethra resulting in bleeding is a wound (*Waltham* (1849) 3 Cox CC 442).

Grievous bodily harm means 'really serious harm' (*DPP v Smith* [1961] AC 290) and is a question of fact for the jury. In *Janjua* [1990] 1 Cr App R 91, the Court of Appeal held that it is a matter for the trial judge in light of the particular facts of the case whether it is necessary to use the word 'really' before 'serious harm'. **Really serious harm can include psychiatric injury** (see *Burstow*, later in this section). While some wounds may also constitute really serious harm, it is clear that the most minor wound, for example a pin prick, falls within s. 20. It is difficult to see why it was thought necessary to specify wounding as a separate head as minor wounds could have been covered by the s. 47 offence. A number of injuries or wounds which individually would not amount to grievous bodily harm may, in total, do so (see *Grundy* [1989] Crim LR 502; *Birmingham* [2002] EWCA Crim 2608). In the latter case D entered a building as a trespasser and inflicted 11 knife wounds on V, together with bruising to her chest. D was charged with aggravated burglary (see **14.3**) which required proof that he had inflicted GBH with a weapon. The wounds were not individually serious but the Court of Appeal relied on *Grundy* to reject D's appeal as the jury were entitled to find that together they amounted to really serious injury.

In determining whether harm is really serious the jury should consider the effect of those injuries on the particular victim, taking into account their age and health (*Bollom* [2003] EWCA Crim 2846).

In *Bollom* V, a child aged 17 months, was found to be suffering from non-accidental bruising and abrasions to her body, arms, and legs. The trial judge directed the jury to take account of the child's age and health when deciding whether the injuries amounted to really serious harm. D argued on appeal that these were not relevant considerations. The Court of Appeal stated that injuries had to be viewed in 'their real context' and there was no need for the harm to be life-threatening, dangerous, or permanent, nor was it a requirement that the victim should require treatment or that the harm should have lasting consequences.

In *Golding* [2014] EWCA Crim 889, the context was that D had infected V with genital herpes, the Court of Appeal holding that V's evidence as to her painful symptoms, the effect at the time, their recurrence, and the prospect of future recurrences was sufficient for a reasonable jury to consider that the infection amounted to really serious bodily harm.

Section 20 refers to GBH being 'inflicted'. This contrasts with s. 18 of the OAPA (see **10.3**) where the relevant word is 'causing' GBH. In a series of cases spread over a century, it had been held that the words 'inflict' and 'wound' require proof of an assault (see *Taylor* (1869) LR 1 CCR 194; *Clarence* (1888) 22 QBD 23 (see **10.7.3.3**); *Springfield* (1969) 53 Cr App R 608; *Snewing* [1972] Crim LR 267; *McCready* [1978] 1 WLR 1383; *Beasley* (1981) 73 Cr App R 44). There were, however, cases in which the requirement for an assault appeared to have been ignored (see *Halliday* (1969) 61 LT 701; *Martin* (1881) 8 QBD 54; *Lewis* [1970] Crim LR 647; *Cartledge* v *Allen* [1973] Crim LR 530). Resolution of this matter became important as s. 6(3) of the Criminal Law Act 1967 provides:

> (3) Where, on a person's trial on indictment for any offence except treason or murder, the jury find him not guilty of the offence specifically charged in the indictment, but the allegations in the indictment amount to or include (expressly or by implication) an allegation of another offence falling within the jurisdiction of the court of trial, the jury may find him guilty of that other offence or of an offence of which he could be found guilty on an indictment specifically charging that other offence.

In *Wilson* [1984] AC 242, the House of Lords was confronted with the question whether on a charge under s. 20 of the OAPA the jury concluded that there had not been a wound or that the injury inflicted did not amount to GBH could they convict of the lesser offence of assault occasioning actual bodily harm contrary to s. 47 of the OAPA? Lord Roskill, with whom all their Lordships agreed, referred to the Australian case of *Salisbury* [1976] VR 452 and stated (at p. 260):

> I am content to accept . . . that there can be an infliction of grievous bodily harm contrary to section 20 without an assault being committed.

Thus an accused could inflict GBH without necessarily committing a technical assault or battery. If the allegation in the indictment for a s. 20 offence does not 'amount to or include' an assault, a conviction for the s. 47 offence as an alternative at that trial would not be possible. If on an indictment for a s. 20 offence the jury are presented with the option of convicting of a s. 47 offence, however, it must be because the prosecution have presented evidence which points to an assault. Lord Roskill stated (at p. 261):

If it be said that this conclusion exposes the defendant to the risk of conviction on a charge which would not have been fully investigated at the trial on the count in the indictment, the answer is that a trial judge must always ensure, before deciding to leave the possibility of conviction of another offence to the jury under section 6(3), that that course will involve no risk of injustice to the defendant and that he has had the opportunity of fully meeting that alternative in the course of his defence.

Wilson **established that 'inflict' has a wider meaning than 'assault'** but did not resolve the question whether it was as wide as 'cause' in s. 18 of the OAPA. Not having to determine the exact meaning of 'inflict' for the purposes of the case before them, their Lordships were content to cite with approval *Salisbury* where it was stated that (at p. 461):

> [G]rievous bodily harm may be inflicted . . . either where the accused has directly and violently 'inflicted' it by doing something, intentionally, which, though it is not itself a direct application of force to the body of the victim, does directly result in force being applied violently to the body of the victim, so that he suffers grievous bodily harm.

In *Savage and Parmenter* [1992] 1 AC 699, the House of Lords followed *Wilson* and arrived at the same conclusion regarding wounding, that is, that an alternative verdict of 'guilty' of the s. 47 offence is permissible on a charge of wounding contrary to s. 20. They accepted that **wounding does not necessarily involve an assault** although they considered that the circumstances in which a wounding might occur without an assault being committed would be 'quite extraordinary'.

> In *Burstow* [1998] AC 147, D was charged with inflicting GBH contrary to s. 20 of the OAPA by means of a campaign of silent telephone calls to V, 'hate' mail, theft of clothing from her washing line, and scattering condoms in her garden all of which led to V suffering severe depression. The defence conceded that depression amounted to GBH and the Crown conceded that there had been no assault or battery as no force had been applied directly to V. The trial judge ruled, however, that the House of Lords in *Wilson* had gone no further than accepting that there can be an 'infliction' without an assault and had not accepted the *Salisbury* judgment in full. Consequently, there was no reason for giving 'inflict' a narrow or restrictive meaning and it should be taken to mean 'impose upon'. In response to this ruling D pleaded guilty and appealed. His appeal was dismissed by the Court of Appeal which certified the following point of law of general public importance for the consideration of the House of Lords:

> > Whether an offence of inflicting grievous bodily harm under section 20 of the Offences against the Person Act 1861 can be committed where no physical violence is applied directly or indirectly to the body of the victim.

Their Lordships answered the question in the affirmative, Lord Steyn and Lord Hope of Craighead delivering speeches. Lord Steyn was of the view that any difference in the language in ss 18 and 20 of the OAPA was not significant. In addition he considered that *Wilson* had not decided what 'inflict' meant before concluding that the only problem remaining was the decision in *Clarence* which Lord Steyn distinguished on the basis that the judges in that case were not concerned with psychiatric injury, opining that the case 'no longer assists'. His Lordship concluded that although the words 'cause' and 'inflict' are not exactly synonymous one could 'quite naturally speak of inflicting psychiatric injury'. Lord Hope also distinguished *Clarence* without overruling it, concluding that the words 'cause' and 'inflict' are interchangeable and that it was entirely consistent in ordinary language to say that D had 'inflicted' psychiatric harm on V. In light of the fact that all their Lordships answered the certified question in the affirmative, *Clarence* is no longer a good authority. In *Dica* [2004] EWCA Crim 1103 (see **10.7.3.3**), where D infected two women with the HIV virus, the Court of Appeal stated that *Clarence* had no continuing relevance in this context and causing someone to suffer GBH through infecting her could amount to an infliction for the purposes of s. 20.

10.3.2 *Mens rea*

D must wound or inflict grievous bodily harm **'maliciously'**. 'Maliciously' does not mean spitefully or with ill-will; rather it **means intentionally or recklessly** and 'recklessly' is given its subjective meaning which requires foresight of a consequence (*Cunningham* [1957] 2 QB 396). What consequence, however, must D be proved to have intended or foreseen?

In *Mowatt* [1968] 1 QB 421, Lord Diplock stated (at p. 426):

> [T]he word 'maliciously' does import on the part of the person who unlawfully inflicts the wound or other grievous bodily harm an awareness that his act may have the consequence of causing some physical harm to some other person . . . . It is quite unnecessary that the accused should have foreseen that his unlawful act might cause physical harm of the gravity described in the section, i.e. a wound or serious physical injury. It is enough that he [foresaw] . . . that some physical harm to some person, albeit of a minor character, might result.

It is important to read Lord Diplock's speech carefully as the issue is not whether he *ought* to have foreseen some harm but rather whether he *did* foresee his act might cause some physical harm. Thus D will be liable where his foresight is of a lesser degree of harm than that which resulted and which is prohibited by s. 20. This was affirmed by the House of Lords in *Savage and Parmenter* [1991] 1 AC 699, 721 (see further *Rushworth* (1992) 95 Cr App R 252; *Pearson* [1994] Crim LR 534). Where the harm alleged is psychiatric, it must be proved that D foresaw harm of that kind.

As with s. 47, s. 20 is a constructive crime. The prosecution need prove only that D foresaw that some physical harm might result from his actions. That is relatively easy to do: the jury or magistrates are unlikely to believe a defendant who claims not to have appreciated that the punches he threw and kicks he landed on V could have caused *some* harm, albeit of a minor character. If the law required the prosecution to prove that D foresaw the actual harm that resulted, convictions would be much harder to secure. While the law thus has practical benefits for the prosecution and may act as a deterrent, it does mean that some people may be convicted under s. 20 when their actions have been relatively minor and by (bad) luck their victim has suffered serious injuries that no reasonable person could have foreseen.

Two final points should be noted. First, an intent to frighten V is not sufficient for the s. 20 offence (*Sullivan* [1981] Crim LR 46) unless such an intent is accompanied by foresight of the risk of psychiatric harm. Secondly, if D honestly, but mistakenly, believes that he is, for example, acting in self-defence he is not intending to wound *unlawfully* or inflict grievous bodily harm.

10.4 Wounding or causing grievous bodily harm with intent

Section 18 of the OAPA provides:

> Whosoever shall unlawfully and maliciously by any means whatsoever wound or cause any grievous bodily harm to any person . . . with intent . . . to do some . . . grievous bodily harm to any person, or with intent to resist or prevent the lawful apprehension or detainer of any person, shall be guilty of [an offence and shall be liable to imprisonment for life].

Beware simply referring to this offence as 'GBH'. Remember that s. 20 also includes the term 'grievous bodily harm'. It is quite common for the media to report that a person is charged with 'GBH', but that could refer to either s. 20 or s. 18.

Actus reus	Mens rea
D unlawfully either: • wounds V; or • causes grievous bodily harm to V.	D does so maliciously, i.e. intentionally, or recklessly, and with intent either: • to do some grievous bodily harm to any person, or • to resist or prevent the lawful apprehension or detainer of any person.

10.4.1 *Actus reus*

'Wound' and 'grievous bodily harm' have the same meaning as in s. 20. **The word 'cause' will be satisfied by proof that D's act was a substantial cause of V's injury** (see **2.6**). One subtle difference between s. 18 and s. 20 is that s. 20 requires the wound or grievous bodily harm to be inflicted on some 'other person' whereas s. 18 only requires that the wound or grievous bodily harm be caused to 'any person'. This raises the interesting possibility that if D caused GBH to himself with intent to do so, perhaps seeking to gain discharge from military service or to enable him to claim disability benefit, he could be charged with the s. 18 offence.

10.4.2 *Mens rea*

There are two elements to the *mens rea* of s. 18. First D must 'maliciously' wound or cause GBH and, secondly, he must do so with an ulterior intent either to cause GBH or to resist or prevent the lawful apprehension or detainer of any person.

10.4.2.1 'Maliciously'

What does 'maliciously' mean in the context of s. 18? Where D is charged with maliciously causing GBH with intent to cause GBH, the word 'maliciously' is superfluous as D can be convicted only where he intended to cause grievous bodily harm. If D is charged with malicious wounding with intent to cause GBH or with malicious wounding (or maliciously causing GBH) with intent to resist arrest the word 'maliciously' requires definition. D may intend to cause GBH without foreseeing a wound. For example, he may administer a karate chop to V intending to break his arm without foreseeing the ensuing wound caused when V falls over cutting his head on the corner of a table. Likewise he may push a police officer intending to resist arrest and not foresee the officer's resultant fall against a hard surface resulting in a fractured skull and cut scalp. If further anomalies are not to be created, 'maliciously' should mean the same in s. 18 as it does in s. 20. In *Mowatt* [1968] 1 QB 421, however, the Court of Appeal stated *obiter* that 'in section 18 the word "maliciously" adds nothing'. As the case concerned a charge of inflicting GBH under s. 20, little weight should be attached to this dictum.

> In *Morrison* (1989) 89 Cr App R 17, D was seized by a police officer who stated she was arresting him. He dived through a window pane dragging her with him as far as the window resulting in her sustaining serious facial lacerations. The trial judge directed the jury that if he intended to resist arrest and was reckless in the *Caldwell* sense as to causing the officer harm, he was guilty of the s. 18 offence. The Court of Appeal quashed the conviction holding that recklessness in the *Cunningham* (subjective) sense was required.

However, the case did not decide what degree of harm D had to foresee to be liable. Under s. 20, foresight of some physical harm is sufficient and this probably suffices for s. 18.

10.4.2.2 The ulterior intent

In respect of the ulterior intent, intention bears the same meaning as for murder—that is, either (i) the consequence (causing GBH or resisting arrest, etc.) was D's aim or purpose or, (ii) if this consequence was not D's aim or purpose, D knew that it was a virtually certain consequence resulting from achieving his aim or purpose, in which case the jury may use this as evidence from which they may find intention proved (see **3.2.3.6**).

10.4.2.3 'Unlawfully'

If D mistakenly believes that he is justified in using force in self-defence or prevention of crime, etc., and he uses reasonable force in the circumstances (as he believed them to be), he would not be guilty of wounding with intent or causing GBH with intent. If D is using force to resist arrest believing the arrest to be unlawful, and it is unlawful, he likewise would not be guilty of the s. 18 offence (*Walker* (1854) Dears CC 358). But if the arrest is lawful, although D honestly believes it is unlawful, he will be guilty of the s. 18 offence (*Bentley* (1850) 4 Cox CC 406; *Lee* [2000] Crim LR 991) as ignorance of the law (in this case the officer's powers of arrest) is no excuse. Thus if D, being innocent of any offence, is arrested by an officer who has reasonable grounds to suspect he had committed an arrestable offence, D would be guilty of the s. 18 offence if he pushed the officer to the ground whereupon he cut his knee (see *Lee*, earlier in this paragraph). If, however, D believed the person arresting him was not a police officer (rather than believing that an officer had no power of arrest in the circumstances) D's mistake being one of fact rather than of law will avail him, under the principle in *Williams* (1984) 78 Cr App R 276 (see **3.6.1.1.2**) (see *Blackburn* v *Bowering* [1994] 3 All ER 380).

10.5 Administering poison

Section 23 of the OAPA provides:

> Whosoever shall unlawfully and maliciously administer to or cause to be administered to or taken by any other person any poison or other destructive or noxious thing, so as thereby to endanger the life of such person, or so as thereby to inflict upon such person any grievous bodily harm, shall be guilty of [an offence] . . . and shall be liable . . . [to a maximum penalty of 10 years' imprisonment].

Section 24 of the OAPA provides:

> Whosoever shall unlawfully and maliciously administer to or cause to be administered to or taken by any other person any poison or other destructive or noxious thing, with intent to injure, aggrieve, or annoy such person, shall be guilty of an [offence] . . . and shall be liable . . . [to a maximum penalty of five years' imprisonment].

10.5.1 *Actus reus*

Both sections require proof that D administered to, or caused to be administered to or taken by, V some poison or other destructive or noxious thing. Thus, D would commit the offence if he fed V with the poison (administered), if he left the poison in V's food and E subsequently fed it to him (caused to be administered), or if he left it in V's food and V subsequently fed himself with it (caused to be taken) (see *Harley* (1830) 4 C & P 369; *Dale* (1852) 6 Cox CC 14). Until V consumes it, however, there is no administration (see *Cadman* (1825) *Carrington's Supplement*) although D's behaviour prior to this could have amounted to an attempt. In *Gillard* (1988) 87 Cr App R 189, the Court of Appeal held that spraying V with a noxious fluid so that it comes into contact with his body amounts to an administration.

In *Kennedy (No. 2)* [2007] UKHL 38, the House of Lords finally sorted out the mess created by the Court of Appeal over a decade in upholding various convictions for manslaughter where heroin-filled syringes had been supplied by one drug addict to another, the recipient self-injecting and dying as a result. In these cases the Crown Prosecution Service charged D with manslaughter on the basis of an unlawful and dangerous act, that act being the s. 23 offence of administering or causing to be administered a noxious thing. The House of Lords confirmed that s. 23 creates three distinct offences as set out earlier, namely administering a noxious thing to another, causing a noxious thing to be administered to another, or causing a noxious thing to be taken by another. Where, however, a person supplies a drug to another who with full knowledge freely and voluntarily self-injects, none of these offences is committed (see **2.6.3.5.4**). In consequence there is no unlawful act and a manslaughter conviction cannot be sustained.

Both sections refer to 'any other person'. Does that include a foetus? The issue arose in *CP (A Child) v Criminal Injuries Compensation Authority* [2014] EWCA Civ 1554.

> CP (aged seven) appealed to the Court of Appeal in a claim for criminal injuries compensation from the Criminal Injuries Compensation Authority (CICA) as a result of being born with foetal alcohol spectrum disorder (FASD) following her mother's excessive drinking during pregnancy. The alcohol consumption had caused intra-uterine damage to CP as a foetus resulting in physical disability and severe learning difficulties. The Court of Appeal dismissed CP's appeal distinguishing *AG's Reference (No. 3 of 1994)* [1998] AC 245 in the process (see **3.6.2.3**). The court ruled that a foetus is not a 'person' and cannot be the victim of an offence under s. 23 of the OAPA 1861. The damage, FASD, while it would amount to GBH, is caused in the womb rather than resulting later when the child is born. *AG's Reference (No. 3 of 1994)* was not apposite as in that case the offence of manslaughter was not complete until death took place, by which stage, the child having been born alive, had achieved legal personality and thus was a person in being. In contrast, a foetus is not a person while in the womb and thus the noxious substance being administered at that stage and the damage being done at that point, the *actus reus* of s. 23 is not complete.

The courts have experienced problems over the definition of 'poison' or 'other noxious thing'. **Ultimately it is for the jury to decide if the substance involved was a poison or noxious thing**. In the context of s. 58 of the OAPA, which relates to the administration of 'poison or other noxious thing' with intent to procure an abortion, the courts have held that the offence may be committed where a 'recognised poison' has been administered although in a quantity too small to be capable of doing any harm (*Cramp* (1880) 5 QBD 307). If the substance is not a 'recognised poison', to constitute a 'noxious thing' it must be administered in such quantity as to be in fact harmful (*Marlow* (1964) 49 Cr App R 49; see also D. C. Ormerod and M. J. Gunn, 'Criminal Liability for Transmission of HIV' (1996) 1 Web JCLI who argue that body fluids infected with the HIV virus are 'noxious' things). The problem with this distinction is that many things which are poisons are beneficial in small doses. For example, strychnine in small doses is used as a treatment to stimulate the respiratory system where a person has been poisoned by depressants of the central nervous system, but larger doses of strychnine are fatal. Similarly, warfarin is used in the treatment of people with certain heart conditions as an anticoagulant to thin the blood. It is also used as rat poison and in larger quantities can kill humans. Are strychnine or warfarin poisons or noxious things? For the purposes of s. 23 it probably does not matter which category they fall into as it appears that the meaning of noxious thing may differ from s. 23 to s. 24. Section 23 requires not only an administration of the poisonous or noxious substance but that the life of V be thereby endangered or that GBH be thereby inflicted on V. If the substance is merely 'noxious' the fact that the life of V has been endangered or he has sustained GBH from its administration demonstrates that it has been administered in sufficient quantity to be harmful. These definitional problems may be relevant, however, where an attempt to commit the s. 23 offence is charged. In *Cato* [1976] 1 WLR 110, D was convicted of manslaughter and an offence under s. 23, having injected V, with his consent, with heroin which caused his death. Lord Widgery CJ sought to distinguish between substances in common use which may be harmful when taken in an overdose and those which are liable to injure in common use. The former are not 'noxious' simply because of their aptitude, whereas the latter are. He placed heroin in the latter category and thus it was always a 'noxious' thing although it may not harm experienced addicts who have a high tolerance to it.

It appears that the GBH or endangerment of life must result from the administration of the substance and would not cover the situation where, for example, the substance causes drowsiness and V falls down a flight of stairs breaking his neck.

There is no requirement in s. 24 for anything other than proof of administration of the poison or noxious thing.

> In *Marcus* [1981] 2 All ER 833, D put eight sedative and sleeping pills into her neighbour's bottle of milk. She was convicted of the s. 24 offence and appealed. On appeal it was argued, relying on *Cato*, that as sleeping tablets are harmless in themselves they could not be regarded as 'noxious' simply because D sought to administer an excess quantity of them. The Court of Appeal explained *Cato* taking the view that Lord Widgery was 'not intending to lay down a general proposition that a substance harmless in itself and in small quantities could never be noxious within s. 24 . . . if administered in large quantities'. In the context of s. 24 'noxious thing' had to be interpreted in light of the requisite intent to injure, aggrieve, or annoy. This involved taking into account 'not only the quality or nature of the substance but also the quantity administered or sought to be administered'. Thus a substance harmless in small quantities could be 'noxious' in the quantity administered. In the context of s. 24, 'noxious' was not to be limited to substances which might cause bodily harm but would also include substances which were hurtful or unwholesome or objectionable.

The Court gave the example of putting a snail in a bottle of ginger beer intending to aggrieve or annoy V. Similarly it would cover putting a large quantity of laxatives in V's milk. In *Marcus*, the sedative quality of the drugs could clearly aggrieve or annoy V but the Court also took the view that they might harm V if, for example, in a sedated condition V were to drive a car or cross a busy street. Thus the 'harmful' quality of the substance may arise indirectly.

10.5.2 *Mens rea*

In both sections the word **'maliciously'** is used which **means intentionally or recklessly in its *Cunningham* sense**; it is the administration which must be intentional or reckless. D will be guilty if he appreciates that the substance might be administered by his actions. In s. 23 no *mens rea* is required with respect to endangering life or inflicting grievous bodily harm; the words 'so as thereby to' indicate that these are matters of causation (see *Cato*).

D cannot be convicted of the s. 24 offence unless the ulterior intent to 'injure, aggrieve or annoy' V is proved. In deciding if D has such an intent, regard is to be had not only to the effect he intends to produce but also to 'his whole object in acting as he has done' (*per* Robert Goff LJ in *Hill* (1985) 81 Cr App R 206). Thus, if D administered a sleeping pill to a woman with intent to rape her when comatose, the tablet would not be intended to produce injury but his 'ulterior motive' would constitute an intent to injure (D would also be guilty under s. 61 of the Sexual Offences Act 2003 of administering a substance with intent to stupefy or overpower C so as to enable D to engage in sexual activity with C). In *Hill*, D gave slimming tablets, which D knew could also produce sleeplessness, to two boys. Keeping someone awake is not necessarily harmful; but it may be depending on whether D's purpose in doing so is benevolent (e.g. to keep the pilot of an aircraft awake) or malevolent (e.g. to carry out a prolonged interrogation). In the instant case D's intention in giving the tablets was to disinhibit the boys and thereby render them more susceptible to his sexual advances; this constituted an intent to injure. A problem with this approach is that Robert Goff LJ proceeded, *obiter*, to provide an example which somewhat stretched the meaning of injury. He stated that if D drugged V with a view to stealing his property while asleep, his intention to deprive V of his property amounted to an intent to injure him. This seems like an intent to 'aggrieve or annoy', but Robert Goff LJ considered that depriving V of his property involved more than simply causing him distress or annoyance but was actually injurious to him.

Section 25 of the OAPA provides that a person charged with an offence under s. 23 may be convicted of an offence under s. 24. In such a case, however, the ulterior intent required for s. 24 must be established.

10.6 Offences involving gunpowder, explosive substances, and corrosive fluids

Section 29 of the Offences Against the Person 1861 provides:

> Whosoever shall unlawfully and maliciously cause any gunpowder or other explosive substance to explode, or send or deliver to or cause to be taken or received by any person any explosive substance or any other dangerous or noxious thing, or put or lay at any place, or cast or throw at or upon or otherwise apply to any person, any corrosive fluid or any destructive or explosive substance, with intent in any of the cases aforesaid to burn, maim, disfigure, or disable any person, or to do some grievous bodily harm to any person, shall, whether any bodily injury be effected or not, be guilty of felony, and being convicted thereof shall be liable [to a maximum sentence of life imprisonment].

As with other offences in the 1861 Act, 'maliciously' means intentionally or recklessly in its *Cunningham* sense. Section 29 is wide-ranging in terms of the types of activity it covers, including causing bombs to explode, sending poisons via the postal system, and throwing acid over other people. The latter type of activity has seemingly grown as a social problem in recent years, with statistics indicating that 'acid attacks' in London using substances such as bleach, ammonia, or sulphuric acid have gone up from 166 in 2014 to 454 in 2016 (*Acid Attacks*, House of Commons

Briefing Paper (2017) CBP 8041). These substances are relatively cheap, easy to obtain, and difficult to trace back to those who use them as weapons. The CPS's prosecution guidance relating to 'Offensive Weapons, Knives, Blades and Pointed Articles' indicates that s. 29 and s. 18 are the most appropriate charges to bring against someone who has thrown acid at another person intending to injure him.

10.7 Consent as a defence to non-fatal offences against the person

It is the essence of offences against the person that what is done is done unlawfully. The main defences which apply in the case of a charge of assault and battery are private defence (e.g. self-defence), acting in the prevention of crime, consent, and lawful correction. For private defence and prevention of crime, see **6.4**. Assaults, batteries, woundings, and even killings in certain circumstances may be performed lawfully as where, for example, D injures or kills V in self-defence. The application of force to another may also be lawful in certain circumstances where it is consented to by the recipient.

There are two main ways of looking at consent in terms of the structure of substantive criminal law. First, the absence of consent may be a definitional element of the offence which the prosecution have to prove to establish guilt. Secondly, the presence of consent may be a fact which D can plead as a defence to a charge of an offence of violence. In *Brown* [1993] 2 WLR 556, the majority in the House of Lords treated consent as a limited defence which could apply in some circumstances. It appears that the absence of consent is not a definitional element of the offence implied by the use of the word 'unlawfully' in the definition of offences of violence; their Lordships have implicitly confined the meaning of 'unlawfully' to justifications such as private defence or prevention of crime.

10.7.1 Consent: the common law before 1993

Prior to the cases of *Boyea* [1992] Crim LR 574, *Aitken* [1992] 1 WLR 1006, and *Brown* the common law provided some piecemeal guidance on the limits of consent; public policy considerations could operate to nullify consent. Thus a person could not consent to being killed nor could he consent to run the risk of being killed by duelling (see e.g. *Rice* (1803) 3 East 581; *Young* (1838) 8 C & P 644; *Cuddy* (1843) 1 Car & Kir 210). A person could not consent to being maimed as this would deprive the Sovereign of an able-bodied man for the defence of the realm (see *Wright* (1603) Co Lit f 127 a–b). The consent of the participants in a prizefight was of no effect on a charge of assault (see *Coney* (1882) 8 QBD 534, CCCR). While consent was generally accepted as an effective answer to a charge of assault, prizefighting was an exception where on grounds of public policy consent was held to be ineffective. In *Coney* the reasons supporting the decisions of the 11 judges were various: prizefighting was unlawful as a breach of the peace so the parties' consent could not render it lawful; it was against the public interest that the participants should risk serious injury or death; and fists are dangerous weapons and prizefighting should be banned for the same reasons as duelling. Consent is an effective answer to a charge arising from an injury incurred in the course of properly conducted games or sports (see *AG's Reference (No. 6 of 1980)* [1981] 2 All ER 1057) which includes sports such as wrestling and boxing. Where, however, parties agree to settle their differences by means of a fight, consent is not effective if the parties intended to and/or did cause actual bodily harm (*AG's Reference (No. 6 of 1980)*). Where, for the purposes of sexual gratification, a person beats another 'with such a degree of violence that the infliction of bodily harm is a probable consequence . . . consent is immaterial' (*Donovan* [1934] 2 KB 498, 507, *per* Swift J). The public interest dictates, however, that consent is effective in the context of reasonable surgical interference, dangerous exhibitions (see *AG's Reference (No. 6 of 1980)*), or rough and undisciplined horseplay (see *Jones* (1986) 83 Cr App R 375).

The cases discussed in this section do not fit together neatly, lacking any clear and coherent articulation of fundamental principles which might govern decisions in new situations, nor is there any clear identification of the public policy considerations which resulted in each decision.

 Questions

Are there sound reasons for the law allowing an individual to consent to run the risk of serious consequences in the context of boxing but not to consent to much less severe injuries in the context of a sexual encounter? Is there a difference between consenting to the risk of injury (even very serious injury) as compared with consenting to the certainty of injury sufficient to constitute actual bodily harm?

With regard to the way in which consent operates, in *AG's Reference (No. 6 of 1980)*, Lord Lane CJ stated that 'it is an assault if actual bodily harm is intended *and/or* caused' (emphasis added) unless there was a 'good reason' for such harm being risked or caused. In such a case consent would be an effective answer to a charge of assault. The implication from this was that consent could only operate as an effective answer to a charge either where the force applied did not create a risk of, nor lead to, actual bodily harm or, if it did (whether because it was intended or it simply occurred without being intended or foreseen) that there was a good reason for allowing consent so to operate.

The House of Lords in *Brown* brought some clarity to this area, although the Lords' reasoning was controversial and raises fundamental questions about the extent to which individuals are free to choose how they behave.

10.7.2 The decision in *Brown* (1993)

In *Brown* the five appellants were convicted of assaults occasioning actual bodily harm contrary to s. 47 of the OAPA. Three were also convicted of wounding contrary to s. 20 of the OAPA. The incidents which led to these convictions occurred in the course of private, consensual homosexual sado-masochistic activities which involved no permanent injuries nor was medical treatment required for any of the participants. The appellants' convictions were upheld by the Court of Appeal where Lord Lane CJ, applying the principle stated in *AG's Reference (No. 6 of 1980)* that 'it is not in the public interest that people should try to cause or should cause each other actual bodily harm for no good reason' concluded that 'the satisfying of sado-masochistic libido does not come within the category of good reason'. The Court of Appeal certified the following point of law of general public importance:

> Where A wounds or assaults B occasioning him actual bodily harm in the course of a sado-masochistic encounter, does the prosecution have to prove lack of consent on the part of B before they can establish A's guilt under s. 20 and s. 47 of the Offences Against the Person Act 1861?

The appellants appealed to the House of Lords which, by a majority of three to two, answered the question in the negative.

The majority started from the premise that the case concerned offences of violence which had a sexual motive, not sexual activity which incidentally involved injury. The language they used throughout their speeches was pejorative about the men's behaviour. Lord Templeman stated (at p. 564):

> In my opinion sado-masochism is not only concerned with sex. Sado-masochism is also concerned with violence . . . . The violence of sado-masochistic encounters involves the indulgence of cruelty by sadists and the degradation of victims. Such violence is injurious to the participants and unpredictably dangerous.

The words 'violence' and 'cruelty' are suggestive of an unwanted application of force resulting in suffering. In a sado-masochistic encounter, however, the force is requested and the pain is desired. But if the encounters were characterised as involving violence and cruelty, then they could be dealt with under a statute, the Offences Against the Person Act 1861, which was designed to protect people from violence and cruelty. This position was summarised perfectly by Lord Lowry who stated:

> What the appellants are obliged to propose is that the deliberate and painful infliction of physical injury should be exempted from the operation of statutory provisions the object of which is to prevent or punish that very thing, the reason for the proposed exemption being that both those who will inflict and those who will suffer the injury wish to satisfy a perverted and depraved sexual desire.

It is difficult to believe that the legislators in 1861 had sado-masochism in mind when they framed ss 18, 20, and 47 of the Act but the majority of the Lords adopted the position that the Act covered such behaviour unless there was clear authority to the contrary. The majority found none either in precedent or policy.

The majority accepted that consent was a defence to a charge of common assault but not to an assault occasioning actual bodily harm or serious bodily harm or a wounding unless a recognised exception applied. These exceptions, according to Lord Templeman, related to 'lawful activities' which carried the risk of harm such as 'surgery . . . ritual circumcision, tattooing, ear-piercing and violent sports including boxing' and 'parental chastisement'. It is arguable that all of these activities *involve* actual bodily harm (at least) albeit that they also harbour a risk of more serious harm. Perhaps his Lordship was seeking to distinguish between harm which is caused deliberately from motives which he found unacceptable (sexual pleasure) and harm which is incidental to some other purpose which he considered acceptable. The appellants had argued that the line between what was lawful and what was unlawful should be drawn at the level of grievous bodily harm (also referred to throughout as GBH) so that the infliction of wounds or actual bodily harm should not be unlawful. The majority, however, accepted that the relevant precedents of *Coney, Donovan, AG's Reference (No. 6 of 1980)*, and *Boyea* drew the line at the level of actual bodily harm. It was, of course, open to their Lordships to consider the issue afresh as none of the authorities they cited was binding on them, but they chose not to do so.

The minority, by contrast, started from the premise that the case concerned activity of a sexual nature which involved the infliction of actual bodily harm or wounds on the other party. Lord Mustill made this point at the outset of his speech, stating (at p. 584):

> This is a case about the criminal law of violence. In my opinion it should be about the criminal law of private sexual relations, if about anything at all.

That the Offences Against the Person Act was used was 'adventitious'. As the activities engaged in by the appellants were atypical of offences charged under s. 18, 20, or 47 of the Act, both Lord Mustill and Lord Slynn of Hadley were anxious to determine whether they rightly fell to be included within the prohibition of those provisions. To this end their Lordships engaged in a careful analysis of the previous authorities, concluding that they were not apposite to the facts of the current case and did not bind the House, leaving it free to decide (*per* Lord Mustill, at p. 599):

> whether the public interest requires section 47 of the 1861 Act to be interpreted as penalising an infliction of harm which is at the level of actual bodily harm; which is inflicted in private . . . ; which takes place not only with the consent of the recipient but with his willing and glad co-operation; which is inflicted for the gratification of sexual desire, and not in a spirit of animosity or rage; and which is not engaged in for profit.

Both their Lordships accepted that a victim's consent to harm amounting to grievous bodily harm was ineffective and, in addition, the public interest might dictate that the law disregards the consent of the victim where other considerations apply. Thus, in contrast to the majority, the minority were looking for reasons why the activities of the appellants should be brought within the prohibition contained in ss 20 and 47 rather than looking for reasons why they should be excluded. The issue was not whether their Lordships were disgusted by the conduct (both indicated that they were), nor whether they were endorsing the conduct as morally right (both indicated that they were not approving the activities), but whether the law should be interpreted to render the appellants' conduct criminal.

Following the decision of the House of Lords three of the appellants complained to the European Commission of Human Rights that their convictions violated their right to respect for private life guaranteed by Art. 8 of the European Convention on

Human Rights. In *Laskey, Jaggard and Brown* v *United Kingdom* (Case No. 109/1995/615/703–705), the European Court of Human Rights held that while the prosecution of the applicants interfered in their private lives, this was 'necessary in a democratic society' in pursuance of a legitimate aim, namely that of the 'protection of health'.

In *Emmett* (a Court of Appeal decision reported in *The Independent*, 19 July 1999), D was convicted of two counts of assault occasioning actual bodily harm arising from consensual sexual activity with his fiancée (involving asphyxiation on the first occasion and the use of lighter fluid on the second) as a result of which she suffered respectively 'subconjunctival haemorrhages in both eyes and some petechial bruising around her neck' and 'a burn, measuring some 6 cm by 4 cm' on her breast. The trial judge ruled that consent was not available as a defence where the parties foresaw the risk of injury arising from their consensual sexual activities. The Court of Appeal saw no reason in principle 'to draw any distinction between sado-masochistic activity on a heterosexual basis and that which is conducted in a homosexual context'. The Court of Appeal stated that the 'actual or potential damage to which the appellant's partner was exposed in this case, plainly went far beyond that which was established by the evidence in *Wilson*'.

10.7.3 Categories of exception

Brown **appears to clarify that consent is a defence to common assault. It is not a defence to assault occasioning actual bodily harm or any more serious offence of violence.** The exceptions to this rule are 'lawful activities' which carry the risk of harm such as 'surgery . . . ritual circumcision, tattooing, ear-piercing and violent sports including boxing' and 'parental chastisement'. The boundaries of these exceptions are poorly defined and lack coherence. In the most recent case on the subject, *R* v *BM* [2018] EWCA Crim 560, the new Lord Chief Justice, Lord Burnett of Maldon, noted that the categories 'do not lend themselves to a coherent statement of underlying principle. They are at best ad hoc, and reflect the values of society recognised from time to time by the judges' (at para. 24).

10.7.3.1 Consent, injury and sport

The Court of Appeal considered the extent of the defence of consent in the context of contact sports in *Barnes* [2004] EWCA Crim 3246. The Court expressed the view that as most organised sports have their own disciplinary procedures and as an injured player could use the civil courts to seek damages, criminal prosecution should be reserved for those situations where the conduct was '**sufficiently grave properly to be categorised as criminal**'. If what occurred went beyond what a player could reasonably be regarded as having accepted by taking part in the sport, this would indicate that the conduct was not covered by the defence of consent.

Whether conduct reaches this level depends on all the circumstances which include the type of sport, the level at which it was played, the nature of the act, the degree of force used, the extent of the risk of injury, and the state of mind of the defendant. In highly competitive sports conduct outside the rules might be expected to occur in the heat of the moment; the fact that such conduct was penalised and even resulted in a warning or a sending off, did not necessarily mean that the threshold level required for it to be regarded as criminal had been reached. In the instant case where V had sustained a serious leg injury as the result of a late tackle by D in a football match, the jury should have been directed to consider whether the contact had been so obviously late and/or violent that it was not to be regarded as an instinctive reaction, error, or misjudgement in the heat of the game.

The Court recognised that 'there will be cases that fall within a "grey area", and the tribunal of fact will have to make its own determination as to which side of the line the case falls'. The test the Court laid down is quite vague, leaving the jury to evaluate whether the conduct was 'sufficiently grave properly to be categorized as criminal', which arguably gives the jury little guidance. Football fans will be familiar with high-profile instances of professional footballers committing acts which, if done outside of a sporting context in the street on a Saturday night, would result in a straightforward conviction for a serious assault. The difficulty with *Barnes* is that while players do consent to the risk of some injury when they play sport, exactly what they consent to is unclear. If a footballer deliberately tackles another with force, aggression, and in full awareness of the possibility of the tackle breaking the opponent's leg, does that necessarily constitute 'sufficiently grave' conduct that can properly be characterized as criminal? The question is circular: in deciding whether the defendant's conduct is criminal, they have to consider whether the conduct is bad enough to be labelled criminal.

10.7.3.2 Branding

The list of lawful exceptions was extended in *Wilson* [1996] 3 WLR 125. At his wife's instigation D branded his initials on her buttocks. The Court of Appeal quashed his conviction for assault occasioning actual bodily harm. Russell LJ stated:

> *Brown* is not authority for the proposition that consent is no defence to a charge under section 47 . . . in all circumstances where actual bodily harm is deliberately inflicted.

The Court considered that the instant case was distinguishable from *Brown* and *Donovan*. The Court based its decision on several grounds, none of which are particularly convincing: Mrs Wilson instigated the branding (but the appellants in *Brown* willingly engaged in the activities there); there was no aggressive intent on the part of D, his desire being not to injure but to assist his wife in what she regarded 'as the acquisition of a desirable piece of personal adornment' (but there was no aggressive intent in *Brown*; the motivation was sexual and sado-masochistic rather than 'artistic'!); the branding was akin to, and no more dangerous or painful than, tattooing (but branding was involved in *Brown* and none of the injuries required medical attention). Adopting an approach similar to the minority in *Brown* the Court asked whether public policy or the public interest demanded criminal sanctions for D's actions, concluding that they did not, Russell LJ stating:

> Consensual activity between husband and wife, in the privacy of the matrimonial home, is not, in our judgment, normally a proper matter for criminal investigation, let alone criminal prosecution.

Herein, it is suggested, lies the real reason behind the decision—the Wilsons were heterosexual and married; Russell LJ's dictum implicitly suggests that even sado-masochism between husband and wife, in the privacy of the matrimonial home, would not be an offence. Would such liberality be shown towards an unmarried homosexual couple? If so, the decision in *Brown* could be seen to be one based more on prejudice than on principle.

10.7.3.3 The transmission of disease

> In *Clarence* (1888) 22 QBD 23, D, knowing he had a venereal disease, had intercourse with his wife, V, resulting in her contracting the disease. It was argued that his concealment of his condition constituted a fraud which vitiated V's consent thereby rendering the bodily contact an assault. The Court held, however, that there was no deception as to the nature of the act, sexual intercourse, and thus there was no assault and, if there was no assault, there could be no infliction of grievous bodily harm contrary to s. 20 of the OAPA.

The court in *Clarence* also took the view that V's consent to sexual intercourse also implied consent to the risk of infection.

The Court of Appeal in the case of *Dica* [2004] EWCA Crim 1103, effectively overruled *Clarence*.

> D, knowing he was HIV+, had unprotected sexual intercourse with two long-term sexual partners from whom he concealed his infection, infecting each of them with the disease. D was charged with unlawfully and maliciously inflicting grievous bodily harm contrary to s. 20 of the OAPA. The trial judge considered (1) that *Clarence* had been undermined as an authority, and (2) that the decision in *Brown* deprived the complainants of the legal capacity to consent to such serious harm with the result that even if they had known of D's condition they could not consent to infection. The Court of Appeal followed the House of Lords' decision in *Ireland; Burstow* [1998] AC 147, which held that the s. 20 offence could be committed without an assault as where, for example, psychiatric injury is inflicted without direct violence or assault. The Court concluded that *Clarence* had no continuing application as assault is not a necessary prerequisite to establishing the s. 20 offence. In ordering a retrial, however, the Court of Appeal confirmed that the issue for the jury was one of consent; while *Brown* prohibited consent to the deliberate infliction of GBH, V could consent to an activity which merely carried the risk of injury or harm. The Court of Appeal distinguished the present situation from *Boyea* and *Emmett* on the basis that those cases demonstrated that:

> > [V]iolent conduct involving the deliberate and intentional infliction of bodily harm is and remains unlawful notwithstanding that its purpose is the sexual gratification of one or both participants. Notwithstanding their sexual overtones, these cases were concerned with violent crime, and the sexual overtones did not alter the fact that both parties were consenting to the deliberate infliction of serious harm or bodily injury on one participant by the other. To date, as a matter of public policy, it has not been thought appropriate for such violent conduct to be excused merely because there is a private consensual sexual element to it. The same public policy reasons would prohibit the deliberate spreading of disease, including sexual disease.

It is interesting that the Court characterised both cases as involving consent to the deliberate infliction of serious harm when this is not how either case was presented before the jury or argued before the Court of Appeal. It is clear that the judiciary still struggle with the notion that people may take sexual pleasure from pain. But, by contrast, the Court of Appeal expressed the view that consensual acts of intercourse were not to be rendered unlawful merely because there might be a known risk to the health of one participant. The Court considered a distinction was to be drawn between those who engage in sexual intercourse knowing there might be a risk and those who are intent on spreading or becoming infected with disease. The Court also noted the higher risks in casual sex between complete strangers as compared to those in 'a long-term and loving, and trusting relationship'. The Court did not wish to criminalise, for example, Roman Catholics who were conscientiously unable to use contraception, but who had sexual intercourse in the knowledge that the healthy partner may become infected. Further the Court did not wish to interfere in the sphere of private relationships.

What was not clear from the decision in *Dica* was whether those who engage in casual unprotected sex, with the risks attendant upon that, are thereby impliedly consenting to the risk of infection such that the reckless infection of such a person by D would not amount to the s. 20 offence. In *Konzani* [2005] EWCA Crim 706, the Court of Appeal held that consent would only operate as a defence where it was 'informed consent'. Where D concealed his disease from his sexual partners he could not seek to rely on a consent implied from the general risk attendant upon sexual intercourse. The Court placed particular emphasis upon the personal autonomy of the victims and indicated that only in rare situations could D rely on the defence of honest belief in consent as silence 'is incongruous with honesty, or with a genuine belief that there is informed consent' (see also *Golding* [2014] EWCA Crim 889). One example given was where D honestly believed V had been informed of his condition by someone else.

It is also unclear from *Dica* and *Konzani* whether D has to have actual knowledge of his infected condition or whether it is sufficient that he realises he might be infected. Recklessness is sufficient for the purposes of proving the infliction of grievous bodily harm contrary to s. 20 of the OAPA. Interesting and difficult issues will arise where D and V are not in a long-term relationship and where D is aware he might be infected with HIV but has chosen not to undergo the necessary testing. Imagine that V, aware that casual, unprotected sex may result in infection, asks D whether he is HIV+, and hears his response ('not to my knowledge') before having unprotected sex with him. It is unclear whether V has given 'informed consent' in this example and whether D's awareness of the possibility of being infected suffices for s. 20.

10.7.3.4 'Horseplay'

Question

Why is rough and undisciplined horseplay, where serious injuries may be sustained by victims whose consent must be seriously in doubt, included in the list of exceptions?

In *Jones* (1986) 83 Cr App R 375, some boys at a youth club tossed two other boys into the air resulting in one suffering a ruptured spleen and the other a broken arm. They were charged under s. 20 of the OAPA. The trial judge declined to direct the jury that the boys were entitled to acquittals if they were only indulging in 'rough and undisciplined horseplay' with no intent to injure and genuinely believed that the victims were consenting. The Court of Appeal held that they ought to have been able to raise the issue of consent as boys have always indulged in rough and undisciplined play among themselves and probably always will.

This case was relied on in *Aitken* [1992] 1 WLR 1006.

The three appellants and V were RAF officers who attended a party where they all became drunk and engaged in horseplay involving setting fire to the fire-resistant suits of two officers who treated it as a joke. Later the appellants, overcoming V's resistance, poured a large quantity of white spirit over his suit and ignited it, severely burning him. At a general court-martial the appellants were convicted of inflicting GBH contrary to s. 20 of the OAPA. On appeal the Courts-Martial Appeal Court quashed the convictions. The Appeal Court confirmed the judge advocate's direction that intoxication was no defence to a s. 20 charge but allowed the appeals on the basis that since the appellants had not intended to injure V, it was arguable both that the pouring of a large quantity of white spirit over him was an accident and that they genuinely believed that V had consented. In effect, the Courts-Martial Appeal Court was holding that V could consent to the risk of serious injury and that an honest belief in such consent negates the element of unlawfulness which had to be proved on a s. 20 charge.

The question which was not answered in *Jones*, *Aitken*, or *Brown* (where their Lordships accepted that rough or undisciplined horseplay was one of the exceptions recognised in the public interest) is, why should the law permit such activities where the injuries risked are life-threatening and where the consents of the victims are highly doubtful? Why should a person be able to consent to the risk of bodily harm (or worse) in the context of horseplay, and another be permitted to risk causing such harm? What public interest is operating here to permit consent (or belief in consent) to operate as an answer to a charge of unlawfully and maliciously inflicting GBH? The fact that 'boys will be boys' hardly constitutes a 'good reason' for permitting a person to risk causing severe injury to another. All the courts turned a blind eye both to the degree of injury risked and the element of peer-group pressure which operates in male community life and which impinges upon the voluntariness of the consent of V. 'Horseplay' may be merely a euphemism for 'bullying'.

In *Aitken* the appellants' honest belief that V was consenting to their horseplay, on a conventional understanding of criminal liability, would not have been an effectual defence to the s. 20 charges as the appellants were drunk at the time. The Courts-Martial Appeal Court confirmed that s. 20 created an offence of basic intent so that it was no defence for the appellants to claim that they were deprived of the ability to foresee or appreciate the risk of harm ensuing from their actions; drunkenness substitutes for the *mens rea* requirement of recklessness (see **5.5.2**). But what if they mistakenly believed that V was consenting, the mistake being a drunken one? Conventional wisdom, based on the precedents, would have suggested that such a belief in a defence of justification would be of no avail (see *O'Grady* [1987] 3 WLR 321; *O'Connor* [1991] Crim LR 135, **5.5.6.3**). If a drunken belief in the need to defend oneself is no defence and a drunken belief in consent in relation to rape is no defence, why should a drunken belief in consent be a defence in respect of a s. 20 charge? No answer is supplied in *Aitken* where no reference was made to *O'Grady* or *O'Connor*. The same error was made by the Court of Appeal in *Richardson and Irwin* [1999] 1 Cr App R 392 (see **5.5.5**).

10.7.3.5 **Consent and medical treatment**

Regarding medical treatment a person may consent to surgery where the operation is for a valid purpose recognised by the law. A person's consent is valid where the operation is for a valid therapeutic purpose. This will cover medically prescribed treatment even though such treatment may involve a risk of harm, provided the possible benefits of the operation outweigh the possible harm from the operation or the failure to perform it. Even a sex-change operation performed for therapeutic reasons would be covered (see *Corbett* v *Corbett* [1971] P 83, 99). However, if a person were to have his hand surgically removed to avoid military service or so that he could claim a disability allowance, his consent would be invalid and the surgeon would be liable at least for assault occasioning actual bodily harm as the operation would have no therapeutic purpose.

10.7.3.6 **Body modification**

 Question

If person A asks person B to modify A's physical appearance, but not for a medical purpose, does A's consent to the modification provide B with a defence to a charge under s. 47, s. 20, or s. 18?

The issue of body modification, including cosmetic surgery, is problematic as it might be viewed as akin to medical treatment, but such operations usually have no medical purpose. It is likely, however, that such operations might have some therapeutic value because of the psychological benefits to the patient. If, however, a person sought to have cosmetic surgery performed on him to change his appearance in the hope of avoiding detection for the offences he had committed, this would not be a therapeutic purpose nor would it be in the public interest so the consent would be invalid.

In *R* v *BM* [2018] EWCA Crim 560, the Court of Appeal was confronted with the issue of body modification undertaken in unregulated contexts by people who have no medical qualifications.

BM was a registered body piercer and tattooist. Three customers separately asked him to perform body modification procedures: one wanted his ear removed, another requested the removal of his nipple, and the final customer asked for his tongue to be split so that it became forked like a reptile's. All had requested and consented to the modifications. BM performed the requested procedures. He was charged with wounding with intent to inflict grievous bodily harm contrary to s. 18, with alternative counts under s. 20. The question arose at a preparatory hearing whether consent could provide a defence, the trial judge determined that it could not. The Court of Appeal dismissed BM's appeal.

BM argued that body modification of this type is akin to tattooing and piercing and that the individuals' personal liberty provided good reason to permit the conduct. The prosecution argued that these were serious, irreversible, unwarranted medical procedures akin to cosmetic surgery. Lord Burnett of Maldon, giving judgment for the Court, started by recognising the difficulties in this area, most noticeably that the exceptions to the general rule confirmed in *Brown* deliver no easily articulated principle by which any novel situation may be judged. To the extent that the case law is principled, he said, they attempt to balance four interests: first, 'a general interest of society in limiting the approbation of the law for significant violence, albeit inflicted with consent'; secondly, the paternalistic need to 'protect from themselves those who have consented', particularly the vulnerable or mentally unwell; thirdly, the 'substantial cost' to society (presumably referring to the health service); and finally, 'the general values of society', by which he meant behaviour that is 'so deeply embedded in our law and general culture that it would require Parliament to render such activities subject to the criminal law'. What is striking here is the absence of 'personal liberty' as a factor that the courts must balance with the others.

Lord Burnett posited that two features underpin the recognised exceptions: discernible social benefit and a (vaguely expressed) sense that it would simply be regarded as unreasonable to criminalise the activity. In the present case the Court of Appeal's conclusion was that the modifications were most properly viewed as surgical procedures carried out by someone without medical qualifications, outside the regulatory framework for cosmetic surgery, and causing very serious harm. Only Parliament, said Lord Burnett, can recognise a new category of exception to the *Brown* general principle.

The emphasis the Court placed on protecting the public suggests the persistence of moral paternalism in these consent cases. The Lord Chief Justice noted the importance of 'protecting the public', by which he meant not only managing the risk of infection or complications arising from this type of surgery, but also the vulnerability of those who request it:

> The fact that a desire to have an ear or nipple removed or tongue split is incomprehensible to most, may not be sufficient in itself to raise the question whether those who seek to do so might be in need of a mental health assessment. Yet the first response in almost every other context to those who seek to harm themselves would be to suggest medical assistance. That is not to say that all who seek body modification are suffering from any identifiable mental illness but it is difficult to avoid the conclusion that some will be, and that within the cohort will be many who are vulnerable.

This seems to suggest that the main reason why BM could not use consent as a defence is either because he was medically unqualified or that those who seek body modification need protecting from their own decisions. In respect of the latter point, the Court noted the serious health risks posed by such procedures as well as expressing concern that some individual customers might be motivated by Body Dysmorphic Disorder to request modification procedures. If the former is the principal reason, would the outcome of BM's appeal have been different if he was a qualified surgeon performing the operations in a hospital? If the latter is the principal reason, might that mean that cosmetic surgeons are potentially liable to conviction under s. 20 or s. 18 if they perform surgery that is not warranted on any medical basis? The judgment makes clear that the argument that personal autonomy must be respected was insufficient to persuade the Court, which was principally concerned with protecting the public (see further Rachel Clement, 'Consent to Body Modification' (2018) CLJ 451–4).

10.7.4 Further issues relating to consent

A number of matters were left unresolved by the decision in *Brown*.

Question

What is the position where actual bodily harm is likely or intended but does not occur?

Dicta in *Donovan* and *Boyea* suggest that consent is negated, although in *Boyea* these dicta were qualified by the requirement that the assault be accompanied by circumstances of indecency. In *AG's Reference (No. 6 of 1980)* it was stated that there would be an assault if actual bodily harm was 'intended and/or caused'. The majority in *Brown*, however, considered that consent is a defence to a charge of common assault. Thus if A and B agree to settle their differences by a fight and are arrested after exchanging a few punches which do not result in any harm, and prosecuted for common assault, they may be successful in raising a defence of consent if the majority in *Brown* are followed on this point, although dicta in the Court of Appeal suggest that the defence should not be available where harm is intended. In *Barnes* [2004] EWCA Crim 3246, the Court of Appeal stated, *obiter*, that 'when no bodily harm is caused, the consent of the victim to what happened is always a defence to a charge'.

Question

What is the position if actual bodily harm was not intended but does occur (unforeseen by the accused); does this negate consent?

In *Boyea* (which was approved in *Brown*) the D's conviction for indecent assault was upheld by the Court of Appeal on the basis of the principle that 'an assault intended or which is likely to cause bodily harm, accompanied by indecency, is an offence irrespective of consent, provided that the injury is not "transient or trifling"' which it derived from *Donovan* and regarded as consistent with the *AG's Reference (No. 6 of 1980)*. The appeal was argued on the basis that D believed V was consenting to his touching of her and that he neither intended to cause actual bodily harm nor foresaw the risk of it occurring. Such a belief, it was believed, would negative the *mens rea* for battery as there would be no intention to apply force unlawfully to another nor would there be recklessness thereto. What then is the *mens rea* for assault or battery in these circumstances? The Court held that intention to touch the other is sufficient if actual bodily harm was likely, albeit unforeseen by D. This conflicts with the statement of principle by Lord Lane CJ in *Gladstone Williams* (1984) 78 Cr App R 276 (see **3.6.1.1.2**) who treated consent as pertinent to the question of unlawfulness which was part of the definitional elements of assault, stating (at pp. 279, 280):

> [W]here the victim consents . . . the application of force to another will, generally speaking, not be unlawful . . . . The mental element necessary to constitute guilt is the intent to apply unlawful force to the victim. We do not believe that the mental element can be substantiated by simply showing an intent to apply force and no more.

This issue was not addressed in *Boyea* or *Brown* but the assumption in *Brown* by the majority is that absence of consent is not a definitional element of the offence and thus this argument about *mens rea* falls by default although, had it been addressed, it would have been difficult to refute. In *Slingsby* [1995] Crim LR 570, however, this approach was rejected.

> D and V engaged in vigorous sexual activity to which V fully consented, in the course of which a signet ring worn by D caused an internal injury to V from which she subsequently died. Injury was neither intended nor foreseen by D or V. D was tried for manslaughter; Judge J (as he then was), ruled that the injury was the accidental consequence of consensual sexual activity and that it would be contrary to principle to treat as criminal an activity which would not otherwise amount to assault merely because an injury occurred.

This approach was endorsed by the Court of Appeal in *Meachen* [2006] EWCA Crim 2414, where D's convictions for inflicting GBH and indecent assault were quashed where unforeseen injury was caused to V in the course of consensual sexual activity. The Court adopted the approach to *Boyea* which had been adopted in *Dica*—namely, that that case was decided on the basis that there was no consent and thus the issue that arose in *Slingsby* and the instant case was not before the Court. Thomas LJ stated (at para. 40):

> It is sufficient for the issue that arises in this case to make clear that if the touching was with consent, then the fact that in the course of the consensual activity some bodily injury, even serious bodily injury, resulted accidentally and unintentionally, then as matter of principle no criminality can attach.

It should be noted that now the relevant sexual offence is sexual assault contrary to s. 3 of the Sexual Offences Act 2003 (SOA) (see **11.4**) which differs from indecent assault as the issue of consent is relevant in every case; if V consented to D's touching in sexual circumstances, that consent will negate liability even if harm resulted. It would be strange in such circumstances if a prosecutor chose to prosecute for assault occasioning actual bodily harm.

Question

What is it that determines that there is a public interest in certain activities being regarded as legitimate?

Why should a religious motive for wounding (as in the circumcision of boys in a number of religions) be regarded as acceptable whereas a sexual motive is not? Why is boxing, involving the intentional injury of an opponent, acceptable whereas settling a dispute by fists is unacceptable? Why is it a 'manly diversion' to bully others whereas sexual deviation is 'unmanly' and deserving of moral and criminal censure? How is the public interest determined? The cases reek of legal paternalism and legal moralism but little reference is made to ideas of personal autonomy or sovereignty. As was evident in *BM* (2018), the Court of Appeal summarily dismissed notions of individual liberty as a factor weighing in their considerations.

10.7.5 What constitutes valid consent?

The fact that V apparently consents to D's act does not mean that the law will treat that apparent consent as valid consent. **If V is a child, or mentally disordered, and the prosecution prove that his understanding and knowledge were such that he was not in a position to decide whether or not to consent, his apparent consent will be invalid** (see *Howard* [1965] 3 All ER 684). The issue is whether he was unable to comprehend the nature of the act.

> In *Burrell* v *Harmer* [1967] Crim LR 169, D was convicted of assault occasioning actual bodily harm arising from tattooing two boys aged 12 and 13 which resulted in their arms becoming inflamed and painful. The Court held that there was no consent as the boys did not understand the nature of the act.

Presumably they understood what a tattoo was but, it would appear, they did not understand the pain it would involve. In the case of a young child the absence of consent may be inferred from his/her age as he/she would not have the intelligence or understanding to give consent (see *R* v *D* [1984] AC 778). In the case of an older child it will be for the jury to decide whether the child was of sufficient understanding and intelligence to give consent and, if so, whether it has been proved that the child did not give its consent (*R* v *D*).

Where V consents only as a result of D's threats or as a result of fear, this will negative consent. It is not entirely clear what kind of threats will suffice; probably threats to dismiss from employment, or falsely to imprison. The issue will have to be determined on the facts of each case, taking into account the nature of the relationship between the parties and then considering whether the threat would be sufficient to overcome the will of a reasonably firm person. In some situations, the threat may be implied from the relationship, for example where D is in a position of authority over V such as a school teacher.

Fraud may vitiate consent where it relates to the nature of the act involved or the identity of the person performing the act, but not if it relates to the surrounding circumstances in which the act is performed. Thus in *Bolduc and Bird*

(1967) 63 DLR (2d) 82, it was held that D, a doctor, was not guilty of assault when he performed a vaginal examination on V, a patient, having told her that E, who was present, was a medical student. E was a voyeuristic musician. This did not vitiate V's consent, however, as D did not deceive her as to the nature of the act. This is undoubtedly a very narrow view as clearly V would not have consented had she known the true circumstances in which the act was to be performed.

> In *Richardson* [1999] Crim LR 62, D was charged with six counts of assault occasioning actual bodily harm arising from her continuing to practise as a dentist while suspended by the General Dental Council. The trial judge rejected a defence submission, inter alia, that the patients had consented to the treatment albeit that they did not know D was suspended from practice. D then pleaded guilty to all six counts and appealed. On appeal it was argued that the patients had been deceived neither as to the nature and quality of the act nor as to the identity of D. The Crown did not take issue on the first point but concentrated on the identity issue. The Court of Appeal allowed the appeal, there being no fraud as the concealment by D of her suspension from practice did not go to identity.

The Court of Appeal was unwilling to extend the concept of 'identity' to cover qualifications or attributes. This seems an unduly narrow approach as consent can only operate as a defence where the activity involved falls into one of the lawful exceptions—in this case reasonable surgical intervention. A person's qualifications to practice medical or dental surgery would seem to be inextricably linked to their identity for the purposes of relying on this exception. Their identity cannot simply consist of their name, age, sex, and race but must, for the purposes of practising medicine or dentistry, include their qualifications so to do.

Question

Would the Court of Appeal have concluded that there was no fraud if Richardson had never been qualified to practise dentistry but had masqueraded as a dentist taking on patients and offering treatment?

If the answer to this question is in the negative it is difficult to find a basis for distinguishing this situation from that in the facts of the case. Further, it is arguable that only a surgeon or dentist can perform a surgical or dental procedure. If performed by someone who is not qualified to practise surgery or dentistry the nature of the act would not be a surgical or dental procedure and thus the actor should be disqualified from relying upon the surgery exception. Clearly the decision in *Richardson* leaves unresolved more problems than it solves.

> In *Tabassum* [2000] Crim LR 686, D carried out examinations of three women's breasts purporting to be carrying out a study on breast cancer. The women believed he was medically qualified and would not have let him examine them had they known he was not. He was convicted on three counts of indecent assault and appealed arguing that consent could only be negatived where there was deception as to identity or where the nature and quality of the act differed from that to which the victim had

consented. The Court of Appeal dismissed the appeal and distinguished *Richardson* noting that the appeal in that case had proceeded solely by reference to the point on identity. In the present case consent to the touching was given as the victims believed it was for a medical purpose—they were not consenting to indecent behaviour. Thus 'there was consent to the nature of the act but not its quality'.

It should be noted that previous cases stated that fraud as to the *nature* of the act would vitiate consent. The Court of Appeal in this case has used the term 'nature and quality' (a term used in the M'Naghten Rules). What the Court seems to mean here is that the nature of the act the victims consented to was a touching but they believed it to be an examination by a medically qualified person and thus to be performed for a medical purpose rather than performed by an unqualified person for an indecent purpose. By focusing on the act the Court negotiated the problem of identity and the relevance of qualifications thereto. *Tabassum* was followed in *Dica* [2004] EWCA Crim 1103, where the Court of Appeal confirmed that D's concealment of his HIV+ status did not negate consent to sexual intercourse, and thus D could not be liable for rape, as his deceit went not to the nature of the act but a quality of the act. It should be noted that for sexual offences, frauds as to the 'nature or purpose' of a relevant act are conclusively presumed to vitiate consent (under s. 76 of the SOA 2003). Frauds as to other matters will only vitiate consent if they negate a person's agreement by choice (see s. 74 of the SOA 2003, **11.2.1.2.1**).

10.8 Necessity

The defence of necessity was examined earlier (see **6.3**). In *re F (Mental Patient: Sterilisation)* [1990] 2 AC 1, Lord Goff of Chieveley stated that the common law principle of necessity could justify action which would otherwise be unlawful where, inter alia, the 'action [was] taken as a matter of necessity to assist another person without his consent'. Thus there would be no assault where D seizes V and forcibly drags him from the path of an oncoming vehicle thereby saving him from injury or death. A problem which frequently arises is the need to provide care or medical treatment for a person who is incapable of giving consent to it—for example, due to mental incapacity or to being unconscious as a result of illness or accident. Lord Goff concluded that it was the principle of necessity which provided a justification for the care or treatment in these cases. Where there is an emergency, a doctor should do no more than is reasonably required in the best interests of the patient, before he recovers consciousness. Where, however, the inability to consent is permanent or semi-permanent, care or treatment which is in the best interests of the person may be administered if 'it is carried out in order either to save their lives, or to ensure improvement or prevent deterioration in their physical or mental health' (*per* Lord Brandon of Oakbrook). Thus the day-to-day care of those who are unconscious or who lack mental capacity to consent is justified by this principle. Lord Brandon made the additional point that it is not only the principle of necessity which justifies treatment where a person is incapable of giving consent; where care has been assumed of a person who cannot consent, there is a common law duty to treat them (see further **2.5.2.2.3**).

One qualification to this point is that 'officious intervention' cannot be justified. Lord Goff stated that intervention would not be justified 'when it is contrary to the known wishes of the assisted person, to the extent that he is capable of rationally forming such a wish'. This raises an interesting problem; suppose P has been diagnosed as terminally ill and he takes an overdose of sleeping tablets leaving a note stating that he cannot face the prospect of a slow and painful death and that he does not wish to be resuscitated. Would D, his medically qualified wife, be guilty of assault if she did resuscitate him? Would D's liability depend on whether P was adjudged rational/irrational or on whether D believed him to be irrational?

10.9 Lawful correction

? Question

May an adult apply force to a child for the purposes of discipline?

It used to be lawful for a parent or other person *in loco parentis* to use reasonable force to discipline their children or charges (see *Cleary* v *Booth* [1893] 1 QB 465; *Mackie* (1973) 57 Cr App R 453) provided the child was old enough to understand its purpose (*Griffin* (1869) 11 Cox CC 402). If corporal punishment was administered out of spite or anger or for gratification, or if the degree of force was unreasonable, it was unlawful (see *Hopley* (1860) 2 F & F 202; *Taylor*, *The Times*, 28 December 1983). Section 58 of the Children Act 2004 now provides clarification of the common law defence of lawful correction. Section 58 provides:

(1) In relation to any offence specified in subsection (2), battery of a child cannot be justified on the ground that it constituted reasonable punishment.

(2) The offences referred to in subsection (1) are—

(a) an offence under section 18 or 20 of the Offences Against the Person Act 1861 (wounding and causing grievous bodily harm);

(b) an offence under section 47 of that Act (assault occasioning actual bodily harm);

(c) an offence under section 1 of the Children and Young Persons Act 1933 (cruelty to persons under 16).

This provision renders any physical punishment of a child an offence if it causes any actual bodily harm (see **10.2.2**) or amounts to cruelty. Cruelty may involve the infliction of unnecessary suffering without any actual injury. It is no defence for D to claim that he did not intend any actual bodily harm as the s. 47 offence does not require *mens rea* in respect of the element of harm (see **10.2.2**). Even if punishment is not cruel and does not cause actual bodily harm, it may still not be lawful if it is not reasonable. Physical punishment of a child for an inability to learn or do something which he could not reasonably be expected to be able to learn or do, is unlikely to be considered reasonable.

10.10 Reform

In November 2014 the Law Commission published *Reform of Offences against the Person: A Scoping Consultation Paper* (LCCP No. 217) which was followed in November 2015 by a Report, *Reform of Offences against the Person* (Law Com No. 361). The Report highlighted the problems with the existing law:

1. There are too many narrowly defined offences about the same subject.

2. Sometimes the same section (e.g. s. 18) lists different but related situations leaving doubt whether the section creates one or several offences.

3. The order and grading of offences by seriousness is unclear and further confused by the sentencing powers (e.g. ss 20 and 47 both of which carry a maximum sentence of five years' imprisonment).

4. The number of obsolete or rarely used offences (e.g. s. 17, under which it is an offence to impede a person endeavouring to save himself from a shipwreck).

5. The use of archaic language (e.g. under s. 26 it is an offence for a 'master or mistress' to fail to provide for any 'apprentice or servant' necessary food, clothing or lodging).

6. The use of words without a clear meaning, e.g. 'maliciously'.

7. References to specific devices and chemicals as means of committing offences means provisions are liable to obsolescence.

8. References to obsolete legal concepts such as felony, misdemeanour, and penal servitude.

9. Penalties for major offences often may only be deduced by reference to other statutes.

The Report recommends replacing the 1861 Act with a new statute which is drafted on similar lines to the draft Offences Bill which was appended to the Home Office Consultation Document of 1998, *Violence: Reforming the Offences Against the Person Act 1861*. A guiding principle is that of 'correspondence', namely that the harm which any offence requires to be intended or foreseen must match the harm done. Some of the main recommendations are:

1. Assault and battery should be replaced by an offence of 'threatened assault' where V is caused to think that violence is imminent and 'physical assault' where violence is inflicted on V. These should be summary offences with a maximum sentence of six months' imprisonment.

2. There should be an offence of 'aggravated assault' where any physical or threatened assault has caused injury to V. This should be a summary offence, with a maximum sentence of twelve months' imprisonment, covering low level injuries which might currently be charged as s. 47 offences which are triable either way.

3. The s. 18 offence should be replaced by an offence of intentionally causing serious injury, triable only on indictment with a maximum sentence of life imprisonment. (There is no separate mention of 'wounding' as a wound can be either a serious injury or an injury.)

4. The s. 20 offence should be replaced by an offence of recklessly causing serious injury, triable either way with a maximum sentence of seven years' imprisonment. This offence requires that D foresaw the risk of serious injury.

5. The s. 47 offence should be replaced by an offence of intentionally or recklessly caus-
    ing injury, triable either way with a maximum sentence of five years' imprisonment.
    This offence requires that D intended injury or foresaw the risk of it but unlike the s.
    47 offence there is no need to prove an assault or battery as any means of causing the
    injury will suffice.

6. The ss 23 and 24 offences should be replaced by an offence of knowingly or recklessly
    administering to, or causing to be taken by, another a substance capable of causing
    injury. This offence would be triable either way with a maximum sentence of five
    years' imprisonment. This offence supplements those in 3, 4, and 5 above as injury or
    serious injury may be caused by any means, including chemical means.

'Injury' includes both mental and physical injury but the Law Commission recommend that only the offence of causing serious injury should be capable of being
committed by the transmission of disease. The Law Commission considered that
the whole topic of transmission of disease was highly complex and merited separate
consideration in a wider review that should involve healthcare professionals and
their professional bodies. Mental injury is confined to psychiatric conditions and
does not include psychological states.

 Key Points

– A technical assault is committed where D intentionally or recklessly causes the victim to
  apprehend immediate and unlawful personal violence (*Fagan* v *MPC* (1969)).

– A battery is the intentional or reckless application of unlawful force by D upon V.

– Where a person commits an offence under s. 20 or s. 47 of the Offences Against the Person
  Act 1861 or common assault, the offence will be aggravated if at the time of committing
  the offence or immediately before or after doing so, D demonstrated towards V hostility
  based on V's membership (or presumed membership) of a racial or religious group (s. 28,
  Crime and Disorder Act 1998).

– Section 47 provides for the offence of assault occasioning ABH. The *actus reus* is committing
  a technical assault or battery that causes ABH (which means any hurt or injury that interferes
  with V's health or comfort: *Miller* (1954)). The *mens rea* is simply that of technical assault or
  battery (*Roberts* (1971)).

– Section 20 provides for the offence of wounding or inflicting GBH. The *actus reus* is causing
  a wound or GBH. Proof that D was aware of a risk of some harm will suffice for the *mens rea*
  for s. 20 (*Savage and Parmenter* (1991)). The prosecution does not need to prove that D
  intended or foresaw wounding or GBH.

– Section 18 requires proof that D intended to do some GBH or to resist or prevent the lawful
  apprehension or detainer of any person, in addition to proof that D wounded or caused
  GBH.

– Consent will, in some circumstances, provide a defence to assault. The leading case is the
  House of Lords' decision in *Brown* (1993): consent is a defence to a charge of common
  assault but not to an offence under s. 47, s. 20, or s. 18 unless a recognised exception
  applies: ➙

→

- Recognised exceptions include surgery, ritual circumcision, ear-piercing, 'horseplay', and sports;

- Behaviour where no recognised exception exists includes: sado-masochistic acts and some types of body modification (*BM* (2018)).

- Section 58 of the Children Act 2004 clarifies the defence of 'lawful correction' of a child: battery of a child cannot be justified on the ground that it constituted reasonable punishment on a charge of s. 47, s. 20, or s. 18 of the OAPA, or on a charge of cruelty to a child.

FURTHER READING

M. J. Allen, 'Consent and Assault' (1994) 58 JCL 183.

B. Bell and K. Harrison, '*R* v *Savage, DPP* v *Parmenter* and the Law of Assault' (1993) 56 MLR 83.

C. M. V. Clarkson, 'Law Commission Report on Offences against the Person and General Principles: (1) Violence and the Law Commission' [1994] Crim LR 324.

S. Cooper and M. James, 'Entertainment—The Painful Process of Rethinking Consent' [2012] Crim LR 188.

C. Elliott and C. de Than, 'The Case for a Rational Reconstruction of Consent in Criminal Law' (2007) 70 MLR 225.

I. Hare, '*R* v *Savage, DPP* v *Parmenter*—A Compelling Case for the Code' (1993) 56 MLR 74.

P. Murphy, 'Flogging Live Complainants and Dead Horses: We May no Longer Need to Be in Bondage to *Brown*' [2011] Crim LR 758.

D. C. Ormerod and M. J. Gunn, 'The Legality of Boxing' (1995) 15 LS 181.

D. C. Ormerod and M. J. Gunn, 'The Second Law Commission Consultation Paper on Consent: Consent—A Second Bash' [1996] Crim LR 694.

D. C. Ormerod and M. J. Gunn, 'In Defence of *Ireland*' (1997) 3 Web JCLI.

J. Rogers, 'A Criminal Lawyer's Response to Chastisement in the European Court of Human Rights' [2002] Crim LR 98.

S. Ryan, 'Reckless Transmission of HIV; Knowledge and Culpability' [2006] Crim LR 981.

S. Shute, 'The Second Law Commission Consultation Paper on Consent: Something Old, Something New, Something Borrowed: Three Aspects of the Project' [1996] Crim LR 684.

J. Stannard, 'Sticks, Stones and Words: Emotional Harm and the English Criminal Law' (2010) 74 JCL 533.

J. Tolmie, 'Consent to Harmful Assaults: The Case for Moving Away from Category Based Decision Making' [2012] Crim LR 656.

M. Weait, 'Knowledge, Autonomy and Consent: *R v Konzani*' [2005] Crim LR 763.

G. Williams, 'Force, Injury and Serious Injury' (1990) 140 New LJ 1227.

11

···

Sexual offences

11.1 **Introduction**

There are numerous sexual offences but for the purposes of this chapter discussion will largely be confined to the main offences of rape, assault by penetration, sexual assault and causing a person to engage in sexual activity without consent, and the main offences relating to children. The Sexual Offences Act 2003 (SOA 2003) reformed the law on sexual offences. It aimed to strengthen and modernise the law to make it both clearer and more coherent. In 1999 the Home Office announced a review of the law relating to sexual offences with the remit of reviewing the existing law and making recommendations that would:

(i)   Provide coherent and clear sex offences that would protect individuals from sexual violation, especially children and the more vulnerable;

(ii) enable offenders to be appropriately punished;

(iii) be fair and non-discriminatory.

The underlying philosophy was that the intervention of the criminal law into private sexual relations would only be justified where there was harm to an individual and generally the activity was non-consensual. The review resulted in the Report, *Setting the Boundaries: Reforming the Law on Sex Offences* (2000) which, in turn, led to the publication of the White Paper, *Protecting the Public* (2002) where the existing law was described as 'archaic, incoherent and discriminatory'. The SOA 2003 repealed most of the Sexual Offences Act 1956 and many other provisions and created a new code of sexual offences. It introduced a number of new offences and redefined existing offences to remove the vestiges of stereotyping of masculine and feminine sexuality and discrimination based upon sexual orientation.

11.2 **Rape**

The Government's *Setting the Boundaries* review described rape as 'the most serious, the most feared and the most debated' of all sexual offences (para. 2.1.1). Parliament and the courts have extended the definition of rape since 1992. In that year, the courts extended the offence to incluce as victims married women who were subjected by their husbands to non-consensual sexual intercourse (see *R v R* [1992] 1 AC 599). Prior to the enactment of the SOA 2003, rape involved vaginal or anal intercourse by D with a person who did not consent to it, D either knowing that s/he did not consent or being reckless thereto. Section 142 of the Criminal Justice and Public Order Act 1994 extended the definition to include anal intercourse, thus recognising the phenomenon of men being raped. Before this change, a man who subjected another man to non-consensual anal intercourse could be convicted only of indecent assault, which carried a maximum sentence of 10 years' imprisonment and a less stigmatising label that many victims felt did not properly recognise and reflect the nature or extent of their experiences. The new offence of rape defined in s. 1(1) of the SOA 2003 further extended the offence of rape to cover other forms of non-consensual penile penetration which are regarded as equally traumatic, abhorrent, and demeaning as vaginal or anal rape. Section 1(1) provides:

A person (A) commits an offence if—

(a) he intentionally penetrates the vagina, anus, or mouth of another person (B) with his penis,

(b) B does not consent to the penetration, and

(c) A does not reasonably believe that B consents.

(Throughout this section the perpetrator will be referred to as A and the complainant as B consistent with the legislation.)

Actus reus	*Mens rea*
• A penetrates B's vagina, anus, or mouth with his penis, and • B does not consent to the penetration.	A: • does so intentionally, and • does not reasonably believe that B consents.

While both males or females may be the victims of rape, the offence remains gender-specific in that it may be committed only by males as principals. A female may aid, abet, counsel, or procure the offence. Where a female causes a male to have non-consensual intercourse with her she may be convicted of the offence of causing a person to engage in sexual activity without consent (SAWC) contrary to s. 4 of the SOA 2003. The maximum penalty for rape is life imprisonment (s. 1(4) of the SOA 2003).

11.2.1 *Actus reus*

In *Setting the Boundaries*, the Government considered the range of acts that should be covered by the offence of rape. The Government considered extending the definition of rape to include all forms of non-consensual sexual penetration, but concluded that this might move the definition too far from the public's understanding of what rape is. While acknowledging that penetration by objects and other body parts can be extremely serious violations, the essence of rape, said the report, is non-consensual *penile* penetration, which carries with it the risks of pregnancy and disease transmission (para. 2.8.4). This argument overlooks of course the fact that not all forms of penile penetration carry the risk of pregnancy and non-penile penetration can carry the risk of disease transmission. Nevertheless, the Government did recognise that forced oral sex, which before 2003 could only be prosecuted as indecent assault, is 'as horrible, as demeaning and as traumatising as other forms of forced penile penetration' and should be included in rape's definition. Section 1 gives effect to that recommendation, leaving other forms of penetration to be covered by a new offence of 'assault by penetration' in s. 2.

11.2.1.1 Penetration

The *actus reus* **of rape consists of the penetration of the vagina, anus, or mouth by the penis.** Section 79(9) of the SOA 2003 defines 'vagina' to include vulva, thereby confirming that the slightest degree of penetration is sufficient to constitute the complete offence. There is no need for the hymen to be ruptured, nor is it necessary for ejaculation to occur. **Penetration is a continuing act from entry to withdrawal** (s. 79(2) of the SOA 2003). Thus if A penetrates B with consent but B withdraws that consent, A must withdraw his penis; to continue to penetrate B would amount to the *actus reus* of rape (see *Cooper and Schaub* [1994] Crim LR 531). Section 79(3) provides that 'references to a part of the body include references to a part surgically constructed (in particular through gender reassignment surgery)' thereby making it clear that the law covers transsexuals—a male–female transsexual may be the victim of vaginal rape while a female–male transsexual may commit the offence of rape as a principal.

11.2.1.2 Absence of consent

A's penetration of B's vagina, anus, or mouth may only amount to rape where B does not consent to that penetration. Before the 2003 Act there was no statutory definition of consent. The leading authority on how juries should be directed on this issue was *Olugboja* [1982] QB 320 where Dunn LJ stated:

> They should be directed that consent, or the absence of it, is to be given its ordinary meaning and if need be, by way of example, that there is a difference between consent and submission; every consent involves a submission, but it by no means follows that a mere submission involves consent . . . . [I]n the less common type of case where intercourse takes place after threats not involving violence or the fear of it . . . [the jury] should be directed to concentrate on the state of mind of the victim immediately before the act of sexual intercourse, having regard to all the relevant circumstances . . . . Where [the line between true consent and mere submission] is to be drawn in a given case is for the jury to decide, applying their combined good sense, experience and knowledge of human nature and modern behaviour to all the relevant facts of the case.

Simon Gardner argued that *Olugboja* possessed 'substantial wisdom' as it recognised that:

> Uniformity and predictability are not prized . . . [the] right course is for the participants to express themselves in all their individuality . . . [T]he right course for the law, in constructing its concept of consent . . . is to accord primary importance to personal make-up and preference. (Simon Gardner (1996) 16(3) *Legal Studies* 275–97)

However, one of the complaints about Dunn LJ's recommended direction was that it left the jury too much leeway and could give rise to inconsistency. As Jennifer Temkin argued:

> Olugboja does little to increase the protection of sexual autonomy. The decision . . . makes for uncertainty . . . . There is no way of telling in advance of a court hearing whether in law consent is present or not. In this way the law fails to meet a minimum requirement of clarity, certainty and comprehensibility. (Jennifer Temkin (2002) *Rape and the Legal Process*, p. 93)

The Government, in *Setting the Boundaries*, recognised the concerns that *Olugboja* meant not only that the meaning of consent was unclear but also that it allowed jurors to apply their own understandings of when someone consents. In turn, that meant that they could be influenced by 'rape myths', misunderstandings, and misconceptions about consent such as, 'It isn't rape if the woman shows no obvious signs of being subject to physical violence.'

In order to address concerns about consent's vague meaning, the 2003 Act provides a statutory definition of consent which is supported further by presumptions, some of which are conclusive that there was no consent and some of which place a burden upon A to raise sufficient evidence as to whether or not B consented. However, despite a statutory definition existing, it is worth bearing in mind that the vast range of situations which involve sex and relationships means that the courts have struggled to provide clear guidance on precisely when someone does not consent and juries can face significant difficulties in deciding that. As Sir Igor Judge said in *Bree* [2007] EWCA Crim 804, the leading case on intoxication and consent:

> Arguments about consent abound just because consent to sexual intercourse extends from passionate enthusiasm to reluctant or bored acquiescence, and its absence includes quiet submission or surrender as well as determined physical resistance against an attacker which might expose the victim to injury, and sometimes death. (at para. 22)

11.2.1.2.1 *The definition of consent*
Section 74 provides:

> For the purposes of this Part, a person consents if he agrees by choice, and has the freedom and capacity to make that choice.

Where the facts of the case do not fall within one of the situations covered by the presumptions, the jury must apply this definition. Often, however, the presumptions will be relevant to the situation. Accordingly, it is important not to consider this section in isolation from the following sections (75 and 76) relating to the presumptions. There are three aspects to this definition of consent which are examined later; these aspects are, however, interrelated and interdependent. It is worth noting at the outset that words such as 'choice' and 'freedom' are philosophically complex. Jurors will have their own notions of 'choice' and 'freedom' deriving from their culture, education, and background. There may be limited common ground between them. The real issue for the jury should not be to struggle to define 'choice' and 'freedom'; rather their focus should be on the issue whether or not B's freedom to choose was in some way constrained.

In the Report, *Setting the Boundaries* (2000), it was recommended that there should be a standard direction given to juries on the meaning of consent. In appropriate circumstances juries should be told not to assume that B freely agreed simply because B did not say or do anything, protest, or resist which might indicate the contrary or that B was not physically injured (see para. 2.11.5 of the Report). The fact that B is frozen by fear of A, and complies with A's demands without resistance, does not mean that B has freely agreed by choice to engage in sexual intercourse with A. A direction along those lines would therefore be appropriate in circumstances such as these to counteract the kind of thinking which considers that if B did not vigorously resist A, B must have been consenting.

 Key Point

Whether B consented to the penetration is a question of fact for the jury, applying s. 74.

(a) *Agreement by choice* **Agreement by choice would seem to imply that B is aware of what the proposed sexual activity is, is aware of who A is, and chooses to agree to that activity with A without any constraint (such as force, coercion, or fraud) impairing that choice.** The previous law clearly established that it is not necessary to prove that B positively dissented, it being sufficient to prove that B did not consent; there was no requirement that the absence of consent had to be demonstrated or that it had to be communicated to A for the absence of consent to exist (see *Malone* [1998] 2 Cr App R 447; followed in *H* [2007] EWCA Crim 2056). In *McAllister* [1997] Crim LR 233, Brooke LJ stated:

> The focus of the inquiry in all these cases is based on the sexual autonomy of the complainant. The circumstances of a possibly reluctant consent may be infinitely varied, and on each occasion the jury has to decide whether an alleged agreement to a sexual act may properly be seen as a real consent or whether it should be regarded as a submission founded on improper pressure which this particular complainant could not reasonably withstand from this particular defendant.

The focus on the particular complainant and particular defendant may be important as the existence of a relationship between them, or the fact of a pre-existing relationship between them, may shed additional light on the issue. For example, B may know from past experience with A that a failure to submit to his sexual demands will result in violence even though no violence is threatened. Ultimately, however, the question of how to characterise B's state of mind is one for the jury.

Question

Should promises of benefit which appeal to B's particular tastes or weaknesses be considered sufficient to vitiate consent? For example, is a young aspiring film actor consenting when she has intercourse with a film's director or producer after he promises her parts in his films? Does the protection of sexual autonomy demand that such a transaction be regarded as non-consensual with the potential of founding a charge of rape?

From one perspective she may be doing something which she finds distasteful and would not otherwise do, but is agreeing to intercourse without any external constraint being imposed upon her. The constraint operating is her own internal ambition; no one is forcing her to be an actor. From another perspective, that analysis of the interaction is too simplistic: although the actor appears to be free to make a simple choice (either secure the role by having sex or walk away), advancement in the film industry for aspiring actors is dependent on the power of (usually male) directors and producers. As has become evident from high-profile cases in the USA such as that of the film producer Harvey Weinstein, who is accused of having raped dozens of women, 'choice' must be seen in the context of power imbalances between the participants. Guaranteeing sex on condition of advancement could be seen as a gross abuse of power, constraining the autonomy of the person who is forced to make a choice that she should not have to make. A jury may conclude, depending on the particular circumstances, that the person did not agree by choice or have the freedom to make that choice.

Threats of detriment of harm may be easier to characterise as removing or restricting B's freedom to make a choice. A threat of violence or false imprisonment clearly bears upon B's freedom to choose and an agreement to intercourse in such circumstances would not amount to consent. But what is the appropriate outcome where the director, faced with reluctance from the actor, tells her that he will ensure she never works in films if she does not have sex with him? There is a threat of detriment which may or may not be an idle one. Balancing the detriment threatened against the detriment of undesired intercourse is thus not a straightforward exercise and how the courts will address the problem of consent is unclear.

If the emphasis under the 2003 Act is upon sexual autonomy, other matters such as the context in which the sexual activity occurs or the consequences of that activity, may have a bearing upon the question whether or not B has truly agreed by choice. **For such a choice to be free and unconstrained, it must be an informed choice.** Concealment of matters relevant to that choice, or deception as to such matters, inevitably impact upon the validity of the agreement which results. For example, in *Linekar* [1995] Crim LR 320, A's conviction for rape was quashed where he had had intercourse with B, a woman working as a prostitute, on the promise that he would pay her £25 which he did not pay. The Court of Appeal considered that A's false pretence did not destroy the reality of B's consent as the only frauds which could vitiate consent were those as to the nature of the act or the identity of the other party (see now s. 76 of the SOA 2003). This situation, however, was covered by the offence of procuring sexual intercourse by false pretences or false representations contrary to s. 3 of the SOA 1956, an offence which has been abolished.

The offence which is meant to replace it, causing a person to engage in sexual activity without consent, faces the same problem as the offence of rape as the same definition of consent applies. The question, therefore, is whether B 'agrees by choice' when she is deceived in respect of the very thing, payment, that B requires before having sex. Section 74 is underpinned by a commitment to protect and uphold individuals' sexual autonomy. In the context of prostitution, where the understanding is that the sexual service offered by B is one for which A will pay, the deception seems to mean that there was no real agreement by B and that her sexual autonomy has been violated.

 Question

If A is infected with a sexually transmitted disease or is HIV+, and does not reveal this when asked by B, is it arguable that B has not agreed to sexual intercourse by choice as she has been deceived as to something fundamental to the conclusion of that agreement?

The law before 2003 did not regard this as a matter which vitiated consent. In *B* [2006] EWCA Crim 2945, the Court of Appeal held that the fact that B had not disclosed that he was suffering from a serious sexually transmitted infection is not relevant to the issue of whether a person with whom he engaged in sexual intercourse had consented to it within the meaning of s. 74 and no issues arose under the presumptions in relation to consent under ss 75 and 76 (discussed later). In particular, s. 76 made reference only to two specific deceptions (as to the nature or purpose of the act or impersonation) which could vitiate consent. (For consideration of liability for inflicting GBH by the transmission of HIV, see *Dica* [2004] EWCA Crim 1103, **10.1.3.1.1(d)**.) Latham LJ said:

> Where one party to sexual activity has a sexually transmissible disease which is not disclosed to the other party any consent that may have been given to that activity by the other party is not thereby vitiated. The act remains a consensual act. However, the party suffering from the sexually transmissible disease will not have any defence to any charge which may result from harm created by that sexual activity, merely by virtue of that consent, because such consent does not include consent to infection by the disease.

This is a difficult decision to support in light of the 2003 Act's aim of upholding sexual autonomy. If B expressly asks A about his HIV status before agreeing to sexual intercourse and A lies, can B be said to be 'agreeing by choice' where she has been deceived in respect of a consideration central to her decision? In *B* the Court expressed the *obiter* opinion that express misrepresentations were no different to implied misrepresentations. Latham LJ did recognise that the issue is a 'delicate matter' that required debate,

> not in a court of law but as a matter of public and social policy. Bearing in mind all the factors that are concerned including the questions of personal autonomy in delicate personal relationships.

His approach in *B* was perhaps rooted in a concern that the label of 'rape' should not be over-extended to cover those who have sex but do not disclose beforehand that they have a sexually transmitted infection. If the Court of Appeal has to address this issue directly, hopefully it will arrive at a different conclusion. In such a situation, if B does not contract HIV, A would not be liable to conviction for an offence under s. 20 of the Offences Against the Person Act 1861 (see **10.3**) and there would be no deterrent to him continuing his dangerous activities if his behaviour is not captured by one of the range of sexual offences.

The deficiencies in the reasoning in *B* have, at least, been recognised by the Divisional Court in *Assange* v *Swedish Prosecution Authority* [2011] EWHC 2489 (Admin) in the context of an appeal against extradition under a European Arrest Warrant (EAW), where the issue was whether conduct alleged to amount to the Swedish offence of sexual molestation was an offence under the law of England and Wales. The crucial issue was whether A would have been guilty of raping B if B had consented only to protected sex, but A, without B's knowledge, did not use a condom, or removed the condom he had initially worn. The Court concluded that the case raised no issue as to the presumptions in s. 76 (see the following extract) because if there was any deception it was not a deception as to the 'nature or purpose of the relevant act'. Sir John Thomas P stated:

> 90 . . . . If the conduct of the defendant is not within s. 76, that does not preclude reliance on s. 74. *B* goes no further than deciding that failure to disclose HIV infection is not of itself relevant to consent under s. 74. *B* does not permit A to contend that, if he deceived [B] as to whether he was using a condom or one that he had not damaged, that was irrelevant to the issue of [B's] consent to sexual intercourse as a matter of the law of England and Wales or his belief in her consent. On each of those issues, it is clear that it is the prosecution case she did not consent and he had no or no reasonable belief in that consent. Those are issues to which s. 74 and not s. 76 is relevant; there is nothing in *R* v *B* which compels any other conclusion . . . .
>
> 91. Thus, if the question is whether what is set out in the EAW is an offence under the law of England and Wales, then it is in our view clear that it was . . .

The Divisional Court was satisfied, quite rightly, that the fact that conduct does not fall within s. 76 (a provision which relates to very limited circumstances in which conclusive presumptions arise) does not preclude reliance upon s. 74. Sir John Thomas P stated (at para. 88):

> It would, in our view have been extraordinary if Parliament had legislated in terms that, if conduct that was not deceptive could be taken into account for the purposes of s. 74, conduct that was deceptive could not be.

Assange was considered in *R (F)* v *DPP* [2013] EWHC 945 (Admin), where the DPP's decision not to prosecute A for rape was successfully challenged in an application for judicial review. While B had agreed to have intercourse with A she had stipulated that he not ejaculate inside her. On penetrating B, A insisted on ejaculating inside her; this was a very different case to one where A intends to withdraw but clumsily fails to do so in time, Lord Judge CJ stating (at para. 26):

What *Assange* underlines is that 'choice' is crucial to the issue of 'consent' . . . . The evidence relating to 'choice' and the 'freedom' to make any particular choice must be approached in a broad common sense way. If before penetration began [A] had made up his mind that he would penetrate and ejaculate within [B's] vagina, or even, because 'penetration is a continuing act from entry to withdrawal' (see s. 79(2) of the 2003 Act) he decided that he would not withdraw at all, just because he deemed [B] subservient to his control, she was deprived of choice relating to the crucial feature on which her original consent to sexual intercourse was based. Accordingly her consent was negated. Contrary to her wishes, and knowing that she would not have consented, and did not consent to penetration or the continuation of penetration if she had any inkling of his intention, he deliberately ejaculated within her vagina. In law, this combination of circumstances falls within the statutory definition of rape.

Assange and *R (F)* were considered in *McNally* [2013] EWCA Crim 1051, where D's convictions for six counts of assault by penetration contrary to s. 2 of the SOA were upheld on appeal.

> A, a female wearing a dildo, tricked B into engaging in sexual acts of penetration, some involving the dildo and some involving digital penetration. B's belief was that A was a boy called Scott. On appeal A argued that deception as to gender could not vitiate consent and that *Assange* and *R(F)* should be distinguished as the deceptions in those cases were not deceptions as to qualities or attributes of the person concerned but as to features of the act itself. The Court of Appeal was of the view that this argument was not sustainable as the wearing of a condom and ejaculation are irrelevant to the definition of rape and are not 'features' of the offence. The Court subscribed to Lord Judge CJ's observation in *R(F)* that the evidence relating to choice and the freedom to make any particular choice should be approached in a common-sense way. They took the view that B's apparent consent was vitiated if she had agreed only because of the deception, Leveson LJ stating (at para. 26):

>> Thus while, in a physical sense, the acts of assault by penetration of the vagina are the same whether perpetrated by a male or a female, the sexual nature of the acts is, on any common sense view, different where the complainant is deliberately deceived by a defendant into believing that the latter is a male. Assuming the facts to be proved as alleged, [B] chose to have sexual encounters with a boy and her preference (her freedom to choose whether or not to have a sexual encounter with a girl) was removed by the appellant's deception.

(b) *Freedom to make the choice* The absence of free choice whether or not to agree to penetration of the vagina, anus, or mouth by A's penis, vitiates consent. Clearly where that agreement is brought about by violence or the threat of force, such freedom to choose is negated. The relationship that exists between A and B may be of particular relevance when considering whether undue pressure or influence has been brought to bear by A upon B to secure apparent agreement to the relevant sexual act. As we saw earlier, the question of whether B 'agrees by choice' will frequently require the jury to consider B's circumstances and the power balance between her and A; the jury will need to consider the extent to which she was free to make an effective and informed choice about whether to have sex.

There are many stories in the news of doctors, psychotherapists, and priests who take advantage of vulnerable patients or parishioners who have looked to them for help and support in times of bereavement, illness, or crisis, and end up having sexual relationships with them. While the SOA 2003 expressly deals with abuse of positions of trust in relation to those under the age of 18 and creates a range of offences to deal with such situations (see ss 16–19), it is unclear to what extent the abuse of a position of trust in relation to an adult of full capacity may be taken into account in considering whether or not there has been consent. Each jury will have to consider the particular facts of the case before it when applying s. 74.

 Question

B suffers a traumatic marital breakdown and looks to her priest, A, for support. Over a period of months, having recognised B's vulnerability and desperation for acceptance and intimacy, A encourages B to pour out her most intimate secrets. He further persuades her that a sexual relationship with him, with no ties or commitment, would assist her in getting over her divorce. B, having been brought up to trust her priest, eventually agrees, after a period of increasing physical intimacy, to engage in full sexual intercourse with A. Several years later, when B has recovered from the trauma of the divorce, she complains that A raped her having abused his position of power, exerted inappropriate influence over her, and taken advantage of her vulnerability for his own purposes. Has A engaged in behaviour such as to negate B's freedom to make a choice?

One view is that while A's actions may attract moral censure, this is not the kind of situation which should fall within the law of rape; ultimately B still made the choice unconstrained by threat, force, fear, or coercion. By contrast, if her psychotherapist had hypnotised her, and when under hypnosis had instructed her to respond willingly to his sexual demands, her apparent willing response subsequently when not under hypnosis may constitute a choice that was not truly free as the decision to agree was involuntary. Another view is that A's behaviour violates the sexual autonomy of a vulnerable person, and that violation is precisely what the legal definition of rape is supposed to capture,

In *Olugboja*, the leading case on consent before the 2003 Act, Dunn LJ stated that juries should be directed that consent, or the absence of it, is to be given its ordinary meaning and if need be, by way of example, that there is a difference between consent and submission; 'every consent involves a submission, but it by no means follows that a mere submission involves consent' (at p. 332). The Court of Appeal approved that direction in *Robinson (Sean)* [2011] EWCA Crim 916. The boundary between consent and submission set in the context of taking unfair advantage of a person in desperate straits, received some attention in *Kirk and Kirk* [2008] EWCA Crim 434.

JM (aged 14) had for many years been sexually abused by P Kirk, her aunt's husband. T Kirk, P Kirk's brother, had also abused her on occasions. She regularly ran away from home because of pressure from her brother who was bullying and blackmailing her over what P Kirk had done to her. JM had been living on the streets for some time. Tired, dirty, and hungry, with nowhere to go, in desperation she went to the minicab office where T Kirk worked, as the only place left where she might get help and something to eat. In return for £3.25 which she used for food, she had sexual intercourse with T Kirk. Years later, having spoken with a counsellor and psychiatrist, JM made a statement to the police about the abuse she had suffered.

The case was left to the jury on the basis that T took advantage of a hungry and vulnerable child whom he knew had been abused by his brother and himself, the prosecution contending that her will was overborne through hunger and desperation such that she submitted but did not consent. The trial judge directed the jury that it was for them to draw the line between submission and consent. The Court of Appeal upheld T's conviction concluding that the trial judge had properly left the issue of submission and consent to the jury against the background circumstances of this case.

The circumstances in which intercourse took place have some similarity to prostitution, in that JM only submitted to sexual intercourse in order to receive some money. However, there were several factors which distinguished JM's situation: there was a history of abuse by T and his brother P (of which T was aware) which created the circumstances giving rise to JM's vulnerability; and JM was a child in desperate circumstances of which T was fully aware. If anything, this case demonstrates the importance which context may play in determining whether in any particular case the agreement to intercourse arises from free choice or constrained choice. T's responsibility for JM's circumstances suggests that any advantage he took of those circumstances for his own gratification would be unfair.

> In C [2012] EWCA Crim 2034, it was alleged that A had sexually abused B, his step-daughter, during her childhood and that he raped her in later years. A argued that there had been no sexual relationship until she turned 16 and thereafter all sexual activity was consensual. In respect of convictions for these rapes the Court of Appeal held that the case could not properly be understood without reference to the past history of childhood abuse and A's apparent dominance and control over B. If the jury were satisfied that the past abuse occurred, this provided context for considering whether, despite appearing to consent, she had not really consented. The case shows that it is possible for a jury to find that a young adult does not consent to sexual acts if she has been scared, conditioned, or 'groomed' into a submissive state (see Andrew Ashworth's case commentary [2013] Crim LR 358–60).

In *Ali* [2015] EWCA Crim 1279, D groomed young and vulnerable girls, plied them with drink, and then allegedly raped them. The question arose whether there was sufficient evidence for the jury properly to conclude that the complainants had not consented. Fulford LJ explained how it should be made clear to the jury in cases involving vulnerable people groomed for sexual exploitation that *apparent* consent (compliance) may not be *real* consent as a young and immature person may not understand the full significance of what s/he is doing. He went on to state (at para. 58):

> Although . . . grooming does not necessarily vitiate consent, it starkly raises the possibility that a vulnerable or immature individual may have been placed in a position in which he or she is led merely to acquiesce rather than to give proper or real consent. One of the consequences of grooming is that it has a tendency to limit or subvert the alleged victim's capacity to make free decisions, and it creates the risk that he or she simply submitted because of the environment of dependency created by those responsible for treating the alleged victim in this way.

Key Point

Whether B has the freedom to choose is a question of fact for the jury to decide. If necessary, the trial judge should direct the jury that there is a difference between real consent and mere submission. The circumstances of the particular case may help to explain why B appears to have given consent, but what appears to be real consent may only be apparent consent. Given those particular circumstances, the jury may therefore find that B was not consenting.

(c) *Capacity to make a choice* If B does not have capacity to make a choice, there can be no consent. Capacity, however, is not defined. **As with the questions of whether B 'agrees by choice' and had the freedom to choose, the jury must decide whether B lacked the capacity to choose.**

Bree [2007] EWCA Crim 804 is the leading case on how trial judges should direct juries on the relevance of intoxication on a complainant's capacity to make a choice and therefore consent.

11.2.1.2.2 *Intoxication and consent*
In *Bree* [2007] EWCA Crim 804, the Court of Appeal provided guidance on how the regularly occurring issue of a complainant's intoxication should be treated. The Court recognised the difficulty of providing precise guidance on when B lacks capacity to consent. Section 75(2)(b) repeats well-established common law principles and acknowledges plain good sense that if the complainant is unconscious as a result of her voluntary consumption of alcohol, there is a rebuttable presumption that she is not consenting to intercourse. Beyond that, the Act is silent about the impact of excessive but voluntary alcohol consumption on the capacity to consent.

The Court held that the essential question is always whether or not B consented; it is not whether alcohol might have removed inhibitions such that B may have done something which she would not have done if sober; nor is it relevant that B later regrets what she did, or that she has little recollection of what precisely happened, or that A or B or both of them were behaving irresponsibly.

On a proper construction of s. 74 the issue was whether or not B had temporarily lost her capacity to choose whether to have intercourse on the relevant occasion; if she had, she was not consenting. The Court said that the phrase 'a drunken consent is still consent', while lacking delicacy, 'provides a useful shorthand accurately encapsulating the legal position' (at para. 33). Sir Igor Judge stated the proper approach that trial judges should adopt in directing juries:

> If, through drink (or for any other reason) the complainant has temporarily lost her capacity to choose whether to have intercourse on the relevant occasion, she is not consenting, and subject to questions about the defendant's state of mind, if intercourse takes place, this would be rape. However, where the complainant has voluntarily consumed even substantial quantities of alcohol, but nevertheless remains capable of choosing whether or not to have intercourse, and in drink agrees to do so, this would not be rape. We should perhaps underline that, as a matter of practical reality, capacity to consent may evaporate well before a complainant becomes unconscious. Whether this is so or not, however, is fact specific, or more accurately, depends on the actual state of mind of the individuals involved on the particular occasion.

Bree is an important decision, as it entrusts juries to decide on the facts of each particular case whether B had the capacity to consent. This faith in the jury is somewhat misplaced, as research evidence indicates many ordinary members of the public think that an intoxicated complainant is partially or totally responsible for being raped because of her intoxication (see the **Law in Context feature, 'Consent in context: rape myths'**). Some critics of *Bree* argue that it would have been more appropriate for the court to make it clear that a person who is very drunk, but short of unconsciousness, cannot give proper consent. Some feel that a more appropriate approach is to use specific levels of alcohol consumption which would determine whether B had the capacity to consent. The Court in *Bree* rejected that argument, noting that experience shows that different individuals have a greater or lesser capacity to cope with alcohol than others, and indeed the ability of a single individual to do so may vary from day to day. The Court recognised that no legislative structure could further define the issue given the infinite circumstances of human behaviour, usually taking place in private without independent evidence and the consequential difficulties of proof to which this gave rise.

In the offence of sexual activity with a person with a mental disorder impeding choice contrary to s. 30(1) of the SOA 2003, a requirement of the *actus reus* is that 'B is unable to refuse because of or for a reason related to a mental disorder'. Section 30(2) provides that:

B is unable to refuse if—

(a) he lacks the capacity to choose whether to agree to the touching (whether because he lacks sufficient understanding of the nature or reasonably foreseeable consequences of what is being done, or for any other reason), or

(b) he is unable to communicate such a choice.

The inability to refuse in either case must be the result of a mental disorder. The phrase 'any other reason' has the potential to be very wide.

In C [2009] UKHL 42, the House of Lords considered that 'any other reason' covered B who suffered from schizo-affective disorder, an emotionally unstable personality disorder, an IQ of less than 75, and had a history of alcohol abuse. Her mental disorder did not mean that she did not understand what was involved when A asked her to perform oral sex on him; however, because of her very unstable condition at the time, which gave rise to an irrational fear, she lacked the capacity to choose. The test is person- and situation-specific in that on a different day, or in a different situation, B may have had the capacity to choose as her mental disorder had a fluctuating impact upon her. The House of Lords rejected the argument that the courts should adopt a status-based approach to consent, by which those diagnosed with specific conditions would be deemed to lack capacity to consent, irrespective of each individual's actual capacity to consent.

The remainder of s. 30(2)(a) relates to whether B has sufficient understanding of the nature of the sexual act involved and what its foreseeable consequences might be: if sexual intercourse, obviously pregnancy; all forms of penetration, the possibility of contracting a STD; if anal intercourse, the possibility of pain and injury. It is submitted that incapacity for the purposes of ss 1–4 of the SOA 2003 is both a broader and a narrower concept. It is a broader concept as matters which may impair a person's capacity to choose are not confined to mental disorders. Clearly a lack of understanding is relevant as a person may not be deceived as to what the sexual act is, but have no comprehension of what it involves, as where, for example, a person has a severe learning disability. By contrast, a person generally may have such understanding but, in a particular circumstance, may lack the capacity to make a choice, as where, for example, s/he is voluntarily intoxicated by drink or drugs or is acting as an automaton in a state of impaired consciousness. It is a narrower concept as an inability to communicate a choice does not prevent a person who understands the nature of the sexual act, and its foreseeable consequences, from positively agreeing to it albeit s/he may be unable to communicate that agreement other than by submitting to the act. If it had been intended that such a person should not be deemed capable of giving consent, this should have been dealt with by means of including in s. 76 a conclusive presumption to this effect. (For a different view see K. Stevenson, A. Davies, and M. Gunn, *Blackstone's Guide to the Sexual Offences Act 2003* (2004).)

11.2.1.2.3 *Consent and presumptions*

In order to provide assistance in determining whether or not B consented to the relevant sexual act, the SOA 2003 created two sets of presumptions, namely conclusive presumptions and evidential or rebuttable presumptions. The presumptions have an impact in terms of both the *actus reus* and *mens rea* elements of the offences in ss 1–4 of the SOA 2003. The 'relevant act', which must be proved by the prosecution before a presumption may arise, is defined in s. 77 of the SOA 2003. In the case of rape the relevant act is the defendant penetrating the complainant's vagina, anus, or mouth with his penis.

(a) *Conclusive presumptions* Section 76(1) of the SOA 2003 provides that where the prosecution prove that the defendant did the relevant act and that one of the two circumstances specified in s. 76(2) existed, it is to be conclusively presumed—

> (a) that the complainant did not consent to the relevant act, and
>
> (b) that the defendant did not believe that the complainant consented to the relevant act.

Paragraph (b) does not create a strict liability offence as the circumstances in s. 76(2) require proof of intention in respect of them on the part of the defendant. The relevant circumstances are that:

> (a) the defendant intentionally deceived the complainant as to the nature or purpose of the relevant act;
>
> (b) the defendant intentionally induced the complainant to consent to the relevant act by impersonating a person known personally to the complainant.

As there must be an intentional deception or inducement, A will have the relevant knowledge about the circumstances. Under the previous law deception as to the nature or purpose of the relevant act negated consent (see *Williams* [1923] 1 KB 340;

Flattery (1887) 2 QB 410). In *Jheeta* [2007] EWCA Crim 1699, the Court of Appeal expressed the view that s. 76 required stringent scrutiny as the presumptions are conclusive on the issue of consent. The Court took the view that s. 76(2)(a) was limited to the nature or purpose of the sexual act involved. The Court cited as examples of cases where the presumption would now arise *Flattery*, *Williams*, *Tabassum* (see **10.7.5**), and *Green* [2002] EWCA Crim 1501. In *Green* a doctor carried out bogus examinations of young men in the course of which they were wired to monitors and asked to masturbate so that he could assess whether they were impotent. The deception related to the 'purpose' of the physical act and therefore his appeal was dismissed. By contrast the Court considered that *Linekar* (see **11.2.1.2.1(a)**)) fell outside the ambit of s. 76(2)(a) as the deception was as to A's intentions rather than the nature or purpose of the act. In *Jheeta* A created a 'bizarre and fictitious fantasy' relating to B's safety and his own suicidal intentions designed to encourage her to have sex with him more often. There was no deception as to the nature (vaginal intercourse) or purpose (sexual gratification) of the act but as to the situation in which she found herself with the result that s. 76(2)(a) had no application. A's deceptions, however, would be relevant evidence for a jury in considering if there was consent under s. 74. (For a bizarre case which appears to have been wrongly decided under s. 76(2)(a) when it more appropriately fell under s. 76(2)(b) see *Devonald* [2008] EWCA Crim 527.)

Section 76(2)(b) is inelegantly worded, particularly in the phrase 'impersonating a person known personally' and potentially unclear in its scope. When is a person 'known personally' to the complainant? Before 2003, impersonation of a woman's husband negated consent for the purposes of rape, but there was doubt whether the impersonation of anyone else did so (see *Elbekkay* [1995] Crim LR 163). Section 76(2)(b) dispels such doubt and includes impersonations of the complainant's partner or family member that induce the complainant to consent. Would impersonation of other people who the complainant knows be included?

 Question

Does the conclusive presumption in s. 76(2)(b) apply in the following examples?

A and B meet in an internet chat room and correspond online, but do not exchange images of each other and do not know what the other looks like. X, B's housemate, logs into the internet chat room pretending to be B and communicates with A. They arrange to meet, A believing that she will be meeting B when in fact she meets X. X continues to pretend to be B and thereby induces A to have sex with him.

C is a well-known 'reality TV' star. He frequents a particular nightclub with friends and he attracts the attention of several women. D admires him from afar in the nightclub. The next weekend, D goes to the same nightclub where Z, a spitting image of C, is pretending to be C in order to induce any woman he can to have sex with him. D genuinely believes that Z is C and they have sex that night.

There are no cases directly on point for these examples. However, it seems clear that the first situation is likely to be covered by s. 76(2)(b) as B is 'known personally' to A despite them never having met and not knowing what each other looks like. In the second situation, D knows who C is but does not know him 'personally' so therefore the conclusive presumption will not apply.

One point worth noting is that these particular deceptions raise a conclusive presumption that consent is negated when arguably more heinous acts, such as the use of violence, or the administration of a stupefying substance, to overcome a complainant's resistance, do not give rise to a conclusive presumption. The legislation is, in this respect, problematic.

(b) *Evidential presumptions* An evidential presumption is a rebuttable presumption. Section 75(1) provides:

> If in any proceedings for an offence to which this section applies it is proved—
>
> (a) that the defendant did the relevant act,
>
> (b) that any of the circumstances specified in subsection (2) existed, and
>
> (c) that the defendant knew that those circumstances existed, the complainant is to be taken not to have consented to the relevant act unless sufficient evidence is adduced to raise an issue as to whether he consented, and the defendant is to be taken not to have reasonably believed that the complainant consented unless sufficient evidence is adduced to raise an issue as to whether he reasonably believed it.

On proof by the prosecution of (a), (b), and (c) the presumption arises and a burden is cast upon the defendant to adduce sufficient evidence (1) to raise an issue as to whether the complainant, despite the existence of the specified circumstances, nonetheless consented, and/or (2) that the defendant reasonably believed the complainant consented. If the judge considers there is sufficient evidence to raise such an issue, he will direct the jury accordingly. If there is not sufficient evidence, upon proof of the necessary facts or circumstances in (a), (b), and (c), the presumption will arise and will be conclusive of a lack of consent on the part of the complainant and a lack of reasonable belief in consent on the part of the defendant.

The relevant circumstances in s. 75(2) are set out in the following paragraphs interspersed with comments.

> (a) any person was, at the time of the relevant act or immediately before it began, using violence against the complainant or causing the complainant to fear that immediate violence would be used against him.

'Violence' is not defined in the SOA 2003. The stereotypical case of rape is that where violence, or threat thereof, is employed by A to overcome B's resistance. While violence, or the fear thereof, will normally impact upon B's freedom to agree by choice, the fact that the presumption is rebuttable allows for the situation where A and B voluntarily engage in sado-masochistic sex. By contrast, the nature of the relationship between A and B may be such that A's apparently innocuous actions are recognised by B as signals of impending violence unless B agrees to A's sexual demands. If A knows that his actions have this effect upon B, the relevant circumstance of 'causing the complainant to fear' would be made out.

> (b) any person was, at the time of the relevant act or immediately before it began, causing the complainant to fear that violence was being used, or that immediate violence would be used, against another person.

Clearly this would cover the situation where violence is used on C to persuade B to consent to A's sexual demands. It would also cover the situation where the relationship between A and B is such that B recognises the signals of A's impending violence against C (perhaps B's child) unless B agrees to A's sexual demands. While there will probably be a relationship between B and C in most circumstances where this presumption is relied upon, there is no requirement for there to be a pre-existing relationship.

> (c) the complainant was, and the defendant was not, unlawfully detained at the time of the relevant act.

A need not be the person unlawfully detaining B, but he has to know of B's unlawful detention. The fact of unlawful detention undoubtedly will impact upon B's ability to make free and unconstrained choices. It is not, however, beyond the bounds of possibility for B to still exercise a free choice to engage in sexual activity with A for which the rebuttable nature of the presumption provides.

> (d) the complainant was asleep or otherwise unconscious at the time of the relevant act.

Under the previous law a person who was asleep was regarded as being unable to provide consent (see *Larter and Castleton* [1995] Crim LR 75). The rebuttable nature of this presumption relating to sleep or unconsciousness leaves A with the opportunity of seeking to rely on reasonable belief in consent despite knowing of B's somnolent or unconscious state. While such might be highly unlikely, it is not beyond the bounds of possibility.

> In *Ciccarelli* [2011] EWCA Crim 2665, A touched B sexually while she was drunk and asleep. A did not know her well having only met her a couple of times before and there had never previously been any sexual activity between them. A nevertheless tried to argue that he had believed she would consent. On appeal from his conviction, Lord Judge CJ explained the operation of s. 75:
>
> > It was suggested that section 75 of the 2003 Act reverses the ordinary principles relating to the burden of proof in criminal cases. We do not agree. Section 75 is an evidential provision. It relates to matters of evidence, and in particular evidential presumptions about consent in circumstances where, as we have already indicated, as a matter of reality and common sense, the strong likelihood is that the complainant will not, in fact, be consenting. If, however, in those circumstances there is sufficient evidence for the jury to consider, then the burden of disproving them remains on the prosecution. Therefore, before the question of the appellant's reasonable belief in the complainant's consent could be left to the jury, *some evidence beyond the fanciful or speculative had to be adduced to support the reasonableness of his belief in her consent.* [Emphasis added]

While A had given evidence to the effect that he did believe she would consent, the trial judge's view was that there was nothing that might even begin to suggest a reasonable basis for such a belief. The Court of Appeal agreed; there was accordingly no evidence capable of rebutting the evidential presumption. Simply asserting a belief (if, indeed, A ever had such a belief) is a long way from providing evidence to support the reasonableness of that belief.

> (e) because of the complainant's physical disability, the complainant would not have been able at the time of the relevant act to communicate to the defendant whether the complainant consented.

Such a presumption may offer protection to those who due to physical disability are unable to communicate. The rebuttable nature of the presumption, however, provides for the situation where despite an inability to communicate, B does consent.

> (f) any person had administered to or caused to be taken by the complainant, without the complainant's consent, a substance which, having regard to when it was administered or taken, was capable of causing or enabling the complainant to be stupefied or overpowered at the time of the relevant act.

There have, in recent years, been widespread fears about the use of drugs, such as Rohypnol and GHB, to stupefy victims for the purpose of having sexual intercourse with them. This provision covers such drugs but would also cover the situation where B's drink is laced with alcohol in sufficient quantity to effect the same purpose. A need not be the person who administers the substance but he has to know of its administration and that it was administered without the complainant's consent. The use of a substance (perhaps alcohol or some other drug) to reduce B's inhibitions to make it more likely that B will agree to sexual activity with A, will not be sufficient to raise the presumption as the drug must be capable of stupefying or overpowering B at the time. This requires that a sufficient quantity is used for that purpose. This provision, however, cannot be intended to require B to be rendered unconscious, this being covered by sub-s. (d) quoted earlier. The effect of some drugs, however, is to impair consciousness rendering B compliant, suggestible, disorientated, and less able to resist demands without being reduced to unconsciousness. It will be necessary for the courts to interpret 'stupefy' and 'overpower' in a way which reflects this or the provision could be rendered nugatory.

11.2.2 *Mens rea*

There are several mental elements which the prosecution must prove. Additional mental elements arise where the prosecution seek to rely on any of the conclusive or evidential presumptions detailed earlier.

11.2.2.1 Intentional penetration

The prosecution must prove that the defendant intended to penetrate the vagina, anus, or mouth of another.

 Question

Is it sufficient that A intentionally penetrates B or must A intend to penetrate a particular orifice?

For example, A and B agree to have vaginal intercourse with A entering B from behind. A is inexperienced and in the dark by mistake slightly penetrates B's anus. On realising his mistake A immediately withdraws. Must the prosecution prove intentional penetration of B's anus or simply intentional penetration of B? Under the previous law, rape was charged as having sexual intercourse with B without consent, there being no need to specify whether intercourse was vaginal or anal. As the definition in s. 1(1) of the SOA 2003 refers to intentional penetration of vagina, anus, or mouth, rather than using a term such as 'sexual intercourse' to embrace all forms of prohibited penetration, it is submitted that the intent must relate to the particular form of penetration.

11.2.2.2 Intention and knowledge in relation to the presumptions

Where the prosecution wish to rely on either of the conclusive presumptions of consent in s. 76 of the SOA 2003, they must prove that either:

(a) the defendant intentionally deceived the complainant as to the nature or purpose of the relevant act; or

(b) the defendant intentionally induced the complainant to consent to the relevant act by impersonating a person known personally to the complainant.

Recklessness as to either of these matters will not suffice. If A is reckless, however, as to either of these matters, this would be a circumstance highly relevant to the consideration of the question whether A does not reasonably believe that B consents.

Where the prosecution wish to rely on any of the evidential presumptions of consent in s. 75 of the SOA 2003, they must prove that A knew of the existence of the particular circumstance in s. 75(2) upon which they are relying to raise the presumption. Recklessness as to those circumstances will not suffice, but again, this would be a circumstance highly relevant to the consideration of the question whether A does not reasonably believe that B consents.

11.2.2.3 Reasonable belief in consent

11.2.2.3.1 *The law before 2003*

In *Morgan* [1976] AC 182 (see **3.6.1.1.1**), the House of Lords held that a defendant could not be guilty of rape where he honestly believed that the woman consented to sexual intercourse, even if he was mistaken in that belief. The belief held by the man did not need to be reasonable, although as a matter of common sense the more unreasonable a belief is the less likely it is to have been honestly held. The decision in *Morgan* was welcomed by subjectivists for its general effects on the criminal law, since it emphasised that people ought to be judged on the facts as they believed them to be, not on facts to which they had not given thought (for discussion see Jennifer Temkin and Andrew Ashworth [2004] Crim LR 328–46).

Following the decision in *Morgan* the *mens rea* for rape was put into statutory form by s. 1 of the Sexual Offences (Amendment) Act 1976 requiring proof either of knowledge that the other person did not consent or recklessness as to their consent. Recklessness was interpreted as covering knowledge that there was a risk that the other person did not consent or indifference whether s/he consents or not—that is, a 'couldn't care less' attitude (see *Kimber* [1983] 1 WLR 1118; *Satnam and Kewal* (1983) 78 Cr App R 149).

There was considerable controversy at the time of the decision in *Morgan* and the subsequent statutory amendment, with the law being described by some as 'a rapist's charter'. By stating that a genuine but unreasonable belief in consent necessarily means that D lacks *mens rea*, the decision encouraged men who were charged with rape (and other sexual offences) to argue that they honestly believed that C was consenting. That meant that if the jury believed D, regardless of how unreasonable his belief was, then he was entitled to be acquitted. The jury's task was to ask, 'Are we sure that he genuinely believed she was consenting?' In turn, that allowed the defence to seek to adduce evidence of anything that might have led D to believe genuinely that C consented. If the basis for the man's genuine belief was that he believed a woman wearing revealing clothing is signalling that she will consent to sex, or that 'women say no when they mean yes', then the jury would acquit if they were sure he honestly believed that C consented, however unreasonable that belief. Defence barristers sought (and were allowed) to question complainants about their past sexual behaviour to persuade jurors that she was the sort of person who was likely to consent to sex and that on this occasion it was not surprising that D genuinely believed she was consenting given the sort of promiscuous or revealingly dressed person she was generally. The law did little to direct juries to assess D's level of blameworthiness, instead shifting attention and intrusive questioning on to the complainant. It was argued therefore that the law reduced the likelihood both of convictions and of victims of rape reporting the offence.

The controversy continued resulting in a change in the law being effected by the SOA 2003. The change requiring reasonable belief in consent is designed to respect and protect sexual autonomy, recognising the serious ramifications for victims where their sexual autonomy is breached. It is worth noting that the change in the law, from an 'honest belief' to a 'reasonable belief' test, was supported by leading criminal law subjectivists, who ordinarily favour a subjective approach to liability and criticise tests for liability based on objectivity (such as one that requires the jury to assess the reasonableness of A's belief as distinct from its genuineness). Andrew Ashworth joined Jennifer Temkin in cautiously welcoming the change, arguing that in the context of sexual offences, the parties' close proximity makes it easy for one person to take steps to ensure that B is consenting; given that B's sexual autonomy is at stake it is fair to demand that A be responsible and do what reasonable people would do in the circumstances (A. Ashworth and J. Temkin, 'The Sexual Offences Act 2003: (1) Rape, Sexual Assaults and the Problems of Consent' [2004] Crim LR 328–46). After all, it is not difficult to ask, 'Are you sure this is what you want?' However, whether the change will break down outmoded and offensive attitudes about the nature of sexual relationships, which are sometimes deeply culturally rooted, only time will tell.

11.2.2.3.2 *Reasonable belief in consent*
In ss 1–4 of the SOA 2003 the prosecution must prove that B did not consent to the relevant sexual activity involved and that 'A does not reasonably believe that B consents'. Subsection (2) of each of those sections provides:

> (2) Whether a belief is reasonable is to be determined having regard to all the circumstances, including any steps A has taken to ascertain whether B consents.

Key Point

As with the question whether B did not consent, the question whether B did not reasonably believe that B consented is for the jury to decide on the particular facts of the case.

The steps that A has taken to ascertain whether B consents are relevant when deciding whether A had a reasonable belief in B's consent. Requiring the jury to consider the steps that A has taken is an important reform. It will be more difficult to argue that A's belief is reasonable where he has taken no steps to ascertain whether B consents. Where A does enquire, and B says 'No', it will also be difficult for A to argue that his belief that 'women always say no when they mean yes' was reasonable.

However, what is meant by the phrase 'all the circumstances'? An issue which the courts will have to resolve is whether 'all the circumstances' include the defendant's characteristics—such as his mental capacity.

> In *Braham* [2013] EWCA Crim 3, A was charged with rape and sought to claim he believed B had consented because of his delusions induced by his paranoid schizophrenia. The Court of Appeal ruled that this could not in law render reasonable a belief that was otherwise completely unfounded. The Court held that where A suffers from some mental or personality disorder which gives rise to delusional beliefs, he will be judged by objective standards of reasonableness rather than account being taken of his disorder which induced a belief which could not reasonably have arisen without it.

Question

Do 'circumstances' embrace A's culturally conditioned beliefs and views of sex based on the inferior position accorded to women within his culture and the view that it is their duty to submit to men's sexual desires?

Of course, the interplay with the evidential presumptions should not be ignored. Where the cultural conditioning of women involves the use of violence to enforce those cultural norms regarding their position vis-à-vis men, it may be that A's sexual advances were causing B to fear that immediate violence would be used against her if she did not comply with A's demands (see s. 75(2)(a) of the SOA 2003).

We live in a society with diverse cultural traditions which include varying cultural norms about the way in which sexual relationships are conducted and the respective roles and duties of men and women. If the dominant culture seeks to promote the equality of the sexes and the need for respect for individual autonomy and freedom of choice (values which seem to underpin the SOA 2003), should A be able to place reliance on the fact that he belongs to a different cultural tradition where the position of women is totally subservient to that of men and where a married woman's duty is to comply with the sexual demands of her husband? In *The Government Reply to the Fifth Report from the Home Affairs Committee Session 2002–2003* HC 639: *Sexual Offences Bill* (Cm 5986, 2003) the Government stated (at para. 3):

[I]t is for the jury to decide whether any of the attributes of the defendant are relevant to their deliberations, subject to directions from the judge where necessary.

In determining this matter a relevant consideration will be the Human Rights Act 1998 and the rights protected by the European Convention on Human Rights. A defendant may argue that his Art. 8 right to respect for his private and family life is engaged. Of course this right is not absolute but is subject to limitations which are necessary in a democratic society in the interests of 'the prevention of . . . crime, . . . or for the protection of the rights and freedoms of others'. Article 14 seeks to secure that the rights and freedoms guaranteed are enjoyed without discrimination. A relevant consideration would be the State's obligation to protect its citizens from 'inhuman or degrading treatment' (see *A* v *UK* (1999) 28 EHRR 603). If victims are to be provided equal protection under the law, it is difficult to see, in this light, that a defendant's cultural conditioning could be regarded as a relevant circumstance.

A further undetermined issue is whether 'all the circumstances' includes B's behaviour, whether at the time or previously. Will A be permitted to tender evidence, or cross-examine B, about his and B's prior relationship to provide support for his reasonable belief in consent? As the words 'at the time of the relevant act' are not included in sub-s. (2), this would seem to be permissible (see the **Law in Context feature** at the end of this chapter for more information on evidence and procedure in rape trials).

 The law in context

Consent in context: 'rape myths'

For many sexual offences the jury has to decide whether the prosecution have proved beyond reasonable doubt that the complainant did not 'consent'. How do they make that decision? How closely do they follow the direction of the trial judge?

In *DPP* v *Morgan* [1976] AC 182 (see **3.6.1.1.1**), Lord Cross said that 'rape is not a word in the use of which lawyers have a monopoly'. Insights from *criminology* help us to understand the social context in which rape's legal definition exists. You may have your own image of who a 'rapist' is and in what situation rape is most likely to occur. We know from research into the views of ordinary members of the public that many people have particular stereotypes of rape: that it is committed by strangers, at night, in remote public spaces, with the use of physical violence (e.g. S. Estrich, *Real Rape* (1988)). These views might stem from the coverage of rape in the media. We tend to hear about rapes that fit that stereotype. However, look again at the legal definition of rape. It says nothing about *where* the incident occurs, *who* commits it (other than it must be a man), what *time of day* it takes place, or what the relationship is between the defendant and the complainant.

The images that we have of a crime such as rape can be important. Stereotypes can lead to 'rape myths', beliefs about what rape is that are not actually part of substantive law. For example, one term that frequently appears in the media is 'date rape'. This suggests that there is a separate, secondary category of 'rape' that applies when the defendant and complainant are known to each other. However, there is no separate category in English law of 'date rape' (the Government considered this in its comprehensive review of sexual offences, *Setting the Boundaries* (2000), but concluded that having such a separate category would create the

➜

impression that rapes committed by acquaintances and intimates were not 'real' rapes). Criminological research indicates that most rape victims know the offender, most victims are raped by either current or former partners, and rapes tend to occur in the home of the offender or victim (Ministry of Justice, Home Office and ONS, *An Overview of Sexual Offending in England and Wales* (2013), p. 15).

There are numerous other commonly held beliefs, ideas, or explanations about rape that arise from and reinforce our prejudices and stereotypes. For example: 'Women provoke rape by the way they dress or act'; 'Women who drink alcohol or use drugs are asking to be raped'; 'Rape is a crime of passion'; 'You can tell if she's "really" been raped by how she acts'; 'Women cry rape when they regret having sex or want revenge'; 'Prostitutes cannot be raped'; 'If the victim didn't complain immediately it wasn't rape' (CPS *Rape and Sexual Offences: Legal Guidance*, https://www.cps.gov.uk/legal-guidance/rape-and-sexual-offences-chapter-21-societal-myths).

Such 'rape myths' may influence, consciously or subconsciously, decisions in the criminal justice system made by complainants, the police, the CPS, and members of the jury. There is evidence that some people who have actually been the victims of rape do not define themselves as such, partly because of their own misunderstandings of what rape is (Myhill and Allen (2002), *Rape and Sexual Assault of Women: The Extent and Nature of the Problem*, p. 53). That is important as the criminal process will never be engaged if complainants do not report what has happened to them. Research indicates that a significant number of rape victims do not report the offence to anyone (Myhill and Allen, p. 45).

Even if the victim does report the offence, the police might be influenced by perceptions of what constitutes 'real rape' when investigating the offence and deciding whether to charge a suspect. There is some evidence that many years ago a 'culture of disbelief' prevailed amongst officers. For example, Temkin reports a police officer in 1975 saying that, '[r]ape is . . . unlikely to have been committed against a woman who does not immediately show signs of extreme violence. If she complains of rape with no such signs of violence she must be closely interrogated. Allow her to make a statement to a policewoman and then drive a coach and horses through it' (Temkin, *Rape and the Legal Process* (2002), pp. 4–6). Such views were rooted in a rape myth: that 'real rape' involves physical violence beyond the inherent violence of the non-consensual penetration. Police attitudes today have (generally) moved on since then. Indeed, it is possible that pressures on the police to deal compassionately with rape allegations might have led some police officers to be too accepting of complainants' narratives. Police officers face the difficult task of dealing sensitively with rape allegations while probing witnesses to establish exactly what happened.

Rape myths might also influence how members of the jury decide whether a defendant is guilty. In its legal guidance to prosecutors for prosecuting rape and sexual offences, the CPS states that:

> It is an unfortunate fact that myths about rape and sexual violence are brought into the jury room, and form an obstacle to obtaining convictions. It is therefore imperative that we recognise these myths and challenge them at every opportunity. (CPS *Rape and Sexual Offences: Legal Guidance* https://www.cps.gov.uk/legal-guidance/rape-and-sexual-offences-chapter-21-societal-myths)

Research into actual jurors' decision-making is prohibited by s. 20D of the Juries Act 1974 (as amended by the Criminal Justice and Courts Act 2015). However, we know from studies of attitudes of ordinary people (and after all, juries are composed of people randomly drawn from the electoral register) that views on what constitutes 'consent' are far from unified and may indicate the continuing prevalence of 'rape myths'. For example, in a study conducted by Amnesty International in 2005, ordinary people were asked about the extent to which a

> →
>
> woman was responsible for being raped in a range of scenarios. Twenty per cent of interviewees said that a woman was partially responsible if she was 'wearing sexy/revealing clothing' and 6 per cent said that she was *totally* responsible in that situation (Amnesty International (2005) *Sexual Assault Research*). Twenty-six per cent said that a woman was partially responsible if 'she was drunk' and 4 per cent said that she was *totally* responsible. The Crime Survey for England and Wales in 2013/14 examined public attitudes to sexual violence and found that the majority of people thought that victims were not responsible for someone sexually assaulting or raping them when they were drunk (66 per cent), under the influence of drugs (60 per cent), or if they had been flirting heavily beforehand (56 per cent). However, some people thought that the victim was 'completely' or 'mostly' responsible for a sexual assault or rape by someone they had been flirting heavily with beforehand (9 per cent), when they were under the influence of drugs (8 per cent), or while drunk (6 per cent). Significant numbers thought that a victim was 'a little bit responsible' when they have been flirting heavily beforehand (27 per cent), were drunk (20 per cent), or under the influence of drugs (23 per cent) (ONS (2015) Violent Crime and Sexual Offences—Intimate Personal Violence and Serious Sexual Assault, https://www.ons.gov.uk/peoplepopulationandcommunity/crimeandjustice).
>
> Such research evidence should make us think carefully about how ordinary jurors might interpret and apply the legal meaning of consent as contained in s. 74 when they have to decide whether the complainant agreed by choice and had the freedom and capacity to make that choice, as well as deciding whether the defendant lacked a reasonable belief in the complainant's consent. Jurors may be influenced in their decision-making by their own pre-existing views of what constitutes 'consent' and when a belief in consent is 'reasonable' and those views may undermine the 2003 Act's aim of protecting sexual autonomy.
>
> The continuing prevalence of 'rape myths' has led the Judicial College to remind trial judges, if they consider the circumstances require it, to caution the jury against making unwarranted assumptions about the complainant's behaviour or demeanour. Trial judges are reminded that it is their responsibility to warn the jury against the unfairness of approaching the evidence with *any* pre-formed assumptions about the nature of the offence of rape (Judicial College, *The Crown Court Compendium: Part I—Jury and Trial Management and Summing Up*, Part 20-I Sexual Offences—The Dangers of Assumptions). However, we do not know the extent to which jurors pay attention to and follow these directions.

11.3 Assault by penetration

The Review concluded in *Setting the Boundaries* that the offence of indecent assault, for which the maximum sentence was 10 years' imprisonment, did not adequately reflect the gravity of a range of serious assaults involving penetration of the complainant by objects or parts of the defendant's body other than his penis. The new offence of assault by penetration contrary to s. 2 of the SOA 2003 carries a maximum sentence of life imprisonment. The Sentencing Council's definitive guidelines for sexual offences indicates a sentencing offence range from a high-level community order to 15 years' custody (Sentencing Council, *Sexual Offences Definitive Guideline* (2014)), reflecting the wide range of circumstances that s. 2 covers.

> The offence is defined as follows:
>
> (1) A person (A) commits an offence if—

(a) he intentionally penetrates the vagina or anus of another person (B) with a part of his body or anything else,

(b) the penetration is sexual,

(c) B does not consent to the penetration, and

(d) A does not reasonably believe that B consents.

Actus reus	Mens rea
• A penetrates B's vagina or anus with a part of his body or anything else, • the penetration is sexual, and • B does not consent to the penetration.	A: • does so intentionally, and • does not reasonably believe that B consents.

11.3.1 *Actus reus*

11.3.1.1 **Penetration**

Penetration of the vagina or anus of another must be proved. Vagina includes a surgically constructed vagina (s. 79(3) of the SOA 2003). Penetration is a continuing act from entry to withdrawal (s. 79(2)). The slightest degree of penetration is sufficient. The penetration may be by a part of the body—such as, a finger, or by an object.

11.3.1.2 **Penetration which is sexual**

The penetration must be sexual. Section 78 defines sexual as follows:

penetration, touching or any other activity is sexual if a reasonable person would consider that—

(a) whatever its circumstances or any person's purpose in relation to it, it is because of its nature sexual, or

(b) because of its nature it may be sexual and because of its circumstances or the purpose of any person in relation to it (or both) it is sexual.

This is a somewhat awkwardly worded provision. It excludes from liability, for example, bona fide medical examinations and surgical procedures; but as such procedures or examinations would be covered by consent or necessity (see *re F* [1990] 2 AC 1, **6.3.1** and **10.8**) it might be considered superfluous. The complexity arises from the inclusion in the definition of the offence the requirement that the penetration be sexual. Where A's purpose is not sexual gratification but to demean and humiliate B, this could present a problem. (From B's point of view the trauma of the assault would not seem to differ whether A's purpose is sexual gratification of himself or humiliation of B.) The solution in the legislation is to create an objective definition of 'sexual' based upon a reasonable person's view which in sub-s. (a) focuses on the nature of the act and takes no account of A's purpose. Undoubtedly the vast majority of reasonable people would regard the non-consensual penetration of another's vagina or anus as a sexual act. In sub-s. (b) the circumstances in which the act is committed and the purpose of A may convert an act which might not appear sexual into one which is. In this situation A's purpose may be sexual gratification—for example, where a doctor performs an intimate examination not because this is necessary but because he derives sexual gratification from it. However, in such a case his deception as to the purpose of the act negates consent under the conclusive presumption in s. 76 and thus, again, the complexity of s. 78 serves no purpose. Arguably, the requirement in s. 2 for penetrative assaults to be sexual is unnecessary. It may be that for the offences in ss 3 and 4 of the SOA 2003 the requirement that the assault or activity be sexual does serve a purpose and that the definition of 'sexual' in s. 78 is necessary to deal with acts which may be ambiguous. Penetration of another's anus or vagina without their consent, it is submitted, permits of no such ambiguity and the combination of s. 2(1)(b) and s. 78 makes for the very complexity and confusion which the new law was meant to counteract.

11.3.1.3 Absence of consent

See **11.2.1.2**.

The presumptions in ss 75 and 76 apply to this offence. The 'relevant act' which must be proved under s. 77 is:

> The defendant intentionally penetrating, with a part of his body or anything else, the vagina or anus of another person ('the complainant'), where the penetration is sexual.

11.3.2 *Mens rea*

See **11.2.2**.

The presumptions in ss 75 and 76 apply to this offence.

11.4 Sexual assault

The maximum sentence for this offence is 10 years' imprisonment. Sexual assault is the second offence which covers activities previously covered by indecent assault. It will cover non-penetrative touchings of another which are sexual. Penetrative touchings of B's mouth with anything other than a penis may fall within this offence. Indecent assault did not require touching (battery), as a technical assault (causing B to apprehend being touched) in circumstances of indecency would suffice. While s. 3 has the heading 'sexual assault' the definition of the offence does not refer to assault but to 'touching' and thus the offence is narrower than the offence of indecent assault. The offence of causing a person to engage in sexual activity without consent contrary to s. 4 will catch many situations previously falling within indecent assault where there was no touching involved (see e.g. *Sargeant* [1997] Crim LR 50). Requiring B at knife-point to undress for A's sexual gratification would have been an indecent assault; it will not be a sexual assault as there is no touching and it will only amount to the s. 4 offence if B does undress and the court concludes that this activity does amount to a sexual activity. If B does not undress there is only an assault.

Section 3 of the SOA 2003 provides:

(1) A person (A) commits an offence if—

    (a) he intentionally touches another person (B),

    (b) the touching is sexual,

    (c) B does not consent to the touching, and

    (d) A does not reasonably believe that B consents.

Actus reus	Mens rea
• A touches B,	A:
• the touching is sexual, and	• does so intentionally, and
• B does not consent to the touching.	• does not reasonably believe that B consents.

11.4.1 *Actus reus*

11.4.1.1 Touching

Section 79(8) of the SOA 2003 provides:

Touching includes touching—

(a) with any part of the body,

(b) with anything else,

(c) through anything,

and in particular includes touching amounting to penetration.

Touching a person with an object or through their clothing is included.

11.4.1.2 Touching which is sexual

The House of Lords identified three situations which could pertain which determined whether or not the assault was indecent for the purposes of the now-repealed offence of indecent assault (*Court* [1989] AC 28). First, the act and its surrounding circumstances when viewed objectively could not be considered indecent by right-minded persons; in such a situation it did not matter that A had a secret indecent motive. Thus in *George* [1956] Crim LR 52, there was no indecent assault where A attempted to remove B's shoe even though this was something A found sexually gratifying, as there were no circumstances of indecency. Secondly, when viewed objectively, an incident could be inherently indecent regardless of D's purpose or motives. An example given was of a man stripping a woman of her clothing against her will. Thirdly, an incident might be capable of being indecent in which case the crucial factor would be A's motive. The instant case fell within this category where A had spanked B, a 12-year-old girl, across the seat of her pants.

When asked by the police why he had done so, he replied 'I don't know, buttock fetish.' A's motive converted an incident which was capable of being indecent into an indecent assault.

A touching can only support a conviction for sexual assault where the touching is 'sexual'—the term preferred by the legislature in place of 'indecent'. While the overlap between these terms is substantial, it may be the case that the word 'sexual' will embrace situations not caught by the word 'indecent'. 'Sexual' is defined in s. 78 of the SOA 2003 (see **11.3.1.2** and the discussion thereafter). The test is objective and depends upon the reasonable person's assessment of the situation. A touching may be sexual under sub-s. (a) where a reasonable person would consider that because of its nature it is sexual regardless of its circumstances or the purpose with which it is done. This seems to suggest that some touchings, by their very nature, are inherently sexual even though A may not have as his purpose sexual gratification. This would seem to cover any touching of another's genitals. It is not immediately clear, however, that stripping someone of their clothing is necessarily sexual, although it may be indecent. If A is doing so to humiliate B rather than for personal sexual gratification, his actions—if not caught by sub-s. (a)—would not fall within sub-s. (b). Secondly, a touching may be sexual under sub-s. (b) because a reasonable person would consider it has the potential to be sexual and, because of its circumstances and/or the purpose with which it is done, it is sexual. In this situation context and purpose become crucial. A coach patting a player on the buttocks when he comes off the pitch to say, in effect, 'well done', may not be regarded as sexual. Where the patting, however, is done by an adult stranger, in a park to a teenager, the context may convert this potentially sexual touching, in the eyes of a reasonable person, into a sexual touching. If A says something at the time of patting B to indicate his sexual motives, his purpose will combine with the circumstances to inform the decision on its sexual nature.

In *H* [2005] EWCA Crim 732, the Court of Appeal emphasised that s. 78(b) creates a two-stage process. In considering the first question, whether because of its nature the touching may be sexual, the jury has to do so without taking any account of the circumstances before and after the touching and any evidence as to A's purpose. In the instant case A had approached B, a stranger, and asked her, 'Do you fancy a shag?' This question by A would have to be discounted by a jury when considering whether the touching he subsequently performed was capable of being sexual. When B had sought to walk away, A had grabbed her by her trouser pocket and sought to pull her towards him covering her mouth with his hand. As all kinds of acts are capable of having sexual significance for those performing them, it is arguable that the ambit of the first category in *Court* (acts which could not be considered indecent) has been greatly narrowed. An alternative way of putting this is that the ambit of the new offence of sexual assault is potentially broader than the offence of indecent assault.

 Question

Might a reasonable person consider that touching another's foot is capable of being sexual?

If A obtains particular sexual gratification from such an act, his purpose would seem to have the potential to render his act 'sexual' when it might not be indecent (cf. *George*, earlier in this section). The Court of Appeal avoided providing an answer to this conundrum in *H* stating that this would be a matter for a jury to determine. Whether a jury could exclude from their minds A's expressed motive when considering the first question is open to doubt.

11.4.1.3 Absence of consent

See **11.2.1.2**.

The presumptions in ss 75 and 76 apply to this offence. The 'relevant act' which must be proved under s. 77 is:

> The defendant intentionally touching another person (the complainant), where the touching is sexual.

11.4.2 *Mens rea*

The *mens rea* is an intention to touch and an absence of a reasonable belief that B consents. See **11.2.2**. The offence, however, is one of basic intent and A is unable to rely on intoxication in his defence (see *Heard* [2007] EWCA Crim 125, **5.5.3**).

The presumptions in ss 75 and 76 apply to this offence.

While it has to be proved only that A intended to touch B, and not that he intended to touch B sexually, A's purpose in touching B may be crucial to the determination whether or not the touching was sexual (see **11.3.1.2**).

11.5 Causing a person to engage in sexual activity without consent

Before the 2003 Act, the law did not catch all the various forms of compelled sexual activity that might arise. In *Setting the Boundaries* it was recommended (at para. 2.20.4) that a new offence be created of compelling another to perform sexual acts. This was intended to cover, inter alia, cases of women forcing men to have sex with them, forcing others to perform sexual acts together, and forcing a person to perform a sexual act on himself or with an animal. Section 4 of the SOA 2003 provides:

> (1) A person (A) commits an offence if—
>
>   (a) he intentionally causes another person (B) to engage in an activity,
>   (b) the activity is sexual,
>   (c) B does not consent to engaging in the activity, and
>   (d) A does not reasonably believe that B consents.

Actus reus	Mens rea
• A causes B to engage in a sexual activity, and • B does not consent to engaging in the activity.	A: • does so intentionally, and • does not reasonably believe that B consents.

The maximum sentence for this offence is 10 years' imprisonment, unless the activity caused falls within s. 4(4) in which case it is life imprisonment. The activities in s. 4(4) are:

(a) penetration of B's anus or vagina,

(b) penetration of B's mouth with a person's penis,

(c) penetration of a person's anus or vagina with a part of B's body or by B with anything else, or

(d) penetration of a person's mouth with B's penis.

There are several anomalies arising from this provision. If B is compelled to submit to penetration of his anus by an animal's penis, the maximum sentence is life imprisonment. But if he is compelled to submit to penetration of his mouth with an animal's penis, the maximum sentence is 10 years. Likewise, if B is compelled to penetrate another person's anus or vagina with his penis or other part of his body, or is compelled to penetrate another's anus or vagina with an object, the maximum sentence is life imprisonment. But if B is compelled to penetrate an animal with his penis the maximum sentence is 10 years. It is difficult to understand how such distinctions have arisen. It is submitted that those activities which attract only a 10-year maximum penalty are every bit as abhorrent, and doubtless cause to B every bit as much trauma, as those for which the maximum penalty is life imprisonment.

11.5.1 *Actus reus*

For discussion of the meaning of 'sexual' see **11.3.1.2** and **11.4.1.2**. If A compels B to take off his clothes, this is not necessarily a sexual activity. A's purpose, if it is one of sexual gratification, may make it so, but if it is simply to humiliate B, will not.

For a discussion of causation see **2.6**. A may cause B to engage in the sexual activity with himself (A), or with another (C), or to perform the act on himself (B) (e.g. masturbation), or with an animal. There must be a direct causal link between A's actions and the activity which B performs or submits to. If B is compelled by threats, sufficient to amount to duress, to commit a sexual act with C who is not consenting, B, as well as being a victim of the offence, will have a defence in so far as he has perpetrated an offence upon C. But if the threats are not of death or serious injury, albeit that they are sufficient to vitiate B's consent, B would not have a defence if charged in respect of the offence he commits on C.

11.5.1.1 **Absence of consent**
See **11.2.1.2**.

The presumptions in ss 75 and 76 apply to this offence. The 'relevant act' which must be proved under s. 77 is:

The defendant intentionally causing another person ('the complainant') to engage in an activity, where the activity is sexual.

11.5.2 *Mens rea*

The *mens rea* is an intention to cause B to engage in a sexual activity and an absence of a reasonable belief that B consents. See **11.2.2**.

The presumptions in ss 75 and 76 apply to this offence.

A's purpose may be crucial to the determination whether or not the activity he has caused B to engage in is sexual (see **11.4.1.2**).

Where A visits a brothel suspecting that the prostitutes are girls held there against their will and forced by threats and violence to offer sexual services to those who frequent the brothel, A's visit to the brothel and payment for the relevant sexual services will have a causal connection to the performance of that activity by B, and A could be liable for the s. 4 offence as his knowledge or suspicion would be relevant to the consideration whether he reasonably believed that B consented to the sexual activity. If A has actual knowledge of the circumstances in which the prostitutes operate, this could give rise to one of the evidential presumptions in s. 75(2)(a) or (c) being raised.

11.6 **Offences against children**

The 2003 Act created five new categories of offences, in addition to the offences in ss 1–4 of the SOA 2003, to protect children. The statutory scheme is complex, the offences overlap, and it is not clear whether some are or are not offences of strict liability. The age of consent to sexual activity remains at 16 such that any sexual activity with a child under that age remains unlawful. There is an assumption underlying the SOA 2003 that children under the age of 13 are incapable of giving consent but this is not actually expressed in the Act. Those between the ages of 13 and 15 may give consent but where the other person is aged 18 or over such consent will not prevent the other being liable for a range of offences. In addition, the offences relating to those under the age of 16 and 13 or over do not require proof of the absence of consent. Consensual acts by teenagers or pre-teens are caught by the legislation. It would have been possible to draft the legislation to exclude from liability consensual acts between those of a similar age but the Government was adamant that all consensual acts involving children should in principle be criminal with it being left to the Crown Prosecution Service to ensure by written guidelines that there were no oppressive prosecutions. The legislation therefore criminalises acts which the Government does not wish to have punished. This smacks of exceedingly muddled thinking. If it is possible to draw up guidelines relating to the circumstances in which prosecutions should or should not be pursued, it is equally feasible to draft the legislation in the first place to exclude the need for such guidelines. The breadth of these offences also offends against the principle in *Tyrrell* [1894] 1 QB 710, under which a child victim could not be convicted as a participant in the offence of unlawful sexual intercourse (see **7.1.6**). Now if two 12-year-olds engage in sexual intercourse they both may be prosecuted.

The prosecution of children for offences against other children where the activity was consensual raises the question whether this could amount to a breach of their Art. 8 right to respect for their private life. This question was answered negatively by the House of Lords in *G* [2008] UKHL 37 (see **4.2.6**).

11.6.1 **Offences against children under 13**

11.6.1.1 **Rape of a child under 13 (s. 5 of the SOA 2003)**

A's intentional penetration with his penis of B's vagina, anus, or mouth, where B is under 13, is an offence with a maximum sentence of imprisonment for life. The offence is one of strict liability as to age (see *G* [2008] UKHL 37; cf. *K* [2001] UKHL 41, **4.2.3.1**). It had been contended in *G* (2008) that as the acts covered by s. 5 are also covered by s. 9, which is a strict liability offence in respect of children under 13 but requires proof of an absence of a reasonable belief that B is 16 or over where B is under 16 but 13 or over, and carries a lesser sentence (14 years maximum), the more serious offence created by s. 5 is one requiring *mens rea* as this is normally read in where the statute is silent (see further J. R. Spencer, 'The Sexual Offences Act 2003: (2) Child and Family Offences' [2004] Crim LR 347; see also **4.1.2**, **4.2.3**, and **11.6.2.1**). This argument failed to persuade the House of Lords. The absence of consent is not an element of this offence and thus belief in consent is irrelevant.

> In *R* v *G* [2006] EWCA Crim 821, A, aged 15, had sexual intercourse with B, aged 12. He was charged with the s. 5 offence and pleaded guilty on the basis that he believed B was 15 as she had told him she was, and that B had willingly agreed to sexual intercourse. A appealed his conviction on the basis that if s. 5 could not be read down by inclusion of a defence of reasonable belief that B was over 13, it was incompatible with Art. 6(2) of the European Convention on Human Rights. Further, that the conviction and sentence (a 12-month detention and training order), constituted a disproportionate interference with respect for his private life under Art. 8 of the ECHR. He drew attention to the contrast between conviction for the s. 5 offence as compared to conviction for the s. 13/s. 9 offence. Under s. 5 he could be liable to a sentence of detention for life and would be subject to notification requirements as a sex offender being labelled a child rapist. Under s. 13 the maximum sentence would be detention for five years, there would be no notification requirement unless the sentence imposed was for more than 12 months, and the label applied to him would be that of a child who had had sexual activity with another child. A contended that it was inappropriate to prosecute a child for the s. 5 offence where intercourse had been consensual relying on a statement during the passage of the bill that one would not expect the full weight of the criminal law to be used against children where sexual activity took place with mutual consent. To rely on the discretion of prosecutors not to prosecute was not consonant with the rule of law.
>
> The Court of Appeal refused to read down s. 5, finding that the presumption of *mens rea* was negatived by necessary implication arising from the express references in other sections to reasonable belief. Strict liability offences did not breach Art. 6(2) as that article was concerned with procedural fairness and not with the substantive law. As for Art. 8, while prosecution could produce consequences that interfered with a child's rights under Art. 8(1), where the facts turned out to be less serious than anticipated when the charge was preferred, a judge could reflect this in sentencing to ensure that there was no interference with the defendant's rights that could not be justified under Art. 8(2); he was not, however, under a duty to substitute a lesser charge if the prosecution, themselves, did not seek leave to withdraw the s. 5 charge in favour of a s. 13/s. 9 charge. On further appeal the House of Lords endorsed the decision of the Court of Appeal.

The fears of many about the oppressive potential of the Sexual Offences Act when it is brought to bear upon child defendants are all too sadly justified by this decision. If the prosecution decide to over-charge by pursuing a s. 5 prosecution rather than a s. 13/s. 9 prosecution, or no prosecution at all, or, on discovering the true facts refuse to withdraw the s. 5 charge, the courts will stand back and do nothing to protect the child defendant other than to reduce their sentence. In the instant case, A having served five months in detention, had his sentence reduced to a conditional discharge. While he avoided the notification requirements as a sex offender, he remains labelled a child rapist. This outcome seems a disproportionate response to what the prosecution accepted was a case of consensual sexual activity where A believed B was over 13. An attempt to apply to the European Court of Human Rights alleging breaches of Arts 6 and 8 was ruled inadmissible (see *G* v *UK* [2011] ECHR 1308).

11.6.1.2 **Assault of a child under 13 by penetration (s. 6 of the SOA 2003)**

A's intentional penetration with a part of his body or anything else of B's vagina or anus, is an offence where the penetration is sexual and B is under 13. The maximum sentence is life imprisonment.

For the meaning of 'sexual' see **11.3.1.2**.

The absence of consent is not an element of this offence and thus belief in consent is irrelevant. As this offence overlaps with the offence in s. 9 (see **11.6.2.1**) it will probably be held to be one of strict liability (see *R* v *G*, **11.6.1.1**).

11.6.1.3 **Sexual assault of a child under 13 (s. 7 of the SOA 2003)**

A's intentional touching of B where B is under 13 and the touching is sexual is an offence carrying a maximum sentence of 14 years' imprisonment.

See **11.4.1.2** for the meaning of 'sexual touching'.

While it has to be proved only that A intended to touch B, and not that he intended to touch B sexually, A's purpose in touching B may be crucial to the determination whether or not the touching was sexual (see **11.4.1.2**). The absence of consent is not an element of this offence and thus belief in consent is irrelevant. As this offence overlaps with the offence in s. 9 (see **11.6.2.1**) it will probably be held to be one of strict liability (see *R* v *G*, **11.6.1.1**).

11.6.1.4 **Causing or inciting a child to engage in sexual activity (s. 8 of the SOA 2003)**

A's intentional causing B to engage in sexual activity or inciting B to do so where B is under 13 is an offence (see s. 8(1)). The maximum sentence for inciting or causing non-penetrative sexual activity is 14 years' imprisonment, but where the activity caused or incited falls within s. 8(2) the maximum is life imprisonment. The activities in s. 8(2) are:

(a) penetration of B's anus or vagina,

(b) penetration of B's mouth with a person's penis,

(c) penetration of a person's anus or vagina with a part of B's body or by B with anything else, or

(d) penetration of a person's mouth with B's penis.

For a discussion of the meaning of 'Causing another person to engage in a sexual activity' see **11.5**. The absence of consent is not an element of this offence and thus belief in consent is irrelevant. As this offence overlaps with the offence in s. 10 (see **11.6.2.2**) it will probably be held to be one of strict liability as regards the element of the age of the child (see *R* v *G*, **11.6.1.1**).

The differential sentencing structure means that the section creates four separate offences: (1) intentionally causing, or (2) intentionally inciting, non-penetrative sexual activity; and (3) intentionally causing, or (4) intentionally inciting, penetrative sexual activity (see *Grout* [2011] EWCA Crim 299). Where the offence is charged as 'inciting' a child to engage in sexual activity, there is no need to prove that any sexual activity occurred. It is sufficient that A incited B so to do. The Court of Appeal has adopted a wide interpretation to incitement, holding in *Walker* [2006] EWCA Crim 1907 that the essence of the offence of incitement is encouragement. This has to be intentional or deliberate and there is no need to prove that A intended that any sexual activity should actually happen. This has been confirmed by *Jones* [2007] EWCA Crim 1118.

> A wrote graffiti on toilet walls seeking girls aged 8–13 for sex in return for payment and left his mobile number. B, a police officer, pretending to be aged 12, contacted A and he incited her to penetrative sexual activity. A was arrested when he turned up to a meeting arranged with her. In upholding A's conviction for attempt to incite based on the text messages, the Court observed that the offence could be committed by general statements, such as the graffiti, which were not made to any specific or identifiable person.

11.6.2 Offences against children under 16

There are two common elements in the offences which follow (ss 9–12 of the SOA 2003). First, B is under 16 and A does not reasonably believe that B is 16 or over. Thus, with regard to the age of B, the offence is not one of strict liability. However, where B is under 13 the necessary implication of the drafting is that the offence is one of strict liability as to age. Secondly, A must be aged 18 or over to be liable to conviction for one of these offences. By a strange piece of legislative drafting, however, s. 13 of the SOA 2003 provides that the activities comprised in ss 9–12 amount to offences when committed by A who is under 18, the only difference being that the maximum sentence is five years whereas the maximum sentence for the offences under ss 9 and 10 is 14 years and for those under ss 11 and 12 is 10 years.

11.6.2.1 Sexual activity with a child

Section 9 of the SOA 2003 provides:

> (1) A person aged 18 or over (A) commits an offence if—
>
>   (a) he intentionally touches another person (B),
>   (b) the touching is sexual, and
>   (c) either—
>
>   (i) B is under 16 and A does not reasonably believe that B is 16 or over, or
>   (ii) B is under 13.

While the heading in the legislation for this offence refers to 'sexual activity', it is, in fact, limited to sexual touching.

For discussion relevant to the *actus reus* of this provision see **11.4**, **11.4.1.1**, and **11.4.1.2**. Touching includes penetration.

The *mens rea* is an intention to touch.

While it has to be proved only that A intended to touch B, and not that he intended to touch B sexually, A's purpose in touching B may be crucial to the determination whether or not the touching was sexual (see **11.4.1.2**).

If B is under 13, strict liability as to age applies. Where B is 13 or over but under 16 the prosecution have to prove either that A did not believe that B was over 16, or if he did, that that belief was not reasonable.

It is worth noting that two 14-year-olds engaging in mutual consensual petting would commit this offence subject to the maximum penalty of five years under s. 13 of the SOA 2003.

11.6.2.2 Causing or inciting a child to engage in sexual activity

Section 10 of the SOA 2003 provides:

> (1) A person aged 18 or over (A) commits an offence if—
>   (a) he intentionally causes or incites another person (B) to engage in an activity,
>   (b) the activity is sexual, and
>   (c) either—
>   (i) B is under 16 and A does not reasonably believe that B is 16 or over, or
>   (ii) B is under 13.

For a discussion of the meaning of 'Causing another person to engage in a sexual activity' see **11.5**. For the meaning of 'inciting' see **8.2**.

Where the offence is charged as 'inciting' a child to engage in sexual activity, there is no need to prove that any sexual activity occurred. It is sufficient that A incited B so to do.

If B is under 13, strict liability as to age applies. Where B is 13 or over but under 16 the prosecution have to prove either that A did not believe that B was over 16, or if he did, that that belief was not reasonable.

It is worth noting that A, a 14-year-old who suggests to B, another 14-year-old, that they remove their clothes to see each other's genitals, would commit this offence subject to the maximum penalty of five years under s. 13 of the SOA 2003, even before an item of clothing is removed. Similarly, if A describes to B the mechanics of masturbation and suggests he do it when he gets home, A and B both being under 16, A would commit this offence even if B did nothing pursuant to A's encouragement. One cannot help but feel that the breadth of the law is much greater than is necessary to deal with the evils of child sex abuse.

11.6.2.3 Engaging in a sexual activity in the presence of a child

Section 11 of the SOA 2003 provides:

> (1) A person aged 18 or over (A) commits an offence if—
>   (a) he intentionally engages in an activity,
>   (b) the activity is sexual,

(c) for the purpose of obtaining sexual gratification, he engages in it—
  (i) when another person (B) is present or is in a place from which A can be observed, and
  (ii) knowing or believing that B is aware, or intending that B should be aware, that he is engaging in it, and
(d) either—
  (i) B is under 16 and A does not reasonably believe that B is 16 or over, or
  (ii) B is under 13.

This is another example of a complex piece of drafting. The purpose in sub-s. (c) of obtaining sexual gratification links to the fact that it is done in circumstances where B may observe it. In fact it is sufficient that A believes B is aware of the sexual activity or intends that B should be aware of it, even though B may not become aware of it. For example, if A engages in a sexual activity in B's presence, intending B to be aware of this but B, unknown to A is blind, A will nonetheless commit this offence. (On sexual gratification, see *Abdullahi* [2006] EWCA Crim 2060, **11.6.2.4**.)

While this offence is aimed at those who may seek to corrupt children by exposing them to inappropriate sexual behaviour by adults, or even sexual behaviour by children directed by adults, the offence is wide enough to catch other situations. For example, A and B masturbate in each other's presence, both being under the age of 16. They would commit this offence subject to the maximum penalty of five years under s. 13 of the SOA 2003.

If B is under 13, strict liability as to age applies. Where B is 13 or over but under 16 the prosecution have to prove either that A did not believe that B was over 16, or if he did, that that belief was not reasonable.

11.6.2.4 Causing a child to watch a sexual act

Section 12 of the SOA 2003 provides:

(1) A person aged 18 or over (A) commits an offence if—
  (a) for the purpose of obtaining sexual gratification, he intentionally causes another person (B) to watch a third person engaging in an activity, or to look at an image of any person engaging in an activity,
  (b) the activity is sexual, and
  (c) either—
    (i) B is under 16 and A does not reasonably believe that B is 16 or over, or
    (ii) B is under 13.

For the definition of 'sexual' see **11.3.1.2**.

Section 79(4) defines 'image' to mean 'a moving or still image and includes an image produced by any means and, where the context permits, a three-dimensional image'. Section 79(5) states that references 'to an image of a person include references to an image of an imaginary person'. Thus the offence may be committed where the child is shown a live sexual activity involving a third party, or a video, picture, or photograph of a sexual activity; or computer-generated images, pseudo photographs, or even a hologram.

The causing of the child to watch such a sexual activity must be intentional.

If B is under 13, strict liability as to age applies. Where B is 13 or over but under 16 the prosecution have to prove either that A did not believe that B was over 16, or if he did, that that belief was not reasonable.

A problematical requirement of the offence, however, is that A must cause the watching of the sexual activity 'for the purpose of sexual gratification'. This suggests that it must be proved that A sought to obtain sexual gratification from causing B to watch the activity. The main menace to children, which the offence might be thought to be designed to deal with, is that of predatory paedophiles who seek to groom children over a period of time to render them more susceptible to their sexual advances. Often this process involves giving children alcohol and cigarettes and permitting them to watch pornographic videos. A may not be present during the watching of the videos; paedophiles often allow their houses to become gathering places for children and teenagers where the rules which parents might impose are not observed. A may obtain no sexual gratification from B actually watching the pornographic video, but his aim ultimately is to bring B to the point where B's view of sex has become distorted, his inhibitions have been worn away, and his trust for A developed such that he will consent to engaging in sexual activity with A. This is virtually the situation which pertained in *Abdullahi* [2006] EWCA Crim 2060. The Court of Appeal held there is nothing to suggest that the offence would only be committed if the sexual gratification and the causing of the child to watch the sexual act are simultaneous, contemporaneous, or synchronised. The Court further stated that sexual gratification may take any of the myriad forms which sexual pleasure or indulgence may take, and it may simply involve the defendant enjoying the sight of the child watching the sexual act. Whatever form it takes, however, there is no temporal restriction which operates so as to stop the section applying to a longer-term plan to obtain further or greater sexual gratification in the form of the eventual working out of a particular sexual fantasy or activity involving the child.

11.6.2.5 Arranging or facilitating commission of a child sex offence

The maximum sentence for this offence is 14 years' imprisonment. Section 14 of the SOA 2003 provides:

> (1) A person commits an offence if—
>   (a) he intentionally arranges or facilitates something that he intends to do, intends another person to do, or believes that another person will do, in any part of the world, and
>   (b) doing it will involve the commission of an offence under any of sections 9 to 13.

Once again an offence is created in language which is opaque. The offence is essentially a preparatory offence aimed at criminalising behaviour which is carried out for the purpose of enabling a child sex offence to be committed by A or by another anywhere in the world. It is aimed at those who procure children for sexual abuse or prostitution or those who avail of their services. The offence could be committed by something as simple as A permitting C to use his mobile phone to contact B who A believes is a child with whom C is planning to commit a child sex offence.

There is a defence to this offence set out in sub-ss (2) and (3) as follows:

(2) A person does not commit an offence under this section if—

    (a) he arranges or facilitates something that he believes another person will do, but that he does not intend to do or intend another person to do, and

    (b) any offence within subsection (1)(b) would be an offence against a child for whose protection he acts.

(3) For the purposes of subsection (2), a person acts for the protection of a child if he acts for the purpose of—

    (a) protecting the child from sexually transmitted infection,

    (b) protecting the physical safety of the child,

    (c) preventing the child from becoming pregnant, or

    (d) promoting the child's emotional well-being by the giving of advice,

and not for the purpose of obtaining sexual gratification or for the purpose of causing or encouraging the activity constituting the offence within subsection (1)(b) or the child's participation in it.

This defence (which overlaps with that in s. 73, see **11.6.2.8**) will cover, for example, police officers using a child as a decoy to seek to catch child sex offenders. It will also cover healthcare workers providing advice on contraception and sexually transmitted diseases and, in addition, providing contraceptives to children under the age of 16 (cf. discussion of *Gillick* at **3.2.3.8**, **6.3.1**, and **6.3.3**). But for this defence, the healthcare worker, for example, who provides contraceptives to two 15-year-olds who are having a sexual relationship, would be facilitating the commission of a child sex offence. Of course, the two 15-year-olds will have to rely on the good sense of the Crown Prosecution Service not to prosecute them.

11.6.2.6 Meeting with a child following sexual grooming

Section 15 of the SOA 2003 (as amended by the Criminal Justice and Immigration Act 2008, sch. 15, para. 1 and the Criminal Justice and Courts Act 2015, s. 36(1)), for which the maximum sentence is 10 years' imprisonment, provides:

(1) A person aged 18 or over (A) commits an offence if—

    (a) A has met or communicated with another person (B) on one or more occasions, and subsequently—

        (i) A intentionally meets B, or

        (ii) A travels with the intention of meeting B in any part of the world or arranges to meet B in any part of the world, or

        (iii) B travels with the intention of meeting A in any part of the world,

    (b) A intends to do anything to or in respect of B, during or after the meeting mentioned in paragraph (a)(i) to (iii) and in any part of the world, which if done will involve the commission by A of a relevant offence,

    (c) B is under 16, and

    (d) A does not reasonably believe that B is 16 or over.

A 'relevant offence' is any offence under Part 1 of the SOA 2003; one of a specified range of traditional sexual offences in Northern Ireland; or any conduct done outside England, Wales, or Northern Ireland which would be an offence if done in England and Wales (s. 15(2) of the SOA 2003). The original meetings, subsequent meeting, communications with B, and intended location for the 'relevant offence' may be in any part of the world. Thus, for example, A, a British citizen resident in England, would commit this offence where he twice contacts over the internet B, a child aged 13 resident in Thailand, and arranges to meet B when he travels to Thailand intending to have sex with B. The offence is complete as soon as A sets off on his journey to Thailand.

Section 67A of the Serious Crime Act 2015 inserted a new s. 15A into the SOA 2003, creating the offence of 'Sexual Communication with a Child'. It is an offence for a person (A) aged 18 or over to intentionally communicate with a person (B) under the age of 16 for the purposes of sexual gratification when the communication is sexual or is intended to encourage (B) to make a communication that is sexual (whether to (A) or another) and (A) does not reasonably believe that (B) is 16 or over.

11.6.2.7 Offences outside the United Kingdom

Section 72 of the SOA 2003 (as substituted by s. 72 of the Criminal Justice and Immigration Act 2008), which replaces s. 7 of the Sex Offenders Act 1997, extends the jurisdiction of courts in England and Wales, and Northern Ireland to cover sex offences against children committed abroad. It covers not just British nationals or residents but also persons who subsequently become nationals or residents. Under s. 72(1) a United Kingdom national will be guilty of an offence if he does an act abroad which is an offence covered by s. 72. Previously it had to be proved that the act was also an offence in the country where it was committed but this requirement has been dispensed with in the new s. 72. Where a person who is a United Kingdom resident does any act abroad which is an offence in that country and would be an offence if done in England and Wales, or in Northern Ireland, he is also guilty of an offence in that part of the United Kingdom (s. 72(2)). If a person who is not a United Kingdom national or resident does an act abroad which is an offence in that country and would be an offence if done in England and Wales, or in Northern Ireland, and he subsequently becomes a United Kingdom national or resident, he may be prosecuted for that offence (s. 72(3) and (4)). The acts covered are any of the offences under ss 5–19, 25, 26, and 47–50 of the SOA 2003; any offence under ss 1–4, 30–41, and 61 where the victim of the offence was under 18 at the time of the offence; and a range of other offences including abuse of a position of trust, offences against persons with a mental disorder, prostitution offences, certain offences relating to pornography, and administering a substance with intent where, again, the victim is under the age of 18.

11.6.2.8 Exceptions for aiding, abetting, and counselling

Section 73 provides a defence which gives statutory effect to, and extends the law deriving from, the decision in *Gillick* v *West Norfolk and Wisbech AHA* [1986] AC 112 (see **3.2.3.8**, **6.3.1**, and **6.3.3**).

The defence applies, inter alia, to offences under ss 5–7, 9, and 13 where the act would be an offence under s. 9 if the offender were aged 18. A person will not be guilty of aiding, abetting, or counselling the commission of such an offence against a child where he acts for the purpose of:

> (a) protecting the child from sexually transmitted infection,
> (b) protecting the physical safety of the child,
> (c) preventing the child from becoming pregnant, or
> (d) promoting the child's emotional well-being by the giving of advice,
>
> and not for the purpose of obtaining sexual gratification or for the purpose of causing or encouraging the activity constituting the offence within subsection (1)(b) or the child's participation in it.

11.6.3 Abuse of a position of trust

Sections 16–24 of the SOA 2003 create four offences of sexual offences with children by persons who are in a position of trust. These offences are essentially those that are provided for under ss 9–12, the only essential differences being that A is in a position of trust in relation to B and B may be up to 18 years of age instead of under 16 as required by ss 9–12. The sections are unnecessarily convoluted, complex, and complicated. All that would have been necessary to achieve the same result would have been one section defining 'position of trust' and one section stating that where a position of trust existed the age limit in the offences under ss 9–12 should be 18 rather than 16. Once again the aim of making the law clearer and more coherent has not been achieved.

As the maximum penalty for any of these abuse of trust offences is five years' imprisonment it is clear that where B is under 16 the offences under ss 9–12 would be charged as the maximum sentence is much greater. The purpose of the offences, therefore, is to protect those between the ages of 16 and 18 from abusive or predatory sexual behaviour by those in a position of trust in relation to them. Of course, the 17-year-old pupil at a college may be the one seducing the young teacher; such a fact will not stop his sexual activity with her from constituting an offence. Again the law is drafted so broadly that it catches situations which involve no abuse.

The range of situations where a position of trust will be deemed to exist is set out in s. 21 of the SOA 2003. The following is a non-exhaustive list of the main situations. A is in a position of trust in relation to B if A looks after persons under 18 who are:

- detained by virtue of a court order and B is so detained (e.g. a young offender institution);
- resident in a home or other place where accommodation is provided under the Children Act 1989 or the Social Services and Well-being (Wales) Act 2014 and B is resident in that place;
- accommodated and cared for in a hospital, independent clinic, care home, residential care home, children's home, private hospital, community home, voluntary home, residential family centre, or a home provided under s. 82(5) of the Children Act 1989, and B is accommodated and cared for in that institution;
- receiving full-time education at an educational institution, and B is receiving education at that institution.

Many people who might generally be regarded as being in a position of trust such as doctors and healthcare employees outside of residential units, priests and clergymen, youth leaders, and child-minders are not covered by s. 21 leaving one to question what the real purpose of the section is.

If B is under 13, strict liability as to age applies. Where B is 13 or over but under 18, A will be taken not to have reasonably believed that B was 18 or over unless sufficient evidence is adduced to raise an issue whether A reasonably believed B was 18 or over.

In the main situations detailed earlier it must be proved that A knew, or could reasonably be expected to have known, that he was in a position of trust in relation to B where A adduces sufficient evidence to raise an issue as to whether he knew or could reasonably have been expected to have known this fact.

There are two defences which A may rely upon and the burden of proving them rests on him. The first under s. 23 is that B is over 16 and A and B are lawfully married. The second under s. 24 is that prior to the position of trust arising a lawful sexual relationship existed between A and B. For example, in the teacher/pupil example given earlier there would not be an offence if A and B had a sexual relationship while A was training to become a teacher which relationship they continued when A, upon qualifying, obtained employment at the school which B attended.

11.7 **Familial sex offences**

Under the SOA 1956 there were two offences relating to incest. Section 10 made it an offence for a man to have sexual intercourse with a woman he knew to be his granddaughter, daughter, sister, or mother. Section 11 made it an offence for a woman aged 16 or over to permit a man whom she knew to be her grandfather, father, brother, or son to have sexual intercourse with her. The offences did not depend upon the absence of consent and made no distinction based on age other than the limitation in s. 11 on the age of the woman. The offence was also limited to vaginal sexual intercourse. The SOA 2003 has replaced these offences with four offences; first, under s. 25 sexual activity with a child family member; and secondly, under s. 26 inciting a child family member to engage in sexual activity. The sexual activity covers both penetrative sexual acts and sexual touching and may be homosexual. The person touched or incited (B) must be under 18. The range of relationships covered (see s. 27 of the SOA 2003) is greater including adopted children, half-brother and half-sister, aunt and uncle, and foster-parent. It also covers, in certain situations, step-relationships and cousins as well as situations where A lives in the same household as B and is regularly involved in the care of B.

Penetrative sexual acts between persons in prohibited degrees of relationship are covered by two offences created by ss 64 and 65. Section 64 covers the situation where A, aged 16 or over, sexually penetrates B, aged 18 or over, while s. 65 covers the situation where A, aged 16 or over, consents to being sexually penetrated by B, aged 18 or over. In each case there is an offence if A and B are related as parent (including adoptive parent), grandparent, child (including adopted child), grandchild, brother, sister, half-brother, half-sister, uncle, aunt, nephew, or niece.

11.8 **Offences against persons with a mental disorder**

The SOA 2003 creates three sets of offences where the victim is a person with a mental disorder. Sections 30–33 create four offences mirroring the child sex offences in ss 9–12, dealing with aspects of improper sexual activity with people with a mental disorder impeding choice. Sections 34–37 create four offences, again mirroring ss 9–12, but relating to persons with a mental disorder which does not impede choice such that they are capable of deciding whether to engage in sexual activity, but their agreement in the particular case is obtained by inducement, deception, or threat. Sections 38–41 create four offences relating to the same activities but where the defendant is a care worker and the offence may be committed regardless of consent.

11.9 **Preparatory offences**

Three offences seek to address behaviour which is engaged in with the intent of committing a sexual offence.

11.9.1 **Administering a substance with intent**

Section 61 of the SOA 2003 creates an offence aimed at dealing with the phenomenon of drug-assisted rape. The offence is drafted in broad terms and covers any form of sexual activity providing much greater protection than s. 4 of the SOA 1956 which it replaces, which only covered administering a drug to a woman to enable a man to have unlawful sexual intercourse with her. Section 61(1) provides:

> A person commits an offence if he intentionally administers a substance to, or causes a substance to be taken by, another person (B)—
>
> (a) knowing that B does not consent, and
>
> (b) with the intention of stupefying or overpowering B, so as to enable any person to engage in a sexual activity that involves B.

This is an offence of ulterior intent which is complete upon the substance being administered with the necessary intent, it being unnecessary to prove that any sexual activity actually took place. In most cases, however, proof of sexual activity at least being attempted will be the most straightforward way of establishing the prohibited intent. A must know that B does not consent. B's lack of consent relates to taking the substance by which A is seeking to stupefy or overpower him, rather than to the sexual activity which A intends to enable to take place. The offence would cover putting a drug, such as Rohypnol, into B's drink or putting, for example, vodka into B's orange juice with the necessary intent. For the definition of 'sexual activity' see s. 78 of the SOA 2003, **11.3.1.2.** The maximum sentence for the offence is six months on summary conviction and 10 years' imprisonment following conviction on indictment.

11.9.2 **Committing an offence with intent to commit a sexual offence**

Section 62 of the SOA 2003 provides:

> (1) A person commits an offence under this section if he commits any offence with the intention of committing a relevant sexual offence.

'Relevant sexual offence' means any offence under Part 1 of the SOA 2003 including aiding, abetting, counselling, or procuring such an offence. The primary offence that might be thought to be covered by this offence would be kidnapping and false imprisonment. If such an offence is committed with the requisite intent the maximum sentence is life imprisonment. In respect of other offences committed the maximum sentence is six months' imprisonment on summary conviction and 10 years following conviction on indictment. The main purpose behind the offence would appear to be to enable the offender to be categorised as a sex offender with the consequence of being placed on the Sex Offenders' Register.

11.9.3 **Trespass with intent to commit a sexual offence**

Formerly the offence of burglary included entering a building, or part of a building, as a trespasser with intent to rape any person therein (s. 9(1)(a) of the Theft Act 1968). Section 63 of the SOA 2003 replaces this form of burglary with a more broadly drafted offence. Section 63(1) provides:

> A person commits an offence if—
>
> (a) he is a trespasser on any premises,
>
> (b) he intends to commit a relevant sexual offence on the premises, and
>
> (c) he knows that, or is reckless as to whether, he is a trespasser.

'Relevant sexual offence' means any offence under Part 1 of the SOA 2003 including aiding, abetting, counselling, or procuring such an offence. For the meaning of 'trespasser' see **14.2.1.2**. Unlike burglary, it is not necessary for A to enter the premises as a trespasser: it is enough that he has become a trespasser—for example, by the removal of permission to be there or the breach of any implied condition attaching to that permission. Thus, where B invites A back for coffee following their meeting at a disco, and A starts to act in a way which makes B feel uncomfortable such that she tells A she is not attracted to him and she asks him to leave, an attempt by A to touch B sexually could amount to this offence provided A has the necessary intent and is at least reckless as to his status as a trespasser. 'Premises' includes a structure or part of a structure; 'structure' includes a tent, vehicle, vessel, or other temporary or movable structure. In the previously used example, if A was in B's car when he was asked by her to leave, his remaining with the necessary intent could amount to this offence. The maximum sentence is six months' imprisonment for summary conviction and 10 years for conviction on indictment.

11.10 **Other sexual offences**

The SOA 2003 creates a range of other offences which are listed without further exposition as follows:

- indecent photographs of persons aged 16 or 17 (ss 45–46)
- abuse of children through prostitution and pornography (ss 47–51)
- exploitation of prostitution (ss 52–54)
- trafficking for sexual exploitation (ss 59A–60)
- exposure (s. 66)
- voyeurism (ss 67–68)
- intercourse with an animal (s. 69)
- sexual penetration of a corpse (s. 70)
- sexual activity in a public lavatory (s. 71).

 The law in context

Procedure and Evidence in Rape Trials

Securing convictions for sexual offences can be challenging for the prosecution. For decades the conviction rate for rape, as a percentage of all allegations of rape that are reported to the police, has been in single digits. Part of the difficulty in securing convictions can be the reluctance of complainants to attend court and give evidence in an adversarial courtroom heavily imbued with legal tradition. A rape complainant will typically have to give evidence about what happened and be cross-examined extensively by the defence barrister. That questioning can be intrusive, humiliating, and frightening. The defence barrister will seek to plant in jurors' minds the notion that the complainant was consenting and/or the defendant had good grounds for believing that she was consenting. The questioning is often designed to undermine the complainant's claim to be a victim of the offence and to portray her as a willing participant in all that is alleged to have happened. Unsurprisingly, many complainants do not want to give evidence in court.

In 1998, the report of the Interdepartmental Working Group on the Treatment of Vulnerable or Intimidated Witnesses in the Criminal Justice System, entitled *Speaking up for Justice*, recommended the court procedures and rules of evidence be changed better to protect vulnerable or intimidated witnesses (not only those in sexual offence cases). Many of these recommendations were implemented by the Youth Justice and Criminal Evidence Act 1999 ('the 1999 Act'). Sections 16–33 introduce 'special measures' for such witnesses. These are intended to ease the burden of giving evidence. Where a complainant in respect of a sexual offence is a witness in proceedings relating to that offence, the witness is eligible for special measures as of right. The court then decides which, if any, of the special measures would be likely to improve the quality of evidence given by the witness (s. 19), taking into account the views of the witness and considering whether the measure(s) might tend to inhibit such evidence being effectively tested by a party to the proceedings (most obviously the defendant).

The special measures include positioning a screen in the courtroom so that the witness cannot be seen by the defendant (s. 23), enabling the witness to give evidence via live link from another room outside of the courtroom (s. 24), ordering the public gallery be cleared so that the witness can give evidence in private (s. 25), requiring the barristers and judge to remove their wigs and gowns (s. 26), and allowing as admissible evidence-in-chief a video recording of the witness's statement (s. 27). The most radical of the special measures (currently

→

→

being piloted in three Crown Court areas) is allowing pre-recorded cross-examination and re-examination of the witness to be admitted as evidence (s. 28). When implemented nationally, that will mean many complainants will not have to enter the courtroom at all. The 1999 Act also prohibits a defendant charged with a sexual offence from cross-examining in person the complainant (s. 34). The latter measure was a direct response to some notorious cases, including that of Ralston Edwards in 1996. Before 1999, a defendant could personally question the complainant in court. Edwards, who was not legally represented, cross-examined the complainant in person over several days wearing the same clothes he wore when he raped her, causing her great distress. His intention seemed to be to derive pleasure from forcing her to relive her experiences of being raped (see *Speaking up for Justice*, para. 9.28).

The 1999 Act also restricts the questioning of complainants about their previous sexual behaviour. Under the Sexual Offences (Amendment) Act 1976, the defence could only question the complainant about her sexual experiences other than with the defendant, or adduce evidence of such experiences, if the trial judge was satisfied that it would be unfair to that defendant to refuse to allow the evidence to be adduced or the question to be asked (s. 2). Despite the 1976 Act's aim of restricting intrusive, upsetting questioning, judges routinely allowed such questioning to take place and many rape complainants felt that they were the ones on trial. The Government's response was s. 41 of the 1999 Act, which tightens the restrictions on adducing evidence about the complainant's 'sexual behaviour' so that it is only permissible if the purpose of the evidence falls into one of four categories (for detailed analysis of s. 41 see R. Munday, *Evidence* (OUP: Oxford, 2017), 4.76–4.96). The evidence or question must relate to a specific instance or specific instances of sexual behaviour and should not be permitted if the purpose or main purpose for which it would be adduced or asked is to establish or elicit material for impugning the credibility of the complainant as a witness (s. 41(4)).

Are these measures controversial? From a victim's perspective, they appear to be progressive steps that the criminal justice system has taken to reduce the emotional burden of having to give evidence and to prevent complainants experiencing secondary victimisation by the criminal justice system itself. However, juries may be swayed by the mere fact that the special measures are being used: why does the witness need such sensitive treatment if there is no basis to her allegation? The law recognises this possible effect on juries and s. 32 requires the trial judge to give such warning to the jury as he considers necessary to ensure the fact that special measures are being used does not prejudice the accused.

The law on cross-examination about the complainant's sexual behaviour in s. 41 can be criticised for restricting the defendant's ability to test properly the prosecution case. For example, by limiting questions to those that relate to the alleged rape itself and behaviour at or about the same time (s. 41(3)(b)) or to similar behaviour to that which is the subject of the charge, the defence is unable to put a full and proper defence to the jury that enables them to consider all relevant information. However, there are a range of safeguards in place to ensure that questions that are relevant can be put. Questions are permitted if they relate to an issue that 'is not an issue of consent' (s. 41(3)(a)), which means, amongst other things, that questions can be put if they relate to the defendant's belief in consent (s. 42(1)(b)). Questions are also permitted if they go no further than is necessary to explain or rebut evidence adduced by the prosecution (e.g. if the prosecution suggest the complainant was a virgin at the time of the alleged rape). The trial judge may only grant leave in relation to any such evidence or question if he is satisfied that refusing to grant leave might have the result of rendering unsafe a conclusion of the jury or (as the case may be) the court on any relevant issue in the case (s. 41(2)). The House of Lords in *R v A (No. 2)* [2001] UKHL 25 considered s. 41 in light of its interpretative obligation under the Human Rights Act 1998. The Court held that evidence of a complainant's previous sexual history is admissible where that evidence, and questioning concerning it, was so relevant to the issue of consent that to exclude it would bring into question the fairness of the trial. These safeguards go a significant way towards ensuring defendants can properly test the case against them.

Key Points

- The Sexual Offences Act 2003 is the key piece of legislation on sexual offences, covering a wide range of offences.

- Rape is defined in s. 1. A commits rape when he intentionally penetrates the vagina, anus, or mouth of B who does not consent and A does not not reasonably believe that B consents. The central issues in most contested rape trials are whether B consented and whether A lacked a reasonable belief in consent.

- Many of the main offences in the SOA 2003 contain 'consent' and 'reasonable belief' as key elements.

- For those offences in which consent is an element, s. 74 provides the applicable definition: a person consents when he agrees by choice and has the freedom and capacity to make that choice.

- Whether B consented is a question of fact for the jury applying that definition. The trial judge can provide some assistance by explaining that there is a difference between submission and real consent.

- Whether A lacked a reasonable belief in consent is a question of fact for the jury, taking into account any steps A has taken to ascertain whether B consents.

- Research evidence suggests that 'rape myths' persist amongst ordinary people and that these may therefore impact on jury deliberations in rape cases.

- 'Assault by penetration' (s. 2) includes acts of non-consensual, sexual penetration that are not included in rape's definition.

- 'Sexual assault' (s. 3) covers non-consensual, non-penetrative sexual touching.

FURTHER READING

E. Finch and V. E. Munro, 'Intoxicated Consent and Drug Assisted Rape Revisited' [2004] Crim LR 789.

K. Laird, 'Rapist or Rogue? Deception, Consent and the Sexual Offences Act 2003' [2014] Crim LR 492.

C. L. Saunders, 'Rape as "One Person's Word Against Another's": Challenging the Conventional Wisdom' (2018) 22(2) E&P 161.

A. Sharpe, 'Criminalising Sexual Intimacy: Transgender Defendants and the Legal Construction of Non-Consent' [2014] Crim LR 207.

O. Smith and T. Skinner, 'How Rape Myths Are Used and Challenged in Rape and Sexual Assault Trials' (2017) 26(4) Social and Legal Studies 441.

J. R. Spencer, 'Child and Family Offences' [2004] Crim LR 347.

J. Temkin and A. Ashworth, 'Rape, Sexual Assaults and the Problems of Consent' [2004] Crim LR 328.

S. Wallerstein, ' "A Drunken Consent Is Still Consent"—or Is It? A Critical Analysis of the Law on a Drunken Consent to Sex Following *Bree*' (2009) 73 JCL 318.

12

Offences under the Theft Acts 1968
and 1978: Theft and related offences

12.1 Introduction

The Theft Act (hereafter referred to as the TA 1968) swept away the previous law creating a new range of offences which were framed, so far as possible, in simple language to avoid the technicality and complexity of the old law. The Theft Act 1978 (hereafter referred to as the TA 1978) was passed to replace s. 16(2)(a) of the TA 1968 which had proved highly unsatisfactory. The TA 1978 also contains other provisions to fill some gaps left by the TA 1968. In 1996 the Theft (Amendment) Act (hereafter referred to as the TAA 1996) was passed inserting new ss 15A and 15B into the TA 1968 to fill further gaps in that Act.

While the TA 1968 and TA 1978 aimed to avoid technicality, problems have materialised. The Acts use words, like 'dishonestly', which the courts have left to juries to define. This creates a potential problem of inconsistency. A second problem is of the relationship between theft and the civil law. Theft and related offences are concerned with interferences with the rights and interests others have in property. It would seem first to be necessary to determine to whom the property belonged; this cannot be done without reference to the civil law. However, the criminal courts have often disregarded the civil law in a misplaced desire to keep the criminal law simple. The result is that the law relating to offences against property remains somewhat confused and inconsistent.

In **Chapter 13** we will examine fraud. The Fraud Act 2006 (hereafter referred to as the FA 2006) has repealed various sections of the TA 1968 and TA 1978, replacing a number of individual offences based on deception with a new offence of fraud which may be committed in three ways. It also creates a new offence of dishonestly obtaining services to replace the offence of obtaining services by deception under s. 1 of the TA 1978. These new offences are designed to overcome problems in the old law and to simplify the law. On occasions in both this chapter and the next chapter it will be necessary to refer to the old law.

One final preliminary point is that many offences of dishonesty involve schemes or activities which cross international borders. Reference should be made to **8.5** where this topic is dealt with. Briefly, theft, blackmail, handling, and fraud may be prosecuted in England and Wales where at least one element of the offence (an act, omission, or the result) occurs in England and Wales.

12.2 Theft

Section 1(1) of the TA 1968 provides that:

> A person is guilty of theft if he dishonestly appropriates property belonging to another with the intention of permanently depriving the other of it; and 'thief' and 'steal' shall be construed accordingly.

The maximum penalty on conviction on indictment is seven years' imprisonment (s. 7 of the TA 1968, as amended by s. 26(1) of the Criminal Justice Act (CJA) 1991).

Five facts must be proved to lead to a conviction for theft; three relate to the *actus reus* and two to the *mens rea*.

Actus reus	Mens rea
• appropriation	• dishonesty, and
• of property	• intention to permanently deprive the other of the property.
• belonging to another.	

These five elements of theft will be examined separately for convenience, but it should be noted that they are interconnected and sometimes difficult to separate.

12.2.1 *Actus reus*

12.2.1.1 Property

Conduct which may constitute 'appropriation' must occur in relation to 'property belonging to another'. The property which may be the subject of theft is defined by s. 4 of the TA 1968. Section 4(1) defines property to include **'money and all other property, real or personal, including things in action and other intangible property'**. This is a sweeping definition subject to some limitation in the ensuing subsections relating to land, things growing wild on land, and wild creatures. Subject to these exceptions, however, the only limitation is whether the property is capable of being appropriated; and it does not matter that the person from whom the property is appropriated is unlawfully in possession of the property (see *Smith* [2011] EWCA Crim 66 where drugs were stolen from a drug dealer and it was unsuccessfully argued on appeal that items unlawfully possessed could not constitute property).

12.2.1.1.1 *Corpses and body parts*

One important exclusion should be noted. **At common law neither a corpse, nor parts of a corpse, could be stolen as there was no property in a corpse** (see *Sharpe* (1857) Dears & B 160). The Court of Appeal confirmed this point in *Kelly* [1998] 3 All ER 741, making it clear that only Parliament could change this principle. However, Rose LJ went on to state (at p. 749) that:

> [P]arts of a corpse are capable of being property within s. 4 of the Theft Act, if they have acquired different attributes by virtue of the application of skill, such as dissection or preservation techniques, for exhibition or teaching purposes.

The Court confirmed the convictions for theft of K, an artist, and L, a junior technician employed by the Royal College of Surgeons. L had removed, at K's request, 35 to 40 body parts which were used by doctors training to be surgeons. K made casts of the parts and used the casts in an art exhibition. He retained some of the parts but disposed of others. Rose LJ went on to say (at p. 750):

> [T]he common law does not stand still. It may be that if, on some future occasion, the question arises, the courts will hold that human body parts are capable of being property for the purposes of s. 4, even without the acquisition of different attributes, if they have a use or significance beyond their mere existence. This may be so if, for example, they are intended for use in an organ transplant operation, for the extraction of DNA or, for that matter, as an exhibit in a trial.

12.2.1.1.2 *Money and cheques*

Money refers only to current coins and banknotes. If D steals a cheque for £100 that I have made payable to X, D has not stolen any money. He has stolen the cheque, which is a piece of paper; he only steals £100 if he manages to cash the cheque and receives coins or notes to that value (see *Davis* (1988) 88 Cr App R 347). The property in the bank in which I have a proprietary right or interest is not £100 in money but rather a debt of £100 owed to me by the bank; a debt is a 'thing in action', which is part of the definition of property in s. 4. A cheque authorises the drawer's bank to pay the sum specified on it to the payee. If the cheque is given for valuable consideration it will create a thing in action, namely a debt between the bank and the payee which the payee could enforce by legal proceedings (see **12.2.1.1.3**). The debt in such a case is property but it belongs to the payee not the drawer (see *Preddy* [1996] AC 815).

A cheque can constitute property in another sense: Professor Smith in 'Obtaining Cheques by Deception or Theft' [1997] Crim LR 396, 400, describes a cheque as not just a piece of paper but as a piece of paper which has 'special properties'—'it is an effective key to the drawer's bank account', a 'valuable security' (see s. 20(3) of the TA 1968). When a cheque is paid it reverts to being just a piece of paper as it then loses its 'special properties' and can no longer be used to instruct the bank to pay money to a payee. For example, V draws a cheque for £50 in favour of D to pay D for tidying his garden and leaves it on the kitchen table intending to pay D when the work is completed. D sees the cheque and enters the kitchen and takes it and leaves without finishing tidying the garden. D has appropriated a piece of paper and a valuable security, the cheque, which at this point still belonged to V although the thing which the cheque represents, a debt between the bank and the payee, D (a thing in action, see **12.2.1.1.3**), would belong to D.

12.2.1.1.3 *Things in action and other intangible property*

A thing in action is intangible property but not all items of intangible property are things in action. **A 'thing in action' is a personal right of property which can only be claimed or enforced by legal action and not by taking physical possession** (see *Torkington* v *Magee* [1902] 2 KB 427). Examples of things in action are debts, a right under a trust, a copyright or a trade mark, a credit balance in a bank account, and a contractual right to overdraw the account.

For example, If D, an accountant authorised to draw cheques on X Co.'s behalf, takes a cheque from X Co.'s chequebook and makes it payable to himself for the sum of £100, when he pays this cheque into his own bank account he will be appropriating a thing in action, namely the debt which the bank owes to X Co. (see *Kohn* (1979) 69 Cr App R 395). On the other hand, if D knows that his own account is not in credit and he has no overdraft facility (or if he has exceeded the limit of his overdraft facility), and he writes a cheque for £50 on his own account made payable to X and backs it with a banker's card so that the bank is obliged to meet the cheque, D does not commit theft. Although the bank's funds will be diminished by this transaction, D has not appropriated a thing in action; he has not taken for himself or another someone else's right to sue as, prior to the cheque being written, there was no specific debt of £50 (or any greater amount of which it formed a part) owed by the bank to anyone (see *Navvabi* [1986] 3 All ER 102; but D may be liable for fraud (see **Chapter 13**)).

 Question

Where a cheque is drawn by P in favour of D, the thing in action which the cheque represents, namely a right in the payee to sue the drawer for £x, belongs to D and thus cannot be stolen by D. However, if D presents the cheque for payment, the effect of this is to diminish by £x (or destroy) P's credit balance in his bank account. Could D be guilty of stealing this?

In *Williams (Roy)* [2001] 1 Cr App R 362:

> D ran a building business and targeted vulnerable, elderly householders. D's practice was to charge a modest sum for an initial piece of work to gain the customers' trust and then to charge exorbitant sums for subsequent work. D was charged with several counts of theft of the customers' credit balances by causing cheques to be drawn in his favour and then presenting them for payment. The trial judge directed the jury that the prosecution had to prove that D had appropriated the credit balances of the customers stating, 'If you get a householder to draw a cheque on a bank or building society and cause the cheque to be presented, you cause the householders' credit balance to be diminished, and accordingly take that credit balance for your own use.'

In upholding D's convictions the Court of Appeal referred to *Kohn* and *Graham* [1997] 1 Cr App R 302, emphasising that nothing it said should cast doubt on *Kohn* and 'the principle that theft of a chose in action may be committed when a chose in action belonging to another is destroyed by the defendant's act of appropriation' (see also *Burke* [2000] Crim LR 413).

The drafting of the indictment is particularly important in cases involving bank accounts. In *Darroux (Pamela)* [2018] EWCA Crim 1009 the defendant was charged with stealing 'monies' belonging to a Housing Association but no cash was involved; she was alleged to have submitted falsely inflated overtime/on-call claims and claims in lieu of holiday entitlement, receiving payments into her bank account from the Association. Davis LJ said (at para. 21):

> While in lay terms it is commonplace to talk of money in the bank, it is in legal terms elementary that a bank account constitutes a chose in action, representing the debt due from the bank to the account-holder. So on any view the counts were incorrectly particularized.

By s. 30 of the Patents Act 1977, a patent, or an application for a patent, is declared not to be a thing in action but it is personal property; it is 'other intangible property' and thus is capable of being stolen. Confidential information, such as the questions on an examination paper, is not 'property' (see *Oxford* v *Moss* (1978) 68 Cr App R 183), and by analogy, trade secrets are not property. If D, however, takes the document on which the information is written, he may be guilty of theft of the document. By contrast, s. 7(2)(b) of the Patents Act 1977 treats an invention for which no patent has been granted or applied for as intangible property. As an invention is essentially information it is difficult to see why confidential information cannot constitute property; the information has value and that value will be lost or diminished if its confidentiality is lost. It is arguable that if D takes that information (e.g. by making a copy of the document), while he does not deprive P of the information he does deprive him of its secrecy which is an intangible quality giving the information value. It is argued by E. Griew, *The Theft Acts 1968 & 1978* (7th edn, 1995), that confidential information is not capable of being appropriated (paras 2–144). To read confidential information, however, is to assume a right of an owner as it is the right of the owner to determine who should have access to it; it is arguable, therefore, that confidential information should be regarded as property which may be appropriated (see further **12.2.1.4.1**).

It appears that electricity is not 'other intangible property' as s. 13 of the TA 1968 creates a specific offence of dishonestly using, wasting, or diverting electricity (see *Low* v *Blease* [1975] Crim LR 513). Thus, if D dishonestly reconnects his electricity supply after it has been cut off for non-payment of his electricity bill, he will commit this offence. Using a private telephone without authority also falls within the scope of this offence, as would switching on the appliances in P's home, when he is away, with the intention that he should incur higher electricity bills.

12.2.1.1.4 *Limitations on the theft of land*
Section 4(2) provides that, subject to certain exceptions, a **'person cannot steal land, or things forming part of land and severed from it by him or by his directions'**. Thus, as a general rule, land is not stealable. If I dishonestly move my boundary fence to incorporate part of my neighbour's garden within my own garden, this will not constitute theft. Land for the purposes of s. 4(2), however, does not include incorporeal hereditaments. Thus **easements, profits, and rents are all capable of being stolen by anyone.**

There are three exceptions to the general rule where land may be stolen. First, under s. 4(2)(a), **a person may steal land**:

> when he is a trustee or personal representative, or is authorised by power of attorney, or as liquidator of a company, or otherwise, to sell or dispose of land belonging to another, and he appropriates the land or anything forming part of it by dealing with it in breach of the confidence reposed in him.

For example, if D is authorised as a trustee to sell 100 acres of land and he sells 99 acres and appropriates the remainder for himself, he would be guilty of theft of that acre of land. In *Gimbert* [2018] EWCA Crim 2190 D's cousin was mentally incapacitated at all relevant times. An enduring power of attorney, which she purported to sign but without capacity, was null and of no effect. D was not therefore authorised by power of attorney and could not fall within the s. 4(2) exception. The Court of Appeal held there was no sufficient justification for writing in the words 'is (or purportedly is) authorised' or 'is (or believes himself to be) authorised' into s.4(2). Where no conspiracy to defraud was involved, most cases of the instant nature would probably fall within the ambit of the Fraud Act 2006, whether as involving fraud by misrepresentation or fraud by abuse of position.

Secondly, under s. 4(2)(b), **a person may steal land**:

> when he is not in possession of the land and appropriates anything forming part of the land by severing it or causing it to be severed, or after it has been severed.

This provision is subject to s. 4(3) quoted in the succeeding paragraph. The difficulty with it is in determining when something forms part of the land. If it is growing on the land or is a permanent structure or integral part of such a structure or a fixture it is part of the land. Thus, if I dig up my neighbour's rose bushes to plant them in my garden, I will be appropriating them by severing them from the land. If my neighbour digs up his rose bushes to move them to another part of the garden and I remove them, I will be appropriating something that has been severed. Likewise I will be appropriating property by severing it from the land where I remove the tiles from his roof or the topsoil from his garden. If, however, I am in possession of the land as a tenant or a licensee and I remove the topsoil or the rose bushes I will not be guilty of theft (but see s. 4(2)(c), later).

A further gloss has been added to this second exception by s. 4(3) which provides:

> A person who picks mushrooms growing wild on any land, or who picks flowers, fruit or foliage from a plant growing wild on any land, does not (although not in possession of the land) steal what he picks, unless he does it for reward or for sale or for other commercial purpose.
>
> For purposes of this subsection 'mushroom' includes any fungus, and 'plant' includes any shrub or tree.

If I uproot a sapling growing wild on my neighbour's land I will not be within this subsection as I am not picking from a plant but rather taking the whole plant; if done dishonestly this is theft. If I pick from plants growing wild—for example, taking blackberries or mistletoe or flowers, or picking mushrooms—this will not be theft subject to a further exception. If I pick these items for a commercial purpose this will be theft provided dishonesty is also proven. If D picks blackberries growing wild along a hedgerow to make blackberry jam to sell at a charity 'Bring and Buy Sale', the picking would be 'for sale' and D will be guilty of theft provided dishonesty is proved. Of course, a jury would be unlikely to find D dishonest in this case as the sale is in aid of charity, but if D is a market trader picking wild mushrooms, mistletoe, or blackberries for sale on his stall, his enterprise being of a more commercial nature may persuade a jury to find that this is dishonest.

Question

D, a famous celebrity chef, likes to forage for ingredients for his restaurant and promotes his restaurant on the basis that he uses 'fresh, locally sourced, seasonal and wild ingredients'. D visits a woodland near his restaurant and picks wild mushrooms to serve in a risotto, various leaves to serve in a 'wild salad', and blackberries and elderberries to serve in a summer pudding. Can D be liable for theft?

Thirdly, under s. 4(2)(c), **a person may steal land**:

when, being in possession of the land under a tenancy, he appropriates the whole or part of any fixture or structure let to be used with the land.

If I am the tenant of the property and appropriate a fixture, such as a washbasin or a fireplace or the fitted kitchen cupboards, I will be guilty of theft. However, I will not be guilty of theft if I remove the topsoil or rose bushes. If a person in possession of the land as a licensee appropriates fixtures he will not be guilty of theft as he is not within the provision, but, if a licensee appropriates a greenhouse, as this is not part of the land, he will be guilty of theft. The distinctions highlighted here are fine and technical and reflect no distinction in culpability. It appears that the differences in liability between licensees and tenants are the result of legislative oversight rather than legislative intent.

Section 4(4) deals with the position of wild creatures. It provides:

Wild creatures, tamed or untamed, shall be regarded as property; but a person cannot steal a wild creature not tamed nor ordinarily kept in captivity, or the carcase of any such creature, unless either it has been reduced into possession by or on behalf of another person and possession of it has not since been lost or abandoned, or another person is in course of reducing it into possession.

The effect of this provision is to limit the circumstances in which theft of wild creatures may occur to the following cases:

Key Point

(1) If a creature is tamed or ordinarily kept in captivity it may be stolen. Thus animals kept in a zoo or wildlife safari park may be stolen, even if they escape, as they are ordinarily kept in captivity. If P tames a wild animal it may be stolen.

(2) Other wild creatures, including game, while at large are not owned by anyone, not even the landowner or someone with shooting rights on his land. But once an animal, or its carcass, has been reduced into possession by or on behalf of another, or while it is being reduced into possession, it may be stolen. If D takes a pheasant shot by P—for example, before P's dog retrieves it or from the back of P's vehicle—this will be theft. If D, P's gamekeeper, shoots pheasant on P's instructions and keeps one for himself, this will be theft as he has reduced the pheasant into possession on behalf of another. If, after a day's shoot, a grouse is not retrieved and D finds it, this will not be theft as possession has been lost or abandoned.

12.2.1.2 Belonging to another

In order to be the subject of theft, the property D appropriates must, at the time of the appropriation, belong to another. The Theft Act protects rights of ownership in property and other interests in property. Accordingly s. 5(1) defines 'belonging' for the purposes of theft:

> Property shall be regarded as belonging to any person having possession or control of it, or having in it any proprietary right or interest (not being an equitable interest arising only from an agreement to transfer or grant an interest).

We will examine separately the different elements of this definition.

12.2.1.2.1 Possession or control

(a) *Possession* In the normal case a person who owns property also has possession of it.

Example

P owns a tool hire business storing the tools at his shop. If D enters the shop and dishonestly appropriates a power drill he will be stealing from P, the owner who has possession of the power drill at that moment.

If P hires a lawnmower to Q, P retains the ownership of the lawnmower but Q has possession of it. If D dishonestly appropriates the lawnmower from Q's garage he will be stealing from both Q who has possession of it and P who has ownership of it. If Q's son R is mowing the lawn when D seizes the lawnmower from him, he will be stealing from R who has control of the lawnmower, if not possession of it, as well as from P and Q.

The inclusion of 'possession and control' in the definition of 'belonging' serves two purposes. First, if someone has possession or control of the article it absolves the prosecution from having to prove who the legal owner was at the moment of appropriation. Secondly, a person with a greater interest in property may steal from a person with a lesser interest. If during the period of hire, P had removed the lawnmower from Q's garage he could be convicted of theft provided he had done so dishonestly.

In *Turner (No. 2)* (1971) 55 Cr App R 336, the Court of Appeal extended liability further.

> D left his car at P's garage for repair. When he completed the repair P parked the car on the road outside the garage. D, using his spare key, removed it without paying for the repair. P had a lien on the car entitling him to retain possession of it until the repair bill had been paid. The judge directed the jury to ignore the question of liens and D was convicted of theft.

The Court held that the words 'possession or control' were not to be qualified in any way. However, this is problematic; if lien was ignored, P was a bailee at will. Bailment at will may be terminated at any time by the bailor. A bailor may be liable for theft of his own goods if he terminates a bailment at will by dishonestly removing the goods from the bailee's possession, even though the bailee could not have prevented the bailor from doing so had he done it openly (cf. *Meredith* [1973] Crim LR 253).

In *Kelly* [1998] 3 All ER 741, the Court of Appeal confirmed that **the word 'lawful' is not to be read into s. 5(1).** Thus, property may be stolen from a person who is not in lawful possession of it; for example, a drug user may steal drugs from his dealer, the dealer being in sufficient possession thereof to satisfy the requirements of the Theft Act even though his possession of proscribed drugs is unlawful (see *Smith* [2011] EWCA Crim 66). In *Smith* the Court of Appeal recognised the havoc that might ensue were they to construe the Act so as to permit drug users to steal from dealers with impunity, Lord Judge CJ stating (at para. 10) that 'the criminal law is concerned with keeping the Queen's peace, not vindicating individual property rights'.

(b) *Control* The problem sometimes arises of determining whether property belongs to anyone. **A person may be in control of property without knowing that he possesses it.** Generally the owner of land is in 'control' of any property on his land even if he does not know it is there. Thus, for example, golf balls lost on a golf course will ordinarily be considered as belonging to the club that owns the course (see *Hibbert* v *McKiernan* [1948] 2 KB 162; *Rostron* [2003] EWCA Crim 2206).

> In *Woodman* [1974] QB 754, English China Clays (ECC) sold all the scrap metal on its site to another company which removed the bulk of it but left some behind which was too inaccessible to remove economically. ECC erected a barbed-wire fence and notices warning trespassers to keep out. D entered the site and removed the remaining scrap metal. D was convicted of theft. The Court of Appeal upheld that conviction as there was ample evidence that ECC were in control of the site, had sought to exclude trespassers, and thus were in control of property on the site.

(c) *Abandonment* If property is lost, P continues to possess it until someone else assumes control of it. For example, if P's wallet falls out of his jacket pocket, the wallet still belongs to P and may, in certain circumstances, be stolen by a finder (see **12.2.2.2.1**). The position is different, however, if P abandons his property—for example, where P buys a new wallet and throws his old wallet into a hedge the old wallet ceases to belong to anyone and thus cannot be the subject of theft. **Property will be regarded as abandoned only when the owner is indifferent as to what becomes of it.** Abandonment is not readily inferred by the courts. The fact that P has no further use for it is not conclusive. Placing the wallet in a dustbin rather than throwing it away would not be abandoning it as he would be putting it there expecting it to be collected by the refuse collectors rather than for others to take it (see *Williams v Phillips* (1957) 41 Cr App R 5).

12.2.1.2.2 *Proprietary right or interest*

A full examination of the civil law relating to property would be necessary to explain proprietary rights or interests; this is outside the scope of this book. We will examine briefly some of the situations which may arise.

(a) *The owner* **A person with a proprietary right or interest in property includes the legal owner of the property but this concept is wider than that of ownership.** If a co-owner sells property without the other co-owner's consent, or if a partner sells partnership property without his partner's consent, this will be theft as each co-owner or partner has a proprietary right in the property which is defeated by such a sale (see *Bonner* [1970] 2 All ER 97).

(b) *Equitable interests* **While a trustee is the legal owner of property, the beneficiaries under the trust have equitable interests in the property.** Thus, if a trustee dishonestly appropriates trust property this will be theft from the beneficiaries as persons with proprietary interests (see *Clowes (No. 2)* [1994] 2 All ER 316). Similarly, if an executor dishonestly appropriates property under a will, this will be theft from the legatee(s) (see *Sanders* [2003] EWCA Crim 3079).

Section 5(1) excludes from the meaning of property belonging to another 'an equitable interest arising only from an agreement to transfer or grant an interest'. For example, D contracts to transfer shares to P who pays for them. Before the transfer is effected D transfers the shares to Q. As P, until the transfer is executed, has only an equitable interest in the shares, D is not guilty of theft of the shares. Depending on what D has done, or intends to do, with the money P has paid him, he may be guilty of theft of the money or fraud.

12.2.1.3 **Special cases**

Although s. 5(1) of the TA 1968 is quite widely drafted there are certain cases which it has been considered appropriate to label as theft, even though the property in question does not belong to another. In these cases, others either suffer loss or D makes an unconscionable gain, although technically the property with which D is dealing legally belongs to him.

12.2.1.3.1 *Trust property*

Section 5(2) provides:

> Where property is subject to a trust, the persons to whom it belongs shall be regarded as including any person having a right to enforce the trust, and an intention to defeat the trust shall be regarded accordingly as an intention to deprive of the property any person having that right.

Under s. 5(1) property in a trust is regarded as belonging to both the trustees and the beneficiaries. However, there are some trusts which do not have specific beneficiaries. Charitable trusts do not have specific beneficiaries who could enforce the trust so, if trustees dishonestly appropriated the property of the trust, it would not be property belonging to another. Charitable trusts are enforceable, however, by the Attorney General and thus this provision deems him to have a beneficial interest in the trust property so that theft by a trustee is theft from him (see *Dyke and Munro* [2001] EWCA Crim 2184, [2002] 1 Cr App R 30).

12.2.1.3.2 *Property received under an obligation*
Section 5(3) provides:

> Where a person receives property from or on account of another, and is under an obligation to the other to retain and deal with that property or its proceeds in a particular way, the property or proceeds shall be regarded (as against him) as belonging to the other.

This provision is designed to deal with the situation where D receives property from or on account of P and, in so doing, he obtains not only possession but also legal ownership of the property. It may be that P retains an equitable interest (see **12.2.1.2.2**) but the subsection is designed to avoid the necessity for complex technical analysis. Thus cases which fall within s. 5(3) are probably also covered already by s. 5(1). Section 5(3) would apply where D receives property from P who attaches to it a requirement that he use it in a particular way.

 Example

P employs D to paint his house and gives him a cheque for £50 to buy paint. D obtains possession and ownership of the cheque but he is under a legal obligation to use the 'proceeds' of that cheque to buy paint. If D cashes the cheque and uses the proceeds to bet on a horse he will be guilty of theft. Alternatively, if he cashes the cheque, buys the paint, and uses it to paint his own house, while he has applied the money for the correct purpose of buying paint, he has appropriated the proceeds of the original cheque by using the paint on his own house. By contrast, if P had paid D a deposit of £50 without imposing any obligation on D on how this money was to be used, D would be free to do with it whatever he liked. Even if he never painted P's house he would not be guilty of theft as there was no legal obligation to use that money or its proceeds in a particular way, although if it was his intention at the outset not to paint the house this might be theft or the offence of fraud.

In *Hall* [1973] QB 126, D, a travel agent received deposits and payments from clients who had booked air trips to America. D paid the money into the firm's general account but never arranged the trips and was unable to repay the money. His conviction for theft was quashed, however, as it was not proved that he was under an obligation to the clients to retain and deal with the money in a particular way.

It would have been different if D had been under an obligation to preserve the money in a separate fund (see *Brewster* (1979) 69 Cr App R 375). **The crucial question is what the clear understanding of the parties to the transaction was.** It is necessary for the prosecution to prove that both the accused and the client clearly understood that the client's money was to be kept separate from the accused's business money (see *McHugh* (1993) 97 Cr App R 335).

> In *Klineberg and Marsden* [1999] 1 Cr App R 427, Powerhouse Canaries Ltd, a company operated by the appellants, sold timeshare apartments in Lanzarote to customers in England. The purchasers paid over the purchase price on the understanding that the money would be held by an independent trust company, Timeshare Trustees International (TTI), which would act as stakeholders to protect the purchaser until the apartment in question was ready for occupation. Between October 1990 and November 1991, 237 people paid over £500,000 to Powerhouse in connection with intended purchases of timeshares but only £233 found its way to TTI. The appellants' convictions for theft were upheld as there was a legal obligation imposed on them to deal with the intending purchasers' property in a particular way which they had breached (see also *Kumar, Re* [2000] Crim LR 504; cf. *Floyd* v *DPP* [2000] Crim LR 41 and commentary thereon).

In some situations it may be unclear in which sense 'property belonged to another', whether under s. 5(1), (2), or (3), or whether it was the original property which D appropriated dishonestly or the proceeds thereof. It will still be possible to secure a conviction for theft, however, where it is clear that whatever category the property fell into it belonged to V and D had, with the requisite *mens rea*, appropriated it (*Hallam and Blackburn* [1995] Crim LR 323).

Section 5(3) also covers the situation where D receives money on account of P.

> In *Lewis* v *Lethbridge* [1987] Crim LR 59, D obtained sponsorship for a particular charity to be paid if X ran the London Marathon. D collected the sponsorship money but did not pay the charity. It was held that there was no obligation upon D to maintain a fund consisting of the money collected or its proceeds; his relationship with the charity was merely that of debtor and creditor.

This case has been overruled by the Court of Appeal in *Wain* [1995] 2 Cr App R 660.

> W organised various events to raise money for 'The Telethon Trust', a charitable body created by the Yorkshire Television Company. With the permission of a representative of the company he transferred the money he had raised from a special bank account into his own personal account. He then dissipated the credit in his own account and was charged with theft of £2,833.25, the amount he had originally raised. The Court of Appeal considered that the Divisional Court had overlooked the trust aspect of the facts in *Lewis* v *Lethbridge*.

McCowan LJ stated:

> [B]y virtue of s. 5(3), [W] was plainly under an obligation to retain, if not the actual notes and coins, at least their proceeds, that is to say the money credited in the bank account which he opened for the trust with the actual property. When he took the money credited to that account and moved it over to his own bank account, it was still the proceeds of the notes and coins donated which he proceeded to use for his own purposes, thereby appropriating them.

It is difficult to formulate any general rules in relation to s. 5(3) as each case will hinge upon its own particular facts. **The obligation upon D, however, must be a legal obligation existing at the time that D dishonestly appropriates the property or its proceeds** (see *Gilks* (1972) 56 Cr App R 734; *Mainwaring* (1981) 74 Cr App R 99).

12.2.1.3.3 *Property 'got' by another's mistake*
Section 5(4) provides:

> Where a person gets property by another's mistake, and is under an obligation to make restoration (in whole or in part) of the property or its proceeds or of the value thereof, then to the extent of that obligation the property or its proceeds shall be regarded (as against him) as belonging to the person entitled to restoration, and an intention not to make restoration shall be regarded accordingly as an intention to deprive that person of the property or proceeds.

This provision is designed to cover the situation where P transfers property to D under a mistake which does not operate to prevent ownership of the property passing to D. In many cases this provision is not necessary.

In some situations, however, P's mistake will not prevent legal ownership in the property passing to D. In such a situation D may commit theft of the property, its proceeds or value thereof, if he dishonestly appropriates it being under a legal obligation to restore it to P.

An example of a situation covered by s. 5(4) would be that disclosed by the facts in *Moynes* v *Cooper* [1956] 1 QB 439.

> D, having received a partial advance on his week's wages, was paid his full wages by the wages clerk. When D opened his wage packet he discovered the mistake but decided to keep the money he had been overpaid. D was acquitted of larceny. The wages clerk had transferred ownership of the money to D so D could not steal what was his own property.

Under s. 5(4), D would be guilty of theft as he would be under a legal obligation to make restitution of the part, or value thereof, overpaid. In *AG's Reference (No. 1 of 1983)* [1985] QB 182, this provision was held to cover the case where an employee received an overpayment of wages by means of a direct debit transaction between the employer's account and the employee's account. In this case, the thing in action, the debt owed by the bank to D, to the value of the overpayment, had been 'got' by the employer's mistake, and D was under an obligation to make restitution of that amount to her employer. If D had spent all the money in her account on drinking and gambling before realising that she had been overpaid, a subsequent refusal to restore the sum overpaid to the employer could not amount to theft as there would no longer be property (in this case a thing in action in the form of the debt owed by the bank to D) which D could appropriate. If, however, D had bought jewellery this would represent the proceeds of the overpayment in which the employer would have a proprietary interest and which D could steal.

D will be guilty of theft only where there is a legal obligation to make restitution; a moral obligation will not suffice.

In *Gilks* (1972) 56 Cr App R 734, D had won £10.62 betting on horses. When he claimed his winnings the betting shop manager paid him £117.25 mistakenly believing he had backed one more winner than he had. D realised the mistake but decided to keep the overpayment. He was convicted of theft. The Court of Appeal held that the conviction could not be sustained under s. 5(4) as 'obligation' meant 'legal obligation' and gaming transactions were not legally enforceable. The Court upheld the conviction, however, stating that, as the property had been transferred under a mistake, ownership did not pass, so the property belonged to the betting shop when D decided to keep it.

12.2.1.4 **Appropriation**

The definition of theft requires that D appropriate property belonging to another. In most cases, it suffices to treat 'appropriating' as meaning 'taking'. The simplest example of appropriation is where D surreptitiously removes P's wallet from his pocket.

It is not every appropriation, however, which amounts to theft; **the appropriation must be accompanied by dishonesty and an intention to deprive the owner permanently of the property.** Thus the pickpocket who intends to spend the money he finds in P's wallet would have the necessary *mens rea*. By contrast, if D is P's son, and is removing the wallet as an April Fools' Day prank, with no intention to deprive his father of it permanently, there would be no theft, not because of a lack of appropriation, but because of the absence of *mens rea*.

When the Criminal Law Revision Committee, in its *Eighth Report, Theft and Related Offences* (Cmnd 2977, 1966), framed the concept of 'dishonest appropriation' it did so in the hope and belief that this concept would be easily understood without the aid of further definition (see para. 34). Unfortunately, during 50 years of judicial consideration involving four decisions of the House of Lords, the meaning of appropriation has proved controversial. Since the last pronouncement of the House of Lords in *Hinks* (see **12.2.1.4.3**) it has been a very broad term that even encompasses situations where a person can be deemed to have appropriated property in situations where he has acquired it lawfully, including where the victim has given the property to the defendant.

12.2.1.4.1 *Assuming the rights of an owner*
Section 3(1) of the TA 1968 provides:

> Any assumption by a person of the rights of an owner amounts to an appropriation, and this includes, where he has come by the property (innocently or not) without stealing it, any later assumption of a right to it by keeping or dealing with it as owner.

For the moment we are concerned only with the first part of this definition; cases of later assumption of rights to property will be dealt with later (see **12.2.1.4.4**). **The phrase 'any assumption of the rights of an owner' suggests that he is taking to himself rights which he does not have and that he is dealing with the property as if he were the owner.** As the word 'assume' may be defined to mean 'to usurp, to arrogate, to seize', **the idea sought to be conveyed is the ousting or supplanting of the owner's property rights** as D seeks to occupy the owner's place in relation to his property. Seen in this light the word 'assumption' (or 'assume') has a pejorative connotation and is not a value-neutral word. **The suggestion is that D is asserting a right, which he neither has, nor has authority to assert, over the property of another.** The principal rights of the owner are, for example, to possess, use, consume, sell, hire, lend, or destroy his property. The paradigm case of theft is that of D, a pickpocket, removing a wallet from P's pocket. In taking the property D is clearly assuming and exercising rights which he does not have to the property. But theft may occur in many and varied situations and the act of stealing itself may not be physical but mental in the sense of a decision made in respect of property (as envisaged by the second part of s. 3(1)).

 Example

P lends D a book for a week but at the time of taking possession of it D intends to sell it. In this situation P is permitting D to take possession of the book for a limited period; D, however, in taking the book is taking it to dispose of outright and thereby is, in his mind, assuming rights of ownership over the book which P had not transferred to him. It would not be inaccurate to say in this situation that D is arrogating to himself rights which P had not granted, or that he is usurping P's rights.

Of course, in the context of the statutory definition, appropriation is inextricably linked to the concept of dishonesty. **Theft, consequently, is concerned with dishonest appropriations.** But an issue which arises is whether all the mischief with which the offence of theft is concerned is locked within the concept of dishonesty or whether some of it is to be found in the concept of appropriation. There is a danger that if the meaning of appropriation is too broad and value-neutral, actions which do not fit paradigms of theft may be sucked within the boundaries of theft by juries (or magistrates) determining, as a moral reaction, whether what D did was dishonest.

A problem which s. 3(1) presents is that it states that any assumption by a person of 'the rights of an owner' amounts to an appropriation. In some cases, however, only one such right is assumed, namely possession. In *Morris* [1984] AC 320, two appeals were heard by the House of Lords relating to dishonest shoppers in supermarkets:

> D and E switched the price labels on goods intending to buy the goods at a lower price at the till. D was arrested after paying the lower price while E was arrested before he paid the lower price. Both D and E were charged with theft. It was clearly one of the owner's rights to fix the price at which his property would be sold. Switching the price labels was an assumption of this right and it did not matter that the dishonest shoppers had not yet assumed all the owner's rights.

Lord Roskill stated (at pp. 331, 332) that **it is sufficient to prove that an accused assumed *any* of the rights of an owner.** This is a necessary construction of the provision as there are cases where D has clearly not assumed some of the owner's rights. For example, D may appropriate property without ever being in possession of it, as where D offers to sell, without authority, P's goods to Q; at that point D is assuming a right of the owner, namely to sell his property (see *Pitham and Hehl*

(1976) 65 Cr App R 45). In such a case the theft is committed at the time of the offer to sell; it does not matter that P was never deprived of his property (although it must, of course be proved that D intended to deprive P of his property permanently).

The decision in *Morris* has important implications relating to when and where theft is committed. In the stereotypical case of shoplifting from a supermarket, where D takes a bottle of whisky from the shelf, puts it in his coat pocket and leaves the store without paying, at what point does he appropriate the property? Taking physical possession of the bottle is assuming one of the rights of the shop-owner, so the appropriation occurs at that point, and if the appropriation was dishonest and D intended permanently to deprive the shop of the bottle, theft is committed. In terms of proving theft, the store detective will wait until the person has passed beyond the checkout before challenging the person; that provides more robust *evidence* of theft than would an earlier intervention even though the elements of theft are all satisfied at the moment that D takes physical possession.

12.2.1.4.2 *Consent and appropriation*

The major problem in relation to appropriation has been whether there could be an appropriation where the owner of the property had consented to the 'taking' of it by the alleged thief. It is important to remember that the Fraud Act 2006 (**Chapter 13**) now provides suitable offences for situations where D deceives C into parting with property or abuses his position to induce C to part with property. In these situations, C may consent to D acquiring the property but only because of D's deception or abuse of position. The leading cases on consent and appropriation all pre-date the Fraud Act 2006.

In *Gomez* [1992] 3 WLR 1061, as with *Lawrence* [1972] AC 626 and *Dobson* v *General Accident Fire and Life Assurance Corporation plc* [1990] QB 274. the owner consented to the taking of the property but only because of a deception practised upon him by the rogue. While these facts could have supported, at the time, a conviction for the offence of obtaining property by deception contrary to s. 15(1) of the TA 1968 (and now, fraud), would they also enable a conviction to be obtained for the simple offence of theft contained in s. 1(1)? *Lawrence* suggested an affirmative answer while *Morris* had been construed in several Court of Appeal decisions as suggesting the contrary.

> In *Gomez*, D was the assistant manager of an electrical shop. X approached him seeking to acquire goods from the shop in exchange for two building society cheques which were stolen. The cheques were undated and bore no payee's name. D approached the manager seeking his authorisation for a sale totalling the amount of £7,950, the amount of one of the cheques. The manager instructed him to confirm with the bank that the cheque was acceptable. D later falsely told the manager that the bank had said the cheque was 'as good as cash'. The sale was authorised and the goods were duly supplied to X. A few days later D presented the manager with the second cheque which was in the amount of £9,250 in support of a further sale and again this transaction was authorised by the manager and the goods supplied to X. Several days later the cheques were returned marked 'Orders not to pay. Stolen cheque'. D was convicted of theft. The Court of Appeal quashed his conviction holding that there was no appropriation at the moment when X took possession of the

goods because he was entitled to do so under a contract of sale (which although voidable had not been avoided at the time). The Court considered that the manager's consent and authority negated the element of appropriation.

The House of Lords heard the Crown's appeal on the following point of law of general public importance:

> When theft is alleged and that which is alleged to be stolen passes to the defendant with the consent of the owner, but that has been obtained by a false representation, has (a) an appropriation within the meaning of s. 1(1) of the Theft Act 1968 taken place, or (b) must such a passing of property necessarily involve an element of adverse interference with or usurpation of some right of the owner?

By a majority of four to one (Lord Lowry dissenting) their Lordships allowed the appeal and approved *Lawrence*, answering the certified question (a) in the affirmative and (b) in the negative. The leading speech was delivered by Lord Keith of Kinkel, who reviewed the earlier decisions of the House in *Lawrence* and *Morris* and highlighted the conflict to which the two decisions gave rise.

In *Lawrence*, D, a taxi-driver, was convicted of theft where he represented to P, his Italian passenger, that the £1 tendered was insufficient to cover the fare and removed a further £6 from the passenger's wallet, the true fare for the journey being 52p. D argued on appeal that the conviction for theft of this £6 could not stand as P had consented to him taking it. D was seeking to have the words 'without consent of the owner' implied into s. 1(1) of the TA 1968. The House of Lords rejected this argument stating that there may be an appropriation 'even though the owner has permitted or consented to the property being taken'. At the time D removed the money from the wallet, it was property belonging to P. In removing it D was doing something which only an owner could do. His removal of the money constituted an appropriation. Whether this was theft would hinge on whether D was dishonest. He would not have been dishonest if he believed that P, knowing the circumstances (i.e. that he was being charged a fare far in excess of the legal fare) consented to his appropriation of the money. Viscount Dilhorne stated (at p. 632):

> Belief or the absence of belief that the owner had with such knowledge consented to the appropriation is relevant to the issue of dishonesty, not to the question whether or not there has been an appropriation.

When D took the £6 from the wallet he appropriated it whether or not P consented to him taking it. D was dishonest because he did not believe that P knew the circumstances and, with that knowledge, consented to the £6 being taken. The transaction was one coloured by D's fraud (and indeed it would now be a simple case of fraud under s. 2 of the 2006 Act).

Viscount Dilhorne's view finds support in s. 2(1)(b) which provides that an appropriation of property belonging to another is not to be regarded as dishonest:

> (b) if D appropriates the property in the belief that he would have the other's consent if the other knew of the appropriation and the circumstances of it.

The section contemplates that an appropriation may be consented to. Viscount Dilhorne expressly stated in *Lawrence* (at p. 632):

> [A] person is not to be regarded as acting dishonestly if he appropriates another's property believing that with full knowledge of the circumstances that other person has in fact agreed to the appropriation.

In *Morris* the House of Lords did not question the decision in *Lawrence*, Lord Roskill taking the view that the facts of the case clearly disclosed a dishonest appropriation. Section 3(1) of the Theft Act 1968 provides that '[a]ny assumption by a person of the rights of an owner amounts to an appropriation . . .'. A question which arose in *Morris* was whether or not D had to assume all the rights of an owner in order to appropriate property. Lord Roskill answered this by stating:

> [I]t is enough for the prosecution if they have proved . . . the assumption . . . of any of the rights of the owner of the goods in question . . .

In *Gomez*, after approving this dictum, Lord Keith proceeded to label as unnecessary and incorrect certain of the observations which Lord Roskill had made in his speech in *Morris*.

First, Lord Roskill gave **the example of the practical joker** who switches price labels on items in a supermarket concluding that this act, without more, would not amount to an appropriation. Lord Keith was of the opinion that label switching in itself constitutes an appropriation as it involves an assumption of one of the rights of the owner irrespective of whether or not it is accompanied by some other act. **It is, accordingly, the absence of dishonesty and an intention to deprive the owner permanently of the property which renders the practical joker not guilty of theft.**

Secondly, **Lord Roskill defined 'appropriation' pejoratively**, stating that it 'involves not an act expressly or impliedly authorised by the owner but an act by way of adverse interference with or usurpation of those rights'. There would have been no real problem with Lord Roskill's dictum if he had excised from it the words 'not an act expressly or impliedly authorised by the owner' as the essential point was that an appropriation is something adverse to the owner, something which usurps the owner's rights. The shoplifter clearly seeks to do so whereas the honest shopper intends nothing adverse to the owner's interests. **The context in *Lawrence* was one of consent or authorisation being induced by fraud; P was consenting to D taking the correct fare whereas D was taking more than the correct fare;** his act was not truly consented to by P. **Likewise, in *Morris*, there was fraud** as D was seeking to deceive the shop assistant as to the correct price for the goods. While the shop owner consented to shoppers taking goods from the shelves for the purpose of purchasing them, he did not consent to them changing price labels to purchase them at a lower price. In response to Lord Roskill's dictum, Lord Keith stated (at p. 1076):

While it is correct to say that appropriation for purposes of section 3(1) includes the latter sort of act, it does not necessarily follow that no other act can amount to an appropriation and in particular that no act expressly or impliedly authorised by the owner can in any circumstances do so. Indeed, *Lawrence v Commissioner of Metropolitan Police* is a clear decision to the contrary since it laid down unequivocally that an act may be an appropriation notwithstanding that it is done with the consent of the owner. It does not appear to me that any sensible distinction can be made in this context between consent and authorisation.

Following *Gomez*, accordingly, **appropriation was seen as something which could be done even though the owner apparently consented to the act.** In *Gomez* the shop manager was only consenting to D taking the goods in return for full payment. There was no actual consent (based on full knowledge of the facts) to what the thief was actually doing. **The problem with *Gomez*, however, is that their Lordships also answered the second part of the certified question in the negative, holding that appropriation is not necessarily something adverse to the owner's rights or something which usurps the owner's rights.** By losing sight of this idea, the Lords made appropriation a value-neutral word stripped of pejorative connotations.

This leaves then the question whether consent, which is not induced by fraud (or some other circumstance which might render the transaction voidable), is relevant to the question of appropriation.

It was clear following the decision in *Gomez* that the degree of overlap between theft contrary to s. 1 and obtaining property by deception contrary to s. 15 of the TA 1968 was considerable (see further *Atakpu and Abrahams* [1994] Crim LR 693). For practical purposes most s. 15 offences also amounted to thefts. This gave the prosecution considerable discretion in deciding which charge to level. Given that consent is irrelevant, it was easier to prove theft than to prove the s. 15 offence which required the prosecution to prove that P was deceived by D into parting with his property. The offence of fraud, which replaces the s. 15 offence, is a conduct crime rather than a result crime and does not require any proof that P is deceived (see **13.1**). While the overlap between fraud and theft remains as great as that between theft and s. 15, there is no particular benefit to the prosecution charging theft in the situation which arose in *Gomez* rather than the new fraud by false representation offence.

12.2.1.4.3 *Appropriating gifts*

A problem arose in several cases involving purported gifts which highlighted a weakness in the reasoning in *Gomez* and *Lawrence*. In both of those cases the consent of the owner had been obtained by deception. In *Gomez* the title D obtained to the property he took from the shop was voidable due to the deception. The same applied in *Lawrence*. **Could a theft occur where there is no false representation and the property D receives indefeasibly belongs to him?**

In the context of the law of gift, if a donor who has capacity makes a gift to a donee, the donor thereby transfers ownership of the property to the donee. If the donor lacks capacity, the transaction is void and the donee would not become the owner of the property. However, if there is coercion, undue influence, or fraud, the transaction is merely voidable—that is, it may be avoided by the donor.

> ### **?** Question
>
> Could D be considered to have committed theft by accepting a gift from P who had capacity, even though there was no coercion, undue influence, or fraud on the D's part albeit that D is manipulative and takes advantage of P's gullibility or vulnerability?

One view is that it would be undesirable for the criminal law to find D guilty of theft where the civil law would find that a valid gift had been made and that the allegedly stolen property belonged to D. However, the House of Lords took a different view in the leading case, *Hinks* [2000] 3 WLR 1590.

> D befriended P, a man of low IQ, and over a period of eight months accompanied him to his building society on most days where he made withdrawals totalling £60,000 which were deposited in her account. In addition he gave D a television. There was evidence that D had encouraged, coerced, or influenced P to make these gifts and that he was naive and trusting and had no idea of the value of his assets. The trial judge, however, did not clearly put to the jury the question whether P either lacked capacity to make the gifts or had been unduly influenced or coerced by D, leaving everything to be considered under the question of dishonesty, namely whether P was 'so mentally incapable that the defendant herself realised that ordinary and decent people would regard it as dishonesty to accept that gift from him?' This left the possibility that D could have been convicted of theft of valid gifts on the basis solely of the jury's view on dishonesty. The Court of Appeal dismissed her appeal taking the view that the validity or otherwise of the gifts was irrelevant to the question whether there had been an appropriation.

This involves treating 'appropriation' as a completely value-neutral word. The problem this gives rise to is that if the gift is valid, D has acquired indefeasible title to the property; the transaction is neither void nor voidable. That being so, how could D appropriate (assume the rights of the owner to) property which was her own? The Court of Appeal certified a question for consideration of the House of Lords:

> Whether the acquisition of an indefeasible title to property is capable of amounting to an appropriation of property belonging to another for the purposes of section 1(1) of the Theft Act 1968.

Controversially, **by a majority of four to one, their Lordships answered the question in the affirmative**. Thus D's receiving of a gift can amount to an appropriation; guilt of theft will hinge on whether the jury consider she was dishonest to accept the gift. The majority took this issue to have been settled by *Gomez*. Lord Steyn, with whom Lords Slynn and Jauncey agreed, considered that the judgments in *Gomez* did not 'differentiate between consent induced by fraud and consent given in any other circumstances'. **'Appropriation'**, in their Lordships' view, **was a totally value-neutral word.** Lord Steyn approved of a dictum of Lord Browne-Wilkinson in *Gomez* that the word **'appropriation' is 'an objective description of the act done irrespective of** the mental state of either the owner or the accused'. Lord Steyn stated (at p. 1599) that *Gomez* treated the word 'appropriation' as 'a neutral word comprehending "any assumption by a person of the rights of an owner"'.

This is controversial because a donor making a valid gift divests himself of all title to the property gifted in favour of the donee; the donee, in accepting the gift, receives her own property to which she has indefeasible title. She is not assuming the rights of an owner—she *is* the owner so there is no assumption. She is not supplanting the owner or arrogating to herself any rights which the owner has not, with full knowledge and consent, transferred to her.

Such arguments, however, had no effect on the majority who were even unconcerned that their decision would create inevitable conflict between the criminal law and the civil law, Lord Steyn considering it a great virtue to seek to eliminate civil law concepts from the deliberations of juries. This means that what the civil law permits may yet constitute theft if 12 people in a jury, or a magistrate on summary trial, consider that D's behaviour is morally reprehensible and therefore dishonest.

In his dissenting speech Lord Hobhouse sought to negotiate the interrelationship of the different elements of the offence while respecting the civil law of property as, in using terms such as 'belonging to another', the Act presumes the existence and relevance of the civil law. He highlighted an anomaly to which the decision of the majority gave rise; s. 5, which builds upon the civil law and is concerned with deeming property to belong to another in circumstances where D has acquired legal title (albeit that his title is defeasible), makes no provision for the situation where D 'has been validly given the property' and in such a situation D 'can no longer appropriate property belonging to another . . . . There is no law against appropriating your own property as defined in s. 5'.

It was not only s. 5 which led Lord Hobhouse to his conclusion. He also considered ss 2, 3, and 6. On the relationship of appropriation to dishonesty, he looked at the wording of s. 2 relating to belief in a right to deprive another of property or belief in consent to the appropriation of property, which both serve to negate dishonesty, and asked (at p. 1614):

[H]ow can it be said that [D's] knowledge that he has such a right or the actual consent of the person to whom the property belongs is irrelevant? How can it be said that the right of the defendant to accept a gift is irrelevant—or the fact that the transferor has actually and validly consented to the defendant having the relevant property?

In the context of a gift, the property once gifted by the donor belongs to the donee. Even if acceptance of a gift could be an appropriation (which Lord Hobhouse strenuously contested), difficulties arise in relation to s. 2(1)(a). His Lordship stated (at p. 1615):

The defendant did have the right to deprive the donor of the property. The donor did consent to the appropriation; indeed, he intended it. There are also difficulties with s. 6 as she was not acting regardless of the donor's rights; the donor has already surrendered his rights. The only way that these conclusions can be displaced is by showing that the gift was not valid. There are even difficulties with s. 3 itself. The donee is not 'assuming the rights of an owner': she already has them.

Lord Hobhouse's speech failed to persuade the majority. Receiving that which the donor wishes her to receive may nonetheless be theft if 12 people conclude she should not have accepted it. **Appropriation, therefore, is a value-neutral term. Thus any dealing with property or any exercise of a right of an owner (even the exercise of that right with the owner's express authorisation in a situation where the owner has full knowledge and there being no circumstances which might render the transaction voidable) amounts to an appropriation.**

12.2.1.4.4 *Appropriation by keeping or dealing*

The second part of s. 3(1) of the TA 1968 deals with the situation where D originally comes by property without stealing it. A later assumption of a right to the property by keeping or dealing with it as owner amounts to an appropriation.

 Example

> If P lends D his book for a week, D obtains possession of it but he is not a thief if he has no intention of depriving P of it. If, however, D subsequently decides to keep the book permanently or if he subsequently sells it (dealing with it), this conduct represents an appropriation as D is assuming the rights of an owner. The same would apply where D receives property as a result of a mistake by P of which D was unaware at the time. For example, P agrees to lend D his books on criminal law. He gives D a pile of books which D later discovers contains a book on contract. If D decides to keep this or otherwise deal with it he would be appropriating it at that time. Similarly if D finds a book and has no means of discovering its owner at the time this would not be theft. If, however, P later tells D that he has lost a book and the facts revealed indicate that the book lost was the one D found, a decision by D at that time to keep it would be an appropriation.

12.2.1.4.5 *Excluding the bona fide purchaser from liability*

Section 3(2) provides:

> Where property or a right or interest in property is or purports to be transferred for value to a person acting in good faith, no later assumption by him of rights which he believed himself to be acquiring shall, by reason of any defect in the transferor's title amount to theft of the property.

This provision excludes from liability bona fide purchasers who otherwise might be guilty of theft under s. 3(1) (see **12.2.1.4.4**).

 Example

> If D buys a car from E in good faith believing that E has good title to the car, D's subsequent discovery that E had stolen the car from P will not render D liable to conviction for theft if he then keeps the car. The relevant moment when considering D's belief is when he purchased the property (see *Adams* [1993] Crim LR 72).

Should D in this example decide to sell the car and then advertise it for sale, impliedly representing thereby that he has good title to it, he would be liable for fraud by false representation contrary to s. 1 of the Fraud Act 2006. This exception under s. 3(2) does not apply to anyone who does not acquire the property in good faith and for value. Thus, where E merely gave the car to D as a gift, he would be liable under s. 3(1) if, on discovering that the car was stolen, he decided to keep it.

12.2.2 *Mens rea*

The *mens rea* of theft is made up of two elements: an intention of permanently depriving the owner of his property and dishonesty. The prosecution must prove both these states of mind. Importantly, while most thieves steal property for personal gain, this is not an element of the offence. Section 1(2) of the TA 1968 provides that 'it is immaterial whether the appropriation is made with a view to gain, or is made for the thief's own benefit'. If P is simply deprived of the property without D benefitting—for example, D throws P's jewellery into the Thames—that may be theft if D's appropriation was dishonest.

12.2.2.1 With the intention of permanently depriving the other of it

There is no requirement that P be actually deprived of his property permanently; the crucial question is what was D's intent at the time he appropriated the property? As a general rule, an intention to borrow the property cannot amount to an intention to deprive permanently. If, however, D takes P's money, intending to return to P an equivalent amount, D does have the requisite intention as he does not intend to return to P the exact coins or notes he removed (*Velumyl* [1989] Crim LR 299). Where P has only a limited interest in the property—for example, where P has hired a lawnmower from Q for the weekend and D takes it knowing of P's limited interest and intending to return it on Monday—this would amount to an intention to deprive P permanently of his interest in the property. In this example, D steals from P because he intends to deprive P of his limited interest in the property; he does not steal from Q because there is no intention permanently to deprive Q of it. If D did not know the facts and, thinking that P owned the lawnmower, he took it intending to keep it for a week, this would not be theft even though P was permanently deprived of his interest in it.

In most cases, D's intention may be inferred from the circumstances. For example, if D takes P's wallet and spends the contents, or if he takes P's DVD player and sells it, or if he takes P's sandwiches and eats them, there is clear evidence of an intention permanently to deprive P of his property. In other cases, however, the correct inference to draw from the facts will not be so obvious. For example, if D removes P's book from his bag and is found reading it in the library, or if D removes P's bicycle from the cycle stands and is found riding it home, it is far from clear whether D was merely borrowing P's property or whether he intended to deprive P of it permanently. Further evidence would be necessary to found a charge of theft.

The issue of intention may usually be left to the jury without too much elaboration. Section 6 of the TA 1968, however, provides a partial definition of 'intention of permanently depriving'.

Key Point

Section 6 operates to deem a person's intention to amount to an intention to deprive permanently even though he may have intended to return the property or even had returned the property. The section should not be referred to if the issue of D's intention may be resolved without reference to it; it should be referred to in exceptional cases only (see *Lloyd* [1985] QB 829).

There are two reasons for this: first, the section is only a partial definition designed to deal with a particular form of mischief; secondly, the section is particularly obscurely drafted. Regarding this latter point it should be noted that the section refers to 'property' and 'the thing itself', but appears to mean the same by both terms. In s. 6(1) the word 'meaning' is used as well as 'intention'; it appears that 'meaning' was used in the sense of 'intending'.

12.2.2.1.1 *Section 6(1)*

Section 6(1) provides:

A person appropriating property belonging to another without meaning the other permanently to lose the thing itself is nevertheless to be regarded as having the intention of permanently depriving the other of it if his intention is to treat the thing as his own to dispose of regardless of the other's rights; and a borrowing or lending of it may amount to so treating it if, but only if, the borrowing or lending is for a period and in circumstances making it equivalent to an outright taking or disposal.

This provision may be divided into two parts which we will examine separately.

(a) *Disposing of the property regardless of the other's rights* 'A person . . . is . . . to be regarded as having the intention of permanently depriving the other of it if his intention is to treat the thing as his own to dispose of regardless of the other's rights.' In such cases, D may intend the property to be returned to P so that P is not actually deprived of it. **D will be deemed to have the requisite intention, however, on the basis of his treating the property as his own to dispose of regardless of P's rights.**

Several situations may fall within this provision. If D takes P's property intending to sell it back to P (the 'buy-back principle'), D will not intend to deprive P of it permanently, but he will be treating the property as his own to dispose of regardless of P's rights; it is one of the rights of the owner to sell his property (see *Hall* (1849) 1 Den 381, and most recently *Raphael* [2008] EWCA Crim 1014). The same principle may be applied where D removes a ticket from a booking office for a pop concert. The organisers of the concert own the ticket which will be returned to them by D when he hands it to the door steward to gain admission to the concert. The organisers, however, are effectively paying for the return of the ticket by providing D with admission. Similarly, if D takes P's property intending to return it only when P pays for it or fulfils some other condition (the 'ransom principle'), he will again be treating the property as his own to dispose of regardless of the other's rights: only an owner may attach conditions to the use or possession of his property (but cf. *Coffey* [1987] Crim LR 498). In *Lloyd* (see **12.2.2.1**), the Court of Appeal affirmed that these situations fell within s. 6(1). The Court, however, considered that s. 6(1) should be given a restricted meaning stating that they would endeavour to interpret the section so that **'nothing is construed as an intention permanently to deprive which would not prior to the 1968 Act have been so construed'**. It was a requirement of larceny at common law and under the Larceny Act 1916 that D have an intention of permanently depriving P of his property.

In *Fernandes* [1996] 1 Cr App R 175, the Court of Appeal provided, it is submitted, the correct interpretation of s. 6, stating (at p. 188):

> In our view, section 6(1) . . . is not limited in its application to the illustrations given by Lord Lane CJ in *Lloyd*. Nor . . . did Lord Lane suggest that it should be so limited. The critical notion . . . is whether a defendant intended 'to treat the thing as his own to dispose of regardless of the other's rights'. The second limb of subsection (1), and also subsection (2), are merely specific illustrations of the application of that notion. We consider that section 6 may apply to a person in possession or control of another's property who, dishonestly and for his own purpose, deals with that property in such a manner that he knows he is risking its loss.

In *Marshall* [1998] 2 Cr App R 282, the Court of Appeal applied *Fernandes*.

> The Ds obtained used, but unexpired, tickets from passengers leaving London Underground stations and sold them on to other travellers thereby depriving London Underground of revenue. They appealed against convictions for theft. The Court dismissed their appeals holding that the tickets belonged at all times to London Underground which had the exclusive right to sell tickets. By acquiring and reselling the tickets Ds had the intention to treat the tickets as their own to dispose of regardless of London Underground's rights.

This decision has been subjected to fairly rigorous criticism by Professor Smith in 'Stealing Tickets' [1998] Crim LR 723, who counsels that the answer will not necessarily be the same for all tickets as the question whether the original vendor of the ticket retains property in the ticket will depend on the terms of the contract.

In certain circumstances D's borrowing of P's property may fall within the second limb of s. 6(1). If D borrows P's book to read on a train journey and, having read it, abandons it in the station at his destination, his abandonment would tend to show an indifference as to whether P recovers the book, particularly if there is little likelihood of P recovering it. He is dealing with it in a way in which only an owner may do and is treating it as his own to dispose of regardless of the owner's rights. In a case such as this there would not appear to be any need to resort to the second part of s. 6(1).

> In *DPP v J and others* [2002] All ER (D) 260, the Administrative Court held that snatching V's headphones and breaking them before returning them to him provided evidence from which the justices could have inferred an intention permanently to deprive. The Court considered that this action amounted to a disposal of the property and was no different from an action which risked the loss of the article.

In *Mitchell* [2008] EWCA Crim 850, a violent carjacking was held not to amount to robbery as D intended only to use the car to make his getaway before abandoning it.

It is important, however, in dealing with cases under the first part of s. 6(1) that meaning is attributed to all the words. It is not enough that D 'treat the thing as his own'; **some meaning must be given to the further requirement 'to dispose of regardless of the other's rights'.** In *Cahill* [1993] Crim LR 142, the Court of Appeal approved the following passage in Professor Smith, *The Law of Theft* (6th edn, 1989), p. 73:

> It is submitted, however, that an intention to use the thing as one's own is not enough and that 'dispose of' is not used in the sense in which a general might 'dispose of' his forces but rather in the meaning given by the *Shorter Oxford Dictionary*: 'To deal with definitely: to get rid of; to get done with, finish. To make over by way of sale or bargain, sell.'

Unfortunately, in *DPP* v *Lavender* [1994] Crim LR 297, the Divisional Court, without referring to *Cahill*, ruled that the dictionary definition of 'dispose of' was too narrow and a disposal could include 'dealing with' property.

> D was charged with theft of two doors which he had removed from a council property undergoing repair and used to replace damaged doors in his girlfriend's council flat. The justices had dismissed the information. The Divisional Court allowed the prosecution's appeal and remitted the case to the justices with a direction to convict.

The Divisional Court's substitution of 'deal with' for 'dispose of' greatly widens the ambit of s. 6(1). If 'dispose of' means 'deal with', it is submitted that the words are superfluous as they simply repeat the previous phrase 'to treat the thing as his own'. If the words are not superfluous they can only mean what the Court of Appeal in *Cahill* accepted they meant and, in line with precedent, the decision in *Cahill* should be followed.

(b) *Borrowing or lending* The second part of s. 6(1) simply expands on the first part; a borrowing or lending of P's property by D may amount to an intention to treat the thing as his own to dispose of regardless of P's rights if 'the borrowing or lending [of it] is for a period and in circumstances making it equivalent to an outright taking or disposal'. In *Lloyd* (see **12.2.2.1**), Lord Lane CJ stated (at p. 836) that this provision:

> is intended to make clear that a mere borrowing is never enough to constitute the necessary guilty mind unless the intention is to return the thing in such a changed state that it can truly be said that all its goodness or virtue has gone.

This was a statement of the **'essential quality principle'**. If D takes P's railway season ticket, intending to return it to him after it has expired, P will receive back a worthless piece of paper. Similarly if D borrows P's battery and uses it, only returning it to P when it is exhausted, the thing returned will be deprived of all virtue. If D returns the season ticket one day before the expiry date, or returns the battery with a little power remaining in it, the question will be whether this is equivalent to an outright taking. It could be argued that not all 'its goodness or virtue' has gone.

In **12.2.1.1.3** the question arose whether confidential information or trade secrets could constitute property. In *Oxford* v *Moss* (1978) 68 Cr App R 183, it was held that confidential information in a university examination paper was not 'property'. It was submitted that the secret quality of the information was a form of intangible property; by reading it D was assuming the right of an owner and permanently depriving the owner of the secrecy of the information. It is further submitted that a person borrowing a document containing confidential information so that he may copy it, or even simply to read it, could be held to intend to deprive the lender of it permanently; the document, when it is returned, has lost its virtue, namely its confidentiality, the very thing which gave it, or enhanced, its value. Thus it is submitted, even if confidential information is not to be regarded as a form of intangible property, D may be guilty of the theft of documents containing confidential information where he only borrows such documents.

12.2.2.1.2 *Section 6(2)*
Section 6(2) provides:

> Without prejudice to the generality of subsection (1) above, where a person, having possession or control (lawfully or not) of property belonging to another, parts with the property under a condition as to its return which he may not be able to perform, this (if done for purposes of his own and without the other's authority) amounts to treating the property as his own to dispose of regardless of the other's rights.

This section covers both the situation where D is the bailee of P's property or where D surreptitiously borrows P's property. In either case if D pledges the property as security for a loan, even though he intends to redeem it and return it to P, he will be deemed to intend to deprive P of the property permanently. It is obvious that at the time of pledging the property D cannot be certain that he will be able to redeem it. If D foresees the slightest possibility that he may not be able to perform the condition, he will fall within the section. It is only where D honestly believes that there is no possibility of him being unable to fulfil the condition that he will not be deemed to have had the necessary intent.

12.2.2.1.3 *Conditional intent*
Will a conditional intent suffice for theft? For example, D takes P's handbag intending to search through it and steal any money he may find; upon finding no money he replaces the handbag where he found it. In such a case D has no intention to deprive P of the handbag, and the property of which he seeks to deprive P does not exist so there is no appropriation of money. He is, however, guilty of attempted theft as a conditional intention suffices for attempt (see **8.4.2**).

12.2.2.2 **Dishonesty**
The final element of theft which must be proved is that at the time D appropriated property belonging to another intending permanently to deprive the other of it, he did so dishonestly. As the concept of appropriation has been stripped of all

pejorative connotations and is a neutral word (see the discussion of *Hinks*, **12.2.1.4.3**), this means that dishonesty has become the crucial concept in theft used to discriminate between those appropriations which may amount to theft and those which may not. This being the case, it might be considered important that there be a clear definition of dishonesty. However, there is **no such definition in the Theft Act. The leading authority is now the Supreme Court's decision** in *Ivey* v *Genting Casinos UK Ltd (t/a Crockfords Club)* [2017] UKSC 67, **which holds that whether D is dishonest is a question of fact for the jury or magistrates: once they have established what D's actual state of mind is, meaning his knowledge or belief as to the relevant facts, the question whether his conduct was honest or dishonest is to be determined by the fact-finder by applying the (objective) standards of ordinary decent people.** Arguably, the trust placed by the Supreme Court in the jury or magistrates to decide when conduct is dishonest, rather than providing a technical precise definition, means that the concept of dishonesty in English law continues to lack clarity. Rather than provide a definition, **s. 2 of the TA 1968 specifies three situations in which D's appropriation is not to be regarded as dishonest** (s. 2(1)) **and one situation in which it may be regarded as dishonest** (s. 2(2)). If D raises a defence which falls within s. 2(1) he will be entitled to an acquittal unless the prosecution disproves his alleged belief beyond reasonable doubt.

12.2.2.2.1 *Section 2*

Section 2 provides:

> (1) A person's appropriation of property belonging to another is not to be regarded as dishonest—
>
>   (a) if he appropriates the property in the belief that he has in law the right to deprive the other of it, on behalf of himself or of a third person; or
>   (b) if he appropriates the property in the belief that he would have the other's consent if the other knew of the appropriation and the circumstances of it; or
>   (c) (except where the property came to him as trustee or personal representative) if he appropriates the property in the belief that the person to whom the property belongs cannot be discovered by taking reasonable steps.
>
> (2) A person's appropriation of property belonging to another may be dishonest notwithstanding that he is willing to pay for the property.

(a) *Belief in a right to deprive* **If D believes he has a legal right to appropriate P's property he is not dishonest no matter how unreasonable his belief may be** (*Bernhard* [1938] 2 KB 264). If D believes the property is his own, there is no intention to deprive another of the property permanently. Section 2(1)(a), however, relates to mistakes as to the law. For example, if D sells and delivers goods to P and P fails to pay for them, D may wrongly believe he has the right in law to take possession of the goods. In such a case D may rely on s. 2(1)(a). If E, D's employee, is instructed to seize the goods from P for non-payment and believes that D has a legal right to them, he similarly may rely on s. 2(1)(a) if charged with theft. D's belief must be in his legal right to deprive; s. 2(1)(a) will not apply merely because D has an honest belief in his moral right to deprive (*Harris* v *Harrison* [1963] Crim LR 497).

(b) *Belief in the other's consent* D, who is hungry and has no money, enters P's house using a key P gave him to check on the property while P is on holiday. D takes food from P's cupboards believing P would have consented to him doing so had he known the circumstances. If such a belief is honestly held, D is not dishonest.

(c) *Belief that the owner cannot be found* Although s. 2(1)(c) does not refer to 'finding' property this is the situation which most clearly falls within this provision. Where D finds property and honestly believes that the owner cannot be discovered by taking reasonable steps, D's appropriation of the property will not be dishonest. In considering what steps would be reasonable regard would be paid to the nature of the property, whether there were any identification marks or distinguishing features, the nature and value of the property, and the place where it was found; but, it must be stressed, ultimately the question is what was D's belief. If D honestly believed there were no reasonable means of discovering the owner he will not be dishonest even if the reasonable person would have recognised an obvious and simple means of tracing the owner. If, after finding the property and concluding that the owner cannot be traced, D discovers who the owner is, or how he may be traced, any subsequent keeping or dealing with the property as owner by D would amount to theft (see s. 3(1), **12.2.1.4.4**).

(d) *Willingness to pay* Section 2(2) states that D's appropriation of property may be dishonest even though D is willing to pay for it. A wide variety of situations may arise, hence the provision is framed in permissive rather than mandatory terms. For example, P has a valuable painting which D covets but P refuses to sell to him. D removes the painting leaving a sum in excess of the value of the painting. In this case D's willingness to pay would have to be set in the context of P's clear unwillingness to sell and it is submitted that this should be regarded as dishonest.

In *Wheatley* v *Commissioner of Police of the British Virgin Isles* [2006] UKPC 24 the Privy Council held that although in most cases of theft there would be an original owner of money or goods who would be poorer because of the defendant's conduct, the prospect of loss was not determinative of the dishonesty necessary to establish the offence.

12.2.2.2.2 *Situations not covered by section 2*
The fact that D cannot rely on any of the provisions in s. 2(1) does not mean that D is necessarily dishonest; his case will be considered under the general test of dishonesty. As the Act only gives a partial definition one might have expected the courts to provide a general definition of this concept and then leave it to the jury in each case to determine whether the facts fall within this definition. The courts, however, have adopted the contrary approach, determining that what is 'dishonest' is not a question of law but a matter for the tribunal of fact. In *Ivey* v *Genting Casinos UK Ltd (t/a Crockfords Club)* [2017] UKSC 67, the Supreme Court held that the jury or magistrates must first decide what was D's actual state of mind as to knowledge of or belief in the relevant facts and then decide whether D was dishonest according to:

> the objective standards of ordinary decent people. There is no requirement that the defendant must appreciate that what he has done is, by those standards, dishonest. (at p. 74)

In most cases there will be no dispute regarding dishonesty; if D is shop-lifting, or robbing a bank, or breaking into and stealing from houses, it would be impossible to argue that this was not dishonest according to ordinary standards of reasonable honest people, or that D did not realise it was dishonest. There are, however, some situations which may give rise to difficulty. The three key cases are *Feely* (1973), *Ghosh* (1982), and *Ivey* (2017).

12.2.2.2.3 Feely *(1973)*

In *Feely* [1973] QB 530, the manager of a betting shop took £30 from his employer's safe, a practice which the employer had prohibited. When charged with theft he claimed he had only borrowed it and was going to replace an equivalent sum. His conviction was quashed as the trial judge had ruled that this did not amount to a defence. **The Court of Appeal held that the question of what was dishonest was for the jury to determine, applying the current standards of ordinary decent people.**

Where an employee borrows his employer's money an infinite variety of circumstances may arise: the employer may have expressly prohibited such a practice in all circumstances; the amount taken may be large or small; the period for which it is taken may vary; D's likelihood of paying it back may vary; D may or may not leave an 'IOU'; D may take the money because some unforeseen emergency has arisen or he may take it for some less creditable reason such as betting on a horse race. The approach of the Court of Appeal in *Feely* enabled one simple test to apply across the enormous range of situations in which theft, and other offences incorporating dishonesty, occur. It also entrusted juries (or magistrates in summary trials) to use their experience as ordinary people to decide whether the particular defendant deserved to have their conduct labelled as dishonest. In that respect, fact-finders were entrusted to do justice in the particular case. Jurors have to decide in their everyday lives what is dishonest and they can bring that understanding to bear on the present case.

However, entrusting fact-finders with the task of deciding whether conduct is dishonest is problematic. As the situations vary so may the conclusions of different juries in similar cases. Entrusting fact-finders with the responsibility for deciding what is dishonest rests on an assumption that there are common standards of honesty in our society and that juries and magistrates can be expected to reach consistent and just decisions. That assumption is perhaps a fiction that glosses over the wide variety of views that jury members in particular might have: jurors are drawn at random from the electoral register, the main qualification being that the juror is between 18 and 75 and has been ordinarily resident in the UK for at least five years since the age of 13 (Juries Act 1974, s. 1; see also ss 9–10 and sch. 1 concerning disqualifications from jury service). There may be different views amongst jurors depending on the juror's age, class, cultural background, and so on. Even judges have been known to differ greatly.

In *Sinclair v Neighbour* [1966] 2 QB 279, D removed money from his employer's till to bet on a horse race. The trial judge thought that this was reprehensible conduct but that it was not dishonest. In the Court of Appeal, Sachs LJ considered that the conduct was dishonest while Sellers LJ considered that views as to the honesty of the conduct might differ.

If judges, who arguably share the same or similar class, cultural, educational, and professional backgrounds cannot agree on what is dishonest, how can we hope for consistency from juries in an increasingly heterogeneous society? At least if judges make errors on questions of law these may be rectified on appeal and a body of precedent is thereby built up to guide future decisions. Jury decisions on questions of fact are not amenable to rectification nor do they provide any guide for the future. In the situation given earlier it is arguable that if D, when removing the money, did not believe that he would have had his employer's consent (s. 2(1)(b)) he should not be allowed by other means to raise a defence. It is arguable, therefore, that the decision in *Feely* promoted inconsistency.

In addition, Griew suggests that many ordinary people have committed minor acts of theft and fraud, such as taking stationery from work or inflating expenses claims. It is possible that jurors will demand of defendants higher standards than jurors themselves will abide by. Alternatively, those jurors might, by applying their own standards of honesty, acquit in cases where there have been infringements of property rights that should be criminalised rather than being deemed innocent acts by ordinary dishonest jurors (see E. Griew, 'Dishonesty: The Objections to *Feely* and *Ghosh*' [1985] Crim LR 341–54, 348).

12.2.2.2.4 *The* Ghosh *test for dishonesty*

Until the Supreme Court's judgment in *Ivey*, the leading case on the test for dishonesty was *Ghosh* [1982] QB 1053.

> G was a surgeon acting as a locum consultant at a hospital. It was alleged that he had falsely represented that he had carried out a surgical operation or that money was due to him or an anaesthetist for such an operation; in fact, the operation had been carried out by someone else, and/or under the National Health Service provisions. He was charged with four counts under the Theft Act 1968, including obtaining money by deception and attempting to procure the execution of a cheque by deception, offences that include dishonesty as an element. G argued that there was nothing dishonest about his conduct as the sums were owed to him for consultancy fees. The trial judge directed the jury on the meaning of dishonesty in accordance with *Feely*.
>
> In the Court of Appeal, Lord Lane CJ laid down a two-part test to be applied by juries, holding that dishonesty could not be established independently of the knowledge or belief of the defendant:

> If we are right that dishonesty is something in the mind of the accused . . . , then if the mind of the accused is honest, it cannot be deemed dishonest merely because members of the jury would have regarded it as dishonest to embark on that course of conduct. So we would reject the simple uncomplicated approach that the test is purely objective . . .
>
> **In determining whether the prosecution has proved that the defendant was acting dishonestly a jury must first of all decide whether according to the ordinary standards of reasonable honest people what was done was dishonest. If it was not dishonest by those standards, that is the end of the matter and the prosecution fails. If it was dishonest by those standards, then the jury must consider whether the defendant himself must have realised that what he was doing was by those standards dishonest.**[Emphasis added]

The Court of Appeal held that 'dishonestly' was not intended to characterise D's conduct but his state of mind which cannot be established independently of his knowledge and belief. The test must therefore include some reference to D's mental state, which the *Feely* test did not. Examining s. 2(1), the Court found that the matters covered related to the accused's belief which could only be established subjectively. It is important therefore to determine what his state of mind was, and for the jury then to determine if this is dishonest. Under s. 2(1), if D claims he believed he had a right to take the property, or that he believed the owner would have consented to his taking it, or that the owner could not reasonably have been found, the jury would find him not dishonest if he may have had that belief.

The second question in *Ghosh* only needed to be posed where there was some evidence to suggest that D believed that what he did was honest by ordinary people's standards (see *Roberts* (1987) 84 Cr App R 117; *Price* (1989) 90 Cr App R 409; *Squire* [1990] Crim LR 341).

One of the problems with *Ghosh* was that it raised the questions, why should being out of touch with normal standards of honesty generally held in the community avail D, and why should D's characterisation of his state of mind be relevant? The Court of Appeal did not address these issues. Indeed the creation of the second question appears to have been based on a misconception. The Court provided the following example (at p. 1063):

> [A] man . . . comes from a country where public transport is free. On his first day here he travels on a bus. He gets off without paying. He never had any intention of paying. His mind is clearly honest; but his conduct, judged objectively by what he has done, is dishonest. It seems to us that in using the word 'dishonestly' in the Theft Act 1968, Parliament cannot have intended to catch dishonest conduct in that sense, that is to say conduct to which no moral obloquy could possibly attach.

If one ignores the fact that there is no offence under the Theft Acts of which such a visitor could be convicted, this example is riven with misconceptions. How can D's conduct, judged objectively by what he has done, be dishonest if one of the objective facts is that he did not believe a fare had to be paid? If there was any offence with which D could be charged and the jury had to consider whether he was dishonest, the first question would be whether what he had done was dishonest by the standards of ordinary honest people. The ordinary honest person would have to be placed in the situation as D believed it to be. To frame the test thus exposes the ludicrous nature of the example. This was a case of simple mistake of fact, not one of conflicting beliefs as to what is or is not honest. Because the Court of Appeal wrongly adjudged their alien objectively dishonest they then had to create the second question to render him honest. The second question, thus, appears to have been an unnecessary construct. No moral obloquy ever attached to his conduct because he acted in furtherance of a mistake as to facts; his mistake did not relate to his assessment of what ordinary people would regard as dishonest.

The first limb of the *Ghosh* test was considered by the Court of Appeal in *Hayes* [2015] EWCA Crim 1944.

> In *Hayes*, D, a trader employed by a large bank, was charged with conspiracy to defraud on the basis that he had conspired with others to manipulate the LIBOR lending rate. (LIBOR is the London Interbank Offered Rate which is the average of the rates London lending banks would charge each other on commercial loans in the London market.) Manipulating the market was designed to produce large profits for the conspirators' banks and, in turn, large bonuses for themselves. At his trial it was argued that the judge should modify the first (objective) limb of the *Ghosh* direction to invite the jury to

consider not just the standards of honest and reasonable people generally, but the standards set by the particular market or business in which D was operating as his behaviour was typical of those operating in that market. D's submission was rejected by the trial judge and, in turn, by the Court of Appeal, Lord Thomas CJ stating (at para 32):

> The history of the markets have shown that, from time to time, markets adopt patterns of behaviour which are dishonest by the standards of honest and reasonable people; in such cases, the market has simply abandoned ordinary standards of honesty. . . . [T]o depart from the view that standards of honesty are determined by the standards of ordinary reasonable and honest people is not only unsupported by authority, but would undermine the maintenance of ordinary standards of honesty and integrity that are essential to the conduct of business and markets.

D, of course, was able to provide evidence regarding the morality of the market to support a contention under the second limb of *Ghosh* (below) that he had so imbibed the market ethos that he did not realise that what he was doing was dishonest by the standards of reasonable honest people. The jury, clearly, had not believed him.

The two-part *Ghosh* test has been subject to repeated criticism, particularly as the test was not clear or easy for jurors to understand and its potential to lead to acquittals in cases where D has a warped sense of what is acceptable. In 2017 the Supreme Court revisited the test for dishonesty.

12.2.2.2.5 *The Supreme Court's decision in* Ivey *(2017)*
In *Ivey*, the Supreme Court ruled that the second limb of the *Ghosh* test did not correctly represent the law and directions based on it should no longer be given. *Ivey* is a civil case and its pronouncements on dishonesty are *obiter*, but the Divisional Court in *DPP v Patterson* [2017] EWHC Admin 2820 (*per* President QBD) held that given the terms of the unanimous and unequivocal observations of the Supreme Court that *Ghosh* does not correctly represent the law, it is difficult to imagine the Court of Appeal preferring *Ghosh* to *Ivey*.

> In *Ivey*, a professional gambler appealed against a decision that the respondent casino had been entitled to refuse to pay him winnings of £7.7 million on the basis that he had cheated. Ivey played a card game of chance, Punto Banco, and used the technique of 'edge-sorting', which relied on noting tiny physical differences in the cards' edges. By claiming to be superstitious, he persuaded the croupier to use the same pack of cards and to turn 'lucky' cards around, enabling him to use the edge-sorting technique. That increased his odds of winning. The gambler believed edge-sorting was an honest technique. He sued for his winnings. Ivey argued that he had not cheated; cheating inevitably involves dishonesty and as he did not consider what he did to be cheating, the second limb of the *Ghosh* test had not been made out. The judge held that although the gambler was genuinely convinced that what he had done was not cheating, he had in fact and in law cheated under s. 42 of the Gambling Act 2005, thus breaching the implied term against cheating in the contract he had with the casino.

In a unanimous judgment, the Supreme Court held that whether a person's behaviour amounts to cheating is a jury question to be determined objectively; the claimant's actions in taking steps to fix the deck in a game which depended on random delivery of unknown cards was, inevitably, cheating, and the judge had been correct to rule that Ivey was not entitled to the money. The Court held that it was not necessary to add to the value judgement whether conduct was cheating a similar value judgement as to whether it was also dishonest. However, the Court undertook a detailed review of *Ghosh*, using the opportunity provided by the case to disapprove the two-part test that the Court of Appeal in *Ghosh* had set out. Lord Hughes stated that:

> The test of dishonesty is as set out by Lord Nicholls in *Royal Brunei Airlines Sdn Bhd* v *Tan* [(1995) 2 AC 378] and by Lord Hoffmann in [*Barlow Clowes International Ltd* v *Eurotrust International Ltd* [2006] 1 WLR 1476]. When dishonesty is in question the fact-finding tribunal must first ascertain (subjectively) the actual state of the individual's knowledge or belief as to the facts. The reasonableness or otherwise of his belief is a matter of evidence (often in practice determinative) going to whether he held the belief, but it is not an additional requirement that his belief must be reasonable; the question is whether it is genuinely held. When once his actual state of mind as to knowledge or belief as to facts is established, the question whether his conduct was honest or dishonest is to be determined by the fact-finder by applying the (objective) standards of ordinary decent people. There is no requirement that the defendant must appreciate that what he has done is, by those standards, dishonest.

Lord Hughes JSC set out six problems with *Ghosh*. First, it has the unintended effect that the more warped the defendant's standards of honesty are, the less likely it is that he will be convicted of dishonest behaviour. **If D was totally out of touch with ordinary community standards, the *Ghosh* direction dictated that he be acquitted.** For example, if D, a latter-day Robin Hood who is incensed by the plight of the homeless, decides to steal from the rich who can easily afford it and give the money to charities for the homeless, and he honestly believes that no ordinary reasonable person would regard his charitable activities as dishonest, he was entitled to be acquitted (although strangely, Lord Lane CJ thought that the *Ghosh* test would not avail such a person). In such a case there is no claim by D of a belief that he had a legal right to take the property or that he believed the owners would have consented to him taking their property; on the contrary he is well aware of the fact that he is depriving them of what is rightfully theirs. Lord Hughes JSC stated (at para. 59):

> [I]t is not in the least unusual for the accused not to share the standards which ordinary honest people set for society as a whole . . . There is no reason why the law should excuse those who make a mistake about what contemporary standards of honesty are, whether in the context of insurance claims, high finance, market manipulation or tax evasion. The law does not, in principle, excuse those whose standards are criminal by the benchmarks set by society, nor ought it to do so. On the contrary, it is an important, even crucial, function of the criminal law to determine what is criminal and what is not; its purpose is to set the standards of behaviour which are acceptable.

Secondly, the second-limb of the *Ghosh* test was based on the premise that it was necessary in order to give proper effect to the principle that dishonesty, and especially criminal responsibility for it, must depend on the actual state of mind of the defendant. The second-limb is not necessary to preserve this principle. In order to decide whether the person who comes from a country where public transport is free is dishonest when he travels on a bus here without paying, it is necessary to understand his own actual state of belief about how public transport works. As he genuinely believes that public transport is free, there is nothing objectively dishonest about his not paying for the bus. As Lord Hughes put it:

> '[D]ishonestly' . . . is indeed intended to characterise what the defendant did, but in characterising it one must first ascertain his actual state of mind as to the facts in which he did it. It was not correct to postulate that the conventional objective test of dishonesty involves judging only the actions and not the state of knowledge or belief as to the facts in which they were performed. What is objectively judged is the standard of behaviour, given any known actual state of mind of the actor as to the facts.

In one sense of course, following *Ivey* there is still a two-part test for juries and magistrates to apply, but the two tests are now clearer and more apposite. The jury or magistrates must first understand what D knew or believed about the relevant facts. Only by taking that first step can the fact-finder then make the necessary judgement about whether D was dishonest by the standards of ordinary people.

 Example

D takes a loaf of bread from a shop without paying and is charged with theft. The jury or magistrates will have to understand what the person was thinking at the time in order to evaluate whether D's actions were dishonest by the standards of ordinary decent people. The fact-finders' evaluation will likely differ in the following circumstances, even though the act of appropriation is the same:

a) D was absent-minded and had not appreciated that he had put bread in his shopping bag;
b) D was fully aware of his failure to pay and had no reason other than greed for taking the bread;
c) D was fully aware of his failure to pay but was desperate and hungry;
d) D was fully aware of his failure to pay but wanted to get revenge on the supermarket, which had sacked him the week before.

Ivey makes a difference in cases where D argues that he honestly believed that other people would consider his actions to be honest. Following *Ivey*, there is no requirement that D must appreciate that what he has done is dishonest by the standards of ordinary people. The fact-finders will convict if they think that D was dishonest by those standards. Under *Ghosh*, the fact-finders' task was more confusing, having to assess D's understanding of those standards and acquitting him if D did not realise that what he was doing was dishonest by those standards.

Thirdly, Lord Hughes stated that jurors and others often find the *Ghosh* test puzzling and difficult to apply. He did not cite any empirical evidence to support this claim. It is possible that jurors found it difficult but that is hard to assess given the prohibition on doing research into juror deliberations (Juries Act 1974).

Fourthly, *Ghosh* created a divergence between the test for dishonesty in criminal proceedings and the test of the same concept in the context of civil actions. Lord Hughes stated (at para. 63):

> there can be no logical or principled basis for the meaning of dishonesty (as distinct from the standards of proof by which it must be established) to differ according to whether it arises in a civil action or a criminal prosecution . . . It would be an affront to the law if its meaning differed according to the kind of proceedings in which it arose.

Fifthly, *Ghosh* represented a significant departure from the law before the Theft Act 1968, when there is no indication that such a change had been intended. In its eighth report, the Criminal Law Revision Committee had recommended that 'dishonestly' would be readily understandable by lay fact-finders and the public generally, and there was no suggestion in its report that whether a person was dishonest should depend on his own view of his behaviour.

Finally *Ghosh* was not compelled by authority. As Lord Hughes put it (at para, 57):

> Although the pre-*Ghosh* cases were in a state of some entanglement, the better view is that the preponderance of authority favoured the simpler rule that, once the defendant's state of knowledge and belief has been established, whether that state of mind was dishonest or not is to be determined by the application of the standards of the ordinary honest person, represented in a criminal case by the collective judgment of jurors or magistrates.

Since *Feely*, there was only one pre-*Ghosh* case which raised the relevance of the defendant's own view as to the honesty of what he had done, *R* v *Gilks*, the facts of which the Supreme Court regarded as 'a powerful demonstration of the perils of the second leg of the Ghosh test' (*per* Lord Hughes at para. 73).

After 35 years, the *Ghosh* test is no more. Following *DPP* v *Hutchinson* [1990] 2 AC 783, it seems clear that *Ivey* has settled the legal test for 'dishonesty' that magistrates and juries must apply. *Ivey* simplifies the law, lays down an appropriate means by which to incorporate and reflect D's mental state in the fact-finders' evaluation of his conduct, promotes consistency between civil and criminal law, and puts the criminal law back on the correct path in line with authorities and the intentions of those who drafted the Theft Act 1968.

Inevitably, however, the debate continues as to what the test for dishonesty should be and whether *Ivey* has in fact adopted the correct approach. Determining whether D is dishonest remains a question of fact for the jury or magistrates, which means the law remains unclear and liable to result in inconsistent verdicts. Is a modern-day Robin Hood dishonest? While a person's deeply held belief in the honesty of their actions, and their belief in other people's belief in the honesty of their actions, does not protect them from being found guilty, ultimately the question is for the magistrates or jury to decide, applying their understanding of the standards of ordinary, decent people. This is problematic if we expect the law clearly to state what is acceptable behaviour rather than leaving undefined such vitally important terms that apply across a range of offences. Different jurors are likely in some cases to diverge in their views of what is dishonest. Similarly, if magistrates are drawn from a homogenous group, in summary trials the concept of dishonesty may come to have meanings that reflect the values and beliefs of that group. The deeper issue here is whether we can place faith and trust in the jury and magistrates appropriately to ensure that only behaviour to which moral obliquy should attach is labelled as criminal.

One solution to the problem of a vague test that leaves the fact-finders to interpret and define the term is for Parliament to provide a legal definition of dishonesty. There is little prospect of this happening, but one possible approach was provided by Professor Smith, *The Law of Theft* (8th edn, 1997). He suggested (at para. 2–124) that a better approach would be to reinterpret 'dishonestly' to mean 'knowing that the appropriation will or may be detrimental to the interests of the owner in a significant practical way'. This would remove the risk of inconsistency between juries and would also negate the defence which the latter-day Robin Hood might raise. Regardless of his or the jury's assessment of what may or may not be regarded as dishonest by ordinary people, he would know that taking another's property may be detrimental to the owner's interests. Another approach would be to adopt the definition of 'dishonestly' in s. 217 of New Zealand's Crimes Act 1961: 'dishonestly, in relation to an act or omission, means done or omitted without a belief that there was express or implied consent to, or authority for, the act or omission from a person entitled to give such consent or authority.'

12.3 Robbery

Section 8(1) of the TA 1968 provides:

> A person is guilty of robbery if he steals, and immediately before or at the time of doing so, and in order to do so, he uses force on any person or puts or seeks to put any person in fear of being then and there subjected to force.

Both robbery and assault with intent to rob are punishable with life imprisonment (s. 8(2)).

Actus reus	Mens rea
(a) stealing property,	(a) dishonesty,
(b) belonging to another, and	(b) intention to appropriate the property
(c) immediately before or at the time of stealing, and in order to do so	(c) intention to permanently deprive the other of the property, and
(i) using force on any person, or	(d) intention or recklessness as to the use of force.
(ii) putting or seeking to put any person in fear of being then and there subjected to force.	

Assault with intent to rob involves all the above except that D does not succeed in appropriating the property as where, for example, D punches V demanding his mobile phone and V retaliates punching D, who runs off.

12.3.1 The need to prove theft

As robbery is an aggravated form of theft the prosecution must prove theft. For the offence of assault with intent to rob it is necessary to prove an intent to steal. If D has not committed a theft—for example, because he believes he has a right to the property—he cannot be convicted of robbery even though he used force to deprive P of the property and even though he knew he was not entitled to use force (see *Robinson* [1977] Crim LR 173). Similarly, if D uses force to deprive P of his property temporarily, thus lacking the intention to deprive P of his property permanently, there is no theft. In either case, of course, D could be charged with the appropriate offence against the person arising from his threat or use of force.

Robbery is complete when the theft is complete—that is, when D has appropriated the property (see **12.2.1.4**). It can apply where the enterprise may be unsuccessful. In *Corcoran* v *Anderton* (1980) 71 Cr App R 104, the Divisional Court found there to be a robbery where D tugged a handbag from a woman's grasp, although he then dropped it and made off without it. The Court said that taking hold of the bag could be an appropriation. But if D does not have the intent permanently to deprive at the time force is used in order to take V's property, even though he may form that intent subsequently and his actions then may amount to appropriation and the completed offence of theft, he has not committed robbery (see *Vinall* [2011] EWCA Crim 6252).

12.3.2 The need to prove force or threat of force

12.3.2.1 Force on a person

In *Dawson and James* (1976) 64 Cr App R 170, D and E jostled P so that he lost his balance which enabled F to take his wallet. The Court of Appeal held that 'force' was an ordinary word and that the trial judge was correct in leaving it to the jury to determine whether jostling P constituted force. This approach was confirmed in *Clouden* [1987] Crim LR 56.

Prior to the TA 1968, robbery required that the force be used to overpower P or to make him give up his property; it was not sufficient if the force was applied to the property to wrench it from P's possession. In *Clouden*, however, the Court of Appeal held that the Act had removed all such distinctions. In this case D approached P from behind and wrenched her shopping basket from her grasp. In using force on the property, force was also applied to P and the judge was correct in leaving the question to the jury whether D had applied force to a person in order to steal. By contrast, in *DPP* v *RP* [2012] EWHC 1657 (Admin), where D had snatched a cigarette from V's hand and was convicted of robbery by the youth court, the Administrative Court allowed the appeal (substituting a conviction for theft) as there had been no direct contact between D and V and it could not be said that the minimal amount of force required to remove the cigarette from between V's fingers sufficed to amount to the use of force on V.

12.3.2.2 Threat of force

It is sufficient that D 'puts or seeks to put any person in fear of being then and there subjected to force'. A threat of future force will not suffice (but this may constitute blackmail; see **14.4**). While most cases will involve awareness on P's part of D's threat to use force, the provision also covers the situation where D seeks to put P in fear of being subjected to force but P remains oblivious to the threat. Thus D would be guilty of robbery where he waved a knife at P and issued verbal threats in order to steal P's property but P, unknown to D, was deaf and blind. If P is aware of D's threat of force (whether express or implicit) but is not put in fear thereby, D will nonetheless be liable to conviction as it is D's intention that matters (see *B and R* v *DPP* [2007] EWHC 739 (Admin)).

12.3.2.3 **On any person**

In most cases, the force, or threat of force, will be used against P, the person in possession or control of the property. D will be liable for robbery, however, where the force, or threat, is used or issued against another in order to steal. For example, D breaks into P's house and is disturbed by the cat-sitter, Q. D knocks Q unconscious and proceeds to steal P's computer. Similarly, if D holds a knife to Q's throat threatening to cut it if P does not hand over the contents of his safe, this would fall within s. 8(1).

12.3.2.4 **Immediately before or at the time of the stealing**

In the previous example of the attack on the cat-sitter, D used force immediately before he appropriated the computer. The phrase, however, may be interpreted expansively to cover a wider range of situations. It is submitted that it would cover the case where D uses force on Q at the house to acquire the keys to P's shop or factory from which D then steals property.

If Q had disturbed D as he was leaving P's study with a computer and D had knocked Q unconscious, the question would arise whether the force was used at the time of the stealing. Appropriation was complete when D laid hands on the computer. For these purposes, however, appropriation is treated as a continuing act (cf. rape, **11.2.1.1**). This problem arose in *Hale* (1978) 68 Cr App R 415. D and E entered P's house and, having taken her jewellery box, tied her up. It was submitted that the theft was complete when they laid hands on the jewellery box and thus they did not use force at the time of stealing. Eveleigh LJ stated (at p. 418):

> To say that the conduct is over and done with as soon as he lays hands upon the property, or when he first manifests an intention to deal with it as his, is contrary to common-sense and to the natural meaning of words . . . the act of appropriation does not suddenly cease. It is a continuous act and it is a matter for the jury to decide whether or not the act of appropriation has finished. Moreover, it is quite clear that the intention to deprive the owner permanently . . . was a continuing one at all times . . . . As a matter of common sense the appellant was in the course of committing theft; he was stealing.

This case rectifies a flaw in the statute so that the whole course of conduct is regarded as stealing rather than the act which satisfies the minimum requirement for appropriation. A line must be drawn somewhere, however, and it would appear that it would be drawn at the point where D ceases to be engaged in removing the property from P (see also *Atakpu and Abrahams* [1994] Crim LR 693). For example, if D had reached the street with the jewellery box before being confronted by P, it is submitted that the stealing would have been completed prior to this point.

12.3.2.5 In order to steal

The force or threat of force must be used or issued in order to steal. For example, if D uses force to rape P and then, having committed the rape, makes off with P's handbag which she had dropped, this would not be robbery as the force was used in order to rape rather than to steal. The force, or threat of it, need not be used only to remove the property from P; it is sufficient if it is used to enable D to commit the theft more safely—for example, where he knocks unconscious a night-watchman before stealing from a factory, in case the watchman might discover him and raise the alarm.

12.4 Taking a conveyance without authority

Where D takes a vehicle it is often difficult to prove an intention of permanently depriving the owner of it; D may take a car—for example, to joyride or to use on a criminal enterprise or to use for his own convenience. Whatever the reason, such behaviour may create a social nuisance, a public danger, and personal inconvenience for the person temporarily deprived of his vehicle. Section 12 covers such taking of motor vehicles and also covers the taking of other conveyances such as boats or bicycles.

Section 12(1) provides:

> [A] person shall be guilty of an offence if, without having the consent of the owner or other lawful authority, he takes any conveyance for his own or another's use or, knowing that any conveyance has been taken without such authority, drives it or allows himself to be carried in or on it.

Actus reus	Mens rea
Either,	For (a), intention to take the conveyance.
(a) without the consent of the owner or other lawful authority D takes a conveyance for his own or another's use, or	For (b), knowledge that the conveyance had been taken without consent or lawful authority.
(b) D drives or allows himself to be carried in or on a conveyance taken without the consent of the owner or other lawful authority.	In either case there is no offence if D acted in the belief he had lawful authority to do so, or that he would have had the owner's consent if he had known what D was doing and the circumstances in which he was doing it (see s. 12(6)).

This section creates two summary offences punishable with a fine not exceeding level five on the standard scale or up to six months' imprisonment or both (s. 12(2) as amended by s. 37(1) of the CJA 1988). On a trial on indictment for theft, a jury may return a verdict of guilty of the s. 12(1) offence if they are not satisfied that the accused is guilty of theft but it is proved that he committed this offence.

12.4.1 Definitional elements

A 'conveyance' is something 'constructed or adapted for the carriage of a person or persons whether by land, water, or air' excluding a vehicle where the person controlling it is not carried in or on it (see s. 12(7)(a)). Implicit in the definition of the offence in s. 12(1) is the requirement that it be a conveyance which can be driven. Thus the vehicle, vessel, or aircraft must be one which carries its 'driver' on it. This is a broad definition and covers cars, lorries, motor-cycles, boats, and aircraft. The definition is wide enough to cover a 'soap-box', a wheelchair, a rowing-boat, or a hang-glider but it would not cover roller skates or skis (*McDonagh* [1974] QB 448).

A person 'takes' a conveyance when he (1) assumes possession or control of it and (2) intentionally causes it to move or be moved (see *Bogacki* [1973] QB 832). There is no need for D to ride on or 'drive' the conveyance; thus the offence was committed where D took a boat, loaded it on a trailer, and drove away (*Pearce* [1973] Crim LR 321).

The taking of a conveyance must be purposive; that is, D must take it for his own or another's use as a conveyance. Thus the conveyance must either be used as such while it is being taken, as where D, or another, rides in or on it as it moves or is being moved (see *Bow* (1976) 64 Cr App R 54), or D must take it intending it to be used in future as a conveyance (see *Pearce*, earlier; *Marchant and McCallister* (1984) 80 Cr App R 361). Pushing a car down a hill as a prank, or to remove an obstruction it is causing, would not amount to using it as a conveyance.

The taking of the vehicle must be without the consent of the owner or other lawful authority. The latter phrase will cover, for example, cases where the police or local authority have a statutory power to remove vehicles. It is no answer to a charge under s. 12(1) that the owner would have given consent had he been asked (*Ambler* [1979] RTR 217). Consent obtained by intimidation or force is not true consent (see *Hogdon* [1962] Crim LR 563).

Section 12(6) provides:

> A person does not commit an offence under this section by anything done in the belief that he has lawful authority to do it or that he would have the owner's consent if the owner knew of his doing it and the circumstances of it.

This provision is similar to s. 2(1)(a) and (b) relating to dishonesty for the purposes of theft. D must adduce evidence of his belief but, having done so, the burden is on the prosecution to disprove that belief beyond reasonable doubt (*McMinn* v *McMinn and another* [2006] 3 All ER 87, QBD).

As it would be unlikely in most cases that the employer would have insurance cover for non-employees to drive his vehicles, the prospects of a defendant being able to raise a reasonable doubt that he did not know or believe his employer would not permit the driving would appear to be very slim.

Where a conveyance has been taken by another without lawful authority (this covers theft or the s. 12 offence; see *Tolley* v *Giddings* [1964] 2 QB 354), and D knows this (wilful blindness will probably suffice), he will be guilty of the second offence created by s. 12(1) if he drives the conveyance or allows himself to be carried in or on it. If D aids, abets, counsels, or procures the taking of the vehicle by E he will be liable as an accessory to E's offence of taking. This second offence created by s. 12(1) extends the ambit of secondary liability. If E takes a car and then meets D and offers him a ride, D would commit the s. 12(1) offence if, knowing that E had taken the car without lawful authority, he accepted the offer and was carried as a passenger in the vehicle. He would not, however, be guilty of aiding and abetting the original taking by E, as this offence was complete prior to D being offered a ride.

12.4.2 Aggravated vehicle-taking

In many cases of joyriding the vehicle involved ends up being damaged. If several individuals were involved it might prove difficult to establish which of them caused the damage. To counter this and other problems the Aggravated Vehicle-Taking Act was passed in 1992. This inserts a new s. 12A into the Theft Act 1968 which provides:

(1) Subject to subsection (3) below, a person is guilty of aggravated taking of a vehicle if—

    (a) he commits an offence under section 12(1) above (in this section referred to as the 'basic offence') in relation to a mechanically propelled vehicle; and

    (b) it is proved that, at any time after the vehicle was unlawfully taken (whether by him or another) and before it was recovered, the vehicle was driven, or injury or damage was caused, in one or more of the circumstances set out in paragraphs (a) to (d) of subsection (2) below.

(2) The circumstances referred to in subsection 1(b) above are—

    (a) that the vehicle was driven dangerously on a road or other public place;

    (b) that, owing to the driving of the vehicle, an accident occurred by which injury was caused to any person;

    (c) that, owing to the driving of the vehicle, an accident occurred by which damage was caused to any property, other than the vehicle;

    (d) that damage was caused to the vehicle.

(3) A person is not guilty of an offence under this section if he proves that, as regards any such proven driving, injury or damage as is referred to in subsection (1)(b) above, either—

    (a) the driving, accident or damage referred to in subsection (2) above occurred before he committed the basic offence; or

    (b) he was neither in nor on nor in the immediate vicinity of the vehicle when that driving, accident or damage occurred . . .

The maximum penalty on conviction on indictment is two years' imprisonment but if it is proved that, in circumstances falling within sub-s. (2)(b) cited earlier, the accident caused the death of the person concerned, the maximum is 14 years (increased from five years by s. 285 of the Criminal Justice Act 2003).

Upon proof of the basic offence in relation to a mechanically propelled vehicle under s. 12(1) of the TA 1968, guilt of the aggravated offence will be established on proof of one of the three circumstances specified in s. 12A(2). Proof of a certain degree of fault is required in respect of driving dangerously in that it must be proved that 'it would be obvious to a competent and careful driver that driving in that way would be dangerous' (s. 2A(1)(b) of the Road Traffic Act 1988). As regards the conditions in (b), (c), and (d) the normal rules of causation apply so that D will not be convicted of the aggravated offence where the harm or damage occurs owing to no fault on his part. This is confirmed by the decision of the Supreme Court in *Taylor* [2016] UKSC 5.

D, whilst driving a tipper truck on a country lane without the consent of the owner, was involved in a collision with a scooter rider, V, resulting in the death of V. It was accepted that D's driving was not at fault. He was, however, charged with the s. 12A(1) offence on the basis that 'owing to the driving of the vehicle, an accident occurred by which injury was caused' to V (s.12A(2)(b)). The trial judge applied the reasoning of *Hughes* [2013] UKSC 56 (see **2.6.3.1**) and ruled that fault was required to be proved. The Crown appealed and the Court of Appeal allowed the appeal relying on *R v Marsh* [1997] 1 Cr App R 67, in which it was held that no element of fault was required in the offence of aggravated vehicle-taking. The Court certified a question for consideration of the Supreme Court which allowed the appeal holding that fault had to be proved, Lord Sumption stating (at paras 22–23):

> [T]he essential point made in *Hughes* is common to both offences. The phrase 'caused the death of another person by driving a motor vehicle on a road' (section 3ZB of the Road Traffic Act 1988) and the phrase 'owing to the driving of the vehicle, an accident occurred by which injury was caused to any person' (section 12A(2)(b) of the Theft Act 1968) both posit a direct causal connection between the driving and the injury. If the requirement of causation is satisfied by the mere fact that the taking of the vehicle accounted for its being in the place where the accident occurred, then all of the anomalous consequences which this court regarded as extraordinary in *Hughes* apply equally to the offence under section 12A. It means that the defendant is liable to be convicted and sentenced to a long period of imprisonment on account of an aggravating factor for which he bears no responsibility.
>
> . . . The Crown's argument effectively invites the court to treat the section as imposing strict liability for the aggravating factors which differentiate this offence from the basic offence under section 12, in circumstances where that course is neither necessary nor war-ranted by the language of the Act.

The Supreme Court overruled the earlier decision of the Court of Appeal in *Marsh* [1997] 1 Cr App R 67, which had imposed liability where the accident which had occurred involved no fault on the part of D, Lord Sumption explaining the require-ments of the offence (at para. 32):

> There must be 'at least some act or omission in the control of the car, which involves some element of fault, whether amounting to careless/inconsiderate driving or not, and which contributes in some more than minimal way to the [accident]'.

 The law in context

'Freeganism' and theft

'Freeganism' is both an ideology and type of behaviour that calls into question the boundaries of property offences. It involves 'urban foraging' or 'dumpster diving' to recover waste food or salvageable items from commercial or private bins, skips, and rubbish heaps. Freeganism is part of a broader anti-consumerist social movement that campaigns against excessive waste. Are 'freegans' guilty of theft (for a detailed analysis see S. Thomas, 'Do Freegans Commit Theft?' (2010) Legal Studies 98–125)?

Given the breadth of its meaning, there is no doubt that taking food or other items (which are 'property' within s. 4 of the TA 1968) from dustbins and skips amounts to 'appropriation' (the courts having interpreted that term very broadly) and that the 'freegan' intends perma-nently to deprive, given that the food will be eaten or redistributed and salvageable items kept and re-used (Thomas, p. 104). However, the prosecution must prove that the property belonged to another at the time of appropriation and that the appropriation was dishonest.

Thomas doubts that freegans are thieves, given that the goods they appropriate have been abandoned and therefore do not belong to anyone (p. 198). As Thomas acknowledges though, the case law on abandonment is 'too opaque to allow for a clear assessment of the criminal status of a freegan bin-diver' (p. 114). We saw earlier that courts are reluctant to find

➡

→

that property has been abandoned so as to exculpate the appropriator (*Williams v Phillips* (1957) 41 Cr App R 5 and *R (Ricketts) v Basildon Magistrates' Court* [2010] EWHC 2358 (Admin)).

The key issue is whether a freegan is dishonest and the moral ambiguity surrounding this type of behaviour is reflected in English law's lack of precision on this point. Thomas argues that freegans will best defend themselves by arguing that their behaviour is not dishonest (p. 124). It is difficult to see how any of the statutory provisions in s. 2 of the TA 1968 about when a person is *not* dishonest could be utilised by a freegan, although Thomas suggests that he might be able to argue that he honestly believed that he has 'in law the right to deprive the other of it' (s. 2(1)(a)). However, that honest belief must be of a *legal* right to deprive and not simply a *moral* right (such as a belief that the practice is acceptable on environmental grounds).

Applying the *Ivey* test for dishonesty, there seems to be significant scope for appealing to jurors' sympathy, as there is in criminal damage cases where environmental protesters have argued they had 'lawful excuse' for damaging property (see **Chapter 15**). Are 'freegans' dishonest according to the current standards of ordinary decent people? One can imagine the range of arguments that could be deployed by someone charged with theft of food from a skip in the grounds of a supermarket or from a domestic waste bin left out on a pavement to be collected by the local authority. The jury would hear of anti-consumerist or anti-capitalist values of the freeganism movement, challenging the morality of society's excessive waste (see Thomas, p. 99).

Whether these arguments would persuade a jury is, of course, impossible to predict, and it is this very uncertainty in the law that has led many scholars to criticise English law's approach to defining dishonesty (whether the *Feely* and *Ivey* objective tests or the two-part *Ghosh* test) as vague, productive of inconsistencies between similar cases, and based on the false assumption of community norms. As Griew noted, that assumption glosses over differences of age, class, and cultural background that undermine the myth of a generally shared sense of the boundary between honesty and dishonesty (E. Griew, 'Dishonesty: The Objections to *Feely* and *Ghosh*' [1985] Crim LR 341–54, 344). There is unlikely to be consensus amongst jurors about a freegan's objective dishonesty, given the range of popular perspectives on social and environmental issues such as climate change, recycling, and waste management.

Under the second limb of the *Ghosh* test for dishonesty, if the jury were not convinced that the freegan's behaviour was honest according to their standards, they had to consider whether the defendant must have realised that what he was doing was by those standards dishonest. Following the Supreme Court's disapproval of *Ghosh* in *Ivey*, now a jury or magistrates will first have to ascertain the actual state of the freegan's knowledge or belief as to the facts, then decide whether the conduct was honest or dishonest by applying the objective standards of ordinary decent people. This too produces no clarity for the freegan on trial. No doubt the freegan will argue that he believed that what he was doing was not dishonest and that others would feel that his behaviour was morally acceptable. *Ivey* perhaps provides no clearer answer than *Ghosh* on the question of the freegan's guilt, other than to say that there is no requirement that D appreciates that what he was doing was dishonest by the standards of ordinary people. The freegan is likely also to argue that he honestly believed that the property had been abandoned. As the Court of Appeal held in *Wood (Peter)* [2002] EWCA Crim 832, if the defendant had an honest belief that the property was abandoned then the jury should acquit (Thomas, p. 124). Yet everything hinges on the personal views of the magistrates or those who sit on the jury.

There are two procedural issues to note concerning the potential prosecution of freegans for theft. First, the uncertainty in the law as to whether a freegan is dishonest makes difficult the CPS's decision to prosecute. Is it in the public interest to prosecute someone who has taken food that was destined to be destroyed or otherwise thrown away and is there sufficient

→

→

evidence of *dishonesty* for there to be a realistic prospect of conviction? Neither question is easily answered in cases of freeganism.

The second point is that the uncertainty in the law of theft means the CPS might have to use other, more obscure laws that do not include dishonesty within their substantive definitions. In 2014 three 'freegans' were charged in relation to taking tomatoes, mushrooms, cheese, and cakes from the dustbins behind a branch of a high-street food retailer (*The Guardian*, 'Three Charged with Stealing Food from Skip behind Iceland Supermarket' 28 January 2014). Stating there was 'significant public interest' in prosecution, the CPS charged them under the Vagrancy Act 1824 rather than the TA 1968. Section 4 of the Vagrancy Act 1824 states: 'every person being found in or upon any dwelling house, warehouse, coach-house, stable or out-house, or in any enclosed yard, garden or area, for any unlawful purpose . . . shall be deemed a rogue and vagabond' and liable to up to three months' imprisonment. Arguably this would have had the advantage for the prosecution of the freegans being tried by the magistrates and not by a potentially sympathetic jury, given that s. 4 is a summary-only offence. However, the prosecutions were eventually discontinued after intervention by the supermarket's management and an internal review of the CPS decision to prosecute (*The Guardian*, 'Prosecutors Drop Case against Men Caught Taking Food from Iceland Bins' 29 January 2014). The law remains unclear as to whether a freegan is a thief (or a rogue and a vagabond).

 Key Points

- Theft is defined in s. 1 of the Theft Act 1968: a person commits theft if he dishonestly appropriates property belonging to another with the intention permanently to deprive the other of it:

  - 'Property' is defined broadly in s. 4.

  - 'Belonging to another' is defined in s. 5. Within the definition, property is regarded as belonging to another when the person has possession or control of it.

  - Appropriation is defined in s. 3 to mean any assumption by a person of the rights of an owner. It is a value-neutral word. The House of Lords has considered the meaning of appropriation on several occasions, holding that it is sufficient to prove that D assumed any of the rights of the owner (*Morris*), that there may be an appropriation even when V has consented to D taking the property (*Lawrence* and *Gomez*) and when D has acquired indefeasible title to the property, such as through a valid gift (*Hinks*).

  - 'Intention permanently to deprive' is defined in s. 6 and is usually a simple question for the jury or magistrates.

  - Dishonesty is not defined in statute, although s. 2 does specify three situations in which D is not dishonest.

  - The leading case on the meaning of dishonesty is *Ivey* v *Genting Casinos UK Ltd* (2017). The Supreme Court held that *Ghosh* is no longer good law.

  - The test for dishonesty is: once the jury or magistrates have established what D's actual state of mind was, the question whether his conduct was honest or dishonest is to be determined by applying the standards of ordinary decent people.

- A person is guilty of robbery under s. 8 of the Theft Act 1968 if 'he steals, and immediately before or at the time of doing so, and in order to do so, he uses force on any person or puts or seeks to put any person in fear of there and then being subjected to force':

  - The prosecution must prove theft and the use or threat of force.

  - The force or threat of force must be used or issued in order to steal.

FURTHER READING

A. Ashworth, 'Robbery Re-assessed' [2002] Crim LR 851.

A. L. Bogg and J. Stanton-Ife, 'Theft as Exploitation' (2003) 23 LS 402.

C. Clarkson, 'Theft and Fair Labelling' (1993) 56 MLR 554.

S. Cooper and M. Allen, 'Appropriation after *Gomez*' (1993) 57 JCL 186.

N. Dent and A. Kervick, ' *Ghosh*: A Change in Direction?' [2016] Crim LR 553.

D. W. Elliott, 'Dishonesty in Theft: A Dispensable Concept' [1982] Crim LR 395.

S. Gardner, 'Is Theft a Rip-off?' (1990) 10 OJLS 441.

S. Gardner, 'Property and Theft' [1998] Crim LR 35.

E. Griew, 'Dishonesty: The Objections to *Feely* and *Ghosh*' [1985] Crim LR 341.

A. Halpin, 'The Test for Dishonesty' [1996] Crim LR 283.

R. G. Hammond, 'Theft of Information' (1984) 100 LQR 252.

K. Laird, case comment on *Ivey* v *Genting Casinos UK Ltd* [2018] Crim LR 395.

E. Melissaris, 'The Concept of Appropriation and the Offence of Theft' (2007) 70 MLR 581.

S. Parsons, 'Dishonest Appropriation after *Gomez* and *Hinks*' (2004) 68 JCL 520.

S. Shute, 'Appropriation and the Law of Theft' [2002] Crim LR 450.

S. Shute and J. Horder, 'Thieving and Deceiving: What is the Difference?' (1993) 56 MLR 548.

A. T. H. Smith, 'Shoplifting and the Theft Acts' [1981] Crim LR 586.

J. N. Spencer, 'The Aggravated Vehicle-Taking Act 1992' [1992] Crim LR 699.

13

....

Fraud

13.1 **Fraud Act 2006**

13.1.1 **Introduction**

The Theft Acts 1968 and 1978 created a range of offences which contained the common element that the proscribed consequence is brought about as a result of D's dishonest deception. These offences, which were result crimes, covered obtaining property, services, or a pecuniary advantage by deception and evading liability by deception.

In 2002 the Law Commission in its Report, *Fraud* (Law Com No. 276) recommended the creation of a unitary offence of fraud which could be committed in three different ways. The aim was to simplify and rationalise the law with the creation of this **conduct crime**, designed to avoid the complexity of the existing law and its difficulty in being adapted to ever-changing technology which was being exploited to deceive people to hand over their property or financial information. The offence of fraud was to be supplemented by a new offence of obtaining services dishonestly to replace the offence of obtaining services by deception in s. 15 of the Theft Act 1968 and cover both the prevalent behaviour of deceiving a machine, which the existing offence did not cover, and other forms of dishonest conduct where a service was obtained without anyone being deceived.

In 2004 the Government issued a Consultation Paper, *Fraud Law Reform: Consultation on Proposals for Legislation* (2004), followed by its response to the consultation in *Fraud Law Reform: Government Response to Consultations* (2005). The Fraud Act 2006 (hereafter referred to as the FA 2006) largely adopted the Law Commission's recommendations with the exception that it did not abolish the common law offence of conspiracy to defraud because of concerns expressed in the consultation as to limitations on the scope of statutory conspiracy which meant that certain types of secondary participation in fraud might only be caught by the common law offence. The FA 2006 repealed the deception offences in ss 15, 15A, 16, and 20(2) of the Theft Act (TA) 1968 and ss 1 and 2 of the TA 1978. The FA 2006 also creates ancillary offences of possession of articles for use in frauds (s. 6), making or supplying articles for use in frauds (s. 7), participating in fraudulent business carried on by sole trader (s. 9), and participating in fraudulent business carried on by a company (s. 10). The FA 2006 also creates a new offence of obtaining services dishonestly; this is a result crime like the offence of obtaining services by deception which it replaces but it is not limited by the concept of a deception.

13.1.2 Fraud

Section 1(1) of the FA 2006 creates the general offence of fraud which is committed where a person breaches ss 2, 3, or 4 which provide for different ways of committing the offence. These modes of committing the offence of fraud are considered in **13.2**, **13.3**, and **13.4**; ancillary offences are considered in **13.5**; the separate offence of obtaining services dishonestly is considered in **13.6**. On summary conviction the maximum sentence is six months' imprisonment or a fine up to the maximum or both. Following conviction on indictment the maximum sentence is 10 years' imprisonment or a fine or both for fraud and five years' imprisonment or a fine or both for the ancillary offences and obtaining services dishonestly.

In the text which follows reference will be made to cases under the Theft Acts as these are still relevant when construing some of the terminology and considering some of the concepts in the FA 2006.

13.2 Fraud by false representation

Section 2(1) provides that a person is in breach of s. 2 if he:

> (a) dishonestly makes a false representation, and
> (b) intends, by making the representation—
> > (i) to make a gain for himself or another, or
> > (ii) to cause loss to another or to expose another to a risk of loss.

Actus reus	Mens rea

D makes a false representation.	(a) dishonestly, and
	(b) intends by making it—
	   (i) to make a gain for himself or another, or
	   (ii) to cause loss to another or to expose another to a risk of loss.

13.2.1 *Actus reus*

 Key Point

Fraud is a conduct crime which means that there is no need to prove that any particular result ensued. The *actus reus* consists of the making of a false representation. There is no requirement that anyone should actually believe or act upon the representation.

The offence of fraud is complete upon a false representation being made with the requisite *mens rea*. Thus, for example, D would be guilty of fraud where he writes a letter to V, his elderly aunt, falsely stating that he is penniless and asking her for a loan, even though the letter is lost in the post and never delivered to V. There is no requirement to prove that D obtained anything as a result of the false representation, although this may be D's purpose when making the false representation. This offence, consequently, has the potential to criminalise many commercial practices which exploit the gullibility of consumers. In effect misleading or exaggerated advertising claims, which clearly have a financial motive in boosting sales, have the potential to found convictions for fraud where everything would hinge on a jury's assessment of dishonesty. Much, ultimately, will depend on the discretion of prosecutors in determining which cases to prosecute. Undoubtedly they will place considerable store on the question whether or not a gain or loss has arisen even though this need not be proved as an element of the *actus reus*.

13.2.1.1 What is a representation?

Section 2(3) of the FA 2006 defines 'representation' as meaning:

> any representation as to fact or law, including a representation as to the state of mind of—
>
> (a) the person making the representation, or
>
> (b) any other person.

A **representation may arise from words or conduct and**, as s. 2(4) makes clear, **may be express or implied.** For example, if D offers to sell a painting (even though he does not own it), he is impliedly representing that he has a right to do so.

What s. 2(3) does not define, of course, is what amounts to a 'representation' albeit that this word is in everyday usage and 'misrepresentation' is a familiar civil law concept. **The provision, rather, seeks to define what the representation must be about, namely any fact, law, or state of mind.**

A representation as to law would cover, for example, the situation where D misrepresents to P the legal effect of a document P is executing. Representations, however, generally relate to facts whether past or present. A straightforward representation of fact would be, for example, 'this bracelet is solid 24 carat gold' when D knows it is only gold-plated. Such representations of fact are unlikely to be problematic. A problem arises, however, in relation to statements of opinion. It is the practice of those selling goods or supplying services to make extravagant claims about those goods or services. How many times do secondhand car salesmen seek to induce sales by declaring, 'this car is a good little runner' or 'a genuine bargain'? While this is a statement of opinion, it is also an implied representation of fact, namely that it is D's opinion honestly held. If D knows that the car in question has several mechanical defects which cause it to stop regularly or break down and which would necessitate a considerable expenditure of money to rectify, it would not be his honest opinion that the car is either a 'good little runner' or 'a genuine bargain'. Thus, if D's opinion is not honestly held, his statement, although appearing to be one of opinion, is, in reality, a false representation of fact because he does not hold the opinion expressed.

A statement of present intention is a representation as to state of mind and is also a statement of fact. For example, if D asks P for money to fund his university course, his intention being to use the money to bet on a horse, he would be falsely representing his state of mind (i.e. his intention). A statement of intention may be implied from D's conduct as in *DPP* v *Ray* [1974] AC 370.

> D ordered a meal in a restaurant intending to pay for it. After eating the meal he decided not to pay and sat at his table until the waiter left the room at which point he departed without paying. The House of Lords held that there was a deception. Lord MacDermott concluded that the initial representation that he would pay, implied from ordering a meal, was a continuing one which remained live and operative and became false upon his change of mind. Lords Morris and Pearson considered that by remaining at the table after he had changed his mind he continued to make from moment to moment, but now falsely, the representation that he intended to pay.

The principle in *Ray* has wide application.

 Example

> P telephones D, in response to D's advertisement that he has a cooker for sale, and D represents that it is in good working order. The representation D made was true when he made it, but D subsequently discovers that the oven is not working. When P inspects the cooker, which is disconnected, and agrees to buy it, D may be guilty of fraud by false representation either on the basis that the original representation was a continuing one which remained live and operative until the contract was concluded, or that, while negotiations were being conducted, D continued to make from moment to moment, but now falsely, the representation that the cooker was in good working order.

In effect, in situations such as this D is under a duty to correct P's misapprehension as soon as the situation has changed such that the earlier representation is falsified. *Ray* was applied in *Rai* [2000] 1 Cr App R 242.

> D applied to the council for a grant to provide a bathroom downstairs in his house for the use of his mother who was infirm. The grant was approved but two days later his mother died. D did not inform the council and the building work went ahead. D was convicted of obtaining services by deception contrary to s. 1(1) of the Theft Act 1978. The Court of Appeal held that D's acquiescence in letting the work be done amounted to deception by conduct as the local authority continued to believe the property would be occupied by his mother.

D's offence now would be fraud by false representation. Similarly, if D asks P for a loan he impliedly represents that he will repay it by using the term 'loan' rather than 'gift'. If it is not his present intention to repay he will be guilty of fraud by false representation. If D's intention at the time of his request was to repay the loan, but having received the loan, D decides not to repay it, he will not be guilty of fraud by false representation as his representation was not false at the time of making it and the representation is not of a continuing nature. Of course, if D makes some further false representation to P to seek to discourage P from enforcing the debt, he would at that point be liable for fraud.

Generally, where contracts for services or for the sale of property are involved, the provider of the service or vendor of the property may charge whatever he likes. An excessive quotation, however, may constitute a false representation where a situation of mutual trust exists between D and his customer or, perhaps, where D knows that his customer is naive or inexperienced and is relying on D's expertise and honesty.

> In *Silverman* [1987] Crim LR 574, D, a builder, had done work for two elderly sisters for many years charging them grossly excessive prices. In this situation of mutual trust, the implied representation was that his charge was fair and proper, which D knew to be untrue. The Court of Appeal found that 'his silence on any matter other than the sums to be charged was as eloquent as if he had said that he was going to make no more than a modest profit'. (See further *Jones, The Times*, 15 February 1993.)

The use of cheques, cheque cards, and credit cards has presented the courts with particular problems. Where D draws a cheque in favour of P—for example, in payment for property supplied by P—the act of drawing the cheque involves certain implied representations. First, D is representing that he has an account with the bank upon which the cheque is drawn; if D has stolen the cheque his conduct in drawing it in favour of P will involve a false representation. In many cases, however, the problem is not that D does not have an account, but rather relates to the state of the account he does have. Secondly, where D draws a cheque in favour of P he is representing that the present facts are such that, in the ordinary course of events, the cheque will be honoured by the bank when presented (see *Metropolitan Police Commissioner* v *Charles* [1977] AC 177). This representation will be true provided either (i) D believes that there are currently sufficient funds in the account to meet the cheque; (ii) he intends to pay in sufficient funds; (iii) he believes a third party will pay in sufficient funds (e.g. his employer may pay his salary directly into his account); or (iv) in the case of a post-dated cheque, he believes that by the time the date for presenting the cheque arrives his account will contain sufficient funds to meet the cheque (see *Gilmartin* [1983] QB 953). If D does not have such a present intention or belief, his drawing of the cheque amounts to a representation of a present fact (his intention or belief) which is untrue.

 Question

What happens if D presents a cheque guarantee card along with the cheque as this ensures that V, in accepting the cheque, will not suffer any loss?

Where a cheque is supported by a cheque card, the situation is not quite so straightforward. Provided the conditions on a cheque card are observed, the bank is legally bound to honour the cheque even though D's authority to use the card may have been withdrawn or D has neither sufficient funds in his account nor sufficient overdraft facility to cover the cheque. When a person presents a cheque card he makes a contract on behalf of the bank with the payee to the effect that the bank will honour the cheque.

> In *Charles* (earlier), D obtained gambling chips at a casino in return for 25 cheques for £30 each, all supported by a cheque card. D knew his account was overdrawn and that he had no authority to overdraw and thus no authority to draw further cheques.

The conditions on the card, however, had been observed so D could not be guilty of a deception in representing that each cheque would be honoured by his bank. In upholding D's conviction for obtaining a pecuniary advantage by deception contrary to s. 16(1), the House of Lords held, however, that D's presentation of the cheque card involved the implied representation that he had the authority of the bank to use the card so as to create a contractual relationship between the bank and the payee.

In a prosecution for fraud by false representation, the same implied representation could be relied upon.

The principle in *Charles* was extended to credit cards in *Lambie* [1982] AC 449. Suppliers of goods and services accept credit cards in pursuance of agreements they have entered into with the credit card companies under which the companies agree to honour credit card transactions provided the supplier complies with certain conditions relating to the validity of the card.

> In *Lambie* D's credit card limit was £200. Knowing she had exceeded this limit and that authority to use the card had been withdrawn, D purchased goods from a shop using the card. The shop complied with the relevant conditions so that a valid transaction was concluded which the credit card company was bound to honour. The House of Lords held that in presenting the credit card D was representing (falsely) that she had the authority of the credit card company to use the card.

The Explanatory Notes to the FA 2006 provide a contemporary example of false representation, 'phishing' (para. 16):

> where a person disseminates an email to large groups of people falsely representing that the email has been sent by a legitimate financial institution. The email prompts the reader to provide information such as credit card and bank account numbers so that the 'phisher' can gain access to others' assets.

13.2.1.2 When is a representation false?

Section 2(2) provides that **a representation is false if (a) it is untrue or misleading and (b) D knows that it is or might be so**. This provision contains an element of the *actus reus* in (a) and an element of the *mens rea* in (b). The representation must be either untrue as a matter of fact or misleading. In their 2005 response to the consultations, the Home Office provided the following explanation of 'misleading' as meaning '**less than wholly true and capable of an interpretation to the detriment of the victim**' (para. 19).

 Example

D drafts an email with the heading 'Sponsored Swim to Support Cancer Research' and sends it to family, friends, and neighbours. D carries out the swim, collects the sponsorship money from those who responded to his email, donates 5 per cent to Cancer Research and keeps the rest. While D has carried out the swim and money he has collected has been donated to support Cancer Research, it is likely that a jury would consider his email to be misleading.

13.2.1.3 When is a representation made?

Ordinarily a representation will be made when D communicates it to the person he is seeking to deceive. The Act, however, does not impose any requirement that the representation be heard or received by another. Thus if D speaks to V and makes a false representation with the necessary *mens rea*, the offence is complete even though V is deaf and did not hear D's representation. Likewise, if the representation is made in a letter, the offence will be complete on D posting the letter even if it never reaches the addressee.

Section 2(5) makes express provision for the situation where the representation D makes is made to a machine and no human agent is involved in receiving or perceiving it.

Section 2(5) provides:

> For the purposes of this section a representation may be regarded as made if it (or anything implying it) is submitted in any form to any system or device designed to receive, convey or respond to communications (with or without human intervention).

The Explanatory Notes to the FA 2006 (at para. 17) express the main purpose of this provision to be to cover the situation where D makes a representation to a machine and a response can be produced without any need for human involvement. An obvious example would be where D acquires V's cashcard and PIN and uses them at a cash machine (ATM) to obtain money. The cash machine responds to the insertion of the card, accompanied by the correct PIN, and responds to the request for cash without any human agent playing a part in the process before the cash is dispensed. Section 2(5) is not confined to situations involving modern technology. As the Explanatory Notes make clear it covers the situation where 'a false statement is submitted to a system for dealing with communications but is not in fact communicated to a human being (e.g. postal or messenger systems)'. Similarly, a message left on an answerphone or voicemail system would be covered.

13.2.2 *Mens rea*

There are three elements to the *mens rea* of this offence, namely knowledge, intention, and dishonesty. They will be considered in turn.

13.2.2.1 Knowing the representation is or might be false

As stated earlier, liability can only arise where the representation made is actually false in the sense of being untrue or misleading. For D to be found guilty it must be proved that he either knew that the representation he made was untrue or misleading or he knew that it might be so (s. 2(2)(b) of the FA 2006). What is required is either actual knowledge or a recognition that the representation might be untrue or misleading and a decision to make it nonetheless. While the latter state of mind is akin to recklessness, it is not entirely the same as recklessness; recklessness involves taking a recognised risk where it is unreasonable in all the circumstances to do so. There is no element of unreasonableness for the jury to consider under s. 2(2)(b) but, of course, the element of dishonesty will be crucial in the ultimate assessment of guilt. In *Augunas* [2013] EWCA Crim

2046, the Court of Appeal quashed the appellant's conviction because the trial judge had told the jury that they could convict if they considered that D ought to have known that his representation was false or misleading. McCombe LJ stated:

> What is required is that the accused person knows that the representation is, or might be, misleading. It is not enough that a reasonable person might have known this; what matters is the accused person's actual knowledge. In our judgment, it not good enough for the prosecutor to satisfy the jury that the accused ought to have appreciated that the representation made by him was or might be untrue or misleading, nor is it enough that the circumstances must have given rise to a reasonable suspicion that the representation was, or might be, untrue or misleading. Of course, if an accused person wilfully shuts his eyes to the obvious doubts as to the genuineness of the misrepresentation that he is making, then he knows that it might be untrue or misleading and he would be guilty of the offence.

In the Consultation concern was raised over art sales as there is always a risk that a painting either may be incorrectly attributed to an artist or be a fake. The Government's *Response to Consultations* states (at para. 18):

> An example was given of a seller of a Renoir painting which turns out to be incorrectly attributed. It was argued that, given the inevitable uncertainties in such areas, the seller would only be able to protect himself from a fraud charge if he had said 'I honestly believe this to be a Renoir' rather than 'This is a painting by Renoir'. We do not agree as the 'dishonesty' requirement will assist in drawing the line in marginal cases. But if the consequence were that sellers became more cautious in their statements this does not seem an undesirable result.

13.2.2.2 Intending to make a gain or cause a loss

The offence is one of ulterior intent. Section 2(1) provides that a person is in breach of the section if he:

> (b) intends, by making the representation—
>   (i) to make a gain for himself or another, or
>   (ii) to cause loss to another or to expose another to a risk of loss.

 Key Point

As the *actus reus* is complete upon a false representation being made, there is no need that anyone suffer any loss, or be exposed to the risk of loss, or that D, or another, actually make any gain. What is crucial is that D's intent in making the false representation must be that of making a gain or causing a loss or exposing another to the risk of loss.

This provision is similar to blackmail under s. 21 of the TA 1968 where an unwarranted demand with menaces is made 'with a view to gain for himself or another or with intent to cause loss to another'. The term 'with a view to' is difficult to distinguish from intent. Blackmail lacks, however, the alternative element of exposing another to a risk of loss.

This provision was introduced at the recommendation of the Law Commission to cover situations where V's economic interests are imperilled such as occurred in *Adams* v *The Queen* [1995] 1 WLR 52, *Allsop* (1976) 64 Cr App R 29, and *Wai Yu-tsang* v *R* [1991] 4 All ER 664 (see **8.3.4.1.1**). These cases involved conspiracy to defraud but the same activities carried out by an individual would now fall under the offence of fraud. The provision is included largely out of an abundance of caution as the purpose of most schemes promoted by false representations is to make a gain for someone. It will be rare, indeed, for a scheme to involve only the risk of loss without there also being an intent for someone to make a gain.

Section 5 defines 'gain and loss'.

 Example

D falsely represents to V that he has inside information and that a particular horse is a certain winner and encourages V to bet £100 on it. If the horse wins, V will suffer no loss—indeed, he will make a considerable gain. D's intent, however, is to expose V to the risk of loss. Whether or not he is acting dishonestly will be a matter for the jury.

Even in this example, there is a gain to someone if the bet fails, namely the bookmaker, and the concept of oblique intent could readily be applied to satisfy the requirement of an intention to make a gain for another as, while that may not be D's direct intent, it is an inevitable consequence if the horse loses. Indeed, as a gain need only be temporary, there is a gain to the bookmaker upon receipt of the bet.

s. 5(2) 'Gain' and 'loss'—

  (a) extend only to gain or loss in money or other property;

  (b) include any such gain or loss whether temporary or permanent;

and 'property' means any property whether real or personal (including things in action and other intangible property).

This definition is consistent with that of 'property' in s. 4(1) of the TA 1968 (see **12.2.1.1**).

The gain or loss must be in money or other property.

In *Gilbert* [2012] EWCA Crim 2392, D used a false representation in order to open a bank account. D's conviction for fraud by false representation was quashed on appeal, however, as the bank account itself was not 'money or other property'. While D might have used the account in the future to transact business and make a financial gain from such activity, the link between any such gain and the false representation was too tenuous to support a conviction.

> s. 5(3) 'Gain' includes a gain by keeping what one has, as well as a gain by getting what one does not have.
>
> s. 5(4) 'Loss' includes a loss by not getting what one might get, as well as a loss by parting with what one has.

'Gain' and 'loss' are defined consistently with s. 34(2)(a) of the TA 1968 (see **14.4.4**). If D uses false representations with the intention of obtaining from V what V already owes him (and thus D is only seeking to acquire that to which he has a lawful claim), this may nevertheless fall within s. 5 of the FA 2006. In *Lawrence and Pomroy* (1971) 57 Cr App R 64, the Court of Appeal assumed that such would be the case in a blackmail case (see **14.4.2**).

> In *Parkes* [1973] Crim LR 358 (Sheffield Crown Court), D was charged with blackmail having demanded with menaces money owed to him by V. It was submitted that to demand what is lawfully owing to you was not a demand 'with a view to gain'. Judge Dean QC ruled that by demanding money lawfully owing to him D did have a view to gain as 'gain' included 'getting what one has not'. By intending to obtain hard cash as opposed to a mere right of action in respect of the debt, D was getting more than he already had.

13.2.2.3 Dishonesty

This is a crucial element in the offence. Section 2(1) provides that a person only commits the offence of fraud by false representation where he 'dishonestly makes a false representation'. Both the Law Commission and the Home Office considered that the *Ghosh* test applies, that is first whether D's conduct would be regarded as dishonest by the ordinary standards of reasonable and honest people, and secondly, whether D was aware that his conduct would be so regarded (see **12.2.2.2** noting that s. 2 of the TA 1968 does not apply to fraud offences). However, following the Supreme Court's ruling in *Ivey* v *Genting Casinos UK Ltd* [2017] UKSC 67 and the Divisional Court's in *DPP* v *Patterson* [2017] EWHC 2820 (Admin) stating that it is difficult to imagine the Court of Appeal preferring *Ghosh* to *Ivey* in future, the test for dishonesty for fraud has been amended. The fact-finding tribunal has first to ascertain the actual state of the individual's knowledge or belief as to the facts, then the question whether the conduct was honest or dishonest is to be determined by applying the objective standards of ordinary decent people (see **12.2.2.2**).

13.3 Fraud by failing to disclose information

Section 3 of the FA 2006 provides:

> A person is in breach of this section if he—
> (a) dishonestly fails to disclose to another person information which he is under a legal duty to disclose, and
> (b) intends, by failing to disclose the information—
>   (i) to make a gain for himself or another, or
>   (ii) to cause loss to another or to expose another to a risk of loss.

Actus reus	Mens rea

D fails to disclose to another person information which he is under a legal duty to disclose.	(a) dishonestly, and
	(b) intends by the failure—
	    (i) to make a gain for himself or another, or
	    (ii) to cause loss to another or to expose another to a risk of loss.

The Law Commission recommended in its Report, *Fraud* (Law Com No. 276, paras 7.22–7.34) a wider offence which would have incorporated situations falling short of a legal duty of disclosure where there was a moral duty to do so because V trusted D to make disclosure of information and it was reasonable to expect him to do so. The Law Commission provided the following example (at para. 7.33):

> For example, a dealer buying an antique is guilty of fraudulent nondisclosure if she knows that the seller is trusting her to disclose any marked discrepancy between the price offered and the true value of the item, *and* it is reasonable to expect her to do so. This is a question of degree. If the dealer knows that she can resell the item for £10,000, but does not disclose this and offers only £2,000, it would be open to a jury to conclude that her failure to disclose the true value was unreasonable. It would be otherwise if she did not expect to be able to resell the item for more than, say, £4,000, because it is not reasonable to expect a dealer to disclose the full extent of the reasonable profit she hopes to make, and such a mark-up would be within the bands of what is reasonable. In such a case we would expect the court to direct an acquittal, on the basis that no reasonable jury could be sure that it was reasonable to expect the defendant to disclose the information in question.

There would be a large number of imponderables in this situation which a jury would be left to determine before convicting the antique dealer. The Law Commission identified these (para. 7.34):

> Whether the defendant is trusted to make disclosure, and if so whether a failure to disclose the information in question is unreasonable, will depend on a variety of factors— for example, whether the defendant is believed by the other to have special expertise, and if so whether the defendant has induced the other to believe this; whether the other has such expertise; the value of the transaction, from the other's point of view; whether the other is in receipt of legal, financial or other advice; and so on. A trial judge would of course remind a jury of any such factor that may have particular relevance to the facts of the case.

The Government in its response to the consultation concluded that this proposal would create an undesirably wide offence with the potential for conflict between the civil law and criminal law as it would become criminal to fail to provide information which D was not under any civil law duty to provide. Such a conflict would mirror that which already exists in theft following the decision in *Hinks* (see **12.2.1.4.3**). In extreme cases, in any event, it may be possible to charge fraud by false representation where D's conduct involves an implied representation (see *Silverman*, **13.2.1.1**). In this case, however, a crucial factor was the course of previous dealing which had built up an expectation on the part of V that D would quote a fair price for any work done.

13.3.1 *Actus reus*

The *actus reus* comprises a failure to disclose to another information which D is under a legal duty to disclose. The mischief which is targeted is that of V acting, or omitting to act, to his economic detriment in reliance upon his trusting D to disclose to him information relevant to his decision and D failing to make such disclosure. The Law Commission provided the following explanation which is reproduced in the Explanatory Notes to the FA 2006 (para. 18):

> 7.28 . . . Such a duty may derive from statute (such as the provisions governing company prospectuses), from the fact that the transaction in question is one of the utmost good faith (such as a contract of insurance), from the express or implied terms of a contract, from the custom of a particular trade or market, or from the existence of a fiduciary relationship between the parties (such as that of agent and principal).
>
> 7.29 For this purpose there is a legal duty to disclose information not only if the defendant's failure to disclose it gives the victim a cause of action for damages, but also if the law gives the victim a right to set aside any change in his or her legal position to which he or she may consent as a result of the non-disclosure. For example, a person in a fiduciary position has a duty to disclose material information when entering into a contract with his or her beneficiary, in the sense that a failure to make such disclosure will entitle the beneficiary to rescind the contract and to reclaim any property transferred under it.

The Explanatory Notes give the following examples (at para. 19):

> For example, the failure of a solicitor to share vital information with a client within the context of their work relationship, in order to perpetrate a fraud upon that client, would be covered by this section. Similarly, an offence could be committed under this section if a person intentionally failed to disclose information relating to his heart condition when making an application for life insurance.

> In *Firth* (1990) 91 Cr App R 217, D, a consultant obstetrician, referred private patients to an NHS hospital for treatment, omitting to declare that they were private patients. D was convicted of obtaining an exemption from liability to make payment contrary to s. 2(1)(c) of the TA 1978. The Court of Appeal affirmed the conviction as D was under a duty to give the relevant information to the hospital. By deliberately and dishonestly refraining from so doing, with the result that no charge was levied on himself or his patients, he had obtained the exemption by deception.

The relevant offence now would be fraud under s. 3 by failing to disclose information. It is arguable that D's act of sending the patients to an NHS hospital would also amount to an implied false representation that they were NHS patients bringing D also within the offence of fraud by false representation.

In an era where inflated claims within, and omissions from, CVs have become almost *de rigueur*, *Razoq* [2012] EWCA Crim 674 is a timely reminder that such actions may amount to crimes.

> D, a doctor suspended from practising, applied for, and obtained, several locum positions failing to disclose his suspension, and falsely claiming qualifications and experience he did not have. He was convicted of seven offences involving breaches of ss 2 and 3. As regards the s. 3 offences, as the contractual documents relating to each position required disclosure, his failure to disclose his suspension breached an express legal duty arising under contract.

Even if the contracts had not contained such express terms, it would have been open to the jury to convict if satisfied that the legal duty arose (1) as an implied term of the contract and the conditions under which the doctor was registered with the General Medical Council, or (2) because the contracts into which he entered were contracts of utmost good faith.

13.3.2 *Mens rea*

The *mens rea* for this offence is (1) an intention to make a gain or cause a loss (or expose to the risk of loss) as for fraud by false representation, and (2) dishonesty. There is no requirement that D should know that he is under, or might be under, a legal duty to disclose information. D's ignorance of such a legal duty, however, will be highly relevant to the question whether or not he was dishonest.

13.4 **Fraud by abuse of position**

Section 4 of the FA 2006 provides:

> (1) A person is in breach of this section if he—
>   (a) occupies a position in which he is expected to safeguard, or not to act against, the financial interests of another person,
>   (b) dishonestly abuses that position, and
>   (c) intends, by means of the abuse of that position—
>   (i) to make a gain for himself or another, or
>   (ii) to cause loss to another or to expose another to a risk of loss.
> (2) A person may be regarded as having abused his position even though his conduct consisted of an omission rather than an act.

Actus reus	Mens rea
D, while occupying a position in which he is:	(a) dishonestly, and
• expected to safeguard, or	(b) intends by means of the abuse of position—
• not act against,	(i) to make a gain for himself or another, or
the financial interests of another person, by act or omission abuses that position.	(ii) to cause loss to another or to expose another to a risk of loss.

This provision aims to deal with the mischief where V has voluntarily placed D in a privileged position in relation to V's financial interests such that D is able to act in relation to those interests without reference to V. The Law Commission provided (at para. 7.36) the example of an 'employee who, without the knowledge of his employer, misuses his or her position to make a personal profit at the employer's expense'. For example, the cinema employees who lent films temporarily to S so that he could make copies of them to sell would now be guilty of the s. 4 offence (see *Scott v Metropolitan Police Commissioner* [1975] AC 819, **8.3.4.1.1**). In such a situation of trust D will be expected to safeguard V's financial interests or not act against them. The Law Commission explained its thinking (at paras 7.37–7.38):

> Such an expectation to safeguard or power to damage may arise, for example, because the defendant is given authority to exercise a discretion on the victim's behalf, or is given access to the victim's assets, premises, equipment or customers. In these cases the defendant does not need to enlist the victim's *further* co-operation in order to secure the desired result, because the necessary co-operation has been given in advance.
>
> The necessary relationship will be present between trustee and beneficiary, director and company, professional person and client, agent and principal, employee and employer, or between partners. It may arise otherwise, for example within a family, or in the context of voluntary work, or in any context where the parties are not at arm's length. In nearly all cases where it arises, it will be recognised by the civil law as importing fiduciary duties, and any relationship that is so recognised will suffice. We see no reason, however, why the existence of such duties should be essential. This does not of course mean that it would be entirely a matter for the fact-finders whether the necessary relationship exists. The question whether the particular facts alleged can properly be described as giving rise to that relationship will be an issue capable of being ruled upon by the judge and, if the case goes to the jury, of being the subject of directions.

13.4.1 *Actus reus*

The offence may be committed both by act or omission. The question whether or not D is in the necessary position in relation to V and his financial interests is initially one for the judge who will determine whether the relationship is capable of falling within the section, and then it is for the jury to determine whether or not it does. The Explanatory Notes to the FA 2006 provide the following examples (at paras 22 and 23):

> An employee of a software company who uses his position to clone software products with the intention of selling the products on would commit an offence under this section.
>
> Another example covered by this section is where a person who is employed to care for an elderly or disabled person has access to that person's bank account and abuses his position by transferring funds to invest in a high-risk business venture of his own.

In the first example, if D went ahead with his scheme he would hold the profits on constructive trust for his employer, but there is some doubt whether or not he could be convicted of theft of those profits (see *AG's Reference (No. 1 of 1985)* [1986] QB 491). The care assistant, however, could be convicted of theft of V's credit balance (cf. *Williams (Roy)* [2001] 1 Cr App R 362 at **12.2.1.1.3**). The advantage of the fraud offence, of course, is that it may be charged when D first acts to abuse his position before any loss might be suffered by V. In *Doukas* [1978] 1 WLR 372, D, a hotel waiter, was found in possession of bottles of wine which he intended to substitute for his employer's bottles when a customer ordered wine. He would then make out a separate bill and pocket the money paid by the customer. D would now be guilty of fraud by abuse of position.

The Explanatory Notes provide the following example of a commission of this offence arising from an omission (at para. 21):

> [A]n employee who fails to take up the chance of a crucial contract in order that an associate or rival company can take it up instead at the expense of the employer, commits an offence under this section.

In *Valujevs and Mezals* [2014] EWCA Crim 2888, the Court of Appeal allowed the prosecution's appeal against the trial judge's ruling of no case to answer in a case involving unlicensed gangmasters who had abused their position by exploiting migrant workers, making unwarranted deductions from their wages, charging them excessive rental payments and imposing unwarranted fines on them. Fulford LJ stated that it is clear from the wording of s. 4 that Parliament did not intend to restrict the section's operation to those situations in which D owes a fiduciary duty to the alleged victim:

> In our view, at the very least, it is open to the jury on the evidence to decide that these defendants had gone beyond merely supplying workers and instead they had assumed control of and/or responsibility for collecting the wages of the workers or they controlled the amounts that the workers would be allowed to retain at the moment the wages were handed over. On either basis, the prosecution are able to contend that the defendants had taken on the obligation of paying the wages of the workers, and it is inherent in that commitment that the wages received by the workers will not be reduced by unwarranted financial penalties or deductions, unlawful demands for the repayment of suggested fines, or artificially inflated rental payments.
>
> . . .
>
> Although the statute does not provide any assistance on the issue, in our view the 'expectation' in section 4 of the 2006 Act is an objective one. It is for the judge to assess whether the position held by the individual is capable of being one 'in which he is expected to safeguard, or not to act against, the financial interests of another person'. If it is so capable, it will be for the jury thereafter to determine whether or not they are sure that was the case. It would be untenable to suggest that the expectation should be that of either the potential victim (the test would, in all likelihood, be too low) or the defendant (the test is likely to be set too high). Therefore, this is an objective test based on the position of the reasonable person.

13.4.2 *Mens rea*

The *mens rea* for this offence is (1) an intention to make a gain or cause a loss (or expose to the risk of loss) as for fraud by false representation, and (2) dishonesty. There is no requirement that D should know that he is in a position of trust in relation to V, although it is difficult to believe a judge would leave to a jury such a relationship if there was no evidence of knowledge on D's part. In any event, D's ignorance of the position of trust, however, will be highly relevant to the question whether or not he was dishonest.

13.5 **Ancillary offences**

Section 6 of the FA 2006 creates the offence of possession of articles for use in fraud. This replaces the offence of going equipped to cheat under s. 25 of the TA 1968. The latter offence has been amended to become the offence of going equipped for burglary or theft.

Section 6(1) provides:

> A person is guilty of an offence if he has in his possession or under his control any article for use in the course of or in connection with any fraud.

This is potentially a very wide offence and could cover possession of pen and paper to write a letter containing a false representation, or possession of something as sophisticated as a cloning machine to clone credit cards. Mr Doukas, on his way to work in possession of the bottles of wine he intends to use to sell to customers in the restaurant, would now commit this offence (see *Doukas*, **13.4.1**). There is no need to prove that D possessed the relevant article to be used in the course of or in connection with a specific fraud, it being sufficient to prove that he had a general intention (see *Ellames* (1974) 60 Cr App R 7). This will be easier to do, however, where the relevant article has no legitimate purpose—for example, the credit card cloning machine.

Section 8 defines 'article' to include 'any program or data held in electronic form'. D's draft email in the Example at **13.2.1.2** would clearly fall within this provision as would his possession of the email program on his computer and the computer itself.

Section 7 of the FA 2006 creates the offence of making or supplying articles for fraud. Section 7(1) provides:

> A person is guilty of an offence if he makes, adapts, supplies or offers to supply any article—
>
> (a) knowing that it is designed or adapted for use in the course of or in connection with fraud, or
>
> (b) intending it to be used to commit, or assist in the commission of, fraud.

For example D would commit this offence if, knowing E intends to seek to defraud customers in his pub, he makes E a fake charity collection box to place on his counter, E intending to keep the proceeds himself. Likewise D would commit this offence where he supplies a credit card cloning machine to E. The Explanatory Notes to the FA 2006 give as an example a person who makes devices to attach to electricity meters to cause them to malfunction and not record the electricity used.

13.6 **Obtaining services dishonestly**

Section 11 of the FA 2006 creates the offence of obtaining services dishonestly to replace the offence of obtaining services by deception contrary to s. 1 of the TA 1978. The maximum penalty on summary conviction is the same as for fraud but on conviction on indictment the maximum penalty is five years' imprisonment (s. 11(3) of the FA 2006). Unlike the offence of fraud, **this is a result crime** as it must be proved that the services have actually been obtained. Unlike the offence of obtaining services by deception, this offence does not require there to be any deception and thus there is no need to prove that the provider of the service has been deceived. The Explanatory Notes to the FA 2006 give the example of D climbing over a wall to watch a football match without paying the entrance fee. D does not deceive anyone in order to gain admission to the ground, but he does obtain a service which is provided on the basis that people pay for it. The absence of requirement that anyone be deceived also catches the situation where D engages in a transaction resulting in the obtaining of a service without any human agent determining that the service should be provided to D. The Explanatory Notes give the example of D using false credit card details to obtain data or software via an automated process over the internet where that data or software is made available only to those who have paid for access rights to that service. A further example given is that of D attaching a decoder to her television to enable viewing access to cable/satellite television channels for which she has no intention of paying.

Section 11 of the FA 2006 provides:

(1) A person is guilty of an offence under this section if he obtains services for himself or another—

  (a) by a dishonest act, and

  (b) in breach of subsection (2).

(2) A person obtains services in breach of this subsection if—

  (a) they are made available on the basis that payment has been, is being or will be made for or in respect of them,

  (b) he obtains them without any payment having been made for or in respect of them or without payment having been made in full, and

  (c) when he obtains them, he knows—

    (i) that they are being made available on the basis described in paragraph (a), or

    (ii) that they might be,

but intends that payment will not be made, or will not be made in full.

Actus reus	Mens rea
• D by an act obtains services for himself or another; • the services are made available on the basis that payment has been, is being, or will be made for or in respect of them; and • he obtains them without any payment having been made for or in respect of them or without payment having been made in full.	• D acts dishonestly; • knowing either that the services are being made available on the basis that payment has been, is being, or will be made for or in respect of them or that they might be being made available on that basis; and • intends that payment will not be made, or will not be made in full.

13.6.1 *Actus reus*

13.6.1.1 Dishonest act

The offence requires that there be a dishonest act—thus it cannot be committed by omission—resulting in D or another obtaining services. In the earlier example of the football match, the act would be climbing into the ground. If the relevant act is a false representation—for example, D says to the turnstile operator at the football ground that the person behind is paying for him—D could also be liable to conviction for fraud by false representation. If D is stopped immediately after he goes through the turnstile and before he has an opportunity to view the football match, he would not have obtained any service at that point but would have committed the fraud offence.

Dishonesty is a *mens rea* element.

13.6.1.2 Obtains

It must be proved **that as a result of D's dishonest act he obtained a service** to which the section applies. If, for example, owing to someone else's mistake, D is given access to satellite television channels which are only available to customers who have paid in advance for them, D's use of the channels would not amount to an offence as he has not performed any act which led to the obtaining of them. His omission to inform the provider of their mistake cannot amount to a dishonest act. Of course, a convoluted argument could be constructed that each time D switches to the relevant channel there is a separate obtaining. Everything would then hinge on whether or not a jury would be satisfied that tuning into that channel was a dishonest act and that it was done with the requisite knowledge and intent.

13.6.1.3 Services

The offence only applies to **services which are made available on the basis that 'payment has been, is being or will be made for or in respect of them'**. If the services are obtained on the understanding that no payment will be made for them, D cannot be guilty of this offence. For example, if D approaches a taxi and falsely represents to the driver that she has been robbed and is unable to pay for the fare and he agrees to drive her to her destination for no charge, she has not obtained 'services' under s. 11 as the service was not made available on the basis that it would be paid for. D could be liable to conviction for fraud by false representation. By contrast, if D orders a taxi intending not to pay the fare and, when it arrives, she gets into it and is driven to her destination where she then runs off without paying, D will have obtained services dishonestly. She would also be liable to conviction for fraud by false representation as by getting into the taxi she impliedly represents she is an honest customer who will pay for the fare. In addition, she could be convicted of making off without payment (see **14.1**).

'Services' are not defined in the Act which leaves room for argument over what constitutes a service. Where a credit card is obtained or bank account opened as a result of a false representation, the card or account does not, itself, amount to a service but rather provides access to a range of facilities which underlie the card or account (see *Sofroniou* [2004] 1 Cr App R 35). This participation in the banking system is a service (*Sofroniou*) and could support a conviction for the s. 11 offence provided there is some charge for the service whether through an annual fee or other bank charges. It is arguable that the low interest rate on a current account or the higher interest rate on a credit card (and the commission fee levied on shops and businesses) means that these services are made available on the basis that payment has been or will be made for them. Thus inducing a bank to open an account with the intention of running up an overdraft on it and not repaying it, or to issue a credit card with the intent of spending up to the credit limit and not paying off the debt thereby incurred or interest charges on that debt, could constitute obtaining services dishonestly provided D had the necessary knowledge and intent.

13.6.1.4 Payment

The services which may be the subject of the s. 11 offence must be services made available on the basis that payment has been, is being, or will be made for or in respect of them. **D must obtain the relevant service either without paying for it or without paying in full for it.** If D obtains a service by means of a false representation but pays for it in full, he would not appear to commit this offence. For example, D, aged 14, gains access to a cinema to watch an 18-plus film by convincing the sales assistant that he is 18. D pays for his ticket and watches the film. D does not commit the offence of fraud by false representation as he does not make a gain in terms of property or cause any loss to the cinema operator. D would have committed an offence under s. 1 of the TA 1978. The Law Commission in its Report of 2002 provides a further example where an offence would not be committed which would have been an offence under s. 1 of the TA 1978, namely 'where parents, who have every intention of paying all relevant fees, lie about a child's religious upbringing in order to obtain a place at a fee paying school'. Both the Law Commission and the Home Office in its *Response to the Consultations* considered that this type of behaviour should not be covered by the new offence which should be confined to situations where there is an intention not to pay.

13.6.2 *Mens rea*

There are three elements to the *mens rea* for this offence.

13.6.2.1 Dishonesty

In determining whether D's act was dishonest, the *Ivey* test applies. The fact-finding tribunal must first ascertain (subjectively) the actual state of the individual's knowledge or belief as to the facts. When once his actual state of mind as to knowledge or belief as to facts is established, the question whether his conduct was honest or dishonest is to be determined by the fact-finder by applying the (objective) standards of ordinary decent people (see **12.2.2.2** noting that s. 2 of the TA 1968 does not apply to this offence).

13.6.2.2 Knowledge

D must know either that the services are being made available on the basis that payment has been, is being or will be made for or in respect of them, or that they might be being made available on that basis.

13.6.2.3 Intention

D must intend either not to pay for the service or not to pay in full for it. This intention must exist at the point that D obtains the service. It would appear, however, that the intent should also exist when D does the relevant act which leads to the obtaining if that act is to be considered dishonest. If D has the intent to do the dishonest act but changes his mind before the obtaining occurs, he will not be liable for the s. 11 offence although, of course, he may be liable for attempt.

It is not clear whether the intent not to pay means an intent never to pay as opposed to an intent not to pay at the time when payment is due. By analogy with making off without payment, it is assumed that an intent never to pay is what is required (see *Allen* [1985] AC 1029, **14.1.2**).

 The law in context

Complex fraud trials: are they fair for defendants and jurors?

Fraud is a broad category of offence. It covers a spectrum from minor acts of dishonest misrepresentation to highly complex commercial transactions (as in *Hayes* [2015] EWCA Crim 1944). One key issue in cases of complex fraud is whether trial by jury is a suitable mechanism for deciding whether a defendant is guilty. There have been high profile cases that have dragged on for months, involving significant cost and placing a significant strain on the jury (Home Office (1998) *Juries in Serious Fraud Trials* (HMSO, London) p. 5). For example, the Court of Appeal quashed convictions in the 'Blue Arrow' case (a complex case of alleged conspiracy to defraud involving millions of pounds worth of shares: *Cohen and others* (1992) 142 New LJ 1267), commenting that the case had become unmanageable and there was a significant risk of a miscarriage of justice from the volume and complexity of the issues presented to the jury. In 2003, a case involving alleged corruption concerning the extension to the Jubilee Line of the London Underground collapsed after 21 months and several million pounds in legal fees (*The Guardian*, 'Jury Protest Forces Fraud Trial Collapse After 2 Years' 23 March 2005), with jurors complaining about the hardships they had experienced, including negative effects on relationships and careers.

In 2001 Lord Justice Auld published his *Review of the Criminal Courts of England and Wales*, and summarised the arguments for and against dispensing with jury trial in complex fraud cases (http://webarchive.nationalarchives.gov.uk/+/http://www.criminal-courts-review.org.uk/auldconts.htm, Chapter 5, para. 181).

In favour of reform, Auld LJ noted that if jurors are truly to be regarded as the defendant's peers, they should be experienced in the professional or commercial discipline in which the alleged offence occurred. The volume and complexities of the issues and evidence, especially in specialist market frauds involving futures or derivatives trading, may be too difficult for jurors to understand or analyse appropriately so as to enable them to determine whether there has been dishonesty. While the issue of dishonesty might be easy for judges to explain to juries (by setting out the test from the Supreme Court's decision in *Ivey*), that can only be properly and fully assessed by a jury if the associated circumstances, which might be very complex and intricate, are understood by the jury (Home Office, *Juries in Serious Fraud Trials: A Consultation Document* (1998), p. 6). A defendant's attempts to conceal his behaviour will exacerbate that complexity. In addition, the length of such trials, sometimes of several months, is an unreasonable intrusion on jurors' personal and working lives, going way beyond the typical requirement for jurors to serve for two weeks (Auld, para. 181). Such long trials are also a great personal strain and burden on defendants, victims, and witnesses. It is arguable that judges, with their legal and forensic experience, and/or specialist assessors would be better equipped to deal justly and more expeditiously with such cases. Auld LJ noted that that would have the benefit of greater openness, since there would be a publicly reasoned and appealable decision instead of the simple verdict of the jury (which he described as 'inscrutable and largely unappealable' (para. 181)). In addition, the length of jury trials in complex fraud cases is very costly to the public and also, because of limited judicial and court resources, unduly delays the efficient disposal of other cases waiting for trial.

The arguments in favour of continued use of juries are that jury trial is a cornerstone of our legal system and a citizen's right in all serious cases, including complex frauds. Random selection of jurors ensures fairness and independence. Juries have 12 members who come from a

→

→

wide variety of backgrounds. As most fraud trials will hinge on the question of ordinary peo-ple's standards of honesty, juries are as well (or better) equipped than a judge sitting alone or a tribunal of professionals with expertise in commercial transactions, to assess the reliability and credibility of witnesses and to decide whether the defendant's behaviour was dishonest. The jury's likely inexperience of complex commercial transactions also encourages open and transparent justice, by requiring lawyers to present their cases in a simple and easily digestible form. Arguably, the solution to complexity lies not in abolishing juries but in improving law-yers' abilities to present their cases well (Auld, para. 181).

Those who defend jury trial in complex fraud cases highlight the lack of empirical evidence, such as research into how juries understand and apply the judge's directions on dishonesty, to support the assertion that juries cannot cope with long and complex cases or that their deci-sions in them are contrary to the evidence (Auld, Chapter 5, para. 181; s. 20(D) of the Juries Act 1974 prohibits research into the deliberations of real juries). Lloyd-Bostock conducted interviews with jurors who had sat on the 21-month-long Jubilee Line case and found that jurors felt they actually had a good understanding of the evidence and had no problem with technical language or documents (S. Lloyd-Bostock, 'The Jubilee Line Jurors: Does Their Experience Strengthen the Argument for Judge-Only Trial in Long and Complex Fraud Cases?' [2007] Crim LR 255, 259). Some had found it more challenging but the main problem iden-tified by the jurors was that the trial's pace was extremely slow and parts of the defence were extremely tedious and boring (at p. 262).

Auld's conclusion was that the 'burdensome length and increasing speciality and complex-ity of these cases, with which jurors, largely or wholly strangers to the subject matter . . . put justice at risk . . .' (Auld, para. 183). He recommended a trial judge should be empowered to direct the trial by himself sitting with lay members or, if the defendant opts for trial by judge alone, by himself alone.

There have been many proposals over the years, such as those in the *Report of the Fraud Trials Committee* (the 'Roskill Report') in 1986, which led to reforms in the Criminal Justice Act 1987, including the establishment of the Serious Fraud Office with responsibility for investi-gating serious or complex frauds. Section 7 of the 1987 Act also introduced reforms to pre-trial procedure (particularly the introduction of preparatory hearings) to focus on helping the jury's comprehension of the issues and expediting the proceedings before them. Roskill also recommended the replacement of juries with fraud trial tribunals, consisting of a judge and a small number of specially qualified lay members.

Auld's recommendations morphed into s. 43 of the Criminal Justice Act 2003, which pro-vided for trial by judge alone in serious and complex fraud cases where 'the complexity of the trial or the length of the trial (or both) is likely to make the trial so burdensome' to the jury that 'the interests of justice require that serious consideration should be given to the question of whether the trial should be conducted without a jury'. However, that provision proved so con-troversial inside and outside of Parliament that the provision never came into force (despite the Government's attempts to bring it into force in the Fraud (Trials without a Jury) Bill 2007) and was repealed by the Protection of Freedoms Act 2012. Other reforms have been introduced though, including allowing trial by jury of sample counts only (if certain conditions are ful-filled), with the remaining counts to be tried by judge alone (ss 17–21 of the Domestic Violence, Crime and Victims Act 2004). In addition, the Lord Chief Justice issued a protocol in 2005 summarising good practice in managing complex cases. The protocol reminds judges and lawyers that trials must be kept within proper bounds in terms of time and money to ensure the jury can retain and assess evidence and to make proper use of limited resources (2005: *Control and Management of Heavy Fraud and Other Complex Criminal Cases—Criminal Procedure Rules*, http://www.justice.gov.uk/courts/procedure-rules/criminal/pd-protocol/pd_protocol).

Key Points

- Section 1 of the Fraud Act 2006 creates the general offence of fraud.

- Fraud by false representation (s. 2) makes it an offence to dishonestly make a false representation and intend, by making the representation, to make a gain for himself or another or to cause loss to another or expose another to a risk of loss:

  - A 'representation' is defined in s. 2(3) as meaning any representation as to fact or law, including a representation as to the state of mind of the person making the representation or any other person.

  - A representation is 'false' if it is untrue or misleading and D knows that it is or might be so (s. 2(2));

  - The *mens rea* is knowledge that the representation is or might be false and dishonest. Dishonesty has the meaning set out in *Ivey* v *Genting Casinos UK Ltd* (2017): once the jury or magistrates have established what D's actual state of mind was, the question whether his conduct was honest or dishonest is to be determined by applying the standards of ordinary decent people.

- Fraud by failing to disclose information is an offence under s. 3 of the Fraud Act 2006:

  - The *actus reus* is failing to disclose to another person information which he is under a legal duty to disclose.

  - The *mens rea* is dishonesty and intending by the failure to make a gain for himself or another or to cause loss to another or to expose another to a risk of loss.

- Fraud by abuse of position is an offence under s. 4 of the Fraud Act 2006:

  - The *actus reus* is abuse, by act or omission, by D of a position in which he is expected to safeguard or not act against the financial interests of another person.

  - The *mens rea* is dishonesty and intending by means of the abuse of position to make a gain for himself or another or to cause loss to another or to expose another to a risk of loss.

- Section 6 of the Fraud Act creates the offence of possession of articles for use in fraud.

- Section 11 of the Fraud Act creates the offence of obtaining services dishonestly to replace the offence of obtaining services by deception in s. 1 of the Theft Act 1978.

FURTHER READING

J. Collins, 'Fraud by Abuse of Position: Theorising Section 4 of the Fraud Act 2006' [2011] Crim LR 513.

C. Monaghan, 'School Application Forms and the Criminal Law' [2015] Crim LR 270.

R. Sullivan, 'Fraud—The Latest Law Commission Proposals' (2003) 67 JCL 139.

14

....

Further offences under the Theft Acts

14.1 Making off without payment

There are certain situations where D obtains property or services, or seeks to evade his liability to pay, which do not fall within the offence of theft or fraud offences (examined in **Chapter 13**). For example, if D honestly obtains ownership and possession of property from P and then decides not to pay, he is not guilty of theft as the property belongs to him (see *Edwards* v *Ddin* (1976) 63 Cr App R 218). If D makes no false representation to obtain the property he is not guilty of fraud by false representation. If D makes off from the place where he obtained the property and where payment was due—for example, by simply driving away from a self-service filling station without any false representation—he does not commit fraud. Section 3 of the Theft Act (TA) 1978 was enacted to cover situations such as these where a debtor, seeking to avoid paying his debt, removes himself from the scene where his liability was incurred. Such conduct is commonly referred to as 'bilking'. Section 3 does not require proof that the property involved belonged to another, or that there was any false representation practised.

Section 3(1) of the TA 1978 provides:

> Subject to subsection (3) below, a person who, knowing that payment on the spot for any goods supplied or service done is required or expected from him, dishonestly makes off without having paid as required or expected and with intent to avoid payment of the amount due shall be guilty of an offence.

Actus reus	Mens rea
• without paying,	• D makes off dishonestly,
• D makes off	• knowing payment on the spot is required or expected of him, and
• from the spot	• intending to avoid payment of the amount due.
• where payment is required or expected of him	
• for any goods supplied or service done.	

The offence is punishable on conviction on indictment with up to two years' imprisonment (s. 4(2)(b)), and on summary conviction with up to six months' imprisonment and/or a fine not exceeding £2,000 (s. 4(3)).

14.1.1 *Actus reus*

14.1.1.1 **Goods supplied or service done**

The goods must be supplied. This is satisfied either by P delivering the goods to D or D being permitted to take them—for example, by filling his petrol tank at a self-service filling station or by taking goods from a supermarket shelf. If D takes goods from a shop which is not self-service he does not commit this offence although he may commit theft. If he takes goods in a self-service supermarket he may be guilty of both offences.

Where services are involved the service must be 'done'. Mending D's shoes, letting a room in an hotel, supplying a meal in a restaurant, or hiring D a car are all examples of a 'service done'. The latter two examples also, incidentally, involve the supply of goods. The use of a facility which P provides—for example, using a car park—would also be regarded as a 'service done' so that D would commit this offence if he drove out without paying the charge due. By contrast, if D surreptitiously enters P's theatre, watches a performance, and leaves without paying, it would be difficult to construe the performance as a 'service done' as P has not permitted D's entry in the way entry is permitted to a car park.

Section 3(3) provides that:

> Subsection (1) above shall not apply where the supply of the goods or the doing of the service is contrary to law, or where the service done is such that payment is not legally enforceable.

The supply of goods would be contrary to law—for example, when P sells prohibited drugs to D, or serves alcohol to D who is under 18. Likewise the supply of the service may be contrary to law—for example, in a brothel or an unlicensed casino. Finally, payment for the service may not be legally enforceable—for example, gaming debts. Further, a prostitute cannot sue her client for payment for her services.

14.1.1.2 **Making off**

 Question

Can there be more than one 'spot' or can the spot be geographically extensive?

D must make off from the spot where payment is required (*McDavitt* [1981] Crim LR 843). There may be more than one 'spot' or the 'spot' may cover a very wide area; where a passenger on the underground fails to buy a ticket, the spot where he commits the offence includes the exit barrier to the underground and is not confined to the place where a ticket should be bought before the journey commences (see *Moberly* v *Alsop*, *The Times*, 13 December 1991, DC; see further *Aziz* [1993] Crim LR

708). If D is caught climbing through a window to leave a hotel he will not have made off but he may be guilty of attempt. 'Makes off' is a broad term which will cover the situation where D leaves by stealth or where he openly runs off—for example, by jumping out of a taxi and running away when it stops at his destination.

In *Morris* [2013] EWCA Crim 436, the Court of Appeal considered *Aziz* [1993] Crim LR 708, where it was held that the relevant spot where payment is required is the place where the taxi is standing and that 'payment might be made while sitting in the taxi or standing by the window'. This is the usual situation but in *Morris* (see **6.4.2.3**) Leveson LJ suggested (at para. 17):

> To apply the words 'in the case of a taxi, payment might be made while sitting in the taxi or standing by the window' too literally would be to misunderstand the legislation. Thus, if a passenger were to explain (honestly) to the taxi driver that he had to enter his house in order to obtain the fare, the moment for payment would be deferred for him to do so. A decision not to return to the taxi would mean that, from that moment, the passenger is making off without payment. The taxi driver would never be in a position to know precisely when the passenger decided not to pay and, in our judgment, must be able to follow the passenger to challenge him in an attempt to prevent the commission of the offence.

This is very much an *obiter* comment and would create difficulties in trying to determine where the 'spot' was. It cannot be inside the house as the expectation of the taxi-driver remains that he will be paid in his taxi when the passenger returns. If the passenger decides not to return but to remain indoors where the taxi-driver consented to him going, he cannot be said to have 'made off' as his departure from the 'spot' was not dishonest at the time he left. Nor can he be said to have committed the offence of fraud if his intention when obtaining the permission of the taxi-driver to go into his house had been to return. If at the time he obtained permission to enter his house his intention was not to return, the passenger would have committed the offence of fraud; but that offence would be complete at the point permission is obtained and therefore not amenable to prevention thereafter.

It was suggested at one time that there could not be a 'making off' where P consented to D's departure as a result of a deception by D—for example, D tells the hotel manager that he has settled the bill with the receptionist and is then assisted into his taxi by the manager. The Court of Appeal in *Brooks and Brooks* (1983) 76 Cr App R 66, did not accept that the term was limited in this way taking the view that 'makes off' means 'departs' regardless of how that departure is effected. The Court emphasised that the crucial consideration was whether the 'making off' was dishonest.

14.1.1.3 Without having paid as required or expected

Payment on the spot for the goods or services must be required or expected. Section 3(2) provides that '"payment on the spot" includes payment at the time of collecting goods on which work has been done or in respect of which service has been provided'. D's departure must be made without paying in the way required or expected. Where D, by false representation, obtains the agreement of the person to whom payment is owed to his paying at some later date, the s. 3 offence is not committed as the requirement or expectation of payment on the spot no longer exists and the court should not explore whether that agreement was induced by deception (see *Vincent* [2001] EWCA Crim 295). The appropriate offence to charge in such a case is fraud by false representation. If D gives forged banknotes he does not pay. Where D pays by means of a worthless cheque the appropriate charge again would be fraud by false representation. The offence under s. 3 should not be charged. Where the cheque is supported by a cheque card, even though there are no funds in D's account, he will have paid P as the bank will be obliged to honour the cheque. Similarly, where D pays by credit card P will be paid as required or expected even if D uses it without authority (whether because his authority has been revoked or it is stolen) (see *Re Charge Card Services Ltd* [1988] 3 All ER 702). In these situations the appropriate charge is fraud by false representation.

14.1.2 *Mens rea*

The making off must be dishonest. In addition it must be proved that D knew that payment on the spot was required or expected of him. If D honestly believed that the goods were supplied or the service done on credit and that he would be invoiced later he would not be guilty. Similarly, if D believed that someone else had paid or was going to pay, he would not be guilty.

It was originally believed that the offence was committed where D's intention in making off was merely to avoid payment on the spot at that time, even though he may have intended to pay later. In *Allen* [1985] AC 1029, the House of Lords held that an intention to permanently avoid payment was required.

14.2 **Burglary**

Section 9 of the Theft Act (TA) 1968 provides:

(1) A person is guilty of burglary if—

   (a) he enters any building or part of a building as a trespasser and with intent to commit any such offence as is mentioned in subsection (2) below; or

   (b) having entered any building or part of a building as a trespasser he steals or attempts to steal anything in the building or that part of it or inflicts or attempts to inflict on any person therein any grievous bodily harm.

(2) The offences referred to in subsection (1)(a) above are offences of stealing anything in the building or part of a building in question, of inflicting on any person therein any grievous bodily harm, and of doing unlawful damage to the building or anything therein.

(3) A person guilty of burglary shall on conviction on indictment be liable to imprisonment for a term not exceeding—

   (a) where the offence was committed in respect of a building or part of a building which is a dwelling, fourteen years;

   (b) in any other case, ten years.

(4) References in subsections (1) and (2) above to a building, and the reference in subsection (3) above to a building which is a dwelling, shall apply also to an inhabited vehicle or vessel, and shall apply to any such vehicle or vessel at times when the person having a habitation in it is not there as well as at times when he is.

Actus reus	Mens rea

s. 9(1)(a):
 • D enters
 • any building or part of a building
 • as a trespasser.
	s. 9(1)(a):
	 • D knows he is, or is reckless as to whether he is, entering as a trespasser; and
	 • D intends:
	   (i) to steal anything in the building or part thereof,
	   (ii) to inflict on any person therein any grievous bodily harm, or
	   (iii) to do unlawful damage to the building or anything therein.

s. 9(1)(b):
 • having entered
 • any building or part of a building
 • as a trespasser D:
   (i) steals or attempts to steal anything in the building or that part of it; or
   (ii) inflicts or attempts to inflict on any person therein any grievous bodily harm.
	s. 9(1)(b)
	 • D knew or, was reckless as to whether he was, entering as a trespasser; and
	 • has the necessary *mens rea* for the ulterior offences specified in s. 9(1)(b).

Section 9 creates two separate offences of burglary. The first offence under s. 9(1)(a) requires proof of entry as a trespasser and of the ulterior intent at that time to commit one of the three offences specified in sub-s. (2). (Subsection (2) used to include a fourth offence of rape; rape was removed from the list by the Sexual Offences Act 2003 which creates a much broader offence of trespassing on any premises with intent to commit a relevant sexual offence (s. 63(1)).) **The second offence requires proof of entry as a trespasser and of commission of theft or inflicting grievous bodily harm or an attempt to commit either of these offences.** In most cases where the second offence is committed D will also have committed the first offence at an earlier stage. The two offences in sub-s. (1), however, are separate and on an indictment for one there can be no conviction for the other (*Hollis* [1971] Crim LR 525). The second offence, however, also covers cases where D entered as a trespasser without having the requisite ulterior intent at that time but subsequently did commit theft or inflict grievous bodily harm or attempt to do so.

14.2.1 Entry as a trespasser

14.2.1.1 Entry

In *Collins* [1973] QB 100, D climbed a ladder and observed P lying naked on her bed asleep. He descended, stripped naked, and ascended again stopping on the window sill. P, thinking D was her boyfriend, beckoned him in and they had sexual intercourse before she discovered her mistake. D was convicted of burglary on the basis that he entered as a trespasser intending to commit rape. One of the issues in the case was whether D had entered before P beckoned to him. Edmund-Davies LJ stated that the prosecution had to prove that D had made 'an effective and substantial entry' before consent had been apparently given.

This appeared to abandon the old common law rule that insertion of any part of the body, however minimal, was sufficient to constitute an entry whether the purpose of the insertion was to commit the ulterior felony or merely to effect entry (see *Bailey* (1818) R & R 341). In *Brown* [1985] Crim LR 611, **the Court of Appeal took the view that all that was required was that the entry be 'effective' and that the question was one of fact for the jury**. In the instant case the jury were entitled to find that there had been an effective entry where D was found with the top half of his body inside a shop window rummaging for goods. **As a burglary is complete when D has entered with the ulterior intent whether or not he commits the ulterior offence, it would seem to be going too far to require that his entry be sufficient to effect that purpose.**

> In *Ryan* [1996] Crim LR 320, D was found trapped with his head and arm inside a window. He was convicted of burglary but appealed, contending that his actions could not constitute an 'entry' as he could not have stolen anything; he was firmly stuck. The Court of Appeal held, following *Brown*, that entry of part of his body could constitute an entry and it was irrelevant whether or not he was capable of stealing anything. The Court did not go so far as to declare that the insertion of any part of D's body is sufficient to constitute an entry preferring to leave the matter to juries to decide.

A further problem relates to the insertion of instruments into a building either to effect the ulterior offence or to facilitate entry. At common law, if the instrument was inserted to effect the ulterior offence, this constituted an entry whereas, if it was inserted to facilitate access, this did not constitute entry. This probably remains the case. Where the instrument is used to facilitate access there will certainly be an attempt. If it is used to effect the ulterior offence—for example, to grab goods—it can be regarded as an extension of D's body.

If D uses an innocent agent to enter the building it is submitted that D commits trespass by that means. There is no reason in principle why burglary should be excluded from the principles relating to the commission of offences by means of innocent agents.

14.2.1.2 **As a trespasser**

In establishing whether a person enters as a trespasser, three questions arise: (1) what is trespass for the purposes of burglary; (2) did the person entering have permission to enter; (3) had he exceeded the limits of that permission?

14.2.1.2.1 *What is trespass for the purposes of burglary?*

Trespass is a civil concept; it is committed where D intentionally, recklessly, or negligently enters a building in the possession of another without either permission to do so or a legal right to enter. D's entry must be voluntary. There would be no trespass where D tripped and stumbled into a building or where he was dragged unwillingly into it.

Mere proof of a trespass for the purposes of civil liability is not sufficient, however, for burglary. In tort trespass may be committed negligently whereas **for burglary *mens rea* must be proved.** In *Collins* (see **14.2.1.1**), Edmund-Davies LJ stated (at p. 105):

> [T]here cannot be a conviction for entering premises 'as a trespasser' . . . unless the person entering does so knowing that he is a trespasser and nevertheless deliberately enters, or, at the very least, is reckless as to whether or not he is entering the premises of another without the other party's consent.

'Reckless' for these purposes has its '*Cunningham*' meaning (see **3.4.2.1**). It was not clear whether Collins was on the inside window sill when P beckoned to him; if he was he had already entered as a trespasser. On the assumption that he was outside, his conviction had to be quashed as the trial judge had directed the jury that a civil trespass was sufficient for the purposes of burglary and thus the question of D's *mens rea* had not been left to the jury. **If D does not enter as a trespasser, he cannot, generally, commit burglary. The exception is where P requests D to leave; if he does not do so within a reasonable time he becomes a trespasser and thus would commit burglary if he then entered another part of the building and, for example, stole P's purse.**

14.2.1.2.2 *Permission to enter*

The person who is in possession of a building or a part of it is the person who may give permission to others to enter. Thus it is the tenant of a flat who may give that permission and not the landlord who owns the property. A lodger or a guest in a hotel, however, is not in possession of his room but is a mere licensee so that permission may only be given by the licensor, in this case the landlord or hotelier. The person in possession, however, may authorise others to give permission to enter. For example, parents who own the family home expressly or impliedly authorise their children to invite others into the home. Similarly, they may forbid the entry of certain persons—for example, their daughter's boyfriend, D. If the daughter invites D into the house and he enters knowing his entry is forbidden, or being reckless thereto, and then steals, he will be guilty of burglary as he entered as a trespasser.

It was suggested in *Collins* that if a person enters having been given permission by one who has no authority to do so, he is not in fact a trespasser for the purposes of burglary. It is submitted that this is wrong. If D enters without the permission of the occupier, this is trespass for civil purposes but only becomes trespass for the purposes of burglary where D knows he does not have the occupier's permission in the circumstances or is reckless thereto. Where the parents had changed their minds and, unknown to D, had given their daughter permission to invite him into the house, if D entered believing he was forbidden from entering and then stole, he would be guilty of theft and attempted burglary (cf. **8.4.4**).

14.2.1.2.3 *Exceeding permission*

A problem which may arise, however, is that of a person exceeding the permission granted. For example, if D had permission to enter but entered intending from the outset to steal, would this nevertheless be burglary on the basis that his permission was impliedly limited to lawful purposes?

> In *Jones and Smith* (1976) 63 Cr App R 47, S had general permission to enter his father's house. On the occasion in question he entered with J to steal a television set. The Court of Appeal upheld his conviction for burglary on the basis that the jury were entitled to find that in entering his father's house with the intent to steal, S had knowingly exceeded the permission given to him.

Thus a person who is given permission to enter a building for one purpose and enters for another will be a trespasser. For example, if P gives a key to D to enter her house and water her plants while she is on holiday, and D enters to steal her video recorder, he will be trespassing and guilty of burglary (see *Barker* v *R* (1983) 153 CLR 338, High Court of Australia). Similarly, if D has permission to enter one part of a building and enters another he will be trespassing. For example, if D is invited into P's house to mend her television in the living room and enters P's bedroom to search for her purse to steal it, he would commit burglary as he has entered this part of the building as a trespasser.

Question

How far does this principle extend? Will D necessarily become a trespasser when he enters with one of the requisite ulterior intents on the basis that this exceeds the permission granted?

Jones and Smith would suggest that this is the case, even though the permission granted to Smith had not been expressly limited to a specific purpose. The decision in *Collins* appears to contradict this. It would defy credulity if D had pleaded that he believed P had authority to permit persons to enter to commit rape. But the Court of Appeal quashed Collins's conviction, which might tend to suggest that entry in excess of permission does not negative that permission. It is submitted that, as the effect on permission of an ulterior intent was not directly adverted to in *Collins*, the case cannot be considered an authority on this point; it should be seen as a case relating to the requirement of *mens rea*. **Thus, if a person enters with an ulterior intent, the entry will generally be trespassory unless the occupier has granted permission to enter for that purpose.** For example, if P invites D into his house to beat up his lodger, D would not enter as a trespasser. It would be burglary, however, where D enters a shop intending to steal at the outset. The permission the shop-keeper gives to the public is impliedly limited to entry for the purpose of inspecting or purchasing goods; that is implicit in the decision in *Jones and Smith* and, it is submitted, rightly so. Thus a person should be regarded as a trespasser where he enters with an intention contrary to the purposes for which permission to enter was granted. If the shopper enters without an intent to steal, but then forms that intent inside the shop, this is not burglary, even if he then proceeds to steal, as the initial entry was not a trespass.

14.2.2 Any building or part of a building

14.2.2.1 'Building'

For the purposes of burglary the trespassory entry must be made into a building or a part of a building. The maximum sentence varies depending on the type of building entered. Section 26 of the Criminal Justice Act (CJA) 1991 introduced a two-tier system, substituting new sub-ss (3) and (4) into s. 9 of the TA 1968. If the building burgled is a 'dwelling', the maximum penalty is 14 years' imprisonment, whereas it is 10 years for any other building. **There is no definition of 'building' but it appears that it must be a fairly permanent structure.** Thus a temporary prefabricated structure (such as a school temporary classroom) would be a building but whether transportable containers connected to an electricity supply on a fairly permanent site are buildings is not yet settled (cf. *B and S* v *Leathley* [1979] Crim LR 314 and *Norfolk Constabulary* v *Seekings and Gould* [1986] Crim LR 167). **A tent is not a building.** It is not clear when a structure in the process of erection becomes a building. If D enters a structure which is complete apart from the roof, doors, and windows, with intent to cause criminal damage, has he entered a building? As yet there is no answer to this problem (cf. *Manning* (1871) LR 1 CCR 338).

An inhabited vehicle or vessel is a building (s. 9(3)). Thus both caravans and house-boats are buildings provided they are occupied, although the occupier does not have to be in at the time D enters it as a trespasser. Problems, however, may arise in defining the limits of 'inhabited'. Is a caravan inhabited when left on a site over the winter months when P does not use it? Is a 'dormobile' inhabited when P is using it simply as a vehicle and not as a holiday home? It is likely that neither of these cases would be covered as P is not actively inhabiting the vehicle. The extension to the meaning of 'building' which s. 9(4) provides is a limited one. It would not cover, for example, a mobile library or shop, or a mobile blood transfusion unit, or a mobile army recruitment office, all of which are essentially vehicles converted for a particular purpose but which are not 'inhabited'. Thus, if D enters a mobile library intending to set fire to the books, he would not be guilty of burglary although if he entered a library building with the same intent he would. The mischief involved would not seem to be any different but Parliament has ordained that the offence of burglary should be restricted. If D is to be liable for burglary where he enters a vehicle or vessel it will have to be proved that he knew that it was inhabited or was reckless thereto.

Just as there is no definition of 'building' there is also no definition of 'dwelling', this being an issue for the arbiter of fact (see *Flack* [2013] EWCA Crim 115). Crucial to such a decision should be the purpose behind the amendment of s. 9, namely a recognition of the sense of violation, distress, and fear caused to residential occupiers by burglaries. It is submitted that if such effects could not arise—as, for example, where a new-build house is burgled before it is sold to a residential occupier and the builder's tools are stolen—the building should not be regarded as a dwelling. Interesting distinctions could arise, for example, where hotel rooms are burgled where one has a permanent resident treating the room as his home and another is occupied by a businessman on an overnight stay. One room, a part of the building, should be regarded as a dwelling while the other should not be so regarded.

14.2.2.2 'Part of a building'

For the purposes of burglary it is sufficient that D enters part of a building as a trespasser. Thus while D may have permission to be in certain parts of the building there may be other parts to which his permission does not extend. For example, a guest in a hotel has permission to enter his own room and communal rooms, but has no permission to enter another guest's room or parts of the building exclusively for the use of hotel staff. **If D, in the hotel bar, goes behind the counter to steal from the till he will be guilty of burglary; the same applies to a customer who goes behind the counter in a shop to steal** (see *Walkington* [1979] 2 All ER 716). The intent, however, must be to commit the ulterior offence in that part of the building which he has entered as a trespasser. If D hides between several racks of clothes in a shop waiting for it to close before removing items of clothing, he would not be guilty of burglary as he has simply remained in a part of the shop which he entered with permission. Of course, if at the time of his original entry into the shop he intended to steal, he would have committed burglary at that point.

14.2.3 The ulterior offence

As we have already seen, burglary is committed either (1) where D enters the building or part of it as a trespasser with intent to commit one of the offences in s. 9(2) (s. 9(1)(a)), or (2) having entered the building or part of it as a trespasser he steals or attempts to steal or he inflicts grievous bodily harm on any person therein or attempts to do so (s. 9(1)(b)).

14.2.3.1 Section 9(1)(a)

Under s. 9(1)(a) it is necessary to prove an ulterior intent to commit one of the three offences specified in s. 9(2). A conditional intent is sufficient (*AG's References (Nos. 1 and 2 of 1979)* [1979] 3 All ER 143). Thus, if D enters as a trespasser intending to steal anything of value he might find, and there is nothing there, he will have a sufficient intent for burglary. In the case of these ulterior offences it must be proved that D *intended* to commit the relevant offence.

The Act speaks of entering a building and stealing anything in it or inflicting grievous bodily harm (GBH) upon a person 'therein' or doing unlawful damage to the building or anything 'therein'. The word 'therein' is ambiguous as it could mean simply performing the act on a person inside the building (this would cover the case of D dragging P into a building with intent to inflict GBH on her), or it may mean with intent to inflict GBH upon a person already in the building before D enters it as a trespasser. As the purpose of burglary is the protection of persons or property in a building it might be suggested that the latter interpretation is the correct one.

14.2.3.2 Section 9(1)(b)

Under s. 9(1)(b), the theft, infliction of GBH, or attempt to commit either of these offences must be proved. This requires that both the *actus reus* and *mens rea* of these ulterior offences must be proved. 'Inflicting grievous bodily harm' would appear to cover the offences under ss 20, 18, or 23 of the Offences Against the Person Act 1861. Recklessly inflicting GBH would be sufficient for this form of burglary. Presumably if D murders P he will also be guilty as the commission of GBH is a step on the way to causing death and it would be ludicrous to suggest that D intended to kill but did not intend to inflict GBH. If D took property intending only to borrow it, there would be no theft and thus no burglary. It is submitted that D in *Dobson* v *General Accident Fire and Life Assurance Corp plc* [1990] QB 274 (see **12.2.1.4.2**) committed burglary as his permission to enter was on the basis that he had come to purchase P's jewellery; his intention was to steal it from the outset. When he appropriated it he committed theft, therefore, having entered the building as a trespasser.

If D has a defence to any of these offences he will not be guilty of burglary. For example, if D enters a building as a trespasser intending to shelter from the rain and P, the occupier, attacks him with an axe seeking to eject him, D would not be guilty of burglary if he inflicted GBH on P in reasonable self-defence. Likewise, if D takes property believing he has in law a right to it, he would not commit theft and therefore would not be guilty of burglary.

14.2.3.3 Intoxication

Where D is intoxicated this will be of no relevance in relation to the question whether he knew he was trespassing or was reckless thereto. Intoxication may be relevant, however, in respect of the ulterior offence. Where D is charged with burglary with intent to steal, this is an offence of specific intent (see *Durante* [1972] 3 All ER 962; see also **5.5.3**). It is submitted that all forms of burglary under s. 9(1)(a) are offences of specific intent. Where D is charged with burglary contrary to s. 9(1)(b) on the basis of theft, this is an offence of specific intent as theft is such an offence (see *Ruse* v *Read* [1949] 1 KB 377). Where D is charged with burglary on the basis of inflicting GBH, however, it would appear that the offence is one of basic intent as the *mens rea* for inflicting GBH is intention or recklessness. If the burglary charge is based upon an attempt to steal or to inflict GBH, it is an offence of specific intent as attempt is an offence of specific intent.

14.3 **Aggravated burglary**

Section 10 of the TA 1968 provides:

> (1) A person is guilty of aggravated burglary if he commits any burglary and at the time has with him any firearm or imitation firearm, any weapon of offence, or any explosive; and for this purpose—
>
> > (a) 'firearm' includes an airgun or air pistol, and 'imitation firearm' means anything which has the appearance of being a firearm, whether capable of being discharged or not; and
> >
> > (b) 'weapon of offence' means any article made or adapted for use for causing injury to or incapacitating a person, or intended by the person having it with him for such use; and
> >
> > (c) 'explosive' means any article manufactured for the purpose of producing a practical effect by explosion, or intended by the person having it with him for that purpose.
>
> (2) A person guilty of aggravated burglary shall on conviction on indictment be liable to imprisonment for life.

The element of aggravation in this offence is the fact that D at the time has with him a firearm or imitation firearm, a weapon of offence, or an explosive. Whether something is an imitation firearm will be a question of fact for the jury (cf. *Morris and King* (1984) 79 Cr App R 104). 'Weapon of offence' is a wider term than 'offensive weapon' under s. 1(4) of the Prevention of Crime Act 1953 as it includes items not only made or adapted for use for causing injury or intended for such use but also items made or adapted for use for incapacitating a person or intended for such use. For example, a broken bottle would be an item adapted for use for causing injury, while a hammer could be an item intended for such use. Handcuffs are items made for incapacitation while a rope or a cloth soaked in chloroform could amount to an item intended for use to incapacitate a person, where, for example, D intends to incapacitate the security guard at a factory. If a question arises whether an article is made or adapted for use for causing injury or incapacitating a person, it will be for the jury to decide (*Williamson* (1977) 67 Cr App R 35). But, with certain items which have no other purpose—for example, a flick-knife or knuckleduster—the jury must take judicial notice that it is so made (*Simpson* [1983] 3 All ER 789). If an article is made or adapted for use for causing injury or incapacitating a person, it is offensive per se and it will be sufficient for the prosecution to prove that D had it with him even if he did not intend to use it. If an article is not offensive per se, but may be used to cause injury or incapacitate a person, the prosecution must prove that D intended it to be used for such purpose.

D must have the firearm, weapon of offence, or explosive with him at the time he commits the burglary. It is not enough that an accomplice who remains outside the building has a weapon with him (see *Klass* [1998] 1 Cr App R 453; *Wiggins* [2012] EWCA Crim 885). 'Has with him' requires that D knows that he has an article of aggravation with him (cf. *Cugullere* (1961) 45 Cr App R 108), so that if D is unaware of the fact that there is a flick-knife in his tool bag, or if he does not know his accomplice is carrying a weapon, he will not be guilty of aggravated burglary. If D has forgotten that he has, for example, a flick-knife in his bag, he does not know that he has it with him (*Russell* (1984) 81 Cr App R 315). D will have an article with him where he has custody of it or where he knows that an accomplice has custody of it and is carrying it into the building.

The meaning of 'at the time of committing the burglary' depends on whether burglary is committed contrary to s. 9(1)(a) or s. 9(1)(b). Under s. 9(1)(a) the relevant time is the time when D entered the building as a trespasser. Under s. 9(1)(b) burglary is committed where D, having entered as a trespasser, commits an ulterior offence; he must have the weapon, etc. with him at the time of committing this offence (*Francis* [1982] Crim LR 363). Thus, if D enters as a trespasser, picks up a knife from the kitchen, and then commits the ulterior offence, he would be guilty of aggravated burglary (see *O'Leary* (1986) 82 Cr App R 341). If D enters carrying with him, for example, a rope to tie together items he intends to steal and, upon being disturbed by the householder, uses it to tie him up, does he commit aggravated burglary—that is, does he have with him at the time of committing the burglary an article intended for use to incapacitate a person? The authorities under the Prevention of Crime Act 1953, on the question whether a person has with him in a public place an offensive weapon, suggested that the person must have formed the intention to use the article for the purpose of causing injury at some time before the occasion for that use occurred (see *Ohlson* v *Hylton* [1975] 2 All ER 490; *Humphreys* [1977] Crim LR 225). These cases can be distinguished, however, as in both cases D was in a public place lawfully going about his business carrying the relevant article without any criminal intent. In the burglary example, D is already engaged in an unlawful purpose and is carrying that article to effect that purpose which he then uses for an additional unlawful purpose. It is difficult to make out a case for extending the reasoning of those two cases to burglary and thus it is suggested that s. 10 should be construed strictly: at the time of committing the ulterior offence did D have the article in his custody intending it for use to cause injury or to incapacitate at that time regardless of any intention in respect of it he may previously have had? The Court of Appeal adopted this position in *Kelly* (1992)

97 Cr App R 245, holding that the screwdriver D used to break into a house became an offensive weapon when he used it to threaten the occupier who disturbed him, as he intended to use it at that time for causing injury to or incapacitating her.

14.4 Blackmail

Section 21 of the TA 1968 provides:

(1) A person is guilty of blackmail if, with a view to gain for himself or another or with intent to cause loss to another, he makes any unwarranted demand with menaces; and for this purpose a demand with menaces is unwarranted unless the person making it does so in the belief—

   (a) that he has reasonable grounds for making the demand; and
   (b) that the use of menaces is a proper means of reinforcing the demand.

(2) The nature of the act or omission is immaterial, and it is also immaterial whether the menaces relate to action to be taken by the person making the demand.

(3) A person guilty of blackmail shall on conviction on indictment be liable to imprisonment for a term not exceeding fourteen years.

Actus reus	Mens rea
D makes:	• D has a view to gain for himself or another or intent to cause loss to another;
• an unwarranted	• and if D contends the demand was not unwarranted, either
• demand	(i) that D did not believe he had reasonable grounds for making the demand, or
• with menaces.	(ii) that D did not believe that the use of menaces was a proper means of reinforcing the demand.

14.4.1 Demand

D must, expressly or impliedly, make a demand of P to do or refrain from doing something. The nature of the act or omission demanded is immaterial (s. 21(2)).

In *Collister and Warhurst* (1955) 39 Cr App R 100, two police officers intimated to P that he would be prosecuted for an offence and arranged to meet him the following day intimating that the report of the offence would be held up and was to be filed only if P failed to keep the appointment. At that meeting W asked P if he had brought anything with him, and P handed him £5. C and W were convicted of demanding money with menaces contrary to s. 30 of the Larceny Act 1916, the judge having directed the jury that they did not need to be satisfied that there had been express threats or demands it being sufficient that:

> [T]he demeanour of the accused and the circumstances of the case were such that an ordinary reasonable man would understand that a demand for money was being made upon him and that that demand was accompanied by menaces . . . so that his ordinary balance of mind was upset . . . .

> In *Lambert* [2009] EWCA Crim 2860, V owed D money. D pretended to be V and rang V's grandmother claiming he was tied up and the people holding him wanted £5,000. The Court of Appeal held that this was capable of being an unwarranted demand and it did not matter whether D was pretending to be the victim or the person holding the victim. A demand did not have to be made in terms of a requirement or obligation. Indeed, the more suave and gentle the request, the more sinister it might be in the circumstances.

It is enough that the demand is made regardless of whether P complies with it. A problem may arise, however, in deciding when or where a demand has been made. Is, for example, the posting of a letter, the sending of a fax, the speaking of words, a demand at that point or only when received or heard by P?

> In *Treacy* v *DPP* [1971] AC 537, D posted a letter in England containing a demand to P in Germany. D argued that the demand was made in Germany when P read the letter and thus she was not triable in England. The House of Lords held, by a majority, that the demand was made when the letter was posted.

The same would apply to a telex or fax. Where D makes a verbal demand, it is made when he utters the words even though P is deaf. If D posts a letter abroad addressed to P in England the offence will be committed when it is delivered to P (see *Treacy* and cf. *Baxter* [1972] 1 QB 1).

14.4.2 Menaces

As with the demand, the menaces may be express or implied from the circumstances (see *Lawrence and Pomroy* (1971) 57 Cr App R 64). 'Menaces' is not defined in the Act but it had developed a wide meaning under the former law. In *Thorne* v *Motor Trade Association* [1937] AC 797, Lord Wright stated (at p. 817):

> I think the word 'menace' is to be liberally construed and not as limited to threats of violence but as including threats of any action detrimental to or unpleasant to the person addressed. It may also include a warning that in certain events such action is intended.

It is immaterial whether the menaces do or do not relate to action to be taken by the person making the demand (s. 21(2)); thus it is sufficient that the act may be carried out by someone else. Further, it does not matter that D is in no position to carry out the menace (*Lambert*). The threats, however, must cross some threshold of seriousness to constitute 'menaces'. In *Clear* [1968] 1 QB 670 (a pre-1968 Act case; see also *Lawrence and Pomroy*) Sellers LJ stated (at p. 679) that **the threat must be 'of such a nature and extent that the mind of an ordinary person of normal stability and courage might be influenced or made apprehensive so as to accede unwillingly to the demand'**. Thus in *Harry* [1974] Crim LR 32, Judge Petre directed the jury to acquit as 'menaces' was a strong word and could not be established on the evidence in the case. D was the organiser of a Student Rag Appeal who had written to shopkeepers offering immunity from any 'inconvenience' arising from Rag activities.

As blackmail is committed when the demand with menaces is made, it does not matter that P is not actually intimidated if the threats would have affected

the mind of an ordinary person of normal stability (see *Garwood* [1987] 1 All ER 1032, 1034). If, however, P is unusually timorous and would be intimidated by threats where a person of normal stability and courage would be unmoved, this will only constitute 'menaces' if 'the accused . . . was aware of the likely effect of his actions on the victim' (*Garwood*).

14.4.3 Unwarranted demand

If D demands from P that to which he is legally entitled—for example, payment of a debt or the return of bailed property—and threatens to institute legal proceedings to enforce the demand, this would not constitute an 'unwarranted' demand as D is simply seeking to do that which he is legally entitled to do. By contrast, if D demands something to which he is not entitled accompanied by menaces, or demands something to which he is entitled but threatens action which he is not legally entitled to use to enforce the demand, his demand may be found to be 'unwarranted'. **Whether or not a demand is unwarranted depends on D's belief. The prosecution must prove beyond doubt either (1) that he did not believe he had reasonable grounds for making the demand or (2) that he did not believe that the use of menaces was a proper means of reinforcing the demand.** The question is 'what was D's subjective belief?' If D does not introduce any evidence that he had both these beliefs, the judge need not direct the jury on this issue (see *Lawrence and Pomroy*). The relevant beliefs will be examined separately.

14.4.3.1 Belief in reasonable grounds for making the demand
The question is not whether there were reasonable grounds for making the demand but rather whether D believed there were reasonable grounds for making the demand. Many situations may arise where D could have such a belief. For example, P may owe him money, or P may have committed a tort and D may believe he is entitled to compensation. D may believe that a demand for payment in these circumstances is reasonable. He may have that belief even though it is founded upon a mistake as where, for example, he believes that Q broke his window and he mistakes P, Q's twin brother, for him. The mistake D makes may be an unreasonable one but this will not matter provided D's honest belief is that he has reasonable grounds for making the demand (see *Harvey* (1981) 72 Cr App R 139).

D's belief need not relate to the law. In the examples given earlier he may have believed that he was legally justified in demanding payment but D's belief may be that he is morally justified in demanding something. For example, Q dies without leaving a will and D, a neighbour who is not entitled to inherit anything on the intestacy, demands from P, Q's daughter, some property from the estate believing that she is morally justified in doing so in recognition of all the help she rendered Q. If D honestly believes that the help she rendered provides reasonable grounds for her demand, the requirements of s. 21(1)(a) are satisfied. In all cases, however, D must also have the belief specified in s. 21(1)(b). This is a provision which it is more difficult to satisfy.

14.4.3.2 Belief that menaces are a proper means of reinforcing the demand
While D may plausibly say that he believed P owed him money, or that he believed he was entitled to certain property, credulity is much more likely to

be strained when he states he believed he was entitled to threaten P with violence or defamatory disclosures to enforce the demand. If the jury consider that D may possibly have believed that the menaces he used were a proper means of reinforcing the demand, they must acquit. To this extent, the standard against which the appropriateness of the menaces is measured is D's understanding of what is morally and socially acceptable in English society.

> In *Harvey* (see **14.4.3.1**) D, E, and F paid £20,000 to S for what was thought to be a consignment of cannabis but which turned out to be a load of rubbish. They kidnapped S's wife and child and told S they would rape, maim, and kill them unless he gave them their money back. The judge directed the jury that threats which were to commit what everybody knew were serious criminal offences could not be proper. D, E, and F were convicted of blackmail and appealed. The Court of Appeal upheld their convictions, Bingham J stating (at p. 142):

> > 'Proper' . . . is, however, plainly a word of wide meaning, certainly wider than (for example) 'lawful'. But the greater includes the less and no act which was not believed to be lawful could be believed to be proper within the meaning of the subsection. Thus no assistance is given to any defendant, even a fanatic or a deranged idealist, who knows or suspects that his threat, or the act threatened, is criminal, but believes it to be justified by his end or his peculiar circumstances.

In the circumstances of this case there was no room for doubt in light of the crimes actually threatened. If what D threatens is not known to him to be a crime, he may still be convicted if he did not believe it to be socially and morally acceptable as a means of enforcing his demand. For example, D demands payment from P of a debt threatening to post on Facebook photographs of P performing a sexual act if P does not pay. D may believe that he has reasonable grounds for making the demand. D may not know that posting the photograph may constitute the offence of disclosing private sexual photographs with intent to cause distress contrary to s. 33 of the Criminal Justice and Courts Act 2015. If he believed that posting the photographs was not unlawful, he could only be convicted of blackmail if it was proved that he did not believe that this would generally be regarded as morally and socially acceptable. However, if D, for example, is a person of limited intelligence and from a social background where it is generally accepted that debts may be enforced by threats, he may genuinely believe his threat to be proper, in which case he would have to be acquitted.

14.4.4 With a view to gain or intent to cause loss

In s. 34(2)(a) of the TA 1968 **'gain' and 'loss' are defined as being limited to gain or loss of money or other property, whether temporary or permanent.** Many demands may be regarded as improper but they will found a charge of blackmail only if made by D 'with a view to gain for himself or another or with intent to cause loss to another'. Thus, for example, if D threatens to expose P's adultery to her husband unless she has sexual intercourse with him, this is not blackmail as it does not involve any gain in money or property to D or similar loss to P. By contrast if D's demand had been for money or property in return for not revealing P's adultery, this would found a charge of blackmail.

Section 34(2)(a) further provides:

(i) 'gain' includes a gain by keeping what one has, as well as a gain by getting what one has not; and

(ii) 'loss' includes a loss by not getting what one might get, as well as a loss by parting with what one has.

The following examples may serve to illustrate what is covered by s. 34(2)(a), the threat in each case being to expose P's adultery, P being his secretary:

Example

(a) D demands that P allow him to keep the camera she has lent him (see (i) in the list above).

(b) D demands that P forgo her salary for a month (see (ii) in the list above).

(c) D demands that P repay a loan he made to her (see (i) in the list above: this is a gain even though D is legally entitled to repayment of the loan; see *Lawrence and Pomroy*).

(d) D demands that P lend him her car for the weekend (both a gain to D and a loss to P).

(e) D demands that P withdraw her writ for damages for injuries sustained due to D's negligence (D has a view to keeping what he has and P will sustain loss by not getting what she might get).

(f) D demands that P destroy photographs of D in a compromising situation which she has (see (ii) in the list above).

(g) D demands that P feature in a pornographic video he is making and proposing to sell (D has a view to gain, i.e. the proceeds of sale of the video).

(h) D (who has a grudge against Q) demands that P set fire to Q's car (this constitutes a 'loss to another'; there is no requirement that the loss be caused to the person against whom the threats are made).

14.5 Handling

Section 22 of the TA 1968 provides:

(1) A person handles stolen goods if (otherwise than in the course of the stealing) knowing or believing them to be stolen goods he dishonestly receives the goods, or dishonestly undertakes or assists in their retention, removal, disposal or realisation by or for the benefit of another person, or if he arranges to do so.

(2) A person guilty of handling stolen goods shall on conviction on indictment be liable to imprisonment for a term not exceeding fourteen years.

Actus reus	Mens rea
Otherwise than in the course of the stealing, D: (i) receives stolen goods; or (ii) undertakes the retention, removal, disposal, or realisation of the goods for the benefit of another person; or (iii) assists in the retention, removal, disposal, or realisation of the goods by another person; or (iv) he arranges to do (i), (ii), or (iii).	• D knows or believes the goods to be stolen, and • acts dishonestly.

A person who handles stolen goods may also, incidentally, commit theft if his act involves an appropriation. The offence of handling, however, is regarded as more serious than theft, as the maximum sentence available indicates. The existence of professional handlers (commonly referred to as 'fences') helps to generate thefts; many thieves might not be so keen to steal if they did not have a person readily available who was prepared to dispose of their goods.

The offence of handling is quite complex as it may be committed in many different ways. In addition terms like 'stolen' and 'goods' have their own definitions.

14.5.1 *Actus reus*

14.5.1.1 'Stolen'

The goods handled must be 'stolen' goods at the time of the handling. If the handler believes the goods to be stolen but they are not, he will not be guilty of handling (see *Haughton* v *Smith* [1975] AC 476) but he may be guilty of attempted handling (see *Shivpuri* [1987] AC 1). For example, goods would not be 'stolen' if the alleged thief believed he had a claim of right to the property. If, however, the alleged thief successfully pleaded the defence of duress on his trial for theft, this would not avail the handler as the defence of duress only operates as an excuse; D admits to committing the offence but is excused from the consequences of conviction and punishment due to the duress operating upon him. If the alleged thief has been tried and acquitted, this is not necessarily inconsistent with a conviction of the handler as, for example, the evidence against the handler may be much stronger than that against the alleged thief. If the thief has been convicted, the alleged handler may, nevertheless, dispute that the goods were stolen, in which case he will have to prove on a balance of probabilities that the thief's conviction was wrong (see s. 74(2) of the Police and Criminal Evidence Act 1984). If the alleged thief has not been tried or, if tried, has not been convicted, the question whether the goods were stolen must be decided on the basis of the evidence produced pointing to that fact in the trial of the alleged handler. The handler's belief that the goods were stolen does not constitute proof that they were (see *AG's Reference (No. 4 of 1979)* [1981] 1 All ER 1193) but D's admissions in respect of facts within his knowledge (such as the circumstances in which he acquired the goods) may provide a legitimate basis for inferences to be drawn by the jury that the goods were stolen (see *McDonald* (1980) 70 Cr App R 288; *Barnes* [1991] Crim LR 132).

For the purposes of the offence of handling, 'stolen' has an extended meaning to include goods obtained by blackmail or by fraud contrary to s. 1 of the Fraud Act 2006 (see s. 24(4)). The words 'steal', 'theft', and 'thief' are also to be construed accordingly.

The goods must remain stolen at the time of the handling. Section 24(3) provides:

> But no goods shall be regarded as having continued to be stolen goods after they have been restored to the person from whom they were stolen or to other lawful possession or custody, or after that person and any other person claiming through him have otherwise ceased as regards those goods to have any right to restitution in respect of the theft.

This provision relates to the two situations dealt with in the following paragraphs.

14.5.1.1.1 *Restoration of goods*

When do goods cease to be stolen? This problem arises most often when the owner (or his agent) or the police repossess the goods and then return them to the thief to entrap the handler. **If the police take possession of the goods this constitutes 'other lawful possession or custody'. In these situations the handler generally will not be guilty of handling as the goods will have ceased to be stolen** (see *Haughton* v *Smith, ante; Dolan* (1855) 6 Cox CC 449; *Schmidt* (1866) LR 1 CCR 15; *Villensky* [1892] 2 QB 597). There is one situation where the handler may be convicted, however, namely where it is alleged that he 'arranged' to handle the goods provided that the arrangement was made after the goods were stolen and before they were restored to lawful possession. For the goods to cease to be stolen there must be an act by the owner, etc. amounting to the deliberate exercise of control over the goods. Simply to mark goods which have been stolen for the purpose of identifying them later when transferred by the thief to the handler does not constitute the exercise of control over the goods (see *Greater London Metropolitan Police Commissioner* v *Streeter* (1980) 71 Cr App R 113).

In deciding whether goods have been restored to lawful possession, the question whether a person has taken possession of goods for this purpose depends primarily on his intentions when he acted (see *AG's Reference (No. 1 of 1974)* [1974] QB 744). In this case a police officer correctly suspected that goods in a car were stolen. He immobilised the car by removing the rotor arm and kept watch. When D returned to the car he questioned him and then arrested him. The Court of Appeal (at p. 753) held that:

> [I]f the jury came to the conclusion that the proper explanation of what had happened was that the police officer had not intended at that stage to reduce the goods into his possession or to assume the control of them, and at that stage was merely concerned to ensure that the driver, if he appeared, could not get away without answering questions, then in that case the proper conclusion of the jury would have been to the effect that the goods had not been reduced into the possession of the police . . . .

14.5.1.1.2 *The right to restitution has ceased*

Goods cease to be stolen when the person from whom they were stolen, or any person claiming through him, no longer has any right to restitution of the goods. For example, if E deceives P into agreeing to sell him property, this is a voidable contract of sale. If P discovers the deception but decides to ratify the contract by delivering the property to E, the goods cease to be stolen. Thus, if E sells the property to D who believes that it is stolen, there is no offence of handling as P's right to restitution of the property ceased upon ratification of the voidable contract.

14.5.1.2 **Goods and their proceeds**

Section 34(2)(b) defines 'goods' to include 'money and every other description of property except land, and includes things severed from land by stealing'. The definition of 'goods' is largely coextensive with that of 'property' for the purposes of theft with the exception that land, if it is to be the subject of handling, must be severed. The requirement of severance acts as a limitation in respect of property obtained as a result of deception or blackmail.

Section 24(2) provides:

> [R]eferences to stolen goods shall include, in addition to the goods originally stolen and parts of them (whether in their original state or not)—
>
> (a) any other goods which directly or indirectly represent or have at any time represented the stolen goods in the hands of the thief as being the proceeds of any disposal or realisation of the whole or part of the goods stolen or of goods so representing the stolen goods; and
>
> (b) any other goods which directly or indirectly represent or have at any time represented the stolen goods in the hands of a handler of the stolen goods or any part of them as being the proceeds of any disposal or realisation of the whole or part of the stolen goods handled by him or of goods so representing them.

The effect of this provision is to extend the range of property which may be regarded as 'stolen' for the purposes of supporting a charge of handling. Thus, if the thief or the initial handler converts the stolen goods into money or other property (i.e. 'proceeds' of the disposal or realisation of the stolen goods), these proceeds are also regarded as 'stolen' so that anyone who knowingly handles them will be guilty of handling. This can lead to considerable multiplication of the 'goods' which may be regarded as 'stolen' for the purposes of handling.

14.5.1.3 Handling

'Handling' may be committed in one of four basic ways provided that the conduct involved takes place 'otherwise than in the course of stealing'. There is, however, only one offence (see *Griffiths* v *Freeman* [1970] 1 All ER 1117; *Nicklin* [1977] 2 All ER 444), and 'handling' is simply a generic term to cover the various ways in which the offence may be committed. Accordingly, an indictment which simply alleges 'handling' is not bad for duplicity but the better practice is to particularise the form of handling alleged (see *Griffiths* v *Freeman*, above; *Alt* (1972) 56 Cr App R 457). If one particular mode of handling is alleged, such as 'receiving', D cannot be convicted on the basis of a different mode (see *Nicklin*, earlier). In any case where there is uncertainty as to the appropriate mode to allege, the indictment should contain separate counts alleging different modes (see *Sloggett* [1972] 1 QB 430).

 Key Point

The four basic modes of committing the offence are:

(1) *receiving* stolen goods or
(2) *undertaking* the retention, removal, disposal, or realisation of the goods for the benefit of another person or
(3) *assisting* in the retention, removal, disposal, or realisation of the goods by another person or
(4) *arranging* to do (1), (2), or (3).

Two points in particular should be noted. **First, in all cases the goods must be stolen at the time the receiving, undertaking, assisting, or arranging takes place.** If, for example, D arranges with A to receive goods which A is going to steal, D is not guilty of handling as there are no goods then stolen, but he may be guilty of conspiracy to handle stolen goods. **Secondly, apart from receiving or arranging to receive, the other forms of handling are subject to a qualification: in (2) the acts must be done 'for the benefit of another person' and in (3) the handler must assist another person to do the relevant acts. If D is charged with arranging to undertake or assist the same qualification applies.**

14.5.1.3.1 *Receiving and arranging to receive*

Receiving involves D in taking possession or control of the stolen goods either alone or with others, which may include joint possession with the thief. It is a finite act so that, where D receives on different occasions goods from different thefts, these occasions must be specified as separate counts on the indictment (see *Smythe* (1980) 72 Cr App R 8). If D's agent takes possession of stolen goods with his authority this will constitute receiving by D (see *Miller* (1854) 6 Cox CC 353). **There is no requirement that D should receive the goods to keep or otherwise dispose of them nor that he should gain any profit or other benefit from their receipt.** Possession or control is sufficient even if D is only receiving them temporarily to hide them (see *Richardson* (1834) 6 C & P 335). There must be evidence, however, that D has possession or control. If D is merely inspecting the goods in the thief's presence during negotiations, he has neither possession nor control of them. Helping a thief to remove stolen goods from a lorry does not amount to receiving (see *Hobson* v *Impett* (1957) 41 Cr App R 138) although it may amount to one of the other forms of handling. If D finds stolen goods and takes possession of them this does not amount to receiving (see *Haider*, unreported, 22 March 1985) although this may amount to theft (see **12.2.2.2.1**).

Negotiating with the thief to purchase stolen goods is not itself a complete act of arranging to receive. When agreement is reached that D will receive the goods, this will constitute the offence of arranging to receive. The arrangement need not be made with the thief; an arrangement made with a person innocently in possession of stolen goods would suffice provided D knew the goods were stolen. Although an agreement may not be concluded, an offer by D to receive stolen goods may constitute an attempt to handle.

14.5.1.3.2 *Undertaking or assisting*

There are four activities which may constitute handling where either D undertakes those activities for the benefit of another, or D assists another to perform those activities or arranges to undertake or assist in those activities. In *Bloxham* [1982] 1 All ER 582, the House of Lords held that 'the other person' must have the same meaning whether it is alleged that D assisted or undertook the relevant activity. Thus something may only be undertaken for the benefit of another if that other person could have done the act himself.

> In *Bloxham*, D, believing that a car he had bought was stolen, sold it to E. He was charged with handling stolen goods on the basis that he had undertaken the realisation of the car for the benefit of another person, namely E. The House of Lords was of the view that the person for whose benefit this transaction was undertaken was D and not E. E's purchase of the car may have been of benefit to him, but this was irrelevant as it was D's act of sale (realisation) which was required to have benefited him. D could only be convicted where the sale was for the benefit of another person as where, for example, he was selling the car as an agent for C (the thief or another handler of it).

Furthermore, the act of sale of the car (realisation) was not one which could have been performed *by* E as he did not possess the car. Where A and B are jointly charged in one count on an indictment with handling 'by or for the benefit of another person', the other person must be someone other than the co-accused (see *Gingell* [2000] 1 Cr App R 88).

The four activities involved each have a separate meaning and appear to cover all the various things a person may seek to do with stolen goods.

(a) *Retention* In *Pitchley* (1972) 57 Cr App R 30, **the Court of Appeal defined 'retain' to mean 'keep possession of, not lose, continue to have'.** A person undertakes the retention of stolen goods where, for example, he stores the goods for the thief or another handler. As retention is a continuing activity, D may commit the offence where, after taking possession of property to retain for another, he discovers that it is stolen. By continuing to keep possession of it he would be undertaking to retain it (but cf. *Pitchley* where the Court of Appeal appears to have treated this as assisting in the retention of stolen goods). D will be guilty of assisting another to retain stolen goods where he does something 'intentionally and dishonestly, for the purpose of enabling the goods to be retained' (*per* Cantley J in *Kanwar* [1982] 2 All ER 528). Examples of such conduct would be where D helps to hide the goods or he puts the thief in touch with someone else who agrees to store them, or where he tells lies to make it more difficult for the police to find or identify the goods (see *Kanwar*).

 Example

If E is a thief and the police visit E's flat seeking particular goods and D tells the police that items fitting the description of the stolen goods in fact belong to him and he lent them to E, D would be assisting E to retain those goods. By contrast, however, if D is, for example, a lodger in E's flat and knows where the stolen goods are hidden, but simply refuses to answer any police questions (as opposed to giving untruthful answers), this does not constitute assisting (see *Brown* [1970] QB 105).

In *Brown*, the Court of Appeal took the view that to hold that a failure to answer questions amounted to 'assisting' would encroach on the principle that a person is not bound to answer police questions. If, however, the stolen goods were hidden in D's room, this would be circumstantial evidence which may point to him having permitted them to be hidden there initially and thus may support a charge of handling on the basis of undertaking to retain the stolen goods.

It appears that D will be convicted only where a purposive intent is proved. In *Kanwar*, D's husband brought home stolen goods which D used to furnish the home being aware of their provenance. Cantley J stated that D would not be guilty of handling where 'she was merely willing for the goods to be kept and used in the house and was thinking it was nice to have them there, although they were stolen goods'. Similarly a person does not assist in the retention of stolen goods merely by using them (see *Sanders* (1982) 75 Cr App R 84).

(b) *Removal* **This involves transporting or carrying stolen goods.** If D transports stolen goods for E's benefit he will have undertaken their removal; if he assists E to transport goods—for example, by lending him a van—he will have assisted in their removal.

(c) *Disposal* **This covers destroying, dumping, giving away, or transforming stolen goods.** An example of transformation would be where D melts down stolen silver items. The fact that D benefits from a disposal of stolen property does not, in itself, amount to assisting in its disposal; assisting requires an act of helping or encouraging (see *Coleman* [1986] Crim LR 56). In *Coleman*, D and his wife purchased a flat in their joint names; the wife, to D's knowledge, used stolen money to pay some of the fees involved. While the purchase of the flat benefited D, this did not establish that he had assisted her; there had to be proof that D encouraged her to do so or agreed to her doing so. On a proper direction, however, a jury may have inferred this from the facts.

(d) *Realisation* **Realisation involves the selling of stolen goods or their exchange for anything else of value.** If D sells stolen goods as agent for E (the thief or another handler) he undertakes their realisation for the benefit of another. If D introduces a purchaser to E who is seeking to sell stolen goods, he assists in their realisation. If D arranges a meeting between D and E he would be arranging to assist in the realisation of stolen goods.

14.5.1.3.3 *Otherwise than in the course of the stealing*

This limitation in s. 22(1) protects the original thief from liability for handling in respect of the course of conduct which constituted the original theft. This is necessary where two or more persons participate in the original theft. As theft is committed as soon as D appropriates property, subsequent acts to remove the property might otherwise amount to handling but for this limitation (see *Gregory* (1981) 77 Cr App R 41). For example, D and E agree to burgle a house. D enters and passes property through the window to E outside. D and E then carry the goods to a van to transport them to a fence who will pay them for the property. If s. 22(1) did not contain this limitation, E would be guilty of receiving when D hands him the goods and both D and E would be guilty of assisting each other to remove the goods and to realise them. The phrase 'course of the stealing' extends beyond the time of the appropriation of the property. **The difficulty, however, is determining when the course of the stealing ends** (*Pitham and Hehl* (1976) 65 Cr App R 45). For example, if D removes a statue from P's house and hides it in P's shed to return later with E to remove it from the premises, it is submitted that 'the course of the stealing' was over when D first removed the statue so that when E later assisted D to remove it from the shed he was assisting another to remove stolen goods. By contrast, if E had accompanied D and waited in the shed to help D, the whole transaction would have been a continuing one and E would have been an aider and abettor to the burglary or theft rather than a handler. It is, essentially, a question of fact when a course of stealing ends.

Where D is found in possession of stolen goods several days after the theft it may not be clear whether he is the thief or a handler.

 Question

If D is charged with handling, must the prosecution prove that he came by the goods 'otherwise than in the course of the stealing'?

The Court of Appeal held in *Cash* [1985] QB 801, that unless there was some evidence pointing to D being the thief, the jury were entitled to infer from the evidence of recent possession that he was the handler and, in such a case, the words 'otherwise than in the course of the stealing' should not be mentioned to the jury.

Once the 'course of the stealing' is over a thief may be guilty of handling the goods he has stolen—for example, by helping a receiver of the goods to move them or dispose of them. Similarly, if D is an accessory to the theft and several days later another party to the theft delivers to him his share of the items stolen, D will be guilty of receiving stolen goods.

It is worth noting that a handler generally commits a separate offence of theft by means of his subsequent dealing with the goods as virtually any act of handling (apart from the 'arranging' cases) will amount to an appropriation of property with the intention of permanently depriving the owner of it.

14.5.2 *Mens rea*

D will be guilty of handling only where he knows or believes that the goods are stolen goods at the time when he does the act which constitutes handling. In the case of receiving or arranging to receive or to do any of the other prohibited acts, this knowledge or belief must exist at the time D receives the goods or makes the arrangement (see *Brook* [1993] Crim LR 455). Where D's acts constitute *undertaking* or *assisting* in the prohibited acts, D will be liable if he learns the truth and continues to undertake or assist in, for example, the disposal of the stolen goods even though his initial participation in this activity was innocent. If D comes by the stolen goods innocently as a bona fide purchaser, his subsequent dealing with the goods, after he learns of their provenance, cannot amount to theft (see s. 3(2) of the TA 1968, **12.2.1.4.5**) but there is no similar provision excluding liability for handling. If, for example, D subsequently assisted E to sell the goods he would appear to have assisted another to realise the goods. By contrast, if D initially received the goods as a gift his keeping of or dealing with them after discovering their provenance would amount to theft (see s. 3(1) of the TA 1968, **12.2.1.4.4**); any dealing with the goods thereafter may also constitute handling.

14.5.2.1 What constitutes knowledge or belief?

Actual knowledge or belief on the part of D must be proved; it is not sufficient that any reasonable person would have realised that the goods were stolen (see *Atwal* v *Massey* (1971) 56 Cr App R 6). It is enough that D knows or believes in the existence of facts which render the goods 'stolen' in law. D need not know the law and, indeed, it would not avail him if he believed the goods had been stolen when, in fact, they had been obtained as a result of blackmail. **In addition, D need not know the nature of the goods**; if he takes possession of a suitcase having been told that it contains stolen goods, he will be guilty of handling if it does contain stolen goods even though they differ from the goods which D believed the case contained (see *McCullum* (1973) 57 Cr App R 645).

If D has direct evidence as to the provenance of the goods—for example, he witnesses the theft or the thief tells him the goods are stolen—he 'knows' the goods are stolen (*Hall* (1985) 81 Cr App R 260). **'Belief' that goods are stolen**, according to Boreham J in *Hall* (at p. 264):

may be said to be the state of mind of a person who says to himself: 'I cannot say I know for certain that these goods are stolen, but there can be no other reasonable conclusion in the light of all the circumstances, in the light of all that I have heard and seen'.

Suspicion, on the other hand, that goods are stolen is not sufficient (see *Hall; Grainge* (1974) 59 Cr App R 3; *Pethick* [1980] Crim LR 242), nor does foresight that goods are probably stolen constitute belief (*Reader* (1977) 66 Cr App R 33). Similarly, wilful blindness does not amount to knowledge or belief, although the fact that D suspects that goods are stolen and deliberately shuts his eyes to this is evidence which may point to him having the requisite knowledge or belief—that is, it is evidence from which knowledge or belief may be inferred (see *Griffiths* (1974) 60 Cr App R 14; *Moys* (1984) 79 Cr App R 72). This latter proposition, which was approved in *Forsyth* [1997] 2 Cr App R 299 (where it was stated that the *Hall* dictum was confusing), is difficult to follow; if the jury conclude that D suspected the goods were stolen, and suspicion does not constitute knowledge or belief, how can they infer from this knowledge or belief? The only way to avoid problems is for the judge to refuse to elaborate on the meaning of 'belief' and leave it to the jury to define as an ordinary word with the warning that suspicion, however great, is not belief.

14.5.2.2 Proof of knowledge or belief

The prosecution may be assisted in their task of proving knowledge or belief by the common law doctrine of '**recent possession**' and by s. 27(3) of the TA 1968. **Where D is found in possession of recently stolen goods and offers no explanation for his possession, or the jury are satisfied beyond reasonable doubt that any explanation offered is untrue, the jury** *may* **infer guilty knowledge from this fact** (see *Abramovitch* (1914) 11 Cr App R 45). The jury are not obliged to draw such an inference and should convict only where satisfied beyond reasonable doubt that D had such knowledge or belief (*Abramovitch*). There is no particular magic in this doctrine; it is, in fact, simply an example of circumstantial evidence.

Section 27(3) is very different. This provision permits the admission of evidence which may have little or no probative value but will have a highly prejudicial effect upon the accused's case. Where D is charged with handling *and* evidence has been given of his having performed an act which could amount to handling, then for the purpose of proving that D knew or believed the goods to be stolen, **two classes of evidence may be admitted:**

    (a) evidence that he has had in his possession, or has undertaken or assisted in the retention, removal, disposal or realisation of, stolen goods from any theft taking place not earlier than twelve months before the offence charged; and

    (b) (provided that seven days' notice in writing has been given to him of the intention to prove the conviction) evidence that he has within the five years preceding the date of the offence charged been convicted of theft or of handling stolen goods.

This subsection is strictly construed. Under (a) it is only permissible to tender evidence of the actual handling; no evidence as to D's state of mind nor as to the circumstances in which D came into possession of them, is admissible (*Bradley* (1979)

70 Cr App R 200). This has the potential of wreaking injustice; the other incident of handling may not have constituted an offence as D may not have known or believed the goods to be stolen. Thus, if D had innocently bought stolen goods and been acquitted on a charge of handling and then is subsequently found in possession of stolen goods, the other incident may be proved. The only purpose of proving it is to try to persuade a jury to conclude that it is stretching credulity to believe that both incidents are innocent. D may simply have been unfortunate, however, rather than dishonest. The trial judge, of course, has a discretion to refuse to admit evidence under (a) which the prosecution might tender (see *Rasini*, *The Times*, 20 March 1986).

Under para. (b) the prosecution may merely prove the fact of D's previous conviction (*Fowler* (1988) 86 Cr App R 219), but again the risk of prejudice is obvious (see *Hacker* [1994] 1 WLR 1659).

14.5.2.3 Dishonesty

The test of dishonesty is the same as for theft (see **12.2.2.2**). Obviously, if D receives stolen goods to hand them back to the owner or the police, he would not be dishonest.

14.6 Dishonestly retaining a wrongful credit

Prior to the decision of the House of Lords in *Preddy* [1996] AC 815, a credit balance obtained by deception from another account would have constituted 'stolen goods' for the purposes of the offence of handling. The Law Commission, *Offences of Dishonesty: Money Transfers* (Law Com No. 243, para. 6.2) states:

> On this assumption, the offence of handling would be committed if, knowing or believing the funds to be stolen goods, a person dishonestly receives them or deals with them in any of the other ways set out in section 22(1). According to *Preddy*, however, the funds are not obtained in the circumstances described in section 15(1); therefore they are probably not stolen goods, and subsequent dealings with them fall outside section 22(1).

The Theft (Amendment) Act 1996 created the offence of obtaining a money transfer by deception to cover the lacuna in s. 15 resulting from *Preddy* (since abolished by the Fraud Act 2006 and now covered by the offence of fraud contrary to s. 1 of that Act). A second offence was created by s. 2 inserting a new s. 24A into the TA 1968, making it an offence dishonestly to retain a wrongful credit. This offence is analogous to handling, but it goes further than simply restoring the status quo as it was prior to *Preddy*, as certain conduct is made criminal which was not previously criminal. Section 24A of the TA 1968 provides:

> (1) A person is guilty of an offence if—
>
>   (a) a wrongful credit has been made to an account kept by him or in respect of which he has any right or interest;

    (b) he knows or believes that the credit is wrongful; and

    (c) he dishonestly fails to take such steps as are reasonable in the circumstances to secure that the credit is cancelled.

(2) References to a credit are to a credit of an amount of money.

Actus reus	Mens rea
• A wrongful credit having been made to an account kept by D or in respect of which he has any right or interest; • D fails to take such steps as are reasonable in the circumstances to secure that the credit is cancelled.	• D knows or believes the credit is wrongful; and • he dishonestly fails to act.

This offence will cover a person whose account is credited with any wrongful credit as defined in s. 24A(2A). Thus D who obtains a wrongful credit by fraud commits this further offence if he dishonestly retains that credit. This stretches liability beyond that which exists for the offence of handling. Liability is further extended by the definition of 'wrongful credit' in s. 24A(2A). For example, if D steals £100 and places it in his own money box he cannot be convicted of handling stolen goods by retaining it (see **14.5.1.3**). By contrast, if D deposits the £100 in his bank account, this amounts to a wrongful credit and he will be guilty of the s. 24A(1) offence if he does not take reasonable steps to cancel that credit by returning £100 to his victim. (The same would apply if D had obtained the £100 by fraud or by blackmail.) If D had deposited the £100 in E's account, E would commit the s. 24A(1) offence if he knew or suspected that this was a wrongful credit and did not take reasonable steps to divest himself of it.

A person guilty of an offence under s. 24A is liable on conviction on indictment to imprisonment for a term not exceeding 10 years (s. 24A(6) of the TA 1968).

 The law in context

Sentencing burglars

What should happen to someone who is guilty of burglary? Research has found that many offenders convicted of acquisitive crimes are motivated by an addiction, often to illegal drugs, alcohol, or gambling. Of those arrested for domestic burglary, three times more are drug misusers than are not (Sentencing Advisory Panel, *Advice to the Sentencing Guidelines Council: Sentencing for Domestic Burglary* (2010), p. 23). The sentencing guidelines have changed in the last 20 years, with the Court of Appeal shifting position from focusing on crime prevention to prioritising the loss and suffering of victims.

The maximum sentence for domestic burglary is 14 years' imprisonment. Guidance from the Court of Appeal in *Brewster* [1998] 1 Cr App R 220 stressed that burglary is a serious offence, but whether a custodial sentence was required, and if so its length, depended heavily on the aggravating and mitigating features of the offence. For example, domestic burglaries were more serious if they were of occupied houses at night; if they were the result of professional organisation; targeted at the elderly, the disabled, or the sick; committed by persistent offenders; or if accompanied by vandalism or wanton injury to the victim. Mitigating features

→

→

included a plea of guilty, particularly at an early stage, and hard evidence of genuine regret and remorse, but there was no mitigation in drug addiction as the motivation for crime.

The Sentencing Advisory Panel in 2002 issued advice to the Court of Appeal on sentencing for burglary, which the Court in *McInerney* [2002] EWCA Crim 3003 only partially followed. In a controversial judgment, the Court issued new guidance for sentencing burglars. Lord Woolf CJ stressed that courts have to take into account the need to promote public confidence in the criminal justice system and the financial cost of different sentences and their relative effectiveness in preventing reoffending. At a time when there was significant judicial concern at overcrowding in prisons, the Court recommended a move away from the use of short custodial sentences for burglary, stating that there was little empirical evidence to suggest they are effective in preventing reoffending. Lord Woolf said that for offences that would otherwise have attracted a sentence of 18 months' imprisonment or less, the courts should impose a community sentence instead. He doubted the effectiveness of deterrent sentencing, and noted both the high recidivism rates for offenders receiving short prison sentences and the high financial cost of those sentences. The Court therefore recommended community sentences for a 'standard domestic burglary' committed by a first- or second-time burglar, subject to the proviso that the community sentence should be an effective punishment and one tackling the causes of the offender's criminal behaviour, such as drug addiction.

The judgment met with a swift and hostile response in the media and Parliament, to the extent that Lord Woolf took the unusual step of issuing a statement clarifying the meaning of *McInerney*, stressing that it presented only a slight change of emphasis rather than a dramatic alteration to existing guidelines (Lord Chancellor's Department Press Notices, 10/03, Statement by the Lord Chief Justice, 14 January 2003, para. 12).

In 2009, a differently constituted Court of Appeal in *Saw* [2009] EWCA Crim 1 criticised Lord Woolf's approach and issued fresh guidance, placing much greater emphasis on the experiences of burglary victims than Lord Woolf had done. Lord Judge CJ emphasised that what Lord Woolf had characterised as a 'standard domestic burglary' would frequently have a significant impact on the victim. He stated (at para 6):

> The starting point must always—we emphasise, always—be that burglary of a home is a serious criminal offence. The principle which must be grasped is that when we speak of dwelling house burglary, we are considering not only an offence against property, which it is, but also, and often more alarmingly and distressingly, an offence against the person. There is a longstanding, almost intuitive, belief that our homes should be our castles. . . . Something precious is violated by burglary of a home, and those who perpetrate this crime should be sentenced and punished accordingly.

Courts, he said, must address both the overall criminality of the defendant, in the light of his previous convictions, and second, 'the true impact of the offence on the victims'. He emphasised that burglary can have devastating consequences for victims even if the monetary cost of the loss is minimal, particularly if items of sentimental value have been taken. Following *Saw*, a standard domestic burglary attracted a custodial sentence, a significant shift away from Lord Woolf's more liberal approach to sentencing in *McInerney*.

It is noteworthy that Lord Judge emphasised the impact on the victim as a particularly important factor in sentencing. In virtually all criminal cases, victims now have the opportunity to complete a Victim Personal Statement in which they can detail how they have suffered physically, emotionally, psychologically, and financially (2013, https://www.gov.uk/government/publications/victim-personal-statement). Courts should consider and take the

→

→

statements into account before sentencing (*Criminal Practice Directions 2015* [2015] EWCA Crim 1567; *Code of Practice for Victims of Crime* (2015) https://www.gov.uk/government/uploads/system/uploads/attachment_data/file/476900/code-of-practice-for-victims-of-crime.PDF p. 21).

In 2011 the Sentencing Council published its definitive guideline on burglary (Sentencing Council, Burglary Offences: Definitive Guideline (2011) http://www.sentencingcouncil.org.uk/wp-content/uploads/Burglary_Definitive_Guideline_web_final.pdf). This explicitly lists victim-related factors (e.g. 'Theft/damage to property causing a significant degree of loss to the victim (whether economic, sentimental or personal value)', 'Trauma to the victim, beyond the normal inevitable consequence of intrusion and theft', p. 8) as ones that could take the burglary into a higher offence category, making it more likely that a custodial sentence will be imposed.

In addition, burglary is one of the offences in English law (alongside repeat trafficking of Class A drugs and some offences related to unlawful possession of knives or offensive weapons) that carries a mandatory minimum sentence for repeat offences. Introduced by the outgoing Conservative Government in the Crime (Sentences) Act 1997 and now consolidated in s. 111 of the Powers of Criminal Courts (Sentencing) Act 2000, a court must impose a minimum sentence of three years' imprisonment for anyone over the age of 18 who is convicted of domestic burglary if, at the time of committing that burglary, he had two other convictions for burglary. The minimum does not apply if there are particular circumstances that relate to any of the offences or the offender that would make it unjust in all the circumstances to impose the mandatory minimum. In *McInerney* (2003) Lord Woolf interpreted the section to mean that judges had a 'fairly substantial degree of discretion as to the categories of situations where the presumption can be rebutted' (para. 16). He said that there might be 'particular circumstances' if the first and second burglaries were committed many years before the third, or the offender has made real efforts to reform or address drug or alcohol additions but 'personal tragedy triggers the third offence'. From one perspective, this was a judicial 'flexing of muscles': the judiciary has tended to be resistant to government attempts to restrict their discretion by *requiring* them to impose sentences of imprisonment, pushing back against the requirements by interpreting the provisions in such a way as to take back discretion. However, the Court of Appeal has shown itself willing, on numerous occasions, to rule as unduly lenient departures from the mandatory minimum for repeat burglars (e.g. *AG's Reference (No. 17 of 2014)* [2014] EWCA Crim 842; *AG's Reference (No. 118 of 2015)* [2016] EWCA Crim 1108).

 Key Points

– Making off without payment is an offence under 3 of the Theft Act 1978:

  – The *actus reus* is complete when D makes off without paying from the spot where payment is required or expected for any goods supplied or services.

  – The *mens rea* is dishonesty, knowledge that payment on the spot is required or expected of him, and intention to avoid payment of the amount due.

– Burglary is defined in s. 9 of the Theft Act 1968:

  – The *actus reus* is complete when D enters a building or part of a building as a trespasser (s. 9(1)(a)), or having entered any building or part of a building as a trespasser he steals or attempts to steal anything in the building or inflicts or attempts to inflict on any person therein any GBH (s. 9(1)(b)).

→

→

– The *mens rea* is intention to commit theft, criminal damage, or to inflict GBH (s. 9(1)(a)) or simply the *mens rea* for theft or inflicting or attempting to inflict GBH (s. 9(1)(b)).

– Insertion of any part of the body may constitute 'entry'. Whether D has 'entered' a building is a question of fact for the jury or magistrates.

– Under s. 9, a person enters as a 'trespasser' when he enters in excess of the permission granted to him by the owner or occupier of the building. D must know that he is entering the building without permission or a legal right to do so, or be reckless as to whether he is.

– Aggravated burglary is an offence under s. 10 of the Theft Act 1968. It is committed when D commits a burglary and at the time has with him any firearm or imitation firearm, any offensive weapon, or any explosive.

– Blackmail is an offence under s. 21 of the Theft Act 1968:

– The *actus reus* is making an unwarranted demand with menaces.

– The *mens rea* is having a view to gain for himself or another or intent to cause loss to another, and if D contends the demand was not unwarranted, either a lack of belief on the part of D that he had reasonable grounds for making the demand or a lack of belief that the use of menaces was a proper means of reinforcing the demand.

– Handling stolen goods is an offence under s. 22 of the Theft Act 1968:

– The *actus reus* is, otherwise than in the course of the stealing, i) receiving stolen goods; ii) undertaking the retention, removal, disposal, or realisation of the goods for the benefit of another person; iii) assisting in the retention, removal, disposal or realisation of the goods by another person; iv) arranging to do any of those three things.

– The *mens rea* is knowledge or belief that the goods are stolen and acting dishonestly.

FURTHER READING

P. Alldridge, 'Attempted Murder of the Soul: Blackmail, Piracy and Secrets' (1993) 13 OJLS 368.

K. Laird, 'Conceptualising the Interpretation of "Dwelling" in Section 9 of the Theft Act 1968' [2013] Crim LR 656.

J. R. Spencer, 'Handling, Theft and the Mala Fide Purchaser' [1985] Crim LR 92 and 440.

15

Criminal damage

15.1 Introduction

The Criminal Damage Act 1971 contains the main offences involving damage to property. The Act is mainly the result of work by the Law Commission (see in particular Law Com No. 29). Criminal damage is a very common offence; in the year ending 2018 the police recorded more than half a million incidents of criminal damage and arson, while the Crime Survey for England and Wales estimates that there were more than 1.1 million offences of that type (Office for National Statistics, *Crime in England and Wales: Year Ending June 2018*, https://www.ons.gov.uk/peoplepopulationandcommunity/crimeandjustice/bulletins/crimeinenglandandwales/yearendingjune2018).

15.2 Destroying or damaging property belonging to another

Section 1(1) of the Criminal Damage Act 1971 provides:

> A person who without lawful excuse destroys or damages any property belonging to another intending to destroy or damage any such property or being reckless as to whether any such property would be destroyed or damaged shall be guilty of an offence.

Actus reus	Mens rea
D: • without lawful excuse, • destroys or damages • property • belonging to another.	D does so: • intentionally, or • recklessly.

The maximum punishment for this offence following trial on indictment is 10 years' imprisonment (s. 4(2)). Where, however, the offence is committed by fire it is charged as arson and the maximum punishment is life imprisonment (ss 1(3) and 4(1)). This reflects the extra danger arising from fire-raising. In 2018, the Sentencing Council published a consultation and draft guideline on sentencing for criminal damage offences (https://www.sentencingcouncil.org.uk/publications/item/arson-and-criminal-damage-consultation/).

15.2.1 *Actus reus*

15.2.1.1 **Destroy or damage**

Whether property is damaged is a question of fact and degree (see *Cox* v *Riley* (1986) 83 Cr App R 54). Few appellate cases have provided clear guidance on precise tests for deciding whether the acts alleged constitute 'damage', the Court of Appeal and Divisional Court repeatedly holding that 'damage' is a question of fact for the jury or magistrates. In *Roe* v *Kingerlee* [1986] Crim LR 735, the Divisional Court held: 'What constitutes criminal damage is a matter of fact and degree, and it is for the justices, applying their common sense to decide whether what occurred was damage or not ...' Sir Igor Judge in the Court of Appeal, in *Fiak* [2005] EWCA Crim 2381, held that the trial judge's direction to the jury that a person damages property if he 'render[s] it imperfect or inoperative' accurately described the constituent of criminal damage. However, Sir Igor Judge indicated that a trial judge should not direct the jury to find 'damage': '[W]e would expect an issue of this kind to be resolved by the jury.'

Damage includes physical harm, whether permanent or temporary, and the permanent or temporary impairment of the value or usefulness of property. Physical harm may result to property in many ways. Trampling down grass, or other vegetation, may constitute damage (see *Gayford* v *Choulder* [1898] 1 QB 316). The Crown Court, in *Hardman* v *Chief Constable of Avon and Somerset Constabulary* [1986] Crim LR 330, held that drawing or painting on a pavement using water soluble chalks or paints constitutes damage where the local authority is involved in expense in cleaning the pavement.

Spitting on a policeman's coat, however, does not constitute damage where the spittle can be removed with a damp cloth (*'A' (a juvenile)* v *R* [1978] Crim LR 689). **The requirement appears to be that if expense on the part of the owner of the property is incurred to restore it to its previous condition a jury or magistrates may conclude that damage has been caused** (see *Roe* v *Kingerlee* [1986] Crim LR 735). Had the policeman's coat required dry cleaning, for example, the result might have been different. The nature of the property involved may also be relevant in addition to the degree of harm caused. In *Morphitis* v *Salmon* [1990] Crim LR 48, the Divisional Court held that a scratch to a scaffold bar could not constitute damage as it involved no impairment of its value or usefulness since scratching was a normal incident of scaffolding components. By contrast, a scratch to the bonnet of a car could constitute damage as this would involve expense on the part of the owner in remedial work albeit that the secondhand value of the car might not be affected. Of course, if the damage to the paintwork is substantial this might also affect the value of the vehicle. **There is no need for the property to be rendered useless if the damage involves diminution in its value.** For example, if water is added to beer its value is diminished but it is not useless; this amounts to damage (see *Roper* v *Knott* [1898] 1 QB 868).

 Question

Do graffiti artists such as Banksy 'damage' the property on to which they spray tags, throw-ups, stencils, and so on?
    (For discussion, see: I. Edwards, 'Banksy's Graffiti: a Not-so-simple Case of Criminal Damage? (2009) 73(4) J Crim L 345–61.)

Damage arising from the impairment of the usefulness of property occurs where, for example, a machine is dismantled or tampered with so that it will not work (see *Fisher* (1865) LR 1 CCR 7; *Getty* v *Antrim County Council* [1950] NI 114). Where a part is removed or a machine dismantled, D should be charged with damaging the machine and not the parts unless these have also been damaged (see *Woolcock* [1977] Crim LR 104 and 161; *Morphitis* v *Salmon*, earlier). Simply to deny P the use of his property—for example, by placing a wheel clamp on his car—does not amount to damage (*Lloyd* [1992] 1 All ER 982).

In *Cox* v *Riley* (1986) 83 Cr App R 54, erasure of the programmes on a printed circuit card used to control a computerised saw was held to be damage to the card (affirmed in *Whiteley*, *The Times*, 6 February 1991). The Police and Justice Act 2006 added a subsection to s. 10 of the 1971 Act, so that it now provides:

(5) For the purposes of this Act a modification of the contents of a computer shall not be regarded as damaging any computer or computer storage medium unless its effect on that computer or computer storage medium impairs its physical condition.

The accused in *Cox* v *Riley* and *Whiteley* would now be guilty of the offence in s. 3 of the Computer Misuse Act 1990 of '[u]nauthorised acts with intent to impair, or with recklessness as to impairing, operation of computer, etc.'.

Section 10(5) does not affect the authority of *Cox* v *Riley* and *Whiteley* insofar as they are appropriate to other situations where information is stored in electro-magnetic form. For example, if D alters or erases P's audio tapes or video tapes, this would constitute damage even though the physical nature of the tapes had not been altered: what needs to be proved is that tangible property has been damaged, not necessarily that the damage is tangible.

Criminal damage is also committed where D destroys property—for example, by demolishing a building, breaking up a machine, killing an animal, laying waste crops (e.g. by mowing a field of wheat, or spraying it with herbicide), incinerating books, etc. It is difficult to envisage a case where damage will not be done to the property in the process of destroying it.

15.2.1.2 Property

Section 10(1) provides:

> In this Act 'property' means property of a tangible nature, whether real or personal, including money and—
>
> (a) including wild creatures which have been tamed or are ordinarily kept in captivity, and any other wild creatures or their carcasses if, but only if, they have been reduced into possession which has not been lost or abandoned or are in the course of being reduced into possession; but
>
> (b) not including mushrooms growing wild on any land or flowers, fruit or foliage of a plant growing wild on any land.
>
> For the purposes of this subsection 'mushroom' includes any fungus and 'plant' includes any shrub or tree.

There are some differences between this definition of 'property' and that in s. 4 of the Theft Act (TA) 1968, necessitated by the differing mischief to which each Act is directed. First, land may not be stolen but it may be damaged or destroyed; indeed arson is generally committed against land in the form of buildings. Secondly, 'property' is confined to tangible property in the Criminal Damage Act. Thirdly, wild mushrooms, flowers, fruit, or foliage cannot be the subject of criminal damage although they may, in certain circumstances, be the subject of theft.

In *Cresswell* v *DPP* [2006] EWHC 3379 (Admin), the Divisional Court held that badgers which the Government was seeking to cull as part of research into the link between badgers and bovine tuberculosis were not property for the purposes of s. 10 or at common law. Accordingly individuals who destroyed badger traps had neither a defence of lawful excuse under s. 5 nor the common law defence of protection of property.

15.2.1.3 Belonging to another

Section 10 provides:

> (2) Property shall be treated for the purposes of this Act as belonging to any person—
>
> (a) having the custody or control of it;
>
> (b) having in it any proprietary right or interest (not being an equitable interest arising only from an agreement to transfer or grant an interest); or
>
> (c) having a charge on it.
>
> (3) Where the property is subject to a trust, the persons to whom it belongs shall be so treated as including any person having a right to enforce the trust.
>
> (4) Property of a corporation sole shall be so treated as belonging to the corporation notwithstanding a vacancy in the corporation.

Again these provisions are broadly similar to s. 5 of the TA 1968. In s. 5 of the TA 1968 theft may be committed where a person has 'possession or control' of property; the equivalent words in s. 10(2) are 'custody or control' suggesting that P must have physical custody of it; these words were used to provide a clearer concept than the word 'possession' which is a technical term sometimes giving rise to difficulty (see *Warner* v *Metropolitan Police Commissioner* [1969] 2 AC 256).

Property may be the subject of criminal damage, therefore, where some person has custody or control of it or a proprietary right or interest in it. As with theft, where D may steal property he owns if another also has a proprietary right or interest in it or possession or control of it, a person may cause criminal damage to property he owns if another has such an interest in it. For example, if D hires a vintage car to P and then removes the rotor arm from it rendering it inoperable, he may be guilty of criminal damage. In cases where D is alleged to have damaged property in which he has a proprietary interest, proof of *mens rea* or disproof of lawful excuse may be difficult. If D destroys his own property for a dishonest purpose—for example, to make a fraudulent insurance claim—this is not an offence under s. 1(1) despite D's dishonesty, as an insurance company has no proprietary interest in property it insures. But if D mistakenly believes property is his when it is not he may be liable for criminal damage if he also believes someone else has a proprietary interest in it (see *Seray-Wurie* v *DPP* [2012] EWCH 208 (Admin)).

15.2.2 *Mens rea*

The destruction or damage to property belonging to another amounts to an offence only if it is done intentionally or recklessly and without lawful excuse.

15.2.2.1 **Intention and recklessness**

As to the meaning of intention see 3.2. If D is charged with intentionally damaging property belonging to another, it must be proved that he intended to cause damage by his act (or omission) and that he intended to damage property belonging to another. If D mistakenly believes that the property he is damaging or destroying is his own, he will lack the requisite intention (but if he believes another also has a proprietary interest in the property his mistake will not save him—see *Seray-Wurie*, **15.2.1.3**).

> In *Smith (David)* [1974] QB 354, D, not knowing property law, damaged fixtures he had installed in the flat of which he was a tenant when removing wiring for his stereo equipment. He believed that the fixtures belonged to him when, in law, they belonged to the landlord. His conviction for criminal damage was quashed, James LJ stating (at p. 360):

>> Applying the ordinary principles of *mens rea*, the intention and recklessness and the absence of lawful excuse required to constitute the offence have reference to property belonging to another. It follows that in our judgment no offence is committed under this section if a person destroys or causes damage to property belonging to another if he does so in the honest though mistaken belief that the property is his own, and provided that belief is honestly held it is irrelevant to consider whether or not it is a justifiable belief.

In this case D's mistake was one of law; it would make no difference if the mistake was one of fact. For example, after his exams D burns a textbook believing it is his when, in fact, it is his flatmate P's textbook which he has picked up by mistake. It is also not necessary to prove that D knows or realises that what he is doing to the property of another constitutes 'damage' in law. In *Seray-Wurie* (see **15.2.1.3**) D wrote on a parking notice with a black marker pen, something which amounted in law to damage even though he may not have believed it did. D agreed he wrote on the notice, intending to do so; his motives for doing so could not alter the fact that his action amounted to damage and his action was intentional.

Question

If a graffiti artist such as Banksy was charged with criminal damage, what would be the effect of him arguing that he honestly believed that his graffiti is not damage but is great art appreciated by lots of members of the public?

Recklessness in the context of criminal damage was originally defined by the House of Lords in *Caldwell* to include inadvertence to an obvious risk of damage to property. In *G* [2003] UKHL 50, the House of Lords reversed *Caldwell* and provided the following fully subjective definition for recklessness (for detailed discussion of the meaning of recklessness, see **3.4**):

A person acts recklessly within the meaning of section 1 of the Criminal Damage Act 1971 with respect to—

(i)   a circumstance when he is aware of a risk that it exists or will exist;

(ii) a result when he is aware of a risk that it will occur;

and it is, in the circumstances known to him, unreasonable to take the risk.

A person will be deemed reckless if he is aware of a risk but then closes his mind to the possibility of damage. In *Booth* v *Crown Prosecution Service* [2006] EWHC 192 (Admin), B was drunk and ran across a road without looking to see whether it was safe to do so, colliding with and denting a car. He was charged with criminal damage. The magistrates found that although he was aware of the risks he deliberately closed his mind to those risks and ran out in front of the car. They also found that the damage was an obviously foreseeable consequence of B's actions. On appeal, B argued that the magistrates had reverted to an objective test which was no longer applicable following *G*. The Divisional Court held that the magistrates had been entitled to find that B was reckless; in crossing the road the risk uppermost in one's mind would be the risk of personal injury, but that does not mean that they were not entitled to conclude that he did in fact appreciate the risk to property. However, it is unfortunate that the Court characterised B's argument as 'an overcritical textual analysis' of the wording used by the magistrates; there is a fundamental difference between finding that a person would have appreciated a risk had they given thought to the possibility and finding that a person did in fact appreciate the risk. That difference is at the heart of the House of Lords' judgment in *G*.

Where D is charged with recklessly damaging property the offence is one of basic intent. If D is charged in the alternative, that is intentionally *or* recklessly damaging property, he will also be denied the possibility of raising intoxication as a factor relevant to his state of mind as criminal damage where recklessness is charged is an offence of basic intent but where the aggravated offence is charged under s. 1(2) (see **14.3**) it is an offence of specific intent (see **5.5.3**).

15.2.2.2 **Lawful excuse**

Section 5(2) provides a partial definition of 'lawful excuse' (see s. 5(5)). Thus D may also avail himself of any other defence, such as duress, prevention of crime, arrest of offenders, and self-defence.

 Example

Where D is being attacked by P he may damage property to defend himself where, for example:

(i)   he jumps through a window, breaking it, in seeking to escape from P;
(ii) he pushes P through the window;
(iii) he hits P over the head with a vase belonging to X and breaks it.

In (i) D's defence would be duress of circumstances and in (ii) and (iii) it would be self-defence. In each case D will succeed provided the measures he took were objectively reasonable in the circumstances.

Section 5 provides:

(2) A person charged with an offence to which this section applies shall, whether or not he would be treated for the purposes of this Act as having a lawful excuse apart from this subsection, be treated for those purposes as having a lawful excuse—

(a) if at the time of the act or acts alleged to constitute the offence he believed that the person or persons whom he believed to be entitled to consent to the destruction of or damage to the property in question had so consented, or would have so consented to it if he or they had known of the destruction or damage and its circumstances; or

(b) if he destroyed or damaged or threatened to destroy or damage the property in question or, in the case of a charge of an offence under s. 3 above, intended to use or cause or permit the use of something to destroy or damage it, in order to protect property belonging to himself or another or a right or interest in property which was or which he believed to be vested in himself or another, and at the time of the act or acts alleged to constitute the offence he believed—

(i) that the property, right or interest was in immediate need of protection; and

(ii) that the means of protection adopted or proposed to be adopted were or would be reasonable having regard to all the circumstances.

(3) For the purposes of this section it is immaterial whether a belief is justified or not if it is honestly held.

(4) For the purposes of subsection (2) above a right or interest in property includes any right or privilege in or over land, whether created by grant, licence or otherwise.

15.2.2.2.1 *Lawful excuse: belief in consent (s. 5(2)(a))*

Section 5(2)(a) is equivalent to s. 2(1)(b) of the TA 1968 (see **12.2.2.2.1**). The only issue is whether D's belief was honestly held regardless of whether or not it was reasonable. It does not even matter that D's mistake was a drunken one (see *Jaggard v Dickinson* [1980] 3 All ER 716, **5.5.6.4**).

> In *Jaggard* v *Dickson*, J was drunk and caused damage to windows and a curtain whilst attempting to break into a house which she mistakenly believed to be her friend's house. The friend allowed the defendant to treat the house as her own. J was convicted of causing criminal damage, the justices ruling that she was not entitled to rely upon the defence under s. 5(2) and (3) of the Criminal Damage Act 1971 (that she honestly believed the friend would have consented to her actions) since that belief was induced by intoxication. The Divisional Court allowed her appeal. Section 5(2) was concerned with the actual state of mind of the defendant at the time of commission of the offence, whether or not that state of mind was induced by drunkenness.

The burden is on the prosecution to prove beyond reasonable doubt the absence of lawful excuse once D has adduced some evidence to raise the issue. D's mistake may relate to one of several matters (or to a combination of these matters): (i) D may mistakenly believe that he has been told to damage or destroy the property, (ii) D may mistakenly believe that the person telling him to damage or destroy the property (or whom he believes is telling him to do so) is the person entitled to consent to its damage or destruction, (iii) D may mistakenly believe that the person entitled to consent to the damage or destruction of the property would do so if he knew of the circumstances in which D has damaged or destroyed it, (iv) D may believe that the person whom he mistakenly believes is entitled to consent to the damage or destruction of the property would do so if he knew of the circumstances in which D has damaged or destroyed it.

If D honestly believes that the owner of property (or some other person entitled to give consent) has consented to his damaging the property, the reason for the damage is irrelevant even if it is for the purpose of perpetrating a fraud. This results from the fact that criminal damage is not an offence of which dishonesty is an element.

> In *Denton* [1982] 1 All ER 65, D, who was employed at a cotton mill, set fire to the mill and machinery in it because he thought his 'employer' T had asked him to do so in order to make a fraudulent claim against the insurers. Indeed, it appeared that T had asked D to do so. The Court of Appeal quashed his conviction, Lord Lane CJ stating (at p. 68):
>
>> [O]ne has to decide whether or not an offence is committed at the moment that the acts are alleged to be committed. The fact that somebody may have had a dishonest intent which in the end he was going to carry out, namely a claim from the insurance company, cannot turn what was not originally a crime into a crime. There is no unlawfulness under the 1971 Act in burning a house. It does not become unlawful because there may be an inchoate attempt to commit fraud contained in it; that is to say it does not become a crime under the 1971 Act, whatever may be the situation outside the Act.

If T had asked D to set fire to the mill for the purpose of making a fraudulent insurance claim, both D and T could have been convicted of conspiracy to defraud. But where D claims 'God' commanded him to damage the property, 'God' is not a 'person' capable of giving such consent (see *Blake* v *DPP* [1993] Crim LR 587).

15.2.2.2.2 *Damaging property in order to protect other property (s. 5(2(b))*

Section 5(2)(b) provides that D has a lawful excuse where he believes his property or that of another (or property which he believes is his property or another's) is in need of immediate protection and he damages or destroys property in order to protect property belonging to himself or another believing that this is reasonable in all the circumstances. D will satisfy the requirement of immediacy in s. 5(2)(b) if the threat to his property has already materialised. In *Chamberlain* v *Lindon, The Times,* 6 April 1998, the Queen's Bench Division upheld the decision of Nuneaton Justices to acquit D of criminal damage where he had demolished a wall built by C on C's land as D honestly believed such action was necessary to protect his right of vehicular access across C's land and that delay would prejudice his rights.

Whether or not D believed the means he adopted to protect the property were reasonable is a subjective question and not a matter of objective fact (see *Jones (Iorwerth)* [2003] EWCA Crim 894). The objective element of this defence, however, is whether what D did could be said to have been done 'in order to protect property'. This assessment is made on the basis of the facts as D believed them to be (see *Jones and others* [2004] EWCA Crim 1981). If D's purpose is something other than the protection of property this defence will not be available (see *Hunt* (1978) 66 Cr App R 105; *Hill and Hall* [1989] Crim LR 136). Having determined what D's purpose was, it is for the court to rule as a matter of law whether this amounts to a purpose of protecting property; the cases hold, however, that the fact that D believes he is protecting his property is irrelevant. The approach adopted in the cases is open to criticism as what D's purpose was would appear to be something which may only be determined by examining his subjective state of mind. Whether the means he chose to effect his purpose were capable of doing so is, strictly speaking, irrelevant. While the efficacy of the means chosen may be circumstantial evidence which may help the jury determine what his purpose was (namely the less likely the means chosen were to be effective, the less likely it is that the protection of property was D's purpose), the fact of their inefficacy should not be determinative of that issue. If D honestly believed that what he was doing would protect the property, no matter how unreasonable that belief might be, he was acting 'in order to protect property'. Section 5(3) states this clearly: it is immaterial whether a belief is justified or not if it is honestly held.

The courts' approach, however, is to impose an objective test on this defence. In *Hill and Hall*, the Court of Appeal created a judicial filter in a move that seemed designed to prevent some lawful excuse defences from going before a jury.

> In *Hill and Hall*, D and E, members of the Campaign for Nuclear Disarmament, believed that, by cutting the fence surrounding a United States naval base at Brawdy, they would protect their homes. Their reasoning was that if the Russians attacked this nuclear base, their homes would be damaged by the blast or fall-out from a nuclear attack. If enough people breached the perimeter fence the Americans might decide to remove the base and thereby remove the threat of nuclear attack. The trial judge's conclusion was that D's and E's purpose was to encourage the Americans to leave and this was not a purpose of protecting their property.

The Court of Appeal affirmed that he had adopted the correct approach which was to decide (i) what was in D's mind (the subjective test) and (ii) whether it could be said, as a matter of law, on the facts as believed by D, that cutting the strand of wire could amount to something done to protect her home or those of others (the objective test). Thus, the question whether property is damaged or destroyed by D 'in order to protect property belonging to himself' is one of law and not a matter of D's belief. The trial judge had also concluded that D and E had not adduced any evidence that they believed that their property was 'in immediate need of protection'. The Court of Appeal held that he was correct in withdrawing this part of the case from the jury. This decision was followed in *Blake* v *DPP*, earlier, where the Divisional Court ruled that it was for the court objectively to decide whether, on the facts believed by the accused, the action taken did protect, or was capable of protecting, property. D, a vicar, protesting outside Parliament against the use of force by the allies in Iraq and Kuwait, wrote a biblical quotation on a concrete pillar. The Court ruled that he could not rely on s. 5(2)(b) as the damage done was not capable of protecting property in the Gulf States as it was too remote. (See also *Johnson* v *DPP* [1994] Crim LR 673.)

> In *Jones (Iorwerth)*, D, in a roof-top protest over planning permission for a lorry park which he believed would lead to further diminution in the value of his bungalow adjacent to the lorry park, caused £65,000 worth of damage to council offices. Upholding his conviction, the Court affirmed the objective nature of the test stating (at para. 19):

> > The court has to decide whether what the appellant claims to be doing can be characterised in law as the protection of property. That, as it seems to us, is no different from, for instance, the court having to decide whether, when a person says that their intent was to break the victim's nose, that in law amounts to an intent to cause grievous bodily harm.

The Court explained its reasoning on the basis of the purpose behind the legislation (at para. 22):

> > Although we have, of course, approached section 5 on the basis of its plain wording and not sought to reflect upon its reasons or motivation, we have no doubt at all . . . that it was not intended . . . to encompass a deliberate and lawless attack on a person's property, with a view to attempt to make him change his mind. It was intended to excuse interference with one part of property that was directly and proximately threatening the property of the appellant.

An important point to note is that the jury plays a crucial role in deciding whether the lawful excuse defence is successful, once the judge has ruled that the damage was capable of protecting other property in immediate need of protection. The defence has been used by political protesters, particularly those seeking to raise awareness of environmental issues by damaging genetically modified crops or painting slogans on power-stations. Jury sympathy can be important in deciding whether defendants are found not guilty (see for example, 'Greenpeace wins key GM case' *The Guardian*, 21 September 2000, https://www.theguardian.com/environment/2000/sep/21/activists.gmcrops).

Question

There has been much public discussion of the impact of hydraulic fracturing, or 'fracking', on property in the area where the activity takes place. Fracking is a technique used to extract gas and oil from shale rock. Some argue that fracking damages property in the vicinity. If a group of protesters damaged or destroyed equipment used for fracking, would they be able successfully to plead lawful excuse under s. 5?

15.3 Destroying or damaging property with intent to endanger life

Section 1(2) of the Criminal Damage Act 1971 provides:

A person who without lawful excuse destroys or damages any property, whether belonging to himself or another—

(a) intending to destroy or damage any property or being reckless as to whether any property would be destroyed or damaged; and

(b) intending by the destruction or damage to endanger the life of another or being reckless as to whether the life of another would be thereby endangered; shall be guilty of an offence.

Actus reus	Mens rea
D:	D does so:
• without lawful excuse,	• intentionally, or
• destroys or damages	• recklessly; and
• property	• intending by the destruction or damage to endanger the life of another, or
• whether belonging to himself or another.	• being reckless as to whether the life of another would be thereby endangered.

The maximum punishment for this offence is life imprisonment (s. 4(1)). In many cases where D damages property and endangers life he will do so with the specific intent to kill and would be liable to conviction for attempted murder. This offence, however, is wider in some respects than attempted murder, as it is sufficient that D is reckless whether life will be endangered (but attempted murder does not require proof of damage to property). This offence avoids the difficulties of proving that D has done a 'more than merely preparatory act'.

15.3.1 *Actus reus*

The meaning of 'damage', 'destroy', and 'property' is the same as for s. 1(1). **There is a major difference, however, in that the property destroyed or damaged need not belong to another; D may commit this offence where he destroys or damages his own property if he does so with intent to endanger life or being**

reckless thereto. For example, if D, a landlord wishing to evict a squatter who is refusing to leave, throws a petrol bomb into the house thereby damaging the property, he is liable to conviction for the s. 1(2) offence if he had the requisite *mens rea* specified in s. 1(2)(b). There is no need to prove that a life was in fact endangered (*Parker* [1993] Crim LR 856).

15.3.2 *Mens rea*

D must intend to damage or destroy property or be reckless thereto. In addition, **D must intend by that damage to endanger life or be reckless thereto**.

> In *Steer* [1987] 2 All ER 833, D fired a shot through a window pane behind which P and Q were standing. It was accepted that he did not intend to endanger their lives. The question remained, however, whether he damaged property being reckless as to whether the life of another would be endangered. D was convicted and appealed submitting that it had to be proved that the endangering arose from the damage to the window and not the act which caused the damage to the window (i.e. the firing of the bullet which smashed it). The House of Lords affirmed the decision of the Court of Appeal allowing his appeal as it was the shooting which endangered the lives and not the breaking of the window.

This requirement has been reiterated in the two cases which follow where the Court of Appeal, by a process of intellectual gymnastics, managed to uphold the convictions.

> In *Asquith, Webster, and Seamans* [1995] 1 Cr App R 492, the appellants had pushed a coping stone from a bridge on to a train passing below. It hit a carriage showering the passengers with debris from the roof but it did not fall into the carriage. In the conjoined appeal of *Warwick* [1995] 1 Cr App R 492 the appellant was the passenger in a stolen car who hurled bricks at a police car, smashing a window and showering the officers with glass. The stolen car also rammed the police car and another brick was thrown which hit an officer. Lord Taylor CJ conceded that s. 1(2)(b) can produce some anomalous distinctions. He emphasised that the issue was not whether and how life was endangered but rather 'whether and how it was intended to be endangered or there was a . . . risk of it being endangered' of which D was aware (see G, **15.2.2.1**). In addition, the reference in s. 1(2)(b) to 'destruction or damage' referred to 'such destruction or damage as the defendant intended'. Lord Taylor CJ stated (at p. 497):

>> [I]f a defendant throws a brick at the windscreen of a moving vehicle, given that he causes *some* damage to the vehicle, whether he is guilty under s. 1(2) does not depend on whether the brick hits or misses the windscreen, but whether he intended to hit it and intended that the damage therefrom should endanger life or whether he was reckless as to that outcome. As to the dropping of stones from bridges, the effect of the statute may be thought strange. If the defendant's intention is that the stone itself should crash through the roof of a train . . . and thereby directly injure a passenger or if he was reckless only as to that outcome, the section would not bite . . . . If, however, the defendant intended or was reckless that the stone would smash the roof of the train or vehicle so that metal or wood struts from the roof would or . . . might descend upon a passenger, endangering life, he would surely be guilty. This may seem a dismal distinction.

The Court of Appeal proceeded to uphold the conviction in *Warwick* as the broken glass, or ramming of the vehicle, could have caused the driver to lose control thereby endangering the lives of the driver and passengers and there was adequate evidence from which the jury could infer an intention to endanger life in this way or recklessness thereto. In *Asquith* the Court of Appeal quashed the conviction as it was based on an erroneous direction that an intent to endanger life by the stone falling on a passenger would suffice. The Court, however, substituted a conviction based on recklessness, Lord Taylor CJ stating (at p. 498):

> However, the jury's finding of an intent by each appellant to endanger life ... must, in common sense, carry the implication that they were each reckless as to endangering life (by whatever damage the stone might do) when it fell. If the intention was for the stone to penetrate the roof, there was clearly an obvious risk that it might endanger life by bringing parts of the roof down into the compartment, quite apart from other obvious risks such as derailment if it fell in front of the train or struck the driver's cab incapacitating him or the controls.

Following the House of Lords' decision in *G* (see **15.2.2.1**) the test now is not whether the risk was obvious but rather whether D was aware of the risk and unreasonably took it. The unreasonableness of taking a risk is assessed in light of the circumstances known to D (see *Castle* [2004] All ER (D) 289 (Oct.)). Following *Heard* [2007] EWCA Crim 125, the s. 1(2) offence is one of specific intent as the element of intent or recklessness as to endangering life is an ulterior *mens rea*. Thus D may rely on his intoxication if it is such that he did not form the requisite intent or did not appreciate the risk to life (see **5.5.2**).

In *Wenton* [2010] EWCA Crim 2361, D's conviction, for damaging property being reckless whether life was endangered, was quashed. D had first broken a window using a brick; he then threw a container of petrol into the house with a lighted piece of paper but the petrol did not ignite. The Court of Appeal considered *Asquith* and *Warwick*, and pointed out, somewhat exasperatedly, that the act which caused the damage was throwing the brick whereas the act which caused the endangerment was throwing the petrol container and lighted paper into the house, the two acts being unrelated. Had the petrol ignited and had damage been caused by the fire, D could have been convicted of arson being reckless whether life was endangered (see *Dudley* [1989] Crim LR 57).

The fact that lives are not in fact endangered is irrelevant if it was D's intention by the damage to endanger life (see *Dudley*, earlier) or he was reckless thereto (*Sangha* [1988] 2 All ER 385).

> In *Dudley*, D threw a fire bomb and set fire to P's house but P and his family quickly extinguished the fire and only trivial damage was caused. D's conviction for arson being reckless whether life would be endangered was affirmed by the Court of Appeal. The relevant time was when D did the act which caused the damage; if at that time he was aware of a risk of danger to life or if he intended to endanger life, he had the requisite *mens rea*.

15.3.3 Without lawful excuse

'Without lawful excuse' in s. 1(2) does not have the same meaning as for s. 1(1). **The definition in s. 5 does not apply to offences under s. 1(2).** Thus, even though D may have P's consent to damage his property, if he does so intending to endanger the life of another or being reckless thereto, he will be guilty of the s. 1(2) offence. In *Merrick* [1996] 1 Cr App R 130, in the process of carrying out approved work to underground cabling, D briefly exposed an electrical cable for a few minutes before rendering it safe. Counts of simple criminal damage were dismissed on the basis of lawful excuse but the trial proceeded for the counts under s. 1(2) where, according to the Court of Appeal, 'the defence of lawful excuse did not apply'. The trial proceeded on the basis that the householder owned the cabling and could consent to its removal. When, however, the trial judge ruled that any precautions designed to eliminate the risk of endangering life had to be taken before the damage was actually caused, D changed his plea to guilty. If, however, the householder could consent to removal of the cabling, D was not placing reliance on s. 5(2)(a) but rather on the fact of consent which is an 'excuse apart from this subsection' (see *Denton*, **15.2.2.2.1**; Professor J. C. Smith, Commentary, *Merrick* [1995] Crim LR 804). The suggestion is that more should have been made of the excuse point on appeal in *Merrick* and that the dictum of the Court of Appeal is *obiter* and wrong.

The limited circumstances in which D would have a lawful excuse appear to be confined to situations where he damages property to prevent crime or defend himself or apprehend an offender and the reasonable force he uses endangers life. For example, if E is attacking D with a hatchet and D smashes P's vase over E's head to defend himself, intending to kill E, D will have damaged property belonging to another intending to endanger the life of another. If the force used, however, was reasonable in the circumstances, D will have been acting with lawful excuse in damaging the property and thereby endangering life.

15.4 Threats to destroy or damage property

Section 2 of the Criminal Damage Act 1971 provides:

A person who without lawful excuse makes to another a threat, intending that that other would fear it would be carried out—

(a) to destroy or damage any property belonging to that other or a third person; or

(b) to destroy or damage his own property in a way which he knows is likely to endanger the life of that other or a third person;

shall be guilty of an offence.

Actus reus	Mens rea

D:
 • without lawful excuse,
 • makes to another a threat, either
   (a) to destroy or damage any property belonging to that other or a third person, or
   (b) to destroy or damage his own property.
	D does so:
	 • intending that that other would fear the threat would be carried out;
	 • and, for the purposes of a charge under s. 2(b), knowing that the way he proposes to destroy or damage the property is likely to endanger the life of that other or a third person.

On conviction on indictment the maximum punishment for this offence is 10 years' imprisonment (s. 4(2)).

The threat may be made by any means. The Law Commission stated that 'the only limitation that needs to be imposed is that the threats should be intended to create fear that what is threatened will be carried out' (Law Com No. 29, para. 55). There is no requirement that D intend to carry out the threats; the essence of the offence is the intention to create fear. If P is not, in fact, put in fear as he does not believe D would carry out the threat, this will not avail D provided it is proved D intended to cause fear in P.

The conduct threatened must be an offence under s. 1 of the Act. If D threatens an offence under s. 1(1), the definition of 'without lawful excuse' in s. 5 applies, but if he threatens an offence under s. 1(2) this definition is inapplicable.

15.5 Possessing anything with intent to destroy or damage property

Section 3 of the Criminal Damage Act 1971 provides:

A person who has anything in his custody or under his control intending without lawful excuse to use it or cause or permit another to use it—

(a) to destroy or damage any property belonging to some other person; or

(b) to destroy or damage his own property in a way which he knows is likely to endanger the life of some other person; shall be guilty of an offence.

Actus reus	Mens rea
D has anything in his custody or control.	Intending, without lawful excuse, to use the thing or cause or permit another to use it: • to destroy or damage any property belonging to some other person; or • to destroy or damage his own property in a way which he knows is likely to endanger the life of some other person.

On conviction on indictment the maximum punishment for this offence is 10 years' imprisonment (s. 4(2)).

It is necessary to prove a purposive intention, that is that D possessed the item for the purpose of committing an offence under s. 1 himself or for another to use it to commit such an offence. A conditional intention, to use the item to cause damage should it prove necessary, will suffice (*Buckingham* (1976) 63 Cr App R 159). 'Without lawful excuse' applies in the same way as for the s. 2 offence (see **15.3.3**). D must have actual custody or control of the item at the time he formulates the intention. If, for example, D gives E a brick and subsequently suggests to him that he should use it to damage P's property, D has the necessary intention but he does not have custody or control of the brick (he would, however, be liable to conviction for incitement). By contrast, if D picks up a brick intending to give it to E so that he can damage P's property, D will have custody and control of the brick with the intention to permit E to use it to cause criminal damage.

There is no definition of 'anything'; the essence of the offence is D's intent. If D has the requisite intent it does not matter what the thing is which he has in his custody or control.

15.6 **Racially or religiously aggravated criminal damage**

Section 30 of the Crime and Disorder Act 1998 provides for the offence of racially or religiously aggravated criminal damage (see s. 30). Criminal damage is racially or religiously aggravated where a person commits criminal damage, and:

(a) at the time of committing the offence, or immediately before or after doing so, the offender demonstrates towards the victim of the offence [i.e. the person to whom the property belongs or is treated as belonging] hostility based on the victim's membership (or presumed membership) of a racial or religious group; or

(b) the offence is motivated (wholly or partly) by hostility towards members of a racial or religious group based on their membership of that group. [See ss 28(1) and 30(3).]

The maximum penalty for criminal damage is increased to 14 years where the offence is racially aggravated. For further analysis of this offence see R. Leng, R. Taylor, and M. Wasik, *Blackstone's Guide to the Crime and Disorder Act 1998* (1998) (for the meaning of 'racial group' or 'religious group' see **10.2.1**).

The tendency for the CPS to charge racially or religiously aggravated offences where the actual reason for the offence has nothing to do with race or religion, and for courts to uphold convictions in such circumstances, risks bringing these laws into disrepute. In *DPP* v *Green* [2004] EWHC 1225 (Admin), the Divisional Court considered *DPP* v *Woods* (see **10.2.1**) and confirmed that an offence may be considered racially or religiously aggravated if accompanied by any racial or religious abuse even where the defendant does not in fact act from any racial or religious motive. In *DPP* v *M* [2004] EWHC 1453 (Admin), D, who was involved in a dispute over payment in a Turkish kebab shop, broke a window in the course of the argument and muttered the words 'bloody foreigners'. The offence was charged as racially aggravated criminal damage and, although the justices found as a fact that the cause of the dispute was an argument over money, the Divisional Court held that the words 'bloody foreigners' were capable of describing a racial group by reference to nationality and the word 'bloody' could demonstrate hostility. The term 'foreigner' lacks specificity; to what nationality is reference being made? Such an argument, however, fell on deaf ears in *Rogers* [2007] UKHL 8 where the same epithet, 'bloody foreigners', was used by D to a group of Spanish women who got in his way as he rode his mobility scooter along the pavement. One view of these cases is that they extend the notion of racial or religious aggravation too far: had Mr M and Mr Rogers simply uttered the words 'bloody chefs' or 'bloody pedestrians' there would have been no offence under s. 30. Another view is that these cases appropriately recognise that hostility can be manifested in passive-aggressive language that does not explicitly reference the person's real motivation or hatred but it is language from which it is reasonable to infer racial or religious hostility (see further **10.2.1**). The simple offence of criminal damage (or indeed assault etc.) is more serious when such hostility is evident, explicitly or implicitly.

The law in context

Criminal damage, lawful excuse, and environmental protest

Environmental groups such as Greenpeace have used the defence of lawful excuse in several cases of political protest involving damage to property. These first-instance cases highlight the central role of the jury in this area of law. For example, in 2007 six Greenpeace climate change protesters entered the Kingsnorth power station. They admitted trying to shut the power station down, by occupying the smokestack and writing a slogan on its side (*The Guardian*, 'Not Guilty: the Greenpeace Activists Who Used Climate Change as a Legal Defence' 11 September 2008). They were charged with criminal damage to the smokestack and argued that they had lawful excuse under s. 5(2)(b) of the Criminal Damage Act 1971. They argued that painting on the chimney protected property belonging to themselves or to others, and that they believed that other property was in immediate need of protection and the means adopted were reasonable. Their defence was that they were acting to protect property around the world, including the Siberian permafrost, public and private property in Bangladesh, and property belonging to the Inuit people of the Arctic. Their argument focused on the environmental impact of coal-fired power stations such as Kingsnorth. By closing the power station, even for a short time, they were protecting property around the world. Leading climate change scientists testified to the environmental impact of climate change. The prosecution's case was simply that the defendants had gone too far in their protest: 'There are things you can lawfully do in making a protest but there's a line which has to be drawn. When the defendants caused damage to that chimney, it's the line that they crossed' (*The Guardian*, 11 September 2008).

In 2000, 28 Greenpeace protesters were charged with causing criminal damage to a field of genetically modified (GM) maize (*The Guardian*, 'Greenpeace Wins Key GM Case' 21 September 2000). They entered fields on a farm that was being used for a trial of GM crops and dug up all the maize plants, which were about to flower. At trial they argued that they acted to protect other property, namely crops in surrounding fields, that was in immediate need of protection from cross-contamination and that the means adopted were reasonable.

In both cases, all of the Greenpeace protesters were acquitted. Why? We cannot know why the jury reached verdicts of not guilty, but in both cases it is likely that jury members were sympathetic to the defendants' arguments about why they were damaging the particular property and about the reasonableness of the means they adopted. As we have seen throughout the book, English law entrusts the jury with deciding what is 'reasonable' and when lawful excuse is pleaded in criminal damage cases defence counsel will seek directly to engage their personal and political sympathies.

This is not to say that the lawful excuse defence is a 'sympathy lottery', devoid of any clarity. We saw earlier that the Court of Appeal in *Hill and Hall* imposed an objective limit on this defence, namely the trial judge must decide whether it could be said, as a matter of law, that the defendant's acts could amount to something done in order to protect property or whether they were too remote. The defendant must show that the act of damaging property was done

→

→

in order to protect property belonging to himself or another. *Kelleher* [2003] EWCA Crim 3525 illustrates this. D decapitated a statue of former Prime Minister Margaret Thatcher that was on display in a London art gallery. He claimed lawful excuse on the basis that her economic policies had promoted materialism and global corporations' influence over democratic governments, which were 'leading the world towards its eventual destruction' (para. 18). However, the trial judge withdrew the defence from the jury, a decision that was approved by the Court of Appeal, because D had not damaged the sculpture *in order to* protect property, but rather to express anger and frustration. It is worth noting though that Kelleher was convicted at a retrial, the jury in his first trial being unable to reach a verdict. The Court of Appeal reiterated the crucial point of English law that a trial judge is not entitled to direct the jury to convict a defendant. The jury remains at the heart of such trials, even when the facts (here, the obvious damage to property!) seem to point to a guilty verdict.

The availability of the lawful excuse defence to a charge of criminal damage can influence prosecutorial decisions. Aggravated trespass under s. 68 of the Criminal Justice and Public Order Act 1994 can be a more attractive charge for the CPS, as it is triable only summarily (although the maximum sentence is only three months' imprisonment, a factor which might lead the CPS to prefer a charge under s. 1 of the 1971 Act). The s. 68 offence is committed if:

> [a] person trespasses on land and, in relation to any lawful activity which persons are engaging in or are about to engage in on that or adjoining land, does there anything which is intended by him to have the effect (a) of intimidating those persons or any of them so as to deter them or any of them from engaging in that activity, (b) of obstructing that activity, or (c) of disrupting that activity.

This might be preferable for the CPS if no criminal damage has resulted or even if criminal damage has resulted, as the case will not be heard by a jury and will, arguably, be likely to result in the magistrates convicting the defendants (as was seen in the case of the 'Plane Stupid' climate change protesters who were convicted under s. 68 after chaining themselves together on a runway at Heathrow Airport: '"Heathrow 13" Climate Change Protesters Avoid Jail' BBC News Online, 24 February 2016, https://www.bbc.co.uk/news/uk-england-london-35651166).

 Key Points

- Whether property has been damaged is a question of fact for the jury or magistrates. The courts have held that property is 'damaged' if expense would be incurred by the property's owner to restore the property to its previous condition.

- 'property' is defined in s. 10(1) and 'belonging to another' in s. 10(2).

- The *mens rea* of criminal damage is intention or subjective recklessness. The leading case is the House of Lords' decision *R v G* (2003), which reversed *Caldwell*.

- The defence of lawful excuse in s. 5 is available when:

  - a person honestly believes the property's owner had or would have consented to the property's damage or destruction; or

  - a person destroys or damages the property in order to protect other property that he honestly believes is in immediate need of protection and he honestly believes that the means used were or would be reasonable.

→

→

- The Court of Appeal in *Hill and Hall* (1989) held that the question whether property is destroyed or damaged 'in order to protect property' is one of law for the trial judge to determine.

- Jury sympathy can play an important role in cases where lawful excuse is pleaded, as shown by some cases involving political protesters seeking to raise awareness of environmental issues.

- For the offence under s. 1(2), D must at least be reckless as to whether the life of another would be endangered by the property's destruction or damage.

FURTHER READING

K. Amirthalingam, 'Caldwell Recklessness Is Dead, Long Live Mens Rea's Fecklessness' (2004) 67(3) MLR 491–500.

I. Edwards, 'Banksy's Graffiti: a Not-so-simple Case of Criminal Damage? (2009) 73(4) J Crim L 345–61.

D. W. Elliott, 'Endangering Life by Destroying or Damaging Property' [1997] Crim LR 382.

INDEX